Praise for *Eighty Days*

"A page-turner . . . Matthew Goodman brings to life the two women, [the] fast-changing times and the v⸻⸻⸻⸻ in their parallel adventures." ⸻⸻⸻*ne*

"Compelling narrative nonfiction ⸻⸻⸻⸻⸻t-ing ride." ⸻⸻*y*

"Goodman's truly exciting account of [Bly and Bisland's] journeys . . . is also quite a fun trip for his readers. He has the gift of turning meticulous research into vividly imagined details. . . . A fully satisfying portrait of the era." —*Bust* magazine

"Delightful . . . History lovers will eat it up." —*Library Journal*

"The true story of Nellie Bly and Elizabeth Bisland, two journalists racing to see who could circle the globe first—and faster than any man before them—is as riveting now as it was when it captivated the nation in 1889." —*Parade* (Top Pick)

"Reading *Eighty Days* . . . is like taking your own journey around the world in 1889–90. . . . Well-researched tales of the trips and the times make for enjoyable reading." —*The Christian Science Monitor*

"Terrifically engaging . . . What Goodman is writing about more than anything . . . is the round-the-world voyage as a cultural phenomenon, and his book functions exceedingly well on this level. (His pages are consistently informed by close and judicious use of all relevant sources and a commitment to lapidary narrative. His digressions are never too digressive; his transitions never jolt or jar.)" —*Los Angeles Review of Books*

"It's a wonderful story, made all the more compelling by fine writing and exceptional historical detail." —*Maclean's*

"Brilliantly researched and detail-packed . . . marvelous . . . an armchair journey you don't want to miss." —*Columbia Daily Tribune*

"[*Eighty Days* is] a dazzling tour of the world at a time when travel routes were just opening up; a look at sensationalist journalism and pop culture in pre-Kardashian America; and testimony to how hard women had to fight to get work and achieve respect as journalists." —*BookPage*

"The story's engaging, the writing gripping, and the treatment—how Bly and Bisland are praised for combating sexism and denigrated for ignoring classism and embracing imperialism—is as clear-eyed as you can get. Well worth a read." —*The Literary Omnivore*

"[Goodman] draws fascinating portraits of two self-made women who captured America's imagination by defying its gender stereotypes. . . . Deftly mixing social history into an absorbing travel epic, [he] conveys the exuberant dynamism of a very unfusty Victorian era obsessed with speed, power, publicity, and the breaking of every barrier." —*Publishers Weekly*

"A richly detailed double narrative of the adventures of two young women journalists in a race against time . . . entertaining and readable throughout." —*Kirkus Reviews*

"What a delight to circumnavigate the globe with pioneering journalists Nelly Bly and Elizabeth Bisland. Matthew Goodman's lively writing and detailed research bring the story of these two remarkable women to life as they race around the world, full steam ahead, giving us an intimate look at a late-nineteenth-century world that is suddenly shrinking in the face of rapid technological change. Only one of these two remarkable women can win the race around the world, but the reader of this fascinating tale will be certain of a reward." —ELIZABETH LETTS, author of *The Eighty-Dollar Champion*

Eighty Days

BY MATTHEW GOODMAN

Eighty Days: Nellie Bly and Elizabeth Bisland's
History-Making Race Around the World

The Sun and the Moon:
The Remarkable True Account of Hoaxers,
Showmen, Dueling Journalists, and
Lunar Man-Bats in Nineteenth-Century New York

Jewish Food: The World at Table

Eighty Days

Nellie Bly and Elizabeth Bisland's HISTORY-MAKING RACE AROUND THE WORLD

MATTHEW GOODMAN

BALLANTINE BOOKS TRADE PAPERBACKS NEW YORK

2014 Ballantine Books Trade Paperback Edition

Copyright © 2013 by Matthew Goodman
Maps copyright © 2013 by David Lindroth, Inc.
Reading group guide copyright © 2014 by Random House LLC.

Published in the United States by Ballantine Books,
an imprint of The Random House Publishing Group,
a division of Random House LLC,
a Penguin Random House Company, New York.

BALLANTINE and the HOUSE colophon are
registered trademarks of Random House LLC.
RANDOM HOUSE READER'S CIRCLE & Design
is a registered trademark of Random House LLC.

Originally published in hardcover in the United States
by Ballantine Books, an imprint of The Random House Publishing
Group, a division of Random House LLC, in 2013.

"Fame is a bee" is from *The Poems of Emily Dickinson,*
edited by Thomas H. Johnson (Cambridge, MA: The Belknap Press
of Harvard University Press), copyright © 1951, 1955, 1979, 1983
by the President and Fellows of Harvard College

LIBRARY OF CONGRESS CATALOGING-IN-PUBLICATION DATA

Goodman, Matthew.
Eighty days : Nellie Bly and Elizabeth Bisland's history-making race
around the world / Matthew Goodman.
p. cm.
Includes bibliographical references and index.
ISBN 978-0-345-52727-1 (pbk.) — ISBN 978-0-345-52728-8 (eBook)
1. Bly, Nellie, 1864–1922—Travel. 2. Bisland, Elizabeth,
1861–1929—Travel. 3. Women journalists—United States—
Biography. 4. Voyages around the world. I. Title.
G440.B67136G66 2013
910.4'109252—dc23   2012046344

Printed in the United States of America on acid-free paper

www.randomhousereaderscircle.com

4 6 8 9 7 5

Book design by Barbara M. Bachman

For Vivian,
who has traveled widely
in Brooklyn

"You have a strange way, Ralph, of proving that the world has grown smaller. So, because you can go around it in three months—"

"In eighty days," interrupted Phileas Fogg.

—JULES VERNE, *Around the World in Eighty Days*

CONTENTS

—

PROLOGUE *xiii*

CHAPTER 1 | A Free American Girl *3*

CHAPTER 2 | The Newspaper Gods of Gotham *17*

CHAPTER 3 | The Secret Cupboard *40*

CHAPTER 4 | "How Quick Can a Woman Go Around the World?" *57*

CHAPTER 5 | "I Think I Can Beat Phileas Fogg's Record" *69*

CHAPTER 6 | Living by Railroad Time *92*

CHAPTER 7 | A Map of the World *116*

CHAPTER 8 | "Et Ego in Arcadia" *139*

CHAPTER 9 | Baksheesh *161*

CHAPTER 10 | An English Market Town in China *184*

CHAPTER 11 | "The Guessing Match Has Begun in Beautiful Earnest" *197*

CHAPTER 12 | The Other Woman Is Going to Win *215*

CHAPTER 13 | The Temple of the Dead *235*

CHAPTER 14 | The Mysterious Travel Agent *255*

CHAPTER 15 | The Special Train *282*

CHAPTER 16 | "From Jersey to Jersey Is Around the World" *307*

CHAPTER 17 | Father Time Outdone *324*

EPILOGUE *355*

ACKNOWLEDGMENTS *377*
NOTES *381*
SELECTED BIBLIOGRAPHY *415*
ILLUSTRATION CREDITS *425*
INDEX *427*
A READER'S GUIDE *451*

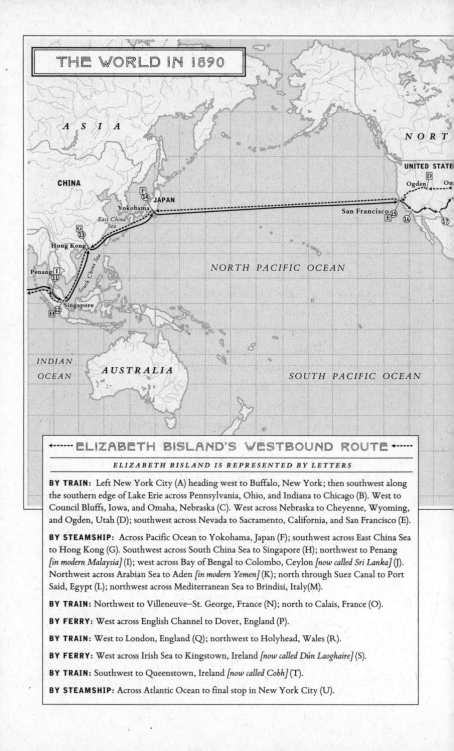

THE WORLD IN 1890

ASIA

NORTH

CHINA

UNITED STATES

F 14

JAPAN

Ogden

D

On

Yokohama

East China Sea

San Francisco

E 15

16

17

G 13

Hong Kong

Penang I 11

South China Sea

NORTH PACIFIC OCEAN

Singapore H 12

INDIAN OCEAN

AUSTRALIA

SOUTH PACIFIC OCEAN

◄------ ELIZABETH BISLAND'S WESTBOUND ROUTE ◄------

ELIZABETH BISLAND IS REPRESENTED BY LETTERS

BY TRAIN: Left New York City (A) heading west to Buffalo, New York; then southwest along the southern edge of Lake Erie across Pennsylvania, Ohio, and Indiana to Chicago (B). West to Council Bluffs, Iowa, and Omaha, Nebraska (C). West across Nebraska to Cheyenne, Wyoming, and Ogden, Utah (D); southwest across Nevada to Sacramento, California, and San Francisco (E).

BY STEAMSHIP: Across Pacific Ocean to Yokohama, Japan (F); southwest across East China Sea to Hong Kong (G). Southwest across South China Sea to Singapore (H); northwest to Penang *[in modern Malaysia]* (I); west across Bay of Bengal to Colombo, Ceylon *[now called Sri Lanka]* (J). Northwest across Arabian Sea to Aden *[in modern Yemen]* (K); north through Suez Canal to Port Said, Egypt (L); northwest across Mediterranean Sea to Brindisi, Italy(M).

BY TRAIN: Northwest to Villeneuve–St. George, France (N); north to Calais, France (O).

BY FERRY: West across English Channel to Dover, England (P).

BY TRAIN: West to London, England (Q); northwest to Holyhead, Wales (R).

BY FERRY: West across Irish Sea to Kingstown, Ireland *[now called Dún Laoghaire]* (S).

BY TRAIN: Southwest to Queenstown, Ireland *[now called Cobh]* (T).

BY STEAMSHIP: Across Atlantic Ocean to final stop in New York City (U).

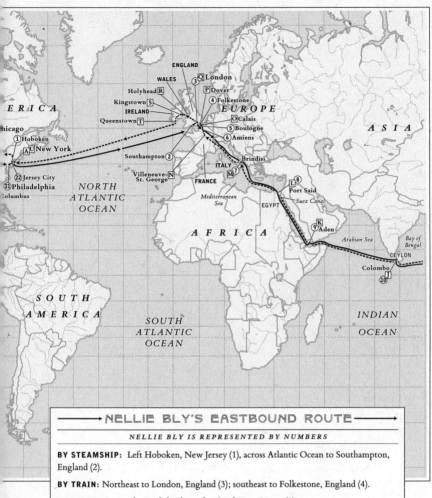

NELLIE BLY'S EASTBOUND ROUTE

NELLIE BLY IS REPRESENTED BY NUMBERS

BY STEAMSHIP: Left Hoboken, New Jersey (1), across Atlantic Ocean to Southampton, England (2).

BY TRAIN: Northeast to London, England (3); southeast to Folkestone, England (4).

BY FERRY: Across the English Channel to Boulogne, France (5).

BY TRAIN: Southeast to Amiens, France (6); then southeast to Brindisi, Italy (7).

BY STEAMSHIP: Southeast across Mediterranean Sea to Port Said, Egypt (8); south through Suez Canal to Aden *[in modern Yemen]* (9); southeast across Arabian Sea to Colombo, Ceylon *[now called Sri Lanka]* (10). East across Bay of Bengal to Penang *[in modern Malaysia]* (11); southeast across South China Sea to Singapore (12); northeast across South China Sea to Hong Kong (13). Northeast across East China Sea to Yokohama, Japan (14); east across Pacific Ocean to San Francisco (15).

BY TRAIN: South to Mojave, California (16); east across central Arizona to Albuquerque, New Mexico (17); northeast to La Junta, Colorado (18). Northeast across Kansas, Missouri, southeastern Iowa, and northern Illinois to Chicago (19). Southeast to Columbus, Ohio (20); east to Philadelphia, Pennsylvania (21); northeast to final stop in Jersey City, New Jersey (22).

PROLOGUE

—

SHE WAS A YOUNG WOMAN IN A PLAID COAT AND CAP, NEITHER TALL nor short, dark nor fair, not quite pretty enough to turn a head: the sort of woman who could, if necessary, lose herself in a crowd. Even in the chill early-morning hours, the deck of the ferry from New York to Hoboken was packed tight with passengers. The Hudson River—or the North River, as it was still called then, the name a vestige of the Dutch era—was as busy as any of the city's avenues, and the ferry carefully navigated its way through the water traffic, past the brightly painted canal boats and the workaday tugs, the flat-bottomed steam barges full of Pennsylvania coal, three-masted schooners with holds laden with tobacco and indigo and bananas and cotton, hides from Argentina and tea from Japan, with everything, it seemed, that the world had to offer. The young woman struggled to contain her nervousness as the ferry drew ever closer to the warehouses and depots of Hoboken, where the Hamburg-American steamship *Augusta Victoria* already waited in her berth. Seagulls circled above the shoreline, sizing up the larger ships they would follow across the sea. In the distance, the massed stone spires of New York rose like cliffs from the water.

For much of the fall of 1889 New York had endured a near-constant rain, endless days of low skies and meager gray light. It was the sort of weather, people said, good only for the blues and the rheumatism; one of the papers had recently suggested that if the rain kept up, the city would be compelled to establish a steamboat service up Broadway. This morning, though, had broken cold but fair, surely a favorable omen for anyone about to go to sea. The prospect of an ocean crossing was always an exciting one, but bad weather meant rough sailing, and also brought with it the disquieting awareness of danger. Icebergs broke off from Greenland glaciers and drifted dumbly around the North Atlantic, immense craft sailing without warning lights or whistles and never swerving to avoid a collision; hurricanes appeared out of nowhere; fires could break out from any of a hundred causes. Some ships simply disappeared, like Marley's ghost, into a fog, never to be heard from again. The *Augusta Victoria* herself was lauded in the press as "practically unsinkable"—the sort of carefully measured accolade that might well have alarmed even as it meant to reassure. A twin-screw steamer of the most modern design, the *Augusta Victoria* had broken the record for the fastest maiden voyage only six months earlier, crossing the Atlantic from Southampton to New York in just seven days, twelve hours, and thirty minutes. Arriving in New York, she was greeted by a crowd of more than thirty thousand ("The Germans," *The New York Times* took care to note, "largely predominated"), who swarmed aboard to get a closer look at the floating palace, taking in her chandeliers and silk tapestries, the grand piano in the music room, the lavender-tinted ladies' room, the men's smoking room swathed in green morocco. Transatlantic travel had come a very long way in the half century since Charles Dickens sailed to America, when he eyed the narrow dimensions and melancholy appointments of his ship's main saloon and compared it to a gigantic hearse with windows.

Dockside, the minutes before the departure of an oceangoing liner always had something of a carnival air. Most of the men were dressed in dark topcoats and silk hats; the women wore outfits made complicated by bustles and ruching. On the edges of the crowd, peddlers hawked goods that passengers might have neglected to pack; sweating, bare-armed stevedores performed their ballet of hoisting and loading around the ropes and barrels that cluttered the pier. The rumble of carts on cobblestones blended with a general hubbub of conversation, the sound, like thunder, seeming to come at once from everywhere and nowhere. Somewhere inside the milling crowd stood the young woman in the plaid coat. She had been born Elizabeth Jane Cochran—as an adolescent she would add an *e* to the end of her surname, the silent extra letter providing, she must have felt, a pleasing note of sophistication—though she was known to her family and her old friends not as Elizabeth or as Jane but as "Pink."

To many of New York's newspaper readers, and shortly to those of much of the world, her name was Nellie Bly.

For two years Nellie Bly had been a reporter for *The World* of New York, which under the leadership of its publisher, Joseph Pulitzer, had become the largest and most influential newspaper of its time. No female reporter before her had ever seemed quite so audacious, so willing to risk personal safety in pursuit of a story. In her first exposé for *The World,* Bly had gone undercover (using the name "Nellie Brown," a pseudonym to cloak another pseudonym), feigning insanity so that she might report firsthand on the mistreatment of the female patients of the Blackwell's Island Insane Asylum. Bly worked for pennies alongside other young women in a paper-box factory, applied for employment as a servant, and sought treatment in a medical dispensary for the poor, where she narrowly escaped having her tonsils removed. Nearly every week the second section of the Sunday *World* brought the paper's readers a new adventure. Bly trained with the boxing champion John L. Sullivan; she performed, with cheerfulness but not much success, as a chorus girl at the Academy of Music (forgetting the cue to exit, she momentarily found herself all alone onstage). She visited with a remarkable deaf, dumb, and blind nine-year-old girl in Boston by the name of Helen Keller. Once, to expose the workings of New York's white slave trade, she even bought a baby. Her articles were by turns lighthearted and scolding and indignant, some meant to edify and some merely to entertain, but all were shot through with Bly's unmistakable passion for a good story and her uncanny ability to capture the public's imagination, the sheer force of her personality demanding that attention be paid to the plight of the unfortunate, and, not incidentally, to herself.

Now, on the morning of November 14, 1889, she was undertaking the most sensational adventure of all: an attempt to set the record for the fastest trip around the world. Sixteen years earlier, in his popular novel, Jules Verne had imagined that such a trip could be accomplished in eighty days; Nellie Bly hoped to do it in seventy-five.

Though she had first proposed the idea a year earlier, *The World*'s editors, who initially resisted the notion of a young woman traveling unchaperoned, had only just consented to it. The previous three days had been a blur of activity, mapping out an itinerary, visiting ticket offices, assembling a wardrobe, writing farewell letters to friends, packing and unpacking and packing again. Bly had decided that she would take but a single bag, a small leather gripsack into which she would pack everything, from clothing to writing implements to toilet articles, that she might require for her journey; being able to carry her own bag would help prevent any delays that might arise from the interference or incompetence of porters and customs officials. As her traveling dress she had selected a snugly fitted two-piece garment of dark blue broadcloth trimmed with camel's hair. For warmth she was taking a long black-and-white plaid Scotch ulster coat, with twin rows of buttons running down the front, that covered her from neck to ankles; and rather than the hat and veil worn by most of the fashionable oceangoing women of the time, she would wear a jaunty wool ghillie cap—the English-style "fore-and-aft" cap later worn by Sherlock Holmes in the movies—that for the past three years had accompanied her on many of her adventures. The blue dress, the plaid ulster, the ghillie cap: to outward appearances it was not an especially remarkable outfit, but before long it would become the most famous one in all the world.

ON THE MORNING OF NOVEMBER 14, Nellie Bly had awoken very early—she always hated to get up in the morning—turned over a few times, dozed off again, and then woke with a start, wondering anxiously if she had missed her ship. Quickly she made her bath and got dressed. (There was no need for her to spend any time applying makeup, as only women of abominably low morals, or unimpeachably high social standing, dared paint their faces.) She tried to choke down some breakfast, but the earliness of the hour, and her anxiety, made eating impossible. The hardest thing of all was saying goodbye to her mother. "Don't worry," Bly told her, "only think of me as having a vacation and the most enjoyable time of my life." Then she gathered up her coat and her gripsack and made a blind rush down the stairs before she could too deeply regret the journey that was only just beginning.

Their apartment was on West Thirty-fifth Street, near Broadway; at Ninth Avenue, Bly paid her nickel and boarded a downtown streetcar. The car was dirty and poorly ventilated, and the straw spread on the floor smelled of the recent rains. The street was choked with horse traffic; on the tracks overhead an El train screeched past. It was only seventy-five days, Bly kept reminding herself, and then she would be back home again. She got off at the corner of Christopher Street and Greenwich Avenue, at the edge of a maritime district, where the low, irregular buildings grew up like toadstools along the water's edge: rigging warehouses and sail lofts, junk shops with their mysterious curios brought in from all over the world, the grim boardinghouses and brutal-looking taverns of the sailors. At the Christopher Street depot she caught the ferry—she needed only a one-way ticket, three cents—that carried her across the Hudson River to the pier at the foot of Third Street in Hoboken, New Jersey. There she was met by two agents of the Hamburg-American Packet Company; they well understood how important it was to the company that Nellie Bly be delivered on time. The two men accompanied their new passenger aboard the *Augusta Victoria* and presented her to the ship's captain, Adolph Albers, explaining to him the special purpose of her trip. An especially popular commander, Albers had a full beard and a genial manner that inspired confidence. He assured Bly that he would do everything in his power to see that the initial part of her complex journey was a complete success. He was certain, he said, that he could put her ashore in Southampton the following Thursday evening; she could then get a good night's sleep in one of the city's hotels and be up in time to catch one of the trains that ran each morning from Southampton to London.

"I won't take any sleep until I am in London," replied Nellie Bly, "and have made sure of my place in the bakers' dozen who go from Victoria Station on Friday night."

Her voice rang with the lilt of the hill towns of western Pennsylvania; there was an unusual rising inflection at the ends of her sentences, the vestige of an Elizabethan dialect that had still been spoken in the hills when she was a girl. She had piercing gray eyes, though sometimes they were called green, or blue-green, or hazel. Her nose was broad at its base and delicately upturned at the end—the papers liked to refer to it as a "retroussé" nose—and it was the only feature about which she was at all self-conscious. She had brown hair that she wore in bangs across her forehead. Most of those who knew her considered her pretty, although this was a subject that in the coming months would be hotly debated in the press.

Before long some friends and colleagues came aboard to bid her goodbye and Godspeed. The theatrical agent Henry C. Jarrett presented her with a bouquet of flowers and a novel; reading, he advised, was the best preventive of seasickness and ennui. Julius Chambers, *The World*'s managing editor, was there as well, and had brought along with him a timekeeper from the New York Athletic Club. As the city's leading amateur sports club, the New York Athletic Club often provided timekeepers for bicycle races, swimming races, and events of track and field; this was the first recorded instance of the club's providing a timekeeper for a race around the world.

Nellie Bly had made her career by training herself to remain calm in difficult situations, and now, too, she managed not to betray the nervousness that she felt; the next day's issue of *The World* would pronounce that she had demonstrated "not a wince of fear or trepidation, and no youngster just let loose from school could have been more merry and lighthearted." While they waited, Bly asked one of her colleagues from *The World*, "What do you think of my dress?" Her tone seemed cheerful enough, but when he hesitated she demanded of him, "Well, a penny for your thoughts."

The reporter eyed the dark blue gown with the camel-hair trim, beneath the checked overcoat; he noted aloud that she was planning to sail past Egypt, and if one of Joseph's descendants there didn't take that dress for his coat of many colors, then—but he was interrupted before he could complete the thought. "Oh, you spiteful thing," Bly said dismissively, with a theatrical toss of her head. "I take back my penny offer for such an opinion as that."

Though *The World* chose not to see it, her impatience was surely indicative of the complicated mix of emotions she was feeling: the intense desire to get going at last, regret at leaving behind friends and family, excitement and anxiety about the strangeness of everything she was about to encounter—strange countries, strange foods, strange languages (for Nellie Bly was attempting to navigate the world speaking only English). This day had dawned bright and beautiful, but she could not help but wonder about the seventy-four yet to come, and the twenty-eight thousand miles that lay ahead of her. If all went well, she would be spending her Christmas in Hong Kong, and her New Year's somewhere in the middle of the Pacific Ocean.

On the front page of that morning's *World,* a map stretching across five columns of type showed "The Lines of Travel to be Followed by *The World*'s Flying Representative." The line began in New York, extended across the Atlantic Ocean to England, moved down through Europe to

Nellie Bly in her famous traveling outfit

the Mediterranean, continued south through the Suez Canal to the Arabian Sea along the northeast coast of Africa, then shifted eastward past Ceylon and up to Hong Kong and Japan, crossed the Pacific Ocean to San Francisco, and concluded through the northern part of the United States and back to New York. It all looked very well thought out, but her itinerary, Bly knew, was not nearly as firm as that solid black line made it seem. It was not clear, for instance, whether the mail train from London to Brindisi, Italy (about which she had been so insistent to Captain Albers), actually left every Friday night or not. A more irregular train schedule could mean a missed connection with the steamship leaving from Brindisi, and from there the delays would cascade, leading inexorably to the collapse of her trip. She understood that she was setting out at the worst time of year, when the Atlantic storms were at their fiercest and snow often blockaded train tracks across the American West. Moreover, she would be racing not just through space but also, in a sense, through time: during the seventy-five days of her trip she would experience the weather of all four seasons. It was a commonplace of world travelers' tales that extreme change in temperature provided the perfect breeding ground for illness. Fever lay in wait everywhere; there was grippe in Europe, malaria in Asia. Storms, shipwreck, sickness, mechanical breakdown, even just a slackening of pace by an uncooperative railroad conductor or ship's captain: any one, by itself, could prove fatal to her plans.

She couldn't bear the thought of returning home a failure; later on she would tell the chief engineer of one of her ships, in full seriousness, that she would rather die than arrive late in New York. She hadn't built her career, hadn't made it from Pennsylvania coal country to the headlines of New York's largest newspaper, by losing. What Nellie Bly did not know, though, as she set out on her journey (and indeed would not know for many weeks to come), was that she might well lose her race, not to the calendar or to Jules Verne's fictitious traveler Phileas Fogg, but to a very real competitor. For, as it turned out, there was not just one young female journalist setting out from New York that day to race around the world—there were two.

ON THE MORNING OF NOVEMBER 14, as Nellie Bly made her way to the Hoboken docks, a man named John Brisben Walker was on a ferry headed in the opposite direction, bound from Jersey City to Cortlandt Street in lower Manhattan. Walker was the wealthy publisher of a high-toned monthly magazine called *The Cosmopolitan* (in later years it would be purchased by Joseph Pulitzer's rival William Randolph Hearst and subsequently assume a very different character), and as the ferry crossed the river he read *The World*'s front-page article revealing Nellie Bly's plan to race around the world. Instantly he recognized the publicity value of such a scheme, even as it occurred to him that a world traveler might do better by heading west rather than east as Bly was planning to do. At once an idea suggested itself: *The Cosmopolitan* would sponsor its own competitor in the around-the-world race, traveling in the opposite direction. Of course, *The Cosmopolitan*'s circumnavigator would have to be, like Bly, a young woman—there was a pleasing symmetry to the notion, and in any case a man racing against a woman would never win anyone's sympathy—and she would have to leave immediately, if she was to have any chance at all of returning to New York before Nellie Bly. After a quick conference at the office with his business manager, John Brisben Walker sent him off to a travel agency to prepare an itinerary, and at half past ten he sent a message to Elizabeth Bisland's apartment, only a few blocks away in Murray Hill. It was urgent, he indicated; she should come to the office at once.

Elizabeth Bisland was twenty-eight years old, and after nearly a decade of freelance writing she had recently obtained a job as literary editor of *The Cosmopolitan,* for which she wrote a monthly review of recently published books entitled "In the Library." Born into a Louisiana plantation family ruined by the Civil War and its aftermath, at the age of twenty she had moved to New Orleans and then, a few years later, to New York, where she contributed to a variety of magazines and was regularly referred to as the most beautiful woman in metropolitan journalism. Bisland was tall, with an elegant, almost imperious bearing that accentuated her height; she had large dark eyes and luminous pale skin and spoke in a low, gentle voice. She reveled in gracious hospitality and smart conversation, both of which were regularly on display in the literary salon that she hosted in the little apartment she shared with her sister on Fourth Avenue, where members of New York's creative set, writers and painters and actors, gathered to discuss the artistic issues of the day. Bisland's particular combination of beauty, charm, and erudition seems to have been nothing short of bewitching. One of her admirers, the writer Lafcadio

Hearn, whom she had befriended in New Orleans, called her "a sort of goddess" and likened her conversation to hashish, leaving him disoriented for hours afterward. Another said, about talking with her, that he felt as if he were playing with "a beautiful dangerous leopard," which he loved for not biting him.

Bisland herself was well aware that feminine beauty was useful but fleeting ("After the period of sex-attraction has passed," she once wrote, "women have no power in America"), and she took pride in the fact that she had arrived in New York with only fifty dollars in her pocket, and that the thousands of dollars now in her bank account had come by virtue of her own pen. Capable of working for eighteen hours at a stretch, she wrote book reviews, essays, feature articles, and poetry in the classical vein. She was a believer, more than anything else, in the joys of literature, which she had first experienced as a girl in ancient volumes of Shakespeare and Cervantes that she found in the library of her family's plantation house. (She taught herself French while she churned butter, so that she might read Rousseau's *Confessions* in the original—a book, as it turned out, that she hated.) She cared nothing for fame, and indeed found the prospect of it distasteful. So when she arrived shortly after eleven at the offices of *The Cosmopolitan* and John Brisben Walker proposed that she race Nellie Bly around the world, Elizabeth Bisland initially told him no. She had guests coming for tea the next day, she explained, and besides, she had nothing to wear for such a long journey; but the real reason, she later admitted, was that she immediately recognized the notoriety that such a race would bring, "and to this notoriety I most earnestly objected." However, Walker (who by this time had already made and lost more than one fortune) was not a man who was easily dissuaded, and at last she relented.

At six o'clock that evening, Elizabeth Bisland was on a New York Central Railroad train bound for Chicago. She was eight and a half hours behind Nellie Bly.

ON THE SURFACE THE TWO WOMEN, Nellie Bly and Elizabeth Bisland, were about as different as could be: one woman a Northerner, the other from the South; one a scrappy, hard-driving crusader, the other priding herself on her gentility; one seeking out the most sensational of news stories, the other preferring novels and poetry and disdaining much newspaper writing as "a wild, crooked, shrieking hodge-podge," a "caricature of life." Elizabeth Bisland hosted tea parties; Nellie Bly was known to frequent O'Rourke's saloon on the Bowery. But each of them was acutely conscious of the unequal position of women in America. Each had grown up without much money and had come to New York to make a place for herself in big-city journalism, achieving a hard-won success in what was still, unquestionably, a man's world. More than anything else, of course, the two women were to be linked forever by unique shared experience: partners, in a sense, in a vast project that for months would captivate the United States, and much of the world besides.

Bly and Bisland raced around the globe on the most powerful and modern forms of transportation yet created, the oceangoing steamship and the steam railroad, sending back messages to waiting editors by means of telegraph lines that had—in the expression of the period— annihilated space and time. They sailed across the breadth of the British Empire, from England in the west to Hong Kong in the east, their ships carrying the tea and cotton and opium and other valuable goods that helped sustain the imperial economy. They traveled through a world defined by custom and deformed by class, in every country they visited, and even on the ships and trains they used to get there.

Nellie Bly and Elizabeth Bisland were not only racing around the world; they were also racing through the very heart of the Victorian age.

THE *AUGUSTA VICTORIA* WAS scheduled to depart at nine-thirty in the morning; shortly before that a long blast from a horn sounded, warning all who were not to sail that it was time to go ashore. "Keep up your courage," one of Nellie Bly's friends said, giving her hand a farewell clasp. Bly did her best to smile, so that her friends' last recollections of her would be cheering ones. Her head felt suddenly dizzy, and her heart, she would say later, felt as if it were about to burst. Her friends moved slowly away, joining the line of other well-dressed people making their way down the gangplank. From the railing of the ship she could see for miles; out toward the horizon the water turned imperceptibly from blue to gray. The world seemed to have lost its roundness, become a long distance with no end. The moment of departure was at hand. Solemnly Nellie Bly and the man from the New York Athletic Club synchronized their watches.

Eighty Days

CHAPTER I

A Free American Girl

NELLIE BLY WAS BORN ELIZABETH JANE COCHRAN IN WESTERN PENNSYL-vania on May 5, 1864, though confusion about her exact age would per-sist throughout her life—a good deal of that confusion engineered by Bly herself, for she was never quite as young as she claimed to be. When she began her race around the world, in November of 1889, Bly was twenty-five years old, but estimates of her age among the nation's news-papers ranged from twenty to twenty-four; according to her own news-paper, *The World,* she was "about twenty-three."

The town in which she grew up, Apollo, Pennsylvania, was a small, nondescript sort of place, not much different from countless other mill towns carved out of hemlock and spruce, unassuming enough that even the author of a history of Apollo felt obliged to explain in the book's foreword, "It is not necessary to be a city of the first class to fill the niche in the hearts of the people or the history of the state. Besides it is our town." On its main street stood a general store (where one could buy everything from penny candy to plowshares), a drugstore, a slaughter-house, a blacksmith shop, and several taverns; the town would not have a bank until 1871. In the winters there was sledding and skating, and when the warmer weather came the children of the town liked to roll barrel hoops down the hill to the canal bridge and to fish the Kiskiminetas River, which had not yet been contaminated by runoff from the coal mines and iron mills being built nearby.

Elizabeth was born to Michael and Mary Jane Cochran, the third of five children and the elder of two daughters. She was known to everyone in town as "Pink"; it was a nickname she came by early on, arising from her mother's predilection to dress her in pink clothing, in sharp contrast to the drab browns and grays worn by the other local children. Pink seems to have been a high-spirited, rather headstrong girl, though much of what is known of her early years comes from her own recollections in publicity stories written after she became famous, at least some of which seem designed mainly to burnish the already developing legend of the intrepid young journalist. One story published in *The World,* for instance (the headline of which claimed to provide her "authentic biography"), told how she was an insatiable reader as a girl, and how she herself wrote scores of stories, scribbling them in the flyleaves of books and on whatever scraps of paper she could find. Nights she lay awake in bed, her mind aflame with imagined stories of heroes and heroines, fairy tales and romances: "So active was the child's brain and so strongly her faculties eluded sleep that her condition became alarming and she had to be placed under the care of physicians." *The World*'s professions of Bly's childhood love for reading and writing, though, are not to be found in other accounts, and in the family history, *Chronicles of the Cochrans: Being a Series of Historical Events and Narratives in Which the Members of This Family Have Played a Prominent Part,* one of her relatives commented somewhat tartly that among the teachers in Apollo's sole schoolhouse, Pink Cochran "acquired more conspicuous notice for riotous conduct than profound scholarship."

Pink's father, Michael Cochran, had become wealthy as a grist mill proprietor and real estate speculator, and he was prominent enough to have been elected an associate justice of the county, after which he was always known by the honorific "Judge." (The nearby hamlet of Cochran's Mills, where Pink lived for her first five years, was named after him.) When Pink was six years old, though, Judge Cochran suddenly fell ill and died, without having left behind a will; according to Pennsylvania law, a wife was not entitled to an inheritance without being specifically named in a husband's will, and by the time his fortune had been parceled out among his heirs (including nine grown children from a previous marriage), Pink's mother, Mary Jane, ended up with little more than the household furniture, a horse and carriage, and a small weekly stipend. Now raising five children on her own, she embarked on an ill-conceived marriage to a man who turned out to be a drunkard and an abuser. After five miserable years Mary Jane took the highly unusual step of filing for divorce; Pink herself testified on her mother's behalf, recounting for the court an awful litany of her stepfather's offenses against her mother. At only fourteen years of age, she had learned all she needed to know about what could befall a woman who was not financially independent.

Pink was determined that one day she would support her mother and herself, and the next year she was sent to a nearby boarding school that specialized in training young women to be teachers. For the fifteen-year-old, the school must have been a welcome opportunity to create a new identity for herself—it was there that Pink Cochran added the silent *e* to the end of her surname—but unfortunately her mother was forced to withdraw her after only a single semester; the family simply did not have enough money for Pink to continue her schooling. This fact seems to have been embarrassing to Nellie Bly, and she omitted it from her own stories about herself. That "authentic" biographical story in *The World,* presumably based on information provided by Bly, asserted instead that she had left "on account of threatening heart disease": even one more year of studies, her physician was said to have advised her, could come at the cost of her life. "She was anxious to continue her studies," *The World* solemnly explained, "but she didn't want to die."

In 1880, when Pink was sixteen, Mary Jane Cochran moved with her children to Pittsburgh, some thirty-five miles away. She was hoping to leave behind the death and divorce with which she had come to be associated in Apollo, but Pittsburgh must at times have seemed a hard bargain. Anthony Trollope once called Pittsburgh "without exception, the blackest place which I ever saw." It was a city given over almost entirely to manufacture, where within a few dozen square miles nearly five hundred factories turned out the steel, iron, brass, copper, cotton, oil, and glass hungrily consumed by an industrializing nation. On the horizon, in every direction, smoke poured from unseen furnaces. At night the sky burned yellow and red. The city's wind carried flecks of graphite; the air smelled of sulfur, and a long walk brought a taste of metal on the tongue. There were unexpected showers of soot. In a neighborhood with a skyline of steeples and onion domes, where railroad tracks wound through backyards, Mary Jane bought a small row house for her family; eventually, like many of the city's homeowners, she earned a bit of extra income by renting out a room to boarders. For the next four years Pink helped support the family by taking whatever positions she could find, including as a kitchen girl; she may also have found work as a nanny, a housekeeper, and a private tutor. (Her older brothers, having even less education than she, found jobs as a corresponding clerk and the manager of a rubber company.)

Though Pittsburgh's population at the time was only about 150,000, the city was able to support ten daily newspapers, more than any other American city of its size. Pink Cochrane was a regular reader of one of them, the *Pittsburg Dispatch,* where the most popular columnist was Erasmus Wilson, who wrote under the name "The Quiet Observer," or simply "Q. O." Wilson was a courtly older gentleman, and in his "Quiet Observations" he liked to espouse what he saw as traditional Victorian values. In one column he took to task modern women "who think they are out of their spheres and go around giving everybody fits for not helping them to find them." A "woman's sphere," he bluntly concluded, "is defined and located by a single word—home."

The column, with its high-flown disregard for the realities of women's lives, outraged Pink Cochrane, and she sat down and composed a long letter to the editor of the *Dispatch.* As was then the custom among those who wrote letters to newspapers, she signed it with a pseudonym: "Lonely Orphan Girl." (It was perhaps an odd choice of name—her mother, after all, was still alive—but it was a poignant reminder of the impact of her father's death, a blow from which the family had never recovered.) The letter caught the attention of the paper's new managing editor, George A. Madden, who placed a notice in the next issue of the *Dispatch* asking "Orphan Girl" to send him her name and address.

The very next afternoon the writer herself unexpectedly arrived at the *Dispatch* office. She was twenty years old but looked even younger; Erasmus Wilson would recall her from that morning as "a shy little girl." She was slimly built, of medium height, with large, somewhat mournful-looking gray eyes and a broad mouth above a square-set chin. She wore a long black cloak and a simple fur hat; her hair, which she had not yet taken to wearing up, fell in auburn curls around the shoulders of her coat. The young woman was plainly uncomfortable in her surroundings, intimidated by her first visit to a city newsroom. In a voice that barely rose above a whisper, she asked an office boy where she might find the editor.

"That is the gentleman," the boy said, and he pointed toward Madden sitting a few feet away.

Seeing the dapperly mustached young editor, she broke into a smile, revealing a physical detail often remarked upon by those who met her: a dazzlingly white set of teeth. "Oh, is it?" she exclaimed. "I expected to see an old, cross man."

George Madden told her that he was not going to print her letter; instead, he said, he wanted her to write an article of her own on the question of "the woman's sphere." Neither Bly nor Madden ever recorded her immediate reaction to his request, but the prospect of actually writing for a newspaper, after four years of tramping Pittsburgh's soot-darkened streets in pursuit of menial work with little hope of ever finding anything better, must have meant everything to her; within the week she had turned the article in to Madden. Her grammar was rough, her punctuation erratic (for years George Madden was heard to complain about the amount of blue pencil he had expended on her pieces), but the writing was forceful and her voice clear and strong. She had chosen to address the question from the perspective of those women who did not have the privileges "Q. O." had summarily granted them: poor women who needed to work to support their families. It was an impassioned plea for understanding and sympathy, into which she must have poured some of her own despair at the conditions of her life and that of her mother:

> Can they that have full and plenty of this world's goods realize what it is to be a poor working woman, abiding in one or two bare rooms, without fire enough to keep warm, while her threadbare clothes refuse to protect her from the wind and cold, and denying herself the necessary food that her little ones may not go hungry; fearing the landlord's frown and threat to cast her out and sell what little she has, begging for employment of any kind that she may earn enough to pay for the bare rooms she calls home, no one to speak kindly to or encourage her, nothing to make life worth the living?

So Elizabeth Cochrane came to be hired as a reporter for the *Dispatch,* at a salary of five dollars a week. Before her next article was published (this one on divorced women, another subject close to her heart), George

Madden called her into his office and informed her that she needed a pen name. At the time, it was considered uncouth for a woman to sign her own name to a news story. The *Dispatch*'s own Elizabeth Wilkinson Wade wrote as "Bessie Bramble"; in New York, Sara Payson Willis was "Fanny Fern"; in Boston, Sally Joy (which itself sounded like a pen name) was known instead as "Penelope Penfeather." He was looking for a name, George Madden said, that was "neat and catchy." Together the two considered several possibilities, but none seemed quite right. It was late in the afternoon; the light from the gas lamps cast flickering shadows on the wallpaper. From upstairs an editor called for his copy. An office boy walked by whistling a popular tune of the day, written by the local songwriter Stephen Foster:

> *Nelly Bly! Nelly Bly! Bring de broom along,*
> *We'll sweep de kitchen clean, my dear,*
> *And hab a little song.*

The name was short, it was catchy, and best of all, the public already liked it. Madden instructed the typesetter to give the story the byline "Nelly Bly"—but the typesetter misspelled the first name, and as a result of the erratum she was forever after Nellie Bly.

OF THE 12,308 AMERICANS listed as journalists in the 1880 U.S. census, only 288—just over 2 percent—were women. The number whose writing appeared in the news sections of the newspaper, as Nellie Bly's would in the *Dispatch,* was far smaller still. By the 1880s many American papers, recognizing that women were an as yet untapped market, had created a separate women's page, featuring articles devoted to the topics in which women were thought to be most interested: fashion, shopping, recipes, homemaking, child rearing, and the doings of high society. Articles discussing the medicinal uses of arrowroot, or the proper sequence of brown and white sauces in a formal dinner, or the gowns worn at a recent cotillion, or why women were afraid of mice—the women's page was where they would appear, written in a suitably cozy tone, and likely interspersed with earnest couplets about love or the weather, and perhaps a review of a new romantic novel or volume of poetry. The articles were not only directed at women but were overwhelmingly written by them;

male editors justified their reliance on female contributors to fill this section by explaining that it was where their natural aptitude lay—as, for instance, the editor of the *New York Telegram,* who once pointed out that in reporting on society functions, "A man must examine minutely a woman's costume in order to describe it, where a woman would take the whole thing in at a glance."

For some female journalists it was where they felt most comfortable, but for others the banishment to the women's page brought only boredom, frustration, and despair at the waste of their talents. In an 1890 *Harper's Weekly* article entitled "A Woman's Experience of Newspaper Work," a reporter who gave her name only as J.L.H. described her long and fruitless effort to escape society reporting. "I think there is no class of employment in the world which I would have liked less than professional intrusion upon the august movements of the élite," she wrote; "but again it was no question of choice. I was obliged to accept the position of society reporter because managers stoutly maintained that there was nothing else about a newspaper office which a woman could do." The year before, in an article for *The Journalist,* the newspaper writer Flora McDonald likewise bemoaned the sorry lot of the intelligent, ambitious female reporter forced to attend one dreary society event after another. "Life," wrote McDonald, "becomes to her one long-drawn-out five o'clock tea of somebody else. She is in the swim, but not of it, and, recording the flops and flounders of the big fish, she in time descends to a state of mental and moral petrifaction that is simply awful. One woman says 'society reporting is prostitution of brains.' Oh, that it were no worse! It is prostitution of soul, too."

The female contributors to the women's page rarely appeared in the newspaper office itself; far more often they wrote their pieces at home and sent them in by mail. Like the saloon or the voting booth, the newsroom was considered an improper place for a woman, as it naturally included a good deal of cigar smoking and tobacco chewing, the occasional slug from a bottle or flask, and copious use of what were then termed Anglo-Saxon words. In 1892 a shocked editor was heard to exclaim, when asked if he would ever hire a woman to work in his newsroom, "A woman—never! Why, you can't say d—— to a woman!" The newsroom was a place where men could smoke and drink and swear without fear of a woman's disapproval, and also without fear of corrupting her character, as exposure to the harsh realities of big-city newspaper life was generally believed to erode the qualities in women most prized by men. "I have never yet seen a girl enter the newspaper field but that I have noticed a steady decline in that innate sense of refinement, gentleness and womanliness with which she entered it," observed one male newspaper editor. "Young womanhood," rhapsodized another, "is too sweet and sacred a thing to couple with the life of careless manner, hasty talk, and unconventional action that seems inevitable in a newspaper office."

For all of the airy talk, though, exclusion from the newsroom had very real and damaging effects on the chances of a woman's career success. As journalism schools did not yet exist, young reporters traditionally learned their trade in what was called the school of experience—one that female reporters found almost impossible to enter. Routinely a young man was brought into a newspaper office to serve as an office boy (the very term indicated who was expected to occupy the position), where he swept the floor, delivered copy, ran errands, learned what an editor expected of his reporters and subeditors, and watched how stories were written and rewritten, over time gaining increasingly greater responsibilities, which, if all went well, ultimately led to his being allowed to try his hand at reporting. When his work was found to be lacking, the offense was most often met not with an editor's gentle admonishment but with long and fluent tirades of abuse, punctuated by curses and threats against his health, the type of rough instruction that had long been understood to be the most effective means of imparting newspaper wisdom, but that most editors would not dare impose on more delicate female sensibilities. And so the young newspaperwoman was left to ply her trade on teas and trousseaux while the rest of the world went on without her.

"A great deal of the practical training of a newspaper office is beyond the sphere into which a woman can enter," The Epoch pointed out in 1889, "and the scope of her work, no less than the fullness of her information, must be limited by this fact." It simply would not do to ask a woman to perform the tasks routinely asked of male reporters—to travel by herself at night, and in all kinds of weather; to pursue stories wherever they led, into tenements and dance halls and barrooms and gambling dens; to consort with criminals and policemen alike; to be present at riots and strikes and fires and other municipal disturbances; to uncover the lies spoken and misdeeds committed by men who held positions of power.

For a woman to engage in such behavior was not only risky, it was also improper, undignified, and unseemly: in a word, unladylike.

Of course, there were notable exceptions to the rule, women who proved themselves to be outstanding journalists, such as the political reporter Jane Grey Swisshelm. A feminist and abolitionist, Swisshelm was also a contributor to Horace Greeley's *New York Tribune*. In 1850, during a brief visit to Washington, she came to call on Vice President Millard Fillmore, asking him to assign her a press seat in the Senate gallery. "He was much surprised and tried to dissuade me," Swisshelm recalled later; the vice president said that she would attract unwanted attention, that "the place would be very unpleasant for a lady." But Swisshelm was persistent, and finally Fillmore relented. The next day she observed Senate proceedings from a seat in the gallery—the first woman ever to do so. In one of her columns Jane Grey Swisshelm ridiculed the scorn and consternation directed at women who had decided that they wanted to go into journalism, or any other intellectual profession:

> They plough, harrow, reap, dig, make hay, rake, bind grain, thrash, chop wood, milk, churn, do anything that is hard work, physical labor, and who says anything against it? But let one presume to use her mental powers—let her aspire to turn editor, public speaker, doctor, lawyer—take up any profession or avocation which is deemed honorable and requires talent, and O! bring cologne, get a cambric kerchief and feather fan, unloose his corsets and take off his cravat! What a fainting fit Mr. Propriety has taken! Just to think that "one of the dear creatures"—the heavenly angels—should forsake the sphere—women's sphere—to mix with the wicked strife of this wicked world!

In the United States, of course, the press had always been one of the centers of social power, the so-called fourth estate, and throughout the nineteenth century the near-total segregation of women within it was justified as being for their own good (by not exposing them to coarse male behavior) or, conversely, by their own fault. Though women writers were widely acknowledged to possess wit, imagination, liveliness, and sympathy in abundance, they supposedly lacked other qualities—good judgment, lucid thinking, and clarity of prose—that were essential for proper journalism. "Women enjoy a reputation for slipshod style," the British writer Arnold Bennett observed in his 1898 book *Journalism for Women: A Practical Guide*. "They have earned it." Among the weaknesses that Bennett diagnosed in women's writing were wordiness, overuse of metaphor and simile, and, more generally, "gush and a tendency to hysteria." It was an opinion not infrequently shared by women who had succeeded in other fields of writing, such as, for instance, the renowned poet Julia Ward Howe, who in the pages of *The Epoch* advised newspaper editors not to employ "women of fluent pen and chaotic mind, who can furnish a farrago of sentiment or of satire upon a variety of topics without any availing perception of judgment regarding any one of them." In the monthly *The Galaxy,* another poet and essayist of the day, Nelly Mackay Hutchinson, took women writers to task for slovenliness, spitefulness, and a "jelly-like inaccuracy of thought and expression." Before a woman could be entrusted with a responsible position on a newspaper, pronounced Hutchinson, "both the nature and social position of woman must be transformed. . . . She must have constant practiced political experience. And she must never let her sympathies, prejudices, and antipathies run too violently away with her. While woman is woman I'm afraid that this latter requirement will not be met."

Unprotected by either a union or a press club—the Women's Press Club was not founded until 1889—women reporters had to pursue their trade in a work environment that all too often included unwanted sexual advances (one anonymous female journalist of the time attested, "Women in absolutely every other line of work are not assailed to such an extent by individuals of the opposite sex as is the newspaper woman") and salaries much lower than those earned by their male colleagues. In *Harper's,* J.L.H. noted that she was often not paid at all for her published work, while another writer said that she was paid in "compliments" rather than cash. Another estimated that she wrote for more than two years before she ever received her first five-dollar payment.

The female journalist who resisted these inequities, who defied social convention, who endured despite the many obstacles placed in her way, was a kind of pioneer, marking out new territory in a forbidding landscape with few protections and few companions to share the load. As late as 1889, the year that Nellie Bly and Elizabeth Bisland set off around the world (by which time enough women had entered the field that *The Journalist* published a "special women's issue" celebrating the work of female journalists, Bly and Bisland among them), Flora McDonald could still point out that for "any well-balanced woman who works among newspaper men, one thousand and one causes make hers the miserable experience of a freak—the 'only and original one of its kind on earth.'" The successful female journalist, McDonald suggested, should be composed of "one part nerve and two parts India rubber."

IN HER FIRST MONTHS at the *Dispatch,* Nellie Bly produced an eight-part series on the working conditions faced by women in Pittsburgh's factories. It was the sort of piece she did best: about people much like her, working people, especially women, who tried to maintain their dignity, perhaps even have a bit of fun, in the face of hardship. At the *Dispatch* she wrote about clerks and chorus girls, servants and religious sectarians. She advocated the establishment of a women's version of the Young Men's Christian Association, where "poor girls" would find "a place that will offer and give assistance." Bly did all she could to resist being confined to the women's page; she was, as she would later write, "too impatient to work along at the usual duties assigned women on newspapers." Still, George Madden insisted, and eventually she found herself writing articles on topics including ladies' hair care, rubber raincoats, and a local minister with a collection of fifty thousand butterflies.

One evening, about nine months after she had started work at the *Dispatch,* Bly was listening to two of her family's boarders, young railroad workers, discuss their plans someday to travel to Mexico; it was possible, they said, to take a train the whole way there. That night she was too excited to sleep; early the next morning she hurried into the *Dispatch* office and begged George Madden to allow her to become the paper's correspondent in Mexico. Madden replied that the idea was out of the question. It was far too dangerous, he said; too many Americans had traveled below the border and simply disappeared. Still Bly persisted, and eventually, possibly by enticing the editor with the prospect of the circulation gains that might be gotten, she managed to win Madden over.

Bly was thrilled by the prospect of the new journalistic enterprise that awaited her, but shortly before her departure she experienced an uncharacteristic loss of nerve at the prospect of traveling alone and asked her mother if she would like to come along as a chaperone. By this time

Nellie's four siblings were either working or married, and her mother agreed to join her. Bly secured railroad tickets for them, and together they set off for Mexico.

The trip south was dreamlike, full of unexpected vistas. One evening as they went to bed the surrounding hills were covered with snow; the next morning, when they arose from their bunks, the world was warm and in bloom. From the train's observation car the two women gazed awestruck at the vast expanses of land. They passed cotton fields that, waving in the breeze, looked like foaming breakers rushing toward the shore; they inhaled the perfume of immense, gaudily colored flowers. After three days they reached the town of El Paso, where, with some regrets at the prospect of the trip's end, they boarded an overnight train for Mexico City.

Nellie Bly spent five months in Mexico. Seemingly unhampered by what she admitted was her "very limited Spanish," she brought the *Dispatch*'s readers along with her to bullfights, theaters, historic tombs; in Mexico City she found a street, apparently unknown to Americans, on which there was nothing but coffin manufacturers. Time and again, in her wandering, she encountered something that surprised or delighted her: the wreaths woven of honeysuckle and roses worn by native women on the Feast of the Flowers; ice cream made by pouring sweetened milk over snow brought down from a nearby volcano; teenage boys calling up to the balconies of their beloved, like a scene out of *Romeo and Juliet*. She observed how in Mexico it was considered polite, even complimentary, for a man to stare at a woman on the streets—"I might add," she wrote, "that the men, by this rule, are remarkably polite." She visited remote villages patrolled by their own armies, where the soldiers smoked cigarettes made from an herb called marijuana, each taking a draw and blowing the smoke into the mouth of the man sitting next to him; the intoxication was said to last five days, "and for that period they are in Paradise."

The longer she spent in Mexico, the more clearly she could see that almost everything Americans thought they knew about the country was wrong. The Mexicans she had met, Bly told her readers, were in the main not malicious, quarrelsome, dissolute, or dishonest; in fact, the worst purveyors of untruths about Mexico—the colony of expatriate Americans living there—were the very ones who treated the natives the most shabbily, who took kindnesses as insults and addressed faithful servants as beasts and fools. Nor during her time in Mexico had she ever experienced the dangers about which she had been so fulsomely warned, all the lazy-minded American clichés about how thieves and murderers lurked around every corner. She wrote, "The women—I am sorry to say it—are safer here than on our streets, where it is supposed everybody has the advantage of education and civilization."

Bly was sending her reports regularly back to Pittsburgh, where they were published in the *Dispatch;* eventually word of one of her articles, about the arrest of a local newspaper editor who had dared to criticize the government, came to the attention of some Mexican government officials. Before long they were threatening to arrest her for violating Article 33 of the country's constitution, which barred foreigners from participating "in any way" in Mexico's politics. Facing the prospect of an extended stay in a Mexican jail, Bly returned to Pittsburgh with her mother, one month earlier than they had intended. Back home, she lashed out at the corruption of the Mexican political system, which she derided as "a republic only in name, being in reality the worst monarchy in existence." One of her articles described how the recently retired president Manuel González had enriched himself by some $25 million during his four years in office; another criticized Mexico's newspapers as little more than "tools of the organized ring." The Mexican people themselves understood how newspapers were complicit in their exploitation, and as a consequence it was possible to travel all day in Mexico and never see a man reading one. "They possess such a disgust for newspapers," Bly observed, "that they will not even use one of them as a subterfuge to hide behind in a street car when some woman with a dozen bundles, three children and two baskets is looking for a seat."

At the age of twenty-one Nellie Bly had proven herself resilient enough to subsist for months on a monotonous, unfamiliar diet, sleeping on mattresses infested with bedbugs; had overcome all the obstacles thrown up by a foreign language; had been astute enough, and courageous enough, to stand up for herself when crooked hotelkeepers and street vendors tried to cheat her. She was proud of herself for demonstrating, in her words, that "a free American girl can accommodate herself to circumstances without the aid of a man." George Madden had now raised her salary at the *Dispatch* to fifteen dollars a week, but Bly simply could not bear the thought of returning to the women's page; for three months after coming home she fought with the city editor over the stories assigned to her.

Nellie Bly had once told Erasmus Wilson that she had four goals in life: to work for a New York newspaper, to reform the world, to fall in love, and to marry a millionaire. The first, at least, seemed immediately attainable. One day in April she simply did not show up for work; no one in the office knew where she was, until someone found the note she had left for Wilson. *Dear Q. O.,* she had written,

I am off for New York. Look out for me.
                                    BLY.

CHAPTER 2

The Newspaper Gods
of Gotham

ONE AND A HALF MILLION PEOPLE, MORE OR LESS, WERE THEN LIVING on the island of Manhattan, and the greater metropolitan area was home to roughly four and a half million people—about one-fifteenth of the population of the United States as a whole, or one out of every three hundred people then living in the entire world.

Half of all the commerce that entered the United States came through New York, and three-quarters of the immigrants; the clerks of the city's post office handled more than a billion letters each year, and another forty thousand tons of newspapers. Around Manhattan, local branches of the Western Union telegraph company were connected to the main office on Broadway by a series of pneumatic tubes. Every day at noon a ball was dropped from a flagpole in front of the Western Union office; a few minutes before that, a crowd of onlookers began to gather, all waiting to set their watches. On the streets everyone seemed to be late for an appointment. The opening page of a tourist guide to New York promised "the crush of carriages, drays, trucks, and other vehicles, private and public, roaring and rattling over the stone-paved streets; the crowds of swiftly-moving men walking as if not to lose a second of time, their faces preoccupied and eager." Visiting the city, the British philosopher Herbert Spencer warned its inhabitants that "Immense injury is done by this high-pressure life" and counseled what he called "the gospel of relaxation." The latest style of men's canes had watches concealed in their handles. Few restaurants in commercial areas could prosper that did not offer the so-called quick lunch for their patrons, and recent years had brought an even more startling development: "lunches sent out," as the new culinary fashion was called, meals delivered on trays directly to the work desk, so that a banker or broker might snatch a few quick bites of his sandwich without missing even a single minute of work. "A life-curtailing habit it is no doubt," editorialized the *Tribune,* "but it illustrates the high voltage system under which business is done in this, the world's busiest commercial centre."

Overhead, electric wires strung from poles formed an intricate web carrying power for the city's lights, telephones, telegraphs, ticker tapes; the wires ran in heavy strands from pole to pole, giving New York the appearance of being permanently draped in black bunting. In the evenings, incandescent light poured from streetlamps, from hotel lobbies and the windows of department stores, the individual splashes of light pooling into a pale radiant haze that hung over Broadway from Union Square up to the midtown theater district. In less heavily trafficked areas, tall standards erected in the center of squares threw down beams of light that gave trees an eerie shimmer and turned the world the black and white of a photograph.

From the streets came an incessant drumming of iron on stone, hooves pounding on paving blocks. Untold thousands of horses pulled the carts, carriages, hansom cabs, omnibuses, and streetcars of the city. When it rained, the horses' manure slicked the cobblestones with a stinking brown ooze; in drier months the pulverized manure formed clouds of dust that blew through the air to join the blacker smoke produced by the engines of the Elevated Railway. *What is there dirtier than some streets in New York?* went the joke making the rounds. *Why, other streets in New York, of course.*

In the summer of 1881 a journalist for *Scientific American* magazine reported that during a single day in the city he had made a dozen office visits, all but one of which required the use of an elevator; by the end of the day, he calculated, he had been lifted sixty-two stories, or more than eight hundred feet into the air. The invention of the elevator had changed everything in New York (sometimes in unpredictable ways: a currently debated etiquette question was whether a gentleman should remove his hat in an elevator in the presence of a lady), and the city, which from its inception had spread inexorably across the land mass of Manhattan Island, was now extending itself into the as yet unconquered geography of the sky. Slender, extravagantly decorated skyscrapers—*sky-piercers,* as they were sometimes called then—rose in hues of red and brown and white, their shafts clad in sandstone and marble and granite, stones dug from the earth and piled ever higher into the air.

Along Park Row, the heart of New York's newspaper district, a line of tall buildings, many of them topped by mansard roofs, seemed to form the dark battlement of a medieval fortress. The Tribune Building's clock tower soared 285 feet into the sky, higher even than the steeple of Trinity Church, the quaint spire that had long dominated the downtown skyline. Nearby, at the *Times,* the paper's owners wanted a taller office tower; not finding an available location that was as desirable as the present one on Park Row, they decided to build the new tower around the old one. It was a highly impressive feat of engineering, made all the more so by the fact that the paper had kept on publishing all the while, not missing a

Park Row in the 1890s. The World Building, with its golden dome,
is at the left of the photo; the Tribune Building is at the center,
and the New York Times Building at the right.

single day's issue in the process. The *Sun*'s offices were in an older five-story building on the corner of Spruce and Nassau Streets, but the relative modesty of the structure was at least partly compensated for by its legacy as the former clubhouse for Tammany Hall. Near the end of 1889 Joseph Pulitzer's four-year-old son, Joseph Jr., would dedicate the cornerstone for *The World*'s new office building on Park Row, one destined to reach the never-before-seen height of eighteen stories, its brick and sandstone body topped by a gilded copper dome that could be seen for miles in any direction. From his sickbed in Wiesbaden, Joseph Pulitzer sent a message that *The World*'s soaring tower was an ideal representation of a newspaper "forever rising to a higher plane of perfection as a Public Institution"; a rather less elevated notion came from the editors working on the building's eleventh floor, who delighted in the fact that they could lean out a window, if they ever felt like it, and spit on the *Sun*.

IN THE SPRING OF 1887, wearing a flowered hat she had bought in Mexico, Nellie Bly arrived in New York. She took a small furnished room in a building on West Ninety-sixth Street; it was at the upper reaches of settled Manhattan, where Broadway was known as Western Boulevard, a name that befitted the frontier feel of the neighborhood. This far north the boulevard was just a dirt road that the city would not get around to paving for another three years; the skyline was low and distinctly gap-toothed in appearance, forlorn houses poking up between vacant lots where goats foraged among the rocks. For the first time in her life, Bly was living by herself; she had left her mother behind in Pittsburgh, with the promise that she would send for her when she found regular work in New York.

Her room on Ninety-sixth Street was about as far from the newspaper district in lower Manhattan as it was possible to be. The trip downtown began with a half-hour ride aboard one of the steam locomotives of the Ninth Avenue Elevated Railway, from the Ninety-third Street station six miles south to Barclay Street; from there she still had a long walk due east to Park Row, the little street that ran diagonally northeast from lower Broadway, fronted on its western side by the greenery of City Hall Park. (A one-sided street, the city's wags liked to remark, provided the perfect home for one-sided newspapers.) She had with her a letter of in-

troduction from Edward Dulzer, a Pittsburgh acquaintance whose influence could not have been as great as Bly had hoped, for despite all her
efforts she didn't manage to obtain even a single interview with anyone
connected with a New York newspaper. Her savings, and her hopes,
began to dwindle. She spent much of the summer supporting herself as
best she could by writing freelance articles for the *Dispatch,* precisely the
type she hated most: Sunday style pieces on the latest fashions worn by
the women of New York. One day she received a letter forwarded to her
by the *Dispatch;* it had been sent by a young woman in Pittsburgh who
hoped to become a journalist and wondered if New York was the best
place for a woman to do so. Nellie Bly knew that she had nothing but
discouragement to offer her correspondent. Was there in fact a place for
a woman journalist in New York? Pondering the question, she was struck
by an idea for a story and suddenly felt the twinge of excitement, at one
time so familiar to her, that she had not felt in a long while: presenting
herself as the *Dispatch*'s New York correspondent, she would arrange to
meet with the editors of the city's six most influential newspapers to interview them on that very subject. She wanted, as she would later write,
"to obtain the opinion of the newspaper gods of Gotham."

The first newspaper she went to was the *Sun.* Bly climbed a spiral
staircase up a lightless shaft to the third-floor city room, where Charles A.
Dana, the paper's powerful editor and publisher, had his office. To an
unsuspecting visitor the city room seemed a kind of bedlam, a thunder of
loud conversations and barked epithets; the band of worried-looking office boys rushing from editor to reporter and back again gave the scene
the frantic topsy-turvy of a music hall farce. At inclined tables, reporters
wrote out their stories longhand, in pencil, seemingly oblivious to the
commotion swirling around them. Sunlight from the overhead windows
was refracted through a blue haze of cigar smoke. Nearly everyone, it
seemed, wore a hat, a tradition dating back to New York journalism's
more raffish early days, when wearing one's hat at all times was the surest
method of preventing it from being stolen. In deference to the summer
heat, suit coats and vests had been removed to the backs of chairs, revealing white shirts with high celluloid collars and dark trousers held up by
white suspenders. The older men wore beards, the younger ones mus-
taches; there were no women in the city room. Charles Dana preferred
men for the *Sun,* and not just any men but college men, and ideally col-

lege men with a classical background. "If I could have my way," he once remarked, "every young man who is going to be a newspaper man, and who is not absolutely rebellious against it, should learn Greek and Latin after the good old fashion." He believed he could find no better man to cover a prizefight or spelling bee than one who had read Tacitus and Sophocles and could scan the odes of Horace. Abhorring nothing as much as a typographical error, he sought to make his newspaper stand as a daily testimonial to correct English usage. Once a writer for another paper sent him a sheaf of his best articles, in hopes of obtaining a job at the *Sun;* later the writer was surprised to find that the editor had returned the copy unmarked and uncommented upon, other than a single thick black line inscribed under the offending phrase *none are.*

Charles Anderson Dana was sixty-eight years old, with a bald head and the long white beard of a biblical patriarch. Ushering Nellie Bly into the relative quiet of his office, he offered her a rickety wooden chair and then took a seat in his own leather-bound one. The room was small and cluttered with the emblems of responsibility. The top of the black walnut desk was nearly hidden beneath piles of articles and correspondence yet to be attended to; it held an inkpot and pen, a pair of scissors, and a revolving bookcase for handy consultation of reference books, atop which stood, incongruously, a large stuffed owl. There was an umbrella rack, a Turkish rug, and a horsehide-covered lounge chair in the event the editor ever felt the need for a nap. Above the mantel hung portraits of Jefferson, Jackson, and Lincoln.

Dana regarded Nellie Bly carefully from behind his gold-rimmed spectacles. Seven years after this interview, he would tell a group of students at Cornell University that the problem with hiring women, especially pretty ones, was that too often they got married and quit—"and there the poor editor is left, helpless and without consolation." Now the editor considered the question that Bly had put to him. "I think if they have the ability," he said slowly, "there is no reason why they should not do the work as well as men. But I do not think they can, as a class, do equally good work, for the very reason that women have never been educated up to it in the same manner as men."

Bly asked, "Are you opposed to women as journalists, Mr. Dana?"

"No. If a woman can do assigned work as well as a man, there is no reason why there should be discrimination to her disfavor. And yet, while a woman might be ever so clever in obtaining news and putting it into words, we would not feel at liberty to call her out at one o'clock in the morning to report at a fire or a crime. In such a case we never hesitate with a man. That is why the latter is preferable."

To this Nellie Bly made no reply. She could feel the room tremble with the vibrations of printing presses working beneath the street. "Accuracy," Dana continued expansively, "is the greatest gift in a journalist. It is difficult for most people, when told that two and two make four, not to write that they make five, or three, or anything except the exact truth. Women are generally worse than men in this regard. They find it impossible not to exaggerate."

"Have you many women applicants for positions on the *Sun*?"

"Not very many. We have a great number of men, but not women."

"Then you think women have a chance in the journalistic field?"

"Anyone with ability has a chance. There is always a demand for people who have ability or talent, and I presume it would be appreciated in a woman as well as a man; but men are preferable because they are educated up to the business."

Finally Nellie Bly came to the question with which she herself had been struggling all summer. She asked, "How do women secure positions in New York?"

At this she observed that Dana's eyes seemed to twinkle behind his glasses, as though amused by the absurdity of the question. "I really cannot say," was his only reply.

The editor of the *Herald,* the Reverend Dr. Hepworth, informed Nellie Bly that the public was unfortunately interested in scandal and sensation, and "a gentleman could not in delicacy ask a woman to have anything to do with that class of news." Mr. Miller of the *Times* said that he could not with any accuracy describe the feelings of the profession regarding female journalists, because during his years at the paper he had never discussed the matter with his colleagues. "Women are invaluable to a newspaper," insisted Mr. Coates of the *Mail and Express;* although their dress, habits, and constitution prevented them from the routine work of reporting, they were perfectly suited for "society, fashion, and general gossip." This point was echoed by Mr. Morris of the *Telegram.* Women, he acknowledged, were more ambitious than men, and had more energy, but an editor couldn't very well send a woman out on an emergency story, where she might have to slide down a banister or run up several flights of stairs four steps at a time: "That's where a man gets the best of her as a New York reporter."

At *The World,* John Cockerill explained that the problem, as he saw it, was that women didn't want to do the sort of work they were most suited for—fashion and society reporting. "What they are fitted for," he said, "is so limited that a man is of far greater service." He hastened to add, however, that *The World* did have two women on its staff—"So you see we do not object personally."

Later, Nellie Bly would sum up the views of the newspaper editors she had interviewed that day. "We have more women now than we want," she wrote. "Women are no good, anyway."

NELLIE BLY'S ARTICLE for the *Dispatch,* entitled "Women Journalists," earned an approving mention in *The Journalist,* the industry's trade magazine, which noted that "Miss Nellie Bly . . . came here from Pittsburg[h] where she made name and fame and cash." In New York, however, Bly could not find work. The low point arrived in a single, heart-stopping moment in September, when she discovered that her purse had been stolen. The purse contained one hundred dollars, her entire life's savings. She stood still for a moment, trying to regain her bearings. The sun beat down; a white haze rose from the pavement like a wraith. She knew she could not return to Pittsburgh, admitting by her presence that the great city of New York had proven unconquerable. There was a maxim by which she had always tried to live, *Energy rightly applied and directed will accomplish anything,* and now, at her lowest ebb, the saying rose again into her mind. Rallying herself, she walked home, borrowed ten cents' carfare from her landlady, and then rode all the way back downtown to the World Building at 31-32 Park Row. On the thumb of her left hand she wore a slender gold ring; that ring, she had always believed, brought her good luck, something she was very much in need of now.

Somehow Nellie Bly managed to get past the security guard at the front door—"I had to do a great deal of talking," was all she ever said about those desperate moments—and into the building's lobby, where an elevator carried her up to John Cockerill's office. But his door was closed, and the clerk who sat outside it informed her in no uncertain terms that the editor in chief was not to be disturbed. Bly, though, would not be

Nellie Bly

denied; she took a seat in the outer office and waited. Somewhere below her was a large room where a hundred compositors converted columns of manuscript into columns of lead; in a subterranean chamber ribbons of paper unspooled from immense cylinders into presses that dropped out printed sheets as smoothly as grains of sand in an hourglass; on a loading dock, mailbags were being tied up for delivery to the Post Office, the hulking gray structure that loomed over the park and threw the World Building into shadow each afternoon. Nearby, in a silk-curtained atelier, artists with steel-tipped pens were bringing crime scenes to life. Men hurried past her brandishing important-looking pieces of paper; these were, she knew, telegrams, cabled in to the office from the paper's correspondents around the world. Still she sat. She had a very important story to propose, she insisted to the clerk, and if the editor of *The World* would not see her, then she had no choice but to go to some other paper and give it to them. Perhaps Bly added a bit of spurious veracity by mentioning the names of the editors she had recently interviewed; in any event, the threat succeeded, for at last the door was opened and she found herself standing before the desk of *The World*'s editor in chief.

It was not a spot where many people felt comfortable. Colonel Cockerill, as he was generally known (this was an honorary title, for he had risen no higher than private during his Civil War service), was an imposing man, over six feet tall, with a massive head and the solid bulk of a stevedore. He had a drooping walrus mustache and black hair just beginning to gray. More often than not a cigar could be seen poking out from beneath that bushy mustache; over the course of a day ashes accumulated like snowdrifts in the folds of his waistcoat. Cockerill could be brusque to the point of rudeness, and he took criticism of his newspaper as a personal affront. Once, when a minister wrote a letter objecting to what he considered an "irreligious" cartoon that had appeared in *The World,* Cockerill wrote a letter of reply that read in its entirety: "My Dear Sir: Will you kindly go to hell?" Around Park Row, his gift for profanity was legendary; he was reputed to be able to swear for ten minutes straight without repeating himself. His specialty was the placement of oaths inside otherwise respectable words—"The problem with that man," he would bellow to an underling, "is that he's too *indegoddampendent*"— which was a trait that he shared with his boss, Joseph Pulitzer. Otherwise the two men, Pulitzer and Cockerill, were constitutionally mismatched. Pulitzer was by nature an introvert and an intellectual; he loved chess, political memoirs, and the novels of George Eliot, and was so sensitive to noise that even the crackling of a piece of paper could cause him physical pain. Cockerill enjoyed the late-night attractions offered by the big city, and after work was often to be found buying rounds for companions at the Rotunda Bar of the Astor House or one of the newspaper district's other watering holes, where he was widely admired for his ability to hold his liquor. Pulitzer had been elected to Congress from New York's Ninth District, but he gave up his seat after only thirteen months when he realized he was more powerful as a publisher than as a politician; Cockerill was the sort of man, a *World* staffer once remarked, who would be selected as an Exalted Ruler of the Elks.

Still, each respected the other's considerable talents, and over the years the two had negotiated an exceedingly successful working relationship. In 1879 Pulitzer had hired Cockerill, then an editor for a Cincinnati newspaper, as managing editor for his *Post-Dispatch* in St. Louis, where Cockerill served for four years, until the Slayback scandal. A St. Louis attorney by the name of Alonzo W. Slayback, incensed by a series of editorials that he believed had impugned the honor of his law partner, burst into the editor's office one evening with a pistol in his hand; when Slayback paused to take off his coat, Cockerill pulled a revolver from his desk drawer and shot him in the chest, killing him. The grand jury declined to indict Cockerill, but more than two thousand St. Louisans canceled their newspaper subscriptions and Pulitzer decided that his position there was no longer tenable. After a decent amount of time had passed, Pulitzer hired Cockerill again to run the paper he had recently purchased in New York, *The World,* and there they resumed their collaboration where it had left off. Pulitzer would later admit to an employee that the way Cockerill had "so coolly killed" Slayback filled him at times with admiration and at other times with repulsion; Cockerill was heard to remark that Pulitzer was "the best man in the world to have in a newspaper office for one hour in the morning" but a "damned nuisance the rest of the day."

Colonel Cockerill did not like ever to be distracted from his work, and Nellie Bly sensed immediately that she should waste none of his time. She presented her idea to him: a trip to Europe, with a return trip in steerage, so that she might describe firsthand for *The World*'s readers the dirty, overcrowded conditions endured by immigrants on their crossing to America. It was an ambitious story, but one that she felt confident she could accomplish, combining the skills she had gained reporting on the working conditions of Pittsburgh factory girls with the foreign reporting she had done in Mexico.

The previous year *The Journalist* had called Cockerill "unquestionably the best news editor in the country," in large part due to his eye for talent, and he must have seen something that he liked in this determined young woman. He gave her twenty-five dollars as a retainer for her services and told her that he would discuss her idea with Joseph Pulitzer. She should come back again later, after he had spoken with the publisher, and he would give her their decision.

Bly returned at the appointed time. John Cockerill informed her that Mr. Pulitzer had rejected the idea about returning from Europe in steerage; for a writer who was new to the paper, Cockerill explained, they preferred a story that was more local in nature. However, Pulitzer himself had suggested a different idea. *The World* had received a tip that the staff of the Blackwell's Island Insane Asylum, on New York's East River, was mistreating the female patients. The paper, though, had been continually frustrated in its efforts to determine if the stories were accurate; the doctors and nurses refused to speak to journalists, and their practices were hidden from view behind barred windows and locked doors. The editors were looking for a female reporter who would feign insanity and allow herself to be remanded to Blackwell's Island, so that she could report firsthand the inner workings of the asylum.

It was the sort of story, ingeniously exposing official misconduct, in which *The World* had come to specialize. It was also the sort of story—one offering at least the possibility of help for a vulnerable, exploited population—that appealed to Nellie Bly.

"Do you think you can work your way into an insane asylum?" Cockerill asked her now.

"I can try," Bly said simply.

"You realize that it is a difficult thing to do. The slightest false move means exposure and failure. The doctors are all clever experts. Do you think you can feign insanity well enough to pass them?"

"Yes, I believe I can." She considered this for a moment. "At least I can make the attempt. I don't know what I can do until I try."

The two decided that she would use the name Nellie Brown; it would be natural for her to answer to her own first name, and the initials *N.B.* would match those already on her linen. Cockerill would do what he could to keep track of her while she was inside. He thought a week's time would be sufficient for her to gain a clear understanding of the asylum's practices. With that Nellie Bly got up to leave; at the door a thought occurred to her, and she turned back to Cockerill. "How will you get me out?" she asked him.

"I don't know," he answered grimly. "Only get in."

ON THE MORNING OF SEPTEMBER 23, 1887, a young woman calling herself Nellie Brown, dressed simply but prettily in a gray flannel dress and a black sailor's hat with a gray veil, appeared at the door of the Temporary Home for Females on Second Avenue. She had hardly slept the night before, having stayed up making faces at herself in the mirror, practicing the wide-eyed, unblinking stares she hoped were indicative of insanity;

when she wasn't staring into the mirror she was reading ghost stories in the dim gaslight, trying to put herself in a properly unnerved frame of mind. All the way downtown she had done her best to affect the dreamy gaze she had seen on romantic maidens in magazine illustrations. After arranging to rent a thirty-cent room, she passed most of the day sitting listlessly in the parlor, barely engaging in conversation with any of the boarders other than to deliver the occasional pronouncement that every-one in the house seemed crazy to her. When the maid came in to an-nounce that it was time for bed, Nellie Brown protested that she was too afraid to sleep and that she preferred just to sit on the stairs; only at the maid's insistence did she finally allow herself to be escorted to her bed-room. That night she again stayed awake (the more sleep she lost, she reasoned, the more insane she would seem to the doctors) and the next morning loudly refused to emerge from her room, insisting that she had lost her trunks and demanding that they be returned to her. When she could not be quieted, policemen were summoned to the house; the two officers accompanied the distraught young woman to the local station house, and from there to the Essex Market Police Court, where the ques-tion of her sanity was to be taken up.

The courtroom was crowded with people dressed in shabby clothes; some talked animatedly with friends, others sat alone, gazing at nothing in particular. The sprinkling of uniformed officers all wore looks of im-mense boredom. From behind his high desk Judge Duffy looked kindly down at the young woman in the docket (her heart sank at his kindness, fearing that he would not send her where she wanted to go) and listened to the story, recounted by the policemen and the assistant matron of the home, of how oddly she had behaved the night before, how she would say nothing of herself other than her name, how she had not slept a wink, how she had concocted a plainly ridiculous tale about lost bags. To this the young woman would only repeat that she wanted her trunks, and that these policemen had promised to help her find them. For some time the judge considered the information that had been presented to him. Finally he ordered the young woman to be sent to his chambers, where he would speak to her in private.

When they were seated, Judge Duffy gently asked her if she was per-haps from Cuba. "Sí, señor," she answered with genuine delight, recall-ing some of the Spanish she had picked up in Mexico. "How did you know?" She told him that she had been born on a farm there, and her real name was Nellie Moreno, but she always used the English "Nellie Brown." Beyond that she could not remember anything. "I have a headache all the time," she said sadly, "and it makes me forget things. I don't want them to trouble me. Everybody is asking me questions, and it makes my head worse." This much, at least, was true, for she had not slept in two nights.

"Well, no one shall trouble you any more," Judge Duffy said. "Sit down here and rest awhile."

The judge was now of the firm belief that Nellie Brown had been drugged and brought by someone to New York; after some time, he returned in the company of an ambulance surgeon, instructing him to be kind in his examination of this poor girl. The doctor asked her to stick out her tongue; he felt her pulse and listened to the beating of her heart, then peered for a long while into her eyes. "I believe she has been using belladonna," he presently announced, and after writing something down in a notebook he indicated that she should be transported to Bellevue Hospital, to receive further examination at the hospital's new pavilion for the insane.

There were two days at Bellevue, all of that time filled with the dread that someone would see through her ruse and send her home. Doctors asked her if she saw faces on the wall, if she ever heard voices calling her name. They asked her to stretch her arms, to move her fingers, to open and close her eyes. When the tests had been completed, the doctors pronounced her insane. "Softening of the brain," one of them murmured to a nurse.

On the afternoon of the third day Nellie Brown was dispatched with four other patients into an ambulance, its back door locked behind them as if they were prisoners. At an East Side pier they were dragged up a plank to a waiting boat, where in a stifling lower cabin they were guarded by two female attendants, coarse, massive women who spat tobacco juice on the floor. When the boat landed, more guards shoved them into another ambulance. "What is this place?" she asked one of them.

"Blackwell's Island," he told her, "an insane place, where you'll never get out of."

Soon the low stone buildings of the asylum had come into view. The guard's chilling promise continued to sound in her mind as they were led up a flight of steep, narrow steps into a small receiving room. The first of the patients to be examined was a woman who spoke only German, and, as there was no interpreter present, the doctor ordered her to be admitted without further questioning. She was but one of many immigrant women Nellie Brown would meet in the asylum who had been locked up, probably for life, simply because they could not make themselves understood to authorities—landlords, policemen, judges, doctors. It was better to be a murderer, she thought, and at least have the chance of trial, than to be declared insane without any hope for escape. Her own examination determined that she stood five feet five inches tall and weighed 112 pounds. She was, she claimed, nineteen years old and originally from Cuba; she insisted that she was not sick and did not belong in the hospital. "No one has a right to shut me up in this manner," she said, but the doctor was writing in his notebook and took no more notice of her.

Later she was taken to a cold, wet bathroom and ordered to undress. When she refused, the nurses pulled off her clothes, piece by piece, until she was wearing only a single undergarment. "I will not remove it," she protested, but to no avail; privacy, she understood at once, was a right she had given up. Naked, she plunged herself into the freezing water of the tub. An old, mumbling woman, obviously another patient, dipped a rag into a pan filled with soft soap and furiously scrubbed until Nellie Brown's teeth were chattering and her limbs were blue. Without warning, three buckets of ice-cold water were poured over her head in quick succession; the water filled her eyes, ears, nose, and mouth, and for a terrifying moment she had the sensation of drowning. Sightless, gasping, and shivering, she was jerked up from the tub—the thought flashed through her mind that now she might well look insane—and a cotton slip was roughly pulled over her; then she was hurried off to a small cell furnished only with a narrow iron bed wrapped in a rubber sheet. She lay down and tried to warm herself with the blanket that had been provided, but found that it was not large enough even to cover her from shoulders to feet.

Despite her exhaustion she could not sleep, and she lay in bed picturing the horrors that would occur in the event of fire: three hundred women were kept in that one building alone, all of its windows barred and each room locked separately. From somewhere she could hear the sounds of women crying, women swearing, women praying for their release. She fell asleep with the first gray shimmer of dawn; at five o'clock the cell door was unlocked and a voice commanded her to get up. She was tossed a plain white calico dress, with the instruction to get dressed;

then she followed a line of women to the bathroom, where fifty patients washed their faces at four basins, drying themselves on two shared towels.

For breakfast, each patient was given a bowl of cold tea, a slice of buttered bread, and a bowl of oatmeal with a spoonful of molasses on it. The butter was rancid; the oatmeal was equally wretched, and she could not bring herself to choke it down. Even the tea, of an oddly pinkish hue, was barely drinkable. Lunches inside the asylum turned out to be more meager still, consisting merely of tea and another slice of bread; dinner was a chunk of boiled meat or fish with potatoes. The deprivation was intensified by its proximity to relief: on the wards the nurses snacked on apples, melons, and grapes brought in by the kitchen staff, just as they wore heavy clothing and coats while they refused the patients' cries for shawls. The cold turned out to be as merciless an enemy as hunger. At times the superintendent of Blackwell's Island strode through the dining hall inspecting the patients. Later, when Nellie Brown asked some of them why they didn't tell the superintendent how they suffered from the cold, they said that the nurses would beat them if they ever dared complain.

The beatings were common, and were administered with fiendish imagination: patients were pummeled with broom handles, pulled by the hair, choked with bedsheets, held underwater until nearly drowned. All of the women were bathed in cold water once a week, and their clothes were changed but once a month, unless they were scheduled to receive a visitor. The clothes had been made by the saner patients among them, who did most of the work of the asylum, which included cleaning the nurses' bedrooms and tending the beautiful lawns that were the face the asylum presented to the world. In the mornings, when the weather was fair, the fifteen hundred women of the asylum were taken on a brief promenade around those lawns, looking like a defeated army on field parade, the patients in rows two or three abreast, all of them dressed exactly alike, in plain calico dresses and cheap straw hats, some chattering to themselves, others screaming, crying, singing, or just staring straight ahead—an unbroken line of misery as far as the eye could see. Worse still were the hours that followed the morning walk, when the patients were forced to sit on benches all day in the "sitting-hall." If they tried to talk, they were told to shut up; if they tried to change position, they were told to sit up straight; if they tried to stand, they were told to be still. "What, excepting torture, would produce insanity quicker than this treatment?" Nellie Bly would later write.

> Here is a class of women sent to be cured. I would like the expert physicians . . . to take a perfectly sane and healthy woman, shut her up and make her sit from 6 A.M. to 8 P.M. on straight-back benches, do not allow her to talk or move during these hours, give her no reading and let her know nothing of the world or its doings, give her bad food and harsh treatment, and see how long it will take to make her insane. Two months would make her a mental and physical wreck.

Bly had resolved to act completely sane once she was inside the asylum, but the more she tried to assure the doctors of her sanity, the more they doubted her. She urged the doctors to try every test on her, to ask any question they wished; she insisted that she was sane and had always been so, that they had no right to keep sane people there, and that many other women there were also sane. "Why can't they be free?" she would ask the doctors.

"They are insane and suffering from delusions," was the inevitable reply.

To her growing horror, it was becoming clear that without the intercession of *The World* she would indeed never leave Blackwell's Island. What if they were not able to procure her release? Colonel Cockerill had suggested that a week inside the asylum would be sufficient, but after seven days there was still no word from the outside world. Finally, on the tenth day, the newspaper managed to get an attorney inside the asylum, who assured the authorities that Nellie Brown would be cared for by friends in the city; she eagerly gave her consent, and then awaited her release.

It came during the morning promenade, as she was helping a patient who had fainted while being compelled by the nurses to walk. She had so desperately looked forward to leaving, and yet now that she could she felt a deep sadness about the women who still remained; it seemed, as she later wrote, "intensely selfish to accept freedom while they were in bondage." For a moment she had the quixotic impulse to refuse her release—but only for a moment. She stepped outside, shutting the door behind her; soon she was crossing the river back to the city.

Afterward, Nellie Bly would call her time on Blackwell's Island "the ten longest days of my life." Even a year later, she was still haunted by thoughts of the companions she had left behind, still tormented by memories of the place that she variously termed a den of horror, a human rat trap, and hell on earth.

ON SUNDAY, OCTOBER 9, less than a week after her release, *The World* unveiled the first part of Nellie Bly's exposé of the Blackwell's Island Insane Asylum, entitled "Behind Asylum Bars," followed the next Sunday by "Inside the Madhouse." It was, trumpeted *The World,* a "remarkable story of the successful impersonation of insanity" undertaken by "a courageous and clever young woman . . . whose pluck and alert intellectual facilities peculiarly fitted her for the work." The story was reprinted in newspapers around the country (shortly afterward it would be issued in book form under the title *Ten Days in a Mad-House*), creating, as *The World* was happy to report, "an immense sensation everywhere." In New York, the district attorney's office convened a grand jury to investigate the asylum, and Bly herself was invited to testify. After giving her testimony she led the jurors on a tour of Blackwell's Island, where she was surprised to discover that, virtually overnight, long-standing abuses had been miraculously corrected: the halls were clean, the bathrooms had shiny new basins, and the bread, previously hard and blackened, was now "beautifully white"; best of all, several of the wrongly committed immigrant women, seemingly doomed to a life behind bars, had been either transferred from the asylum or discharged.

There was no doubt, given the acclaim that had greeted her first production for *The World,* that Nellie Bly would be hired as a full-time staff reporter. Joseph Pulitzer himself, interviewed by an enterprising reporter for the *Dispatch* while waiting for a train in Pittsburgh, praised his new reporter as "very bright" and—the adjective that would forever after be associated with her—"very plucky." Said Pulitzer, "She is well-educated and thoroughly understands the profession which she has chosen. She has a great future before her." (He did not fail to mention that he had rewarded her excellent work with "a handsome check.") Just two weeks after the publication of the second installment of her Blackwell's Island exposé, Nellie Bly was already writing regularly for *The World*—not fashion or society pieces, for which John Cockerill had earlier pronounced women reporters most fit, but investigative journalism, often going undercover again to experience firsthand the subjects about which she wrote. "I had some faith in my own ability as an actress," she had written of her daring imposture as Nellie Brown, and the success of her Blackwell's Island exposé emboldened her for further impersonations.

Answering a "suggestive advertisement" in *The World,* she assumed the role of a new mother and applied to an agency that would, for a small fee, sell her unwanted baby for her. ("A girl?" said the man at the agency. "Too bad. They are very hard to get rid of. Now, if it was only a boy you would have had more chance.") She got herself hired in a paper-box factory, where young women worked all day for low pay in an unventilated room reeking of glue. Once she received a tip from a reader about a man who drove a carriage around Central Park each day to prey on unaccompanied young women, whom he ordered into his carriage under threat of arrest; he had bought the complicity of the local policemen with regular gifts of beer. Dressing herself as a "country girl," Bly stationed herself on a park bench and allowed herself to be picked up by the man, who drove her to an uptown roadhouse where he attempted to ply her with spiked lemonade; with the help of a *World* reporter and photographer, she was able to identify the man by name, and then published in the newspaper his home address and place of employment. In one of her most ambitious exposés, she posed as the wife of a seller of patent medicines, who hoped to kill a bill coming up for consideration by an Assembly committee. She visited the hotel room offices of Edward R. Phelps, the "Lobby King" of Albany, who grandly assured her that for as little as one thousand dollars he could purchase the votes of a majority of the committee members, going so far as to place a pencil mark by the names of the members he promised he could buy. After *The World* published Bly's article about her meeting with Phelps (complete with a facsimile of his annotated list), public condemnation of the Lobby King's corrupt influence was so sharp and immediate that within the week Phelps fled Albany: the King, crowed *The World,* had been "driven from his throne." Before long, Nellie Bly had become so renowned for her undercover work that the humor magazine *Puck* was advising its readers, "When a charming young lady comes into your office and smilingly announces that she wants to ask you a few questions regarding the possibility of improving New York's moral tone, don't stop to parley. Just say: 'Excuse me, Nellie Bly,' and shin down the fire-escape."

Just a few years before, Pink Cochrane had been tramping the streets of Pittsburgh looking for work; now Nellie Bly was a popular reporter for New York's most widely read newspaper. Thanks to Bly's new financial security, her mother was able to join her in New York; with her growing success the two women moved ever farther downtown, in 1888 to West Seventy-fourth Street and the following year to West Thirty-fifth Street, between Broadway and Seventh Avenue, in the heart of the theater district known as "the Rialto." Now, in the evenings, Mary Jane and her daughter could join the well-dressed crowds hurrying by on their way to a show, or just stroll the avenue at a more leisurely pace, past the gleaming black carriages and the restaurant windows shining with golden light, and contemplate how far they had come from the grist mills and tallow candles of Apollo.

In 1889, Nellie Bly was twenty-five years old. She had changed her hairstyle from her Pittsburgh days and was now wearing it pinned up in the back, with rounded bangs that gave her a more girlish appearance. Her figure was slender, made shapely by a narrow waist corseted punishingly tight. She liked to dress stylishly, in high-collared blouses with brooches at the throat, or floor-length satin gowns that she selected in the parlors of the most fashionable dressmakers. Bly took great care with her personal appearance, both because she enjoyed the attentions of men and because she believed that a woman should use pretty clothing as a means of advancing herself. "Dress is a great weapon in the hands of a woman if rightly applied," she would write. "It is a weapon men lack, so women should make the most of it." She was greatly disturbed, covering the National Woman Suffrage Convention for *The World,* that the female delegates seemed to be "neither men nor women." When she met Susan B. Anthony, president of the convention, she did not hesitate to tell her that "if women wanted to succeed they had to go out as women. They had to make themselves as pretty and attractive as possible."

An item in *The Epoch,* New York's weekly cultural magazine, about "the enterprising and remarkable member of the *World* staff" noted that Bly "eschews all the literary 'sets' of society, and is to be found neither in the parlors of Bohemia nor in the drawing-rooms of the wealthy and lion-hunting." Still, given her personal attractiveness and her rising visibility in the city, it is not surprising that her name was romantically linked with at least two prominent men, including Dr. Frank G. Ingram, the young assistant superintendent of the Blackwell's Island Insane Asylum, who was the only sympathetic official that Bly had found during her confinement there. A more serious suitor was James Metcalfe, the drama critic for the satirical magazine *Life,* whom she had met when he helped her up after she slipped on an icy sidewalk during the great blizzard of 1888. Metcalfe, a Harvard graduate, was famously handsome—few accounts of the time failed to mention his violet eyes—successful enough as a journalist not to be intimidated by her success, and amusing in a sardonic sort of way; Bly, who tried not to take herself too seriously, must have enjoyed how free he felt to poke fun at her more high-minded exploits. Metcalfe himself was sufficiently taken with Nellie Bly that he published a poem in *Life* inspired by their first meeting, an awkward bit of verse that ran in part:

> *When first you dropped upon the pave and I came walking by*
> *I picked you up and looked at you with far from eager eye.*
> *But this soon changed to interest and then to something more*
> *Until at last, I now must own, a woman I adore!*

Often, of an evening, James Metcalfe could be found escorting Nellie Bly around town, perhaps to a play at the nearby Madison Square Theatre, famous for its "double stage" that was raised and lowered by hydraulic pressure and was at least as much of an attraction as the show itself; or, if they were in the mood for lighter fare, to a performance at Dockstader's Minstrel Hall on Broadway. On warm afternoons they shared picnics in the English gardens of Riverside Park and stately trips by horse-drawn stagecoach up Fifth Avenue to the Metropolitan Museum of Art.

All this time Bly maintained a grueling work pace, often turning out a new adventure every week. Early in her career at *The World* an editor had counseled that the public liked her in part because she was young and pretty and lively; if she wrote only critical, moralistic stories, he said, people would eventually forget about those other qualities and grow bored with her. Bly considered this for a while and decided that he was right—and so, in addition to her investigative pieces, she brought her readers along as she happily partook of all the variety the city had to offer. She played cornet in a marching band and made friends with the women of a Wild West show. She learned to ice skate and to fence, to ride a bicycle and to dance ballet. She watched, aghast, as "iron-nerved young women" performed human dissections at a women's medical college; she visited Vassar College to ask why men were not allowed to enroll there. She attended the races at Saratoga and spent a day strolling the grounds of a fancy resort in Newport. ("If you are rich and have a place in polite society, by all means go to Newport. . . . If you are poor, go anywhere else on earth instead.")

Bly became so popular that her name appeared not only in the bylines of her stories—in itself an achievement for the time—but in the headlines as well: NELLIE BLY ON THE WING, NELLIE BLY AS A MESMERIST, NELLIE BLY A PRISONER. She received as many as two hundred letters a week; some contained threats, others marriage proposals. When she reported that she suffered from regular headaches, she received bagfuls of letters offering surefire cures, from a cold sponge bath each morning to a raw onion each night. ("I have 700 physicians who diagnose my case and prescribe without charge," she noted gratefully.) In a perverse tribute to Bly's popularity, in October 1889 it was revealed that several young women around the country were impersonating her, running up large tabs with hotels and dressmakers and asking the bills to be sent to *The World* in New York. "I have no way to protect myself or the public against such people," Bly wrote. "I would only say to too confiding business people that I never run up bills, that I never under any circumstances use the name of 'Nellie Bly' outside of print. I live quietly and am only known to the few I have come in contact with in business as 'Nellie Bly.'" That state of affairs, though—her quiet, anonymous life—was about to end.

When Joseph Pulitzer purchased *The World* from the Wall Street financier Jay Gould in 1883, its circulation had stood at about fifteen thousand; by the fall of 1889 the circulation was more than ten times that. In its first five years *The World*'s growth had been nothing short of spectacular, but in recent months, as the paper became a more familiar feature of the New York landscape, there had been first a leveling off, and then a slight dip in total circulation. It was not a situation that Joseph Pulitzer or the men who worked for him took lightly. Each evening the editors of *The World* gathered to discuss possible story ideas. They were looking for something sensational—a story that would rivet the public's attention, and not just for a day or two, but for months on end. One idea after another was discarded, until finally they had found what they wanted. It was the story that Nellie Bly herself had suggested a year before; now, at long last, they were prepared to do it. On the damp, chilly evening of Monday, November 11, 1889, the editors sent Bly a message:

They wanted her to go around the world.

CHAPTER 3

The Secret Cupboard

Tʜʀᴇᴇ ʙʟᴏᴄᴋs ᴇᴀsᴛ ᴀɴᴅ ᴛʜʀᴇᴇ ʙʟᴏᴄᴋs sᴏᴜᴛʜ ᴏꜰ ᴛʜᴇ ᴀᴘᴀʀᴛᴍᴇɴᴛ that Nellie Bly shared with her mother, Elizabeth Bisland had recently moved in to an apartment with her sister. Those few blocks, though—no more than ten minutes' walk—bridged two very different worlds. On West Thirty-fifth Street by Broadway, Nellie Bly was living at the northwest edge of the notoriously louche neighborhood that a New York police captain, in honor of the plentiful opportunities for graft to be found there, had dubbed the Tenderloin ("I've been having chuck steak ever since I've been on the force," he gloated upon his transfer, "and now I'm going to have a bit of tenderloin"). An out-of-town theatergoer making a wrong turn away from the Rialto would find that just to the east, on Sixth Avenue, the lights emanating from the storefronts had become at once dimmer and more lurid, the crowds jamming the sidewalks less expensively dressed and a good deal livelier, the avenue itself lined on both sides with raucous dance halls, gambling parlors, and saloons with names like Paddy the Pig's and the Burnt Rag (each of them, courteously, had a separate Ladies' Entrance), as well as numerous whorehouses more politely termed "houses of assignation." Some of the houses catered to more upscale customers; their front parlors were scented with patchouli and brightened with sprays of fresh-cut flowers, and at midnight the evening's patrons were served an oyster supper.

Across Fifth Avenue, the dividing line between the East and West

Sides, Elizabeth Bisland's apartment was at Thirty-second Street in genteel Murray Hill, long the site of the city's most exclusive clubs and elegant stores. In her walks around the neighborhood, Bisland would have
stopped to browse in the showrooms of the European art importers clustered between Thirty-first and Thirty-third Streets and paused to gaze at
the fine millinery, furs, and jewels displayed in the nearby shop windows.
Though her own apartment was modest and located above a candy store,
an early-morning stroll might allow her to cross paths with Astors,
Vanderbilts, or Rockefellers, and just three blocks away was the home of
the dry goods tycoon A. T. Stewart, the most expensive ever built on the
North American continent, for which the stucco work alone had reportedly cost over a quarter of a million dollars. Fourth Avenue, where she
lived, sloped gently down to the manicured lawns and geometric flower
beds of Madison Square Park, which a contemporary observer noted was
"filled with a better class" than was normally found in a public park, the
pervasive atmosphere of wealth making it "unfavorable to the gathering
together of the tramps and shiftless idlers who may be seen airing their
tattered garments so often in the other parks."

In the warmer months of 1889, Elizabeth Bisland would often have
walked along Madison Square Park, admiring the pleasant scene it presented on a sun-filled day, for catercorner to the park, on Twenty-fifth
Street, *The Cosmopolitan* had its offices. To accommodate his magazine's
rapid growth, publisher John Brisben Walker had leased the entire third
floor of the Madison Square Bank building, between Fifth Avenue and
Broadway; it was, remarked *The Journalist,* "probably the best location
for a magazine that can be found in the whole city of New York." Walker
had recently arrived in the city from Denver, where he had made a fortune in alfalfa, having already made and lost one in iron. He was a millionaire with a social conscience, a former newspaper editor who now
had enough money to buy a magazine of his own, and in January 1889 he
purchased a foundering monthly called *The Cosmopolitan* from a Christian publishing company that had bought it the year before from a manufacturer of office equipment. He imagined a magazine that would
combine aesthetic cultivation and social uplift, intended for the sort of
people he had known out west, the families of the rising middle class in
towns and small cities, who were ambitious enough to want to improve
themselves but not yet too busy to read advertisements. Early issues of
The Cosmopolitan brought readers articles about the application of elec-

tricity in household appliances, the fighting forces of Germany, and the development of men's trousers over the centuries. Responding to the American public's ever-growing interest in travel stories, the magazine emphasized first-person accounts of every manner of foreign adventure— an African elephant hunt, a pilgrimage to Meshed, a train journey across the Russian steppes, an ice whaling expedition among the Eskimos. At least one poem or short story appeared in every issue of *The Cosmopolitan,* as well as an omnibus review of several recently published books called "In the Library."

To serve as the "In the Library" columnist, John Brisben Walker hired the twenty-seven-year-old journalist Elizabeth Bisland. It was an understandable choice on his part: Bisland was highly literary, with refined tastes and wide-ranging interests (the subjects covered in her first few columns included Tolstoy's social gospel, the fourteenth-century tales of Don Juan Manuel, the collected poems of Emma Lazarus, and a new two-volume history of the Vikings by the Norwegian author Hjalmar Hjörth Boyesen), and she had established herself as a frequent contributor to many of the city's leading periodicals. An admiring item in *The Journalist,* published the month before her work began appearing in *The Cosmopolitan,* noted that "her talents have realized for her that recognition of publishers which gladdens the heart and burdens the purse." Like every other contemporary journalistic account about her, this item remarked on her "great beauty," and it also made reference to her "powerful friends" in the city. But it did not mention that Elizabeth Bisland had arrived in New York with no friends at all, and that those she now had scarcely knew how difficult the journey there had been.

ELIZABETH BISLAND'S EARLIEST memories were of water: of waves churning on the Mississippi River in endless permutations of dark and light, rising in gray curls and then sizzling down into white foam, strong enough to rock the steamboat on which she stood watching at the rail. She was four years old and traveling with her family from Mississippi to Louisiana, returning to the sugar cane plantation from which they had fled two years earlier. It was 1865, and the Civil War had just ended. She was with her mother and father, her older sister Mary Louise, whom everyone called Molly, and the baby Thomas Pressley, whom everyone called Pressley; she herself was Elizabeth Ker, and was called Bessie. She watched as the land moved slowly away, until she was surrounded by an immensity of water, a waving blue plain under a blue vault of sky. Then it was night and the sky was sprinkled with stars, and her family was waiting for another boat on the riverbank, her father having built a fire there as a signal. Earlier they had stopped on the porch of an old house, where the owner, wearing a black sunbonnet and black calico dress of mourning, gave them warm saleratus biscuits and buttermilk; it was all she had, she apologized, because of the war. The railroad had been torn up in the fighting; the only way to move now was by water. The moon rose large and orange, as though reflecting the glow of their fire, and after a long time the lights of a steamboat appeared on the horizon. The steamboat sailed through the night and into the next afternoon, dropping them at the mouth of a bayou where four rowboats awaited their arrival, propelled by black men dressed in overalls. When the family decamped for Mississippi the men had been slaves; now they were free, but they still called her father "Master." The boats moved easily through the still brown water of the swamp, only the splash of the oars breaking the silence. Stands of cypress trees rose from the water, forming columns and arches above them, woolly tresses of Spanish moss hanging down below. The thick, hot air shone green in the gathering dusk. Finally the boats emerged into a clearing. In the distance stood a large white house that she did not recognize. Its pillared portico was spotty and charred, the brick chimney jagged at the top. Bullet holes scarred its face like pockmarks after an illness. A log barricade, crudely lashed together, hid most of the front yard; nearby a broken cannon listed uselessly to one side, the eye of its barrel staring unblinking at the sky.

For several months during the war the Bisland family's estate, known as Fairfax, had served as the base of operations for troops under the command of the Confederate general Richard Taylor. On the morning of April 12, 1863, advancing Union forces launched a barrage of artillery fire against Taylor's position; the rebels answered with their cannons. The battle went on until dark and then resumed the next day, now intensified by shelling from U.S. and Confederate gunboats stationed offshore. That night General Taylor, fearing that Union troops were about to cut off an escape route to the rear, ordered an immediate evacuation. The fierce two-day fight had produced hundreds of casualties on both sides, and would come to be known as the Battle of Fort Bisland.

Inside the house, Taylor's men had hastily thrown up barriers to aid their retreat; for the rest of her life Elizabeth Bisland would remember how the family's chairs and sofas were climbing over one another, as if in a panic to escape, against the battered front door. A huge mahogany bedstead, hacked and mangled, had been wedged fast on the front staircase. Paintings hung in grotesque tatters from their frames; torn books, their pages burned, were strewn around the fireplace. Overwhelmed by the devastation, her mother sat on the lowest stair and wept.

That night four-year-old Bessie and her five-year-old sister Molly slept rolled up in shawls on the floor; the South, they agreed, seemed much more interesting than the North, where they had always gone to sleep in a bed. During the war, as Union troops began their advance through Louisiana, their mother had fled with the two girls in an army ambulance, first to the home of her husband's family in Mississippi and eventually to safer territory at her parents' home in Brooklyn, New York, where they stayed for the remainder of the war. Their father had long been away from home, serving as a quartermaster sergeant in the Twenty-Sixth Louisiana Infantry. When the war ended, the Bisland family reunited in Mississippi and then made their way down the river back to Fairfax.

It was a while before even a semblance of order was restored in the house, and for a long time after that the children had to remember to sit carefully on the chairs with mended legs, and not lean too hard on the parlor table or move the little stool that hid the burned place in the carpet. Their father tried to paste the covers back on the damaged books, and he replaced as best he could the pages that had been torn out; those books would prove to be Elizabeth Bisland's best teachers. Her actual schooling was conducted at home by her mother—there were no local schools, and not enough money to send the children away—though often the lessons were interrupted by the reveries about prewar life that now occupied so much of her mother's attention: how her grandfather had owned a stable full of horses in Attakapas, and how they had never spent the hot season on the plantation but had always gone north to Saratoga, and how on her wedding day her father had given her a five-piece silver tea set, each piece engraved with anthemion and morning glories, and all on a silver tray. It was strange, Elizabeth thought as she listened, how a war could change people so completely. Before the war, it seemed, everyone had been good-looking and clever and rich; now there were lots of ugly and stupid people around, and no one seemed to have any money.

Her mother, Margaret Cyrilla Brownson Bisland—she was called Maggie—could trace her family back to the Leicester baronets of England in the early seventeenth century; Elizabeth's great-grandmother on her mother's side had been the second wife of the last Spanish governor of the province of Louisiana. Her father, too, could trace his family back to England, and in 1782 his ancestors had received their first territory in Mississippi as a land grant from the Spanish governor. At one time the Bisland family had owned six plantations and nearly four hundred slaves across Mississippi and Louisiana. Now Elizabeth's father spent a lot of time chewing the ends of his bushy black mustache and looking worriedly up at the sky. One year there was a freak September snowfall, and despite the frantic work by every hand on the plantation to get the cane cut and into the boiling kettles, most of the year's sugar crop was ruined. After that he rode to New Orleans carrying the silver epergnes and salvers and pitchers that had been hidden beneath the floor of the smokehouse during the war; when he returned home his cart was empty. Trained as a doctor, Thomas Shields Bisland had left medicine because he preferred the more leisurely life of a Southern planter, and in 1858 he had spent $112,000—his share of his father's estate—to purchase Fairfax; now he milked the cows and fed the mule, chopped wood and tilled the garden. During the week he wore old checked shirts and cottonade trousers, and on Saturdays Elizabeth and her sister scrubbed his black clothes and filled in the seams with ink so he could wear them in church the next day. The family sewed their own clothes, boiled their own soap, and brewed their own medicines. Most of the time they ate hominy made from whole corn kernels, which they called, in the Louisiana fashion, "big hominy." After suppers came the long evenings sitting out on the gallery, when Tom would lean back in his chair and smoke his meerschaum pipe, brooding about the Yankee carpetbaggers who had let in all that cheap Cuban sugar (never did he begin to suspect that the plantation system—ever so slightly modified after the Southern defeat to include meager wages for its former slaves—might itself be the culprit, that feudalism could never compete with modern capitalism), while Maggie reflected aloud about how that silver tea set had been engraved with her own initials, M.C.B., and how her father had always been able to get money when he needed it, and how Southern men had seemed ever so much more energetic and capable before the war. The only relief came on the nights when they went to dinner at their cousins' house, where there was chicken gravy and sweet potato pone and watermelon pickle, and talk around the table turned to who had really written the *Letters of Junius* and whether, as her father always insisted, English poetry had ended with Byron. "The conversation impressed me," Elizabeth Bisland would later write, "as having risen to the highest levels."

Like many of their neighbors, Tom and Maggie Bisland held strongly to the belief that children were by nature sinful and the proper role of the parent was that of a missionary among pagans. Children should be taught to obey their parents and distrust their native instincts; to be irreverent, or careless, or impatient, or untidy—to be, that is, at all childish—was deemed not just wrong but wicked, and the offender was duly punished, in the time-honored adage, "for your own good." Even the harshest beatings, it was solemnly affirmed, were being delivered in the spirit of loving kindness, and had as their justification infallible scripture, in the injunction from wise King Solomon that to spare the rod was to spoil the child. The Bisland children were ordered to read a chapter from each Testament every morning and evening, and on Sundays secular reading

Mount Repose

of any type was strictly forbidden; instead, the time was spent memorizing selected hymns, psalms, and Bible chapters, and any straying from letter perfection brought corrective discipline. Yet Elizabeth did, in her own way, find escape. From a very young age she was losing herself in the books that she found on the shelves at home, not the didactic children's tales prescribed by her parents but the six thick volumes bound in polished tree calf that contained the complete plays of Shakespeare, and novels by Cervantes and Zola, and a long row of black-bound volumes collectively entitled *The British Poets,* in which she discovered for the first time the work of Pope and Keats and Sir Walter Scott, and committed to memory the whole of Thomas Gray's "Elegy Written in a Country Churchyard" for the sheer enjoyment of it, and marveled to herself at the unexpected pleasure she took in repeating "The mountains look on Marathon—And Marathon looks on the sea." She read every book she could get her hands on, and did not let on to any adults what she was doing. "I was quite old enough to realize that my pastors and masters would be convulsed with horror did they at all suspect what I was at," she would later write. "I had intelligence enough not to chatter about every book I opened."

Each year, it seemed, another child arrived; by 1874 there were nine Bisland children in all, two of whom died of tuberculosis. In 1873, when Elizabeth was twelve years old, her father inherited the house in which he had grown up in Natchez, Mississippi, and the family moved there from Louisiana. Mount Repose was a large, gracious two-story plantation house amid a grove of live oaks. The doorway was hand carved, and inside were numerous historical pieces, including a desk once used by Aaron Burr; on the walls hung portraits of generations of Bislands. The Bisland who oversaw construction of the house in 1824, Tom's father William, had been a great admirer of the Kentucky politician Henry Clay, the longtime Speaker of the U.S. House of Representatives. According to Bisland family lore, William had vowed that his house's front drive would remain unbuilt until Clay was elected president; half a century later, Thomas Bisland and his family, like all other visitors before or since, entered Mount Repose by the side gate.

Perhaps it was the family's increasingly straitened circumstances, now placed in such stark relief by the luxuriousness of their surroundings— and made worse by having to live with those more prosperous Bislands always gazing down at them—but the move to Mississippi seemed only to exacerbate the tension within the family. Maggie wanted to move back to New York, where her father had established himself as a wealthy attorney, but Tom would not hear of it; once an argument grew so heated that she pushed a grandfather clock down the stairs at him. On at least one occasion the couple separated, with Tom going to live with a nephew back in Louisiana.

In her youth Maggie had considered herself a poet; now she began writing poetry for a newspaper that had recently been founded in New Orleans, the *Times-Democrat*. The poems weren't especially good but they helped the family make ends meet. Elizabeth, too, had begun writing poetry, in private. She worked on her poems whenever she could wrest a few minutes from the hours spent helping her mother care for the younger children, writing in the remotest parts of the garden or high in the stable loft, far from the prying eyes of her family, like Jo March in her ink-stained pinafore scribbling away in the garret. When she had to stop, she stored her work in a secret cupboard that she had found in the house; previous occupants had used the cupboard to hide money, and now the poems became for Elizabeth Bisland a valuable cache of her own, concealed from discovery by potential invaders, a bulwark against future uncertainty.

When she was twenty years old, Bisland decided that the time had come to submit her work for publication, and under the nom de plume of B.L.R. Dane she sent a Christmas sonnet to the *Times-Democrat;* to mail it she walked several miles to a neighboring town so that the postmark would not betray the poem's origins. In the days that followed, she eagerly scanned the pages of the newspaper, and one morning she was secretly thrilled to see her poem included in its Christmas edition. Her initial success encouraged her to submit several more poems, also pseudonymous, composed in a variety of poetic forms—including sonnets, villanelles, and a rondeau with the arresting title of "Dead! Dead!":

> *O fierce wild wind that in thy moaning pain*
> *Beats't with wet fingers on my door in vain!*
> *Dost thou come from the graves with that sad cry*
> *That pleads for entrance—that, denied, goes by,*
> *And faints to tears amidst the freezing rain?*
> *In here the glowing fire leaps amain*
> *And from its red heart casts a ruddy stain:*

Here is no thought of death or men that die—
O fierce wild wind!

Why shouldst thou come, then, to my window-pane
To wring thy hands and weep and sore complain
That they alone, and wet, and cold must lie
In dark, deep graves, and we breathe not a sigh?
We had forgot—the quick and dead are twain,
O fierce wild wind!

The newspaper's literary editor, Lafcadio Hearn, thought this poem "exquisite," revealing "a power of weird fancy worthy of any literary celebrity." Edgar Allan Poe was clearly an influence—she was a great admirer of his poetry—but other poems of hers did not lean so heavily on gothic effect, such as a poem in quatrains called "Mardi Gras" that vividly presented a nighttime street carnival as seen from a balcony over-head. Her most ambitious poem was the one entitled "Caged," a four-stanza ballade about a songbird who vainly beats against the bars of her golden cage, longing to feel the "grey and patient sand" and the dawn breezes that "come up across the lea / With wild wet feet." She imagines the thunderous wings of the seabirds over the water and curses the gods for having so confined her, lamenting at the end of each stanza: *"Alas!"* she saith,—*"how sweet the world outside."*

As the poems continued to arrive in the newspaper office, Hearn would later recall, "considerable curiosity was aroused in regard to the personality of the author," so much so that eventually Page M. Baker, the editor in chief of the *Times-Democrat,* wrote to Maggie Bisland to ask if she hap-pened to know of any poets in her area by the name of Dane. When Maggie mentioned the unusual query at supper that night, Elizabeth shyly con-fessed that she was the mysterious poet. Tom and Maggie were astonished—not just by their Bessie's unsuspected talent, but also that she had successfully hidden her literary aspirations for so long—though their astonishment was hardly greater than that of Baker himself, who later admitted that he had imagined B.L.R. Dane to be an elderly man who had once lived in England.

THE ACTUAL B.L.R. DANE was about to turn twenty-one, old enough, she felt, finally to move away from home and get a job to help support the family. Though she hadn't published anything beyond those poems in the *Times-Democrat,* Elizabeth Bisland already recognized herself to be a natural writer, someone who could produce work quickly and with little need of revision; she would later characterize herself as one of a "mob of gentlewomen who wrote with ease." She wrote to the *Times-Democrat* asking about the possibility of obtaining a position on the paper, and she was soon hired. In the winter of 1882 she set off for New Orleans, with the promise that she would send back as much money as she could.

Bisland took a small whitewashed room on the third floor of a cheap boardinghouse on the Rue Royale in the French Quarter, where vacancies were signaled by a sign that read CHAMBRES À LOUER dangling by a string from one of the balconies. The room looked out on a world far removed from any she had known before. The French Quarter was home to the dignified and the disreputable alike, and every block seemed to whisper of secrets: wherever one turned there were shuttered windows, locked gates, narrow alleys, private courtyards. On the famous wrought-iron balconies of the Quarter the metal seemed to come alive with a profusion of vines, flowers, and fruit, the filigree as complex and delicate as lace. Just down the street from her boardinghouse the stately marble-

Royal Street in the French Quarter at the time Elizabeth Bisland lived there

fronted Merchants' Exchange had lately been turned into an immense gambling palace that offered its patrons games from keno to roulette, with no limit placed on bets. There were barrel houses, dance halls, and concert cafés where the din of raucous, drunken laughter competed with a fiddle's wail and the tinkle of a cheap piano, and at the front door, always, bouncers stood guard wearing brass knuckles on both hands. At the intersection of Royal and Canal was Monkey Wrench Corner, a gathering place for local sailors, especially ones who were currently out of work ("monkeys," in the local argot) and looking to borrow money from ("put the wrench on") those fortunate enough to have a ship. She must have felt a sharp pang of memory when she first saw, by that same corner, the twenty-foot-high monument to Henry Clay.

Looking back years later, Elizabeth Bisland would laugh at the attitude that she, "a wretched little provincial," initially assumed on her arrival in New Orleans, "imagining it would appreciate the condescension with which I stepped down from a poor but proud estate." Whatever hauteur she might have brought with her from Mount Repose dissipated very quickly in the French Quarter. She was alone for the first time in her life, in a strange city where a sense of danger seemed to swirl in the air like the fog that drifted in at night from the marshes. She was not used to such a casual mingling of blacks and whites on the street, to the jumble of European and Caribbean cultures, as though the city were a colonial outpost transplanted onto the American mainland. She had learned French to read Rousseau; now she was hearing it spoken all around her, though often in a patois she did not understand. A few blocks toward the river, the stalls of the French Market had tables heaped high with dates and bananas and leathery pomegranates cut open to reveal glistening red seeds packed into pale membranes like rubies in a bed of cotton; from all around came the singsong cries of street vendors wearing dresses the colors of a tropical garden. The city was like a traveling carnival that never moved on, noisy and surprising and disorderly, and, to a young woman newly arrived from a ruined plantation, overwhelming: in the mornings she would linger behind the weather-stained front door that opened onto the Rue Royale, gathering her courage to plunge into the indifferent crowd.

The offices of the *Times-Democrat* were on lower Camp Street, the section of the city known as "Newspaper Row," as thirteen papers— from the *Picayune* and the *Ledger* to the *Jewish South* and the *Southwestern*

Christian Advocate—made their offices there. It was not a long walk from her boardinghouse, just past Canal Street, the city's busiest thoroughfare and its cultural dividing line. (Canal Street, a German visitor to the city once remarked, divided New Orleans as the Straits of Dover divided England from France.) Walking to work Elizabeth Bisland would have passed from the Rue Royale to Royal Street, addressed first as "Mademoiselle" and then, a few blocks along, as "Miss." Across Canal, on Camp Street, the store awnings and ground floor windows advertised the services of print shops and lithographers and paper warehouses and binderies, the businesses that attend a great newspaper district as camp followers accompany an army. The street, alive with carriages and streetcars, was lined on both sides with antebellum row buildings, four and five stories high, in the Greek Revival style; on spring mornings, when the windows were open, Bisland would have heard the satisfying metallic clicks of type being set by hand. In the narrow alley by the Newsboys' Home, clusters of boys, most of them orphans, rolled dice or tossed a ball, waiting to pick up their copies of the latest edition. All around reporters, editors, typesetters, office boys hurried to make a deadline or, having already made it, paused for a moment to chat about the latest news; as in any business district of the time, there were very few women.

Not surprisingly, Elizabeth Bisland was assigned to the women's page of the *Times-Democrat,* for which she wrote about the doings of high society. The New Orleans on which she was now reporting was a far different city from the one she had found in the French Quarter. It was a city of white-pillared mansions on broad, tree-lined avenues, of teas and garden clubs and flower shows, sun-filled afternoons at the Fair Grounds racetrack and glittering evenings at the French Opera: a city ruled by customs and manners, where a young lady could accompany a gentleman for a ride in his carriage but had to be chaperoned to concerts or the theater, where women read the latest books and attended the ballet but professed to be shocked by the use of the word "leg" in conversation.

Her hours, she found, were increasingly filled. There were, for instance, the regular meetings of the literary club that had been organized by the Tulane professor John Rose Ficklen, of which she was an original member (another was Julia Ward Howe, author of "The Battle Hymn of the Republic"), and on Friday afternoons between three and six o'clock there was the salon at the Royal Street home of the poet and novelist Mollie Moore Davis. No invitations to the Royal Street salon were ever sent out, and none needed to be—the right people knew to attend, among them Kate Chopin and Grace King (both of whom would become famous authors), as well as New Orleans's most celebrated writer, George Washington Cable. This salon, as Davis herself characterized it, was "a place of resort for men and women of brains and wit, where fashion is subservient to mind, and where the twaddlers cease to twaddle"—a place that provided exactly the type of intelligent, stimulating talk that Elizabeth Bisland had longed for since those long-ago dinner table conversations about English poetry. Now she could have those conversations again, week after week; in this house on Royal Street she was not the shy country girl cowering behind the door of the cheap boardinghouse but was instead a talkative, self-assured, radiant young woman. One of the salon's participants would later recall how on those afternoons Bisland smiled spontaneously and with delight, seeming to create around her "a little circle of magnetic sunshine."

She was tall and slender and had large, soft brown eyes with long lashes, and a graceful neck, and full lips that turned up slightly at the ends as if she was privately amused about something; her long wavy hair, pinned up in the back, was chestnut-colored, a dark frame for her pale skin. Her voice was soft, her gaze languid, and she had about her the aristocratic manner that other girls paid extravagant sums to be taught in Southern finishing schools. "She is a refined, elegant and accomplished lady," the New Orleans *Daily Picayune* observed, "and one of the most beautiful women of her day."

Another participant in the Royal Street salon, the *Times-Democrat*'s literary editor, Lafcadio Hearn, had already become one of Elizabeth Bisland's closest friends; it was a friendship that would last a lifetime. Bisland had long admired Hearn's lush, poetic, sometimes macabre sketches of New Orleans life, and soon after her arrival in New Orleans she paid a call on him at his home in the Vieux Carré, a little green-shuttered house covered in vines. He proved to be as strange and startling as the city itself. Hearn stood only five foot three, with small feet and delicate hands, but it was his eyes that most compelled attention. As a schoolboy he had injured his left eye, which became infected and then blind; the sightless eye had since turned a milky white, while his right eye, as if in compensation for the other, bulged behind his thick glasses. Dignified, gentle, and extraordinarily sensitive, Hearn would wander about the room during their conversations, softly touching the furnishings, sometimes picking up an object to study with his pocket glass, all the while keeping up a steady stream of talk about voodoo rituals, Creole cookery, Chinese ghost stories, Japanese folk tales. Bisland could scarcely have imagined a wittier or more delightful conversationalist than Lafcadio Hearn, though she quickly realized that "to remain on good terms with him it was necessary to be as patient and wary as one who stalks the hermit thrush to his nest."

As for Hearn, he was simultaneously entranced and repelled by Bisland. She was young and beautiful and knew a great deal about poetry, but she also represented to him the new type of American woman, whom he thought of as cunning, overly ambitious, and, in his characterization, "diamond-hard." To look at her she was a perfect Southern belle, but unlike most of the belles about whom she reported for the *Times-Democrat,* who married young and were proud never to have held a job, Bisland was determined to create a full intellectual and professional life for herself: to read and write as she wished, to earn her own living, to make her opinions known, in public and private alike. In one of his letters Hearn referred to her as *"une jeune fille un peu farouche"*—no other word, he felt, so conveyed her particular combination of shyness and force.

Though she now often found herself in upper-class company, Elizabeth Bisland had years of deprivation in her past, and she well understood that whatever money she made would come by way of her own pen—that she was, in a real sense, living by her wits. Her most valuable lesson had been taught by her mother, after all: her mother, who at the age of eighteen had tied her fortunes to a man from a wealthy family and then, when history turned and the money ran out, was left with few resources of her own, with little to do but write the occasional anodyne poem and complain about the fecklessness of her husband and dream of how things used to be. Bisland was not about to repeat her mother's mistakes. She was a professional woman trying to make her way in a world run almost exclusively by men, and in New Orleans, as her newspaper work took her around the city, she began to notice that other young women, working in a variety of fields, were facing similar challenges. Together, she thought, they might be able to assist one another, and in 1884, at the age of twenty-three, she inserted a notice into the *Times-Democrat* calling for the creation of a new women's organization in the city.

In her notice Bisland reminded the paper's readers that the men of New Orleans had the Young Men's Christian Association and various other benevolent organizations through which they were "elevated financially, socially, and morally"—all of these benefits, she took care to point out, due at least in part to the "gratuitous labor" provided by the women's auxiliaries of these groups. Surely, she wrote, the women of the city deserved such an organization of their own, one that would have as its goals "equal salaries with men whenever women rendered equal services, and assistance when a member was out of work or ill." No comparable organization had ever existed before in New Orleans; the city had numerous women's clubs, of course, but they were devoted to social activities or charitable work, not professional advancement. Hers was an exceedingly daring proposition—it was difficult enough to convince conservative Southerners that women should work outside the home, much less that they should earn as much as men—but on the following Monday evening twelve women showed up in the parlor of the local YMCA, and by the time the meeting was over the New Orleans Woman's Club had been established and Elizabeth Bisland voted in as its first president.

The club's constitution declared that it would be devoted to "breaking down and removing barriers of social prejudice" through both intellectual improvement and practical instruction. As time went on it offered members regular concerts, plays, and lectures on topics ranging from English and Russian literature to Louisiana history and the role of the press in shaping public opinion, as well as classes that taught skills such as typewriting, stenography, telegraphy, needlework, and elocution. A *Daily Picayune* article remarked that, as late as ten o'clock at night, it was not unusual "to see two or more score of husbands amiably cooling their heels in the club halls while their wives in the pretty parlors beyond were listening to literature lectures, to good music, or to practical talk, calculated to make them better homemakers or more sensible women." The club established its own Bureau of Employment, and members took on projects to place matrons in police station houses, provide supplies to the local Woman's and Children's Hospital, and distribute food and clothing to flood victims. A reporter of the time, describing the successes of the New Orleans Woman's Club to the readers of the New York weekly *The Epoch,* declared, "This Louisiana sisterhood . . . owes its existence to one woman—in this case to a journalist, Miss Elizabeth Bisland."

Bisland had provided the club with a solid foundation, but she would not serve out the year as its first president. After three years in New Orleans, she was ready to leave. The world in which she was moving had begun to feel uncomfortably small; the more interesting people, she sensed, the more challenging writing, the more important publications, lay elsewhere. She was increasingly frustrated with what she considered to be the parochialism of the South, its chivalrous men and idealized women, its aggressive religiosity, its insistent focus on the lost glories of the past. As a girl she had imagined herself as a nymph out of Bulfinch's *Mythology,* dancing in the moonlight that silvered the white irises in the garden. Even then literature had been her means of escape. Now she saw herself as the songbird she had dreamed up in a poem years before, beating its wings against the bars of its cage, longing to be part of the wider world.

CHAPTER 4

"How Quick Can a Woman Go Around the World?"

LIZABETH BISLAND ARRIVED IN NEW YORK AT NIGHT, ENTERING HER new home as she had returned to her first one, by water, breathing in the salt air and gazing up at the lights of the skyscrapers that twinkled in the darkness, as bright and distant as stars. She had fifty dollars in her purse.

The first room she found was in a modest five-story stone building on Madison Avenue at the northwest corner of Thirty-first Street. In time she would come to see herself as a kind of naturalized citizen of New York, but first she had to adjust to its strange ways. There was, she was surprised to discover, a reserve among New Yorkers that she had never experienced in the South and that made her uncomfortable. Nor had she quite anticipated how everyone there lived so piled on top of one another. Increasingly the city's residents were taking to a European style of building called an apartment house; in 1869 New York had only a single rental apartment building, but by 1885, the year she arrived, there were three hundred. Some of these buildings had been built to resemble Moorish castles and German châteaus and were as much as fourteen stories tall. "Why not go as high as the strength of materials will permit," suggested an article in the *Real Estate Record and Buildings Guide,* "or until the tenants of the upper stories begin to suffer, like Humboldt in the Andes, from nose-bleed and ringing in the ears." In the upper stories, the tenants reached their apartments by means of a passenger elevator, with a separate elevator reserved for coal, wood, ashes, and freight. Some of the houses offered a kitchen in each apartment; others consisted simply of suites of rooms, and provided, after the fashion of hotels, a restaurant on the ground floor. Her own building had a concierge by the front door, a "large and determined" man who greeted visitors and received packages. Just down the block was a new apartment house called the Hubert Home Club, a massive brick building with gabled roofs; it rose eleven stories high and in the mornings cast the street into shadow. She had never lived in a city this cold, nor one as dark. But gas for the lights turned out to be dreadfully expensive, and coal cost twice as much by the scuttleful as by the half ton: as the saying went, it took money to economize.

Fifty dollars, Bisland knew, would not last long in a city such as this, and so she needed to find work at once. She went first to the offices of the *Sun,* where, thanks to letters of introduction from newspaper friends back in New Orleans, she managed to get an interview with Chester Lord, the paper's longtime managing editor. She told him who she was and what her experience had been, and then asked about the possibility of obtaining writing work. Lord was an exceedingly courteous, mild-mannered man—both unusual qualities in the New York newspaper business—and he listened patiently to Bisland's story; when she was finished he said to her, "My dear little girl, pack your trunk and go back home. This is no place for you."

Bisland, however, was undeterred—she had not come more than a thousand miles only to turn around at the first rebuff—and when she persisted, Chester Lord consented to give her a trial run; she went off and soon returned with a feature article in hand, which she later recalled as being "a little sketch of a negro funeral." Lord was impressed with the quality of writing shown in the article, its appealing mixture of humor and pathos. He published the piece in the *Sun* and then gave her many more assignments, which in turn helped her to place work at other publications. Before long Bisland was regularly writing feature articles for the *Sun* and magazines such as *Harper's Bazaar, Illustrated American,* and *Puck,* and book reviews for a number of newspapers, including *The World,* where Nellie Bly would soon begin work. She also contributed the "New York Letter" to both the *Brooklyn Daily Eagle* and the *Chicago Tribune,* in which she saucily commented on some of the goings-on of metropolitan society life, from Mrs. Cornelius Vanderbilt's innovation of freezing Roman punch in tulip hearts to the use of spirit guides by certain members of the stock exchange. In addition to all this, she wrote the "Literary Bric-a-Brac" column for the *Times-Democrat* of New Orleans. Lafcadio Hearn reported to a friend, "She works for four papers at the same time—a very brave girl: works often eighteen and twenty hours at a stretch, and still keeps fresh and rosy and gracious as a jessamine."

In 1887, Bisland's older sister Molly joined her in New York; the two moved in to an apartment exactly one block west of her previous one, above a candy store on Fourth Avenue between Thirty-first and Thirty-second Streets. As time went on, Bisland became well known among New York's creative set, and by 1889 she was hosting a Sunday afternoon salon in her apartment in which she sought to re-create the intellectually stimulating atmosphere of Mollie Moore Davis's salon on Royal Street. Among those who attended the gatherings were the Shakespearean actor Henry Irving, the actress and elocutionist Sarah Cowell, the war correspondent Archibald Forbes, the poet Clinton Scollard, and the portrait painter William Henry Lippincott; when Coquelin, the leading man of the Comédie Française, was in New York, Bisland's was one of the few salons the actor visited, and the only one in which he gave an impromptu performance. Her knowledge of French must have been an inducement for him to perform, as well as what *The Cosmopolitan* termed "her charm of manner" and, of course, her "considerable personal beauty."

There was simply no avoiding how beautiful she was. Her beauty was remarked upon again and again, in every article in which she was mentioned, its peerlessness presented less as literary flourish than as objective statement of fact. She was, claimed *The Journalist,* "undoubtedly the most beautiful woman in Metropolitan journalism"; an article on "Feminine Bachelors" in the *Philadelphia Inquirer* declared that she was "the prettiest writing woman in New York." A New York friend of Lafcadio Hearn's was at a party one evening when Elizabeth Bisland entered the room. "She was a devilishly beautiful woman," the friend recalled, "and it wasn't a minute before she was the center of a crowd composed of all the men in the room, while the women still sat, lonely sentinels, in every other chair." Hearn himself came once to visit, and decided that Bisland, since arriving in New York, had "expanded mentally and physically into one of the most superb women you could wish to converse with. . . . It now seems to me as I had only seen the *chrysalis* of her before; this is the silkmoth!" He grumbled to friends, though, about how hard it was to get her attention in a crowded room. "She is a witch—turning heads everywhere," he wrote to a friend in Philadelphia; "but some of her best admirers are afraid of her. One told me he felt as if he were playing with a beautiful dangerous leopard, which he loved for not biting him. As for me she is like hasheesh: I can't remember anything she says or anything I myself say after leaving the house; my head is all in a whirl, and I walk against people in the street, and get run over, and lose my way."

Elizabeth Bisland herself could not help but be aware of her own beauty, and the intoxicating effect it seemed to have. She was flattered by the attentions of men, but at the same time she distrusted the way men doted (that was the verb she used) on a pretty woman. She found little appeal, as it turned out, in being cast as a goddess, a devil, a leopard, a witch. It all seemed terribly unreal to her. In later years she would come to prefer the company of European men, who seemed to listen more intently to what she had to say. She wrote, "Mentally American women do not interest American men."

ELIZABETH BISLAND WROTE for several newspapers, but the hectic pace of daily journalism was never exactly to her taste. She much preferred the more deliberate contemplation allowed by a monthly schedule, and the more serious attention many magazines were willing to devote to books and literature. So when John Brisben Walker, who had recently taken over *The Cosmopolitan,* asked her to write feature articles for the magazine and, better still, to take over its "In the Library" column, she happily accepted.

John Brisben Walker was forty-one years old, with wavy black hair and a handlebar mustache; he stood six feet tall and had a barrel chest and the erect bearing of the West Point cadet he once had been. He took great pride in his physical vigor—every year on his birthday, well into his old age, he would leap over a four-barred gate and declare that he was good for another year. Walker had a gift for making money, but his particular genius lay in finding schemes that managed to combine his two greatest passions: social reform and free publicity. His most ambitious venture was *The Cosmopolitan*'s Correspondence University, which offered free study by mail with professors from the nation's most prestigious colleges, in the subjects of "English, Philosophy, Sciences, and Modern and Dead Languages"; within two years more than twenty thousand people had

John Brisben Walker

enrolled, and Walker, overwhelmed by the demand, was forced to discontinue the program. *The Cosmopolitan* once offered a prize of three thousand dollars (equal to more than $75,000 today) to the horseless carriage that would most quickly make the trip from City Hall Park in New York to the town of Irvington-on-Hudson, in Westchester County. On another occasion Walker announced that *The Cosmopolitan* was making plans to assemble a "World's Congress" that would bring together one hundred delegates "representing the highest thought and most practical statesmanship of all nations." Though that foray into international diplomacy never materialized, Walker did once send an emissary to Spain to discuss the possibility of the United States purchasing Cuba's independence for the price of one hundred million dollars. The Spanish government duly refused the offer, but *The Cosmopolitan* had received its publicity.

On the morning of November 14, 1889, John Brisben Walker read the first reports about Nellie Bly's race around the world. There was, he understood at once, a grandeur to this enterprise. The carriage ride from his home in South Orange, New Jersey, to the ferry station in Jersey City had never seemed quite as slow as it did that morning, nor the trip across the Hudson. Disembarking at Cortlandt Street in lower Manhattan, he was carried along by a tide of men in black suits and hats, all of them, like him, bound for the office. In the streetcar all the way up to Madison Square his mind was occupied with thoughts of railroads and steamships. He knew something about world travel; as a young man he had spent some years living in China, serving as an adviser to the Chinese military. *The World,* he believed, had made a grievous error in its planning.

The Madison Square Bank building stood on the northwest corner of the square. Entering the building, Walker strode up the stairs; he had taken the entire third floor for his newly launched magazine and, to the astonishment of the city's publishing industry, had signed a seven-year lease. Gathering his staff around him, Walker asked, "How quick can a woman go around the world?"

The magazine's business manager, A. D. Wilson, replied that Nellie Bly proposed to make the trip in seventy-five days, and had already set sail that morning on the *Augusta Victoria.*

Yes, he had seen the reports in *The World,* Walker said. *The Cosmopolitan,* he now announced, would be sending its own woman reporter to race against Nellie Bly. Their competitor, however, would travel west rather than east—for, as experienced travelers knew, from October through April the winds across the South China Sea blow from the northeast. On her route Nellie Bly would be heading directly into the wind, and as a result she would lose, according to standard calculations, between three and four days; she would also, upon returning to the United States in January, have to contend with the difficulties and delays attendant to a cross-country train trip amid the snows of winter. To demonstrate the confidence he had in his decision, he planned to make a public wager with the publisher of *The World*—his $1,000 against Mr. Pulitzer's $500—about which competitor would arrive home first.

The Cosmopolitan's competitor, however, would have to leave without delay. Walker checked his pocket watch; it was already past ten. He sent Wilson off to the famed travel agency Thomas Cook & Son to determine, as the agency's magazine *Cook's Excursionist* later reported, whether an around-the-world trip could be arranged on such short notice ("This we explained we could readily do") and to purchase the necessary railroad and steamship tickets. Then he dispatched a messenger to Elizabeth Bisland's apartment, only a few blocks away, with the instruction that she should come at once.

At eight o'clock that morning Elizabeth Bisland had been awakened by the maid with the breakfast tray, on which were also the morning newspapers and a pile of letters. Bisland was pleased to see half a dozen acceptances of invitations she had sent out for tea the following day; there were a few notes from friends as well, and a bill, and a notice from her tailor that a dress she had ordered was ready for a final fitting. She had a leisurely breakfast and read the papers. The Madison Square Theatre, just a few blocks away, was beginning matinee performances of *Little Lord Fauntleroy;* the boy playing the title role, in the estimation of the *Sun,* was "a prodigy without the parrot traits so dreaded in children on the stage." The *Times* reported that the previous evening had been "ladies' night" at the New York Press Club—on that night the club's members, all of them men, had been allowed to bring their wives and daughters. That morning's *World* contained another installment of Robert Louis Stevenson's latest novel, *The Master of Ballantrae: A Winter's Tale,* which the paper was trumpeting as "The Greatest Story of Modern Times." If Bisland noticed the news about Nellie Bly's race around the world, she never made any mention of it. She might also have missed the small item about the new fast mail train that had left New York the previous evening for San Francisco, with the goal of cutting a day's time from the delivery of transcontinental mail; in retrospect, it was an article that would have been worth her attention.

At half past ten, the apartment's buzzer rang. A messenger was waiting to pass along the information that John Brisben Walker wished to see her as soon as possible. Bisland pressed him for more details, but he had none to relate; all he could do was repeat Mr. Walker's instructions to come to the office right away.

It was only a few minutes' walk from her apartment to the offices of *The Cosmopolitan.* The morning was chilly but clear, the thin November sunlight a restorative after several days of rain. Bisland, though, would scarcely have noticed, her mind too filled with questions about what might have precipitated such a sudden and mysterious request. John Brisben Walker was known to be a very demanding employer—"the stiffest man in New York to work for," by one account—restless, ambitious, occasionally impulsive. Perhaps her most recent feature article had caused consternation among some of the magazine's more important readers: she had suggested that carefully planned tenement buildings, providing modern hot water plumbing, shared laundry facilities, and a well-stocked reading room and making provision for cooperative marketing and cooking among the tenants—and paid for by charitable millionaires—might "reconcile some of the terrible inequalities that make anarchists among a people with the most liberal institutions, the greatest natural wealth, and the most wonderful industrial development on the globe." It was, of course, possible that some of the magazine's backers were not as forward-thinking as was Mr. Walker himself. By eleven o'clock she had reached the headquarters of *The Cosmopolitan,* where she was immediately ushered into the office of the publisher.

John Brisben Walker wished her a cordial good morning. He asked whether she might leave New York that evening for San Francisco, and then proceed onward from there around the world; if at all possible, he was hoping that she could do it faster than anyone ever had before.

It was some time before Elizabeth Bisland responded to this. At first she thought he was joking; he did not smile, though, or say anything more, and slowly it dawned on her that his request was in earnest. The next half hour was spent with Walker insisting that he wished her to make the attempt, and Bisland insisting with equal vehemence that she meant to do nothing of the sort. To begin with, she said, she had no desire to go around the world, and she was certainly not qualified to make the trip—she had never even been out of the country. Walker brushed that objection aside; the fact that she had never been to foreign lands, he explained, would make her impressions of them all the more fresh and vivid. Bisland protested that she had guests coming the following day, and that she did not have the appropriate clothing for such a long journey.

But these arguments, as she herself well knew, were easily countered and were, in any case, beside the point; her more serious concerns lay elsewhere. From her very first efforts to become a published writer—when she had walked to a neighboring town to mail her poem to the *Times-Democrat*—she had always striven to emphasize her writing rather than her identity. In the words of one who had known her back in New Orleans, she was "the very essence of culture and refinement, and about the last person in the world that one would associate with hoop and spangle journalism." It was all well and good for a sensation writer like Nellie

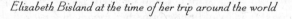

Elizabeth Bisland at the time of her trip around the world

Bly to turn herself into a public curiosity, offering herself up for the amusement of anyone with a few pennies to spend on a paper, but for her this held not the slightest appeal. She had no interest at all in seeing her name in a newspaper headline. Yet this was precisely what lay ahead of her, she knew, if she undertook the race around the world: it was just as certain as any destination on the itinerary.

He was proposing to pay her a handsome salary, said John Brisben Walker; he would bring her on as a full-time employee of *The Cosmopolitan,* amply compensating her for any writing income she might lose while on the trip (one news report put the salary at $3,000 a year for two years "whether she lost the race or won"). It is possible as well that Walker suggested that she would lose her job if she refused his request—all Bisland would ever say about it was that he made "substantial arguments." John Brisben Walker had already amassed fortunes in iron and alfalfa and was in the process of amassing still another, in publishing. In later years he would become the first president of the Automobile Manufacturers' Association and the first president of the American Periodical Publishers' Association; he was a man exceptionally skilled at getting his way, and by the time Elizabeth Bisland left the office she had been persuaded to make the trip.

Bisland left the office in a kind of stupor. She took a cab to a previously scheduled fitting with her tailor (where, after "a vigorous interview," she managed to convince him that she *could* wear that dress at six o'clock that evening), and then returned home. For the next several hours Bisland's apartment was a scene of bustle and confusion. Fifty people had been invited for five o'clock tea the next day; her sister Molly said that she would make the necessary apologies. Two dinner engagements, as well, had to be broken. She had letters to write, maps and schedules to consult, bags to pack. She was having trouble anticipating exactly what lay ahead of her. There would be railway dust, sea damps, tropical heat: that much at least she knew. The thought occurred to her that she could not be both a hard-working bee and, in the saying of the day, a butterfly of fashion, and that helped to simplify matters. She finally settled on two cloth dresses, half a dozen light bodices, and a silk dress for evening wear. She made sure to pack lots of hairpins, as they had always had a way of playing hide-and-seek with her, and she knew that if this happened in a foreign country it would undermine her mood. She packed shoes, and gloves, and underwear (silk, she thought, would not gather dust, nor conduct changes in temperature), and a nightdress and dressing gown, and slippers as well, and toiletries of all sorts, and a sewing case for necessary repairs along the way, and a traveling inkstand for the writing she planned to do, and a supply of books and paper. For colder weather she packed a heavy wool overcoat and a travel rug to wrap herself in while aboard ships and trains; for wet weather, a pair of rubber overshoes and an umbrella. It would not do, she warned herself, to forget anything now, or to make any mistakes, particularly ones that could not be rectified later. She finally managed to get all of her belongings inside a steamer trunk, a Gladstone valise, and a shawl strap that she could sling over her shoulder.

For her traveling outfit she selected a new black dress (the one her tailor had finished that very afternoon) with a newmarket coat, and a glazed black sailor's hat she had never worn before. Outwardly she remained calm, but her mind was racing. She had woken up that morning to her usual routine, and now she was embarking on a trip around the world. As the hour grew later the sensation began to creep over her that she was living inside a nightmare from which she could not awake, and just when she was about to give in to despair the hansom cab arrived to take her to the Grand Central Depot at Forty-second Street. She had a berth reserved on the New York Central Railroad's Fast Western Express, the most popular through train in America.

The traffic moved slowly along Fourth Avenue, but before long the distinctive mansard roofs of Grand Central had come into view. The building was made of brick trimmed with white-painted cast iron, giving it the look of a fancily iced layer cake. The New York Central Railroad occupied most of the western side of the depot, on an avenue named for Cornelius Vanderbilt. Commodore Vanderbilt, as he was called (though his naval service consisted solely of owning a fleet of steamships), had begun buying up New York Central stock in the 1860s, consolidated his hold on the business with bribery and price manipulation, and at the end turned it over to his son William; his dying words to his son were, "Keep the money together, hey. Keep the Central our road."

Inside the station, the atmosphere was one of barely suppressed hysteria. The daily tide was now flowing back out of the city, bound for the

NEW YORK CENTRAL R. R. DEPOT.

New York's Grand Central Depot

quieter towns to the north. A uniformed porter led Bisland past rows of ticket offices and waiting rooms to the train shed at the rear of the depot. Six hundred feet long and two hundred feet wide, the Grand Central train shed was the largest enclosed space in the United States. An arcade of ornately decorated trusses rose up its sides, as in the vault of a medieval cathedral. The ceiling, a soaring dome of glass and iron, glowed purple from the setting sun; it seemed to retain light as the roof of a conservatory retains heat. Twelve tracks ran in parallel lines out of the shed, with elevated platforms between each pair. On one of the platforms a group of friends and colleagues had come to see her off. The last few minutes passed in a blur: there were hugs and kisses farewell, final instructions, a large bouquet of pink roses, everyone talking at once, a trunk bumping up a stair, the musty smell of a sleeping car, a settling back into soft plush, and then a shrill whistle and a jolt as the wheels lurched into motion.

It was six o'clock on Thursday, November 14. Elizabeth Bisland was going around the world.

CHAPTER 5

"I Think I Can Beat Phileas Fogg's Record"

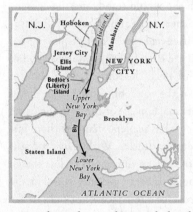

NOVEMBER 14, 1889
New York Harbor

THERE WAS A BLAST FROM A HORN. AT 9:40 A.M., WITH A SUDDEN SHIVER of movement, the *Augusta Victoria* pulled away from the Hoboken pier. Nellie Bly stood at the port rail with the other passengers and waved her cap to those she was leaving behind; she could not help but wonder if she would ever see them again. Seventy-five days, which had seemed so short in the planning, now seemed an age. Smoke poured from the ship's three funnels in thick black columns, then turned an irresolute gray and dissipated into the sky. The timbers of the deck thrummed softly beneath her feet. Behind her, just beyond the greenery of the Battery, the *Tribune*'s brick clock tower, seeming part schoolhouse, part church steeple, rose over the city's newspaper district; before the day was out, Bly knew, her name would be repeated a thousand times there, in every newsroom and beanery and oyster saloon, wherever the men of the press congregated.

In the distance she could see the lighthouse and telegraph station of Sandy Hook; to the east, the morning sun silhouetted the Statue of Liberty. The great lady stood with torch aloft, still the brown of a penny, the copper of her exterior having not yet developed its verdigris patina. Her official name was *Liberty Enlightening the World,* but she was most often referred to simply as "Bartholdi's statue." The Alsatian sculptor Frédéric-Auguste Bartholdi had originally meant for her to stand at the entrance to the Suez Canal, where, in the veil and dress of an Egyptian peasant woman, she would have held up a lantern that symbolized the light of Egypt bringing progress to Asia. That plan, however, had been rejected by Egypt's ruler Khedive Isma'il Pasha as too expensive, and so Bartholdi went back to the drawing board, where he converted progress into liberty. He draped his figure in the robes of ancient Greece and turned the lantern into a torch, and the statue, when it was finally built, became a gift from France to the United States in honor of the American centennial. The U.S. Congress, however, refused to allocate the funds needed to build the granite pedestal on which she would stand, and the centennial came and went without the statue there to commemorate it. Eventually the American fund-raising committee had the idea of displaying the statue's right arm outside Madison Square Park to bring attention to her plight. For seven years, from 1877 until 1884, the immense slender arm had risen gracefully over the treeline of the park, but little progress was made until Joseph Pulitzer issued a personal appeal for funds in the pages of *The World.* From the paper's working-class readers, many of them immigrants, came pennies, nickels, sometimes dollars. Within five months the $100,000 was raised—80 percent of it from donations of less than a dollar—and two years later the Statue of Liberty proudly stood at the entrance to New York Harbor, her presence a testimony not only to the immigrants who were already transforming the life of the city, but also to the seemingly illimitable power of its press.

The *Augusta Victoria* slid smoothly toward the open water of the Atlantic. Some of the passengers began to settle themselves into deck chairs, wrapping steamer rugs around themselves against the chill of the day. Word had begun to circulate among them that the young woman in the plaid coat was the reporter Nellie Bly, embarking on a race around the world. One of the passengers struck up a conversation with her, pointing out that a voyage truly begins only when the harbor pilot disembarks and the captain assumes command of the ship. "So now," he said, "you are really on your tour around the world."

She did not immediately reply. *Tour around the world:* something in his words called up thoughts of seasickness. Never having been on a sea voyage before—and being prone of late to nauseous headaches—she had feared that she would fall victim to the malady known among ocean travelers of the time as "the green monster." Now she began to notice more acutely the humming of the engines, the constant vibrations in her feet, the queasying rise and fall of the ship. Her face must have betrayed her discomfort, for the man asked her, not unkindly, "Do you get seasick?" That was enough; she looked blindly down for a moment, then rushed to the rail and threw up over the side. When she turned back around, wiping the tears from her eyes, she noticed that the passengers nearby were smiling; other people's seasickness, as it turned out, was an endless source of amusement aboard ocean liners. One of the men said dismissively, "And she's going around the world."

Bly joined in the laughter that followed; silently, though, she was marveling at her own boldness.

NELLIE BLY'S JOURNEY to that ship had started almost exactly a year before, in the fall of 1888. Sundays were the days Bly customarily devoted to thinking up ideas for new stories, and though good ones were never easy to come up with, on this particular Sunday she had spent most of the day and half of the night searching in vain for even a single suitable idea. Of late her exhausting work pace had begun to take a toll on her; after a lifetime of near-perfect health, she had started to get migraine headaches, some of them so severe that she was confined to her bed. Now, once again, her head was aching, and the longer she tossed and turned in bed the more frustrated she became. Her want of ideas kept her from getting sleep, and her want of sleep kept her from getting ideas, and by three o'clock in the morning she had decided that she could think of nothing worse than being a newspaper columnist, and at some point the thought occurred to her that she wished she was at the other end of the earth.

That thought brought her up short. She could use a break, that much was certain—in her two years of work as a newspaper journalist, she hadn't taken a single day of vacation—so why *not* a trip around the world? She lay in bed for a while contemplating the prospect of it. Growing up in Pennsylvania, she had heard countless family stories of her great-uncle Thomas Kennedy, who as a young man had traveled around the world. The trip had taken him three years and had ruined his health, but he had done it, and it was what people remembered about him. Of course, she had no intention of spending three years working her way around the world, as her uncle had done; she had always been too restless to sit still for long, too impatient to discover what came next. If she could make it around the world as swiftly as, say, Phileas Fogg had, she would definitely consider doing it. But was it actually possible to make the trip in eighty days, as Jules Verne had imagined it might be? As she pondered that question she could feel her body relax, and before long she had drifted off to sleep, secure in her determination that she would soon know whether she might become a real-life Phileas Fogg.

The next day, Monday, she set off for Bowling Green on lower Broadway; the offices of most of the city's steamship lines were clustered there, in a row of ancient brick houses that had once belonged to the families of wealthy merchants. Bly entered one of the offices and picked out a selection of timetables for ships and trains. With some trepidation at what she might find, she sat down and began to consult them. At first the tables seemed to be nothing more than long columns of random numbers, but little by little she began to piece them together. The regular business of the steamship office went on all around her; well-dressed New Yorkers came in to buy tickets, compare fares for different classes of accommodation, inquire about lost baggage. She stared at the pages spread out before her like a mathematician who has stumbled onto the solution to a long-vexing problem, checking and rechecking her work.

A trip around the world, she now felt sure, could be accomplished in eighty days. With some luck, it might be done in as little as seventy-five.

Excitedly gathering up her papers, Bly left the steamship office and set off for *The World*'s headquarters. At the foot of Park Row stood the *Herald*'s office building, a white marble palace with black walnut doors flanked by six richly ornamented columns. Farther along the street's few short blocks were the offices of the *Mail and Express,* the *Commercial Advertiser,* the *Times* (struggling in its fourth decade, and widely considered too respectable ever to be successful), the *Daily News,* the *Morning Journal,* and, at the end of the street, the *Tribune,* its impressive clock tower facing the statue of Benjamin Franklin at Printing-House Square. *The*

World, where Bly was headed, was midway up the street, at 31–32 Park Row.

John Cockerill, the paper's editor in charge, would have been expecting Bly, as she came to his office every Monday morning to discuss story possibilities. With his large body and massive head, Cockerill seemed scarcely less imposing than he had when she first came to interview him about women journalists. "Have you any ideas?" he asked her as she sat down.

"One," she replied. To this Cockerill said nothing; he played with the pens on his desk, waiting for her to continue. "I want to go around the world," said Bly. "I want to go around in eighty days or less. I think I can beat Phileas Fogg's record. May I try it?"

Cockerill was not enthusiastic; he told Bly that *The World*'s editorial staff had thought of that very idea some time before, and though nothing had come of it, the intention of the editors had always been to send a man. However, Cockerill said, he was not personally opposed to her going, and he suggested that the two of them go talk to the paper's business manager, George Turner.

"It is impossible for you to do it," Turner said firmly when he heard what Bly was proposing. In the first place, he explained, she was a woman and therefore would require a protector to travel with her. *The World* couldn't very well have a young female reporter wandering across the farthest reaches of the globe without a chaperone; it was far too dangerous. Most newspapers were uncomfortable about sending their female reporters around the city, much less around the world. And even if it *was* possible for her to travel unaccompanied, as a female traveler she would require so many bags—probably a dozen trunks or more—that she would never be able to make the rapid changes that this sort of lightning trip would require.

Bly tried to protest, but Turner cut her off. "There is no use talking about it," he said. "No one but a man can do this."

In her year at *The World,* Bly had braved the terrors of an insane asylum, had exposed the corrupt workings of the state's most powerful lobbyist, had put herself at risk to identify a predator when the police themselves had been unwilling to do it. She had proven to her own satisfaction that she possessed as much drive and determination as any male reporter, but she was perfectly willing, if called upon to do so, to prove it once more. "Very well," she said angrily. "Start the man, and I'll start the same day for some other newspaper and I'll beat him."

George Turner looked at her for a moment. "I believe you would."

NELLIE BLY LEFT TURNER'S OFFICE that day having at least obtained the promise that if *The World* was to send anyone racing around the world, it would be she. For the next year the idea was hardly discussed, as Bly and her editors moved on to other stories. Still, they were by no means the only ones who had considered the possibility of such a trip: the notion of a race to beat Phileas Fogg's eighty days around the world was an idea that seemed to be hanging in the air, ready to be plucked. At some point during the course of that year *The World* received a letter from a reader in Toledo, Ohio, outlining such a trip and putting himself forward as the man to carry it out; a similar letter was subsequently received from a reader in Bangor, Maine. That same year a Washington correspondent on the *World* staff proposed to undertake a timed race around the world; he had apparently given a good deal of thought to how it might be done, and was deeply disappointed to learn from his editors that the idea was already under consideration. In the fall of 1889, the New York theatrical agent Henry C. Jarrett was discussing the notion with several other members of the Players Club, a Gramercy Park social club founded by the legendary actor Edwin Booth. Much as Verne had imagined with Fogg at his Reform Club in London, Jarrett's friends at the Players Club stoutly declared that an eighty-day trip around the world was inconceivable—too many things, they insisted, could go wrong—while Jarrett maintained that such a trip could be not only conceived, but accomplished. And as had happened with Fogg and his whist partners, the discussion grew spirited enough that eventually wagers were made on the proposition.

Henry C. Jarrett, as it happened, had already made his mark in the field of record-breaking travel. In 1876 he had organized a cross-country train trip that carried his theatrical troupe from New York to San Francisco in only eighty-three hours—less than half the time such a trip normally required. The consummate impresario, Jarrett had persuaded James Gordon Bennett, Jr., the publisher of the *Herald,* to underwrite half the cost of the trip in exchange for exclusive rights to the story. Now, before he began preparing for an around-the-world journey, Jarrett stopped by

The World's offices to inform the editors of his plans, hoping that the paper would sponsor the trip as the *Herald* had his earlier one. (In the intervening years *The World* had supplanted the *Herald* as the city's most widely read newspaper.) Hearing that the trip had already been promised to Nellie Bly, *The World* later reported, Jarrett "courteously and gallantly gave way to the young lady."

Jarrett had been gracious in stepping aside, but as *The World*'s editors were acutely aware, he could well change his mind and offer his idea to one of the city's other papers, particularly if enough time passed without an announcement of a trip by Bly. And even if Jarrett held to his word, there was no assurance that someone else would not get the same idea. By this point it was clear that a kind of critical mass had been achieved: someone, sometime soon, was going to race around the world. To *The World*'s editors, the prospect of Henry C. Jarrett, or some other would-be circumnavigator, embarking on a well-publicized race under the aegis of a rival newspaper was highly distressing—particularly given their paper's recent downturn in sales—and anxiety seems to have pressed them into action. Late in the afternoon of Monday, November 11, John Cockerill sent Nellie Bly a note requesting that she see him in his office at once.

An urgent editorial summons was an unusual enough event that Bly spent the entire trip downtown wondering just what she had done to bring on a scolding. She entered his office and sat down by his desk, waiting for him to acknowledge her presence. Finally looking up from his writing, Cockerill asked her, "Can you start around the world day after tomorrow?"

"I can start this minute," Bly replied.

The steamship *City of Paris* was leaving New York for Southampton on Wednesday morning, Cockerill said, and it would surely arrive in time to catch the mail train out of London bound for the Italian port city of Brindisi. But the editors of *The World* preferred to book her on the *Augusta Victoria,* leaving Thursday morning; that way she would not have to spend an extra day in London waiting for the Brindisi train and could thus cut a day's travel time from her trip. Still, he warned, there was a risk: if the *Augusta Victoria* was slowed by rough weather crossing the Atlantic, she might fail to connect with the mail train.

"I will take my chances on the *Augusta Victoria,* and save the extra day," she said.

Nellie Bly walked out of Cockerill's office, her head filled with a thousand things. Outside, New York careened around her. Night had fallen, and the electric lights shimmered in the puddles left from the morning's rain. On Park Row white clouds of steam, produced by underground printing presses, wafted up through grates in the sidewalk; the illuminated clock face on the *Tribune* tower shone like a full moon. By the thousands the city's working people, sewing girls, typewriters, clerks, streamed from the buildings into the streets, like her, heading home. Only she among them, though, was about to race around the world. Her astonishment gave everything a soft edge of unreality. It was Monday night; by Thursday she would be crossing the Atlantic Ocean.

That evening she and her mother went to the Broadway Theatre, where Edwin Booth himself was performing as Hamlet. The next morning, sometime after ten o'clock, she set off for the studio of the dressmaker William Ghormley (*Robes et Manteaux*), on Nineteenth Street east of Fifth Avenue, in one of the city's most exclusive commercial districts. Ghormley had opened his shop ten years earlier, and over that time he had become one of the favored dressmakers of New York society, his agents in Paris, Lyons, London, and other European fashion capitals always on the lookout for the latest styles and colors.

"I want a dress by this evening," Bly told him.

"Very well," Ghormley replied unconcernedly, as though a young woman requesting a dress on a few hours' notice was a regular occurrence. Usually one of his creations required at least several days in the making, and this was by no means exceptional. The one hundred fifty gowns ordered by Mrs. Vanderbilt for the female guests of her famous 1883 ball had kept Monsieur Lanouette's one hundred forty dressmakers working around the clock for five weeks.

"I want a dress," she added, "that will withstand constant wear for three months."

William Ghormley brought out several different materials from his storeroom in the back and tossed them onto a small table. He held up the fabrics in front of him to study the various effects in a pier glass on the wall; he performed his examinations as carefully and unhurriedly as a veteran medical man, maintaining a lively conversation all the while but never taking his gaze from the work before him. Within a few minutes he had decided on a plain blue broadcloth and patterned camel's hair as an attractive and durable combination for a traveling gown, and immediately set to work measuring and cutting. By the time Bly left the shop, around one o'clock, the dress had been boned and fitted; she was to return again at five for a final fitting.

Meanwhile, in the *World* offices downtown, furious preparations were being made. To everyone's great dismay, it turned out that Nellie Bly did not possess a passport, and so the editorial writer Edward S. Van Zile had been immediately dispatched to Washington, D.C., to obtain one. Van Zile arrived in Washington late Monday night, and the next morning managed to obtain a meeting with no less a personage than Secretary of State James G. Blaine. Hearing of *The World*'s passport dilemma, . Blaine promised Van Zile that he would personally handle the matter. The secretary of state proved to be as good as his word, and the next day, Wednesday, he delivered a temporary passport for Nellie Bly. At once Van Zile sped back to New York, arriving in the city at four-thirty Thursday morning—exactly five hours before Bly's scheduled departure—with Special Passport Number 247 in hand.

Another member of the *World* staff was sent on a shorter but no less important journey, just across City Hall Park to 261 Broadway, where the leading international travel agency, Thomas Cook & Son, had its New York offices. At Cook's a tentative itinerary for Bly's trip was worked out. If all went according to plan, the *Augusta Victoria* would deposit Nellie Bly in Southampton, England, on November 21. In Southampton she could catch an overnight train to London and then proceed onward by train to Brindisi, Italy, arriving on the twenty-fifth. There she would board the Peninsula and Oriental steamer *Cathay,* bound for points east. Christmas she would spend in Hong Kong, and then, after a three-day layover (one of the very few pauses allowed for in the schedule), she would depart for Yokohama, Japan. On January 7 she would board a Pacific steamship, with the goal of reaching San Francisco by January 22. The last leg of her journey would be a train to New York, which, barring unforeseen delays, would allow her to make a triumphant return to the *World* offices on January 27. Seventy-five days, then, around the world.

The itinerary, *The World* admitted in its announcement of the trip, was "very pretty on paper, but it is a case of man proposes and God disposes." As Henry Jarrett's companions in the Players Club had pointed out, a trip of some thirty thousand miles brought with it nearly as many details, all of them just waiting to go wrong. Nellie Bly, for instance, might become sick en route (this was by no means a remote possibility, given the extreme changes in climate she would endure, from damp, drizzly London to sun-baked Aden), and, as *The World* noted, "a fever-racked patient is hardly a fit subject to play the part of Mercury." She might encounter one of the sea storms called typhoons, or one of the sandstorms called simoons. Icebergs were a constant danger; in the previous eight years three dozen steamships had been damaged by ice on the North Atlantic. There was, literally at every moment, the chance of a mechanical breakdown, which was bad enough if it occurred on land or in port but potentially catastrophic on the high seas. Even a seemingly minor delay could result in a missed connection, leading to further delays, like a boulder gaining speed as it rolls downhill, with disaster the inevitable result.

The World made very clear that Nellie Bly would simply "take her luck as a first-class passenger, using the facilities which are now demanded by travellers." She would not be permitted to hire any chartered locomotives or special boats to help her make especially fast time, for that would undermine the trip's central purpose—to determine how quickly and efficiently a typical traveler could move around the globe using only "the ordinary lines of commerce." Intent on having Bly's trip be seen as more than just a publicity stunt, *The World* was busily promoting it as another instance of public interest journalism, in which Nellie Bly would experience at first hand the latest conveniences and lingering hardships of the modern age of travel. Bly had been instructed to keep her eyes and ears open while she sped around the globe, and *The World* promised its readers that she would return with "suggestions for improvement in travel, in treatment of travellers, in costume and what not, all told in a woman's gossipy fashion."

WILLIAM GHORMLEY HAD made good on his promise to create a traveling gown in a single day; so, too, did Bly's regular dressmaker, Florence Wheelwright, from whom she had ordered a second lightweight dress for warmer weather. On Wednesday night, though, making her final preparations for the trip, Bly discovered that the dress simply would not fit into the traveling bag she had bought. She faced a stark choice: either bring a second bag or go around the world in only one dress. She gave up the extra dress.

Bly was absolutely determined to carry only a single bag on her trip, and not just because she wanted her travel to be reduced to its most efficient possible form, with no need to check trunks or look after wayward bags that might or might not ever catch up to her as she sped around the globe. Just as important, she wanted to give the lie to the timeworn notion that a woman could not travel without taking along several pieces of luggage. (Even *The World,* in its first report of her trip, marveled that Bly was not taking "a Saratoga nor even a thin flat state-room trunk, when many a belle thinks herself going in wretchedly unprovided fashion if she does not take a round dozen of great roomy trunks for a fortnight's stay at a Summer resort.") The year before Bly's trip, the popular travel writer Thomas W. Knox had published *How to Travel: Hints, Advice, and Suggestions to Travelers by Land and Sea All Over the Globe,* which contained a chapter entitled "Special Advice to Ladies." The chapter consisted of nine pages of remarkably specific advice about how to pack one's bags for a transatlantic voyage. It recommended that the female traveler bring a small steamer trunk and satchel into her stateroom, containing all of the items that would be necessary while on board, as well as a larger trunk to be stored in the ship's hold; ideally, that trunk should measure approximately fourteen square feet at its bottom.

For her single carrying bag Nellie Bly chose a sturdy leather gripsack measuring at its bottom sixteen by seven inches. In that small space she managed to pack a lightweight silk bodice, three veils, a pair of slippers, a set of toiletries, an inkstand, pens, pencils, paper, pins, needles and thread, a dressing gown, a tennis blazer, a flask and drinking cup, several changes of underwear (flannel for cold weather, silk for hot), handkerchiefs, and a jar of cold cream to prevent her skin from chapping in the various climates she would encounter. (That jar of cold cream, Bly would later admit, "was the bane of my existence." It was large and bulky and often kept her bag from closing, but she refused to give it up.) With these few provisions she felt confident that she could meet whatever conditions she might encounter along the way. "If one is traveling simply for the sake of traveling," Bly liked to say, "and not for the purpose of impressing fellow travelers, the problem of baggage becomes a very simple one."

There was, of course, the problem of laundry, and this was an issue to which she gave close consideration in the days before her departure. On the railroads, she knew, there would be no laundry service available, but fortunately the longest railway journey of the trip, between San Francisco and New York, was scheduled to last only four days. The transoceanic steamships, though, maintained their own laundries, and Bly had discovered that the steamers that would take her across Asia, though smaller than the ocean liners, produced amounts of washed clothing each day to rival even the largest laundries of New York. Bly had decided not to bring any jewelry other than a thin gold band that she wore on the thumb of her left hand. She believed this ring was a lucky talisman, as she had been wearing it on the day of her interview with *The World* two years earlier, when she had lost all her money and desperately needed a job. She was also bringing with her two self-winding watches, one of them set into a leather band on her wrist (a highly unusual style for the period), to be adjusted to the local time as she traveled, and the other snug in her pocket, this one a beautiful gold-plated 24-hour watch, which, in antici-pation of her return, would remain set to New York time. On Wednes-day night Bly went to the *World* office, where she received £200 in English gold and Bank of England notes as well as $2,500 in American gold and bills that she would attempt to use at the various ports she visited, to test how widely American currency was accepted around the world. The gold she would keep in her pocket, the notes in a chamois leather bag tied securely around her neck.

The next morning, at the pier in Hoboken, Bly received five copies of that day's *World,* the issue announcing her departure aboard the *Au-gusta Victoria;* the papers were not intended to be given as mementos to foreign hosts, but simply to accompany her all the way around the globe, so that on her return they would become, in *The World*'s phrase, "rare souvenirs." Bly stowed the five newspapers at the bottom of her grip-sack, where she also carried the temporary passport that had been so hast-ily obtained by Edward Van Zile. She was not carrying a revolver, though it had been suggested to her as a suitable companion piece for the pass-port. She believed strongly that the world would greet her as she greeted it; and in any case, she insisted, if her conduct was proper she would al-ways find men ready to protect her.

NOVEMBER 14–21, 1889
Atlantic Ocean

The *Augusta Victoria,* of the Hamburg-American Line, had a straight stem and a long graceful body, and its three funnels were the color of heavy cream. It was often referred to as one of the "greyhounds of the ocean." It was a twin-screw steamer, which meant it contained a system of double propulsion—twin engines connected to twin shafts and twin propellers. The two mechanisms, separated by wooden bulkheads running from stem to stern, could be operated independently, so that if one was damaged or otherwise incapacitated, the other, as a Hamburg-American advertising pamphlet noted, "will continue to work and propel the ship with perfect ease." Thus the twin-screw ship could depend for its passage entirely on mechanical power: steam had at last conquered sail. The stand of masts that had defined countless generations of ocean-going ships had now evolved, vestigially, into bare flagpoles, the array of billowing canvas sails giving way to smaller flags of country and company. Four hundred sixty feet long, with four complete decks, the *Augusta Victoria* was the largest ship ever built in a German yard. It had accommodations for 364 first-class and 116 second-class passengers, and another 695 could ride in steerage. Nellie Bly was berthed in stateroom Number 60, on the port side. Like the ship's other first-class accommodations, hers was a pleasant, surprisingly high-ceilinged room, and one with an especially desirable location, as she was directly amidships, the section of the ship least affected by the vibration of the engines and so least likely to bring on attacks of seasickness.

The Augusta Victoria, the steamship on which Nellie Bly crossed the Atlantic Ocean

Bly's first attack had occurred within minutes of the ship's setting sail, and her physical discomfort had been made far worse by the fear that she might be sick for the seventy days of her journey to be spent on the water. It was a reasonable enough concern: she had, after all, never been on a long sea voyage and so had not developed her sea legs, the tolerance to a boat's rocking motion that seemed to build up over time, like a violinist's callus, inuring one to future discomfort. Moreover, it was widely known that women suffered more than men from seasickness, a misery that, like the pains of labor, could never be adequately communicated to those who had not experienced it. The sufferer was liable to feel at once freezing and feverish, unable to sit up without a sickening nausea; even the softest and most innocuous sounds—a creak of a floorboard, the lapping of the waves—reverberated inside the head as loudly and unnervingly as the yowl of an alleycat. The wretchedness of the condition was perhaps best conveyed by the old saying that those suffering from seasickness believe they will die on the first day, are sure they will on the second, and hope they will on the third. After her first voyage to Europe, Harriet Beecher Stowe had written, "I wonder that people who wanted to break the souls of heroes and martyrs never thought of sending them to sea and keeping them a little seasick." Worse still, one could not be sure how long an attack would last, nor that any of the proffered remedies would actually lessen its agonies, for even after millennia of human travel on the water, little was known about the malady's prevention or cure. Those afflicted were variously instructed to lie down and to stand up, to rest and to exercise, to seek out darkness and light. They were advised to drink champagne, port, brandy, rum, or salt water (the latter treatment, it was admitted, "makes the drinker very miserable for a few minutes"); to eat chicken, oysters, celery, marmalade, hot West Indian pickles, or to eat nothing at all. In his *Practical Treatise on Sea-Sickness* (1880), Dr. George M. Beard suggested chloral hydrate—more popularly known as knockout drops—though he cautioned that it was "not recommended for daily or long-continued use."

Lunch was served on the *Augusta Victoria* at one o'clock. On the first day, still weak from her earlier attack of seasickness, Bly made her way to the first-class passengers' dining hall in the ship's deckhouse. It was a large room, decorated in a rococo style that the industry journal *The Marine Engineer* generously termed "mixed Renaissance." Overhead arched a canopy of stained glass; there were bronze statues, gilded mirrors, intricately painted panels done by "the best artists of the German school." Stewards in full dress and white gloves moved noiselessly about, seeming to anticipate passengers' needs before they were spoken. A group of musicians—the stewards of the second-class dining hall, hired in part for their musical skills—played an overture for the passengers as they arrived. As an honored guest, Bly was seated at the captain's table, in the armchair directly to his left. Soon the captain himself, handsome and bearded, took his place at the head of the table. The waiters ladled out the soup; Bly discovered that she had an overwhelming desire not to see, smell, or taste food at least until they had reached land. The passengers began to introduce themselves. To Bly's embarrassment, the others at the table turned out to be old hands at ocean crossings, and she thought she saw indulgent smiles on all their faces when, feeling another attack coming on, she put a handkerchief over her mouth and did her best to excuse herself politely from the table. "Miss Bly," said Captain Albers, "you must come back every time." One of the stewards helped her to a secluded spot on the deck, where again she was sick. Back inside the dining room, she was greeted with a hearty round of congratulations for her fortitude—"The only way to conquer seasickness is by forcing oneself to eat," the captain noted approvingly—but the bravos of her tablemates only made her more conscious of her precarious condition, and when the fish course was placed before her she felt her stomach start to turn, and, choking behind her handkerchief, she was forced to excuse herself to the deck for a second time.

Bly, though, had made up her mind that she could not afford to be seasick, that she would heed as long as she could the captain's advice to keep coming back to the table, and so, like a boxer who returns to the center of the ring after having been knocked down, she returned again, on unsteady legs, to the warmth and murmur of the dining room. She was aware now that every unexpected sensation—the flare of a light, a food's aroma, even the expression on someone's face—could by itself bring on a new wave of nausea. The band still played its distressing tunes. She did her best to focus on the story the captain was telling. Once she caught the eye of a waiter, who seemed to be watching her with an amused gleam in his eye; again Bly felt sick, and for the third time, blindly, despairingly, she rushed out of the dining room. Staggering once more back inside, she now felt that she had already passed over to the third stage of seasickness, in which one hopes for death. Her head was on fire, but her hands and feet seemed to be encased in ice. She tried to keep as still as possible; she felt she could scarcely remember a time when moving had not been a misery. The courses arrived in seemingly endless succession. She spoke little and ate less, and it was all she could do, when at last the final course had been served, to mumble that the meal had been very good and then excuse herself and head wobblingly back to her cabin, where she crawled into bed and almost immediately fell asleep.

She slept all through the night. Later she would recall some dim, awful dreams, and waking up once to take a few sips of tea, but beyond this all was oblivion until she heard a voice calling her name. Opening her eyes, she found a stewardess and one of the female passengers in her cabin and Captain Albers standing at the door. "We were afraid that you were dead," he said jovially.

"I always sleep late in the morning," she said, in as apologetic a tone as she could muster.

"In the morning!" exclaimed the captain with a laugh. "It is half past four in the evening!

"But never mind," he added, "as long as you slept well it will do you good. Now get up and see if you can't eat a big dinner."

Feeling half-drugged with sleep, Bly pulled herself out of bed and drank a cup of tea. When she went back up on deck she found, to her great relief, that she felt perfectly well, and at dinner that evening she did not miss a course.

ON THE OPEN OCEAN, far from the greenery of the land, the air smelled different, clean and crisp and mineral. The sea during that trip was often very rough. The ship's bow plunged into the waves, sending gusts of spray in every direction, gliding beneath the water before rising, like a porpoise, for air, and then diving again. The ship rose and fell, rose and fell without cease; a seat on one of the deck chairs was like a marathon ride aboard the Serpentine Railway at Coney Island. Bly came to enjoy the rhythmic toss of the ship, though in the early days of the voyage she was haunted by the idea that her seasickness would return. Many of the women were indeed sick, and on rough days the men stayed below in the smoking room. Among some of the passengers it became a morbid fascination to observe the twenty feet of new railing near the ship's deckhouse. The rail had been torn away a month earlier by a hurricane that battered the *Augusta Victoria* three days out from England; only by grabbing a steam winch had the ship's chief officer kept himself from being swept overboard in the gale.

On calmer days the passengers of the first and second classes idled on deck. Most spent their time reading, or chatting, or napping, or strolling. Three times another ship was sighted in the distance, and each sighting occasioned a great excitement among the passengers. Almost any break in the endless line of the horizon—a sail, a leaping fish, a seabird—that on land would be given hardly a second thought was treated aboard ship as a major event. There was shuffleboard on deck, and the venerable shipboard game called bull, which consisted of tossing leather-covered lead rings onto a numbered scoreboard. On deck the women wore heavy skirts, as the sea breezes did not respect proper decorum; some had sewn weights, or little packets of coins, into the hems. In the evenings the band played concerts under the stars. After dinner, tea was served in the ladies' saloon, where the furnishings were upholstered in plush of a delicate lavender, while the men took cigars and brandy in the smoking room. The music room, decorated with oil paintings and rich hangings of silk and damask, contained a grand piano, and many evenings were cheerfully passed in group singing. Nellie Bly was not much for singing, and she found the long unfilled hours tiresome—she was anxious to reach England and get on with her trip—but she amused herself by noting the idiosyncrasies of the other passengers. One man, she saw, took his pulse after each meal; another, for some reason, counted the number of steps he took each day. At some point during the voyage Bly discovered that one of the female passengers had not gotten undressed since the ship embarked several days earlier. "I am sure we are all going down," she explained, "and I am determined to go down dressed."

For the first-class passengers, it was possible to spend the entire day eating. Breakfast was served at eight o'clock, lunch at one, and dinner at seven, but platters of fresh fruit were available for the early risers, and cups of bouillon were brought around on trays in the midmorning, followed by sandwiches at noon, ices at three, tea at four, and sweets at five; and at nine o'clock, for those who somehow could still manage an appetite, a late supper was served in the main saloon. For sheer luxury the meals rivaled anything to be found at Delmonico's or the Brunswick, the dishes prepared in the ornate style of the period, strongly French in influence and often named for generals and heads of state. A typical bill of fare for a dinner served on one of the oceangoing steamships of the period offered choices from twenty-nine separate dishes in nine courses, literally from soup to nuts. There was turtle soup to start, and *blanquettes de poulet aux champignons,* and *filets de boeuf* à la Bordelaise, and saddle of mutton with jelly, and ham in champagne sauce, and roast turkey with truffles, and *pommes de terre Duchesse,* and Marlborough pudding, and a great deal more, ending with a selection of fruits and nuts served with the *café noir.* The ship's bakers began work at four in the morning to make the rolls and cakes for breakfast; the cooks, attired in their formal chef's whites, turned out a banquet for hundreds of diners several times a day for a week straight, and did so from galley kitchens that rolled and tossed underfoot, in which the pots and pans had to be fitted into deep grooves to prevent them from sliding off the stove. A near battalion of uniformed household staff was in constant attendance, cooks and stewards and laundresses and chambermaids, transforming the modern steamship, in the much-used phrase of the day, into a floating palace, where guests could live for a week like royalty, with servants who appeared at the press of an ivory button, with a perpetually groaning board, a well-stocked library and an equally well-stocked bar, and a band of ready musicians: all of it helping to divert attention from the dark, churning water outside, from the too-real prospect of lurking icebergs, from the very absurdity of the notion, if one dwelled on it too long, of crossing the Atlantic Ocean in a boat.

For those traveling below, there were no such diversions. The majority of the passengers aboard the *Augusta Victoria* were not fed in grand style at all hours of the day, were not permitted a stroll on the upper deck, could not enter the smoking room or the music room or the library, did not have high-ceilinged staterooms—did not, indeed, have any rooms at all. For the seven hundred passengers traveling in steerage the experience of steamship life was an entirely different one. They slept in large, barracks-like rooms (unmarried men all together in one room, unmarried women in another, and married couples and their families in a third), dark, foul, airless places, blocked off from the rest of the ship by massive iron doors. Bathrooms were widely shared, not the private facilities offered on many of the modern ships. There were never enough sinks, and those that there were had to suffice for all purposes; dishes were washed and clothes cleaned in the same basins used to dispose of vomit. "No sick cans are furnished," a U.S. Immigration Commission would later report, "and not even large receptacles for waste. The vomitings of the sick are often permitted to remain a long time before being removed. The floors, when iron, are continually damp, and when of wood they reek with foul odor because they are not washed." No chambermaids ever descended with fresh linens, as the passengers here had to provide their own bedding, as well as their own plates, cups, and eating utensils; one of the regular sights of the steamship age was the long line of men and women waiting to trudge onto the ship, dressed nearly alike in dark bulky overcoats, lugging their shapeless bundles of bedding and crockery on their backs, like a defeated people in flight from advancing armies.

Breakfast was either bread and butter or oatmeal and molasses; lunch, the main meal of the day, included soup and a serving of meat or fish with potatoes and bread, and on Sundays a dessert; dinner consisted simply of tea with bread and butter, though sometimes there was a second dinner of oatmeal gruel. Unlike the formal service in the dining halls of the upper decks, in steerage the stewards simply set the food down in the middle of the table and left those who were seated around it to fend for themselves. Even this was an improvement over earlier generations of steerage, when the passengers were required to cook their own meals in one of the ship's galleys. "It needs no imagination," noted a magazine writer of the time, "to picture the struggle of immigrants, one against another, for a turn at the fire."

Downstairs they ate their meals and afterward cleaned up as best they could, and they endured the toss of the ship and the loud ceaseless vibrations of the engines, and they talked, and squabbled among themselves over the available food and space, and their children ran and played games in the narrow passages of the lower deck. Even these basic activities served, for the other passengers on the ship, as yet another kind of shipboard recreation. For the passengers of the ship's upper classes, it was a regular form of entertainment to lean over the railing of the top deck and observe those down in steerage, much like the society matrons who would order the drivers of their carriages to make a brief turn through the slum district so they might gain an agreeably shocking glimpse of how, as the journalist and social reformer Jacob A. Riis memorably put it, the other half lived, before hastening back uptown. It was "great fun to watch life in the steerage," recalled one traveler of the time, adding, predictably enough, that "they were a merry lot, although deprived of nearly every comfort." Sometimes, for extra fun, those up above tossed coins or candy to those down below, so that they might feel benevolent while watching the enjoyable scramble that ensued. In 1883 a Bostonian by the name of Fannie A. Tyler was reprimanded by her ship's officers for bringing baked apples from her table to some of the children down in steerage; she had been moved to action by the pity she felt in comparing the happy, capering children at the top of the stairs to the hungry ones below. "The children among us pelt the little ones not so fortunate as they with nuts and raisins," she wrote; "and these look up . . . with such eagerness they remind me of a nest of little birds waiting for the food the faithful mother-bird will surely bring."

More often than not, those traveling in steerage were engaged in far more serious business than a European vacation, or a race around the world. Most were immigrants fleeing the poverty and oppression of their native countries for what they hoped would be a better life in the United States; or conversely, they were returning home with whatever little sums they had been able to save during their time there. The ships' manifests reveal the men to have been policemen, farmers, sailors, waiters, weavers, gardeners, publicans, bricklayers; often they were identified in the most elemental terms, simply as *worker*. The women were generally categorized only as *wife* or *single*. They were, for the most part, people with trades and families, who had been thrown together in overcrowded, unsanitary conditions, without sufficient air and light, made to subsist on fare that was as meager as it was monotonous. For those traveling in steerage, an oceangoing steamship was not a floating palace but a floating tenement: the class system did not stop at the water's edge but was instead perfectly replicated, in miniature, aboard ship.

When Nellie Bly first came to the *World* offices two years before to seek work as a reporter, the story idea she had suggested was to sail back from England in steerage so that she might allow *The World*'s readers to learn about the appalling conditions endured by those below on their journey across the ocean. Now, as a celebrated *World* reporter, she was only a few steps away, but during her time on the *Augusta Victoria* she seems never to have set foot into steerage, and she never wrote a word about it.

NOVEMBER 21–22, 1889
Southampton, England

As the bad weather persisted, Bly grew increasingly nervous about her chances of catching the mail train from London to Brindisi; missing that train, she knew, meant failure, an end to the journey almost before it had begun. She could not help but question her decision to take the *Augusta Victoria* rather than the *City of Paris:* perhaps she had overplayed her hand, dared too much too soon. The *Augusta Victoria* had been due in Southampton at ten in the morning on Thursday, November 21, but it was already past noon before the Scilly Light was sighted to the southwest of Cornwall, the first glimpse of land since leaving New York. When the cry went up the passengers all rushed to the railing to see if they could make out the shore in the distance. It was just a bleak spot of rocky coastline, but at that moment it was, thought Bly, the most beautiful scenery in the world.

As darkness fell, the *Augusta Victoria* continued its path along the jagged southeastern English coast. Just after midnight the lights of Hurst Castle were sighted at the entrance to the Solent, the narrow strait between the English mainland and the Isle of Wight. If the ship could proceed at full speed it might reach Southampton in time for Nellie Bly to catch the one A.M. train to London, but the water continued to be very rough, with a strong wind bearing straight down on the ship, and by the time the *Augusta Victoria* had rounded the long strip of sand that divides the Solent from the Southampton River and finally sailed into port, it was two o'clock Friday morning—sixteen hours past schedule. Still more critical time was lost in waiting for the tugboat to arrive to take off the departing passengers. Several of Bly's companions from the captain's table had stayed up late to see her off, and she spent the last minutes idly chatting with them and nervously walking up and down the deck. Tracey Greaves, *The World*'s London correspondent, was supposed to meet her in Southampton, but the hour was so late that she did not expect Greaves still to be there. Everyone was wrapped in traveling rugs against the night's chill; she could see her breath steam and rise in the air. The minutes dragged on. She felt herself standing at the threshold of a great room, not permitted to enter. Her satchel had been ready since noon.

It was half past two before the tugboat finally pulled up alongside the

Augusta Victoria and a gangplank was set into place. Bly positioned herself near the top of the gangplank. A tall young man stepped up on deck, looking over the waiting passengers in a quick, bright way that made her think he must be the *World* reporter. "Nellie Bly?" he asked.

"Yes," she replied gratefully, holding out her hand, which he gave a cordial grasp while asking if she had enjoyed her trip, and if her baggage was ready to be transferred.

Her baggage, she answered, was already in her hand.

A few more warm handclasps, last best wishes sent all around, a little dry feeling of sadness in her throat, and she hurried down the gangplank onto the tugboat waiting to take the passengers to shore. The boat bobbed maddeningly for a few more minutes on the waves, and then the hum of the engines grew louder and the tug pulled away from the glow of the *Augusta Victoria* toward the darkness of the shore. The cabin was stuffed full of luggage and mail and lit by an old oil lamp with a smoked globe; Bly stood with Tracey Greaves and the other passengers up on deck, shivering in the cold fog.

Greaves turned to her. He had exciting news. "Mr. and Mrs. Jules Verne," he said, "have sent a special letter asking that, if possible, you stop to see them."

"Oh, how I should like to!" Bly exclaimed. Then she thought for a moment. Jules Verne, she knew, lived in Amiens, France. "Isn't it hard," she murmured, half to herself, "to be forced to decline such a treat."

"I think it can be done," said Greaves, "if you are willing to go without sleep or rest for two nights."

The last train, he explained to her, had already left for London, and the next one would not leave until morning. If they had to remain in Southampton all night there would not be enough time to make the detour to Amiens on the way to Brindisi. There was, however, still one hope. He had been talking to the Southampton postmaster and officials of the London Southwestern Railway, and according to post office regulations, if the mails landed on the Southampton dock between one and three o'clock a special train could be ordered for the delivery of mail, and the railway officials had promised that Bly would be provided with a seat on the train. Everything now hinged on whether that mail train would be run. He said grimly, "We shall see when we land what they decide to do."

It was almost three in the morning when the tug pulled up to the

Southampton wharf, as dreary and dingy a place, Bly thought, as ever existed. The Custom House was a large, almost empty shed with a single railroad track running behind it. Greaves took her gripsack and escorted her quickly inside. Dim lights left the corners of the room in shadow; a few sleepy-looking men in rumpled uniforms sat behind long, low tables. "Where are your keys?" one of them asked, taking the bag from Greaves.

"I have none," said Bly. "The satchel is not locked."

The customs officer said to Greaves, "Will you swear that it does not contain any tobacco or tea?"

"Don't swear," Bly told Greaves, and then turned to the official and said, "It's mine."

The officer seemed highly amused by this, and with a broad smile he made a chalk mark on the bag and dismissed them.

Too nervous to remain inside, Bly headed out of the back door of the Custom House and waited in the chilling damp. She looked at her watch. It was just three o'clock. She peered into the distance, as far down the tracks as she could see. Through the fog, like a ghostly rider, the special mail train was moving toward the station.

CHAPTER 6

Living by Railroad Time

NOVEMBER 14, 1889
New York

OUTSIDE THE SKY DARKENED TO
BLACK; IN THE LIGHTED TRAIN COM-
partment the glass slowly turned
from window to mirror. Her face,
Elizabeth Bisland thought, looked
drawn and pale with nerves, but
that new sailor's hat was very be-
coming. If she pressed her nose to the glass she could dimly make out the
contours of the passing landscape. The inky blackness of the night had
blotted out all traces of human activity, so that the land seemed as wild
and unknowable as it must have when Henry Hudson sailed up the river
seeking the passage to Asia. In the distance the cliffs of the Palisades rose
sheer against the sky, like the wall of a massive stone fortress guarding
undreamed-of treasures. She was too exhausted, her thoughts still too
jumbled, to concentrate on the book in her lap. Later, she would have
trouble remembering anything from those first hours. She knew, at least,
that she was on the Fast Western Express of the New York Central Railroad, traveling north along the eastern bank of the Hudson River. If all
went well, she would be arriving in Chicago's Union Depot the follow-

ing evening. From there she would transfer to an Omaha-bound train, and in Omaha connect to a train on the Union Pacific line for San Francisco. The journey from coast to coast would be completed in less than five days, amid a splendor that beggared the imagination. It was as though, in purchasing a ticket, she had been allowed inside one of those grand mansions she passed by on her way to the *Cosmopolitan* offices.

The New York Central Railroad ran out of Grand Central Depot, and the Pennsylvania Railroad out of the Jersey City terminal, and the rival companies had waged a long battle to outdo each other in the amenities they offered their customers (that is to say, their first-class customers—for passengers on trains, like those on steamships, were always divided by class). The very first car produced for the New York Central's Chicago express had been designed by Louis Comfort Tiffany himself, and the subsequent cars were, if anything, even more opulent. The exteriors of the cars were painted the colors of plums and chocolate and olives—dark colors better hid the soot produced by the locomotive— and stenciled with gilt and silver; the interiors had panels of ebony, tiger maple, tulip, amboyna, and other rare woods, combined in ornate decorative patterns. Meticulously turned pieces of wood bloomed into flowers, dragons, winged lions, or whatever else suited the fancy of the craftsman in the railroad shop. New techniques of marquetry were developed; it turned out to be possible, by lightly scorching satinwood in hot sand, to realistically convey the texture of a rose leaf. Individual cars were done in styles suggested by earlier civilizations: English baronial, Italian Renaissance, Spanish mission, Chinese dynasty, ancient Egyptian. A fully equipped train carried not just sleeper cars and a dining car, but also a library car and a smoker car and a parlor car and a barber car; there was talk one day of railroad cars with billiard tables and bowling alleys. Some trains provided stenographers and secretaries for their business travelers. That very morning the Pennsylvania line had announced that it would introduce "ladies' maids" onto its Cincinnati- and Chicago-bound trains. "Their duties will be those of a maid in one's own household," a news story reported, "and they will be particularly charged with the care of ladies traveling alone, ladies with children, and invalids."

The Fast Western Express began its long ascent into the mountains, a single moving light in a world of darkness. The train rolled past the stone redoubt of West Point, past the high country estates of wealthy New Yorkers. There was a low murmur of conversation in the car. Porters moved through the aisle preparing beds for the night. The New York Central Railroad provided actual compartments for passengers in its sleeper cars, not the curtained Pullman sleepers still in use by the Pennsylvania Railroad. A seventy-foot-long car could hold ten compartments; at the ends of the car were three men's and two women's washrooms. Gathering the toiletries case from her Gladstone bag, Elizabeth Bisland used one of the washrooms; then, back at her seat, she climbed up into her sleeper compartment, pulling the door closed behind her, and in that tight space began what she called the "futile wrestlings" with her clothes. Eventually she managed to undress, slipping on her nightgown and then, over it, a warmer dressing gown; it would not do, she told herself, to catch a cold at the very outset of her journey. Her pillow was at the end of the berth toward the front of the train; the window by her feet she cracked open ever so slightly, just enough to allow the free circulation of air in the little compartment without creating a draft.

When she awoke, the train would at last be traveling west.

BY THE NEXT MORNING, New York's newspaper readers had learned that not just one young reporter was racing around the world, but two. In fact, many New Yorkers now believed that there were three, thanks to a story in the *New York Tribune*. "An epidemic of globe-galloping broke out in these parts yesterday," reported the *Tribune,* "and already has three victims trying hard to get home the longest way round in the shortest time." According to the *Tribune,* "it had been whispered in Park Row" that the *Herald* had dispatched its own reporter—a man—around the world on only two hours' notice, with the orders to beat Bly back to New York "by a day, an hour, a minute, anything." The competitor from the *Herald* was said to have "actually taken passage on the *Augusta Victoria* and to have steamed down the bay with his unsuspecting rival."

Fortunately, this particular piece of misinformation was not long lived, as there was never any evidence adduced for it other than the "whispers" supposedly heard by the *Tribune*. The *Herald* itself never claimed to have sent any world traveler, and indeed the paper took no notice of Nellie Bly's trip in its pages, other than a brief satirical piece a few days later, supposedly written by a male reporter named "Very Fly" who had been "summoned to the office yesterday and told to immediately pack my gripsack and start on a trip around Manhattan Island, with the design of breaking the record by accomplishing this wonderful feat in seventy-five minutes." Tossing a second shirt collar into his handbag, he set out on his journey via elevated railroad. Predictably enough, he managed to complete the trip in precisely 74 minutes 59 seconds.

Following the *Herald*'s lead, the *Tribune* ran a whimsical editorial suggesting that a race around the world was old hat ("Everybody has either made the journey himself, or has a friend who has made it") and that a real achievement would instead be a trip to the moon. Even the staid *New York Times,* not willing to ignore the story entirely, ran a paragraph headlined "Flying Trips of Two Young Women" at the bottom of its sports page, just below an item about the second annual Fall Games of the Plainfield, New Jersey, bicycle club.

Those early news reports were rife with mistakes, as Park Row, caught unawares by the story, tried to pin down just who these young female reporters were. According to the *Tribune,* Bisland was twenty-two years old, understating her actual age by six years, while in the *Press* she was twenty-three and Nellie Bly was "in the neighborhood of thirty"—a rather expansive neighborhood, as she was in fact twenty-five. Perhaps the most flagrant error came from the editor of the *Press,* Joseph Howard. The information must have begun to circulate around Park Row that Elizabeth Bisland had written book reviews for *The World,* and, as in the children's game Chinese whispers (later, given technological developments, it became known as "telephone"), the original idea turned out quite different in the retelling. "Miss Nellie Bly and Miss Elizabeth Bisland are the best-known women reporters on the *New York World* staff," Howard informed the readers of the *Press.* "They have both started around the world, and it makes no difference to anybody outside of the *World* office which of the two comes out ahead."

It made a great difference, for one, to John Brisben Walker (who must have been quite taken aback to see his reporter identified as a member of the *World* staff), and on the afternoon following the departures, Walker made good on his original idea and grandly appeared at the *World* offices on Park Row to announce that he would bet $1,000 against *The World*'s $500 on the outcome of the race; to further sweeten the offer he suggested that the winning amount be donated to charity. Walker well understood that a sporting wager between the two publications would be excellent publicity for all concerned, but *The World,* with the vast resources at its disposal, was perfectly capable of generating its own publicity without having to involve *The Cosmopolitan* in the bargain. About Walker's offer *The World* would say simply, "That proposition was declined."

On the day of Bly's departure a reporter from *The World* sought out the mayor of New York, Hugh J. Grant, who gave a statement to the paper complimenting Miss Bly on her "plucky undertaking" and noting that "When you come to think of it, travelling at the rate of 400 miles every twenty-four hours for a period of seventy-five days is enough to take one's breath away. It would be an uncommon task for a man to accomplish, and the mere fact that a young woman attempts the feat is amazing." Mayor Grant, however, was unwilling to take a position on whether Bly would accomplish her goal, stating only, "I shall watch her progress from place to place with considerable interest." Other elected officials were more definitive, among them Congressman Amos J. Cummings, who asked rhetorically, "Do I think Nellie Bly will go round the earth in seventy-five days?" and then answered, "Of course I do, if she keeps her health and strength, and from what I know of Miss Bly, I am satisfied that she will pull through all right." He added, "As an American I am proud that one of our women is brave enough to undertake such a wonderful journey, and as a man I glory in her spunk."

Students at Johns Hopkins University in Baltimore were said to be studying a map of the world in order to calculate the probabilities of success. The travel writer Thomas Knox (who had earlier provided female travelers nine pages of advice for packing their bags) declared that he believed it was theoretically possible to circumnavigate the globe in seventy-five days, though of course "what its practical aspect is remains to be seen"; Knox himself had circled the world twice, and each time the trip took a year and a half. The baseball impresario Albert G. Spalding, who had recently returned from a barnstorming tour of the world with a team of all-star ballplayers, remarked wonderingly, "It took me nearly six months to go around the earth, while she is trying it in one-third of the time. I never met Miss Bly, but I have no doubt she will reach the home-plate on time." Not content with only a single baseball metaphor, Spalding went on to say, "Talk about home-runs around the diamond, why, she is making one round the earth. I hope she will make the full score and win the game."

So the public was presented the views of the race held by politicians, world travelers, and sportsmen. Though little of it ever found its way

into the newspapers, it is not unreasonable to imagine a different sentiment prevailing among the women who worked for the papers, who had
been sharply limited in what they were permitted to write about, who
worked for less pay and less prestige than their male colleagues, and who
understood how little career advancement would likely ever be available
to them, no matter how capably they performed their jobs; it must have
been gratifying to see the names of two female reporters appearing daily
on the front pages of newspapers, on the editorial pages, even on the
sports pages—anywhere but on the style pages. Alone among its contemporaries, the *Philadelphia Inquirer* published a signed editorial about
the race by a female reporter, Dorothy Maddox.

> *The World,* in sending its bright little correspondent upon such a
> novel, yet hazardous mission, has with one unique stroke accom-
> plished more for my sex than could have been achieved in any
> other way in a decade. This odd but clever departure from every
> rule that has heretofore governed the newspaper kingdom is a
> stirring editorial upon woman's pluck and woman's energy and
> swings wide open the door that leads to success in every branch
> of the world of letters. It also goes a long way toward proving
> that the gentler sex, released from depreciating influences and
> given a sound body to co-operate with the divine inspiration of
> the mind, may compete most successfully with the brightest men
> of the day.

NOVEMBER 15–16, 1889
New York to Chicago

Speeding toward Chicago on the Fast Western Express, Elizabeth Bisland
would not have been pleased to know that her name, as she had feared,
was now appearing in the columns of daily newspapers, nor that word of
her race was moving across the United States even more rapidly than she
was. From Buffalo, in upstate New York, her train headed west on the
Lake Shore Railroad line along the southern shore of Lake Erie, passing
through Erie, Ashtabula, Cleveland, and Toledo, the smoky gray industrial cities of Pennsylvania and Ohio eventually giving way to the prai-

ries of Indiana and Illinois, the countryside in mid-November already withered and brown, like a landscape in one of those sepia-toned photographs that had become so popular in recent years, stretching all the way to the horizon and relieved only occasionally by a distant farmhouse or forlorn-looking tree. The bleak, unvarying scenery did nothing to assuage the loneliness she felt, a young woman on a train surrounded by strangers (it was generally considered improper for a single woman to initiate conversation with a man on a train, and risky for her too willingly to accept it), and as the sky began to darken she could not have helped but cast her mind back to the city from which she had been so unexpectedly uprooted and think about the many friends who would otherwise have been arriving just then for Friday afternoon tea.

It was late when the lights of Chicago first came into view as a pale glow on the horizon. Outside the window yellow flickers appeared and disappeared in the darkness like stationary fireflies; they were flames spat out from the tops of high smokestacks. The Union Depot at Van Buren Street was an impressively large limestone building topped by several smaller mansard roofs, much like the Grand Central Depot that Elizabeth Bisland had left behind the day before in New York. The Fast Western Express rolled into the immense shed behind the station and with a last, sighing expulsion of steam came to a halt. Helped by waiting porters, the passengers stepped down from the train and filed slowly into the train hall.

It had been arranged that *The Cosmopolitan* would send someone to meet Bisland at the station; as she entered the hall she looked around expectantly, but no one came forward for her. The other passengers met family with hugs and kisses, friends and associates with handshakes and pats on the back, or simply strode toward the baggage room; they handed over their claim checks to the baggage master, gathered up their belongings, and made their way out to the street. Little by little the group dispersed. With polite thanks she declined offers of assistance from the few remaining porters: she was expecting someone. Silently she waited; the minutes passed, but still no one came to meet her.

Finally, having given up hope that *The Cosmopolitan*'s emissary would ever arrive, Bisland began to wander around the vast, gloomy station, not knowing which direction to go, angry at the unexpected complication, resentful at Walker for having sent her on this ridiculous wild-goose chase, and at herself as well for ever having consented to participate in it.

She felt, all at once, terribly homesick, so far from the cozy apartment where her sister had by now lit the gas jets and prepared a quiet dinner for herself; she remembered that she hadn't eaten on the train and realized that she was very hungry. She passed shuttered newsstands and lunch counters, a waiting room with a few sleepy-looking passengers in it; she could hear her own footsteps echoing in the cavernous hall. On a wing adjoining the main hall a telegraph office was still open: but at this hour, a wire back to *The Cosmopolitan* would do no good. A friendly conductor took pity on her and helped her locate the departure gates for the Rock Island Road, where she would transfer to the train for Omaha, before bidding her, in Bisland's description, "a commiserating adieu." Near the waiting area she found a lunch hall that was open late, and she sat on a high stool at the counter and ate a solitary dinner of ham with a cup of tea. Even this seemingly ordinary act was daring in its way: in New York there was only a single restaurant at which it was considered appropriate for respectable women to sit on stools and eat at a counter on which no cloth was spread. That restaurant was located on Broadway near Twenty-first Street, and Elizabeth Bisland, who worked only a few blocks away, surely knew of it, and had likely eaten there on her way to or from the *Cosmopolitan* offices. Memories of New York would have only exacerbated her sense of loneliness. She was in a nearly deserted train station in a strange city late at night having dinner, unaccountably, by herself. It could not bode well for her trip, she must have pondered, that the magazine had made this mistake at the very first opportunity to do so. As she ate, her every mouthful was regarded with wan interest by the man who oversaw the lunch hall. She finished her meal and hurried out to the train.

The train to Omaha, as it turned out, ran more slowly than the Fast Western Express had, and on far straighter track, so the rocking of the car was gentler, soothing and peaceful and free of sudden sidelong bumps, and Bisland fell asleep right away. After only a few hours she awoke in her berth feeling surprisingly rested and—really for the first time since she had left the *Cosmopolitan* offices two days earlier—in her right mind, no longer afflicted by what she called that "stupefaction of amazement." Pulling up the window curtain, she saw that dawn was just beginning to break. A frost had formed during the night, and the harvested fields glistened with silver and pearl. With delight she watched the silently waking world go by her window, noting the subtle tints of rose and milky blue that spread across the land as the sun made its way above the horizon; she felt herself traveling "for some brief space in a world of intolerable splendor, where innumerable billions of frost crystals flashed back to the sun the reflection of his shining face." In the distance she could make out silver streams running like veins through the countryside, occasionally flanked by willow trees draped in their primeval-looking fringes, shining in the morning light. Here and there the train passed a neatly demarcated square of jet-black loam amid the amber fields, where the ground had been broken by a farmer for winter sowing. Above it the sky was a pale turquoise. It all seemed to her absolutely exquisite. That afternoon she inscribed in her notebook the words "A perfect day."

NOVEMBER 16–17, 1889
Omaha, Nebraska, to Ogden, Utah

By early evening the train had arrived in Omaha. The station there was a hub for several railroad lines, and at this hour it was a hive of activity, passengers rushing from one train to the next, vendors hawking their newspapers and basket snacks, porters lugging Gladstones and hatboxes and rolled-up steamer rugs and, for the Western sportsmen, rifle cases and fishing rods and telescopes, the general hubbub punctuated by shrill train whistles and bells announcing another departure; but somehow, amid that clamor (she herself only ever said that it happened "by chance"), Bisland managed to talk her way aboard a new fast mail train that was about to depart for San Francisco on the Union Pacific line.

The U.S. government's Railway Mail Service hoped to cut the time of the New York to San Francisco trip from 118 hours down to 108; though the difference was only ten hours, by arriving in San Francisco in the morning rather than the evening, the post office would effectively save a full day in the delivery of the mail. The government had offered the Union Pacific and associated railroads a contract worth $750,000 if the trip could be accomplished in that time. The very first run of the transcontinental fast mail train had left New York's Grand Central Depot on the evening of November 14—just three hours after Elizabeth Bisland's Fast Western Express—to determine whether it might be done. The train was carrying a mail car, a baggage car, two sleeper cars, a dining car, and a private car belonging to Edward Dickinson, general manager of the Union Pacific Railroad; the passengers included several railway and postal officials, as well as newspaper reporters from some of the cities along the cross-country route, who were looking to provide their readers with firsthand accounts of the historic trip. Elizabeth Bisland was the only woman aboard the train.

Leaving Omaha the mail train was an hour and a quarter behind schedule; it steamed west across Nebraska, heading toward Cheyenne. The train made a distinctive sight, as all of its cars were painted a stark white and bore the words *The Fast Mail*. Near the front of the train, the mail car was brightly lit by a row of overhead globe lamps. Inside, a dozen clerks wearing green eye shades sorted letters into long pigeonholes, the pile of letters on the distribution tables in front of them constantly replenished by assistants. A clerk would glance briefly at an address on the front of an envelope, then toss the letter into the correct slot with the flick of a wrist. When a pigeonhole was filled the letters inside it were placed in labeled sacks, to be delivered to a connecting train at the appropriate station. The train thus served as a kind of traveling post office; it had left New York loaded with thirty-eight tons of mail, with twenty-five more tons brought on in Chicago and thirteen in Omaha. All of that mail was sorted and bagged in transit. "The letters were dealt out into their proper places almost as rapidly as an expert card player would deal at whist," marveled one reporter, "and this in spite of the physical and mental strain arising from the peculiar conditions under which the operation was performed."

In the other cars the activity was far less organized. To pass the time, some of the men played whist in the general manager's private car. One of the passengers brought a Winchester rifle out to the platform of the rear car and took shots at coyotes and grouse. It was possible to stand on the platform and see all the way to the horizon in any direction. The air shone with a luminous clarity that Elizabeth Bisland did not recognize from the coastal cities, south and north, in which she had lived. Here was the frontier she had read about in childhood stories of pioneer families; it was a windswept, empty place. They rode through vast plains the color of ash. The only water was in feebly trickling streams around which no greenery grew; spavined horses took what little sustenance they could from the barren upland meadows. From time to time the train passed an isolated settlement, usually little more than a few rickety cabins made of rough, unpainted boards, the cabins always tightly shut up and to all indications empty, as though the occupants had fled in advance of an invading army. Only once did she ever see any sign of human habitation around those silent, lonely homes, and that was a tiny pair of light brown wool trousers—butternut trousers, as they were then called—fluttering on a clothesline. As the train continued west the land grew, if possible, even drearier; to Bisland, it began to resemble a kind of prehistoric Sodom sown with salt. There was, she thought, something brutal and hideous in the doom laid upon this unhappy country, "as of a Prometheus chained to his mountain-tops, its blood dried to dust in its veins, and lifting a scarred face of gray despair to the rainless sky."

Near Wyoming the train began a long ascent into the mountains. The train stopped at various stations along the way to pick up and distribute bags of mail and to change engines and crews; whenever the stop was long enough, Bisland made sure to walk around for a few minutes, filling her lungs with the cold air and shaking out her limbs to get the blood moving. The mountain air brought a strange exhilaration, a sense of impending good fortune. "It is," said one of the reporters, "like sublimated champagne." By nightfall the train was approaching the Utah territory. The stars here were not the softly glowing planets she remembered from her girlhood in Louisiana; here they shone as keen and brilliant as swords. Much of the earlier delay had been made up in crossing Wyoming, but at Evanston, near the Utah border, the train was still twenty-eight minutes behind schedule; three-quarters of a million dollars hung on their timely arrival in Ogden. At Evanston a new, more powerful engine was brought on, as was a new engineer. Bill Downing was a mountain engineer, a large, bluff Irishman apparently blessed, or cursed, with a complete absence of fear; among railroad people he was known as Cyclone Bill. He understood that it was his business to get to Ogden on time, and he meant to do it. "It is seventy-six miles to Ogden," he told one of the reporters, "and I will not be happy until I make it in seventy-two minutes."

That kind of speed was impossible down Weber Canyon, the reporter said, but Downing was resolute. He would, he announced with a disarming cheerfulness as he climbed into the cab, "get us to Ogden—or hell—on time." Several times during the course of that ride, Bisland later reported, the betting stood ten to one on Hades.

At precisely 12:55 A.M., Cyclone Bill pulled out the throttle and the train lurched into motion. Using every pound of steam the engine could handle, the train climbed the eastern slope of the Wasatch mountain range, its speed increasing as it neared the summit, where it paused momentarily and then, with a stomach-lurching plunge, began its race downhill. The train careened wildly around the mountain passes, swept across plateaus, shot through tunnel after tunnel, going faster and faster; still the engineer did not ease up on the throttle. The local superintendent for the Railway Mail Service, James E. White, tried to joke that Downing was straightening out all the curves on the line, but there was no laughter in the car. Someone murmured that it would be a terrible thing to run off the track. No one said anything to that—derailments happened more often than anyone in the car cared to think about, and particularly at high rates of speed. An isolated mountain pass late at night, it didn't need saying, would be the worst possible place to derail. To Elizabeth Bisland the train felt like a runaway horse; one of the reporters compared it to "some insane monster striving to free himself." Its roar reverberated like a cannonade off the rocky sides of the canyons. At Devil's Gate, where the track was not as crooked, the train seemed, impossibly, to pick up speed. The car rocked side to side like a ship in a storm, and some of the passengers actually became seasick, turning, in their urgency, to the nearby cuspidors. The warm, crowded car took on an unpleasant aroma. One man began to writhe on the floor in terror and was handed a flask of brandy to calm himself. From the rear platform of the car the passengers could see a shower of sparks trailing behind them; the tracks looked like two lines of fire in the night. "The telegraph poles," Bisland wrote, "reeled backwards from our course and the land fled from under us with horrible nightmare weirdness." She was not sick, but she could feel her nerves beginning to give way. Everyone sitting down held tight to the armrests; those who had mistakenly imagined they might sleep clutched the sides of their berths to keep from falling out. The train passed into the longest tunnel on the road, more than seven hundred feet cut out of hard red clay and sandstone; for endless seconds the blackness outside the windows seemed to grow still blacker. Just beyond the tunnel was the approach to Echo Canyon, where the declivity was 250 feet per mile and the road was said to be as crooked as a ram's horn. Here the tracks hugged close to the hillsides, running along a narrow strip of earth high above the canyon. They could hear the steel wheels grinding on the curves; behind them the double stream of fire was almost continuous. James White got up to check the speed indicator that had been installed in the car and gasped at what he read there. Incredibly, a mile through

Echo Canyon had been run in fifty-two seconds. Ahead lay an even more treacherous bit of road, the reverse loop at Antelope Gap. The train hit the first curve at full speed, and as it did, one side of the car was lifted into the air, so that only one set of wheels still clung to the tracks; there was an awful moment of suspense and then the car managed to right itself, the wheels landing down with a bump, before the train hit the reverse turn and the other set of wheels went up. Finally General Manager Edward Dickinson could take no more. "Let the schedule go!" he shouted to C. E. Brown, the Union Pacific press agent. "Pull the bell rope, Brown, then run forward and tell Downing to stop this if he wants us to reach Ogden alive."

Brown passed the orders up to the engineer, but Bill Downing, checking his watch, replied that he regretted he could not oblige them. When that word came back, Dickinson sprang to his feet, ran to the rear platform of the car, and pulled the brake with all his might. The speed began to slacken.

Still, the fast mail train arrived at Ogden on schedule. The final seventy-six miles had been covered in sixty-five minutes—the shortest time ever recorded on that stretch of track. Having made good on his promise, Cyclone Bill Downing dismounted from his cab; casually remarking that these night rides were prone to give a man a cold, he passed through the swinging doors of a bar on the corner and was not seen again.

JUST FIFTY-THREE MILES west of Ogden stood the railroad station at Promontory Summit, Utah, where only two decades earlier, in 1869, the final spike in the transcontinental railroad, the legendary "Golden Spike," had been hammered into a ceremonial tie of polished California laurel. There the Union Pacific met the Central Pacific, and the nation, only a few years earlier torn apart in civil war, had been joined together by the railroads. A trip across the country from coast to coast, which had previously demanded months of hard travel by covered wagon, or a sail all the way around the tip of South America, could now be completed in less than a week. It was, proclaimed General William T. Sherman, "the most important event of modern times."

As was much remarked upon at the time, before the introduction of the railroad the president of the United States could travel no faster than a Roman emperor had, modern horses being no swifter than those of the ancient world; the steam locomotive, however, was an "Iron Horse," one that could reach speeds upward of sixty miles per hour, and moreover could run through snow and blazing heat, up and down hillsides for hours at a time, and never get tired. There seemed no end to the ways in which it was superior to the domesticated animals of the natural kingdom. "It carries its own food and water, just as a camel carries its spare supplies for the long journey over the sands," noted an awestruck observer in the 1870s. "It can carry greater weight than an elephant, can drag a heavier load than a team of oxen, make a longer journey than a string of camels, and go with its load more rapidly than the fleetest racehorse!" The locomotive was more like some immense, roaring creature out of myth, and indeed some writers of the time, Charles Dickens among them, saw in it not a horse but a fire-breathing dragon.

At the time the transcontinental railroad was completed in 1869, 46,844 miles of railroad track had been laid throughout the United States; just twenty years later that number had nearly quadrupled, to 161,276 miles. Train tracks ran over rivers, across deserts, even through mountains. There seemed no obstruction, natural or human, that could not be conquered. Across the Great Plains, facing hostile Sioux and Cheyenne, the railroad was extended with the help of the U. S. Army. "This railroad will be built . . . and if your young men will interfere the Great Father, who, out of love for you, withheld his soldiers, will let loose his young men, and you will be swept away." So was a gathering of Indian chiefs informed by William Tecumseh Sherman, head of the army, who had been named after a Shawnee warrior of earlier times. "The railroad men in Omaha have an infallible remedy for the Indian troubles," the *Chicago Tribune* would later report. "That remedy is extermination." The Indians hated the railroad in part because it divided the great herd of Plains buffalo, who refused to cross the tracks; the buffalo themselves were wiped out by hunters who shot at them from the train windows as they passed. ("In no parts of the 250 miles ranged by the buffalo are bleached buffalo skulls and bones out of sight from the railroad cars," noted a writer for the Quaker journal *The Friend,* adding, "Their extinction is only a question of time.") Trains brought immigrants from cities to the countryside, and emigrants from the countryside to the cities. They carried coal, lumber, iron, steel: commodities of which the railroad was itself the single largest consumer. By 1880 fully three-quarters of all the steel produced in

America got turned into railroad tracks. The railroad industry was the nation's first big business, the fortunes of men named Vanderbilt, Harriman, Gould, Morgan, and Carnegie tied, directly or indirectly, to its growth. The Pennsylvania Railroad employed more workers than the state of Pennsylvania; some of the larger railroads controlled assets greater than those of the U. S. Treasury. "The railroad kings have of late years swayed the fortunes of American citizens more than the politicians," James Bryce observed in his 1888 book *The American Commonwealth*. "When the master of one of the greatest Western lines travels towards the Pacific on his palace car, his journey is like a royal progress. Governors of States and Territories bow before him; legislatures receive him in solemn session; cities and towns seek to propitiate him, for has he not the means of making or marring a city's fortunes?" Perhaps inevitably, railroad executives began to accord to themselves the sort of language normally reserved for heads of state: they delivered "ultimatums," divided competitors into "enemies" and "allies," negotiated "treaties," launched "wars" to protect their "territory." The president of the Union Pacific Railroad, Edward H. Harriman, was once in Vienna for a meeting with Emperor Franz Joseph of Austria-Hungary; the emperor was late for the appointment, and when an aide offered apologies for the delay Harriman airily brushed them aside, saying, "I, of all people, know the problems of empire."

In 1889, the noted civil engineer Thomas Curtis Clarke wrote, "The world of to-day differs from that of Napoleon more than his world differed from that of Julius Caesar; and this change has chiefly been made by railways." When America still maintained a slower, more agrarian pace, a traveler on a stagecoach or canal boat was deemed to be on time if he arrived on the designated day; in a rapidly industrializing country arrivals were organized by the railroad timetable, the station clock, the conductor's pocket watch. Distances that had always been measured in miles could now be measured in hours and minutes, and though the distance itself was immutable, the time between places could be reduced. New York, of course, had moved no closer to Philadelphia, but a trip that had once taken seven days now required less than seven hours. The country seemed to be growing ever smaller, more tightly knit: everywhere seemed closer than before.

Indeed, time itself had been forever changed by the railroads. Until the latter decades of the nineteenth century, communities had the power to establish their own time zones in what was known as "local mean time," determined by the position of the sun as it passed overhead. The state of Illinois contained twenty-seven different time zones, Wisconsin thirty-eight. In Pittsburgh the train station had six clocks, and each one showed a different time. When a clock struck noon in Washington, D.C., the time was 12:08 in Philadelphia, 12:12 in New York, and 12:24 in Boston. Local mean time was a perfectly fine standard when a day's travel brought one only to a nearby town, but far less so when trains could cover a mile in a single minute and railroad companies operated in several states at once. The B&O Railroad, for instance, ran its eastern trains by Baltimore time, its Ohio trains by Columbus time, and those out west by the time of Vincennes, Indiana. Trains were moving at speeds never before seen, with the ever-present risk of catastrophe if one collided with another, and the widespread confusion about the exact times of arrivals and departures was, if nothing else, a major safety issue (particularly as railroads frequently ran trains in opposite directions on the same stretch of track). In October 1883, representatives of the largest railroad companies met at a General Time Convention in Chicago, at which it was decided to divide the country into four time zones, corresponding to the mean sun time at the meridians near Philadelphia, Memphis, Denver, and Fresno. This action had been taken without the consent of the president, the Congress, or the courts, but almost immediately it became the de facto law of the land. On Sunday, November 18, 1883, clocks across the country were changed to the new railroad standard; that Sunday became known as "the day of two noons." Local mean time was gone; now everyone was living by railroad time. As one Indianapolis newspaper observed in a widely quoted editorial: "People will have to marry by railroad time, and die by railroad time. Ministers will be required to preach by railroad time, banks will open and close by railroad time; in fact the Railroad Convention has taken charge of the time business, and the people may as well set about adjusting their affairs in accordance with its decree."

The locomotive, its plume of smoke trailing behind it like a war pennant, now seemed to be a natural feature of the landscape, and to most Americans it represented progress, modernity, even beauty. In his poem "To a Locomotive in Winter" Walt Whitman extolled the "fierce-throated beauty" of a railroad train. "Type of the modern!" he chanted, "emblem of motion and power! pulse of the continent!" Ralph Waldo

Emerson apotheosized railroad iron as "a magician's rod, in its power to evoke the sleeping energies of land and water." His friend Henry David Thoreau took a different view. "We do not ride on the railroad," he wrote in *Walden;* "it rides upon us."

NOVEMBER 18–19, 1889

Nevada Desert to San Francisco

Elizabeth Bisland had been traveling for less than four days, and already she was exhausted; she had slept poorly since leaving New York, and even now, a day later, she could still feel the terrifying hour at the hands of Cyclone Bill Downing, a shakiness in her muscles like that which remains after a fever. At times, in her seat, she found herself actually shivering with fatigue and "nameless, undefined apprehensions." Her immediate plans were still maddeningly indeterminate. She was due into San Francisco early Tuesday, the nineteenth of November; her Pacific steamship, the *Oceanic,* was not scheduled to leave until Thursday, but John Brisben Walker was at present negotiating with the owners of the Occidental and Oriental Steamship Company to have the departure time moved up two days. She did not know how much he was offering the steamship officials, and there was no word yet on their decision, but Walker was a very persuasive fellow. Those two days saved would lower her final total, of course, but privately Bisland hoped that she might spend her time in San Francisco more in the manner of the lilies of the field, as she had recited so many times as a girl: neither toiling nor spinning. Human beings, she had come to believe, were simply not made to travel a mile a minute. How was it possible to move nearly a hundred feet in a single second? What sort of toll did that take on the nervous system? She wondered how coming generations, who would surely travel one hundred or even one hundred fifty miles an hour, could possibly handle the strain of it. Some process of adaptation to the new environment would doubtless take place: humanity, it seemed, always found a way to bear what had previously seemed unbearable.

The American West was turning out to be a larger and more inhospitable place than she had ever imagined, and gazing out the train window, her traveling rug pulled tight around her, she fondly recalled the tropical climate in which she had grown up, the gardens lush with roses and camellias and black-eyed Susans, so different from this forbidding land-scape, too hard, too drab, too cold, too dry. For long hours through northern Nevada the mail train passed little but sagebrush and sand, mile after mile as barren and lifeless as the photographs she had seen of the surface of the moon. The ground was white with alkali, as if covered in snow; the fine white dust seeped through the windows of the train, mak-ing her skin feel sticky and uncomfortable and reddening her eyes so that reading became difficult. The endless white of the sands was relieved at times by a backdrop of jagged red cliffs, their tops carved by eons of wind and rain into ancient-seeming forms. Dark pools of shade, like a mirage of water, gathered in front of the cliffs. The sun was very bright here, but the air was cold and dry. The only signs of life were the occasional stray jackrabbit or coyote, and unexpectedly, breathtakingly, like a storybook come to life, clusters of tepees.

At every station stop Indians crowded around the train. The women carried their babies strapped on their backs in small wooden crates softly lined with rabbit skins; the mothers turned their backs to the passengers to show off their babies, and then held out their hands hoping for a coin. In the West as in the East, it seemed, there was money to be made in dis-playing oneself for the curiosity of strangers. She thought the Indian children were very beautiful, with smooth tawny skin and long, shining black hair on the boys and girls alike. The old women were impossibly wrinkled; they squatted in the dust, huddled in blankets against the cold, as impassive as idols. A coin dropped in their hand would elicit an indis-tinct mumble and perhaps a glance of acknowledgment, but they seemed not to care much one way or the other, just as the arrival of the fast mail train, gleaming white and altogether modern, did not interest them. It was clear that they had long ago given up any hope of comprehending the vagaries of the white man, and had come to understand, as Bisland noted, that "peace and composure lay only in entirely ignoring him."

Less than a hundred hours earlier Elizabeth Bisland had been lying in bed reading the newspapers; now she was riding on a train in the desert, looking at Indians. Once more she had the sensation she had felt back in her apartment waiting for the hansom to take her to the station: that she was living inside a dream from which she could not awake. As the after-noon drew to a close the train began ascending to higher ground, into the districts of silver and lead, through old mining towns with names like Mirage and Look Out and Miser. The towns seemed to have been rigged up entirely out of canvas and wood, with little more concern for permanence than the weekend camp of a traveling medicine show. What a relief it was that evening, stopped at a little wayside eating station, to make out through the dusk a line of poplars. *The echoing timber,* Gerard Manley Hopkins had called it, full of birdsong that rinses and wrings the ear. The mountain air felt delightfully soft after the aridity of the desert, and in the darkness was a sweet smell that reminded her of white clover, though she knew that there could be no early flowers of grass in November, not in the Sierra Nevada.

Awaking at daybreak, Bisland saw from the window of her berth the Sacramento Valley opening itself up below her, grassy, rounded hills with wisps of mist like whitecaps rolling among them. The sky had now grown cloudy, the light filtered and low across the horizon. She opened the window wider and was startled to see the distinctive spreading canopy of live oaks, unexpected but absolutely unmistakable, and wonderfully reminiscent of her home places of Louisiana and Mississippi. The western edge of America seemed almost to be echoing the eastern, another sign that her cross-country journey was nearing its end. Just after breakfast the train rolled into the Oakland Mole, a pier built fully two miles out into the bay, where the train passengers boarded the ferry to San Francisco. The boat made its way through the choppy waters of the bay toward the narrower strait of the Golden Gate, passing the lighthouse at Alcatraz, the Army barracks of Angel Island, the island itself ringed by cannons. Through the rain and the mist San Francisco rose into view, a vision in white, lines of elegant frame houses spread out over the steep hills, broad streets running up and down between them. Just ahead was the ferry house at the foot of Market Street, a low wooden building on which stood a single clock tower. At a quarter past nine on Tuesday, November 19, the ferry bumped up against the San Francisco wharf: Elizabeth Bisland had traveled coast to coast in only four days, fifteen hours, and fifteen minutes. The mail, too, had arrived on time, and the railroad officials cheered and clasped hands in jubilation and then went to deliver their statements to the reporters. Bisland made her way to the terminal, through the rain and the oozing mud, feeling great pleasure in walking with long strides and swinging arms after days of confinement on the train, delighted to be rid of the roar of the engine in her ears.

NOVEMBER 19–21, 1889

San Francisco

Along with the other passengers from the fast mail train, Elizabeth Bisland would be staying at the Palace Hotel, the most opulent hotel in San Francisco and, with more than eight hundred guest rooms, the largest anywhere in the country. The Palace featured all the latest conveniences, including electric call buttons in every room, more than seven hundred noiseless water closets, and four hydraulic elevators, which the hotel preferred to call "rising rooms." Bisland was not sorry to learn upon her arrival that she would be remaining in the city for the next two days, as John Brisben Walker's efforts to arrange an early departure for the *Oceanic* had fallen through. That afternoon she went out and bought herself some thin shirtwaists to wear in the hotter countries, to supplement the two dresses she had brought along with her. She also bought some silk and worsted for fancywork; she rarely did needlepoint in New York— she just never seemed to have the time—but now she thought it would give her something else to do on board ship. The *San Francisco Examiner* sent a reporter to the hotel to interview her about her trip, a young woman writing under the pen name "Annie Laurie." The reporter's real name was Winifred Black, and she would go on to become one of the most admired journalists in San Francisco; her article about Elizabeth Bisland was the first she ever published in a career that spanned five decades. Bisland did not like to be interviewed; it was something she knew she would never get used to, but it was unavoidable now and the best thing to do was to speak as pleasantly as possible. She fully anticipated, she told Annie Laurie, that she would enjoy her trip, though of course she wished she had more time to spend in the places she would be visiting, especially the Orient. She did not expect to meet Nellie Bly along the way, though it was certainly possible that they might pass each other without knowing, like Gabriel and Evangeline in the Longfellow poem. She would be very glad to return home again.

The next morning Bisland was surprised to see that the *Examiner* had placed its article about her on the front page. "She doesn't look like a very daring creature, this little woman with the gentle voice and appealing dark eyes," the story began. "But she's going around the world in

The marble-floored courtyard of San Francisco's Palace Hotel

seventy-five days, and she's going alone. If this thing can possibly be accomplished she is the very one to do it. It is always these delicate, high-bred women who have unheard of endurance and wonderful pluck." To her great consternation, as a result of the article she had become something of a celebrity in town, and all morning she was interrupted by visitors who sent their cards up to her room bearing urgent messages, but who upon admittance confessed that they had no reason for the intrusion other than a desire to look at her.

Thankfully, that afternoon editors from the *Examiner* took her and some of the other mail-train passengers to lunch at the Cliff House. A steam railway carried them through the city. To Bisland's eyes, grown used to the spires of New York, San Francisco seemed very low in scale, few of the buildings more than three or four stories high. That was because of the fear of earthquakes, her hosts told her; still, in recent years earthquakes had almost entirely ceased, and many of the newer buildings were much taller than the ones they replaced. Even in November, roses climbed up front porches, their heavy blossoms perfuming the damp streets with lovely garden smells. When she closed her eyes she could almost imagine herself back in New Orleans, on just such an expedition to the Spanish Fort by the lakeside, and she was filled with a sense of nostalgia for those earlier times, glad to be free for a few moments of the demands of the race clock, once again amid a cheerful group of witty, good-looking men who would let a day slip away with the carelessness of a spendthrift.

The Cliff House, a grand restaurant perched precariously atop a huge flat rock high above the ocean, was a sight that all visitors to the city wanted to see. Elizabeth Bisland had had quite enough of majestic cliffside views, but this establishment, at least, was stationary. Carriages brought patrons up the long road that led to the restaurant. There was terrapin and frogs' legs, oyster soup and roast chicken and lamb chops. Between courses one could revive an appetite with a promenade on a long balcony facing the ocean. Perhaps two hundred yards away the Seal Rocks jutted up from the waves like three black eggs, where a raft of sea lions played, hobbling from spot to spot on the rocks, then diving into the water with unexpected grace. The ocean breezes felt, somehow, both warm and cool on her cheeks. This was the first time she had ever seen the Pacific Ocean, grand and serene in its immensity, and she surprised herself with the thrill of discovery she felt, the joyous shock of astonishment at the sight. She was reminded of the Keats poem, recalling the lines about Cortez staring "with eagle eyes" at the Pacific; not even he, she thought, who stood "silent, upon a peak in Darien," had felt a more magnificent opening of the spirit than she at that moment. In the distance the curtain of cloud began slowly to raise; low on the horizon, the sun reddened the sky and cast a single, shining beam on the water, as though making a golden road to the west. It was, Bisland's companions assured her, a most promising sign.

The *Oceanic* was scheduled to depart at three o'clock Thursday afternoon. That morning Elizabeth Bisland used her remaining time in San Francisco to make the final preparations for her voyage. She exchanged American banknotes for English gold, read telegrams, wired parting messages to New York, and revised her itinerary. The plan now was for her to sail with the *Oceanic* to Yokohama and then board a train for Tokyo, where she would charter a special steamer to Hong Kong in order to catch the North German Lloyd ship *Prussian,* bound for Genoa. (*The World* had declared that Nellie Bly would not charter any special trains or steamers on her trip, but John Brisben Walker had never made such a stipulation.) In Genoa she would take an express train to Le Havre, where the fast French steamer *La Champagne* was departing for New York. She thought the trip might be accomplished in as little as seventy-two days, though (as she was quick to add to all the reporters who arrived to interview her) there was no predicting the final outcome.

By the time of the *Oceanic*'s departure, several articles about Elizabeth Bisland had appeared in the local newspapers, and the crowd that assembled on the dock that afternoon was much larger than usual to see off a steamship. The *Examiner* reported, "Women jostled and rumpled each other in the effort to crowd aboard the *Oceanic* and catch a glimpse of the adventurous heroine." A few especially determined young women actually did manage to get aboard the ship and into her stateroom, "a delegation," Bisland called them, "who had got wind of my eccentric performance and came with no other credentials than a desire to gape." Two days earlier they had never heard of Elizabeth Bisland, but now she was being talked about in the papers, she was apparently beautiful and clever and daring and she was trying to do something that had never been done before, and if she could find her way around the world they could find their way to her cabin; and they gathered around her in the small, crowded room, peppering her with whatever questions came to mind: *How old are you? Do you expect to be seasick? Have you any limes or lemons? Is this your first trip? Are you afraid of the water? Ain't you got nobody with you?*

Elizabeth Bisland's replies were not recorded, although the *Examiner* reporter on hand did note that Occidental and Oriental officials, having refused John Brisben Walker's offer of money in exchange for moving up the departure time, had at least consented to issue orders to the ship's captain and chief engineer to proceed with all possible speed. "I intend," Bisland said playfully, "to make eyes at the Engineer." (The *Examiner* noted, "This will doubtless insure a trip of unexampled rapidity.") She was being as amusing as she could, but in truth she was feeling especially low at that moment, lonely in an overcrowded room, making awkward conversation with acquaintances, openly stared at by strangers: turned, in her words, into "a sort of inexpensive freak show."

In the future, Bisland silently resolved, she would conduct herself in such a way that journalists never again had reason to put her name in a headline.

At last the ship's bell sounded, and Bisland accompanied her visitors back down to the wharf to say final goodbyes, when to her surprise a handsome gray-haired man handed up to her a bouquet of white chrysanthemums and roses; attached to the flowers was a card printed with the name J. M. Prather, the words *good wishes* and *New Orleans* written in pencil in the corner. He tipped his hat and smiled at her with such friendliness that she felt she was being greeted by a relative. That he had taken the trouble to bid her silent farewell seemed to her a delicate and charming example of chivalry; she felt that she had been entrusted with a memento from an earlier time, and though she never saw Mr. Prather again she did not forget him, nor his kindness, which bore up her spirits as she sailed from American shores.

CHAPTER 7

A Map of the World

NOVEMBER 22, 1889

London

THE SPECIAL MAIL TRAIN FROM SOUTH-
AMPTON ARRIVED IN LONDON'S WATER-
loo Station at five o'clock in the
morning. Nellie Bly and Tracey
Greaves, *The World*'s London correspondent, who would be accompanying her to France, had traveled for
two hours in the train's single passenger car, the locked compartment
heated only by foot warmers and dingily lit by a smoky oil lamp. At that
moment Elizabeth Bisland was beginning her trip across the Pacific
Ocean, but Nellie Bly was unaware of this fact—no one from the *World*
staff had wired the information about Bisland to Tracey Greaves, or if
they had, he had neglected to tell her. As far as Bly knew, she was racing
purely against a timetable established by a fictional character named
Phileas Fogg, and she was thrilled by the opportunity she had now been
given to meet Fogg's creator, the world-famous novelist Jules Verne.

It was some time before the porter came to unlock the doors of the
car. Bly was increasingly anxious to get going—they had, she knew, only

four hours in the city, and much to accomplish while there—but finally he appeared, and the two rushed through the train shed and into the vast, deserted station, Bly struggling to keep up with Greaves's longer strides. Outside, London seemed covered with a sheer scrim, the entire city clothed in heavy gray fog. In front of the station a dozen large carriages were lined up to receive the Royal Mail; they were the only vehicles in sight, other than a solitary hansom cab, a four-wheeled brougham that at first appeared to be empty but upon closer inspection revealed the cabman sleeping inside it. At some length the driver was awakened and persuaded to take on a pair of paying customers, and to make as much haste as he could in the run across the city. He asked where the trunks were, and Bly just smiled and pointed to the gripsack at her feet. The driver looked at Bly for a moment, not saying anything, and it occurred to her that he probably thought she had run away from home. But he did not ask any more questions; he just climbed up onto his seat and lashed the horse, and the carriage set off at a brisk clip, speeding across Waterloo Bridge without Bly getting a glimpse of the Thames flowing beneath it, along the Strand without her seeing any of its famous mansions, past Trafalgar Square without pausing to admire Nelson's Column. "If she attempts any description at all of what she saw in England," Tracey Greaves would write in *The World,* "it will be much the same as a man describing Broadway if he were shot through a pneumatic tube from the Western Union Building to the Twenty-third Street Uptown Office."

Looking up through the carriage's side window, Bly could see the forms of skeletal trees outlined in black against the sky; below, houses glided by like ghosts in the swirling mist. Here and there she could make out a shadowy figure on the sidewalk, on his way to complete some unknowable errand. It was a morning much like those she remembered from her years in Pittsburgh, the fog blurring the gas lamps and softening the edges of the buildings, lending a pleasing air of peace and solemnity to things that in the plain light of day would seem merely commonplace. "How are these streets compared with those of New York?" asked Tracey Greaves, breaking the silence.

"They are not bad," Bly replied, in as offhand a tone as she could manage, turning her face to the window to avoid any further talk on the subject. In fact she had been thinking about how much better the London streets were than the dreadful ones back in New York; she wondered what possible excuse she would make, if anyone dared actually say that to her. She had made up her mind that while on foreign shores she would hear no word spoken against her country.

She settled down deeper into the carriage seat; even in her wool cap and ulster she was shivering in the damp London chill. She had been awake for nearly twenty-four hours, and during that time she had been in a steamship, a tugboat, a train, and now a carriage. She could feel a headache coming on, that familiar dull throb, the world starting to totter around her. The brougham made its way through the gray, silent streets, the only sounds the rumble of the wheels and the clop of the horse's hooves on the pavement. Finally the carriage pulled up at an address in the fashionable West End section of London, the residence of the second secretary of the American Legation, Robert S. McCormick. A light burned in one of the downstairs windows. Tracey Greaves had wired ahead with his special request—Nellie Bly, *The World*'s celebrated globe-trotter, needed a permanent passport to be issued immediately—and so even at this early hour the second secretary was already up and dressed. He was forty years old, with kindly dark eyes and a Vandyke beard with a mustache that curled up at the ends. After warmly welcoming Nellie Bly and congratulating her on the successful completion of the first leg of her journey (and, to Bly's relief, offering his visitors coffee), he ushered them into a large room where he sat down at a desk and began making out the passport. Bly gratefully drank her coffee while McCormick asked her the standard questions: eye color, height, place of birth. Then McCormick asked Greaves to please stand at the other side of the room so that he might ask Miss Bly an important question. Bly had never filled out a passport before, and she wondered nervously what type of secret information might be connected with such official proceedings.

"There is one question that all women dread to answer," Robert McCormick told her—his voice, lightly accented, revealed his Virginia origins—"and as very few will give a truthful reply, I will ask you to swear to the rest first and fill in the other questions afterwards, unless you have no hesitancy in telling me your age."

"Oh, certainly," she said with a laugh. "I will tell you my age, swear to it, too, and I am not afraid. My companion may come out of the corner."

The passport having been completed, McCormick took a moment to discuss the peculiarities of various women he had encountered coming to the Legation for passports. "I remember once," he recalled, "eight or ten girls came at the same time for passports, and each one of them managed to avoid letting any of the others see what her exact age was. There was some maneuvering required to bring that about, I can assure you."

Bly took a last sip of coffee and began drawing on her gloves. "Very entertaining," she said, "but we must be off."

A few moments later she and Greaves were again in a carriage hurrying through the streets of London, first to the *World* offices near Trafalgar Square, where she received the cables awaiting her arrival and the "bon voyages" of the handful of newspapermen gathered there, then back east to the offices of the Peninsular and Oriental Steamship Company on Leadenhall Street to purchase the tickets that would cover her journey from Brindisi, Italy, all the way to Yokohama, and then west again to Charing Cross Station to reserve seats on the morning train running down to Folkestone, the departure point for the ferry across the English Channel to Boulogne. The two had just enough time to bolt down a quick breakfast of ham and eggs with coffee at the Charing Cross Hotel next door and then find their way to the Folkestone train. It was at times like this, rushing madly from place to place, that she was delighted with her decision to carry only a single bag. At last, four hours after arriving in London, all of their business had been transacted and Bly and Greaves could settle in for the ride back to the south of England. The trip to London had taken Bly perhaps fifty miles out of her way, and added a good deal of extra complication when she was already exhausted from lack of sleep, but still, she knew, the trip was a necessary one, for it had allowed her to obtain the passport that would make the rest of her journey possible. That passport, with Second Secretary McCormick's official seal on it, was now safely tucked inside her gripsack. Not until many years later would it be discovered that Nellie Bly had sworn to Robert McCormick that she was twenty-two years old.

She was twenty-five.

IN 1871 JULES VERNE WROTE to his publisher, Pierre-Jules Hetzel, about a new novel on which he was currently at work: "Have I been slaving? Can you doubt it? If you only knew how much this trip around the world in eighty days amuses me in writing it! I dream about it: If only it will amuse our readers as much." By that time the forty-three-year-old

Verne had become the most successful practitioner of the literary genre that would eventually come to be known as science fiction, but in the late nineteenth century was more often called "scientific romance." It was a career for which he had been preparing all his life. Born in Nantes, a harbor town on the north shore of the river Loire, as a boy Jules had spent endless hours sitting on the stone wall that ran along the ancient quay, watching the ships sail in laden with bags and crates marked with thrillingly indecipherable languages: blue-sailed fishing boats, high-masted schooners, and most magical, the pyroscaphe, an experimental form of paddleboat, long and low with an arching beam at its bow like the head of a mythical sea creature, churning up great clouds of foam in its wake as it made its way slowly down the river. Jules loved tales of adventure, devouring the translated novels of Walter Scott and James Fenimore Cooper, *Robinson Crusoe,* and his favorite of all, *The Swiss Family Robinson.* He dreamed of seeing the world for himself, and once, when he was eleven, he managed to talk himself aboard a schooner that needed a new cabin boy. The ship was bound for the West Indies, but Jules made it no farther than the next town along the Loire before the captain discovered his real age and dropped him off on the quay, from where his father brought him back home. In the future, he promised his distraught mother, he would travel only in his imagination.

As a young man Verne moved to Paris and began to study law, with the idea of following his father into the family law practice. But he didn't much care for his studies, and he spent most of his time writing plays and librettos for comic operas. Though he did manage to graduate, in the end he decided to brook his father's disappointment and not take over the practice. "I may become a good writer but I would never be anything but a poor lawyer," he wrote by way of explanation, "since I habitually see only the comic or artistic aspect of things, while their precise reality escapes me." When he was twenty-eight he married Honorine de Viane, a young widow with two children, and to support his new family began working, of all unlikely professions, as a stockbroker. Still, he kept writing, and in 1863 he published his first novel, entitled *Five Weeks in a Balloon;* about a scientific expedition across the African continent. The book did well enough that he was able to quit the brokerage (not surprisingly, he had never been very successful there) and devote himself full time to writing adventure stories that merged fact and fantasy, science and speculation. His early novels, among them *A Journey to the Center of the Earth* and *Twenty Thousand Leagues Under the Sea,* took readers on fantastic trips to undreamed-of places, anticipating twentieth-century technologies such as the rocket ship and the nuclear submarine; the novel about which he wrote to Pierre-Jules Hetzel, however, was very different, for it went no farther than around the world, and involved only technologies—primarily the steamship and the steam locomotive—available to anyone with enough money for a ticket.

That book, of course, was *Around the World in Eighty Days*. Its hero, Phileas Fogg, is the very embodiment of English exactitude. At eleven-thirty each morning he leaves his home on Savile Row, walks the 1,151 steps (576 by his left foot, 575 by his right) to the Reform Club, where he takes his lunch, reads the newspapers until dinner, and afterward plays whist with other club members before returning home precisely at midnight. In his habits he is as regular as clockwork, and the adjective Verne most often uses to describe him is "mathematical." Fogg's predictable routine, however, is disturbed one evening by a discussion around the whist table about the shrinking of the globe in the new age of rapid travel. One player suggests that a complete circumnavigation of the earth might now be made in as little as three months. "Eighty days," corrects Phileas Fogg. The others are skeptical of Fogg's claim—what about unfavorable weather, they ask, or headwinds, or shipwrecks, or derailments? All of those contingencies, Fogg coolly replies, are accounted for in his schedule. That might be well and good in theory, his tablemates insist, but actually putting such an idea into practice is an entirely different matter. Ever the English empiricist, Fogg wagers twenty thousand pounds—half his fortune—that he can complete the trip in eighty days or less ("i.e., in 1,920 hours or 115,200 minutes," he elucidates mathematically). The whist players agree to the bet, and Fogg sets off on his trip that very evening, accompanied by his French manservant Passepartout—and carrying, like Nellie Bly after him, only a single bag.

The novel contains several subplots; one, for instance, involves the pursuit of Fogg around the world by a detective named Fix (who mistakenly believes that Fogg is fleeing the country after robbing a bank of fifty-five thousand pounds), and another the rescue of a widowed Indian princess named Aouda, the intended victim of suttee at her husband's funeral, who will remain with Fogg and Passepartout for the remainder of the trip. (Aouda eventually becomes Fogg's wife, making him, the narrator reports, "the happiest of men.") But the heart of *Around the*

World in Eighty Days is the contest between time and distance: Phileas Fogg's quest to maintain his rigidly plotted-out schedule as the clock grinds relentlessly on. Fogg is a literary expression of the solid Victorian virtues: he is honest, he is rational, he is patriotic, he is courageous, he is chaste. More than anything, though, he is unflappable, and much of the pleasure of the book comes from watching him maintain his composure in the face of the seemingly insuperable obstacles that Verne places in his path. When there turns out to be a fifty-mile break in the Indian railway, Fogg finds an elephant to carry them on to Allahabad; when Fogg and Passepartout are arrested on a trumped-up charge in Calcutta and sentenced to seven days in jail, he pays the £2,000 bail (equivalent to nearly a quarter of a million dollars today) so that they are not late for their China Sea steamship; when a Sioux attack in Nebraska causes them to miss their train, Fogg and the others set out on a sail-borne sled speeding along the railroad tracks to Omaha. When the merchant steamer they have hired runs out of coal before reaching Liverpool, Fogg calmly purchases the ship from its owner and orders that its upper works be hacked apart and the wood used for fuel; eventually the cabins, the masts, the rails, and most of the deck find their way into the furnace, and by the time the ship reaches port it is little more than a floating iron hull.

Still, for all of Phileas Fogg's daring and ingenuity he is unable to keep precisely to his schedule and he arrives back in London five minutes past the agreed-upon time. He has thus lost the £20,000 wager, and has spent the other half of his fortune in pursuing the ill-fated race; he is ruined, and his future seems dark indeed—at least until the following afternoon, when Passepartout realizes that the travelers had actually gained a day in their eastward path around the globe, and that the trip they believed to be eighty days long was in fact only seventy-nine. They hurry to the Reform Club, where they surprise Fogg's clubmates by walking in precisely as the clock strikes the appointed hour. Phileas Fogg has gone around the world in eighty days, has won his bet, and has found a wife in the process. "Truly, would you not," the narrator asks the reader at the book's close, "for less than that, make the tour around the world?"

The idea for the novel seems to have been born in the summer of 1871, when Jules Verne, sitting in a Paris café, noticed a newspaper advertisement for a tourist trip around the world being organized by the British travel agent Thomas Cook. That previously unthinkable notion—that not just a single country or continent but the entire globe might be the subject of a tourist excursion—was itself traceable to the opening of the Suez Canal in November 1869, which established for the first time a direct water route between Europe and Asia. In conjunction with the new transatlantic railroad in the United States (completed just six months earlier), the opening of the canal meant that a traveler could now pursue a more or less direct path around the world via train and steamship. The inevitable next question was how quickly such a trip might be completed, and though no one could yet say for sure, speculation began to center on a period of eighty days. Shortly before the completion of the Suez Canal two French journals published itineraries for an eighty-day trip, and the 1869 volume *L'Année scientifique et industrielle* also imagined the possibility of circling the globe in eighty days. Still, this was no more than a hypothetical construct based on the arrival and departure times of ships and trains. Theory was one thing, as the Reform Club members reminded Phileas Fogg; actual practice was quite another.

The first of the real-life "globe girdlers," in the phrase of the time (a reference to Puck in *A Midsummer Night's Dream,* who claimed that he would "put a girdle round about the earth"), was named, fittingly, George Francis Train. Train was a wealthy businessman who had amassed his fortune, in part, by buying up real estate along the Union Pacific railroad corridor around Omaha. According to *The Biographical Review* he was also "one of the most eccentric men in America." In 1872 he ran for president as "Citizen Train," becoming perhaps the only candidate in American history to charge admission to his campaign rallies. When meeting someone for the first time, Train would shake hands with himself (a practice he claimed he picked up in China); he wrote poetry in alternating lines of red and blue; on at least one occasion he walked down the street stark naked; and in his later years he vowed that he would speak with no one in the world but children. In 1870, however, George Francis Train did complete a circuit of the world—a trip that went relatively smoothly, other than an incident in Marseilles in which he got caught up in an insurrection against the French government, declared himself the liberator of France, and was thrown into prison. Still, he managed to make it around the world in exactly eighty days (that is to say, eighty days of travel time, excluding the time he spent in a French prison), and afterward Train insisted to anyone who would listen that he was the "real" Phileas Fogg.

George Francis Train, however, was not the only man who could legitimately make such a claim. Another possible Fogg antecedent was the Cleveland city official who circled the world during the years 1869 and 1870 and sent back letters chronicling his travels to the *Cleveland Leader* newspaper, which were subsequently collected in a book entitled *Round the World: Letters from Japan, China, India, and Egypt.* He required a good deal longer than eighty days to make it around the world, but his credentials as a source for Verne lay elsewhere: for his name was William Perry Fogg.

Jules Verne himself always insisted that he had never heard of William Perry Fogg, and that his protagonist's name was simply a play on the word "fog," which Verne thought to be emblematic of the character's London home. ("When I found 'Fogg' I was very pleased and proud," he later told a British journalist.) Verne's *Le Tour du monde en quatre-vingts jours* first appeared at the end of 1872 as a serialization in the Parisian newspaper *Le Temps* and subsequently, as *Around the World in Eighty Days,* in English and American newspapers. Appearing in book form in 1873, it quickly became the most beloved of all Verne's novels, selling more than a hundred thousand copies in France during his lifetime and hundreds of thousands of copies more in translation around the world. In 1874 the book was turned into a play; adapted by the French dramatist Adolphe D'Ennery, *Around the World* added not just one but two shipwrecks to the narrative and featured the appearance onstage of a locomotive, a nest of snakes, and, most thrillingly for the audience, a live elephant. Like the novel, the play was both a critical and a popular success, running in Paris for more than two years. Verne himself had been concerned about the play's prospects, and before it opened he invited his friend Félix Duquesnel, a drama critic and playwright, to attend one of the rehearsals. "Between ourselves, a success?" Verne asked him afterward. "No," replied Duquesnel, "a fortune."

Indeed, though later Verne would complain that he had received much less than his fair share for the play, and moreover that he had sold the novel for "a tenth of its value," it was his tale of the circumnavigator Phileas Fogg that finally secured his fortune, and transformed him from a popular adventure novelist into a literary celebrity, an author who could no longer stroll unnoticed amid the Parisian crowds, whose name appeared in society columns and who was deluged with love letters containing locks of his female admirers' hair. Verne already owned a yacht, the *Saint-Michel,* but now he traded it in for a new, larger one, and then another (*Saint-Michel II* and *III*), on which he made tours of northern Africa and Scandinavia. The boat was one of his few indulgences; the mansion in the northern city of Amiens had been purchased at the behest of his wife, who enjoyed far more than he did the bourgeois life of the French provincial city. Verne's own daily routine was near monastic: he slept where he worked, in his little study decorated only with busts of Shakespeare and Molière and a watercolor of the *Saint-Michel* on the wall. Each morning at five o'clock he rose from his narrow iron bed and sat down at the plain writing desk, where he worked through the morning, stopping only briefly to eat the breakfast that Honorine had placed by the door exactly at seven. He was in bed again by eight-thirty each night, often having politely excused himself from one of his wife's many social engagements. And so the novels kept coming, sometimes at a rate of two per year. In 1886 Verne's brilliant but mentally ill nephew unaccountably shot him; he was hit twice, one of the bullets lodging in his ankle. Surgeons were unable to remove the bullet, and for the rest of his life Verne walked with a limp and often suffered a good deal of pain. No longer was he able to sail his yacht; now, as he had promised his mother long before, he could travel only in imagination. The next year he entered local politics, winning a seat on the Amiens city council as a member of the Radical Republican party (both politically and theologically he was a thoroughgoing nonconformist), a position to which he would be re-elected three times.

In the fall of 1889, Robert H. Sherard, *The World*'s Paris correspondent, contacted Verne to ask if he might meet a young female journalist by the name of Nellie Bly, who was setting out to beat Phileas Fogg's eighty-day trip around the world. The paper's managing editor had cabled Sherard from New York with instructions to set up the meeting; Robert Sherard later recalled that the editors thought "it would give a good advertisement" for Bly if she could visit the illustrious writer and, in a sense, receive his imprimatur for her trip. According to Sherard, Verne was initially hesitant about the idea, not understanding what purpose would be served by such a meeting, but after some discussion he agreed to meet the young lady. The news was sent back to Bly via *The World*'s London correspondent, Tracey Greaves, who made the necessary changes in her train schedule to allow for a brief detour on the way from

London to Calais. When Nellie Bly's train rolled into the station in Amiens, Jules Verne and his wife, Honorine, were waiting for her on the platform.

NOVEMBER 22, 1889
Amiens, France

About to meet one of the world's most famous men, Nellie Bly worried that her face might be soot-stained from the train ride, her hair tousled under her cap. It was late Friday afternoon, and she had barely slept since Wednesday. Already that day she and Tracey Greaves had traveled by train from London to Southampton, endured a rough crossing of the English Channel (apparently inured now to seasickness, she had stayed up on deck with the men rather than join the other women below), and then eaten another quick meal at a small, dingy restaurant in Boulogne before boarding the train to Amiens. On the Amiens train she managed a nap at her seat; it was a pleasant sleep, filled with dreams of home, but she woke up feeling chilled and achy, wishing she could stretch out. The compartment's foot warmer was shared by all five of the passengers, and Bly guiltily realized that she must have stepped on some toes while she slept; the man across from her kept giving her angry looks over the top of his newspaper. Her feet were burning hot, but her back was freezing cold. The accommodations here were not at all like those on American trains, where a first-class carriage was as comfortable as a first-class hotel. If she had been on an American train, Bly thought, she would have been able to tidy up en route, but these European trains with their locked compartments were useless for that. On the train to Southampton she had come to understand why English girls needed chaperones, locked away as they were into those private compartments, where they might be knees to knees with a stranger for hours at a time; in the larger American carriages, on the other hand, everyone in the crowd was a potential protector. There was safety in numbers: that was the lesson mothers should be teaching their daughters. She was pondering this as the train pulled in to the station at Amiens.

"There they are," said Greaves, and Bly quickly scanned the platform. Jules Verne looked like one of his own characters, a ship's captain perhaps, with wavy white hair swept back from his forehead and a thick gray beard, barrel-chested and still powerful-looking at the age of sixty-one. He was of average height, standing about five foot five; beside him Honorine was several inches shorter, and stout, wearing a sealskin jacket over a dark watered silk skirt, a small velvet bonnet on her head. Though her hair was as white as her husband's she had a youthful face, with a clear complexion and very red lips. Bly waited with Greaves for the porter to come unlock their compartment, then she gathered up her bag and stepped down from the train. The Vernes strode toward them, calling their greetings; Bly shyly said hello and thanked them for agreeing to meet her. The thin blond man behind the Vernes introduced himself as Robert Sherard, who had arrived earlier from Paris to act as translator. Sherard was twenty-seven years old; he had been educated at Oxford and was a friend of Oscar Wilde and Victor Hugo. In his memoir he did not mention Bly by name, describing her only as "a girl reporter."

Two carriages were waiting for them at the station. Verne turned and led the way (he walked surprisingly quickly despite the evident limp), helping Bly and his wife up into one of the carriages before joining Greaves and Sherard in the other. Though she didn't say anything, Bly felt awkward about being left alone in the carriage with Mrs. Verne—as Honorine Verne's English vocabulary consisted simply of the word "no" and her own French simply of "*oui*," there was little

Jules Verne in 1888

for them to do during the drive but admire the scenery and occasionally smile apologetically at each other. They were riding on a tree-lined boulevard through the center of town, far removed from the large, noisy factories down along the canals of the Somme, where water-powered looms turned out bolts of linen, silk, and velvet. Here was the France that Bly had always imagined: brightly lit shops, a charming park, uniformed nursemaids pushing baby carriages or calling after children who ran ahead on the path. In the distance she could see the immense bulk of the Amiens cathedral glowing a pinkish white in the late-afternoon sun; more than three hundred feet high and nearly as wide, the cathedral dominated the sky the way no single building in New York ever could.

After twenty minutes the carriages pulled up before a high stone wall. Verne opened a door in the wall, revealing a large fieldstone house with a turret running up one side. Honorine led them up a flight of marble steps and through a glass-walled conservatory, filled with beautiful flowers, into the house. Entering the sitting room, she knelt and lit a fire in the open fireplace, then indicated that Nellie Bly should sit closest to the fire, in one of the five easy chairs that formed a semicircle around the hearth. The others sat down as well. On the wall above them hung matching oil portraits of the Vernes. The room had a rich, dark beauty; the chairs were upholstered in brocaded silk, the windows draped with velvet. Two years earlier Bly had been shivering with fear and cold inside a women's insane asylum; now she was sitting in an easy chair by a comfortable fire talking with Jules Verne about her work.

"Many of Monsieur Verne's books have American locales," she said to Robert Sherard. "Has Monsieur Verne been in America?"

He had been there once, Verne answered, but for only a few days. He had managed to see Niagara Falls, though, which was a sight he had never forgotten. He tried to keep up with all the latest news from America, and greatly appreciated the hundreds of letters he received each year from his readers there, many of them addressed simply to *Jules Verne, France*. He had always longed to return, but the state of his health prevented him from taking any long journeys. It had been four years since he had even boarded a train. "I used to keep a yacht," he explained, "and then I traveled all over the world studying locations; then I wrote from actual observation. Now, since my health confines me to my home, I am forced to read up on descriptions and geographies."

Verne was sitting forward at the edge of his chair, his hair artistically disordered, his eyes dark and brilliant beneath heavy white brows. He spoke in a rapid voice, and as he spoke his hands fluttered around his head like birds. When he was especially interested in a subject his nostrils flared; he had, an observer once remarked, "the nose of a sleuth." Now, through Sherard, he asked Bly what her line of travel around the world was to be.

"My line of travel is from New York to London, then Calais, Brindisi, Port Said, Ismailia, Suez, Aden, Colombo, Penang, Singapore, Hong Kong, Yokohama, San Francisco, New York."

Verne considered this for a moment. "Why do you not land at Bombay and travel across India to Calcutta, like Phileas Fogg?"

"Because," Bly replied, "I am more anxious to save time than a young widow."

The Vernes laughed. "You may save a young widower before you return," said Jules Verne.

The room was momentarily quiet. Honorine gently stroked a white Angora cat that had jumped into her lap. Verne said, addressing no one in particular, "It really is not to be believed that this little girl is going all alone round the world. Why, she looks a mere child."

"Yes, but she is just built for work of that sort," remarked Honorine approvingly. "She is trim, energetic, and strong. I believe, Jules, that she will make your heroes look foolish. She will beat your record. I am so sure of that that I will wager with you if you like."

Verne shook his head. "I would not like to risk my money," he said, "because I feel sure, now that I have seen the young lady, that she has the character to do it." He did not address his wife's remark about his heroes being made to look foolish, but he could not have been pleased by it. This warmly furnished sitting room was where, in the evenings, Honorine entertained guests in whom her husband had no interest, where she had given interviews to journalists that ended up embarrassing or upsetting him, as, for instance, when she pointed out how few women characters he had included in his books. Over time it had become clear to him that she did not understand his literary ambitions. At eleven each morning they had lunch together in the small breakfast room next to the kitchen, usually eating in silence while Jules brooded about his latest book. He was increasingly withdrawn; his wife frequently burst into tears, often for reasons he did not comprehend. She resented that he did not like to take her into Amiens society, and complained to friends that "he piles the problems produced by his discouragement onto me." Always on Sundays she wanted him to accompany her to Mass; he had gone at first to appease her and then, after a while, he gave it up for good. Marriage, Verne once wrote in a letter to his brother—meaning the institution in general and his own in particular—constituted "an immense and irreparable folly." Still, the two worked hard to keep up appearances, to be in public the couple the world wished them to be.

It was a pity, said Jules Verne, that Nellie Bly was traveling in winter rather than summer; in the warmer weather she would doubtless have better sea passages and would likely gain an additional day or two. Bly told the Vernes about the rough passage across the Atlantic and the mad scamper, as she put it, around London. It had been only that morning, but it felt like ages ago. She glanced at her wristwatch: the time, she saw, was already growing short. There was only a single train from Amiens to Calais; missing it meant a week's delay, in which case she might just as well turn around and head back to New York the way she had come. She said, "If Monsieur Verne would not consider it impertinent I should like to see his study before I go."

He was only too happy to show it to her, Verne said, and even as his reply was being translated Honorine was standing and had lit a candle. With the candle in hand she led the way out of the room, her husband limping behind her, back through the conservatory to the house's turret, then up a narrow spiral staircase three flights to the top floor. There Honorine paused to light the gas jet in the hallway; Verne opened the door of his study and Bly and the others stepped inside after him.

She was astonished; based on the many descriptions she had read of the studies of famous authors (each time filled with envy, thinking of how scarce and expensive space was in New York), she had imagined a large, richly furnished room, perhaps a hand-carved desk covered with expensive trinkets, rare paintings on the wall. This study, though, was not much larger than her own back in New York. On the desk an ink bottle and a penholder sat alongside a neat stack of white paper—the manuscript of the novel on which he was then at work, *Sans dessus dessous,* about a group of Americans who try to shift the axis of the earth in order to warm the North Pole and gain access to its mineral reserves. "A purely imaginary story," Verne said to her, as though in apology. With a sense of awe Bly picked up a page of the manuscript, and was immediately struck by the exquisite penmanship: the writing looked as much like poetry as prose.

Several sentences had been carefully blotted out, but no new ones had been put in between the existing lines; the great author improved his work, she noted to herself, always by cutting, never by adding.

It was, Verne told her, the tenth draft of the novel. "Often," he said, "I entirely rewrite the whole work when completed. I copy and re-copy even then and make as many corrections as you see there. I don't believe in dashing off things. One can't attain anything in the world without labor and fatigue. I think you will be fatigued, Mademoiselle, before you get to the end of the journey you are undertaking. That picture," he said, pointing to the watercolor on the wall, "is my yacht entering the Bay of Naples. I used to cruise about the Mediterranean a great deal and wish I could do so still." There, again, the flared nostrils: how hard it must be to endure that diminishment, to watch from home as others traveled the world, to be regularly interrupted in his imagining of faraway lands by the whistle of a train he was not allowed to ride. He said, "If you will come into the next room I will show you my books."

Adjoining the study was an enormous library, lined from floor to ceiling with glass-fronted bookcases filled with handsome leather-bound volumes, among them the collected works of Homer and Virgil, Montaigne, Shakespeare, Balzac, and his favorite author, Charles Dickens. There were countless foreign editions of his own novels, translated into languages including Arabic and Japanese. One wall was covered with pigeonholes containing all of the reference notes he had gathered over the years, some twenty-five thousand of them, arranged according to subject. The visitors, all writers, marveled at the literary treasures arrayed before them, until Verne asked the group to follow him out into the hallway, where he stopped before a large map of the world that hung on the wall. Holding up a candle for illumination, he pointed out to Nellie Bly a sequence of blue lines that had been inscribed on the map. This, she immediately understood, was the very map on which he had traced out Phileas Fogg's journey before beginning work on his novel. Now with another pencil Verne lightly marked the places where Bly's route diverged from that of his world traveler. Bly studied the map, comparing the lines of travel. Fogg's moved southeast through the Middle East and across India, veered sharply south to Singapore, and then proceeded northeast to Hong Kong and northwest again to Shanghai, the line resembling the long handle and rectangular bowl of the Big Dipper. Her own was a straighter, more direct path. Aden, Colombo, Penang, Yokohama: all of those unfamiliar names, she knew, would soon enough be made real to her.

Back downstairs, the table had been set with plates of cookies and glasses of wine. Through Sherard's translation Jules Verne explained that although he rarely drank alcohol, on this afternoon he would take a glass of wine so that they might have the pleasure of drinking together to the success of her undertaking. "If you do it in seventy-nine days," Verne told Bly, "I shall applaud with both hands." He reached over to clink glasses with her, and in doing so endeavored, in English, to wish her success. "Good back," he said, "good back."

Everyone laughed and clinked glasses and drank, and Nellie Bly took a moment to tell Jules Verne how much she had enjoyed meeting him and his wife. As they stood up to go, Honorine told Robert Sherard that she would like to kiss Miss Bly goodbye; Sherard translated her request for Bly, adding that it was considered a great honor in France for a woman to ask to kiss a stranger. Nellie Bly was not used to this kind of formality, but she was flattered by the request, and she leaned forward—for she was a good deal taller than Mrs. Verne—as Honorine kissed her in the Gallic fashion, on both cheeks. Bly had a sudden impulse to surprise Honorine with a kiss right on those red lips, but, as she wrote later, "for once I was able to control my mischievousness, which often wrecks my dignity, and take my farewell after her own sweet way."

In spite of the cold weather the Vernes insisted on following their visitors outside to see them off, and they waved and called their farewells as Bly and Greaves got into the carriage that would take them to the nearby train station. When Bly turned for a last look she could still see them waving, the wind tossing their white hair.

The following month, in an interview with the *Pall Mall Gazette* of London, Jules Verne said of Nellie Bly that "what took the hearts of both myself and Mrs. Verne was the complete modesty of the young person," and called her "the prettiest young girl imaginable." In private, he had other thoughts. "My God, what a shame to see such a clever woman treated so badly by nature," Verne wrote about Bly in a letter to a friend, "as thin as a match, neither bottom nor bosom!"

THE INTERVIEW IN the *Pall Mall Gazette* was by no means the only news story about Nellie Bly's meeting with Jules Verne. As the editors of *The*

World had anticipated, the visit with the famous novelist brought new attention to Bly's trip throughout the world—not only in France but all around Europe, and eventually as far as Japan. *The World*'s own article about the Amiens meeting, written by Tracey Greaves, appeared on the paper's front page less than forty-eight hours after Bly took her leave of the Vernes. There would subsequently be a second article by Greaves, as well as a *World* editorial that declared, hyperbolically, that Jules Verne "gave the plucky little traveller no end of encouragement and pronounced her undertaking one of the marvels of American journalism." In the editorial *The World* avowed once more that Bly would employ no special trains or chartered ships during her trip, and noted, in an unmistakable reference to *The Cosmopolitan,* "Imitators may spring up in various quarters, but the fact remains that THE WORLD was the first to put into execution this plan of circumnavigating the globe against time which has excited the admiration and won the unstinted praise of the famous JULES VERNE."

"The Young Lady's Undertaking," *The World* proclaimed in a headline, was "a Constant Subject of Comment," and every day the paper reprinted items about the trip from other newspapers around the country, taking special care to include the items that praised *The World* for its journalistic daring. Much of the time that daring involved the newspaper's supposed insistence that its female reporter travel light. Observed the *Long Island Times,* "The New York World has just surpassed all the former achievements of men by inducing a woman to start off on a journey around the globe without a big trunk and with only one dress to wear. Completing the journey in seventy-five days will not eclipse the feat of getting a woman to travel with so little toggery." In a similar vein, *Cooley's Weekly* of Norwich, Connecticut, praised Bly's "heroic work," which consisted mainly of not bringing along "a four-story Saratoga trunk, such as a lady needs for a three weeks' millinery exhibition at Newport or Long Branch," while the *Reporter* of Towanda, Pennsylvania, chimed in that "the most remarkable feature of this progressive undertaking is that Miss Bly takes only one dress and no trunk."

Less than two weeks into Bly's trip, *The World* appointed an "Excursion Editor" (later called the "European Trip Editor") to oversee the publicity surrounding, as the paper liked to call it, "Nellie's Rush Around." The editor, who was never identified by name, first appeared in a published response to a letter signed "Five Girls in Mount Vernon." It was an unabashed fan letter, containing the sort of breathless prose far more often meant for singers or actresses than newspaper reporters. "Will you tell us about Nellie Bly personally?" the girls pleaded.

> We have read so much about her that we are very anxious to know. Everything she writes is so good and her descriptions of the places she has visited are so perfect and we admire her so much for that ability that we want to know all about her. She is about how old? Tall or short? Dark or light? Handsome, ordinary or plain? (She is so smart she could not possibly be homely.) Tell us all about her. She is a wonder in our minds, and we are waiting to read her description of her trip around the world. The fact is, Mr. Editor, we five girls think we must know more about Nellie Bly. Will you tell us and oblige?

The Excursion Editor answered that "the young lady in question" was "about twenty-three years of age" (Bly was, of course, twenty-five), that she stood five foot three (she was actually two inches taller than that), had dark hair and gray eyes, and was "fairly good-looking. She is quiet and reserved, her manners are genteel, though she is full of determination, and, girls, she does not chew gum."

NOVEMBER 23–25, 1889
Calais, France, to Brindisi, Italy

Nellie Bly and Tracey Greaves arrived in Calais shortly before midnight, with nearly two hours to spare until the departure of the mail train bound for Brindisi, Italy. The glow of the meeting with the Vernes still lingered in Bly's mind, how Jules Verne had traced out her route side by side with that of Phileas Fogg, how Honorine Verne had expressed her confidence that she would beat Fogg's time. All the way to Calais, Greaves later wrote, "Nellie did nothing but talk about the motherly kindness of Mrs. Verne." The Calais agent of the International Sleeping-Car Company met them at the station. Against company regulations he offered to open the train's sleeping car ahead of time, to allow Nellie Bly the opportunity to go to bed, but though she had barely slept in more than forty-eight hours she turned down the offer. "This is the first time since I started when I really felt I had an hour to call my own," she said. "I want to look about a bit."

So Bly and Greaves walked down the pier and out along the shore. The air was cold and fresh, and in the moonlight the sea looked like a sheet of molten silver. Down the beach they paused to admire the Calais lighthouse, a skyscraper rising improbably from the water, thin and white and rounded on top, like a rocket ship that might have been imagined by Jules Verne. After a while they turned and headed back to the station, waiting in its coffee shop until a railway official came in to announce that the boat from England had just arrived; as soon as its mail was transferred from ship to shore, the train for Brindisi would be off. Before long Bly was saying a warm goodbye to Tracey Greaves, thanking him for the many courtesies he had shown her. Then she stepped aboard the train; she was traveling alone once more.

The train from Calais to Brindisi (the India mail train, as it was commonly known) was one of the most famous in the world, despite being designed more for the transport of mail than of people. It carried only a single Pullman sleeper car with twenty-one berths; reservations had to be made no later than twenty-four hours before departure and were usually filled long before then by travelers who wanted an exceptionally fast trip across the Continent regardless of price—it cost more to travel from Calais to Brindisi than from New York to San Francisco. Leaving Calais every Saturday morning precisely at one-thirty, the train sped down France's western coast to Amiens, skirted the suburbs of Paris, and ran through Burgundy to Dijon; crossing the Italian border during the night, the train arrived in Turin around lunchtime, then continued south along the Adriatic coast until it reached the port city of Brindisi, where its mailbags would be unloaded onto ships bound for India and Australia.

Exhausted, Nellie Bly went immediately to bed, and despite the noise and rocking of the train she slept soundly and awoke feeling surprisingly refreshed. The car had only a single washroom, where she cleaned herself as best she could at a washstand piled high with dirty towels. Many of the male passengers were playing cards; the air in the car was already thick with cigar smoke. Breakfast was nothing more than coffee and bread served by the conductor and porter from a greasy portable stove, and lunch was scarcely better. For hours the train rode through wheat fields brown and barren, pastures where red cattle grazed, but Bly could seldom make out much detail; through the begrimed windows of the train the landscape looked blotched and blurry, as in one of the modern French paintings. In the evening a dining car was attached to the train, but some of the other women informed Bly that it was not considered suitable for them to dine in a public car with the men, and so they took dinner in their compartments. When the sun went down the car grew much colder, and Bly put on her ulster and wrapped herself tightly in her traveling rug, yearning again for the luxury of American trains. That night she turned in early; she piled her coat and all of her clothes on top of the berth's single blanket and lay awake half the night shivering and thinking about how fortunate the train's passengers had been the week before. In the very mountains through which they were now passing, the train had been attacked by bandits: those passengers, at least, had been given some excitement to get the blood moving.

The next morning Bly threw open the shade and looked eagerly out of the window for balmy Italy, but she saw there only a dull screen of gray, almost as though the shade had not been lifted. For a confused moment she wondered if, for once in her life, she had risen before the sun, but according to her wristwatch it was ten o'clock. Quickly she dressed and found the porter.

"It is a most extraordinary thing," he said. "I never saw such a fog in Italy before."

There was nothing to do except sit and stare out at the shrouded landscape. Silently she counted the number of days she had been away from New York, subtracting them from the number that would have to elapse before her return; she had, she figured, seventeen thousand miles still ahead of her, and sixty-five days in which to cover them, which came to an average of 261 miles that had to be traveled every day, or somewhat more than ten miles per hour, every hour, for the duration of her trip. When these calculations grew monotonous she thought about how one might go about introducing brown uniforms for railroad employees in the United States (those worn by the conductor and porter, brightened by gold braid on the collars and cuffs, were so much nicer than the plain blue ones found in America), and after a while she began to notice how the train guards signaled the conductor not by pulling a wire inside the car but by blowing a little tune on a bugle, and how the engine whistles were less a nerve-rattling blast than a plaintive appeal, like a shepherd calling after his flock. Somewhere out there the Adriatic lay hidden like a stage set behind a curtain; at times, when the train slowed down, she could hear the beating of the waves. She had seen little of England, less of France, and now was seeing nothing at all of Italy. All day the fog refused to lift; from morning until night she rode through Italy—sunny Italy, as the guidebooks loved to call it—and only once did she get a glimpse of the country she had heard so much about. It was near sunset, and the train had stopped at some station along the line. She went out on the platform to stretch her legs, and as she did the fog dissipated for a moment, and suddenly lying before her was a beautiful beach, the water dotted with fishing boats propelled by red triangular sails that reminded her of monarch butterflies fluttering about in search of nectar.

The India mail train arrived in Brindisi at one-thirty Monday morning, three and a half hours behind schedule, but still more than an hour before the steamship *Victoria* of the Peninsular and Oriental Line was due to depart. The train station was ringed by men loudly offering the use of their carriages, but beyond the station the town was dark and silent. A few ruined houses were all that remained of Brundisium, the great port city of the ancient Romans, where Virgil died after contracting a fever in Greece. Beyond the walls of the town, now, marshes were being drained; the most recent Baedeker guide warned visitors that "the environs are fertile, but malarious." One of the train guards volunteered to escort the female passengers to their ships and make sure that they were not charged more than the correct fare. An omnibus was hired, the sleepy passengers climbed aboard with their luggage, and the carriage set off for the nearby piers, first to the steamer that was soon to depart for Alexandria, and then on to the *Victoria,* which would take Nellie Bly as far as Ceylon.

A long breakwater sheltered the harbor from winds; the night air was chilly but carried a hint of the tropics. The train guard accompanied Bly and the other passengers up the ship's gangplank. With the guard's help Bly located her cabin, but she waited there only long enough to drop her bag. She wanted to cable *The World* to say that she had arrived in Brindisi, and so the two went to ask the purser if there was time to stop by the telegraph office in town before the ship departed. She could make it, the purser told her, adding, "If you hurry."

The train guard took Bly back down the gangplank and into the town. They walked through winding, unlit streets until at last they came to an open door where he stopped; she followed him inside. The room was bare but for a pair of desks, on one of which a sheet of blank paper lay beside a pen and an ancient inkwell. Bly thought that everyone had retired for the night and her cable would have to wait until the next port, but the guard explained that it was customary to ring for the proprietor. He pulled at a bell that hung by one of the desks, and after some time the window opened and a head appeared.

Nellie Bly told the telegraph operator that she wanted to send a cable to New York. That was fine, he replied, but where exactly was New York? Astonished and amused, Bly did her best to explain, and as she did, the operator brought out a pile of books that he consulted to determine what line he should use to send her cable and how much he should charge for it. She wrote out her message on the blank sheet of paper; two days later it would be printed on the front page of *The World,* under the headline NELLIE BLY HEARD FROM:

> *BRINDISI, Italy, Nov. 25.—I reached Brindisi this morning on time after an uneventful trip across the Continent. The railway journey was tedious and tiresome, but I received no end of courtesy from the railway officials, who had been apprised of my coming. In a few hours I will be on the bosom of the Mediterranean. I am quite well though somewhat fatigued. I send kind greetings to all friends in the United States.*
>
> *NELLIE BLY.*

Leaving the telegraph office, Bly was startled by the warning sound of a ship's whistle. She had been so preoccupied with her cable that she had forgotten entirely about the *Victoria*'s impending departure. For a moment her heart stopped beating. She looked at the guard and he looked at her. "Can you run?" he asked.

She said that she could, and the guard took hold of her hand. Down the silent, deserted streets they ran, until at last they rounded a corner and found themselves back at the pier. Bly looked out at the water, straining to see through the darkness. Then she felt she could breathe again.

The ship for Alexandria had gone, but hers still lay safely in port.

CHAPTER 8

"Et Ego in Arcadia"

NOVEMBER 21–25, 1889
Pacific Ocean

SLOWLY AMERICA SANK OUT OF
SIGHT, GREEN HILLS GIVING WAY TO
a rolling blue plain of sea. The White
Star steamship *Oceanic,* of the Occidental and Oriental Line, set sail
from San Francisco at exactly three
o'clock Thursday afternoon, No-
vember 21, with Elizabeth Bisland on board. As of today she had been
traveling for a full week, one quite unlike any other she had ever lived
through, and she was still feeling the effects of that mad rush by train
across the country. Even amid the luxury of the Palace Hotel—with its
marble-paved courtyard and wood-paneled rising rooms and concierges
on every floor, communicating with the front desk via an ingenious series of speaking tubes—she had had little time to rest, what with the final
preparations to be made for her trip, the sightseeing expeditions organized by her newspaper hosts in the city (they had been so gracious she
could not possibly say no), and of course the constant interruptions from
curiosity seekers wanting just to get a glimpse of her, that newfound celebrity, that inexpensive freak show. She was relieved finally to be rid of

them, excited to be leaving her country for the first time, and very much looking forward, on this long voyage across the Pacific, to leisurely meals with congenial companions, to many long hours of reading and writing and many more with no greater obligation than just to gaze at sea and sky: to the opportunity of returning to her senses.

The *Oceanic,* Bisland could tell right away, was a magnificent ship, with its black hull and white body, the single white funnel with black topband and four masts gaily flying the White Star and the O&O house flags under the Union Jack (she thrilled to feel herself, for a time, under English rule). Built by the White Star Line in 1870, the *Oceanic,* an observer had remarked, was "the ship which makes possible the concept of a steamship as a travelling palace." The first-class staterooms all had electric call buttons to summon stewards; water taps replaced the jugs that had been used in the past; and, happily enough, lavatories had been placed near the staterooms, rendering unnecessary those middle-of-the-night treks across the ship to the closest one, or, worse, the resort to chamber pots that sloshed around during the night and could be tipped over by any sudden wave. Downstairs, the ship's steerage was crowded with Chinese immigrants returning to their homeland. "There were," the *San Francisco Chronicle* reported, "424 coolies on board." As the *Oceanic* set sail many of the steerage passengers stood at the lower rail tossing overboard little pieces of paper. It was a Chinese tradition; each of the papers contained a prayer for a safe voyage. The scraps of paper fluttered in the wind like autumn leaves before disappearing into the sea.

The breeze was picking up, the air turning cold. Above her Bisland could see crewmen setting topgallant sails to catch the rising wind. The worrisome news began to circulate among the passengers: a storm was coming. At that she went below to her stateroom to prepare for her first night at sea, which gave every indication of being a rough one. For the next four days Elizabeth Bisland's only memory of the Pacific Ocean was of a foaming flood of emerald water beyond the porthole, which cast the room into a sickening green twilight. Her head pounded and her stomach lurched; lying in her thin berth, eyes shut tight, she could feel herself descending the seven rounds of hell. She did not eat and she barely slept, for the nights were positively terrifying. It seemed as if every plank in the ship groaned, joints racked by dozens of hard ocean crossings; the ship beat ceaselessly up and down with the pulse of the sea. She watched with indifference as her possessions slid like Alpine skiers back and forth across the stateroom floor; the bouquets given her by well-wishers lay tossed about the cabin like sprays scattered over a grave site. It was comforting to remember that her last will and testament had already been written, but hateful to imagine a death at sea. The longest plummet line ever dropped had gone down here and only found bottom at a depth of four thousand fathoms: nearly five miles straight down. *The vast, salt, dread, eternal deep,* Byron had called it. Anyone falling overboard, she mused, would never reach the earth that lay beneath the water, would just float forever in those soundless depths, drifting along in the slow flux of the undersea tides, surrounded by strange, formless protoplasmic life; in those blue solitudes of silence he would lie enclosed through the ages as in a crystal sarcophagus, a burial as splendid and secure as those of the Pharaohs. . . . She tried to will her mind away from morbid thoughts; she counted, again and again, the six wooden slats of the upper berth above her. Later on, she knew, when she remembered nothing else of this room she would still remember those six boards.

Inside her stateroom the air seemed tainted. It was a smell she recognized, the sweet aroma of joss sticks mixed with the bitter fumes of burning opium; she had smelled it for the first time only a few nights before, in the Chinese Quarter in San Francisco, where her hosts in the city had organized a late-night excursion for some of the passengers from the fast mail train. The sensation she had felt as a young woman living in New Orleans—that a foreign city had somehow been transplanted onto the American mainland—struck her even more forcefully in the Chinese Quarter, jostled about by a crowd dressed in loose-fitting black silk, the streets as busy at midnight as at noon. Even at that hour everyone had seemed cheerful and wide awake; their high-pitched chattering reminded her of guinea fowls she had kept as a girl. Upstairs, above the frail-looking balconies, windowsills held jars of chrysanthemums, the blossoms yellow and ragged around the edges like old newspaper. An off-duty detective had been enlisted to show them some of the sights; he led them down rickety, greasy stairs through back corridors hidden from the street, past open doorways that revealed steaming restaurant kitchens where white-aproned cooks barked and cackled at each other, their pots hissing on the stove. Old men squatted on their heels smoking cigarettes. The night air was chill and damp, rank with mysterious, vaguely suggestive smells that seemed to emanate from every grate and doorway. Here and there red light leaked through a shuttered window; it was impossible to know what lay behind those shutters.

Once, as they approached a building, they heard a shout from somewhere and in an instant the street swarmed with men with hands clasped under their blouses. The detective showed them inside the building, where a man, the owner no doubt, sat alone at a long table quietly smoking a cigarette; a minute earlier the room had been filled with gamblers playing fan-tan, but that single call of warning had emptied it out. This was an old building, Bisland reflected, which had long been put to other uses; now it was an illegal gambling parlor. All through the Quarter, Chinese immigrants had gutted houses and reconstructed the interiors to suit their needs. San Francisco was changed by their arrival; they were not. Tens of thousands of them already lived in the city, with untold millions of hungry countrymen waiting behind them. She returned to her hotel feeling that she understood for the first time why California had put an end to Chinese immigration; the Chinese Quarter, she later wrote, was "a place that left a sinister, menacing impression on my mind."

By that time nearly one in three of San Francisco's workers was Chinese. They worked as laundrymen, cooks, waiters, servants, gardeners; they built houses and dug ditches and operated sewing machines. Some of them had started out in the California gold mines, but they soon discovered that Chinese miners were forbidden access to the so-called mother lodes; if they tried to move to a better mine the white workers would as a matter of course beat and rob them, and, for humiliation, cut off their pigtails. The men who committed these crimes were rarely punished, as the Chinese were not allowed to testify in court. They were also not allowed to vote or to obtain citizenship; though they paid school taxes, their children were denied entry into public schools. It was during this period that a new phrase entered the American idiom, referring to a remote possibility of success: "a Chinaman's chance." A Chinese-English phrase book of the period, published in San Francisco, taught English-speaking employers such useful phrases as *Can you get me a good boy? He wants eight dollars per month? He ought to be satisfied with six dollars. When I find him useful, I will give him more. I think he is very stupid. If you want to go out, you must ask me. Brush my clothes. Light the fire. Wash the floor. I want to cut his wages.* Chinese speakers learned: *Yes, madam. Dinner is on the table, sir. When shall I begin? I beg you to consider again. You must not strike me.*

Many of the Chinese immigrants found jobs building the transcontinental railroad, where they became known as coolies. The word "coolie" was derived from an Urdu word referring to unskilled labor; the British had learned it in India and passed it along to the Americans, who applied it out west. The workers on the Union Pacific mostly came from Ireland, but on the Central Pacific, which ran from California to Utah, they were mostly Chinese. The man who oversaw the construction of the Central Pacific line, Charles Crocker, praised the Chinese laborers for their discipline and industriousness, and eventually came to prefer using them for jobs that had to be done quickly. When pressed by doubters, Crocker would point out, "They built the Great Wall, didn't they?"

The Chinese railroad workers prepared for themselves meals involving oysters and cuttlefish and abalone, bamboo sprouts and seaweed and dried mushrooms, strange foods that mystified and repelled the men who mostly ate the boiled beef and potatoes provided by the railroad. The Chinese drank only tea; as it turned out, boiling the water for the tea helped avert the dysentery that afflicted many of the white workers, who drank their water directly from streams. The Chinese used the stream water to wash their clothes and, warmed by a fire, for daily sponge baths; again, this was different from the typical white railroad worker, who, noted one observer, "has a sort of hydrophobia which induces him to avoid the contact of water." They were small (most stood less than five feet tall) and had hairless faces and wore their hair in pigtails, which made them seem, to the other workers, like women. Still, they often did the jobs that the whites were not able, or not willing, to do themselves. At night they wove reeds into baskets in which, during the day, they hung over gorges to place packets full of black powder into crevices dug into the faces of cliffs. When the packet was secure, the Chinese worker lit the fuse and then yelled to a crewman above to haul him up before the powder exploded. This was how railroad beds were carved into the sides of mountains, to make the narrow, vertiginous passes like the one on which Cyclone Bill Downing had set the fast mail train careening. "Good engineers," reported *Van Nostrand's Engineering Magazine,* "considered this undertaking preposterous." It is indisputable that many of the men laying powder in this manner were killed or injured on the job, but the exact numbers will never be known, as the Central Pacific Railroad did not keep records of Chinese casualties. Black powder, of course, was originally a Chinese invention, and the workers did not ask for instructions in handling it. They used the powder, as well, to blast holes directly into mountains, creating tunnels through which the trains would travel. It was an almost unimaginably laborious process of drilling, blasting, scraping, and hauling; the men worked in shifts around the clock, and when the day was over they might have carved away as much as twelve inches.

Elsewhere, on flat land, the Chinese workers cleared forests for railroad tracks. These were primeval trees, often well over a hundred feet tall, with trunks up to eight feet in diameter. The workers would saw the trees down to stumps, then blast the stumps from the ground with black powder. Clearing a good-sized stretch of forest required thousands of barrels of powder; to observers the work sites brought back unhappy memories of Civil War battlefields, the air ringing with explosions, made dangerous by flying rocks and shards of wood turned into shrapnel, and indeed in any given week a railroad crew would set off as much black powder as was used by both Union and Confederate armies during the battle of Antietam.

After the transcontinental railroad was completed in 1869, some of the Chinese railroad workers went back to China, while others fanned out through the West seeking other forms of work. Throughout the 1870s anti-Chinese sentiment grew in the United States, whipped up by politicians who were discovering that no region of the country was immune from racial prejudice, and that even a few thousand votes swayed by fear and hatred could make the difference in a close election. Further, during a time of rising labor unrest (in 1877, for instance, a national strike tied up much of the country's railroad lines), it was helpful to refocus the resentments of American workers away from their employers to a group of working people even more vulnerable and exploited than they were. One of the leaders of the anti-Chinese campaign, Republican senator James G. Blaine of Maine, wrote a letter to the *New York Tribune* in which he characterized Chinese immigrants as "vicious," "odious," "abominable," "dangerous," and "revolting," and asserted that the United States government had the right to bar them just as surely as it had "the right to keep out infectious diseases." George Hazelton, a congressman from Wisconsin, described the Chinese immigrant as a "monstrosity" who "lives in herds and sleeps like packs of dogs in kennels." For his part, Representative William Calkins of Indiana saw Chinese immigrants simply as "a cancer in your own country that will eat out its life and destroy it."

In 1882 the U. S. Congress passed the Chinese Exclusion Act, which barred Chinese immigrants from entering the country for the next ten years; it was the first federal law ever to ban a group of immigrants on the basis of their race or nationality. The stirring words of the poet Emma Lazarus, inscribed on the base of the Statue of Liberty, proclaiming to the rest of the world that the United States would welcome "your tired, your poor / Your huddled masses yearning to breathe free" did not then apply to Chinese; eventually Koreans, Japanese, and Eastern and Southern Europeans would also be barred from entering the United States. In the 1880s America, long a country with a policy of open immigration, began a new tradition of exclusion. "Hereafter," the *Chicago Times* noted approvingly, "we are to keep our hand on the door-knob, and admit only those whose presence we desire."

BEFORE THE *OCEANIC* set sail across the Pacific, Elizabeth Bisland had composed a quick note addressed to her editors at *The Cosmopolitan* and sent it back to shore by pilot boat. She did not mention the low spirits that had afflicted her in her stateroom crowded with strangers, adopting instead the tone of cheerful determination that she would maintain, at least publicly, throughout the trip. She wrote, "Everyone has been charming to me. The officers of the Occidental and Oriental Steamship Company promise to get me through on time. My stateroom is filled with flowers and books, and even strangers sent me great baskets of flowers and came down to the wharf to see me off. Good-bye, I hope to be at The Cosmopolitan office on the 26th of January."

The note appeared in the "In the Library" column of *The Cosmopolitan*'s January 1890 issue, which was published in early December of 1889, while Bisland was still steaming across the Pacific to Yokohama. The column would be taken over by William S. Walsh for the duration of her trip. "Starting from New York at the briefest possible notice," Walsh explained, "she is at this moment nearing the coast of Japan, and is engaged upon a series of articles upon the incidents of the voyage around the world." Despite publisher John Brisben Walker's public wager with *The World* about whose competitor would return first, *The Cosmopolitan*, maintaining a sense of decorum, chose to characterize Elizabeth Bisland's undertaking only as a "voyage," a "trip," and a "journey," never as a "race." Still, no one would have had much difficulty reading between the lines. "Before Miss Bisland started on her westward trip," Walsh wrote, "the New York *World* had sent out its most accomplished correspondent, Miss Nellie Bly, who has rendered valuable services not only to *The World* but to the public on repeated occasions, to make the same journey, traveling eastward. Her start antedated that of Miss Bisland by about nine hours." Nor did *The Cosmopolitan* join *The World* in insisting that the trip would provide an instructive test of modern means of travel and communication. Walsh noted pointedly, "It is, of course, understood that no important results are likely to be attained from such a trip, nor anything of scientific value demonstrated; but, under the sprightly pen of Miss Bisland, the incidents of the journey are likely to prove of a thoroughly entertaining character."

The Cosmopolitan, of course, was a monthly magazine, while *The World* was a daily newspaper; by the time the "In the Library" column about Bisland appeared, *The World* had been promoting—or, in the locution of the period, "booming"—Bly's trip every day for almost a month, often several times in a single issue. And even though Bly was already far better known than Bisland, widely acclaimed for her work as an undercover journalist, none of her earlier successes had brought anywhere near this level of attention. Revealing the crooked doings of corrupt public institutions was one thing; traveling around the world faster than anyone ever had before was something else entirely. The endeavor was daring, it was unexpected, and there was an appealing patriotism in the notion of an American attempting to capture a record held by an Englishman— albeit a fictional one. The laudatory notices soon began to appear everywhere. Nellie Bly, declared the *Boston Herald,* was "not merely a smart girl; she is a mighty brave one." In the *Detroit Commercial* she was "this plucky young woman," and in the *Atlanta Constitution* the "enterprising young lady reporter." "Miss Bly is pretty when she talks and smiles, for then her face brightens up and her eyes sparkle and there is a turn at the corners of her mouth that is very fascinating," observed the *San Francisco Examiner.* "In a word, she is a plain every-day girl, with a wonderful head and warm heart."

Nellie Bly had her detractors, of course, those who considered her headstrong and intemperate and her attempt to outrace Phileas Fogg an absurd endeavor unfit for a woman. Particularly vitriolic was the *Philadelphia Inquirer,* which excoriated her as "a very ordinary, every day young woman, rather slight in form, leaning to eccentricity in dress, masculine in her tastes and ideas, and a man-hater from way back." Overwhelmingly, though, Bly was extolled in the press as a representative young American woman (representative, in any case, of how Americans liked to think of their young women): plucky, bright, courageous, free-spirited, warm-hearted, pretty but not overly beautiful.

Elizabeth Bisland, by contrast, was matinee-girl gorgeous, she was an aesthete and an intellectual, and she seemed to belong—though she had grown up very poor and supported herself entirely by her own writing—to the upper class. Indeed, when *The New York Times* ran a biographical item about Bisland, it appeared not on the news or the arts pages, but in the "Society Topics of the Week" column in the paper's Sunday edition. "Society people are much interested in the westward trip around the world of Miss Elizabeth Bisland, who started last week to surpass the famous record of 'Phileas' Fogg," the *Times* reported. Bisland, the paper informed its readers, was "a New-Orleans girl of excellent social position" and "exceedingly pretty," whose "charms of manner and person have made her most popular, and although her education and surroundings, which have been those of refinement, if not luxury, have hardly fitted her for so arduous a task as to journey unprotected with the utmost haste around the globe, her friends have every confidence that her perseverance and ambition will carry her safely through." It was an assessment strikingly similar to that of the *San Francisco Examiner,* which declared, "Miss Bisland is universally regarded as one of the handsomest women in New York. Hers is a distinctively southern beauty, the soft eyes and long lashes which raise languidly to look at you, the full mouth, the gentle outline of her figure, her dainty small hands and feet all pointing to the South. She has never done anything of the Bly order and a great deal of curiosity and surprise was shown here when it was known that she had started on a trip of this kind. She has a large amount of determination, however, which one does not expect in the beauties of the South, and there is no doubt that it will stand her in good stead."

So it was not very surprising that in early December a brief notice about Elizabeth Bisland appeared in *Town Topics,* New York's powerful weekly magazine of high society gossip. The item was admiring, if somewhat patronizing in tone; after noting that Bisland "is not a creole, as many papers have endeavored to make her out," the magazine observed, "Her home is with her sister in a delightful apartment on Fourth Avenue, where their informal and gracious hospitality is much enjoyed by a chosen few. Her little teas were especially delightful, and when half a dozen bright girls curled upon her roomy divan and drank Oolong, there was sure to be as a result a poem in the *Century* or a good article in one or another of the monthlies, to nearly all of which Miss Bisland is a valued contributor." About Nellie Bly, on the other hand, the magazine was nothing short of contemptuous. Bly, after all, was a muckraking female journalist for a newspaper that was aimed primarily at a working-class audience far removed in all respects from the drawing-room elite who read *Town Topics*. A satiric item in the magazine entitled "Around the Whirled in 60 Seconds" presented the world traveler "Nellie Fly" as a dim-witted, barely literate buffoon who subsisted on beer and corned beef sandwiches and whose work was entirely rewritten by a young man in the *"Whirled"* newspaper office. The article purported to reveal a dispatch that Nellie Fly had wired to her editor in New York, reporting that the *Augusta Victoria* had arrived and she was now in transit for London. The dispatch read in its entirety:

> Yure brave gurl airived hear at ate thurrty this moarning, and emediately took the trane for London. Awl wel and harty.

And this, after editorial revision, was how it appeared in the paper:

> Beneath the sparkling sun of a golden English sky the staunch ship *Augusta Victoria* floated majestically into the harbor of Southampton at half-past eight this morning, and your correspondent stepped ashore a few moments later to begin the second chapter of her swift flight over the earth's surface. The fresh, enlivening odor of the sea overspread the land, the vagrant birds seemed to whistle a chorus of welcome, the very air breathed a perfumed promise of sweet success to this quaintest of all enterprises.

"Limit your cables to ten words," the editor was said to have instructed Nellie Fly in his telegram to London. "Keep up your courage and keep down expenses. If you speak English as well as you write it you will be well understood in China."

NOVEMBER 25–DECEMBER 8, 1889
Pacific Ocean

On the fifth day of the voyage the storm subsided, and Elizabeth Bisland joined the other female passengers straggling back to life up on deck, pale creatures with uncombed hair tied up in lace scarves; they lay in steamer chairs wrapped in rugs and drinking beef tea, indifferent to their appearance and immune to the pleasures of conversation. Bisland spent hours marveling at the ocean. "The blue deepens and deepens," she wrote, "until one finds no words to express, no simile to convey, the intensity of its burning azure." She had never seen anything quite as beautiful, she thought, or as calming to the spirit. Behind the ship, the white foam that curled up from the wake was tinted with blue, like the bluish shadows in snow; up ahead, the prow flung up two delicate plumes of pearl, trimmed by the sunlight with rainbows that vanished as quickly as they appeared. She read, she took notes, she busied herself with the fancywork she had brought along. When she got tired of sitting she wandered the ship, strolling from promenade deck to saloon deck, from saloon deck to upper deck, from upper deck to lower deck.

Aft of the saloon were the steerage compartments that held single women and married couples; forward of the ship's first-class accommodations—and cut off from them by a massive set of iron doors—was the steerage compartment for the unmarried male passengers. Those traveling in steerage had paid about forty-five dollars apiece for their passage. According to one steamship official, the daily cost to feed each steerage passenger was no more than ten cents, as they were "quite content with boiled rice, three times a day, seasoned with a little dried fish or curry"; the result, happily enough, was "a liberal margin for profit to the ship." Down on the lower afterdeck, Elizabeth Bisland watched the raucous games of fan-tan that went on all day among the Chinese, as well as the more contemplative games of chess and dominoes. The forward deck had a space reserved for female passengers, and a cluster of five or six usually gathered there for conversation, gentle, mild

*Elizabeth Bisland
aboard ship*

women who smiled back at Bisland when she smiled at them and exchanged amiable Chinese greetings for hers offered in English. On a bench, placed where he could catch as much of the healthful salt breezes as he could, a young Chinese man, perhaps twenty-five years old, lay motionless all day. His eyes were sunken, his face the color of old wax; he lay on his back with his hands crossed over his chest, as though he were already in the grave. Bisland had heard that it was common among Chinese immigrants to fall sick with consumption and then struggle back like this, so that they could die in their native land. The young man, she noted, "seems afraid to breathe or move, lest he should waste the failing oil or snuff out the dying flame ere he reaches his yearned-for home."

All the while the ship steamed steadily westward, through calm mornings and moonlit nights. The Pacific crossing was the loneliest of all voyages; for thousands of miles one saw neither sail nor shore, the only sign of life the seabirds that seemed to have followed the ship all the way from San Francisco. Out on the ocean for so long, it was possible for the passengers to imagine themselves the lone survivors of a biblical flood, the whole world now covered with water. The initial days aboard ship had brought first wonder, then misery, then relief; as the days passed, Elizabeth Bisland found that at times she felt a kind of despair, waking each morning to the same endless sea, the same horizon, the same birds, each day just like the one before it, with nothing to mark one's progress except the figures marked every day at noon on the map that hung over the companionway on the deck. After a while the eye became desperately hungry for form, yearning for something, anything, to appear on the horizon, something to look at other than the vast disk of water and inverted bowl of sky.

"A ship is a world," Thomas Knox wrote in his guide for travelers, "and the ocean is the measureless azure in which it floats." As the memory of the life they had left behind began to recede, the passengers were thrown upon one another to relieve the monotony of the trip. "Our small, circumscribed world daily grows in importance in our estimation," Bisland recorded. "We know intimately the characters, tastes, and histories of our companions. We take each other's photographs, and exchange warm professions of friendship; we advise each other about the future, and confide the incidents of the past." Up on deck the first-class passengers played draughts and quoits and cards, and gossiped, and flirted, and broke in to the ancient storehouse of nautical jokes: *What colors are the waves and the winds? The waves rose and the winds blew. Why is a fast young lady like a steamer? There is always a swell after her. What is the difference between an auction and seasickness? One is a sale of effects, the other the effects of a sail. Why should a seasick man wear a plaid waistcoat? To keep a check on his stomach.*

In the evenings there was group singing around the piano; some of the other passengers bent over chess and backgammon boards or dealt out hands of whist. In recent years *tableaux vivants* had become an increasingly popular diversion. To perform a *tableau vivant,* participants selected a well-known scene—usually one from a painting, but occasionally from a book or a play—and dressed themselves as the figures portrayed there. They would arrange themselves behind a curtain or folding screen, assuming the positions shown in the *tableau;* then the audience was invited in and the curtain dramatically removed to reveal the scene, the participants remaining perfectly still for as long as possible. Remarkable effects could be accomplished with just a few shawls or cloaks, some wigs, spectacles, cleverly concealed pillows, a bit of burnt cork. "The more complete the transformation the greater the fun," advised Lady Gertrude Elizabeth Campbell in her book *Etiquette of Good Society,* "gentlemen dressed as ladies, children metamorphosed into adults, thin people made up into stout ones—any change, in fact, but that of ladies donning male attire."

Early in the morning of December 8, 1889, one of the sailors pointed to the horizon and announced, "That is Japan." Elizabeth Bisland joined in the excitement among the passengers, though as far as she could tell there was nothing to be seen but the same monotonous sea and sky. After a time a delicate gray cloud could be made out low on the far horizon; as the ship steamed closer the cloud began to assume the shape of a cone, lifting itself ever higher from the sea until it was no longer a cloud at all but a snow-capped mountain, white on top and dark below, spreading out toward the bottom like an inverted fan. Mount Fuji, or Fujiyama, as the Japanese called her, "Mother of Fire" (for it was an active volcano that had last erupted in the year 1707), rose more than twelve thousand feet into the sky, unmarred by any surrounding peaks, isolated in its majesty. Seeing it for the first time, Bisland understood at once how it could figure so strongly in the Japanese imagination, could be worshipped as a sacred place, made the site of countless pilgrimages. She recalled the lines of the ancient Japanese poem: "Wouldst thou of the lofty gods / Know the annals, only Fuji / Can the secret story tell thee." Gazing in silent awe at the mountain glowing pink in the morning sun, she knew it was a sight she would not forget.

Elizabeth Bisland was now twenty-four days out of New York; traveling so long due west, she had at last reached the East.

DECEMBER 8–10, 1889

Yokohama, Japan

The *Oceanic* cruised up the long bay toward Yokohama. The green hills that sloped down to the water were a tonic to eyes long accustomed to seeing only blue, as were the bright red buoys bobbing in the harbor. All around them large ships lay at anchor: oceangoing steamships, British, French, and German merchant vessels, American men-of-war. A cloud of sampans descended on the *Oceanic* as it made anchor well offshore, the native craft looking something like flat-bottomed Indian canoes. The boatmen stood at the front of the sampans, which they propelled with surprising speed by means of a single long pole. They had narrow wrists and delicate hands and wore blue cotton robes that seemed to merge with the sea and sky. The *Oceanic*'s first-class passengers gathered at the gangplank to await a pilot boat; the Chinese in steerage were not allowed to go ashore and would remain on the ship for the two days it was docked in Yokohama. On the ship, Bisland had become friends with a pretty dark-eyed American named Madge, who shared her excitement about Japan; the two young women were privately hoping to be transported to the pier on one of the sampans, but the missionaries had far too much baggage for that, and meekly they relented and joined the others on a more prosaic steam launch. Ascending a flight of stone steps Elizabeth Bisland was, at long last, on solid ground; after sixteen days at sea the ground seemed to sway beneath her.

She stood at the edge of the Bund, the tree-lined esplanade that ran along the waterfront, captivated by the scene: all around her was Japan. Men wearing large mushroom-shaped straw hats trotted by pulling two-wheeled vehicles behind them. These were the famous *jinrikishas*—man-power carriages, in the Japanese—a word sometimes abridged to *'rikishas,* and eventually Anglicized into "rickshaws." Each jinrikisha carried a single passenger, who sat on a high leather seat covered by a retractable hood; it was something like one of the hansom cabs found in New York, though here of course the pulling was done by a man rather than a horse. Bisland noticed a strange quiet on the bustling street, and then realized it was the absence of horse traffic. Teams of porters—coolies, the foreigners called them—carried merchandise on poles strung across their shoulders, chanting a strange song as they walked. Their heads were completely shaven, other than a curious little twist of hair on top. The women wore their hair pulled back from their face in elaborate thick coils gleaming with oil, clasped tightly with pins of ivory or jade; they wore bright silk kimonos and wooden clogs that made a pleasant clicking sound on the macadamized street. Along the esplanade tonsured children in flowered gowns flew box-shaped kites.

Near the pier a group of jinrikisha drivers offered rides to the tourists just off the ships. The men dressed in a style that put Bisland in mind of medieval knights, in pale blue cotton robes like tunics and skin-tight breeches that came down to their knees; their legs, she observed admiringly, were as lean and muscular as those of a thoroughbred horse. They wore straw sandals tied to their feet by a strap around the big toe. An hour on a jinrikisha cost only fifteen cents, and for seventy-five cents one could ride for the entire day. At the end of the day, Bisland reported, the jinrikisha driver "will not be winded at all, and will be in a gay and charming temper." The men ran in sun and rain alike (Yokohama's annual rainfall averaged about sixty inches), in the humidity of summer and the near-freezing temperatures of winter, and were expected to maintain a speed of anywhere from five to seven miles per hour. The exhausting pace of the job, the regular alternation of overheating and sudden cooling, produced chronic ailments of the throat and lungs that frequently led to consumption and then to death; a jinrikisha driver's working life, it was said, rarely lasted more than five years.

Bisland engaged a jinrikisha from one of the men who had smiled at her (she had already come to think of them as the "medieval folk"); he settled himself between its two wooden shafts and, grabbing hold, set off at a brisk trot to her hotel. From here, the trip would cost only a dime. They passed the Yokohama Rowing and Athletic Club, adjoining the French pier; the United Club, a popular stopping place for British visitors to the city; and several hotels, trading houses, and foreign consulates. Four decades earlier Yokohama had been a small fishing village, but in 1858 the Japanese shogun signed a treaty with U.S. consul Townsend Harris that granted the United States the right to trade with the Japanese, and on July 4 of the following year, Yokohama was officially designated as the first foreign port established under the terms of the treaty. By 1889 it was Japan's chief port; the city now had a population of about eighty-five thousand, of whom slightly more than a thousand were foreigners, and was divided into Japanese and European sections. Many of the foreign residents lived in villas on the cliffs that overlooked the water, an especially picturesque area known as the Bluff, surrounded by large gardens and cricket fields, and most of the rest in large stone houses on the Bund.

Bisland was staying at the Grand Hotel, at the southern end of the Bund, a gabled mansion with a courtyard landscaped with flowering trees. Arriving at the hotel she was greeted by a steward in stockinged feet who led her to a large room facing the water; the room, she was surprised to see, had steam heat and electric call buttons. A pair of tall French doors opened onto a wide terrace, where Yokohama Bay spread itself out below her. Darkness closed down swiftly; the moon rose large and yellow, the ships in the harbor outlined in black against the sky as if drawn with a pen. In the evening the jinrikisha drivers hung pink paper lanterns from their vehicles, droplets of colored light streaming back and forth on the Bund. Before long it was time to change for dinner.

The Grand Hotel was owned by two Frenchmen, both of whom had previously worked as professional chefs, and the hotel's dinners were generally regarded as the best in Yokohama. As the waiters spoke nothing but Japanese, patrons ordered their dishes according to the numbers that preceded each listing on the menu: to begin the meal with Fish à la Chambord, for instance, one simply indicated the number two; Snipe à l'Imperiale was four, Roast Truffled Capons eleven, and Pudding à la DuBarry thirteen. Silent waiters dressed in short jackets and tight black leggings provided the service; they were, a guest of the hotel noted appreciatively, "busy, attentive, hurrying little fellows." At dinner Bisland and some of her shipmates made the acquaintance of a Lieutenant McDonald, a paymaster in the American navy, who had been in Yokohama for two years and knew the city well. He offered to be their guide for an evening jaunt through the native town. In the hotel courtyard they found a row of jinrikishas standing in the moonlight, each with its pink lantern swinging. Together they set off through the quiet European town, the office buildings long since closed down for the night, the employees back at their homes on the Bund or the Bluff. They crossed a broad canal to Shichiu, the native town. Here the business day was not yet over; Bisland was reminded of her late-night tour through San Francisco's Chinese Quarter, where midnight seemed as busy as noon. Crowds streamed around the line of jinrikishas; from everywhere came the clacking of wooden clogs. They rode past little stalls where steaming tea was poured out into cups the size of thimbles, and sake from porcelain bottles with long, delicate white necks like those of swans. In the residential areas the houses were long and low, made of wood or bamboo with tiled roofs; from the eaves hung soft bubbles of tinted light, lanterns of every shape and size. Everything seemed to her radiantly clean and inviting. Bands of white-robed policemen patrolled the streets, carrying lanterns and clubs; on the hour they called to one another in high-pitched cries that, like a ship's eight bells, indicated all was well.

Lieutenant McDonald was taking them to the theater, a large and fashionable playhouse boasting some of the finest actors in all of Japan. In the box office were piles of small flat sticks, each painted with a Japanese character; they were, Bisland discovered, shoe checks for the many pairs of sandals hanging on rows of pegs by the door—for in the theater, as in every Japanese house, one entered only in stockinged feet. As foreigners, however, they were permitted to retain their shoes, and inside, in one of the upper viewing galleries, they were given chairs so that they would not have to sit on their heels like the others in the audience. They had entered during one of the play's intermissions. Downstairs, in the pit at the front of the stage, families sat on rugs beside little charcoal braziers that kept their teapots warm; some of the men were smoking or curled up taking a nap, while the women drank tea and chatted and their children romped around happily. From a latticed box on the side of the stage came the plaintive music of Japanese stringed instruments. After a while a gong sounded; the men woke, the children were recalled, and the play continued, the stage curtain pulled aside to reveal the front of a Japanese house.

As the action began, two maids appeared and waited on their hands and knees for the entrance of their mistress, who turned out to be a male actor skillfully painted and gorgeously arrayed. The lady and her maids discussed what were obviously some very unhappy affairs, when next the lord of the house entered, a very aristocratic-looking man in a formal robe with two swords. Bisland, of course, could not understand what he was saying, but judging from his manner she presumed he could add nothing of cheerfulness to the situation. Matters remained at this melancholy pass for a while until a great clash of music startled the audience, a curtain was drawn aside from a little room at the other side of the theater, and the great shogun himself entered, strutting magnificently in his black velvet trousers down a raised pathway to the stage, followed by a retinue of attendants. He was, Bisland reflected, the embodiment of the sterner side of the Japanese character, the aristocratic spirit that kept feudalism alive in Japan long after Europe had abandoned it, the spirit that allowed no military conqueror ever to set foot on Japanese soil and that made the Japanese, to her mind, "the bravest and freest race in Asia." Before exiting, the shogun pronounced his imperious decree, the nobleman bowing his head in calm acceptance and the mistress and her maids expressing extreme displeasure: the shogun seemed to have advised the nobleman that the best solution to his problem was an act of hara-kiri, the "happy dispatch." Soon a talkative old beggar had arrived on the scene—presumably, Bisland figured, to relieve the gloom of the situation and provide the deus ex machina that would avert the tragedy. She would gladly have stayed to see how it all turned out, but by this time her companions were tired and wanted to go home. The next day they would be taking a train to Tokyo.

Back at the hotel, Bisland opened the French doors and walked onto the terrace. The air felt cool and crisp on her cheeks. She realized, to her relief, that all day she had not thought about schedules. She felt deliciously tired, and very pleased to lie in a bed that was large and soft and did not sway with the motion of the waves.

In the morning she and Madge engaged jinrikishas to take them to the main shopping street of the native town. The weather had turned colder; as they strolled about they warmed their hands at the braziers of the food stalls and drank cups of pale tea that washed away all traces of sleep and left their breath smelling like flowers. The Japanese were plump from layers of cotton-padded kimonos, their hands tucked inside the wide sleeves. It was possible, here, to imagine life in Japan before the European and American settlement. As one American visitor of the time observed, "The homes and the habits, the dress and food, the employments and amusements of the natives are here almost exactly what they were before Commodore Perry awakened the country from its long slumbers."

The street was lined with shops selling lacquer work, bronze, ivory, jade, all of the most astonishing craftsmanship. Every shop, it seemed, had a porcelain vase standing in the corner, with a spray of chrysanthemums artfully arranged. The shop fronts were simply bamboo curtains rolled up at the start of the business day; the floors, raised two or three feet from the ground, were covered by a fine white mat on which the shopkeepers sat on their heels, their wares displayed on shelves around them, everything within easy reach. The two women also removed their shoes and sat at the edge of the floor and did their best to communicate in the pidgin English the shopkeepers used and that to Elizabeth Bisland's ears sounded like baby talk. They had been instructed always to bargain and never to pay more than half the asking price, but everything was so inexpensive that they were happy to pay without haggling. They were received everywhere with an air of affectionate friendliness; the shopkeepers always bowed in greeting, encouraging them to look at anything they pleased and never pressuring them to buy. After a lifetime spent amid the fierce suspicions of Americans, who seemed to look on everyone as a would-be swindler, the amiability and trustfulness of everyone here moved Bisland almost to tears. The silk shops, which they were especially eager to see, displayed elegant quilted dressing gowns, pin cushions, pillow cases, embroidered handkerchiefs, but most entrancing were the fabrics themselves. Bisland marveled at crepe of milky opal and dusky azure, crepe with the faint purples and pinks of sunsets, crepe richly patterned with bamboo fronds and chrysanthemum blossoms. In one of the shops the proprietor opened a sweet-smelling wooden box and brought out the most beautiful silk she had ever seen; it was, he told her, the "Garments of the Dawn." The threads shimmered with the silvery white of moonlight, but within the folds the white blushed to rose, paled to blue, deepened to gold. Bisland immediately ordered a gown to be made from that fabric, and several more from some of the others; they would be ready by the following day. It was remarkable, she thought: one had only to say "Let there be a gown," and there it was.

The two of them lingered so long in the shops that they almost missed the train to Tokyo. Bisland spent most of the hour-long trip happily watching the passing countryside. The mist drifted in and out of the valleys between the hills; one moment the hilltops peeked out above it like islands rising from the sea, and the next melted into vapory gray outlines. Amid the fog huge dragon pines clawed the edges of the hillsides, their immense roots winding like tails around the boulders, looking exactly like the mythical creatures for which they had been named. After a time the mist floated away and the landscape became a mass of green velvet. They rode past villages of thatch-roofed farmhouses, past tidy railway stations, latticed teahouses with roofs like pagodas, little roadside temples, plum orchards, water-soaked rice paddies, nothing seeming unnecessary or out of place, everywhere an atmosphere of delicate fantasticality; it occurred to her that the Japanese painters so often derided by Western critics as simplistic and convention-bound had in fact been able to capture with exquisite fidelity, in just a few deft brushstrokes, the world as it actually existed around them.

Their guide to Tokyo was a sweet-mannered Japanese man wearing a gray kimono and a black American hat, who would be taking them to the famous temples at Shiba. At the train station they hired a party of jinrikishas and set off on a broad, smooth road overshadowed by pines. A lacquered gateway led into the temple grounds, where a shaven-headed Buddhist monk led them up a steep hillside to the tomb of Iemitsu, the seventeenth-century shogun who had closed off Japan from the influence of the outside world. The stone steps were covered with moss and strewn with glossy red camellia blossoms. A light breeze brushed their cheeks as they ascended the hill; sunlight filtered through the canopy of pine trees above them. At the top of the hill an avenue of gray stone lanterns led to the shogun's burial place. The tomb was made of dark-hued bronze, the black paneled gates in front decorated with gilded Sanskrit characters. Inside, the walls were a deep red, the color undimmed by the passing of the centuries; the ceiling displayed a magnificent carved frieze on which lacquered and gilded dragons, birds, lotus flowers, chrysanthemums were tangled in intricate profusion. The petals of a giant stone lotus curled up from the mosaic floor. The room seemed to her like an immense and perfect jewel box, gilded and inlaid with precious stones, the richly colored lacquers as hard and polished as gems.

Elizabeth Bisland walked out of the tomb of Iemitsu, squinting in the mild late-afternoon sunshine. She had come from, as she thought of it, "the country of common-sense, of steam-ploughs and newspaper enterprise," to arrive at a land of porcelain and poetry, where even the most commonplace things were beautiful. She turned for one more look at the tomb and was suddenly reminded of Nicolas Poussin's painting (done, as it happened, in Iemitsu's lifetime) depicting shepherds of antiquity outside a tomb inscribed with the epitaph *Et in Arcadia Ego:* "I have been in Arcadia," the idyllic pastoral land of which Virgil wrote. The Buddhist monk had smilingly warned her of the exceeding loveliness of the shogun's tomb, and having seen it Bisland decided that she would forgive fate in advance for any future trick, because it had given her this day of unmarred beauty. "Et ego in Arcadia," she cried to the monk as he walked beside her down the flower-strewn stairway, "I too have been in fairy-land!"

She did not want to leave Japan, and promised herself that someday she would return, but the *Oceanic* was ready the next morning to depart for Hong Kong. The passengers had a last glimpse of Mount Fuji as Japan sank slowly into the distance. It would be a five-day sail southwest across the East China Sea. As the land disappeared, the wind began to pick up; masses of dark cumulus clouds gathered ahead of them. Another storm was brewing. Later that day Elizabeth Bisland heard the news that the silent young Chinese passenger with the waxen face had died. One of the sailors hung a canvas screen across the corner of the steerage deck where he had lain, and the ship's doctor went gravely back and forth from behind it. Though the young man would not be alive to see it, he would nonetheless reach his native land—an agreement between the steamship lines and the Six Companies, a Chinese-American benevolent society, forbade burials of Chinese immigrants at sea. The Six Companies furnished at least a dozen coffins to each Pacific steamer bound for China, as well as a supply of embalming fluid for the ship's doctor. When a Chinese passenger died his body was embalmed and placed in a coffin, which was sealed up and stowed in the ship's hold. In Hong Kong the body was delivered to the Tung Wah Hospital, which arranged for its disposition to family or friends. The expense was paid by voluntary contributions made by the Chinese passengers and crew on the ship, from a dime to a dollar apiece. A pan containing cubes of Chinese sugar was placed beside the coffin, and each of the Chinese on board dropped in a contribution and removed a sugar cube; it was supposed to bring good luck.

CHAPTER 9

Baksheesh

NOVEMBER 25–26, 1889

Mediterranean Sea

NELLIE BLY'S FIRST MORNING ABOARD
THE *VICTORIA* DID NOT GO WELL. THE
night before, after her hurried excursion to the telegraph office in
Brindisi, she had arrived back at her
cabin, crawled exhaustedly into her
berth, and recalled nothing at all
until a few hours later, when she suddenly awoke to find herself standing
upright by the bed, as wet as the proverbial drowned rat. For a few seconds she stood insensible, wondering where she was and how she had
gotten there; then her head cleared and she heard the rasping *swish-swish*
of scrub brushes on the deck above her and she understood at once what
had happened. Before going to sleep she had opened the porthole above
her berth to let a bit of air into the room, and in the morning she had
received the full force of a sailor's scrub water as it sloshed down from the
deck through the open porthole. Now that she was awake, of course, she
might get dressed and go up on deck, but Bly was never one to rise early
if she could avoid doing so, and she had no intention of greeting the
dawn while cruising the Mediterranean with no story deadline and no

editor within thousands of miles of her. So she just dried herself off as best she could (she had not included a change of nightgown in her gripsack) and went damply back to bed.

She had not been asleep long before she heard a man's voice calling her from the doorway. "Miss," he said, "will you have your tea now?" Bly mumbled that she was not in need of any tea, and after the door closed managed again to get back to sleep, but she was shortly awakened by another voice asking, "Miss, will you have your bath now?" A woman in a white cap was standing over her. Bly was tempted to say she had already had her bath that morning—a shower-bath—but she held her tongue and replied only that she would get up in a few minutes.

"Well, you are a lazy girl!" the stewardess exclaimed. "You'll miss your bath and breakfast if you don't get up this instant." For a moment Bly wondered if she were back in boarding school being scolded by the housemistress, but again she kept her thoughts to herself and said only, "I generally get up when I feel so inclined." She intended to sleep, and whether it pleased the stewardess or not mattered little to her. Before long, though, the steward had once more put in an appearance.

"Miss," he said stiffly, "this ship is inspected every day and I must have the cabin made up before they come. The captain will be here presently."

There was, at this point, nothing to do but get up. Bly made her way down the hall to the bathroom, but no matter how she manipulated the faucet she was unable to turn on the water. She asked a steward passing by where she might find the stewardess.

"The stewardess," he told her, "is taking a rest and cannot be disturbed."

Bly was astonished. "The impudence and rudeness of the servants in America is a standing joke," she would later write, "but if the servants on the *Victoria* are a sample of English servants, I am thankful to keep those we have, such as they are."

THE PENINSULAR AND ORIENTAL Steam Navigation Company—the P&O, as it was universally known—had been in operation since 1837, when, as the Peninsular Company, it received a contract from the British government to run mail ships from London to Lisbon and Gibraltar. Very quickly its area of operations was extended to Malta and Alexandria, and in 1840, having now added "Oriental" to its name, the company was incorporated under royal charter to carry the British mails throughout the Far East. In 1887 the P&O celebrated its golden jubilee, which, fortuitously enough, coincided with that of Queen Victoria; to commemorate the double anniversary the company launched four new ships, each of them larger than any it had produced before, and gave them the impeccably patriotic names *Victoria, Britannia, Oceania,* and *Arcadia.*

On the *Victoria,* Nellie Bly put away the woolen traveling dress that she had been wearing since she left New York, exchanging it for a lighter silk bodice. She was delighted to have left behind the rough, choppy waters of the North Atlantic, the cold wind that blew across the English Channel, the fog that had so bedeviled her in Italy. Here passengers in summer clothes lounged on steamer chairs or lazily promenaded on the broad white deck, sheltered from the sun by a canvas awning stretched overhead. Bly had expected that the English passengers would hold themselves aloof from her, but she quickly discovered that many of the women wanted to know all about America, and admired and even envied an American woman traveling on her own. After only a few days one of them confided to her that a rumor had begun to circulate that she was an eccentric American heiress traveling around the world with little more than a hairbrush and a bankbook, as was confirmed when a young man sidled up to Bly on deck and introduced himself as the Honorable Wyndham Curzon of London. He was small and had a bushy red mustache and, Bly decided at once, an unattractive face. Mr. Wyndham Curzon said he had been watching her and had come to the conclusion that she was the sort of girl he liked. He was the son of an earl, he explained, but it was his great misfortune to have been born the second son, and as his older brother would get both the money and the title, his sole ambition in life was to find a wife who would stake him to £1,000 a year. In that regard he wondered whether she might consent to marry him, and he asked flirtatiously what she would do with him if she did. Bly gazed at him; after a moment she replied that she would put him to work—a response that produced, as she had intended, "a rather dampening effect."

Another young man told Nellie Bly that he had been traveling constantly since he was nine years old, and had always suppressed the desire to marry because he did not believe he could find a woman who could travel without innumerable trunks. This, Bly thought, was an especially curious requirement for a wife; she had earlier noticed that this young man always dressed impeccably, changing his outfit several times a day, and now she was curious enough to ask how many trunks he carried with him. "Nineteen," he replied at once, and Bly no longer wondered why he might want to find a wife who traveled light.

When yet another hopeful young man approached her on the subject of marriage she admitted to him—in strictest confidence—that rather than being an American heiress she was, in fact, a beggar; as her health was bad a few charitable societies had raised enough money to send her on a long trip in the hope that she might benefit from the sea air. This news, of course, was promptly spread around the *Victoria,* and the parade of suitors came to an end.

NOVEMBER 27, 1889
Port Said, Egypt

Late in the afternoon of November 27 the *Victoria* anchored at the Egyptian town of Port Said, near the entrance to the Suez Canal, to take on coal. Thirty years before, Port Said had been little more than a strip of bare sand, its only permanent inhabitants some flocks of pelicans and other varieties of water bird. The town had come into existence in 1859, after the French consul in Egypt, Count Ferdinand de Lesseps, persuaded his childhood friend Mohammed Said Pasha, the ruler of Egypt, to provide land for a new canal that would provide the long-dreamed-of bridge between the Eastern and Western worlds. Lesseps needed a port for the northern end of the canal, which in honor of his patron he named Port Said. Painstakingly, Egyptian laborers dredged a deep artificial harbor and built two immense breakwaters, each jutting out more than a mile into the harbor. The breakwaters were made of huge blocks of stone placed atop one another, nearly thirty thousand in all, each of the blocks twelve cubic yards in size and weighing twenty-two tons—a scale of construction not seen in Egypt since the time of the pharaohs.

The silt churning at the bottom of the harbor turned the water an odd brown color, the waves at the breakwater tossed into a thick white foam like the head atop a chocolate soda water. Dozens of steamships from all over the world lay at anchor, some loading coal and others stopping only to discharge or take on passengers. Port Said was one of the largest coaling stations in the world, the harbor workers able to load a vessel at a rate of

Cattle to provide beef for an ocean liner anchored in Port Said

two hundred tons per hour. Still, it would be several hours before the *Victoria* would be ready to sail again, and the ship's passengers prepared for a brief visit to the town, the men arming themselves with canes and the women with parasols—to keep away the beggars, they told Bly. Bly had neither cane nor umbrella with her, and she turned down their offers to provide her with one, "having an idea," she wrote, "probably a wrong one, that a stick beats more ugliness into a person than it ever beats out."

As soon as its ladder was lowered the *Victoria* was besieged by a fleet of small boats, the boatmen jostling for position, yelling, fighting, even pulling one another into the water in their determination to be first in line to receive the ship's passengers. Several clung to the ladder as if it was a matter of life and death and would not relinquish their holds until the captain of the *Victoria* ordered some of the ship's sailors to beat them with long poles. As Bly and the others stepped into the first boat, several members of her party were grabbed by rival boatmen and dragged onto other boats. "The men in the party used their sticks quite vigorously," Bly would later recall, "all to no avail, and although I thought the conduct of the Arabs justified this harsh course of treatment, still I felt sorry to see it administered so freely and lavishly to those black, half-clad wretches, and marveled at their stubborn persistence even while cringing under the blows." Having finally settled into the boats, the passengers ordered the boatmen to head to shore; midway across, however, the boatmen halted their craft, and in forceful and perfectly intelligible English declared that they would not land until they had received payment for the trip. They had long experience in dealing with the English and their sticks, one of them explained to Bly, and had learned never to land an Englishman before he had paid in full.

Bly and the others in her party walked up the beach to the main street of Port Said. At once they were surrounded by groups of men offering their services as guides, others extending handfuls of Turkish candy and cigarettes for sale. Some simply held out empty hands. *Baksheesh,* they cried over and over in the universally understood term for charity, *baksheesh, baksheesh.* Shirtless native boys beseeched the group to ride on the donkeys that waited patiently beside them. Over time the boys had learned to attract attention by calling the donkeys by the names of statesmen or famously beautiful women of whatever country the tourists came from. "Here's Gladstone!" they called to the Englishmen of the *Victoria,* pushing the shy creature forward. "Here's Mrs. Maybrick! Here's Lillie Langtry!" Nellie Bly was no stranger to burros, having lived for several months in Mexico, but they were a novelty among the other passengers, most of whom were eager to take a ride; so several dozen of the passengers rounded up all of the available donkeys, mounted them, and set off laughing and shouting through the town, bouncing up and down in the saddles, while the boys walked behind, urging the animals on with sharp hisses and, when necessary, prodding them with pointed sticks.

In Port Said particles of coal dust floated in the air, and the town wore the gray, greasy look that Bly remembered from coal towns back in western Pennsylvania. On the unpaved sandy streets passed a raffish mix of Arabs, Jews, Russians, Turks, Greeks, Italians, Frenchmen, Englishmen, the crowd like a kaleidoscope rotating endlessly, always turning itself into something new. From all around came a hubbub of unfamiliar languages; inevitably the first-time visitor to Port Said was put in mind of ancient Babel. There were men in turbans and fezzes and planters' hats and pith helmets, in muslin and linen and the coarse blue cloth the sailors called by the Hindi word *dungaree,* all of them walking quickly, speaking in the chummy, confidential tones in which everything sounds like a ne-gotiation. Shadowy figures huddled together in narrow alleyways; painted women looked down languidly from upstairs balconies. White-plastered hotels, their windows curtained against the outside, stood alongside two-story wooden bungalows, billiards parlors, tobacconists, bars, dance halls, *cafés chantants* (one of which, the Eldorado, featured an orchestra composed entirely of young Hungarian women): the sort of establishments, as the wealthy Bostonian Thomas Gold Appleton once observed, not disapprovingly, "indicating a colony from Europe's far West victoriously planted on desert sand." In the town there was a feel-ing of high spirits mixed with depression. Packs of skinny dogs, many nearly hairless and surrounded by a nimbus of flies, lay in the warm sand of the street waiting for scraps tossed out from the cafés. Outside the cafés men sat at tables drinking little cups of black coffee and smoking foul-smelling cigarettes, playing gambling games that Bly did not recog-nize. The sounds of a string orchestra floated out from the open door-ways of the casinos, the music intended as a kind of siren call luring potential gamblers inside. Bly joined a small group in a visit to one of the casinos, where she put down some of her English gold on the roulette wheel that chirped happily as it spun. "I do not think that any one of us knew anything about the game," she would later write, "but we reck-lessly put our money on the table and laughed to see it taken in by the man who gave the turn to the wheel."

Soon night had begun to fall; most visitors considered it foolhardy to wander the streets of Port Said after dark, and the group set off back to their ship. The coaling of the *Victoria* was just being finished as Nellie Bly came aboard, and her last memory of Port Said was of the barge in the fading light: sweating men stripped to the waist, shouting and groaning as they hauled heavy baskets on their shoulders up a steep gangplank. The ship's open hatchway glowed like the mouth of an iron mill; the coal dust that rose from it turned the men's skin from brown to near black. Those who had reached the top of the plank pitched the coal forward, and it clat-tered loudly down the chute. When a stray piece fell into the water, divers plunged in to retrieve it; some bits of coal might bring them a coin later.

IF ALL WENT WELL the *Victoria* would reach the Suez Canal the following night. It was about a day's passage through the canal, after which the ship would sail via the Red Sea to Aden, on Yemen's southern coast, and then head into open waters toward Ceylon, where Nellie Bly was scheduled to arrive on December 10, twenty-six days into her journey. That very same month another ship—this one a yacht—would set out across the Mediterranean toward Port Said, also bound for Aden and points east. The ship's passenger was Joseph Pulitzer, owner and publisher of *The World,* and he was setting out on his own trip around the world, though far more slowly than his star reporter, Nellie Bly, and at the instruction not of editors but of doctors. His health, while never robust, had of late grown increasingly precarious, and his physicians believed that a long, leisurely sail, far removed from the stress of work, might help calm his nerves and restore his fading eyesight. As it turned out, Pulitzer would make it no farther than Constantinople; one afternoon, standing at the rail of the ship, he turned to his English secretary, Claude Ponsby, and remarked, "How suddenly it has gotten dark." Ponsby looked at him in confusion and concern, for the midday sun was very bright. As it turned out, Pulitzer had suffered a detached retina in his left eye (which had been, up until then, his "good" eye), and he was immediately sent back to Europe to receive the care of ocular specialists. He would not return to the United States for another eighteen months.

Joseph Pulitzer stood six feet two inches tall and was rail thin, with long arms and the frail, narrow chest of a tubercular patient, though that was one of the few ailments with which he was not afflicted. He did have asthma, and he loved to sail his yacht not only because he craved the feeling of speed but because the ocean was the only place he felt he could get enough air. The instruction he most often gave his crew was simply, "Find a breeze." He suffered from stomach troubles, insomnia, depression, anxiety, and an extreme sensitivity to noise, all traceable to a nervous disorder that was never adequately diagnosed despite the efforts of world-renowned specialists. Even the smallest sounds—the creak of a floorboard, the crumpling of a piece of paper—could cause him physical pain. Most debilitating of all was his poor eyesight, which would eventually deteriorate to the point that a team of secretaries had to spend hours each day reading aloud to him. Pulitzer wore pince-nez eyeglasses with small oval lenses; behind the glasses his eyes were a watery blue, though over time, as his vision dimmed, they grew clouded and gray. He had black hair swept back from his face, and a thick red-tinged beard that tapered to a point and that led his rivals to compare him to Mephistopheles.

Pulitzer's most prominent feature was his nose, a long, hawkish beak of the sort often featured in anti-Semitic caricatures, which he detested in large part because it gave his enemies ammunition against him. "His face is repulsive," Charles Dana once wrote in a *Sun* editorial, "not because the physiognomy is Hebraic, but because it is Pulitzeresque." Though he would not give his rivals the satisfaction of publicly responding in kind (in his editorial the next day Pulitzer replied, "The editor of *The World* accepts the hatred of Mr. Dana as a compliment"), in private these attacks drove the thin-skinned Pulitzer mad. He had been born into a Jewish family in Makó, Hungary, in the year 1847; both of his parents were Jewish, but Pulitzer did not attend synagogue and never sought to correct the reports, widely circulated, that his mother was a Roman Catholic. His Jewishness, however, did not go unnoticed. Dana taunted him as "a renegade Jew who denies his breed," while Leander Richardson of *The Journalist* referred to him in print as "Jewseph Pulitzer"; in St. Louis, Pulitzer had been known among rival newspapermen, most succinctly, as "Joey the Jew."

Pulitzer's birthday was April 10, and throughout his life he maintained a mystical attachment to the number 10 and tried to incorporate it into all of his dealings. He bought *The World* on May 10, 1883, for instance, as he had earlier consolidated the *Post* and *Dispatch* of St. Louis on December 10, 1878. He bought the property for *The World*'s new Park Row office tower on April 10, 1888, his forty-first birthday, and the cornerstone was laid the following year on October 10. The first house Joseph Pulitzer bought in New York was at 10 East Fifty-fifth Street—the two fives of the street address only added to its appeal—and he later bought one on East Seventy-third Street. That house, designed by the leading New York architectural firm McKim, Mead & White, was not like any other ever seen in the city. Adjoining the main house Pulitzer had a one-story annex built to serve as his study. The walls were packed with mineral wool, the windows insulated with three panes of inch-thick glass, the fireplace chimney lined with thousands of silk threads to muffle all sound; the floor was set on ball bearings to prevent vibrations. According to *The World*'s business manager, "The room was so still as to be uncanny." When Pulitzer traveled in Europe, he directed his secretaries to rent the rooms directly above, below, and on either side of his room; in later years his private yacht, the *Liberty,* was built with the captain's bridge at the back of the boat rather than at the front, as was standard

Joseph Pulitzer in 1888,
at the age of forty-one

practice, so that no one would need to walk above Pulitzer's head as he
sat reading in his library. He had, remarked one of his secretaries, a will
of iron but a nervous system of gossamer.

Pulitzer was famously generous with his employees, paying salaries
that were generally much higher than those of competing newspapers
and supplementing them with unexpected, lavish gifts. He gave bonuses
for work he deemed especially good, and prizes for the best news ideas,
headlines, and editorials. In 1884, when *The World*'s circulation topped
one hundred thousand for the first time, Pulitzer gave each of his editors
a silk top hat; in 1890, as a reward for loyal service, he gave his private
secretary, Edwin Grozier, a purse containing $1,000 in twenty-dollar
gold pieces—the modern version of the bag of gold dreamed of in fairy
tales. His largesse, however, came at a price. Pulitzer was haunted by the
fear of being ruined by a libel lawsuit, and his editors knew that at night
he read every item in the paper with that worry in mind. As the years
went on he became increasingly suspicious of those around him; he often
employed two men for a single job (he believed the rivalry would spur
even greater creativity, but in fact it had the opposite effect, as the competitors either spent their time watching each other or else simply divided up the work between them), and he hired office spies and then paid
additional spies to spy on them. The result, a *World* staffer once remarked,
was "a condition of suspicion, jealousy and hatred, a maelstrom of office

politics that drove at least two editors to drink, one into suicide, a fourth into insanity, and another into banking."

Though the newspaper business had made him a millionaire, though he owned a yacht and a box at the opera, Pulitzer was never embraced by New York's elite and never considered himself part of what he called the "vulgar wealthy" and the "watered-stock aristocracy." Himself an immigrant from Central Europe—he had arrived in New York in 1864 at the age of seventeen, having been recruited in Hamburg to fight for the Union in the American Civil War—Pulitzer had no use for the coats of arms that had begun to appear on the sides of private coaches, for the French chefs and liveried servants in the Fifth Avenue mansions modeled on châteaus and palazzi, for the general fascination with Old World aristocracy that had taken hold among the city's wealthy.

"It was a strange complex," the New York socialite Elizabeth Lehr recalled many years later, "that made us, who belonged to a society so new, seek always inspiration from our ancients in the past! No one would have dreamt of anything so plebeian as modern fancy dress; we had all to be kings and queens and courtiers." At her famous ball of 1883, Alva Vanderbilt dressed herself as a Venetian princess in a cream-colored gown adorned with jewels, around her neck a long strand of pearls that had once belonged to Catherine the Great. At one New York society dinner each lady guest found a bejeweled gold bracelet wrapped in her napkin, and at another the cigarettes passed around with the after-dinner coffee were wrapped in $100 bills: the hosts had, literally, money to burn. The financier Henry Villard, owner of the *New York Evening Post,* built an immense mansion inspired by the Palazzo Farnese in Rome, a structure so large that it required a ton of coal per day to heat. In the Whitney mansion on Fifty-seventh Street at Fifth Avenue, the painted and gilded ceiling of the grand hall had been extracted from an Italian palace of the sixteenth century, and the stone fireplace from a French château of the same period; the walls of the salon were covered in figured Renaissance velvet; the library's marble fireplace had been carved in Italy in the fifteenth century; and on it went throughout the house. All over Europe, Renaissance palaces were being torn down and their paintings and rugs and tapestries and statuary shipped across the Atlantic to fill the modern palaces of New York. The owners of these houses were far more plutocrat than aristocrat—most had amassed their fortunes in the new industries of railroads, steel, oil, and telegraphy, or the slightly older ones of shipping and real estate—but they arrayed themselves in the style of Europe's peerage, with their country estates and stables and game preserves, and shooting parties and fancy dress balls, and yachts and private railroad cars and gleaming carriages attended by coachmen and footmen: "the very carmagnole of display," huffed society writer Constance Cary Harrison, "that in earlier days was supposed to be the appanage of royalty alone."

Jay Gould, the financier and railroad baron who owned *The World* from 1879 until 1883, lived, like many of his contemporaries, in a brownstone mansion on Fifth Avenue; he also owned an immense country house in Westchester built in the style of a Gothic castle, complete with tower and turrets, from which he commuted to his Manhattan office on his 230-foot-long yacht. Before a strike by the workers on one of his railroads Gould boasted that he could "hire one half of the working class to kill the other half," which was a sentiment not far removed from that of the editor of the *New York Tribune,* Whitelaw Reid, who during the 1877 railroad strike had declared that "authority ought not to rest until it has swept down every resisting mob with grape-shot" and that the strike should be crushed "though it cost a thousand bloody corpses." At the *Sun,* editor Charles A. Dana had been a radical in his youth, but as the years went by he became increasingly hidebound, caustically deriding all efforts for meaningful social change; he opposed female suffrage, for instance, because he believed it would introduce "a spitefulness that is peculiarly feminine" into American politics. Dana forbade the use of the term "upper classes" in the *Sun* because he denied the existence of class distinctions in the United States—this at a time when the top 12 percent of American families owned 86 percent of the country's wealth. Joseph Pulitzer, who bought *The World* in 1883 for $346,000 (Gould was happy to unload it, as the paper was reportedly losing $40,000 a year), had a very different idea for his newspaper. On his first day as publisher of *The World,* Pulitzer gathered together all of the employees and made a little speech to them. "Gentlemen," he said in his accented English, "you realize that a change has taken place in *The World*. Heretofore you have all been living in the parlor and taking baths every day. Now I wish you to understand that, in the future, you are all walking down the Bowery."

The Bowery, of course, was the downtown boulevard that ran parallel to Broadway but formed, as a guidebook of the time observed, "a complete antithesis to that splendid thoroughfare." Boisterous and proudly disreputable, it wore its dime museums and dance halls like cheap, flashy jewelry, and was the only avenue in New York on which no church would ever be built. The trains of the elevated railway roared and shrieked overhead, drowning out the conversations that went on below in Yiddish and German and Italian, and an English tinged with memories of Dublin or Donegal. The Bowery was the pulsing artery that ran through New York's immigrant neighborhoods, home to those who brought to the city, in *The World*'s phrase, "strong blood and unlimited possibilities." Four out of five people in New York were either immigrants or the children of immigrants, and they were the people to whom Joseph Pulitzer hoped to sell his paper. "Condense! Condense!" he regularly barked at his editors, urging them to cut extraneous words, to keep sentences short and descriptions vivid, to make the language as accessible as possible to an immigrant new to the country, as he himself had been only two decades earlier. "The first object of any word in any article at any time must be perfect clarity," Pulitzer once said. "I hate all rare, unusual, non-understandable words. Avoid the vanity of foreign words or phrases or unfamiliar terms. Editorials must be written for the people, not for the few."

In his very first editorial for *The World,* Pulitzer declared,

There is room in this great and glowing city for a journal that is not only cheap but bright, not only bright but large, not only large but truly democratic—dedicated to the cause of the people rather than that of purse-potentates—devoted more to the news of the New than the Old World—that will expose all fraud and sham, fight all public evils and abuses—that will serve and battle for the people with earnest sincerity.

"Our aristocracy," he wrote two days later, "is the aristocracy of labor."

When the workers of Jay Gould's Missouri Pacific Railroad went on strike, *The World* supported them, remarking of Gould that "one bottle of his choice wine costs more than a Missouri Pacific laborer can spend for his family for two weeks." *The World* campaigned for a graduated tax on incomes above $10,000 a year and advocated new taxes on luxury items, on monopolies, and on inheritances. An investigation by *The World* exposed fraudulent spending of more than $2 million by the Pacific Railroad; another revealed that William H. Vanderbilt, ex officio president of the New York Central—who possessed a fortune that he himself estimated at upward of $200 million—had avoided paying any income tax at all by claiming that his debts had surpassed his earnings. *The World* stated bluntly, "Wealth escapes taxation." *The World* exposed the police brutality rampant in immigrant neighborhoods; it agitated to reduce the working day of the city's horsecar drivers to twelve hours; it tracked down the sources of tainted milk and sausages made from horsemeat; it shone a light on the squalid, dangerous conditions existing in New York's tenements. Though other papers sometimes published reform-minded articles (Jacob Riis's riveting exposés of slum life, for instance, appeared in the *Sun*), only *The World* consistently and unequivocally spoke out against the enemies of the poor—robber barons, slumlords, corrupt politicians, uncaring bureaucrats. Alone among the daily newspapers of New York, it was *The World,* day after day, that told the city's newest and most vulnerable residents that the conditions in which they lived were not inevitable and were by no means unalterable: that they were not condemned to give their children poisoned food, or to breathe the noxious fumes from nearby slaughterhouses, or fear the policeman's club, or work for pennies, or go to bed wondering if they would be set upon by rats during the night.

Joseph Pulitzer was trying to sell his paper to New Yorkers who had no tradition of reading newspapers, many of whom were barely literate in English and who had to be persuaded to stop as they walked by a corner newsstand or heard a newsboy calling out a headline. This feat would be accomplished by the front page, which functioned for a newspaper much as a display window did for a department store, luring passersby to come inside. (Pulitzer always said that he attracted his readers with the stories on page one so that they would read the editorials on page four.) Under its previous ownership, *The World*'s front page had featured decorous articles with headlines such as *Affairs at Albany, Bench Show of Dogs,* and *Mrs. Vanderbilt's Trip*. No one could possibly confuse them with the articles that immediately began to appear on Pulitzer's front page, full of violence and sex and tragedy, the headlines often running in several decks down the column, claiming one's attention with the brazen urgency of a carnival barker:

INSANE FROM TOBACCO.

A MANIAC IN A HOTEL OVERPOWERS HALF A DOZEN MEN.

HE CHEWED TWO POUNDS OF TOBACCO A DAY.

WENT TO THE PARK TO DIE.

A YOUNG WIFE ENDS HER LIFE WHILE TEMPORARILY

DERANGED. CHRISTMAS WILL BRING NO MIRTH TO

THIS HOUSEHOLD. HER HUSBAND WHILE SEARCHING FOR HER

MET THE OFFICERS BEARING HER LIFELESS BODY—

SHE HAD SHOT HERSELF THROUGH THE HEAD.

SHE CUT OFF HER HAND. AND ALSO SLICED OFF HER TONGUE

WITH A BREAD-KNIFE. AN INSANE WOMAN CRUELLY MUTILATES

HERSELF. SHE DIES A FEW HOURS AFTERWARD—

THE SEVERED HAND FOUND ON THE PARLOR FLOOR.

Crime stories were the staple of the front page (a good crime story, after all, could provide violence and sex and tragedy all in one), but inside, the paper offered a great deal more. A *World* reader might find, for instance, a poignant report about flowers growing in tenement windows. "The woman who bought the flower made shirts," the story noted about one of them. "She finished them at thirty-five cents a dozen. The flower cost fifteen cents and the pot ten. The woman made nine shirts to buy the flower." Joseph Pulitzer understood that his readers wanted the news, but also much more: they wanted the latest fashions in robes and bonnets and trousers, an explanation of how a telephone worked, etiquette lessons, gossip about their favorite theatrical stars, adventure tales of explorers in Africa and stowaways on a tramp steamer. They wanted stories that brought them closer to their city, and stories that allowed them, at least for a while, to escape from it, and that was what they found in *The World:* part carnival, part crusade, and all available for only two cents a day, three on Sunday.

Though their personalities were entirely dissimilar (one scholarly and anxious, the other fun-loving and gregarious), Joseph Pulitzer was in his professional life much like an earlier master of sensation, P. T. Barnum; as Barnum had stuffed the rooms of his American Museum with oddities and wonders from the world over, inspiring shock and horror and joy in his visitors, so too did Pulitzer's *World* give readers stories that made them laugh and cry and shiver and shake their fists. And like P. T. Barnum, who had also arrived in New York as a penniless young man, Joseph Pulitzer achieved success of a kind never before seen in his field. When Pulitzer bought *The World* in May of 1883, the paper's Sunday circulation stood at 15,770; by September it had nearly doubled, to 29,140. *The World*'s growth was so dramatic and so impossible to ignore that the *Times* cut its price from four cents to two, and the *Herald* from three cents to two. Still *The World*'s circulation kept rising; by 1885 it had increased tenfold, to 153,213. To his rivals, Pulitzer's huge and ever-growing readership must have seemed at times like a massed army besieging their citadels on Park Row, a feeling that could only have intensified when in the fall of 1889 the new World Building began to go up, rising to a height of sixteen stories and made even more impressive by the gilded copper dome where Pulitzer had his office, with frescoed ceilings and leather-covered walls and three windows through which he could look down on the rest of the city. The story is told of the *Sun*'s Charles Dana standing at his second story window with his publisher, William L. Laffan, watching Pulitzer's workmen put up the enormous girders for the World Building next door. Dana turned to him and said, "Laffan, that begins to look serious." "A mere episode," the publisher replied, as if trying to convince himself, "a mere episode."

Yet even as its new office tower began to rise over Park Row, *The World*'s remarkable growth had already begun to stall. In fact, the paper's weekly circulation figures for November of 1889 were down by more than 51,000 from September, the first downturn since Pulitzer had taken over *The World*. It was this alarming trend (especially when the paper was footing the bill for a building that would ultimately cost $2 million, twice the original budget) that led to John Cockerill's message to Nellie Bly instructing her to begin immediate preparations for a trip around the world.

Right away the race against Phileas Fogg seemed to be having the desired effect. Just before Bly set out on November 14, *The World*'s weekly circulation was 2,163,210 copies; by December 1 the weekly circulation was up to 2,297,600. There was, however, one problem: the paper's editors were having trouble finding enough news copy to maintain the public's interest in the trip. From Nellie Bly herself there had been only a single brief message via telegraph, reporting her on-time arrival in Brindisi; additional information would have to await the arrival of the international mails by steamship. Bly's first dispatch to *The World,* describing her voyage across the Atlantic on the *Augusta Victoria,* would not appear until December 8, three weeks into her trip. As a result, *The World*'s coverage leaned heavily on laudatory articles reprinted from newspapers around the country, as well as its own editorials touting the significance of Bly's trip. So the days passed in a more desultory fashion than the paper's editors would have preferred, as they anxiously awaited more information from the world traveler herself. How, they must have wondered, could they keep this up for seventy-five days? It was not until November 30, more than two weeks into her trip, that *The World* finally hit on a scheme that would decisively capture the attention of the public and transform Bly's trip from a newspaper publicity stunt into a national sensation.

NOVEMBER 28, 1889

Suez Canal

Although Nellie Bly counted herself among those people "who think that night is the best part of the day and that morning was made for sleep," on the morning of November 28 she got up very early, so eager was she to see the Suez Canal. She rushed up on deck, but the famous canal turned out to look like nothing more than an immense ditch. On both sides the desert stretched away endlessly like a vast tideless sea, the sand glowing a pale pink beneath the violet haze of the sky. Even at this hour the day was already very hot, and to make things worse the *Victoria* seemed to be barely moving; ships on the Suez Canal were not permitted to sail faster than six knots, because greater speed created waves that might erode the sand banks. As a result, the canal, though not even one hundred miles long, required a full day to navigate.

Bly passed much of the morning discussing the history of the Suez Canal with one of her fellow passengers, an older gentleman who had been traveling all his life. Begun in 1859, the canal took ten years to build; it was said that more than one hundred thousand workers had died in the process. The sun blazed in a cloudless sky. By the afternoon the water shone a radiant blue and the sand had turned from a pinkish yellow to a stark white, as if bleached by the sun's rays. The monotony of the landscape was relieved only by the passing stations (called by the French word gares) that the Suez Canal Company had built along the banks of the canal, tidy little houses surrounded by trees and flower gardens: man-made oases grafted onto the desert sands. Bly sat in her steamer chair, the happiness she had felt on the Mediterranean draining away. The heavy, sluggish air provided an ideal breeding ground for mosquitoes; she wished that she had thought to bring a supply of insect repellent in her bag. She worried that the extreme heat would bring on one of her sick headaches. It had been, she realized, only six days since she was freezing in a railroad car headed to Amiens. She felt very far from home—at times she almost trembled when she thought of how many miles still lay ahead of her—and lonesome as well. Her cabinmate, a young Australian woman traveling with her brother, was pleasant, as was the young man who sat next to her at table, who had, as she put it, "large dreamy blue eyes" and the racking cough of a consumptive; he spoke well (she had always liked that in a man) and seemed to have been everywhere. They were the first passengers on the *Victoria* to whom Bly revealed the real purpose of her trip. In general, though, as she would write in a letter to *The World,* "Our passengers are mostly English people and are not the jolliest lot in the world."

The ship's surgeon, fair and fat with a thin ginger mustache over thick lips, had taken a shine to Bly; after every remark of hers he would laughingly reply that she was "pulling his leg," a coarse-sounding expression that she had not heard before. The self-appointed arbiter of all social matters on board the ship was a Mr. Weston-Edwards, who dyed his mustache and spoke through his nose and professed to be fluent in ten languages. Nellie Bly detested him at once. Weston-Edwards solemnly claimed to have a vast knowledge of America and Americans—as, for instance, in his assertion that when an American became famous, he hyphenated his Christian and family names and used the composite as his name, and his children, in turn, adopted the hyphenated name as their own. Thus, he illustrated, Jay Gould was now known in America as Mr. Jay-Gould, and his son as George Jay-Gould. Bly did what she could to contradict him, but he was adamant and at a certain point she decided that there was no use in arguing. Finally it occurred to her to ask, "How much time have you spent in studying the United States?"

Weston-Edwards hemmed and hawed, but Bly, a veteran reporter, insisted on a precise answer. "Well," he said at last, "I stayed an hour in

New York, then rode at night to Buffalo, and crossed over the next day into Canada."

That was the maddening thing about the English, Bly thought: they could spend only a day or two in a place and then claim to be an expert on it.

It seemed to be one of the perquisites of empire, like high wages or cheap tea.

All day the *Victoria* maintained its frustratingly slow pace. Often beggars ran along the canal calling to the ship. Their voices carried through the still air: *baksheesh, baksheesh, baksheesh*. Some of the passengers tossed money, but the distance to shore was too great and most of the coins fell uselessly into the water; the Suez Canal had become like an enormous wishing well. Still the natives kept running in pace with the ship, crying *baksheesh,* until finally they were exhausted and had to give up.

Near nightfall the *Victoria* dropped anchor at Suez, by the entrance to the Red Sea. Instantly the ship was surrounded by small sailboats carrying men who came aboard the *Victoria* to offer fruit, shells and coral, and picture photographs for sale. Though the passengers paid little attention to the vendors, they were very interested in a native conjurer who performed tricks for money. He wore a turban and a sashed robe with a baggy pocket in which he carried two lizards and a rabbit; the rabbit and the lizards would soon appear in his performance, he declaimed to the crowd, but first he wanted to demonstrate what he could do with a simple handkerchief. The conjurer selected Nellie Bly to assist him. First he showed the crowd a small brass bangle, which he deposited inside the handkerchief; then he placed the handkerchief in Bly's hand, telling her to hold it tightly. Bly did as she was instructed, acknowledging that she could feel the bangle very plainly. The conjurer blew on her hand, and then pulled the handkerchief from her grasp and shook it out. To everyone's astonishment the bangle had vanished. Happily the conjurer passed among the crowd collecting the coins offered to him, but while his attention was occupied, some of the passengers managed to steal his rabbit, and in the meantime one of the lizards had also escaped from the pocket of the robe. When the conjurer discovered the loss of his animals he was predictably irate, and he refused to perform any more tricks until they were returned to him. Finally a young man produced the rabbit from his coat pocket; the lizard, though, was not to be found, and as the *Victoria* was about to set sail the conjurer had no choice but to return to his boat without it.

Once the conjurer was gone several of the passengers asked Nellie Bly if she had any idea how the trick with the handkerchief had been done. She explained to them that it was really a very old trick involving two brass bangles. One of them the conjurer had secretly pocketed after he pretended to place it in the handkerchief. The other (the one she had felt in her hand) was actually sewn to the handkerchief; when the conjurer displayed the handkerchief he made sure to keep the bangle always on the side facing him, so that it would not be seen by the audience. One of the men listening became indignant at this explanation, and demanded to know why, if she knew how the conjurer did his trick, she had not exposed him. Bly replied simply—much to the Englishman's disgust— that she had wanted to see the man get his money.

DECEMBER 2, 1889

Aden, Yemen

On the morning of December 2 the *Victoria* reached the town of Aden, on Yemen's southern coast. The steamship had traversed thirteen hundred miles of the Red Sea in four and a half days, which meant that Nellie Bly was now one day ahead of schedule. Since leaving Hoboken she had traveled 6,905 miles—slightly less than one-third of the journey—in only eighteen days. After a brief stop at Aden for refueling, the *Victoria* would sail another two thousand miles across the Arabian Sea to Colombo, on the island of Ceylon, where Bly was scheduled to connect with another P&O steamer, the *Oriental,* which would take her as far as Hong Kong.

Aden, a rocky peninsula some five miles wide, was the most forbidding-looking place Bly had ever seen. The adobe houses of the town rose from inside the crater of a huge extinct volcano, surrounded by craggy mountains of lava that shone black in the sun. Atop the highest of the mountains, a Union Jack flew over a massive fort with battlements outlined against the sky. Half a century earlier, in 1839, two British warships, carrying thirty-eight cannons and seven hundred troops between them, had sailed into the harbor and begun bombarding an ancient fortress occupied by a thousand Arabs armed chiefly with matchlock rifles. Within the hour a ground assault was launched; the fighting was brief but intense, and when it was over Aden had become the first colonial acquisition of Queen Victoria's reign. Since then the port had served as an important coaling station between Suez and Bombay, and as a central link in Great Britain's chain of island colonies that stretched from Gibraltar to Malta and Cyprus and on to Ceylon, Penang, Singapore, and Hong Kong.

The officers of the *Victoria* had warned the passengers not to go ashore because of the intense heat, but Bly, along with half a dozen of the more adventurous among them, hired a boat to town. She was awed by the magnificent stone double gate, guarded by sentinels pacing to and fro, that led up to the British fort, and by the white mansion on the hill used by the British sailors as a clubhouse; bewitched by the local women who adorned all parts of the body with hoops and rings and bracelets and chains; impressed by the grace of the native boys who dived for coins tossed from the ships by tourists and who always emerged miraculously unharmed by the sharks that infested the water. ("They claim that a shark will not attack a black man," Bly observed, "and after I had caught the odor of the grease with which these men anoint their bodies, I did not blame the sharks.") Later, though, in recalling her time in Aden, what Nellie Bly recalled most strongly was that Union Jack flying at the top of the highest mountain, seventeen hundred feet above the sea.

Shortly after the *Victoria* left Aden some of the English women on board performed a series of *tableaux vivants,* one of which was meant to represent the nations of the world. The women had earlier asked Bly if she would agree to represent the United States, but she refused. In her book about the trip, Bly did not explain why she declined to participate; she did, though, express her surprise that the women, who wanted to include several countries' flags in the *tableau,* needed her to tell them what the American flag looked like.

As she traveled among the English, Nellie Bly was becoming increasingly conscious of the peculiar privilege that imperial power conferred upon its citizens: the privilege of insensitivity. They could, if they chose to, carry the empire along with them on their travels, as they sailed on English ships, slept in English hotels, ate English meals, taking little notice of the specific characteristics of the countries through which they passed, much as a rich man, who had all of his daily needs attended to, might know nothing of the personal habits or the likes and dislikes of his servants. From Europe and across the Middle East and Asia, English travelers could use their own currency everywhere they went—Bly had not yet found an establishment that refused English banknotes, nor one that accepted American money—and could get by perfectly well speaking only their own language. The waiters back in Calais had spoken English, as had the telegraph operator in Brindisi, and the boatmen in Port Said, and the vendors in Suez; their livelihoods, after all, depended on it. Even the donkey boys of Port Said knew that Gladstone was prime minister. And while Bly's personal feelings about the English were by no means warmer than before—that hostility would persist to the very end of her life—she was beginning to understand the sense of pride they felt as Britons, citizens of an island nation that ruled an empire many times its size, their money desired everywhere, their flag flying over the most desirable properties, their warships ensuring safe passage from port to port. "As I traveled on and realized more than ever before how the English have stolen almost all, if not all, desirable sea-ports," Bly wrote, "I felt an increased respect for the level-headedness of the English government, and I ceased to marvel at the pride with which Englishmen view their flag floating in so many different climes and over so many different nationalities." Nellie Bly did not like the English, but she had, surprising herself, begun to envy them. As far as she was concerned the United States was the greatest of all nations, but for as long as she could remember it had been led by small men unworthy of their citizens' trust or affection. Of the voyage on the *Victoria,* Bly would later write:

> Though born and bred a staunch American, with the belief that a man is what he makes of himself, not what he was born, still I could not help admiring the undying respect the English have for their royal family. During the lantern slide exhibition, the Queen's picture was thrown on the white sheet, and it evoked warmer applause than anything else that evening. We never had an evening's amusement that did not end by everybody rising to their feet and singing "God Save the Queen." I could not help but think how devoted that woman, for she is only a woman after all, should be to the interests of such faithful subjects.
>
> With that thought came to me a shamed feeling that there I

was, a free-born American girl, the native of the grandest country on earth, forced to be silent because I could not in honesty speak proudly of the rulers of my land, unless I went back to those two kings of manhood, George Washington and Abraham Lincoln.

CHAPTER 10

An English Market Town in China

CHINA

Hong Kong

South China Sea

HAINAN

ON THE EVENING OF NOVEMBER 14, 1889, JUST HOURS AFTER ELIZABETH Bisland set out from New York, *The Cosmopolitan*'s business manager, A. D. Wilson, gave an interview to a reporter from Bisland's hometown newspaper, the New Orleans *Daily Picayune*. In the story, headlined "Woman Against Woman: The World to Be Embraced in a Quick Trip," Wilson laid out the magazine's plan to win the race around the world. Bisland was then crossing the continent on a fast train; on November 21 she would set sail from San Francisco on the steamship *Oceanic,* arriving in Yokohama, Japan, on December 11. According to Wilson, *The Cosmopolitan* had already arranged for a "government boat" (he did not specify which government) to transport Bisland from Yokohama to Hong Kong, at a cost of $8,000; *The Cosmopolitan* expected to make up crucial time against Nellie Bly on this leg of the race, as Bly's schedule required her to wait four days in Hong Kong for the *Oceanic*'s return voyage to San Francisco. (Bly was scheduled to sail east across the Pacific on the very same ship that Bisland took heading west.) "The rest of the journey," Wilson told the *Daily Picayune,* "is comparatively simple for Miss Bisland." Arriving in Hong Kong on December 16, she would set sail the following day on a Peninsular and Oriental steamship bound for Brindisi, Italy. At Brindisi she would board another ship for Marseilles, scheduled to arrive on January 21, 1890. If there was sufficient time, Bisland would that same day catch a steamship of the Compagnie Générale Transatlantique—the French Line—from Le Havre, due to arrive in New York on January 28; if not, she would take a train to Southampton, England, and set sail from there for New York. In either case, *The Cosmopolitan* foresaw an around-the-world trip for Elizabeth Bisland requiring no more than seventy-four days—one better than Nellie Bly's proposed seventy-five-day trip—and very possibly even less.

As it turned out, despite the confidence of A. D. Wilson's assertions, Elizabeth Bisland ended up following almost none of that itinerary. When she arrived in Japan, for instance, Bisland did not take a special "government boat" to Hong Kong; that plan seems to have fallen through while she made her way across the Pacific, as had John Brisben Walker's earlier attempt to bribe officials of the Occidental and Oriental steamship line to move up the *Oceanic*'s departure from San Francisco. Still, the officials did assure Walker that the ship would make all possible haste on Bisland's behalf, and whether it was due to their instructions to Captain Kempson, or simply to the good fortune of favorable weather (or to Elizabeth Bisland's following through on her joking promise to "make eyes at the Engineer"), the *Oceanic* covered the 4,690 miles from San Francisco to Yokohama in only sixteen days, one of the fastest westbound crossings on record for that time of year; the ship arrived in Japan on December 8, three days earlier than *The Cosmopolitan* had accounted for in its itinerary. And though no chartered boat was there to transport Bisland immediately to Hong Kong, the *Oceanic* stopped in Yokohama for only thirty-six hours and then, despite a northwest gale, took no longer than the typical five days to cross the East China Sea, dropping anchor in Hong Kong on Sunday afternoon, December 15.

One month into her trip, Elizabeth Bisland was one day ahead of schedule, and one day ahead of Nellie Bly.

DECEMBER 15–17, 1889
Hong Kong

In Hong Kong Bay the water was a cool emerald green that glittered in the early afternoon sun. Hundreds of Chinese fishing junks, their bamboo masts and flapping sails like the veined wings of giant yellow butterflies, darted amid larger European ships devoted to war and commerce: ghostly white French frigates; three-masted Russian corvettes with Cyrillic letters painted in gold across their bows; long, dark British ironclads bristling with cannons. In the distance a semicircle of hills sheltered the harbor from winds. Thickets of pine trees grew irregularly on the hillsides; from the treeless patches the ground peeked out warm and tawny, like the hide of a lion glimpsed through the forest. Hong—*Kong*! Elizabeth Bisland repeated to herself delightedly, the rhyming syllables sounding to her like two reverberant notes of a gong.

Friends of Bisland, a German couple now living in the city, had agreed to put her up during her stay there, and one of them was waiting on the dock now with two of her personal sedan chairs—comfortably upholstered armchairs trimmed with silver and attached on the bottom to two long bamboo poles. The sedan chair was to Hong Kong what the jinrikisha was to Yokohama, but while a single driver pulled the two-

Buildings along the Hong Kong waterfront

wheeled rikisha, each sedan chair was borne on the shoulders of two men. The four chair bearers on the dock were dressed in loose black trousers and white cotton tunics, and their feet were bare; they wore their hair in long pigtails that were pulled back and twisted into a Psyche knot at the top of the head, much like the style lately favored by American shopgirls. Bisland stared at the foot traffic passing by on the Queen's Road. Hong Kong, it seemed, boasted as many varieties of sedan chair as New York did of carriages. There were chairs made of wicker and wood and bamboo; upholstered chairs and painted chairs; chairs with overhead coverings to protect the occupant from rain or sun; most mysteriously, chairs set inside boxes closed off with bamboo blinds, meant to shield upper-class Chinese women from the gaze of the public. Like many American visitors to Hong Kong, Elizabeth Bisland was at first uneasy about the notion of being carried around on the shoulders of other human beings. "Conveyance in the East is a constant source of unhappiness to me," she later observed. Her friend, though, had come all the way to the dock to meet her, and there was no other option but to walk all the way up the long, steep hill; overcoming her hesitation, Bisland stepped into the chair and sat down. In a single smooth motion the chair bearers lifted the poles to their shoulders and set off at a swift trot; as they ran the chair swayed gently from side to side, and the effect (once one got over the initial fear of tipping over) was as pleasant as swinging in a hammock.

Riding high above the crowd, Bisland was astonished by the variety of life on display around her. Chinese merchants strolled by in exquisitely brocaded silk outfits, their hands tucked away inside loose sleeves. Plump, prosperous-looking men with astonishingly thick beards wore tailored European suits and tall purple satin hats that bulged outward like upside-down coal scuttles; they were Parsees, members of the Zoroastrian faith who had come to Hong Kong from India to pursue entrepreneurial opportunities in the industries of shipping and trade. Stout, ruddy-faced Englishmen rode silently past in their own sedan chairs. Teams of Chinese laborers stripped to the waist knelt as if in supplication, fixing the streets.

Bisland had to make a stop at the local offices of the Great Northern Telegraph Company to inform *The Cosmopolitan* of her arrival. That task completed, the chair bearers set off again, padding up a broad avenue that curled around the hill, up to the English residential section. (Now it had become clear why sedan chairs rather than jinrikishas were used in Hong Kong: it would be impossible to pull a jinrikisha up those steep streets.) Handsome terraced houses rose, tier upon tier, above the street; the houses were made of granite and had arcades and immense verandahs that reminded Bisland of paintings she had seen of the villas of ancient Rome. Her friends lived near the top of the hill, in a two-story stone house with a rear verandah that overlooked the glittering waters of the bay. The chair bearers trotted down a curving flight of steps and deposited the riders at the front door. Down a long, dark hallway, the large drawing room was adorned with potted palms and ferns and massive furniture of Indian ebony and marble, with photographs of the Hohenzollerns, the Prussian royal family, scattered about. Bisland and her friends drank cups of tea brought by a tall pigtailed servant dressed in silk trousers, a black satin cap, and a crisp blue gown that reached nearly to his ankles and rustled as he moved.

On the verandah Bisland gazed down at the harbor below. The shorefront was lined with massive, imposing buildings made from granite taken from the nearby hills; she could see how the water broadened to bays and narrowed to straits between the island mountains. Her friends told her that Hong Kong was considered to be, with Sydney and Rio de Janeiro, one of the three most beautiful harbors in the world. For Great Britain, the strategic importance of Hong Kong—the easternmost of the Crown's possessions—was so great that two full regiments were always garrisoned there, and several warships stationed in the harbor.

A servant showed her to a huge bedroom, which had an attached dressing room as large as her drawing room back in New York. The furniture, of mahogany and silver, had been brought over from Germany two generations earlier. The airy, darkly wooded room reminded her of bedchambers in old plantation houses she had known in the American South. Much here, in fact, reminded her of the South: the cool, shadowy rooms filled with ancestral furniture, the lush foliage, the slow pace, the "careful sweet civility" of the conversation—and of course, though Bisland did not mention this, the constant attentions of dark-skinned servants. Dinner that night was formal, with delicate food and fine wines; it flowed, Bisland wrote, with a "cool and unhasting repose." Perhaps her choice of noun was not inadvertent, for that villa in the hills above Hong Kong must have called to mind thoughts of what her own family's home of Mount Repose would have been like in the years before she was born, when the war had not yet come and it still seemed possible to maintain a European way of life in a tropical place.

The next day her friends took her to the native section of town. The streets were so narrow and the stairs that ran between them so steep that their sedan chairs could barely pass by. More than 160,000 people lived there—an astonishing sixteen hundred people per acre, far denser than even the worst blocks of the Lower East Side—compared to eight thousand or so residents in the entire English section. Elizabeth Bisland found herself repelled by the crowds moving so tightly around her, and almost reflexively she adopted the Western custom of thinking of the Chinese crowd as a swarm, "buzzing and humming like the unreckonable myriads insects breed from the fecund slime of a marsh." Even the children she compared to "flies in number and activity." The air here was at least ten degrees hotter than up on the hill, thick with smells so powerful they were almost dizzying, the bitter, musky scent of burning opium, rows of ducks hanging by their necks in sunlit shop windows, smoky pork and sausages, cut-up bits of chicken and ropy green vegetables and mysterious other foods sizzling in braziers on the street, open jars of pickles and baskets of salted fish: the overall effect was something like moldy cheese aging in a closed cellar. Cauldrons bubbled away in open-air restaurants; out front, men sat at long tables eating their food with chopsticks. They did not sit on the benches placed around the tables, as she would have expected, but instead squatted on them, with their knees up around their chins. The shops were faced in ornate gilded fretwork; hanging outside, long vertical signs displayed black Chinese characters that seemed to her as elaborate and incomprehensible as ancient hieroglyphics. The houses were lime-washed in pale tints of green, gold, crimson, blue; they reminded Bisland of Chinese porcelains on the shelf of an import store, each one tasteful in itself, yet jarring, almost grotesque, when squeezed too tightly together.

Her friends, Bisland noted, were "loath that I should lose a single pleasure," and so they set off again back up the hill. More than one hundred feet above the town they passed the stately Government House, the residence of the colony's governor, and entered the green twilight of the Botanical Gardens.

We pass under the tremulous lacey shadows of ferns twenty feet high, through trellises weighted with ponderous vines that blow myriad perfumed purple trumpets up to the golden noon, and emerge upon sunny spaces where fountains are sprinkling silver rain upon banks of crimson and orange flowers. The flaxen-haired, muslin-clad English children play here, cared for by prim trousered Chinese amahs; and we meet pretty blue-eyed German ladies in their chairs taking this road home.

From far below, Bisland could hear the faint ripples of water lapping at the foot of the hills. The afternoon sun filtered through the pines. Behind a milky-white bungalow young Englishmen in white flannels played tennis on a freshly mown court, the thwack of the ball echoing in the air. In *Around the World in Eighty Days* Jules Verne had written of Hong Kong: "Docks, hospitals, wharves, godowns, a Gothic cathedral, a Government House, and surfaced roads—everything made you think that one of the many market towns in Kent or Surrey had passed right through the terrestrial sphere and popped out at this point in China, almost at the antipodes." On every stone wall and balcony railing stood rows of earthen jars full of greenery and blossom, spiky aloe and cactus, poinsettia, bougainvillea, passion flower, regal orchids blooming in the November sunlight; there was a casual luxuriant beauty here, profusion almost to the point of surfeit, that reminded Bisland of New Orleans. It was at times like this that she felt grateful to John Brisben Walker for insisting on this wild-goose chase; she could do without the whirlwind of the race, of course, that constant pull and hustle, but for someone who had never been out of the United States, for whom New York, only a few years earlier, had been the height of exoticism, it was a splendid opportunity to see the world. She rode for some minutes in a haze of content, gently swaying on a sedan chair several feet above the macadam, feeling herself at one with a little piece of England, the land she had first imagined as a girl in a ruined library, dreaming along with Coleridge as he yearned to see again *shaping in the steady clouds / Thy sands and high white cliffs*, or with Wordsworth, who declaimed *O, England!—dearer far than life is dear / If I forget thy prowess, never more / Be thy ungrateful son allowed to hear / Thy green leaves rustle, or thy torrents roar!* If all went smoothly, in scarcely a month's time she would be seeing it for herself at last, *this other Eden, demi-paradise / this fortress built by nature for herself / against infestation and the hand of war.*

Bisland was jolted from her reverie by the sight of a tall, darkly bearded figure standing at attention by the roadside; he wore a khaki uniform with an intricately folded scarlet turban, and at his side, dramatically, he carried a long sword. Seeing him, Bisland gasped in astonishment. "Is it an emperor?" she called to her friend riding in a chair alongside.

"An emperor? It's only a Sikh policeman. There are hundreds about the place quite as splendid as he." The British had imported them from India to serve as colonial policemen in Hong Kong; the "exceedingly tall" Sikhs, *The Chautauquan* magazine reported that year, "make a figure among the short people of southern China well calculated to strike terror into the hearts of the disobedient." Bisland found it impossible to believe that there could possibly be others, much less hundreds, as noble-looking as this one, and in contemplating this she suddenly recalled a story she had heard about the Egyptian soldiers who had fled before the assault of the Highland Brigade at Tel el-Kebir a few years before. Stunned by the ferocity of the Scottish soldiers in their kilts, the Egyptians were said to have exclaimed, "If these are the Scottish women, what must the men be?" If these are the Sikh policemen, Bisland wondered now, what must their princes be?

Even as she was contemplating this, one of the Highlanders came striding down the hill, a member of the Forty-Second Royal Highland Regiment—the legendary "Black Watch," the Scottish regiment that had helped defeat George Washington on Long Island and Napoleon at Waterloo and had most recently put down native uprisings at Cawnpore and Lucknow in India. Now the Black Watch was garrisoned in Hong Kong. Despite the tropical climate the Highlander was dressed in plumed helmet, scarlet jacket, blue tartan kilt, and long hose, as Bisland later described it, "with six inches of bare stalwart pink legs showing, and a fine hearty self-confidence in his mien that signifies his utter disbelief in the power of anything human to conquer him."

It gives me my first real impression of the power of England, who tames these mountain lions and sets them to do their police duty. It would seem incredible that this rosy commonplace Tommy Atkins who comes swaggering down the street in his scarlet coat can be the weapon that tamed the fine creature in the turban. What is it makes this cheerfully vulgar Anglo-Saxon the lord of the Hindoo? Physically he is not the Sikh's superior, and in profound and passionate sentiment, if one may judge by the countenance, the Hindoo is infinitely above the Briton. Nor is the latter greater in courage or dignity, for these Indians made a noble resistance to English encroachment, and after submission were enrolled in the army of the conquerors as their bravest and most loyal troops. What is the secret? Is it more beef and mutton perhaps—or more of submission to orders and power of self-discipline?

In seeking the "weapon that tamed the fine creature in the turban," Elizabeth Bisland might have looked instead to the fleet of British iron-clads she had seen back in the harbor. After all, machine guns mounted on warships—the fearsome Gatling guns, each capable of firing more than six hundred rounds per minute—had played a decisive role at Tel el-Kebir, where Egyptian soldiers faced a barrage of some forty thousand rounds fired by British sailors at close range. "Round whisked the Gatlings, r-r-r-r-r-rum! r-r-r-r-r-rum!" enthused *The Army and Navy Gazette* in its issue of October 1882, one month after the battle. "The report of the machine guns, as they rattle away, rings out clearly on the morning air. The parapets are swept. The embrasures are literally plugged with bullets. The flashes cease to come from them. With a cheer the blue-jackets double over the dam, and dash over the parapet, only just in time to find their enemy in full retreat. That machine gun was too much for them." The Highlander Regiments, like their fellow infantrymen in Egypt, had been supplied with breech-loading rifles accurate to one thousand yards and loaded with soft-lead slugs, as a chronicler of the Tel el-Kebir campaign noted, that left "wicked wounds. . . . the enemy were usually literally 'blown-away' by sheer fire-power—as was the fate of innumerable Afghans, Afridis, Dervishes, Egyptians, Zulus and a host of other native tribesmen in various Victorian colonial wars."

Though the British imperialists of the time liked to ascribe their conquests to moral superiority over the dark-skinned natives, to the qualities of patriotism, sportsmanship, selflessness, daring, and courage collectively known as "Anglo-Saxon manhood"—much as Elizabeth Bisland herself looked to attributes such as self-confidence and self-discipline—and though it was comforting for the British to tell one another inspirational stories about General Gordon, the devout soldier-saint of the defense of Khartoum, or Bishop Hannington and his missionaries bravely facing the warriors of King Mwanga in Uganda, the real explanation for the dominance of Great Britain (and the other imperial powers) in the colonial world lay elsewhere. "In the final analysis," one military historian has observed, "it was not superior virtue that brought them victory after victory. It was superior firepower."

The late nineteenth century was an age of unprecedented technological advance, when wood gave way to coal, iron to steel, and the horse and the sail to the steam engine; many of the new technologies, not surprisingly, were quickly put to the service of warfare. Powerful steamships—fueled at a far-flung network of coaling stations on fortress colonies—could command the entrances to rivers and harbors, bombard enemy strongholds, and deliver troops by the thousands to the scenes of colonial disturbances halfway around the world. Over land, railroads could transport troops and supplies far more quickly and on a far greater scale than the mules and wagons used by earlier generations of armies. "Ten thousand men with a rail to travel by," wrote a British correspondent for the *Lahore Chronicle* in 1857, "are fully equal, in this country, to thirty thousand by the existing means of conveyance." Thanks to newly laid telegraph wires, generals could issue orders to many battlefields at once, and do so while remaining at a safe distance from the front lines. As a British colonel based in India observed, "It is almost impossible to overestimate the assistance which the telegraph renders, not only in the administration of the country, but in the conduct of every military operation that is undertaken." During the Sepoy Mutiny, for instance, when Indian soldiers based in Meerut rebelled against their British officers, telegraph operators in nearby Delhi were able to transmit news of the uprising to British regiments around the country, allowing them immediately to disarm the local Indian troops. In his report afterward, the judicial commissioner of the Punjab declared, only somewhat hyperbolically, "The electric telegraph has saved India." (By which, of course, he meant the British in India.)

A telegraph message could be sent from London to Bombay, more than four thousand miles away, and a reply received, astonishingly, in less than five minutes. The feat was unlike anything ever seen before, and was performed, in innumerable variations, untold times each day. The distinguished English historian A. W. Kinglake called the telegraph "that new and dangerous magic." Like the best magicians, it produced extraordinary effects by means that few people understood, and indeed, it seemed to have performed the greatest trick of all: making time disappear. Awestruck observers struggled to express the new conditions of the world the telegraph had wrought. "Time itself is telegraphed out of existence," declared the London newspaper called, fittingly enough, the *Daily Telegraph*. "They have killed their father Time," wrote Rudyard Kipling in a poem entitled "The Deep-Sea Cables." Another poem, "The Victory," written in tribute to Samuel Morse, had it that "Science proclaimed, from shore to shore / That Time and Space ruled man no more." At a banquet held at Delmonico's in New York Morse was toasted for having "annihilated both space and time in the transmission of intelligence." The railroad had regulated time; the telegraph seemed to have vanquished it entirely.

DECEMBER 18, 1889

Hong Kong

Elizabeth Bisland was scheduled to leave Hong Kong on December 21, on the Norddeutscher Lloyd steamship *Prussian,* a five-masted single-screw ship notable for having made the fastest time on record between Hong Kong and Ceylon. The *Prussian* would carry Bisland all the way to Genoa, Italy, where it was due on January 23. An arrival on that date would have been too late to get her to New York by January 28, seventy-five days after her departure, but the German government had begun offering financial inducements to its steamship lines to arrive ahead of schedule; as a consequence, noted the *San Francisco Examiner,* "it has been their pleasing custom of late to arrive in Genoa seven or eight days ahead of schedule time, which would make it very delightful for Miss Bisland." And just to be doubly sure, *The Cosmopolitan* sent a cable to the owners of the Norddeutscher Lloyd company offering a substantial reward (the specific amount was never revealed) if the *Prussian* was able to surpass its fastest travel time. Given the incentives to do so, it seems very likely that the *Prussian* would have arrived in Genoa no later than January 17, at which point Bisland could have taken a train to Le Havre, where the fast French Line steamship *La Champagne* was departing on January 18. A typical Atlantic crossing would then have brought Elizabeth Bisland to New York on January 26, resulting in a trip around the world, depending on the exact hour of arrival, of less than seventy-three days.

In Hong Kong, though, Elizabeth Bisland met with unexpected misfortune: as it was entering Hong Kong harbor, the *Prussian* broke its screw.

The loss of a ship's screw—the bladed propeller—was a very common accident of the time (it could be caused, for example, by hitting a piece of floating timber, or a sunken wreck, or a sheet of ice, or a whale), but it was also a very serious one. A contemporary account of steamship travel warned that losing the screw will "render a single screw steamship helpless, and she can only reach port by being towed, or by the very tedious process of sailing under her own canvas." To repair or replace the screw was a major job, and inevitably meant a substantial delay. When she received the distressing news about the *Prussian,* Bisland hurried from her friends' house to the local offices of the Occidental and Oriental Steamship Company (owners of the *Oceanic,* on which she had made such good time across the Pacific), where officials advised her that the *Thames,* of the Peninsular and Oriental line, would soon be departing for Colombo, in Ceylon. At Colombo she could transfer to the *Britannia,* which was—like the *Victoria,* on which Nellie Bly was then en route from Brindisi to Colombo—one of the large modern ships of the P&O fleet. The *Thames,* admittedly, was not as fast as the *Prussian;* moreover, it was a British mail ship, the schedules of which were as regular as the rising of the sun, and just as impervious to financial inducements. However, the *Thames* was leaving Hong Kong three days earlier than the *Prussian* would have, which meant that, barring any more unforeseen developments, Bisland had every chance of meeting *La Champagne* in Havre and arriving in New York ahead of Nellie Bly. (About the transfer to the *Thames,* Bisland herself said only, "I am advised to go in her as far as Ceylon, and I do.") She wired the news back to *The Cosmopolitan:* there had been a change of plans; she would be taking the *Thames* to Colombo, and connect there with the *Britannia* for Le Havre.

So on Wednesday morning, December 18, Elizabeth Bisland found herself on the deck of the Peninsular and Oriental steamship *Thames* with her friends from Hong Kong. The Union Jack flew gaily from the masthead above them. The population of the ship seemed to her as delightfully motley as that of the city she was leaving. As with the other Peninsular and Oriental ships, the crew of the *Thames* was made up mostly of the East Asian sailors called Lascars, distinctive in their blue checked cotton tunics and red turbans. A group of Parsees in their fine clothes and purple hats were bidding farewell to a friend headed home to

India. A member of the Highlander Regiment was also on his way home to Scotland, and several of his fellow soldiers were seeing him off, bearing whisky and bagpipes. A few took up the pipes and played him a last tune; the others linked arms and danced, their faces turning red and sweaty in the heat. Soon the ship's bell had rung, and members of the crew circulated on deck giving the usual warning: "All ashore that's going!" Bisland's friends wished her speed on her journey; she called goodbye to them as they made their way down the gangplank. She wondered when she would see again the beautiful city of Hong Kong; she regretted having to leave, just as she had Yokohama before it. Her next stop, five days and sixteen hundred miles hence, would be Singapore. The rope was cast off, and the *Thames* made its way out of the bay; Hong Kong slowly vanished in a haze of sunlight. The keening of the bagpipes, lively and mournful, still sounded in her ears.

CHAPTER 11

"The Guessing Match Has Begun in Beautiful Earnest"

Madras·

BRITISH INDIA

Bay of Bengal

CEYLON

Colombo·

INDIAN OCEAN

On the morning of Friday, November 29, on an inside page just below an item from Reading, Pennsylvania, about a three-month-old girl who had tragically been suffocated by the family cat (the cat, the story reported, had been found lying across the girl's mouth and nose), *The World* printed a small advertisement announcing the "Nellie Bly Guessing Match," to commence the following Sunday. DON'T FAIL TO ORDER YOUR SUNDAY WORLD AT ONCE, the ad instructed readers, AND FILL OUT A BLANK THEREIN WITH A GUESS AS TO THE TIME OF NELLIE BLY'S TOUR. THE BEST GUESSER WILL HAVE A FREE TRIP TO EUROPE.

The next day's edition included a full article, headlined A GUESS THAT WILL PAY. It began: "Thousands of 'mind's eyes' are now following Nellie Bly in her trip around the world. Interest in her race has been increased by THE WORLD's offer to furnish a first-class trip to Europe, with about a week each in the English and French capitals, and perhaps a run down to historic Rome, all free of cost, to the person who sends to THE WORLD on SUNDAY WORLD blanks the nearest guess to the exact time in days, hours, minutes, and seconds that are required for her globe-girdling tour." Anyone could participate in the guessing match, but there was one important stipulation: all guesses had to be recorded on the official coupons ("blanks," in *The World*'s parlance) that would be printed in Sunday editions of the paper. Only one guess would be permitted per coupon. "Those who wish to guess more than once," *The World* advised readers, "must equip themselves with a number of the Sunday World blanks." (And the only way so to equip oneself, it didn't need to be stated, was to buy multiple copies of *The World*.)

The first coupon for the Nellie Bly Guessing Match appeared in the issue for Sunday, December 1, 1889. It measured about five inches high by two inches wide and featured a drawing of a dark-haired young woman standing amid the clouds, wrapping what looks to be a ribbon of some sort—perhaps it is a measuring tape—around the circumference of the globe. Below were separate boxes for days, hours, minutes, and seconds, as well as lines for the guesser's name and address and for the date on which the guess had been made. Once the coupon was filled out, readers were instructed, it should be clipped and sent to *The World* care of the European Trip Editor. At the bottom of the coupon was a capitalized, bold-faced exhortation: **GUESS EARLY AND OFTEN**!

The accompanying article, entitled "Hints for the Guessers," asked the question that was seemingly on everyone's mind: "When will Nellie Bly actually arrive in New York?" Bly's officially recorded moment of departure from Hoboken, *The World* reminded its readers, was 9:40:30 A.M. on November 14, 1889. As of the first of December her exact whereabouts were unknown, but she was somewhere on the Red Sea, on a steamship sailing eastward toward Ceylon, where she would connect with another steamship bound for Hong Kong. If Bly was able to get to Hong Kong by December 25 to meet the steamship *Oceanic,* and if the *Oceanic* crossed the Pacific Ocean smoothly and delivered Bly to San Francisco on time, she would then depart for New York on January 22 by way of the Central Pacific, Union Pacific, and Pennsylvania Railroads; and if she did not encounter any broken bridges, snow blockades, or derailments Bly would arrive at the Pennsylvania Railroad's Jersey City depot sometime around seven P.M. on January 27, 1890. If she did manage to maintain that schedule the entire way ("the 'if,'" *The World* felt obliged to point out, "is a big one") and arrived on the dot of seven o'clock, the trip would have been completed in precisely 74 days, 9 hours, 19 minutes, and 30 seconds. Those were the basic facts of the journey, but as to the

A World *entry blank
for the Nellie Bly
Guessing Match*

final result, any of the paper's readers knew as much as any of its editors. "Therefore let the guessing proceed," *The World* declared, "always bearing in mind that all guesses must be made on the accompanying blank."

"THE GUESSING MATCH has begun in beautiful earnest," *The World* reported on Tuesday.

The envelopes containing coupons for the Nellie Bly Guessing Match had started to arrive at the *World* offices first thing Monday morning, most of them white or buff-colored, with some of pink or light blue, each bearing one of the newly issued red two-cent stamps that featured the heroic profile of George Washington, or perhaps two of the blue Benjamin Franklin one-cent stamps; some of the envelopes, though, had been affixed with extra postage, for they contained several of *The World*'s coupons, some with as many as twenty, and with accompanying notes from the guessers indicating that they intended to submit just as many coupons the following week, and the week after that, and every week thereafter until the contest was brought to a close. In New York at that time business mail was delivered as many as four times a day, and with each successive delivery the piles grew higher, quickly exceeding the limits of the European Trip Editor's office and seeping ever farther into the hallway, the incoming mail like an avalanche, or a tide that never receded. The guesses were arriving in far greater numbers than even the most optimistic editor could have anticipated; in the face of those colossal numbers, remarked a *World* writer, "it seemed that arithmetic itself must give out and topple over." A kind of lottery fever seemed to have descended on New York, thanks to the unexpected possibility of winning an all-expenses-paid trip to Europe for an initial investment of only a few cents; and what made the prospect especially appealing was the fact that this particular lottery, unlike all others in the city of New York, was perfectly legal. "The match will be the biggest thing that New York has ever seen," *The World* gleefully predicted, noting that copies of the Sunday *World* with unmarked Nellie Bly coupons still in them "are now as eagerly sought as those attached to United States bonds."

By the end of that first day *The World* had received more than one hundred thousand guesses.

"THE GUESSERS," *The World* observed on Wednesday, "adopt queer methods sometimes." Several hundred of them apparently considered 7 to be a lucky number, and had based their estimates on it: thus 77 days, 7 hours, 7 minutes, and 7 seconds, or some variation on the theme. One entrant pointed out that in his guess the numbers of days, hours, minutes, and seconds were each divisible by 7, and the sum of the numbers added together was itself divisible by 7. A guesser from Brooklyn ascribed his use of the mystic 7 to the 7 letters found in the name "Nell Bly." "This, however, is not the young lady's full name," *The World* admonished, "so the application of it in this way is imperfect."

A reader from Troy, New York, explained in a letter that accompanied her coupon that she was sure to win the European trip, as she had obtained the figures in a dream, after a lobster salad supper, lying flat on her back with her hands clasped over her head, and that she "never knew such cause and results to fail me." Another entrant, a woman identified in the paper only as L. N., sent in twenty guesses, and with them four verses of poetry, the final one of which read:

Oh, ma chère Nellie Bly,
You are smart, and you are spry;
Pray, oh, do pray try
And get here just as nigh
Time marked for you to go by.

This was the first example of what would become, for a while, a minor poetic genre: the Nellie Bly around-the-world poem. At least one of the poems sent to *The World* included the poet's guess within it:

Nellie Bly is flying high
On the China Sea;
With her goes the hope of one
Who wants to see Paree;
She'll get here in 74,
Sure as she's alive,
Hours 12, minutes 10 and seconds 25.

A guesser from Wilmington, Delaware, created an astonishingly beautiful entry—"really," *The World* observed admiringly, "a work of art." Across the top of the page a steamship and a railroad train had been painted in watercolors, and below, the days, hours, minutes, and seconds were printed in Roman numerals. There was, however, a serious problem: the guess had not been submitted on an official *World* coupon—thus disqualifying it from consideration—and furthermore, after going to all of that trouble the sender had forgotten to include his or her own name.

A reader in Chicago submitted her guess with a twelve-page letter in which she explained that she had arrived at her decision with the assistance of a clairvoyant who was possessed by the spirit of Marco Polo. The spirit of the dead traveler, she wrote, had revealed that he was accompanying Nellie Bly around the world, and, with the aid of Aristotle, Cicero, and Pythagoras, had figured out that the journey would be completed in one hundred days, ten hours, ten minutes, and ten seconds.

Each day another deluge of guesses descended on the office. "Such great success never before visited a project so suddenly," *The World* exulted on Thursday. "By to-morrow night, if the downpour continues at the present rate, the European Trip Editor will be covered so deep that it will take a snow-plough and a big force of men to find him in the midst of his work." The times of the guesses ranged from sixty to one hundred days; according to *The World,* one entrant had predicted that the trip would never be completed. "I sincerely hope that this guess will not win," he wrote, "but, knowing the uncertainty of life, I think the chance worth taking." As was to be expected, most of the guesses tended to cluster around Nellie Bly's estimated time of arrival, though *The World* took pains to point out that Bly's actual time could easily vary up to five days in either direction. As sixty different guesses were possible for each minute (one for each second), there could be up to 3,600 different guesses to an hour, 86,400 different guesses to a day, and 864,000 different guesses to ten days. And that was simply within the range of easy possibility; beyond those dates the number of guesses—any one of which might turn out to be correct—was practically limitless, especially given the fact that it was permissible within the rules of the contest to divide the seconds themselves into fractions.

The rules of the contest were in fact a subject of ongoing clarification and refinement. In the event of a tie, *The World* declared, the prize would be awarded to the guess that had been mailed first. The winner could embark on the trip at any point during the 1890 travel season. The right to the trip could be transferred by the winner to someone else if circumstances so compelled it, and there might be some allowances made to travel to European capitals other than London, Paris, and Rome. On the other hand, *The World* emphatically refused one reader's suggestion that the winner might instead choose a trip of equal value to California, or perhaps even accept the equivalent in money and simply stay home: "The successful guesser will be awarded a free round trip to Europe— nothing else—and THE WORLD feels assured that the winner of the prize will be so proud of the victory won over so many thousands of other guessers that he or she, as the case may be, will not elect to stay at home, or to dispose of his right, but will set sail triumphantly and see the three most interesting capitals of the Old World."

On Sunday, December 8, at the end of the first week of the Nellie Bly Guessing Match, *The World* reported that the week's total circulation was 2,637,560 copies, an increase of more than three hundred thousand over the previous week. An editorial observed, "It is safe to say that no newspaper in this country ever printed so many copies in one week in the month of December as did THE WORLD last week." Two days later, on

Tuesday, December 10, *The World* abandoned its initial plan to provide coupons only in its Sunday editions, and now—in response, it said, to "numerous requests"—began to include them in each day's issue, as it would until the close of the contest. (Exactly when that would be had not yet been determined.) The around-the-world race had long since grown into the leading topic of conversation in town, discussed in horsecars and on ferries, in factories and the exchanges; it was a subject ready-made for spirited debate, as everyone could support his or her opinion about the outcome of the race with additional opinions about the weather, the state of modern technology, and the constitution of the female traveler. The thousands of New Yorkers who had submitted a guess now had not just a rooting interest but a personal stake in Nellie Bly's trip (the contest of Bly against the calendar had, at least for the contest's entrants, rendered Elizabeth Bisland mainly an afterthought), and they watched her progress around the globe with all the excitement and anxiety of a gambler at a horse race or prizefight; but unlike spectators at a race course, they did not have to cease betting once the race had begun. Indeed, it was now possible to enter new guesses every day rather than have to wait for the end of the week, guesses that might be more optimistic or pessimistic depending on the latest reports or simply on one's mood at the time, and each new coupon could be had for only two cents, three on Sunday, and submitted for just the price of a stamp.

Nor was it only New York that had become transfixed by the race. The astonishing success of the guessing match, *The World* noted, had "set the whole country to talking," including the nation's capital, where, presumably, matters of weightier import were available to occupy residents' attention. The paper's distinguished correspondent Frank G. Carpenter reported that "Nellie Bly's trip around the world excites great interest in Washington. It is one of the common subjects of conversation in the cloak rooms of the House and Senate, in the hotels and at dinners. Miss Bly's course is commented upon, and not a few prominent men try to figure out where she is from day to day."

"The entire press of the country is discussing the trip," agreed *The Journalist*. Accounts of the race appeared seemingly everywhere, in every town large enough to support a newspaper. Many of the articles focused on the competition between two young female reporters, but some mentioned only Nellie Bly, such as the *Free Press* of Waverly, New Jersey, which called Bly "one of the New York World's most brilliant and successful reporters." The *Star* of Wilmington, North Carolina, admired the speed with which Bly was circumnavigating the globe, while cautioning readers that "it does not necessarily follow from this that she is a 'fast' young lady. On the contrary she is a good, well-behaved girl, who crosses her t's and dots her i's."

In the second week of December a New York clothing company announced the production of a new model of ladies' dressing gown. It was to be called "The Nellie Bly."

DECEMBER 8, 1889

Colombo, Ceylon

Nellie Bly herself, of course, had no idea that American women would soon be wrapping themselves in a robe named after her; nor did she know yet that another young woman was racing her around the world; nor had she heard anything of the guessing match that tens of thousands of people had already joined. ("She will hear of it, though," *The World* assured its readers, "and the vastness of the contest which is being waged on her account will fill her soul with wonder.") She was simply traveling eastward, and thus far, having traversed the Atlantic Ocean, Europe, and the Middle East, she had managed to keep to her schedule. Bly may not have liked the crew or the accommodations provided by the *Victoria,* but she could not complain about its speed, for the ship made excellent time across the Arabian Sea and around the southern tip of India, arriving in Colombo, the largest port in Ceylon (later renamed Sri Lanka) on December 8, two days ahead of schedule.

Ringed by coral reefs and covered in waving palm trees, Ceylon was a tropical island so lushly beautiful that Muslim and Christian accounts alike suggested it might be the site of the Garden of Eden; indeed, the tallest mountain on the island—its tip could just be made out above the treeline, glowing purple in the late morning sun—was known as Adam's Peak. Early December was among the best times of year to visit, the island then being free of the monsoons that often arrived in April and October, or the heat of May, or the damp January winds that the older British expatriates called the longshore winds, which they complained brought rheumatism and other ailments but must also have conjured up wistful thoughts of England. Now the breezes that ruffled the ship's flags were warm and fragrant; Bly had never been to a place where the air smelled like a kind of perfume, sweet and musky like powdered cocoa, made spicy with hints of cinnamon and vanilla. Inland, Ceylon's jungles were as crowded as those of the *Peaceable Kingdom* paintings, full of leopards and deer and monkeys and mongoose and little black bears and innumerable other flying and creeping creatures; the trees themselves were rich with mangoes and bananas and breadfruit and figs. Its waters offered up oysters bearing pearls; its earth gave rubies and sapphires. To the Chinese, Ceylon was known as "the island of jewels," and Hindu poets had dubbed it the "pearl-drop on the brow of Ind," while a nineteenth-century British poem praised Ceylon as "the best and brightest gem / in Britain's orient diadem."

Great Britain had taken Colombo in 1796, ousting the Dutch, who had themselves ousted the Portuguese a century earlier. About seven thousand Britons were living in Ceylon, plus another thousand or so of the empire's soldiers, among an island population of nearly three million. They lived in plantation estates and in tidy bungalows that overlooked the water; they drove their carriages on smooth red roads and took their afternoon promenades on a concrete breakwater that extended a mile and a half into the sea, the first stone of which had been laid by the Prince of Wales himself. Nothing that might interfere with the pleasant, orderly progress of life had been left unaccounted for. The island's elephants, who once ran in herds, had been tamed and put to work carrying stones and uprooting trees, while bullocks pulled carts and water buffalo plowed rice paddies. To protect against the sun there was light flannel clothing ("now made in all sorts of tweed-like patterns," one of the local guidebooks noted brightly) and the pith helmets called topees; against the leopards, there were deadfall traps baited with live goats; against the mosquitoes, the mixture of citronella, coconut, and kerosene oils called "Bamber-Green oil," available at all the local chemists' shops. Even the venomous snakes, it was said, showed the proper respect for their colonial masters—they never bit Europeans.

With one of her shipmates, Nellie Bly declined the steam launch provided for the *Victoria*'s passengers and instead came ashore on one of the native outrigger boats called catamarans. The surf crashing against the beach was the pale green of topaz; the earth was an astonishing red, the sky a brilliant blue. After the grim black crags of Aden and the Suez Canal in its various shades of sand and mud, the colors of Ceylon seemed

Street scene in Colombo, Ceylon

heightened, almost unreal. The local Singhalese men wore loose sashed gowns, or were bare-chested with gaily patterned sarongs wrapped around their waists; they had earrings and long, sleek black hair twisted into a chignon in the back and held in place with a tortoiseshell comb. The women wore their hair in the same style, but fastened with a hairpin rather than a comb; golden rings adorned their toes, ankles, wrists, arms, necks, lips, ears, noses. Almost everyone, it seemed, chewed betel leaves, which discolored their teeth and stained their mouths a vampirish red.

Bly gathered up her leather gripsack and set off to her hotel, only a few blocks from the jetty. She passed an open-air marketplace draped in red and gold, the honeycombed stalls offering hand-woven baskets, silk shawls, carvings of ivory, ebony, and tortoiseshell, the simple exotica for which tourists would gladly part with their rupees and pounds without a second thought. Across the street stood the Grand Oriental Hotel, where she would be staying during her two days in Colombo. It was an imposing-looking white building with long rows of handsome windows and the tiled arcades of a Roman bath; the outside shone in the sun but the inside turned out to be shadowy and cool. In an airy, comfortable inner courtyard, guests relaxed in easy chairs with a lime squash or a cup of one of the native teas. Some of the men drank whisky with soda as they perused the daily papers, while the women chatted and read novels and inspected the wares of the turbaned merchants who circulated through the courtyard, snapping open little velvet boxes containing the gems for which Colombo was known the world over, sapphires in blue and in white and in the purple variety known as "Oriental amethyst," orange cat's-eyes, blood-red rubies, the stones having been mined from nearby gravel pits and cut on corundum wheels, then polished to such an alluring sheen that even the men who had waved the merchants away ended up putting down their newspapers and going off with one of the dealers to a dim secluded corridor to see a sapphire gleam in the light of a match and bargain a twenty-pound price down to two or three.

Bly had arrived in time for lunch, which at the Grand Oriental, as in the other hotels of the East, was known by the Indian word *tiffin*. The dining room was a stark, clean white; the small tables were decorated with bowls of brightly colored flowers, the utensils laid out on large green leaves delicately fringed at the edges like lace doilies. Ceiling fans made from strips of embroidered gold cloth attached to bamboo poles revolved above the diners as they ate, kept in motion by silent young men pulling long ropes. The food was served by Singhalese waiters in crisp white jackets and flowing skirts, tall and slender and dignified as bronze statues. Bly soon discovered that the waiters answered to only a single term of address: "We can call 'steward!' 'waiter!' 'garçon!' until we are weary, without any result," she wrote, "but the moment we whisper 'boy!' a pleasant black fellow says, 'Yes, sir,' at our side, and is ready to do our bidding." One of the waiters placed in front of her a large platter of white rice and a strikingly yellow dish called curry, divided into varieties of meat, chicken, and shrimp. Bly was no stranger to exotic food—she knew the sausages and blood puddings of the German rathskellers tucked in amid the newspaper buildings of Park Row, the bagels dangling from metal rods sold by gaunt, bearded vendors on the Lower East Side, the boiled spaghetti served up in the Italian kitchens of Greenwich Village, the chop suey available at all hours of the night in any of the city's eight Chinese restaurants—but curry was a dish entirely unfamiliar to her. Still, she had always prided herself on her adventurousness (whatever she had gotten in life had come from taking risks), and she spooned a mound of rice onto her plate and some shrimp curry over it; she added a dollop of the glistening sweet-and-spicy condiment called chutney, then sprinkled on top a bit of the salted and dried Maldivian fish that smelled like a garbage scow on a hot day but went by the grandly deceptive name of "Bombay duck." As instructed, she mixed everything together and took a bite. The flavor was not like anything she had ever tasted before, it was like pepper and garlic and, somehow, flowers, the heat of the dish subtle at first but stronger with each bite, until it seemed to warm her entire body. Curry, Bly decided, was unsightly but delicious, and during her time in the East she ate it whenever she could, stopping only when, after a particularly hearty meal, its spiciness threatened to give her "palpitation of the heart."

After lunch some of the hotel guests decided to take a ride through the town. It was there, in Colombo, that Nellie Bly first confronted the prospect of the jinrikisha. Like Elizabeth Bisland, Bly was initially reluctant to use one, but soon overcame her hesitation. "I had a shamed feeling about going around the town drawn by a man," she admitted, before adding more facetiously,

> but after I had gone a short way, I decided it was a great improvement on modern means of travel; it was so comforting to have a horse that was able to take care of itself! When we went into the shops it was so agreeable not to have the worry of fearing the horses were not blanketed, and when we made them run we did not have to fear we might urge them into a damaging speed. It is a great relief to have a horse whose tongue can protest.

That evening everyone went for a moonlight ride to the Galle Face, a hilltop promenade overlooking the ocean. They passed beautiful homes set amid cliffside gardens, a scene that reminded Bly of a tropical version of Newport, Rhode Island. Many of the roads were embowered by palm trees, the branches forming an arch of foliage above their heads. At the Galle Face Hotel, Nellie Bly and some of the others relaxed on chaise longues on the tiled verandah. Crickets murmured in the trees; the waves beat rhythmically against the shore like music. From somewhere far away came the melancholy howl of a jackal. Silent couples walked arm in arm along the beach, the moonlight brilliant on the water. The man next to her was saying something, but she was only half-listening. On that picturesque verandah, Bly observed, one could "drift out on dreams that bring what life has failed to give, soothing pictures of the imagination that blot out for a moment the stern disappointment of reality." And when those dreams faded away, she thought, one could drown out the sigh with a sip of lime squash brought by a silent, barefooted waiter. The moon had alchemized the red surface of the road to silver; in the distance the foamy breakers seemed like snowdrifts from a December on the other side of the world. How very far she had come, not just from New York City but from her origins in western Pennsylvania, where no sapphires or rubies were pulled from the ground but only hard anthracite coal. Through the moonlight Bly could make out a native fisherman standing waist-deep in the roaring surf. The fishing was better at night, she knew, but she couldn't help but contemplate how an especially strong wave might wash him away into the black soundless depths, never to be seen again by his loved ones; it was so easy to lose one's footing and disappear forever. She could feel the happiness of earlier in the day draining out of her, the lonesomeness she had felt so acutely on the *Victoria* returning again. Soon, at least, she would be at the halfway point of her trip, and each day thereafter a little closer to home.

Bly watched the jinrikishas come in and out of the gaslit gate of the hotel. Her attention was drawn to an arch of the verandah, where two dark figures, a man and a woman, stood close together, outlined by the lamp of the gate. The woman's face was upturned to the man's; he clasped her hands in his and held them close to his chest. As Bly later recalled, "I felt a little sympathy for them as wrapped in that delusion that makes life heaven or hell, that forms the foundation for every novel, play or story, they stood, until a noisy new arrival wakened her from blissful oblivion, and she rushed, scarcely waiting for him to kiss the hand he held, away into the darkness."

In her account of the trip, that single sentence was Nellie Bly's only allusion, direct or otherwise, to romantic feelings. The "delusion" of love, she tartly noted, formed the foundation of every novel; in her own novel, *The Mystery of Central Park,* one of the minor characters is an editor by the name of John Stetson Maxwell, an obvious reference to James Stetson Metcalfe, the handsome violet-eyed writer often seen squiring Bly around town beginning in the winter of 1888. In the novel, published in October 1889, Maxwell is characterized by the female protagonist as "brutal and unkind." By November of that year Bly and Metcalfe's relationship must have been over, for Bly felt not the slightest hesitation about leaving town for a trip of some seventy-five days, nor was James

Metcalfe among the friends and colleagues who had gathered at the Hoboken pier to see her off. "Have you any reason for feeling depressed, any love affair?" one of the doctors she consulted for her headaches had asked shortly before she left New York. "No," she replied, "I have no love affair."

Bly sighed again and took another sip of her lime squash, and then turned to answer her companion.

DECEMBER 10–13, 1889

Colombo, Ceylon

According to Nellie Bly's itinerary, the stopover in Ceylon was supposed to last only two days, at which point she would set off on another Peninsular and Oriental steamship, the *Oriental,* bound for Penang, Singapore, and Hong Kong. The *Oriental* could not depart, however, until it had received mail and passengers from the steamship *Nepaul* arriving from Calcutta, and to all indications the *Nepaul* was the slowest ship on the ocean. By December 10, the scheduled departure date, it was still nowhere in sight. Soon the bad news had been posted on the blackboard in the lobby of the Grand Oriental Hotel; at once Bly set off to the nearest telegraph office. A telegram from Colombo to New York cost twenty-five cents for eight words, and five cents for each additional word; for urgent messages, however, the price was seventy-five cents for eight words, and ten cents for each word beyond that. For this message, presumably, Nellie Bly spent the extra money.

On Thursday, December 12, a capitalized headline in *The World* announced: NELLIE BLY DELAYED. The newspaper had received a telegram from Bly reporting that she would have to spend five days in Ceylon, three more than had been allotted in her schedule. Bly had offered no explanation for the unexpected delay, saying only that she would be sailing from Ceylon on December 13 rather than December 10.

Nellie Bly was still 3,500 miles from Hong Kong, where the Occidental and Oriental steamship *Oceanic* was due to depart on December 28, in fifteen days' time. As a result of the three-day delay in Ceylon she now had no margin to spare: to lose even a single day anywhere between Colombo and Hong Kong would mean missing the *Oceanic,* a catastrophic outcome, as she would then likely arrive in New York no earlier than

February 3—a trip of eighty-one days. "The monsoons and typhoons of Indian and Chinese waters will have to be agreeable to make the trip come out all right from this point," *The World* noted soberly, adding, "Miss Bly can yet, with fortune favoring her, complete her tour in less than seventy-five days, but it is only fair to everybody to state that the elements are against her in that part of the journey where it is most essential that they should be propitious."

"THE GORGEOUS BUDDHIST temples of the Singhalean will astonish her and fill her with admiration," *The World* predicted in an article about Nellie Bly's stay in Ceylon, and Bly did visit the local temples—but found there "little of interest," she remarked, "and always having to pay liberally for the privilege of looking about." She also stopped into the offices of the two Colombo newspapers, about which she said only that the young Englishmen who ran them were "very clever" and "very kind to strangers." She did not "join in an elephant hunt," as *The World* had suggested she might, nor did she "go berrying in the coffee fields."

Coffee had once been Ceylon's most important export crop, but in recent years a fungus had blighted the fields and increasingly the larger colonial planters were switching over to tea. The families who worked as tea pluckers were not native Singhalese but rather Tamils from the southern part of India, who were thought to be stronger and more willing to work. "The coolie," the director of Ceylon's Royal Botanic Gardens remarked admiringly of the Tamils, "is a very docile and obedient labourer." About the imported workers one of the local guidebooks observed, "Both men and women, to say nothing of the children, may make good wages for work which after all is by no means exhausting, though they work from 6 A.M. to 4 P.M. at a stretch," and additionally noted that while "the rate of wages, being only 30 to 50 cents a day of Ceylon money, or 5d. to 8d. English, may seem to the newcomer mere starvation . . . when one considers that at home the same people would not be able to earn more than about one-third of that, it assumes the guise of actual wealth." (And furthermore, though that same newcomer might blanch at the tiny huts in which the tea-plucker families were forced to live, it was helpful to keep in mind that these huts were "almost palatial compared to their own homes, and that they do not like large and airy quarters.") W. S. Caine, a British member of Parliament who had visited the island two years before Bly, stoutly declared, "To these Tamils Ceylon is a heaven upon earth."

Theological metaphors aside, an investigation into the actual working conditions of the Tamil tea pluckers would seem to be the sort of story Nellie Bly might have been interested to undertake while she waited for the *Nepaul* to arrive, of a piece with her earlier reports about Pittsburgh's factory workers, or Mexico's tortilla makers, or the paper-box girls of New York. Bly, though, did not visit any tea plantations while she was in Ceylon, nor any of the immense cinnamon plantations, nor any of the island's rice paddies, nor any of the other places in which native people lived and worked; and indeed the only subject to which she devoted more than a few sentences in her various accounts of Ceylon was the plot of a show she saw one night at a local theater. On Ceylon, Bly's renowned reportorial instincts deserted her; she found it difficult to concentrate, so focused was she on the need to get moving again. She seemed aware of this, variously describing herself as being in an "ill humor" and a "bad temper." Bly and two shipmates from the *Victoria* took a train one morning to the nearby city of Kandy, an ancient highland city set like a gemstone into the surrounding mountains. With its Hindu and Buddhist temples, palaces, artificial lake, hilltop walks, and botanic gardens surrounded by a lush tropical forest, Kandy was commonly cited by travelers as the most beautiful city in the world; it was "pretty," Bly said dismissively, "but far from what it is claimed to be." After the trip to Kandy she came down with one of her sick headaches, the first she had gotten since she left New York, and went to bed that night without dinner. Bly ascribed the headache to the heat of Ceylon, but Aden and the Suez Canal had been hotter; surely it was due, at least in part, to the anxiety she felt in waiting for a ship that seemed never to come.

The hours went by, the days went by, and still there was no sign of the *Nepaul*. A land often compared to the Garden of Eden was not the most disagreeable place to be held over, but Nellie Bly passed the time in an agony of waiting. At last, on the fourth day, the blackboard in the hotel lobby brought the welcome news that the *Oriental* would be leaving the following morning at eight. Bly was awakened promptly at five o'clock, and she was so anxious to be on her way that she set off for the dock that morning without even stopping to eat the toast and tea that a waiter brought to her room. She was the very first passenger aboard the ship. The only other people on deck were an elderly man with striking blue eyes, who turned out to be the chief engineer of the *Oriental,* and a younger blond man wearing a white linen suit, who was the ship's doctor. The two men strolled along the deck, looking out to sea as they chatted.

Bly tried to untie a steamer chair so she could have someplace to sit while she waited, but grew frustrated as she struggled with this normally simple task; her patience had long since given way under the strain of waiting. The older man came up and offered to assist her; in a moment he had the chair untied.

"When will we sail?" Bly asked him anxiously.

"As soon as the *Nepaul* comes in. She was to have been here at daybreak, but she hasn't been sighted yet. She's a slow old boat."

"May she go to the bottom of the bay when she does get in!" Bly exclaimed. "The old tub! I think it an outrage to be kept waiting five days for a tub like that."

The engineer smiled at her. "Colombo is a pleasant place to stay," he said lightly.

"It may be, if staying there does not mean more than life to one. Really," she said again, "it would afford me the most intense delight to see the *Nepaul* go to the bottom of the sea."

Bly's vehemence surprised the two men, and their surprise in turn amused her, as she thought how little anyone else could understand what this delay meant to her, how she dreaded the thought of being "a forlorn little self creeping back to New York ten days behind time, with a shamed look on her face and afraid to hear her name spoken," and the picture that appeared in her mind—that forlorn, creeping little self—caused her to laugh out loud, and the men looked at her in astonishment and perhaps some concern as well, which made her laugh even harder, and as she did she began to relax and she could feel her better nature returning, and she found herself able to say, "Everything happens for the best," and almost believe it to be true.

In the end, it was Nellie Bly who first spotted the ship. "There is the *Nepaul,*" she called, pointing to a faint wisp of smoke just above the horizon. The two men doubted that she could be right, but after a few minutes the wisp had lengthened into a plume and a small black dot had appeared beneath it, like an exclamation point.

The *Nepaul* did not discharge its passengers to the *Oriental* until nearly one o'clock in the afternoon. Not long afterward the *Oriental* was finally able to set sail, and soon Ceylon was receding behind them, the island's palm trees seeming to wave farewell in the breeze. It was, Bly thought, "a great relief to be again on the sweet, blue sea . . . free from the tussle and worry and bustle for life which we are daily, hourly even, forced to gaze upon on land."

Still, as Bly set out across the Bay of Bengal she could not have been entirely without care. She had been traveling for twenty-nine days and had covered almost exactly nine thousand miles. But for the first time since setting out from New York, she was behind schedule.

CHAPTER 12

The Other Woman Is Going to Win

DECEMBER 18–23, 1889

South China Sea

ON BOARD THE PENINSULAR AND ORIENTAL STEAMSHIP *THAMES* BOUND for Singapore, Elizabeth Bisland slept "the languorous, voluptuous sleep of the tropics." Her stateroom had a comfortable bed with an iron frame, but she preferred the divan that lay beneath the square window that let in warm sea winds and soothing whispers of water as it brushed against the side of the ship. She had never felt quite as happy as she did on board the *Thames*. It turned out that she loved to travel; she took unexpected pleasure in the daily cataloguing of new sights, understood the exultation of Keats's "watcher of the skies / When a new planet swims into his ken." Travel, she had discovered, was a delightful means of gratifying the intelligent curiosity that Dr. Johnson had called the root of all wisdom and culture. "I go to bed exhaustedly happy," she wrote in her notebook, "and wake up expectantly smiling."

At six-thirty each morning a white-capped stewardess brought tea, fruit, and a biscuit; at first Bisland found it odd to eat at this hour, but she quickly learned that in the tropics it was best to eat small meals at numer-

ous times throughout the day. Later she would write in an essay for female travelers, "If one refuses to adapt one's self to this custom, and
insists upon doing in Rome as the Americans do, the result will be a feeling of great exhaustion after dressing that robs one of appetite for breakfast and spoils the day." She could spend hours at a time on one of the
ship's bamboo lounging chairs, with perhaps a book or some sewing in
her lap, watching the sea quiver under the blinding sky. In the afternoon
she bathed in a large marble tub filled with cool salt water, followed by a
nap between the hours of three and four. Other than "a charming little
old lady from Boston," Elizabeth Bisland was the only female passenger
aboard the *Thames;* as a result, she wrote, "the atmosphere has a pronounced masculine flavor; but despite even this limitation it is interesting." All of the passengers traveled first or second class; there were no
accommodations for steerage. The ship was yachtlike in its proportions,
with a saloon of gold and white that extended the length of the ship and
a broad top deck generously shaded by canvas awnings. Cages with ca-
naries in them hung above the deck; the air around the ship was filled
with birdsong as it was scented with coal smoke and lavender water.

The sky stayed always the same clear blue, but the sea was ever-
changing. One day it was speckled like the breast of a peacock, another it
was divided, curiously, into distinct bands of green, blue, and violet. Unlike the Pacific Ocean, where Bisland had spent whole days clutching the
sides of her berth inside a storm-tossed cabin, the sea here was as flat as
the western prairie; it occurred to her that the ship could carry a full glass
of water the entire way and never spill a drop. The evenings brought no
spectacular sunsets, as the sky held no clouds to reflect the light; the sun
simply turned red and fell swiftly toward the horizon, where it was
doused by the ocean like a heated wheel in a blacksmith's trough. Then
just as swiftly the powerful tide of light vanished, and the ship sailed in
phosphorescent water. Overhead, myriad constellations hung in the
boundless black vault of the sky: Cassiopeia, Perseus, Orion, the last of
the old gods who still watched from above. The warm, moist nights, so
reminiscent of those on the bayou, gave heavy, relaxed sleep, and she
awoke refreshed at dawn to a pale lilac sky still glimmering with stars.

"Everything pleases, everything amuses me," Elizabeth Bisland
wrote while at sea; "most of all perhaps the strong British atmosphere in
which one finds one's self on board a P. and O. steamer." On the *Thames*
Bisland delighted in eating the foods she had only ever read about in En-

glish novels. She came to know the difference between the Bath bun and the Scottish scone; she sampled for the first time veal-and-ham pie (the "weal and hammer," as Dickens called it in *Our Mutual Friend*) and an array of sweets royally christened: Alexandra wafers, Beatrice tarts, Victoria jelly roll. She was endlessly fascinated by the variety of English accents on the ship; no two of the men sounded quite alike. The bearded giant who sat by her at table spoke with a broad Scottish burr; the handsome fourth officer with the black eyes and shy ruddy face revealed traces of a Yorkshire accent, a *d* replacing a *th* on the tip of his tongue; the tall young blond arrayed in snowy silk and linen had the superciliously rounded vowels learned at Eton and Oxford. Bisland herself spoke with a gentle Southern drawl, even more unusual here than it was in New York; and though she did not write about this, one can imagine the level of attention that must have been paid, on a ship populated almost entirely by men, to a beautiful young woman traveling unaccompanied around the world.

Nor was she in turn immune to their charms. From captain to cook, she observed admiringly, the men on the ship were "fine creatures": tautly muscled, with curly hair and white teeth and eyes the turquoise of the sea. (Bisland seems to have been especially taken with the ship's doctor. The following year she would write in an article for *Harper's Bazaar,* "There is a sea rumor that candidates for the medical advisorship to the sea-sick undergo a competitive examination, sending in sealed photographs, judged by a committee of young women. But perhaps this rumor is not verifiable. Nevertheless it is a fact that all ships' doctors are beautiful. It is demonstrated on the Atlantic liners, and on the P. & O. ships of the East it is still more supernally true.") Aboard the *Thames* the men were "flat-backed and lean-loined; they carry their huge shoulders with a lordly swagger; they possess a divine faith in themselves and in England." They had a vigor and virility that came from being the stewards of the world's most powerful empire, so markedly different from the Southern men around whom she had grown up, hard and bitter, long marinated in the vinegar of defeat. In an interview with the New Orleans *Daily Picayune,* Bisland marveled at the Englishmen she had met on Peninsular and Oriental ships. "I never saw such splendid figures," she recalled. "Way out there in the east their faces are as rosy as if they had just come from London. They have such superb confidence in themselves, too. I never met anything like it in my life. They own everything.

Anything they have not got you will hear them say in the most careless fashion: 'Oh, we'll be taking that in a few years.'"

Elsewhere Bisland wrote, "Only those who travel to these Eastern ports can form any adequate conception of the ability which has directed English conquest in the Orient." In fact at least one American traveler to Eastern ports would have disagreed with Elizabeth Bisland's interpretation of English conquest—that traveler being, of course, Nellie Bly, who, sailing from Aden, acidly noted that the British had "stolen" the region's best ports. It was just one of the many offenses, large and small, of which Bly found Great Britain guilty during her travels, along with impudent servants and poorly heated railroad carriages. Bly was hardly alone among Americans in her dislike of all things English, and indeed only a few years later the Yale University history professor George Burton Adams would publish a short book with the title *Why Americans Dislike England,* which contained at the very outset this assertion:

> It must be regarded as proved beyond all doubt that there is in the minds of a large proportion of our people, very probably a majority of them, a peculiar feeling of dislike towards England, which they cherish towards no other country, and a peculiar quickness to flame up into open opposition to her whenever she seems to be threatening the slightest encroachment upon our interests. . . . The fact is undeniable that the mass of Americans look upon England alone among all the nations of the world as the one which is naturally unfriendly to us, and which we must always regard with suspicion.

Some of this dislike, Adams continued, arose from the "air of superiority which England has so often assumed towards America, and certain classes of Englishmen towards Americans." One distinguished British observer, the historian and member of Parliament James Bryce, had recently acknowledged that "English travellers and writers used no doubt formerly to assume airs of supercilious condescension which must have been offensive to Americans"; however, Bryce immediately added, "these airs were dropped twenty or thirty years ago." To this George Burton Adams responded simply, "Mr. Bryce is hardly correct in this statement, if numerous stories afloat in this country are to be trusted." (Nellie Bly herself would have concurred with Adams's assessment, and she made her own small contribution to the trove of stories about the smugness and insularity of English travelers.) Still more damaging to transatlantic relations was the widespread belief among Americans that the British government was selfish, unscrupulous, greedy, and bellicose. In its brief history the United States had already gone to war twice with Great Britain, in the American Revolution and the War of 1812—the first time to win its liberty and the second time, in the popular view, to protect it—and further inflaming the tempers of many Americans, during the Civil War, Great Britain had spurned its own antislavery rhetoric and remained neutral as the South seceded and the United States was torn apart. The indictment of Great Britain was succinctly delivered by Senator Joseph R. Hawley of Connecticut: "In every emergency with which the United States has been confronted, the British government has been our enemy."

Though anti-British sentiment could be found everywhere among Americans, it was more widely and passionately held at each descending step on the economic ladder, culminating with the poorer Irish Catholic immigrants, who saw the British government as nothing more nor less than an agent of tyranny and oppression. Upper-class Americans, on the other hand, were by ethnicity overwhelmingly Anglo-Saxon, by religion Episcopalian, and by political outlook congenial to the idea of a traditional aristocratic society sitting atop a relatively immobile class structure. For many of these Americans, Great Britain was not a foe or a despot, but rather the beloved ancestor from which the United States had inherited the "seed of civilization" (to use the highly charged phrase employed by imperialists of the period), the country with which the United States shared a race, a religion, and a language: less a threat than a model for America's own future of imperial expansion. In this view the United States might at times resent Great Britain's superior confidence and strength, as a younger brother might resent an older one and strive to outdo him, but at moments of crisis they inevitably recognized that they were blood relations and closed ranks against any threats from outside.

Andrew Carnegie himself adopted this view in an 1890 magazine article emphatically entitled "Do Americans Hate England? No!" in which he declared, "The Briton and the American are too much alike and too much to each other not to have feelings of rivalry excited as between themselves; but now that all feeling of condescension on one hand and assertion on the other has ceased, and they are recognised equals, every hour taken from the passage between them, every visit paid, draws the two branches closer together, and leads both to feel deep down in their hearts that they are branches of the same great family." By this time, as Carnegie suggested, advances in maritime technology had made the Atlantic crossing far easier than ever before, and for many of those Americans who could afford it Great Britain became a regular travel destination, from which they returned home with a renewed appreciation for English education, English culture, English hereditary titles, and even English-style spelling (such as *honour, centre, fulfil,* or *memorise*), a style that would eventually come to be adopted by, among others, Elizabeth Bisland.

The very different views of Great Britain had been put on vivid display in New York two years before Bly's and Bisland's trips, on June 21, 1887, on the occasion of Queen Victoria's golden jubilee. That morning at the Metropolitan Opera House, its stage bedecked with British and American flags, a large crowd described by *The New York Times* as "prolific in enthusiasm" enjoyed a program of patriotic songs and tributes to the queen by political and religious leaders, among them the former mayor of New York, Seth Low, who proclaimed that "the tangled threads of Anglo-Saxon greatness have become the warp and woof of human progress over a large portion of the globe" and promised Great Britain that "the American people, grateful for her constant friendship, join with you to-day from ocean to ocean in your own prayer, 'God Save the Queen,'" a conclusion that was reportedly met with "prolonged applause and cheers." It was a far more somber scene later that evening, when some 2,500 of the city's Irish immigrants filled Cooper Union Hall for what the event's organizers called "a memorial demonstration in honor of the victims of Queen Victoria's 50 years of misrule." Speaker after speaker catalogued the horrors that English despotism had visited upon the Irish people; the stage was draped in the black crepe of mourning, and from the front of the podium there swung a hangman's noose.

The segment of Americans most resolutely hostile to Great Britain— working-class Northerners, and especially Irish Catholic immigrants— were the very people among whom Nellie Bly had long lived and worked; her own paternal grandparents, Robert and Catherine Risher Cochran, had left Ireland's County Derry and settled in western Pennsylvania in 1804. Elizabeth Bisland, on the other hand, came from Scottish stock, her great-great-grandfather, John Bisland, having been a dry-goods merchant in Glasgow who emigrated to North Carolina shortly before the

American Revolution. "It fills my soul with a passion of pride that I, too, am an Anglo-Saxon," Bisland once wrote. She was, moreover, a Southerner and an Episcopalian, and, though not wealthy herself, she was by disposition entirely comfortable among aristocrats. (In Ceylon, for instance, she would begin a close friendship with Lady Broome, who wrote travel books under the name "Lady Barker.") Perhaps most important of all, Bisland was someone who had fallen in love with books as a young girl, for whom the most beloved literature would always have a distinctively English flavor—or, as she herself preferred, *flavour*.

EVERY HOUR NOW brought Elizabeth Bisland closer to the equator. The *Thames* was sailing south from Hong Kong to Singapore, where it was scheduled to arrive on December 23. At the same time the *Thames*'s sister P&O steamship, the *Oriental,* continued on its path north from Singapore to Hong Kong; it, too, would make port on December 23, Nellie Bly's thirty-ninth day out of New York.

Somewhere on the South China Sea, in the third week of December 1889, Nellie Bly and Elizabeth Bisland passed each other unawares as they made their way around the world.

DECEMBER 13–16, 1889
Straits of Malacca

Nellie Bly was pleased by almost everything about the *Oriental,* by the politeness of the crew, the spaciousness of the cabins, the quality of the food, but most especially by the length of each day's run: when the *Oriental* reached the Straits of Malacca, after crossing the Bay of Bengal, it had already made up much of the time lost in Ceylon. Bly, however, could not say much for the weather, which was so hot and damp that mirrors fogged and cabin keys began to rust. The sultry air brought a laziness to life aboard the ship; little distinguished the passing of the hours, other than an occasional sighting of a sea turtle as it poked its head up to bask in the sun, or a school of flying fish skimming like dragonflies over the surface of the water, or jellyfish drifting slowly around the ship like moons. Unhurriedly the sailors hoisted and pulled sails as they laughed and chatted among themselves, while the passengers lounged on deck watching beautiful green islands slide slowly past, idly speculating about whether they might be inhabited. Some of the passengers told stories about how the straits had once been infested with pirates, and Nellie Bly found herself silently wishing that a few erstwhile buccaneers might reappear and provide a bit of excitement to break up the long uneventful days of travel, much as earlier, while riding the mail train in Italy, she had hoped for bandits.

On the morning of December 16 the *Oriental* anchored for refueling on the island of Penang (or, as the British preferred to call it, Prince of Wales Island), the northernmost seaport on the Malay peninsula; the thirteen hundred miles from Colombo had been covered, remarkably, in only three days. Still, given the long delay in Ceylon, the captain was anxious to make up even more time, and he advised the passengers that the *Oriental* would set sail again in six hours. Pairs of Chinese laborers were already padding up the gangway between ship and shore, hauling baskets of coal suspended from a pole between them. Bly and one of the men from the ship took a sampan ashore, where they hired a jinrikisha to take them into the nearby hills. Here the air was still cool, the woods wreathed in white mist. They rode beneath canopies of coconut palms, past the cozy red-roofed bungalows where the English residents lived nestled into the rocks and foliage, above cascades where clear streams emptied into granite basins. They were headed toward the immense waterfall that supplied the island with its fresh water; Penang's waterfall was a favorite attraction for visitors to the island, but the ennui that Bly had felt during her last days in Colombo seemed to have traveled with her across the Bay of Bengal. "The picturesque waterfall is nothing marvelous," she later remarked. "It only made me wonder from whence it procured its water supply, but after walking until I was much heated, and finding myself apparently just as far from the fount, I concluded that the waterfall's secret was not worth the fatigue it would cost."

By the time they returned to the harbor the sky had clouded over and the water turned rough. Huge waves tossed their sampan as they sailed back out to the *Oriental,* the swell intensified by the rolling of the coal barge alongside the ship. Bly had barely climbed up onto the deck when the barge was ordered to cast off; even as this was being done the *Oriental* was already hoisting anchor and starting on its way. Soon after, several dozen Chinese coal haulers rushed up on deck only to discover that while they were unloading their last sacks of coal in the hold below, the barge had left without them. "There followed," Bly reported, "dire chattering, wringing of hands, pulling of locks and crying after the receding barge, all to no avail."

Hearing their cries, the captain of the *Oriental* told the coal haulers to go off on the pilot boat, the little tug that was escorting the *Oriental* out of the harbor. Not wanting to lose time before the oncoming storm, the captain ordered the pilot boat to be boarded even as the vessels continued to plow through the waves, but one of the Chinese trying to leap from the steamship plunged terrifyingly into the sea and the captain had no choice but to turn off the engines and wait in the harbor until he had been rescued. By now the wind was howling over the water, churning up spray that dangerously slicked every surface. Droplets glistened on the bare backs of the men; their long hair whipped like flags in the wind. Some of the men slowly worked their way down the long cable that connected the *Oriental* to the pilot boat, where their comrades pulled them, wet and frightened, to safety. Others descended the ladder on the side of the steamship, but the ladder ended several feet above the tugboat that beat furiously back and forth on the waves; many a coal hauler, reaching the bottom of the ladder, would cling despairingly to its lower rungs, not willing to loosen his grip and perhaps fall into the waves below, as those already in the boat shouted encouragement and reached for his legs, while the *Oriental*'s officers threatened to knock him off the ladder with poles. To those watching from above, safe on the top deck, the scene looked as amusingly chaotic as a music hall sketch. "We all gathered to

Loading coal onto a steamship

see the sight," Nellie Bly reported of her fellow passengers, "and a funny one it was!"

At long last all of the coal haulers had managed to get aboard and the line was cast off. The *Oriental,* now fully coaled, steamed out of the harbor, while the fierce tide swept the smaller vessel back toward the shore. The pilot boat, Bly noticed, was so overloaded that the men aboard were afraid to move, even to bail out the water that had collected at the bottom of the boat.

DECEMBER 16–17, 1889

Singapore

Nearing Singapore, less than one hundred miles from the equator, Nellie Bly was at the southernmost point of her journey, and exactly halfway around the world. She had reached the midpoint on only her thirty-third day out of New York, but she knew that she could not maintain that pace—the trip across the South China Sea would be against the wind, and she would likely have a long wait for the connecting steamship in Hong Kong—and she was eager to make port in Singapore before night fell. The *Oriental,* though, did not reach Singapore's waters until nearly six o'clock in the evening, and many more long minutes passed before the harbor pilot came aboard the ship to instruct the captain about how to proceed. Anxiously Bly awaited his verdict. The *Oriental,* the pilot finally decided, would have to anchor outside the harbor until morning, it being too dangerous to try to dock the steamship after dark. Bly could barely contain her frustration and rage; in her mind the delay "was the result of slowing down to leave off the coolies at Penang." And this delay, in turn, would lead to an even greater one:

> The mail contract made it compulsory for the ship to stay in port twenty-four hours, and while we might have been consuming our stay and so helping me on in my race against time I was wasting precious hours lying outside the gates of hope, as it were, merely because some black men had been too slow. Those few hours might mean the loss of my ship at Hong Kong; they might

mean days added to my record. What agony of suspense and impatience I suffered that night!

When Bly came up on deck in the morning, the *Oriental* lay alongside the Singapore wharf and was already being refueled. On the native sampans that clustered about the ship—that flotilla of little boats seemed a fixture of steamship travel in the East—peddlers called up to the passengers on the *Oriental,* offering deals on silk, fruit, lace, picture photographs, and, oddly, monkeys.

While they waited for the ship to depart, Bly and a companion, a young Welsh doctor named Brown, hired a gharry to take them into the town. The gharry, Singapore's distinctive vehicle, was a square four-wheeled wagon, something like a New York hansom cab but with Venetian blinds on the windows and pulled by a spotted little horse barely larger than a sheep. The road ran along the sea, skirting the low inland hills; the hills were composed primarily of laterite and many had already been dug up in quarries, the green hillsides turned the rusty red of an old wound.

The gharry driver took Bly and Dr. Brown to the Singapore esplanade, fifteen acres of greensward devoted almost entirely to the pleasures of sport: men dressed in white played vigorous games of cricket and tennis and bowls, cooled by the breezes that swept over the seawall. At the very center of the esplanade stood the imposing bronze statue of Sir Stamford Raffles, the British statesman often described as "the father of Singapore," his arms crossed as though in disgruntlement at the frivolity going on all around him. The two visited the newly opened Raffles Museum, its collections already including thousands of specimens of native plants, animals, and insect life, and then had an early dinner at the popular Hôtel de l'Europe, where they ate at a long table draped in white linen on the verandah facing the sea. The food was French and the waiters Chinese, and around them conversations were going on, it seemed, in all the languages of the world.

After dinner they rejoined their driver, who drove them back toward the center of town. In the distance they heard a clamorous, vaguely musical sound, reminiscent, to Bly, of a political procession on the night of an election.

"That's a funeral," the driver called back to them.

"Indeed!" said Bly. "If that's the way you have funerals here, I'll see one." The driver pulled the gharry to the side of the road, and they waited eagerly for the funeral to pass. First into view was a row of men flourishing black-and-white satin flags, followed by a band of musicians atop small Malay ponies, blowing trumpets, beating tom-toms, striking cymbals, and hammering gongs. Men dressed in white trousers and blue tunics marched by brandishing roasted pigs impaled on spits, while others held aloft Chinese lanterns. Next came the casket draped in scarlet cloth, resting on long poles suspended on the shoulders of some forty pallbearers dressed in black, the rear brought up by mourners in a long line of gharries. The mourners were dressed in white satin from head to toe and were, Bly observed, "the happiest looking people at the funeral." She and Dr. Brown watched intently to the very end, as delighted as if they had seen a circus parade.

"I would not have missed that for anything," said Dr. Brown when it was all over.

"You could not have," Bly replied laughingly. "I know they got it up for our special benefit."

And so they rode back to town, still captivated by a funeral that had for them not the slightest suggestion of death. The gharry driver took them to a small Hindu temple used by the local *dhobies,* or laundrymen; the dhobies were a common sight in the nearby Stamford Canal, bent over their work, rinsing soiled linens in the water and then beating them against a flat stone. At the temple door a priest informed the doctor and the gharry driver that they could come inside if they removed their shoes, but that the lady would not be permitted to enter.

"Why?" Bly demanded at once. She was intent on finding out "why my sex in heathen lands should exclude me from a temple, as in America it confines me to the side entrances of hotels and other strange and incommodious things."

"No, señora, no mudder," said the priest, emphatically shaking his head.

"I'm *not* a mother!" Bly cried so indignantly that her companions burst into laughter. The priest, though, was insistent, and so the three left the temple and walked back down the front path to the waiting gharry.

On their way back to the ship, Bly and Dr. Brown stopped at the home of the gharry driver. His wife, a beautiful young Malay woman, was dressed in several yards of colorful cloth wrapped around her waist and over her right shoulder; she had a large gold ring in her nose and several more on her ears and toes, and bracelets around her ankles. Standing by the door was a macaque monkey, stoutly built and not much more than two feet tall. Nellie Bly had thus far resisted making any large purchases, not wanting the burden of additional baggage, but seeing the monkey's eager, expressive face she felt her willpower begin to melt away. She had, after all, only a few more transfers remaining on the trip, and at each station there would be porters on hand to assist her; the monkey himself would no doubt be an amusing companion and a memorable souvenir of her travel around the world, and if he proved too much trouble she could always donate him to the menagerie in Central Park. After some negotiation, she and the gharry driver agreed on a price of three dollars. Some of the monkeys for sale in the harbor were being offered for as little as fifty cents, but to Bly they looked like puny creatures that would likely die of consumption on the voyage; this particular monkey, on the other hand, seemed "as strong as a man"—an observation subsequently borne out when the monkey grappled with a ship's coxswain one day on the Pacific Ocean and threw him flat on the deck.

Nellie Bly carried the monkey with her in a cage the rest of the way back to New York; he would become, like the ghillie cap and the traveling bag, one of the symbols of her trip, with numerous accounts portraying him as sitting contentedly on her shoulder, an incident that never actually took place, for the monkey had a tendency to scratch and bite and seemed to reserve his fiercest temper for Bly herself, as though blaming her—reasonably enough—for being the one who had uprooted him from his native land. ("It is a savage little fellow," Bly was heard once to remark of the monkey, "but takes to most everybody but me.") She had some trouble deciding what to call him, and during her Pacific voyage she tried out the names Solaris, Tajmahal, and Jocko; eventually, back in the United States, she settled on McGinty, a name suggested to her by a reporter, after a character in a popular song of the time. By that time Bly was telling people that the monkey had been given to her by a rajah in Singapore.

DECEMBER 17–23, 1889

South China Sea

Entering the South China Sea from the Straits of Malacca, the *Oriental* ran into a monsoon. Despite the danger—and the slowing of the day's run—Nellie Bly could not help but think the billowing sea the most magnificent sight she had ever seen. In the afternoon she sat breathless up on deck watching as the bow of the ship lifted upright like a horse rearing on its hind legs, paused at the top of a wave for a queasying moment, and then plunged down again as if heading straight for the bottom of the sea. Despite the spray of the waves, the air was heavy and close, and at times Bly felt almost as if she would smother; most of the passengers preferred to stay below in their cabins, but some of the men lay stretched out on chairs on deck, gasping for air. Once, suddenly, the ship dropped to one side like a wagon that had lost a wheel, tossing Bly from her chair clear across the deck. As she slid, Bly had the presence of mind to grab hold of an iron bar that protruded from the deck; that bar, she realized later, was all that had prevented her from crashing through the skylight into the dining room below.

During that storm one of the men on deck became seasick. As it happens, this particular man had been, in Bly's words, "quite attentive to me," and even in the midst of the storm, his face drawn and pale, he lay on his traveling rug at her feet, gazing miserably up at her and pleading for sympathy. Bly said little to him; she knew that she was being heartless, but she could not bring herself to sympathize with a seasick man, and especially not this one.

"You don't know how nice I can look," the man said to her later, adding that if she would only stay over in Hong Kong for a week she could see for herself.

"Indeed," Bly said drily, "such a phenomenon might induce me to remain there six weeks."

For days her hapless suitor followed her plaintively about the ship, until at last one of the other passengers had the idea to tell him that Nellie Bly was engaged to the ship's chief officer Sleeman and that the chief officer did not approve of her talking to other men; this information, though, seemed only to fuel his devotion. One evening, finding Nellie

Bly alone on deck, he sat down at her feet and asked her, "Do you think life is worth living?"

"Yes, life is very sweet," Bly replied. "The thought of death is the only thing that causes me unhappiness."

"You cannot understand it or you would feel differently. I could take you in my arms and jump overboard, and before they know it we would be at rest."

"You can't tell. It might not be rest," she began to say, but he exclaimed with sudden passion, "I know, I know. I can show you. I will prove it to you. Death by drowning is a peaceful slumber, a quiet drifting away."

A chill began to creep over her as she realized that she was alone on deck with a madman. "It is?" she said, adopting the soothing tones of a policeman coaxing a would-be jumper from the rail of a bridge. "You know, tell me about it. Explain it to me."

Just as the man began to answer, Bly saw Chief Officer Sleeman come up on deck. She dared not call out to him, dared not even smile lest her companion notice and fling them together overboard into an everlasting slumber. The chief officer approached them; he clapped the man on the back and said in amusement, "What a very pretty love scene."

"Come!" Bly shouted at once, grabbing the officer's hand and rushing away before the startled man could react.

Down below, with the chief officer and the ship's captain, she related what had happened. The captain wanted to put the man in irons, but Bly, who felt more sorry for him than anything else, requested that he be left free. Afterward, though, she was very careful not to spend a single moment alone and unprotected on deck.

The *Oriental,* it seemed, had more than its share of the odd characters Bly thought of as "cranks." One morning, for instance, the captain asked one of the passengers, a minister, to lead the Sunday service. The minister agreed to do so, but when the ship reached Hong Kong he handed the captain a bill for two pounds. He had been enjoying a vacation, he explained, and did not propose to work during that time unless he was paid for it. (The P&O paid the bill, Bly reported, but warned the company's officers that in the future ministers could not perform the service unless a price had been agreed upon beforehand.) Another passenger, an Englishman with a strong taste for whisky and soda, prefaced nearly all of his comments with the phrase, "Dear me." (Englishmen always say "Dear me," Bly teased him once, because they think so highly of themselves.) One of the *Oriental*'s female passengers told the chief officer that she wanted a cabin located directly over the ship's screw so that she could always be sure that the ship was moving. She received that cabin, and Bly noted, with evident satisfaction, that this passenger soon developed the worst case of seasickness she had ever seen in a woman.

One day in the dining room, some passengers were discussing the amenities on the ship and Bly said, "Everything is such an improvement on the *Oriental*. The food is good, the passengers are refined, the officers are polite, and the ship is comfortable and pleasant."

Among the other people sitting at the table was a shy young newly-wed, who looked up from her meal and said in a quiet voice, "Yes, everything is very nice. But the life preservers are not comfortable to sleep in."

The other passengers gazed at one another for a moment in shocked amazement before bursting into laughter. The young woman explained that ever since she and her husband had left home on their bridal tour they had been sleeping in their life preservers; they thought it was the thing to do aboard a ship.

DECEMBER 23, 1889
Hong Kong

The *Oriental* entered Hong Kong Bay at seven o'clock in the morning on December 23. Not only had Nellie Bly made up the three days lost in Ceylon, she had arrived in Hong Kong two days ahead of schedule. It was the *Oriental*'s maiden voyage to China, and despite the monsoon on the South China Sea, the ship had broken all records for the fastest passage from Colombo to Hong Kong. (Not surprisingly, perhaps, one of the *Oriental*'s passengers sued the P&O for bringing him to Hong Kong two days early. He claimed that he had purchased his tickets to cover a certain span of time, and if the company got him in before that time expired, then they were responsible for his expenses and had to pay his hotel bill. Bly did not report how that suit turned out.)

With her Welsh friend Dr. Brown, Nellie Bly walked down the *Oriental*'s gangway and to the end of the pier, where the two hired sedan chairs for the ride into town. Bly stepped backward into the chair, as she was instructed, and in an instant the two drivers had hoisted the poles onto their shoulders and she was in the air. They set off at a steady trot that reminded her of the saddle horses she had ridden as a girl back in Pennsylvania. It was a pleasantly lulling motion, and the town drifted by in a comfortable haze. Bly had not gotten much sleep—she had stayed up late the night before, one of two women amid a group of male passengers singing songs and telling stories—but even so she felt elated that morning, thanks to the *Oriental's* record-breaking run: she was only thirty-nine days out of New York, and she was in China.

The sedan drivers followed the road that ran along the shore, passing tall narrow houses crowded with Chinese families. Everything Bly saw from the window of the sedan chair—the road, the houses, the people—seemed to her unclean; even the drivers themselves looked to her like "dirty fellows, their untidy pigtails twisted around their half-shaven heads." She did not, though, pay much attention to the passing scenery; her single desire in Hong Kong was to leave it as quickly as possible.

The sedan drivers turned off the main road onto one of the narrower roads that wound along the hillside; before long they had stopped in front of the offices of the Occidental and Oriental Steamship Company. Hurrying inside, Bly asked the man behind the counter, "Will you tell me the date of the first sailing for Japan?"

"One moment," he said after a small but discernible pause, and then disappeared into an inner office. Soon he had re-emerged with another O&O agent, who introduced himself as Mr. Harmon. Bly repeated her question to him.

"What is your name?" Harmon asked.

"Nellie Bly," she answered in some surprise, wondering why he needed that information to answer her question.

"Come in, come in," he said, ushering Bly and Dr. Brown into his office. The agent, she thought, seemed strangely nervous. Everyone settled into chairs, the men hitching up their trousers, Nellie Bly arranging her skirt. Harmon said, "You're going to be beaten."

"What?" said Bly, her confusion deepening. "I think not. I have made up my delay."

Harmon shook his head. "You are going to lose it."

"Lose it? I don't understand. What do you mean?"

"Aren't you having a race around the world?"

"Yes, quite right," Bly said. "I am running a race with time."

"Time? I don't think that's her name."

"Her?" Bly had begun to think that this Mr. Harmon might perhaps be unbalanced; she briefly wondered if she dared wink at the doctor to suggest the advisability of making good their escape.

"Yes, the other woman," Harmon said. "She is going to win. She left here three days ago."

Bly stared at him. She said, "The other woman?"

"Yes, did you not know? The day you left New York another woman started out to beat your time, and she's going to do it." Her editor, he said, had offered $2,000 to officials of the Occidental and Oriental line to have the *Oceanic* leave San Francisco two days early. The officials had not done so, but they had agreed to do whatever they could to ensure that their steamship reached Hong Kong on time so that she could catch the English mail ship bound for Ceylon. If she had not made that ship she would have been delayed ten days in Hong Kong. "But she caught the boat and left three days ago," Harmon said, "and you will be delayed here five days."

Bly could feel a panic beginning to rise inside her. With great effort she forced herself to smile. She said quietly, "That is rather hard, isn't it?"

"I'm astonished you did not know anything about it," the agent said. "She led us to suppose it was an arranged race."

"I do not believe my editor would arrange a race without advising me. Have you no cables or messages for me from New York?"

"Nothing."

There was a silence in the room; the sounds of commerce drifted in from the outer office. Bly murmured, "I do not understand it." She thought over what the agent had told her. "You say I cannot leave here for five days?"

"No, and I don't think you can get to New York in eighty days." The other woman, Harmon told her, intended to make it there in only seventy. She was carrying letters addressed to steamship officials at every port requesting that they do everything possible to speed her journey. "Have you any letters?" he asked Bly.

"Only one, from the agent of the P. and O., requesting the captains of their boats to be good to me because I am traveling alone. That is all."

Harmon looked at her sympathetically. "Well, it's too bad," he said at last. "But I think there is no chance for you. You will lose five days here and five in Yokohama, and you are sure to have a slow trip across at this season."

Just then a young man in a white uniform walked into the room. Mr. Harmon introduced him as Mr. Fuhrmann, the purser from the *Oceanic,* the steamship on which Bly was scheduled to travel to Japan and the United States. Fuhrmann had black eyes and a pale complexion, and he clasped her hand firmly and said, "I went down to the *Oriental* to meet you. Mr. Harmon thought it was better. We want to take good care of you, now that you are in our charge, but unfortunately I missed you. I returned to your hotel, and as they knew nothing about you there I came here, fearing that you were lost."

"I have found kind friends everywhere," Bly said, gesturing toward Dr. Brown, who had settled back down in his seat; the doctor seemed to have been rendered speechless by the bad luck that had befallen her. "I'm sorry to have been so much trouble to you."

"Trouble!" said Fuhrmann. "You are with your own people now, and we are only too happy if we can be of service." There was, Bly noted, a pleasing softness in his voice. She must not mind, he told her, if someone else got around the world in less time than she did, for everyone knew that the idea had originated with her and that others were simply trying to steal the work of her brain; whether she got in earlier or later, people would still give her the credit for having had the idea in the first place. Bly knew that the purser was trying to be kind, but she could not bear the pity she thought she heard in his words. She had been too proud to reveal to Mr. Harmon her ignorance of a matter of such vital importance; she would not now admit to Mr. Fuhrmann how painful was the thought of losing.

"I promised my editor that I would go around the world in seventy-five days," she said stiffly, "and if I accomplish that I shall be satisfied. I am not racing with anyone. I would not race. If someone else wants to do the trip in less time, that is their concern."

Bly arranged for the transfer of her luggage and the monkey from the *Oriental* to the *Oceanic* and then left for her hotel. Beyond the window of the sedan chair Hong Kong passed in a blur. Five days in the city would be an eternity; then she would depart again for strange lands, on a strange ship, with no assurance of what the future would bring. Her head whirled with unexpected information. She did not believe that the editors of *The World* would have arranged a race without telling her, but at that moment she felt she could be certain of only one thing, which was that as a reporter she had never been bested: not by the keepers of the Blackwell's Island asylum, not by the Lobby King of Albany, not by her headaches, and not by anyone or anything else. Nor would she be now. She would not be turned into that pitiful creature, the also-ran, creeping back too late to New York with a shamed look on her face, afraid to hear her name spoken. The race was only half over, there was an ocean and a continent yet to be crossed, and somehow she would find a way to win.

CHAPTER 13

The Temple of the Dead

DECEMBER 23–24, 1889

Singapore

NEARING SINGAPORE THE MER-
CURY COLUMN IN THE SHIPBOARD THER-
MOMETER registered temperatures in
the nineties, and the air was so heavy
that one seemed instead to be breathing water. The Peninsular and Oriental steamship *Thames* was now less
than one hundred miles from the equator; many of the passengers complained loudly about the weather, but Elizabeth Bisland had decided that
tropical heat was her ideal climate, producing none of the "creeping
chills" that sometimes troubled her in New York. The water was turquoise and so clear that fish of all shapes and sizes could plainly be observed swimming beneath the surface; in the distance the hills were
dazzling green, the line of the sky feathery with palm fronds.

The *Thames* would dock in Singapore overnight to refuel and receive
mail and passengers bound for Penang and Colombo. In the harbor, Bisland came ashore on a steam launch with three other passengers: a Ceylon tea planter, the old lady from Boston, and the tall blond from Oxford,
flawlessly arrayed in white silk and linen, with a wide-brimmed slouch

hat and a floating scarf. At the end of the pier the group hired a gharry to take them to their hotel; the carriage was pulled by a disconsolate-looking pony, and silently Bisland offered "an elaborate apology to this wretched little beast" before she could "reconcile it to my conscience to climb into the gharry, or let him drag me about at a gallop." The road that ran along the water was crowded with people: tall Sikh policemen in khaki uniforms and red turbans, farmers walking alongside heavy-shouldered white bullocks hitched to carts filled with coconuts and pine-apples and mangoes, barefoot Chinese laborers dressed only in short blue breeches, wealthy native merchants riding in jinrikishas, and English of-ficials in gharries. The Malays had silken black hair and very white teeth and skin that gleamed in the sun. Men and women alike had long hair twisted up at the nape of the neck; most wore clothing that consisted of only a few yards of red cotton fabric artistically draped about the body, as though intended more to adorn than to conceal. Emerging from a side street Bisland was startled by the passing sight of a fat old woman just out of a bath, gray hair knotted up carelessly and wearing only a towel; after a moment she was relieved to see that it was in fact an elderly Malay man in conventional businessman's attire.

In town, most of the houses were made of lime-washed brick, and most had been built without windows, to keep out as much as possible of the sun's heat and glare. The inside of Bisland's hotel offered cool, pleas-ing dimness, with cloistered arcades and a loftily vaulted dining hall where potted palms swayed in the breeze made by huge fans revolving overhead. The guests were dressed all in white, like brides or debutantes: tall men in linen suits and pith helmets; slim girls in muslin frocks, their cheeks pink from the heat and their blond hair curled in damp ringlets about their brows and necks; imposing British matrons with the haughti-ness of old Rome in their bearing, who carried themselves as the mothers and wives of conquerors. Bisland arrived during the midday meal called tiffin; young Indian waiters in tunics and turbans brought out rolls on banana leaves and platters of rice and curry that they served with spoons made from large pink shells. She sat with three soldiers, two of them young subalterns with "the sappy red of English beef still in their cheeks" on their first tour of service in the East. Rather than curry they ordered beef with beer; they mopped their faces from time to time with handker-chiefs and listened to the talk of their superior officer, who was dressed much like them but for the gold epaulets on his shoulders. The tropical sun had long ago burned the red English beef out of him, leaving him as dark and lean and dry as jerky; he drank a little iced brandy and soda, ate a bit of curry and a few pieces of fruit, and seemed to pay no attention to the heat. "He has no enthusiasms," Bisland tartly noted, "he has no interests except duty and the service, and he does not think any brown or yellow person in the least pretty or pleasant." His tone was gloomy, full of the disillusionment brought by years of colonial rule, and she could tell that the subalterns listened with respect but not enthusiasm, not wanting anything to dampen the pleasure they took in their own youthful fervor.

Bisland's room in the hotel, at it turned out, was right next to the dining hall. It was a very large but austere room, with a stone floor and the simplest of furnishings; the high iron-framed bed offered only a thin hard mattress, no top sheet, and a pillow filled with straw. One of the two doors opened directly onto the dining hall, the other onto the lawn. The doors were jalousies with wooden blinds and no locks; still, she assured herself, no one would intrude.

But that night, when Elizabeth Bisland got into bed and blew out the candle, she almost immediately thought she heard something moving inside the room. She caught her breath and listened. There was unmistakably a sound, and it was coming from somewhere below her, near the floor; it was a heavy, stealthy, animal rustling. The realization ran through her like an electric current: there must be a tiger in her room. A tiger could simply push open that unlocked door and come in from the lawn; beyond that carefully tended patch of green stretched untold expanses of jungle. It was an axiom often repeated among the British in Singapore that the local tigers killed, on average, one Chinaman per day. The sound was now moving closer to the bed. Her skin felt icy cold; she could barely breathe. Tigers, she knew, did their hunting after dark. She understood that she should not call out or make any sudden moves, but it seemed just as foolhardy to lie defenseless in bed; she did not even have a top sheet to draw over herself. The room was hot and black and perfectly still, other than that ominous scratching on the stone floor and the thudding of her heart against her ribs. Beyond the blinds of her door the hotel was just as dark and silent; for a wild moment Bisland imagined that the tiger had already eaten everyone else in the hotel. The darkness was only to the tiger's advantage, for he could see through it while she could not. She would strike a match, and that way, at least, perish in the light.

Carefully, hardly daring to move, Bisland reached for the box of matches on her bedside table. She struck a match and lit the candle, and found herself staring into the face of a huge gray rat. In New York rats were tossed into pits and killed by fox terriers as a spectator sport, but this creature would surely hold its own against any terrier. It had glossy fur and a big belly and a pointed snout, and its eyes were small and black and unnervingly calm. For a terrifying moment Bisland and the rat stared motionless at each other, each appraising the other's intentions; then the rat turned its attention back to her shoes and stockings, running its snout over each in turn, flicking its long scaly tail behind it like a riding crop. Its examination completed, the rat scurried up her dressing table and began sniffing through her hat and gloves. Bisland watched in mixed horror and relief; the rat presented no mortal danger, she knew, but there was something unspeakably terrible about seeing it paw through her clothes like that. Still, she had no intention of attacking the rat, and the rat, for its part, seemed entirely uninterested in her; so, she finally decided, the best response to an unwelcome guest was simply to ignore him. She blew out the candle and fell asleep to the sound of rustling silk.

THE NEXT DAY ELIZABETH BISLAND and the other three passengers from the *Thames* hired a carriage to take them to the bungalow of the local chief of police, a personal friend of the blond from Oxford. They drove through the hills beyond the town, passing the governor's residence, an immense white palace built by Indian convict laborers on the site of a former nutmeg plantation. The earth along the roadside was a deep red, the trees above it a bright green, and overhead was a sky like blue lacquer; far below them the beaches were frilled with white foam, and palm trees leaned over the water, Narcissus-like, to see their own reflections. Everything around her radiated a brilliance and intensity that she had only ever seen before in precious stones. It was in Singapore that Bisland noticed for the first time how in the tropics the nervous system seemed to become heightened, like a substance expanded by heat: the eyes able to perceive undreamed-of possibilities of hue, the skin sensitive to the faintest movements of the air, the sense of smell so acute that the fragrance of even distant flowers seemed as strong as if they were held in the hand.

The chief of police was dressed in white and was himself as lean and brown as all of the longtime British officers in Singapore; he gave his personal waiter instructions for the tea service in fluent Malay. It was said that no other Englishman in Singapore could equal the police chief in his knowledge of the Malay language, and as a result part of his mandate was to conduct negotiations with the sultan of Jahore whenever the potentate was unhappy about something. None of the chief's subordinates could understand what he said while he was in consultation with the sultan, but he always returned with the desired concessions and was thus presumed to speak the language convincingly and with eloquence. "He has learned in his score of years in the East great gentleness of voice and manner," Bisland would later write, "but underneath it is felt at once the iron texture of this man whom the natives regard with undisguised respect and fear." He was, after all, the man to whom the power of colonial discipline had been entrusted on this island, who possessed the keys to the prisons, who had at his disposal the bamboo canes used for flogging those thought to have disobeyed the Crown's rule.

After a pleasant tea with the police chief, Bisland and the others visited the nearby botanical gardens and then spent a few hours wandering through the town's shops and museums before returning to the ship. In the harbor, a flotilla of native canoes clustered around the *Thames,* their owners offering passengers deals on shells, pineapples, parakeets, monkeys, and other native species; the shell boats were packed with specimens as carefully arranged and attractively displayed as those in a museum case. Some of the smaller canoes contained Malay children dressed in breechcloths, who called up to the ship for coins. "Massa, massa, massa!" they cried in their broken English. "Now, massa! I dive very good, massa!" Some of the *Thames*'s passengers, Elizabeth Bisland among them, had earlier changed a few shillings into native currency, which they now flung by the handful into the waters of the harbor. Bisland delighted in watching the native children "plunge over after these with little splashings like frogs, and wiggle down swiftly to the bottom, growing strange and wavering of outline and ghostly green as they sink. They are wonderfully quick to seize the glinting coin before it touches the sands below, and come up wet, shining, and showing their white teeth. We play this game until the whistle blows, and then sail away."

The *Thames* left Singapore at four-thirty in the afternoon. An hour later the ship was steaming along the palm-fringed coast when up on deck Elizabeth Bisland heard a sudden cry and the sounds of a struggle. She caught a glimpse of the naked back of a young Chinese man with hands manacled behind him; the man tried to wrest himself from a sail-or's grip, and then suddenly, shockingly, he darted to the side of the ship and threw himself overboard. He was a Chinese prisoner, Bisland learned, convicted of forgery, who was being transported to Penang to face the punishment of the native authorities. (In Penang's prisons inmates received no food, and had to depend on the charity of loved ones to keep from starving to death. "If I feed them," the local sultan was said to have remarked, "my whole country will want to go to jail.") Almost as soon as the prisoner plunged into the sea the ship's engines were reversed and a life buoy thrown overboard, but he did not reappear. Long seconds ticked by, the *Thames*'s crew scanning the horizon like seamen on a whaler watching for the telltale plume of spray. Finally a cry went up: in the distance one of the sailors had seen the faint outline of a head bobbing up from the surface and moving rapidly toward the shoreline some four miles in the distance. Evidently the prisoner was a very strong swimmer, and something of a magician besides, for he had managed, while in the water, to slip his handcuffs. A lifeboat full of cheering Lascar sailors, under the command of a "calm and dominant" third officer, was lowered into the water and sent out in pursuit. The sailors rowed in unison, their oars cutting through the placid sea; from the deck of the *Thames,* Bisland watched the dash of the lifeboat slowly converge with the dot of the swimmer. In the distance she could make out some doubling back and forth by the lifeboat, presumably as the officer shouted commands at the man in the water, and then an oar raised menacingly overhead, until at last the fugitive submitted to being pulled into the boat. The trip back to the *Thames* took a good deal longer than the trip out, lacking, as it did, the thrill of the chase.

Elizabeth Bisland was among those standing by the gangway when the Chinese prisoner was brought onto the ship. One of the Lascars gripped him by his pigtail as they mounted the stairs, displaying the beaming self-satisfaction of a fisherman holding up a prize catch for a crowd's approval. The prisoner was naked and shivering, Bisland observed, and wore an expression of stolid despair. He was taken somewhere below, and she never saw him again.

The *Thames* sailed on through clear blue waters toward Penang. Sailors began to drape festive bunting around the ship; down in the galley the cooks were preparing plum cake. It was Christmas Eve.

DECEMBER 23–25, 1889
Hong Kong to Canton

Nellie Bly had five days to spend in Hong Kong while she waited for the steamship *Oceanic* to depart, and though she wanted nothing more than to be setting off for Yokohama, she resigned herself to a few more rounds of sightseeing. The captain of the *Oceanic,* William Smith, came to her hotel to introduce himself; he was a youthful-looking forty-year-old Canadian, tall, slim, and handsome with deep blue eyes and a light brown mustache, and Bly laughed to herself, thinking of the heavyset, gray-bearded man she had envisioned. Captain Smith took her on a jinrikisha ride into the hills outside of town to see "Happy Valley," the beautifully wooded hillside cemetery open to people of all faiths—Presbyterians and Episcopalians lying next to Fire Worshipers, Muslims by Methodists—the shaded walks and beautifully planted shrubs and flowers giving a feel less of a cemetery than a public park; they rode back to town through some of the most densely crowded sections of Hong Kong, where the inhabitants reminded Bly of ants swarming over a lump of sugar.

By her second day in Hong Kong, Bly was already tired of the usual tourist whirl and looking for something more substantive. She was well aware that the Chinese Exclusion Act had sharply restricted Chinese immigration to the United States, and she wanted, she said, "to see all of them I could while in their land. Pay them a farewell visit, as it were!" She returned to the offices of the Occidental and Oriental Steamship Company, where she booked passage to the nearby city of Canton on the *Powan,* a river steamer of the Hong Kong, Canton & Macao Steam-boat Company. The O&O travel agent escorted Bly to the ship (surely not a courtesy extended to many patrons) and placed her in the charge of the *Powan*'s commander, Captain Goggin, a very large, red-faced American with a surprisingly soft voice, who greeted her and welcomed her aboard. Bly looked at the captain's immense round body, his red face embedded in his shoulders and chest apparently without benefit of a neck, and decided that she had never met a fatter man; for a moment she was taken with a wild, unkind inclination to laugh, but then she thought about how pleasant and appealingly bashful Captain Goggin seemed to be, and she thought, too, about herself, and how sensitive she was about her personal appearance:

I have always said to critics who mercilessly write about the shape of my chin, or the cut of my nose or the size of my mouth, and such personal attributes that can no more be changed than death can be escaped: "Criticize the style of my hat or my gown, I can change them, but spare my nose, it was born on me." Remembering this, and how nonsensical it is to blame or criticize people for what they are powerless to change, I pocketed my merriment, letting a kindly feeling of sympathy take its place.

Captain Goggin politely excused himself and left to prepare for the ship's departure. At six o'clock that evening—Christmas Eve—the *Powan* set sail for Canton, some ninety miles up the Pearl River, where it would make port the following morning. The *Powan* was a broad white-painted ship with the multiple arcaded decks of an American riverboat, flying the Union Jack and the white St. Andrew's cross of the Hong Kong, Canton & Macao house flag. Bly visited below decks, where hundreds of Chinese passengers shared a single cabin. The room was large and noisy and reeked of the distinctive smell of opium, something like gunpowder and flowers and the sweaty musk of a horse after a run. Thick clouds of gray smoke hung above the passengers who sat cross-legged and crouching on the floor, reading, talking, playing fan-tan, cooking rice, and brewing tea; some of them even managed to stretch out and sleep amid the clamor. Like immigrants in the steerage of transatlantic steamships, the Chinese passengers had to supply their own beds (really little more than bits of straw matting) and their own food as well. An English traveler on the *Powan* would later write: "These ships carry, each trip, from five hundred to two thousand Chinamen, and the monthly circulation between Hongkong and Canton amounts to over one hundred thousand pigtails. This enables the Company, who practically have a monopoly of the business, to pay a very handsome dividend."

Upstairs, the first-class passengers were served dinner, which was delicious but memorable less for the food than for the swords and rifles that hung from all the walls of the saloon; a sword hung in each cabin as well, and Bly was informed that the captain had a pistol in his bunk. Several years earlier, a band of Chinese pirates had come aboard the *Powan* as passengers, and at a prearranged signal had murdered the crew—thirteen in all—and taken possession of the ship. Still, Bly and the others were assured, there had been no trouble since the company took the precaution of providing weapons for the crew and the first-class passengers; more-over, after nightfall the Chinese cabin would be sealed off from the rest of the ship behind an iron gate guarded by an armed sentry.

After dinner Bly went up and sat by herself on the top deck. Almost imperceptibly the *Powan* made its way up the Pearl River. There was no moon; beyond the water, unseen rice paddies slid by in the darkness. The only sound was the lapping of the waves against the hull; to her that was the most soothing and restful sound in the world, and listening to it she was able to set aside, if only temporarily, thoughts about rivals and itin-eraries and time clocks and allow herself a rare moment of lyrical reflec-tion:

> To sit on a quiet deck, to have a star-lit sky the only light above or about, to hear the water kissing the prow of the ship, is, to me, paradise. They can talk of the companionship of men, the splen-dor of the sun, the softness of moonlight, the beauty of music, but give me a willow chair on a quiet deck, the world with its worries and noise and prejudices lost in distance, the glare of the sun, the cold light of the moon blotted out by the dense black-ness of night. Let me rest, rocked gently by the rolling sea, in a nest of velvety darkness, my only light the soft twinkling of the myriads of stars in the quiet sky above; my music, the sound of the kissing waters, cooling the brain and easing the pulse; my companionship, dreaming my own dreams. Give me that and I have happiness in its perfection.
>
> But away with dreams. This is a work-a-day world and I am racing Time around it.

The *Powan* anchored in Canton before daybreak. The Chinese pas-sengers, their cabin unbarred, disembarked at first light, but the first-class passengers stayed behind to have breakfast and await the arrival of their tour guide. He turned out to be a stout and prosperous-looking older man who introduced himself as Ah Cum and wished them all a merry Christmas. Ah Cum had founded the tour business in Canton more than twenty years earlier, and now he was one of the most well-known men in the city, sought out as a guide, as a British military officer in Bombay once noted, by "princes and statesmen" and "most of the names which are household words in Europe." He wore beaded black shoes and dark blue leggings, and a short quilted silk jacket over a stiffly starched blue tunic. Beneath a round black cap his pigtail, or queue, stretched down his back. He spoke fluent English, having been educated in an American mission in Canton until the age of fourteen, and his manner was stately and dignified. But despite his prosperity, his proficiency in English, his acquaintance with distinguished men from all over the world, he himself had never set foot outside his own city: like Henry David Thoreau and Concord, Ah Cum had traveled widely in Canton.

Ah Cum had arranged for sedan chairs to await their arrival on the pier. The chairs to be used by the members of the tour group were made of plain willow and rested on raw wooden poles; Ah Cum's chair, on the other hand, was all black, the cover draped with black silk with tassels at the bottom and the poles made of black wood finished with brass knobs. The difference in appearance was striking, like a row of hackney cabs lined up behind a millionaire's gleaming black-lacquered private carriage, and all the more so because the tour group's chair bearers wore dark blue shirts and trousers while Ah Cum's had outfits of crisp white linen gaily trimmed in red. Three men carried each sedan chair, two to hold the poles in the front and one in the back. Over time Bly began to notice that one of the bearers at the front of her chair was having trouble with the strap that helped to keep the pole on his shoulder. The strap wrapped around the base of his neck, and the skin there had been inflamed by the constant rubbing; it worried her and she watched the spot all day, wondering if it would blister. Many times during the day coolie number two (as she came to think of him) stopped to shift the position of the strap, each time turning around to indicate with agitated hand gestures that Bly was sitting too far to one side or the other. "As a result," she wrote, "I made such an effort to sit straight and not to move that when we alighted at the shops I would be cramped almost into a paralytic state. Before the day was over I had a sick headache, all from thinking too much about the comfort of the Chinamen."

From the pier the tour group plunged into the narrow streets of Canton, with Ah Cum leading the way. The streets twisted and turned with no discernible regularity or pattern, and following them visitors to the city inevitably felt themselves entering a labyrinth in which every turn seemed to lead away from the exit. There was Longevity Street, Bright Cloud Street, Street of the Ascending Dragon, Street of One Hundred Grandsons, Street of Nine Fold Blessings, Street of One Thousand Fold Peace. The group rode over a bridge across a dull, muddy stream to a little island called Shameen, where the foreign residents of Canton lived, through an entryway guarded by policemen. No Chinese were allowed on Shameen without a pass; at nine o'clock each night a trumpet sounded, a cannon was fired, all of the island's gates were closed, and, in the words of the United States Consul General in Hong Kong, "the foreigner lies down to sleep as safe as though he were in Hong Kong or New York."

Unlike the rest of Canton, Shameen was green and quiet, the paved roadway, shaded by banyan trees, winding past handsome brick houses with small, well-kept gardens. "Having it entirely under their own control," a British missionary in China wrote of the island, "the residents have made roads and planted trees, and made it look as much like a piece of England as they possibly could." They passed an Anglican church, a boathouse, a bicycle track, an athletic club with several tennis courts behind it. Soon Ah Cum had brought them to an official-looking two-story building of brick and stucco, and seeing it, Bly caught her breath for a moment: there, over the gateway in front of the American consulate, the American flag was flying. This was the first time she had seen the flag

Riding in a sedan chair from Shameen into Canton

since leaving New York, and it felt like unexpectedly running into an old friend among a crowd of strangers in a distant city; a sense of pride welled up in her, and also anger at the many slights and insults she had felt from the British among whom she had traveled, anger at how easily they claimed the right to rule the world, and especially at how they looked at the United States as an embarrassing younger brother, overgrown and clumsy and with little education or culture, who too often had to be brought into line. It was strange, she thought, but the farther she went from home the more loyal to her own country she felt. She would hear nothing more against it. Removing her cap, Bly announced to the rest of the group:

"That is the most beautiful flag in the world, and I am ready to whip anyone who says it isn't."

No one said a word. With some satisfaction she noticed that one of them, an Englishman, glanced at the Union Jack flying over the nearby British consulate, but furtively, as if he was afraid to let her see.

AH CUM LED THE GROUP back into the center of Canton. It was a city of more than a million inhabitants, where the main streets were no more than twelve feet wide, the side streets barely allowed the passage of sedan chairs, and the alleys were so narrow that when two people met one of them had to step into a doorway to let the other go by. Horses were unknown on these streets; everything that had to be moved was carried on human shoulders. Thin vertical signs of crimson and gold hung in front of the storefronts, while overhead, awnings stretched along both sides of the street, blocking out the sun; Bly thought at first that she was being carried through the aisles of some great indoor market and was astonished to realize that they were actually outdoors. There was a powerful smell of standing water and rotting fish and decaying vegetables and garbage swept by shopkeepers into the street. Some of the streets were devoted to a single industry, full of jade merchants, silk manufacturers, coffin makers one after another; others were a medley of food stalls selling candy and peanuts and little yellow bean cakes, fishmongers with tubs of live fish in front, butchers' shops that displayed not only pigs and chickens and ducks but also storks and snakes and rats preserved in brine, and, most disturbing to Western eyes, skinned dogs trussed up like roast pigs. (To the shocked tourists among his parties Ah Cum quietly but firmly defended traditional Chinese practices; when asked, for instance, why Chinese women bound their feet he replied simply that European women pinched their waists, which was far more injurious.) Some of the larger and more well-kept curio shops catered exclusively to foreign visitors and were overseen by proprietors with the tact and persuasive powers of diplomats. Still, foreigners were something of a rarity on the streets of Canton, women especially, and often men rushed out of the shops to look at Bly as she passed by; unexpectedly, the Cantonese women seemed very taken with her gloves, some of them bold enough actually to reach out and touch them, gazing in wonder at clothing meant to be worn on the hands.

Soon the group had arrived at a pottery where two women were arranging half-dried pots into rows. Ah Cum instructed the group to dismount from their sedan chairs, and he led them behind the pottery and through a crooked back alleyway that opened into another yard, no more than seventy-five feet long by twenty-five feet wide. This, Ah Cum told them, was Canton's execution ground. Here those condemned to death knelt before the executioner with arms folded and neck extended, much as they might have, under other circumstances, kowtowed before the emperor. Bly noticed that the earth in one section of the yard was colored red.

"It's blood," Ah Cum said, scuffing at the ground with his beaded black shoe. "Eleven men were beheaded here yesterday." Ordinarily, he explained, ten or more criminals were executed at a time; each year some four hundred prisoners were killed. In a single year of the Taiping Rebellion, 1855, more than fifty thousand rebels had been beheaded on that narrow strip of earth; the smell of death was said to have been discernible from half a mile away.

While Ah Cum was talking, Bly noticed some wooden crosses leaning up against a high stone wall; imagining that the crosses were used in religious ceremonies before the executions, she asked Ah Cum about them. When women were condemned to death, he told her, they were bound to those crosses before being cut into pieces. This form of execution was called *ling-chi,* in which the body was sliced apart with a sword, starting with fleshy parts like thighs and breasts, then proceeding to nose and ears, fingers and toes, on and on until only the bleeding trunk remained; in the hands of a skilled executioner the procedure was performed so quickly and deftly that the victim was dismembered and disemboweled while still alive. Male prisoners, said Ah Cum, were beheaded unless they had been convicted of especially serious crimes such as multiple murder or patricide, in which case they were subjected to *ling-chi,* given the death of a woman, to bring them greater dishonor. He asked, "Would you like to see some heads?"

Bly assumed that Ah Cum's question was rhetorical, that he was exaggerating for effect; New York tour guides were renowned for the highly colored tales they told to out-of-town tourists. "Certainly," she replied, affecting a casual tone, "bring on your heads."

Ah Cum indicated that she should give a bit of money to a man standing nearby. Bly did so, and without a word he went over to a large earthen jar and reached in and pulled out a human head. It was an unexpected and gruesome sight, but Bly did not record her reaction to it, noting only, "Chinamen are very indifferent about death; it seems to have no terror for them."

Not far from the execution ground was the jail, where Bly was surprised to see the cell doors left open. Inside, the prisoners had thick, heavy wooden boards fastened around their necks like collars; the boards prevented them from ever lying down or resting their heads on the floor, which inevitably led to exhaustion and, in most cases, death, and they stared at the visitors with glassy, uncomprehending eyes. Bly no longer felt surprised at the unbarred doors; there was no need, she understood now, for locking them. By the jail was the courthouse, an imposing stone building where the group was shown various instruments of punishment and torture, lengths of split bamboo for caning, thumbscrews, pulleys on which prisoners were hanged by their thumbs, each device seemingly more brutal and ingenious than the next. In a small sitting room she was introduced to some judges who appeared to be gambling at fan-tan, while in another room several more judges lounged about smoking opium. Bly made no secret of her shock at what she was seeing, and though she did not mention his response, Ah Cum might well have noted that the opium being smoked by the judges had likely been transported to China on a Peninsular and Oriental ship, much like the one on which Bly herself had arrived in Hong Kong.

The P&O's history, in fact, was intimately bound up with the opium trade, and indeed the company's early expansion into the Far East had been subsidized by a British government looking for efficient means of bringing to China the opium produced in colonial India. At the time

China was almost entirely self-sufficient, having—as the Englishman in charge of the Chinese customs service once remarked—"the best food in the world, rice; the best drink, tea; and the best clothing, cotton, silk, fur," not to mention world-class porcelain, silk, lacquer ware, wallpaper, objets d'art, and handwoven cloth said to rival anything produced by the new mechanized looms of Lancashire. Opium was about the only product that the Chinese wanted and could not provide for themselves, and Great Britain needed it to make up the country's balance-of-payment deficit with China: the opium smoked in Canton would pay for the tea drunk in London. In 1838 the viceroy of Hunan estimated the number of opium smokers in China to be four million (some estimates put the number at twice that), and that year, under the leadership of an aggressive new high commissioner, Chinese authorities began arresting thousands of opium smugglers, brokers, pushers, and addicts. When in 1839 China confiscated and burned chests of opium worth more than £2 million, Great Britain declared war.

It was a war, lamented the educator and historian Thomas Arnold, "so wicked as to be a national sin of the greatest possible magnitude," and he beseeched his countrymen, "Cannot anything be done by petition or otherwise to awaken men's minds to the dreadful guilt we are incurring?" The answer, apparently, was no. Not long after the declaration of war a remarkable flotilla appeared on the Chinese coast, consisting of three 74-gun warships, two 46-gun frigates, five 28-gun frigates, eight corvettes with ten to eighteen guns apiece, and four armed steamers provided by the East India Company, plus twenty-seven transport ships carrying 3,600 soldiers. Against them the Chinese sent out a makeshift army recruited in large part from unemployed tea porters and a fleet consisting of Chinese junks and rented fisherman's boats. The outcome was inevitable, and when the Opium War was concluded in 1842, the Treaty of Nanking gave Great Britain ownership of Hong Kong in perpetuity and opened up five Chinese ports—Canton among them—to British trade.

Though opium remained officially prohibited, after its military defeat the Chinese government could no longer enforce its own drug laws. Traveling in China in 1869, the American William Perry Fogg (the namesake, it was sometimes claimed, of Jules Verne's own Phileas Fogg) noted that Great Britain had "forced the accursed drug upon the Chinese at the cannon's mouth. The Emperor of China, when asked to license its sale, replied in words that should mantle the cheek of every Englishman with shame. 'It is true,' said he, 'that I cannot prevent the introduction of the flowing poison. Gain-seeking and corrupt men will, for profit and sensuality, defeat my wishes, but nothing will induce me to derive a revenue for the vice and misery of my people.' " Fogg concluded disgustedly, "So Christian England deals with heathen China!"

It was impossible to tour Canton without visiting some Buddhist temples; the city had more than eight hundred, the most popular being the Temple of Horrors, located on the Street of Benevolence and Love. Old, sick, palsied beggars cried for alms as the group ascended its stone steps; inside, a courtyard was crowded with peddlers, gamblers, and fortune-tellers, and, oddly, with dentists who advertised their experience by displaying long strings of extracted molars, looking like strange tribal necklaces or the vertebrae of some immense reptile. Inside the temple, a row of brick sheds with wire netting in front displayed carvings representing the punishments of the Buddhist hell that awaited sinners: one man was being sawed in half lengthwise, from his head to his feet; another was strapped to the ground with his feet in the air while a demon bastinadoed him; others were being stabbed with knives, hacked to pieces with swords, boiled in oil.

Later Ah Cum took the tour group to a park with a few feeble, stunted trees in it, where thin black pigs rooted energetically in the ground. They walked through the Gate of Equity into a large quadrangle that looked something like a railroad cattleyard, with long rows of low whitewashed buildings. The buildings were divided into 11,616 cells, each about five and a half feet long by three and a half feet wide and containing one low board for a bed and a slightly higher one for a desk. This was the Examination Hall, where every three years more than eleven thousand students ("all male," Bly noted tartly) underwent the demanding three-day examination in Confucian texts that earned a few of them—sometimes no more than 150—a highly coveted job in the civil service; the many thousands who failed would face another three years of study. Afterward they ate lunch in a nearby temple, to the beat of a tom-tom and the shrill of a pipe; it was, Ah Cum told them, the Temple of the Dead. Not far from the temple he ushered the group past a high wall, where an unexpectedly bucolic sight lay on the other side: a sheet of black water undisturbed by even a breath of wind, in the distance low overhanging trees and a small phalanx of long-legged white storks. It was a pretty scene but also somehow mournful, and as they headed back to the *Powan,* Bly was conscious of what she described as "an inward feeling of emptiness." She supposed that the feeling arose from her regret about not being in New York for Christmas dinner, but there was no denying that it had been a long, difficult day; Ah Cum had led her through a world of beheadings, torture, addiction, destitution, and damnation, her Virgil on a guided journey through a kind of hell, though this journey, unlike Dante's, took place not during Easter Week but on Christmas Day, and this hell was aboveground and all too real.

NELLIE BLY'S CHRISTMAS, *The World* informed its readers, "will be pleasantly spent in Hong Kong." She might even find some turkey and plum pudding, as "there are enough Europeans and Americans to give the good old Yule festival a friendly introduction into the land of the tea chests and red-tongued dragon." A cablegram had been sent to her care of the American consul in Hong Kong, conveying best wishes from the entire *World* staff for a merry Christmas and a happy New Year. As for the readers of *The World,* they "may devote their Christmas to figuring out Nellie Bly's time."

The readers seemed to need no such encouragement, as thousands of guesses continued to pour into the *World* offices each day, some with accompanying letters explaining the methods used to arrive at them. On Staten Island, a reader who signed herself simply "Mrs. C." submitted her guess according to a personal numerology that Joseph Pulitzer himself might have appreciated. "I have been waiting for the 8th of December before guessing on the Nellie Bly tour," wrote Mrs. C., "that date being the anniversary of my wedding day, and No. 88 being the number of the house in New York City where I spent many happy days after the wedding. I have ever since that time called the figure 8 my lucky number, and will try and see how near it will bring me luck in this contest." John J. Blair, a teacher in Winston, North Carolina, reported that forty-three of the eighth- and ninth-grade students in his school were "deeply interested in Miss Bly's trip around the world"; each had made a guess about the exact time in which she would complete her journey, and from those forty-three guesses the average time had been calculated and turned into a single guess. "It was their wish that I, their teacher, should use the guess," Mr. Blair wrote, "and it is needless to say, so great is my confidence in their guessing abilities, that I am looking forward with great pleasure to my trip to Europe next summer."

DECEMBER 26–28, 1889

Hong Kong

After returning from Canton, Nellie Bly still had three days to spend in Hong Kong, and she occupied her time as best she could. One day she went up Victoria Peak, the highest mountain on the island; visitors took a newly opened elevated tramway part of the way up the mountain and then rode in sedan chairs to the top. At a distance of nearly two thousand feet the hundreds of junks and sampans that dotted the bay looked like toy ships in a child's bathtub. The view, though, was said to be even better at night: after dark each of the ships set out its lantern and the black water of the bay glimmered like a sky filled with stars, so that looking down from above, one seemed to be suspended between two heavens.

In town Bly visited the Chinese shops of the Queen's Road; entering each one she felt a little thrill of pleasure at the gold and silver jewelry, the ivory carvings, the painted fans and sandalwood boxes displayed on the shelves. She couldn't help but feel greedy, but she confined herself to only a few purchases. In one of the jewelry shops she had a pin specially made for her, a narrow rectangle—it looked to her something like a slip from a Chinese laundry—imprinted with Chinese ideograms that translated as *Success to your novel enterprise*. Elsewhere she found a huge-legged Chinese temple chair, finished in brass and brilliant red lacquer, that she would carry with her all the way back to New York; by this time, with few connections remaining on her trip, she had clearly given up her intention of traveling with only a single bag. In another shop she was surprised and delighted to find packs of chewing gum for sale, and she bought enough to last for the remainder of her journey. (*The World*'s Excursion Editor had assured Nellie Bly's young admirers in Mount Vernon, "girls, she does not chew gum," but in fact she was an inveterate gum chewer and sought it out wherever she could on her travels.)

At last December 28 arrived and Bly was able to board the Occidental and Oriental steamship *Oceanic*—the very same ship on which Elizabeth Bisland had sailed west from San Francisco—scheduled to arrive in Yokohama, Japan, on January 2, the forty-ninth day of her trip. She would have, maddeningly, five days to wait in Yokohama before the *Oceanic* set sail again for San Francisco. On board Bly was relieved to hear that her monkey had been safely transferred to the *Oceanic* from the P&O ship *Oriental*. Finding the stewardess, Bly asked her about the monkey. The stewardess replied drily, "We have met."

Bly was now alarmed to see that the stewardess's arm was bandaged from wrist to shoulder. "What did you do?" she asked.

"I did nothing but scream," the stewardess replied; "the monkey did the rest."

DECEMBER 31, 1889
East China Sea

Before the *Oceanic* was launched in 1871, the partners of the White Star line had sent a letter to the ship's first captain, Digby Murray, containing this stern instruction: "The most rigid discipline on the part of your officers should be observed, whom you will exhort to avoid at all times convivial intercourse with passengers, or with each other, and only such an amount of communication with the former as is demanded by a necessary and businesslike courtesy." Four years later, though, the White Star chartered the *Oceanic* to a new steamship line, the Occidental and Oriental Steamship Company, and by the late 1880s its captain and crew were renowned for the conviviality and good humor they brought to their ship, qualities that were never more in evidence than on New Year's Eve. Early that evening, Nellie Bly and the other first-class passengers sat with several of the *Oceanic*'s officers in the Social Hall, talking and laughing and telling stories. Captain Smith brought a tabletop organette down to the Social Hall, and he and the ship's doctor took turns cranking out tunes on it. A passenger from Yokohama taught everyone an amusing song with the simplest of lyrics: "Sweetly sings the donkey when he goes to grass, sweetly sings the donkey when he goes to grass, Ee-ho! Ee-ho! Ee-ho!" Bly confided to Captain Smith that before he had arrived at her hotel in Hong Kong she had pictured him as a short, stout old man with an iron-gray beard. "You were so different from what I imagined you would be," she told him.

"And I could not believe you were the right girl, you were so unlike what I had been led to believe," he said with a laugh. "I was told that you were an old maid with a dreadful temper. Such horrible things were said about you that I was hoping you would miss our ship."

Later in the evening everyone repaired to the dining hall, where the purser had punch and champagne and oysters waiting for them. At midnight—eight bells aboard a ship—everyone rose and sang "Auld Lang Syne" with champagne glass in hand, and as the last notes died out they shook hands all around and toasted the start of a new year and a new decade. Not long after midnight the female passengers retired, and Bly went to sleep happily lulled by the sounds of the men singing "familiar negro melodies" in the smoking room beneath her cabin—among those familiar melodies, perhaps, "Nelly Bly" by Stephen Foster, the song that a Pittsburgh office boy happened once to be humming to himself as a girl waited downstairs for a newspaper editor to give her a new name: a girl with few prospects, who had spent years helping her widowed mother support her family, and one day, unexpectedly, had impressed that editor with a letter she wrote, and who could scarcely have dreamed that half a decade later she would be traveling on a steamship on the East China Sea in a dress made just for her, with countless thousands eagerly awaiting her return.

CHAPTER 14

The Mysterious Travel Agent

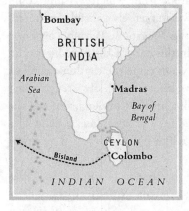

Bombay

BRITISH
INDIA

Arabian
Sea

Madras

Bay of
Bengal

CEYLON

Bisland

Colombo

INDIAN OCEAN

JANUARY 1–8, 1890
*Colombo, Ceylon, to
Aden, Yemen*

In Ceylon, on the first day of
the new year, Elizabeth Bisland
boarded the Peninsular and Oriental
steamship *Britannia,* bound for Brindisi, Italy. Like the *Victoria,* on
which Nellie Bly had sailed east
from Brindisi to Ceylon, the *Britannia* was one of the P&O's "Jubilee"
steamships, launched by the company in 1887 to commemorate the fifti-
eth anniversary of Queen Victoria's coronation. It was a single-screw
steamship with two funnels and four masts, large enough to accommodate 410 passengers and four thousand tons of cargo. Each of the passengers was provided with his or her own bamboo lounging chair, little
table, and tea service for the indispensable ceremony of five o'clock tea.
Three times a week, Bisland learned, the ship's band played for dancing
on deck; the other evenings were filled with *tableaux vivants* and private
theatricals and fancy balls. The days on the water were long and, other
than the occasional cricket match on the afterdeck, uneventful. The sea
rose and fell not in waves, but in steady, almost imperceptible exhala-

tions. Sometimes, toward the end of the day, rosy clouds floated up from the horizon. They were sailing now in the regions that early mapmakers had believed were inhabited by dragons; as far as she could tell, none lurked in these waters, though sometimes a whale surfaced to send up a jet of shining spray, leaving a long green ribbon of wake behind it. Occasionally schools of fish with wings of film rose into the path of the ship, then flitted away like flocks of sparrows. But day after day, little marked the passing of the hours but the coming and going of the light.

Eventually the air became drier, the hills dotting the distant shoreline not as green. This was the Gulf of Aden, along the southern coast of Yemen. Late in the afternoon of January 8, the *Britannia* entered Aden harbor and cast anchor to await recoaling. The harbor was surrounded by jagged masses of black rock. Aden might be a barren volcanic outcropping, but as a coaling station and harbor from which warships could guard the entrance to the Red Sea it was immensely valuable and therefore, Bisland observed, "like Hong Kong, Singapore, Penang, Ceylon—like everything much worth having in this part of the world—it is an English possession." From across the water came the rhythmic clink of sledge and drill and the chants of native laborers endlessly strengthening the town's fortifications; they worked, a visitor to Aden had noted the previous year, "with the persistent industry of coral insects building a reef that shall endure for ever." A white-hulled man-of-war slowly steamed out of the harbor on its way down the African coast to the Transvaal, where the Portuguese were threatening British trade at Delagoa Bay. Near the shore local boys dived for coins tossed by tourists, darting beneath the surface like minnows in search of the slowly sinking money. With their piping broken English and their playful gyrations in the water, they reminded her of the divers she had seen in Singapore just two weeks before. The skin of these boys was darker, and glistened with thick oil meant to ward off sharks, but otherwise they seemed exactly the same.

In the early evening Elizabeth Bisland and some of the other passengers from the *Britannia* hired a boatman to row them to shore. The landing area was separated from the beach by a long black paling; behind the fence stood a crescent of ramshackle two- and three-story stucco houses and the much larger, newly built Bank of Aden. Everything was covered by a layer of coal dust. At the landing, under a corrugated iron roof, sat a group of turbaned carriage drivers, the gharry-wallahs. The passengers hired one to take them to the Tanks, a remarkable system of ancient stone cisterns; it was, they had been told, the only sight in Aden worth seeing. The gharry was a rickety four-wheeled carriage drawn by a sleepy-looking Somali pony. They climbed up into the back of the carriage, the gharry-wallah took his seat just in front of them, and they set out on a sandy road into an astonishingly arid landscape. In three years not a drop of rain had fallen. Nothing green could live in this place; the earth was a dull gray powder that no roots could grasp. Even the rocks were cracked and faded as though withered; they were, Bisland thought, the dust and bones of a dead land.

The road wound upward from the sea to a barrier of rocks; two hundred feet above them was the British army station, a heavily fortified compound of barracks, officers' bungalows, and a telegraph office with lines to Suez, Bombay, and Durban. The carriage rattled through a black echoing pass. On the other side of the hills Aden lay on a plain at the center of a huge volcanic crater. They could see rows of low flat-topped houses made of stone and mud, lime-washed to the whiteness of snow. In the center of town the gharry-wallah stopped the carriage and they got out. On the street, piles of elephant tusks and animal hides waited to be loaded onto camels; there were sacks of coffee beans, tins of frankincense and myrrh. Indians in scarlet and gold robes hurried past, and Parsee shopkeepers wearing the coal-scuttle hats Bisland remembered from Hong Kong. Bearded Arabs gathered at tables in front of cafés, drinking coffee and smoking the water pipes called hubble-bubbles, passing the mouthpiece back and forth. At the cafés, draped in white robes like Shakespearean actors, groups of Africans sat playing dominoes. They came from countries with names that sounded to her like the lands in a children's storybook: Sudan, Zanzibar, Abyssinia. Long trains of camels sauntered by, the creatures' heavy-lidded eyes and wryly smiling mouths giving them, Bisland thought, an air of evangelical superiority. Women drew well water into tall jugs, as if posing for one of the illustrated catechisms she had been made to read as a young girl.

Her carriage passed out of the town and back into the hills. Night was coming on; the disappearing sun turned the air faintly golden-green. Soon the Tanks came into view. Peoples of antiquity had carved immense cisterns out of the tall rock wall to collect rainfall; there were perhaps fifty in all, together able to hold more than thirty million gallons of water but now as dry as a bone. Though the Tanks were the product of unimaginable labor, knowledge of their builders had been lost long ago; the idea for their creation was variously attributed to King Solomon, the Queen of Sheba, the Himyarites, the Phoenicians, the Persians. A broad stone aqueduct conducted rainwater from the surrounding hills down to the cisterns, which were built as a system of terraces so that the overflow from the upper level would fall and be collected by a lower one, and then another, and another; set into the clefts at the foot of the rocks, irregularly shaped masonry bowls stretched enormous thirsty mouths up to the rainless sky. The immense rock wall extended in a sinuous curve, like the belly of some ancient fertility goddess. Unlike the tropics, there was no evening mistiness of vision: the little flat white town in the distance, the turbaned figures in the streets, the sailboats moored on the glassy sea beyond could all be clearly made out through the deepening twilight. *The sun's rim dips; the stars rush out:* of late she often found herself thinking of the Ancient Mariner, telling his unbidden travel stories to indifferent party guests. *At one stride comes the dark.* In an instant, it seemed, the sky had turned black and the stars appeared. She had never seen a sky so thickly studded with stars; there were unimaginable myriads, stars beyond number, so plentiful that in places they became a wash of light, as from an artist's brush. Beyond these high rocks stretched the immense, lonely desert. There was nowhere on earth more distant than this, she knew, no place that could possibly be less like New York.

LATER THAT NIGHT, having returned to the ship for dinner, they hired a gharry to visit the Tanks by moonlight. The moon had risen full and white, bright enough for one to read and even see colors, bright enough to blot out the stars in the sky. In the high thin air it was possible to make out the various figures that had long been read into the shadows on the moon: a frog, a rabbit, a hunchback sitting under a tree, a woman bent over a kettle, a peasant carrying a bundle of sticks on his back. It was banished Cain, some said, made to circle the world forever for his sin, near enough to see his home but never to reach it. Near the Tanks they passed a train of camels lurching away into the desert, driven by lean Arab men draped in white—such a caravan, Bisland thought, as might have gone down into Egypt to buy grain from Pharaoh four thousand years before, with nothing changed in any way. The solemn procession moved silently on. Behind them the town was as white as a pearl in the moonlight. Slowly the Tanks rose against the sky. The group dismounted from the carriage. Their footsteps and voices echoed from the empty cisterns to the surrounding hills, though they walked lightly and spoke in awed whispers. The night was utterly still, with no leaf to rustle nor insect to cry. In the silence the world grew dreamlike and unreal. Bisland thought she would feel no surprise to come suddenly among the rocks upon a gaunt, wild-eyed Hebrew prophet clothed in skins, wrestling with the unsolvable riddles of existence. It was a night and a place for such things as that.

She walked along the Tanks in the moonlight, running her hand along the deep grooves made by some anonymous ancient carver. In her whole life she had never touched anything as old as this. Traveling by locomotive and steamship, she had been brought to the past. Here in the hills she could see for miles, past the town and all the way down to the sea. In the distance the full moon made a rippling band of light on the water; it stretched to the horizon like a silver road, and in imagination it joined with the golden road across the water that had been made by the setting sun back in San Francisco. Her new friends there had called it a sign of good fortune for her trip, and that was what she had received. She could still hear those sea lions barking at the edge of the Pacific Ocean, still see them frolicking on the rocks like playful black piglets. She had tucked that scene away inside her memory, laid it up as her family had once laid up stores of grain against an uncertain future. If she desired, she could close her eyes and see it again, just as she could see the fairy robes of the sampan boatmen, or a patch of blue prairie cornflowers, or a Chinese prayer fluttering in the air, or these ghostly Tanks. It was possible, as with a child's grab bag, to reach in anywhere and pull out a treasure; and to do so with the same sensation of wondrous delight. That was what this trip had given her—the vividness of a new world, where one was for the first time, as Tennyson had written, *Lord of the senses five,* where the light of night and day had a new meaning, where years of indifference could fall away like a dried-up husk and every sense respond with the keenness of faculties newborn. Even much later, she felt sure, not a line would have faded or grown dim; she would be able to recall every impression, every sensation, as though not an hour divided her from it.

It was well, she told herself, to have thus once really lived.

JANUARY 7–14, 1890
Pacific Ocean

The steamship *Oceanic* left Yokohama on a bright sunny Tuesday morning, with all boding well for a pleasant and, most important, rapid voyage. The chief engineer, William Allen, quickly became Nellie Bly's
strongest supporter aboard the ship. Back in November the *Oceanic* had
broken the record for the fastest eastbound Pacific crossing, having sailed
from Yokohama to San Francisco in only thirteen days and fourteen
hours, and Allen was confident that the *Oceanic* could match its record-
setting time and arrive in San Francisco on January 20, two days ahead of
schedule. Indeed, Allen was so confident, and so committed to Bly's successful return, that he ordered a rhyming couplet to be written on the
ship's engines and throughout the engine room:

> *For Nellie Bly,*
> *We'll win or die.*
> *January 20, 1890.*

Initially it seemed a safe enough prediction, for after three days at sea
the *Oceanic* was 110 miles ahead of the pace it had set in November. On
the fourth day, though, the weather turned unexpectedly foul, with tor-
rential rains and fierce winds. Some of the officers tried to reassure Bly,
predicting that the storm would last only a day, but the following day the
weather was even worse. The ship plunged through the wild, roaring sea,
buffeted by mountainous waves, rolling, pitching, the storm never letting up for even a moment. Chief Allen, who had been making the run
from Hong Kong to San Francisco for eleven years, admitted to Bly that
he had never encountered such adverse weather. Hour after hour, day
after day, the rain continued to beat down on the ship. Every day Bly
anxiously waited for noon, when the figures for the most recent 24-hour
run were posted in the dining room; each time she hoped that the ship
would have gained a few miles on the day before, and each time she was
disappointed. The *Oceanic*'s captain, William Smith, had earned the nickname "Typhoon Bill" for the skillful seamanship with which he brought
his ships safely through fearsome storms on the China seas—but even

Typhoon Bill could not maintain full speed in the face of such unrelenting wind.

As the *Oceanic* continued to make its way eastward across the Pacific, the image that had arisen during her delay in Ceylon now began to appear to Bly again, as she pictured herself arriving late at the *World* offices, the famous loser of a famous race, ashamed to show her face in the city or to hear her name spoken. "If I fail, I will never return to New York," Bly would tell the ship's officers despondently, looking at the figures for the previous day's run. "I would rather go in dead and successful than alive and behind time."

"Don't talk that way, child," Chief Allen would always reply. Bly described Allen as "a jolly story-teller, a capital singer and a popular gentleman with both sexes," and he seemed genuinely grieved by her distress. He assured Bly that he was doing everything in his power to help: he had worked the engines as they had never been worked before; he had sworn at the storm until he had no swear words left; he had even prayed—and he hadn't prayed in years—that the storm might pass over so that they could get her in to San Francisco on time.

No, it was hopeless, she would lament, just hopeless.

At this point the ship's doctor might speak up, saying in mock admonition, "Look here, Nellie Bly, if you don't stop talking so, I'll make you take some pills for your liver."

"You mean wretch, you know I can't help being blue. It's head winds and low runs—not liver!" And then she would laugh, and so would they, and Chief Allen, who always urged her to give "one glimpse of that old, jolly smile," would return to his engines content.

In this way Bly was daily coaxed out of her unhappiness.

After four days the storm still showed no signs of relenting. In foul weather everyone on a ship had to work harder, but none more than the ordinary seamen, who had to perform most of their tasks on deck, where the wind hit with the force of a battering ram and the rain stung like bees on every bit of exposed skin and every surface became dangerously slick with spray. A long storm was a kind of siege, against a powerful and implacable enemy attacking from all sides and at every hour of the day and night, and fought with little sleep and no dry clothes. It was enough to try the patience, and the nerves, of even the most experienced sailor, and as the days passed with no break in the weather the idea began to circulate among the crew that the *Oceanic* must have a Jonah aboard—nautical parlance for something, or someone, bringing bad luck to a ship. The question was apparently being extensively discussed, and much to Bly's dismay, it was reported to her that some of the sailors had suggested that the Jonah was in fact her monkey. There was even talk that the best remedy would be to throw it overboard.

Nellie Bly was herself superstitious (she readily admitted that she wore the gold ring on her left thumb as a kind of talisman), but she had never encountered a group as concerned with signs and omens as was a ship's crew. Ever at the mercy of the wind and the water, through their numerous superstitions—the received wisdom of untold generations—sailors sought to make sense of a life filled with random misfortunes. A voyage should not be begun on a Friday, or a nail driven on a Sunday. Sneezing to the left was unlucky, though sneezing to the right was not; this was apparently a very old superstition, as the Athenian general Themistocles was said to have once delayed his ships from sailing into battle for fear of the bad luck brought about by a wayward sneeze. Whistling, when done correctly, could raise a wind, but when done in a wind could bring a hurricane. Cats and ministers were very bad luck: "Always a head wind," sailors liked to say, "when a parson's aboard."

Bly discussed the issue with Chief Allen, who strongly advised her not to surrender the monkey. Just then someone nearby reminded Bly that there were two ministers aboard the *Oceanic*. Bly thought about this for a moment and then declared, in a quiet but firm voice, that if the ministers were thrown overboard she would say nothing about the monkey.

Thus, Nellie Bly reported later, her monkey's life was saved.

WHEN, IN NOVEMBER 1889, the *Oceanic* set the record for the fastest crossing from Yokohama to San Francisco—thirteen days, fourteen hours—it surpassed the record previously held by the White Star steamship *Arabic,* which in 1882 had made the run in thirteen days and twenty-one hours; and in turn the *Oceanic*'s mark would be overtaken the following year by the Pacific Mail steamship *China,* which arrived in San Francisco only twelve days and eleven hours after setting sail from Yokohama. In the latter decades of the nineteenth century, accounts were carefully kept of the fastest crossings between all major ports; record-breaking times were printed in newspapers and almanacs and were well known among the traveling public. Passengers liked the prestige that came with traveling on the fastest ships, and they wanted the shortest possible ocean voyage, despite the fact that the greater speed produced by the engines also produced greater noise and vibration throughout the ship. "It is better to be comfortable for seven days than to be miserable for six," a devotee of the older ships grumbled in 1890, but in this opinion he was decidedly in the minority.

On the North Atlantic, where most of the business was, the competition was especially intense, and a ship that made the fastest crossing was awarded the "Blue Ribbon of the Atlantic," purely an honorary title but one much coveted by steamship lines. When a particular line took the Blue Ribbon, notice was taken in the boardrooms of its rivals and plans quickly drawn up for new and even faster ships. Hulls were streamlined, boilers expanded, engine velocity increased. "To-day," a writer for *Scribner's Magazine* noted in 1891, the naval architect "is faced with a competition that did not exist in the past, and his ears are constantly assailed by the cry for higher speed; and whereas a few years ago it was a common impression that the maximum limit had been reached, we have witnessed, during the past three or four years, performances by ships, both large and small, of speeds then undreamed of." Only two decades earlier, a speed of fourteen knots was considered exceptional; by the late 1880s seventeen and eighteen were standard, and plans were being made for ships with speeds of twenty knots and higher. Modern technology was producing power that would have boggled the minds of earlier generations of seafarers: the 19,500 horsepower of a typical large steamship of the day was equivalent to an ancient galley with 117,000 men working the oars.

The *Oceanic* had been designed to burn 58 tons of coal per day at regular cruising speed; when steaming at full power it required 70. This was by any standard a huge amount, but in fact was highly economical compared to newer ships like the *Augusta Victoria,* which burned an average of 220 tons of coal per day. A *New York Times* editorial called this amount "almost appalling," but even it was modest in comparison to the latest class of ships that regularly consumed 300 tons of coal every twenty-four hours—"and if they could burn more," a correspondent for *The Cosmopolitan* wrote in 1892, "it would be gladly supplied for the sake of an extra knot or two in the day's run." On these ships, as on the railroads, speed was a product of steam, and steam was a product of fire, and fire was a product of coal. Before setting out on its voyage a passenger steamship would be loaded with hundreds of tons of coal, all of it brought aboard by means that had barely progressed since the time of the pyramids. A small coal barge pulled up alongside the steamship; a bucket was lowered from the ship, and men aboard the barge shoveled the coal into the bucket. The bucket was unloaded into the ship's hold, where trimmers delivered the coal in wheelbarrows to bunkers distributed around the ship, and then, when it was needed for burning, brought it from the bunkers to the fire room, in the lowest depths of the ship.

Though Nellie Bly constantly urged the ship's engineer to make more speed, she seems never to have actually gone down to the fire room where workers shoveled the coal that produced that speed—just as, for instance, she never went into steerage to investigate the conditions in which the passengers there had to cross the ocean, the very topic about which she had proposed to write for *The World* when she first sought a job on the paper. By this point in the journey she had essentially stopped functioning as a reporter. Gone were the curiosity, the perceptiveness, the moral sense that had been on such abundant display, for instance, during her months in Mexico, when she used her dispatches to refute all the American clichés about dirty and dangerous peasants and courageously decried official corruption and the press's complicity in perpetuating it. On her race around the world she had neither the time nor, apparently, the inclination to delve beneath surface appearances. Her most passionate and concerted attention was devoted to her own itinerary; and when that itinerary forced her to remain in a place for long, she did not seek out compelling news stories or interview local people of interest, and only reluctantly did she participate in sightseeing expeditions on which, more often than not, she was repelled by what she saw. The Hindu temples of Penang were filthy (they seemed not to have heard, Bly noted drily, that cleanliness was next to godliness); the beggars of Port Said "thrust their deformities in our faces to compel us to give money"; she was "disgusted with all we found worth seeing" in Kandy; the Chinese of Canton and Hong Kong were, in her description, "the dirtiest and shabbiest" people in the world. "The Japanese are the direct opposite to the Chinese," Bly later elaborated. "The Japanese are the cleanliest people on earth, the Chinese are the filthiest; the Japanese are always happy and cheerful, the Chinese are always grumpy and morose; the Japanese are the most graceful of people, the Chinese the most awkward; the Japanese have few vices, the Chinese have all the vices in the world; in short, the Japanese are the most delightful of people, the Chinese the most disagreeable."

Earlier in the trip Nellie Bly had rightfully objected to an Englishman making sweeping generalizations about the United States based on only a single day spent there. This was, it seemed to her, an imperial mind-set, but by the time her trip was over it was one she had claimed for herself.

THOUGH NELLIE BLY never went down to the *Oceanic*'s fire room to watch the stokers at work, plenty of passengers on other steamships did, carefully making their way down iron ladders smeared with oil to prevent corrosion, the sounds of clanging metal growing ever louder, the vibrations stronger, the air hotter with each descending level. In the fire room—or, as it was colloquially known, the stoke hole—one could see, most dramatically, the human costs of the devotion to speed. It was a vast, murky, shadowy space, the dark intermittently broken by silver cones of light from overhead lamps, the air unbearably hot and foul, swirling with smoke and reeking of sulfur. Standing before long rows of massive furnaces, stripped to the waist, their skin blackened by coal dust, dozens of stokers endlessly shoveled coal. The larger and faster steamships of the day required more boilers to deliver steam to the ship's engines, which in turn required more furnaces, making the stoke hole even hotter; the temperature inside the room often rose to 130 degrees and higher, and in at least one case was measured at 167 degrees Fahrenheit. When a stoker opened a furnace door there was a great roar and a bright, scalding tongue of flame leaped out, the furnace like a fire-breathing dragon that had to be constantly appeased. Averting his face as best he could, the stoker would toss in several shovelfuls of coal, rake them to a uniform depth for most efficient burning, remove clinkers and ashes, and then slam the door shut again. Over the course of a four-hour shift the iron shovels themselves grew hot, sometimes hot enough to blister skin; even far from a ship, one could recognize a stoker by the black lines that crisscrossed his hands like a road map, where coal dust had gotten into the blisters as they healed. The trimmers trundled in and out with their barrows, dumping the coal in piles on the iron floor; the stokers called for more coal not by shouting for it— for the shouts would go unheard in the din of the room—but by banging their shovels on the furnace doors. The heat, the fire, the sulfurous smells, the sweating, exhausted men bathed in the flickering light of the flames: it was like a scene from a vision of hell as painted by Brueghel.

Each stoker routinely shoveled two tons of coal a day, stopping every few minutes to gasp for breath under one of the gratings that carried a thin stream of fresh air down from the deck. This luxury was dispensed, though, only when the arrow on the steam gauge allowed it; when steam pressure dropped below a certain level there was no time for rest. The steam must always be kept up, for the sake of the engines and the day's run; and much of the time a member of the crew was behind the stoker shouting at him to work harder: "Shove it back! Shove it back, damn you! You mutton-headed son of a sea cook, shove it back!" The ship's engines needed more coal when operating at full power, and so conditions in the stoke hole were at their worst when the desire for speed was most intense—as when a Blue Ribbon was in sight, or, for example, when the ship's chief engineer had committed himself to bringing one of the passengers into port ahead of schedule. "These are horrible suggestions of ours," *The Engineer* magazine declared in 1890, "but, if every man connected with the management of a steamship had to work one voyage below in the fire-room or the engine-room, they would tell people who shouted for quick passage to go to Davy Jones. . . . Flesh and blood cannot stand it, and this is a solemn fact." Often, when more speed was needed, the stokers worked literally until they dropped. After a record-setting voyage by the new steamship *Majestic,* a *New York Times* article noted, "It was interesting to learn that on the trip not a single fireman had been carried out of the fire room overcome by heat," and further pointed out, "This is an altogether different state of affairs from that usual on board the greyhounds."

Typically stokers worked for four hours and then rested for eight, for the duration of the voyage. At the end of their shift, they would go up on deck for some fresh air, where, amid the passengers in crisp linen and white muslin, they stood by themselves in their dungarees, dark flannel shirts, and heavy boots: exhausted, silent, sullen creatures squinting in the daylight. Nowhere else on earth was the contrast between rich and poor so great, or so sharply delineated, as on the deck of a luxury steamer. Writing about the stokers clustered together at the end of a shift, a steamship passenger observed, "They were tough-looking characters. Their faces, blackened with coal dust, and streaked with sweat, had a dulled, animal-like look, and they seldom smiled. It was killing work." The stokers looked, in fact, very much like the men who had mined the coal they now fed to the furnaces. From digging to burning, coal—the life-blood of the nineteenth century—joined miners and stokers in a desperate cycle of misery and disease. In 1886, Dr. Hobart Amory Hare of the University of Pennsylvania published a book with the provocative title *New and Altered Forms of Disease, Due to the Advance of Civilization in the Last Half Century*. About the stokers on "the large ocean steamships" Dr. Hare noted:

> Working, as these men do, in the hold of a ship and surrounded by fires on all sides, the only ventilation coming from above, it cannot be wondered at that they strip to the waist and fairly drip with sweat, and when relieved go to the deck, there to get a whiff of fresh air, and perhaps a fatal chilling of their bodies. The mortality among these men is frightful, and the writer has been informed by ship's surgeons that few "stokers" live more than two years after entering upon their duties, provided they stay at work with fair regularity.

As early as 1860 the medical journal *The Lancet* was calling the stoke hole "a cavern of torture and a hot-bed of disease." Stokers suffered from heat stroke, muscle cramps (known at the time as "stokers' disease"), rheumatism, pneumonia, pleuritis, catarrh, and a host of other ailments. The stokers lived in a world of coal dust, and the fine gray powder that covered the houses and streets of Aden and Port Said inevitably settled into their lungs as well. Over time many stokers, like miners, developed a continuous hacking cough; those so afflicted, a medical report of the time concluded, were "dyspneic and short lived." Autopsies would find that their lungs were a mottled black and had the texture of old leather. Later the disease would be called black lung, but this was a term that had not yet been invented.

Lung disease was a slow, lingering death; another death well known among stokers was much shorter and less painful, though also of a character that medical authorities might term "occupational." The extreme heat of the furnaces caused some stokers to collapse, but others were instead driven temporarily insane, and when this occurred it was not uncommon for the delirious stoker to rush up on deck and throw himself overboard, his mind filled only with the overpowering desire to relieve the terrible heat of his body. Down he would plunge, from the top deck past the passenger decks and into the cooling sea. Sometimes, if the cry of "Man overboard!" had gone up promptly enough, the captain would order lifeboats to be sent out after the drowning man, but they were rarely able to reach him in time, for the stoker was weak and the steamship moving too fast.

JANUARY 16, 1890

Brindisi, Italy

On January 16, after eight days at sea, the Peninsula and Oriental steamship *Britannia* anchored in Brindisi, Italy. The air here had a crispness that Elizabeth Bisland recalled from autumns in New York, a bracing chill that tingled on the skin without penetrating the bones. Brindisi—the ancient Brundisium of the Romans—was a town more than twenty-five centuries old, but the buildings visible from the wharf seemed merely worn and shabby, with none of the nobility that came with great age. Seeing them, Bisland decided that she couldn't agree with the provincial official in Plutarch's *Lives,* who insisted that he would rather be first in Brundisium than second in Rome. In any case, her efforts were now directed at being the first *out* of Brundisium, as her train was scheduled to depart within the hour. Although the *Britannia* would eventually continue on from Brindisi to Portsmouth, in the south of England, the India mail train (the same train Nellie Bly had taken from Calais to Brindisi after her meeting with Jules Verne) ran straight through Italy and France, in so doing gaining five days in the delivery of the mails. With room for only twenty passengers, space on the train was always at a premium, but it was possible to reserve a berth by cabling ahead. Elizabeth Bisland had done this before boarding the *Britannia* back in Ceylon, and she did not anticipate any problems—provided, that was, that she could get her luggage off the *Britannia* and through customs on time.

This was much easier said than done. The ship was in an uproar that morning, full of noise and activity as might attend the preparations for a small infantry assault. On the top deck, steamship officers were shouting out orders to the crew, directing passengers to the appropriate ship or train or local hotel; a long line of anxious, fidgeting passengers waited with their luggage for the customs officials who had just come aboard and were beginning the process of inspecting the bags and registering them to their final destinations. Porters gathered up the checked and registered bags, hurrying them down the ship's gangway. For those passengers, like Elizabeth Bisland, traveling on the India mail train, their steamer trunks would be sealed and registered through to London. The tickets for the India mail carried these decisively worded instructions: "All baggage by this service must be registered in London through to Brindisi, and vice versa; no luggage *whatever* will be admitted into the cars, except a small handbag and a bundle of rugs. *It has been found necessary to rigidly enforce this rule.*" Once her trunk had been registered, Bisland rushed off to the train station to pick up her tickets and send a telegram back to New York.

JOHN BRISBEN WALKER received the telegram that evening. It said that Bisland would be leaving at 1:45 in the afternoon on the India mail train from Brindisi. The news was cheering, for it meant that she should be able to connect with the steamship *La Champagne* sailing from Le Havre, scheduled to arrive in New York on January 26. *The Cosmopolitan*'s business manager, A. D. Wilson, told a reporter from the *St. Louis Republic,* "The steamer is due in this city the following Sunday and the company has promised us that every effort will be made to secure a quick passage." Wilson said that he now felt confident that Bisland would win the race around the world.

"Nellie Bly, however," the reporter reminded the paper's readers, "is due in San Francisco on the 22nd of this month. It is a four days' ride to New York, which will bring her here on the same day on which Miss Bisland arrives. A few hours either way will, therefore, probably decide the race."

JANUARY 16–18, 1890
Brindisi, Italy, to Villeneuve–St. Georges, France

At the Brindisi train station Elizabeth Bisland bought her tickets and she sent her cable, and she returned to the mail train ten minutes before the scheduled departure—only to discover that her luggage was not there. Rushing back to the ship, she found the missing bags still on deck with an Italian customs official who insisted that they had not yet been properly inspected and demanded the keys from her. She protested that there was no need to examine her steamer trunk, as it was under seal to be sent straight through to England, but the customs man was adamant and she had no choice but to relent.

By now Elizabeth Bisland had been traveling for sixty-three days, and over that time various additions to her wardrobe had so enlarged the contents of her trunk that only by very careful packing, and the ship's stewardess sitting down on the lid, had she managed to shut it at all. Now she needed to unpack it all again, and out it came, the inkstand and the sewing kit and everything else, her dresses and nightdresses and underwear and slippers and shoes, the shirtwaists she had bought in San Francisco and the silk gowns she had bought in Yokohama (the "Garments of the Dawn" did not look quite as lustrous when strewn about the deck of a ship), all of it subject to the scrutiny of the customs officer. "I hope I did not forget the dignity a gentlewoman should preserve under the most trying circumstances," Bisland would later remark, "but I fancy that my tones, while low, were concentrated."

The inspection at last completed, Bisland gathered up her belongings, tossed them into the trunk pell-mell, jumped on it while she snapped the hasp, and ran off with a porter to the train with "blank despair" in her heart, as she knew that she had been detained longer than ten minutes. Fortunately she discovered that Italian trains were not bound by overly narrow interpretations of timetables, and she did manage at last to board the India mail along with "the luggage and some few tattered remnants of a once nice temper."

With her traveling bag and shawl strap safely stowed on the rack above her, Bisland settled back into her seat. She was not used to losing her temper, found it in fact deeply unsettling, and fully an hour passed before the beauty of the countryside began to have its soothing effect on her; she would, she decided, forgive the Italians because of Italy. Outside the window the Adriatic Sea was as blue as lapis lazuli and flecked with white sails. Little cottages perched as delicately as seabirds along the shore. The train rode past gray olive orchards, the trees strangely human in their gnarled grotesqueness; it was not hard for her to imagine how people who lived among olive groves had created a dryad mythology and legends of flying women transformed into trees.

In addition to the engineer and a British postal official in charge of the mails, there was one railroad employee on board, a conductor in an old blue uniform with silver buttons who attended to all the needs of the passengers, serving as porter, steward, cook, and brakeman all in one; at night he also arranged their sleeping berths, and Bisland supposed that he would perform barber duties and assist with their toilets if ever called upon to do so. At mealtimes he retired into a little galley kitchen, and from a space not much larger than a telephone box emerged with delicious soups and salads, well-cooked game, baskets of twisted Italian bread, wine, oranges, and excellent coffee. The British government, Bisland knew, subsidized the Italian government to ensure the rapid passage of the mails, but the conductor apparently had his own ideas on the matter, for at each stop along the route a little crowd of townspeople received him with affectionate enthusiasm; with an unexpected burst of animation he inquired—Bisland imagined—"after each one's kin unto the fourth and fifth generation," gave his careful attention to all the local gossip, and in turn related the information he had gathered at the previous stations. When all of the news had been disseminated he said his warm goodbyes and the train was off again.

In the afternoon of the second day the train began to climb into the mountains, and the car grew much colder. Here vineyards clung precariously to the steep hillsides, propped into place by stone dams that kept the soil from sliding downhill; villages were tucked at impossible angles into clefts in the hills. Before long a pale film of snow appeared on the ground: in scarcely more than a week she had traveled from summer to winter. She caught a glimpse of white heights outlined against blue sky and realized happily that they were approaching the Alps. Suddenly the world became black, the air filled with thundering, clattering echoes— they were passing through the Mont Cenis tunnel—and when they reemerged into daylight they were in France.

Elizabeth Bisland's plan was to take the India mail train to its stop at Villeneuve–St. Georges, a suburb less than ten miles from Paris, and there change trains for the short ride into the city. In Paris she would board another train bound for Le Havre, where the fast steamship *La Champagne* of the Compagnie Générale Transatlantique (the "French Line") was scheduled to depart the following morning, Saturday, at six o'clock. Unfortunately, the India mail train was now running behind time, and unless the French Line would agree to delay the departure of *La Champagne* there was no use in trying to reach Le Havre by then. In that event,

A. D. Wilson had devised an alternate route by which Bisland would continue on with the India mail to Calais, then ferry across the English Channel to meet the Norddeutscher Lloyd steamship *Ems,* which would be sailing from Southampton on Sunday, January 19. There was still a chance, however, that *La Champagne* would wait for her, and sometime after two o'clock that night the train conductor woke Bisland to deliver a telegram instructing her to be ready at four A.M. to board the train for Paris when the India mail arrived in Villeneuve. In Paris a special train had been arranged to take her the 142 miles to Le Havre; the Western Railroad of France estimated that its chartered train could cover the distance in three hours, about twice as fast as a regular train. If the French Line could be induced to hold *La Champagne* for even an hour, Bisland would have a real chance of making the connection. Bisland rose from her sleeping berth and dressed quietly, so as not to disturb her fellow passengers; she wrote notes of farewell to those who had been "especially courteous" and then found her seat in the darkness of the car. At four o'clock she was waiting with her veil and gloves on when the train stopped at Villeneuve–St. Georges.

The train station was nearly deserted. As Elizabeth Bisland stepped down onto the platform a young Frenchman appeared. He was, he told her, an agent from Thomas Cook and Son. He had come from Paris to meet her. He had bad news.

THE THOMAS COOK TRAVEL AGENCY had begun in 1841 when Thomas Cook, an English printer and occasional author of temperance pamphlets, organized a railway excursion from Leicester to Loughborough, having gotten the idea that travel would provide the working class with an invigorating and wholesome alternative to the evils of ale. The excursion proved a rousing success, with hundreds of paying customers, and Cook was encouraged to continue; before long he was devoting all of his time to the travel business, arranging tourist trips first throughout Great Britain, then to continental Europe, and, beginning in the 1870s, around the world. By the time of Thomas Cook's death in 1892 his company had grown into the world's largest travel agency, earning for itself the grandiose title "Booking Clerk to the Empire," an honorific that was borne out in spectacular fashion in 1884, when the company managed to transport eighteen thousand British and Egyptian troops up the Nile to relieve the besieged forces of General Charles Gordon in Khartoum, for a contractually agreed-upon price of twenty-one pounds per soldier. This, of course, was a highly unusual venture; mostly Thomas Cook & Son (as the company became known after Thomas's son John joined it in 1871) arranged group and individual tours, a service for which it became so famous that the phrase "Cook's tour" was adopted into the language. Cook & Son had offices in cities around the world that offered a wealth of services to travelers: they booked steamship and railway tickets (the tickets enclosed in a leather or cloth case with COOK'S TOURIST TICKETS embossed on the cover); arranged hotel reservations; provided accident insurance, foreign exchange, traveler's checks, and letters of credit; sold guidebooks and timetables; and gave sightseeing advice. Cook & Son opened its first Paris office in 1874, moving to larger quarters in August 1889; the office was managed by a M. Georges Lemoinne and had a staff of four employees. Presumably it was one of these men (the Cook's agent never identified himself) who met Elizabeth Bisland at the Villeneuve–St. Georges train station.

The steamship *La Champagne,* the agent told Bisland, would not wait for her. He had done everything he could to get the ship to wait, but the French government simply would not allow it. *La Champagne* was a mail ship and had to keep to its schedule. He was very sorry. Having delivered his message he bade her farewell and good luck, and disappeared.

Elizabeth Bisland had no reason to doubt the agent's word. After all, Thomas Cook & Son was the world's most well-known and reliable travel agency—when John Brisben Walker needed a westbound trip around the globe to be arranged at a moment's notice he went to Cook & Son, just as the editors of *The World* had earlier gone to them for Nellie Bly's eastbound trip. But in fact none of what the Cook's agent had said was true: the steamship *did* wait for her.

As Elizabeth Bisland was making her way across Italy on the India mail train, John Brisben Walker had been frantically cabling the Compagnie Générale Transatlantique to request a delay in the departure of *La Champagne*. After some negotiation the French Line agreed to hold the ship for a price of $2,000; however, as the French government paid for the use of the steamer as a mail ship, the company could not actually do so without the consent of the French minister of posts and telegraphs. At that point Walker cabled the American Legation in Paris, hoping that some of the officials might exert their influence with the French minister. The diplomatic mission apparently met with success, for *La Champagne* waited in Le Havre harbor for more than three hours that morning, and when the low tide made it necessary for the ship to cross the bar it remained off the coast for an additional half-hour, in the hopes that Elizabeth Bisland might still arrive.

Back in Paris, John Brisben Walker had invited several members of the American Legation to meet Bisland and accompany her on the special train to Le Havre—chartered from the Western Railroad at a cost of $300—with breakfast included and all other amenities fully provided for. Walker, as a longtime *Cosmopolitan* editor once remarked, was "a czar in his own world," who was "firm that his orders should be carried out." So it is not difficult to imagine his astonishment and distress when he received a cable from one of the Paris welcoming party informing him that Elizabeth Bisland had not gone to Paris after all, that *La Champagne* had waited at Le Havre until ten A.M. and had finally sailed without her, and that she was now apparently on her way to London.

Later, upon Bisland's return to New York, there would be rumors, accusations, threats of lawsuits. Elizabeth Bisland herself wrote only, "The cause of this false information was never satisfactorily explained."

JANUARY 18–19, 1890

Villeneuve–St. Georges, France,
to Queenstown, Ireland

At half past four in the morning Elizabeth Bisland returned to the India mail train. She was already dressed, too confused and jangled to go back to sleep, so there was nothing to do but throw herself down on her seat and wait for the coming of day. When next the sun went down, she told herself, she would be in London. From London it was but a five-hour train ride to Southampton, where she could catch the fast steamship *Ems* the next day; the *Ems* was due into New York on January 27, making for an around-the-world trip of just under seventy-four days. Outside the sky slowly turned from black to gray. Here and there a thin plume of smoke curled up against the sky from the chimney of a thatched cottage. Peasants who seemed to have stepped out of a Millet canvas trudged along the road in heavy boots and homespun clothing, carrying sticks or baskets of potatoes and turnips. A cart full of milk jugs was being pulled, incongruously, by a large dog, while a woman wearing a cap and tucked-up skirts walked alongside, blowing on her fingers to keep them warm.

It was ten o'clock when the train reached Calais. The ferry for Dover had just left and the next would not leave until one o'clock, so she had time to eat breakfast—a lucky break, as things turned out, for she would not eat again for another forty-eight hours. As she set out on the afternoon ferry the Channel was gray and stormy, the wind brisk, a spatter of rain splashing down every now and again. Some of the passengers, defying the rain, spread themselves out in chaise longues; others turned up the collars of their long coats, thrust their hands in the pockets, and strode along the rolling deck. Later the sun broke through the clouds, turning the sea a stormy gray-green—and there before her, appearing through the mists, were the cliffs of Dover. For a moment she stood transfixed, dazzled by the unexpected whiteness of the stone. The chalk cliffs jutted straight up from the water, as solid and immovable as the sea was restless and shifting, grand and dignified as any national monument. Nothing on this trip had moved her quite as much as that sight; it was worth a journey around the world, she told herself, just to have seen it. Two months earlier she had started out from a continent that English people had claimed as their own, where the English language, English laws and customs reigned from sea to sea; as far as she traveled she had heard that same language, seen the same laws, found the same people. Now at last she was seeing the tiny island that had sprung, as she thought of it, this race of kings. "It fills my soul with a passion of pride," she wrote, "that I, too, am an Anglo-Saxon."

Disembarking from the ferry in Dover, Elizabeth Bisland set foot at last on what she thought of as "the mother soil." Once again she was immediately hurried onto a train, and before she knew it she was sitting in a first-class carriage the pale blue of a lady's boudoir. The train pulled away from the docks, rode through a cleft in the chalk hills, and descended into the English countryside. Here was Kent, the venerable Saxon county, Shakespeare's "civil'st place of all this isle." The scene reminded her of the American South—the neat farms with their carefully hedged borders, churchyards shaded by tall oak trees, ancestral homesteads, red-brick villages nestled into the green hillsides, everything compact, solid, durable. It was a landscape she felt she already knew from books; riding through it she was not learning but remembering. The land seemed to swarm with phantoms from history, poems, stories. They tramped across the fields, peered over the hedges, looked out from every window; she could hear the clang of their armor, their horses' hoofbeats, their voices ringing out a call of welcome in the frosty winter air.

By late afternoon darkness had begun to fall. In the distance Bisland could see a dull bluish haze reflected off the low clouds, indicating the presence of a great gaslit city. The train drove past endless miles of houses, and then suddenly, in a blur, London center flashed past: a huge, shadowy half-globe looming against the sky—the dome of St. Paul's; the vast bulk of the Houses of Parliament; towers and delicate spires with windows shaped like lances; then long serpentine gleams of yellow on black water. That was the river Thames, and a moment later, with a great screeching of wheels and a final exhalation of smoke, the train pulled into Charing Cross Station.

Climbing down from the train, Bisland found a porter for her bags and with the other passengers entered the station. It was an immense space, seemingly far larger than Grand Central Depot in New York. The Saturday evening crowd streamed around her. Porters wheeled trucks piled impossibly high with luggage. "By your leave!" they shouted. "By your leave!" On every side of the station were cloak rooms, refreshment rooms, luggage rooms, waiting rooms, and it was all she could do just to locate the booking office for the next leg of her journey. Bisland had planned to remain overnight in London and the next morning take a train to Southampton to meet the fast Norddeutscher Lloyd steamship *Ems*. But now, in Charing Cross, she was shocked to learn that the *Ems* had been suddenly withdrawn and would not sail again until later in the week. It was, she acknowledged later, "a bitter disappointment." After all this time, having crossed the United States, the Pacific Ocean, the whole of Asia and Europe, she had reached the final leg of her trip, and she could not bear the thought of failing now, not when the end point seemed close enough to touch. New York was right there on the other side of the ocean, just over the horizon; she needed only to find a ship to take her there.

Her last remaining option was to take the night mail train to Holyhead, on the northwest coast of Wales, and from there cross the Irish Sea to meet the Cunard steamship that sailed Sunday from Queenstown, on Ireland's southern coast. Here, too, she received bad news. The Cunard steamer *Etruria* was normally scheduled to leave from Queenstown; the *Etruria* was a sleek modern vessel, so fast that in June of 1888 it had won the Blue Ribbon for the Queenstown to New York run, making the crossing in only six days and five hours. Cunard, though, had pulled the *Etruria* off the line and replaced it with the *Bothnia,* a much slower ship. Indeed, with a cruising speed of under thirteen knots, the *Bothnia* was perhaps the slowest vessel in the entire Cunard fleet. But now it was her only chance.

Charing Cross Station had a telegraph office, but there was no time to send a cable to *The Cosmopolitan* and await instructions. The Holyhead train was scheduled to leave in an hour and a half from Euston Station. She had never been to London before and did not know where Euston was. This station had a bewildering number of platforms, with trains headed seemingly to every town in England. Some were names she recognized, but others, in her exhaustion, broke down into nonsense syllables: Strood, Dorking, Dartford, Wookey. All around her a thousand voices merged into a single roaring chorus. Dimly she registered hurry, clatter, confusion, everyone offering different suggestions and directions. Fortunately a fellow passenger on the India mail train, seeing her difficulties, stepped in with an offer of help. Later, in an essay for solitary woman travelers, Elizabeth Bisland would write, "The woman who knows how to accept a favor frankly and without tiresome protest, and is at the same time gratefully aware that the service is a favor and not a duty, makes every travelling man her faithful servitor." He arranged for her to have dinner at the nearby Grand Hotel with two other train passengers, Sir William Lewis and his daughter; meanwhile he would attend to her new travel schedule.

The Grand Hotel's dining room had marble walls, electric lights in the gilt chandeliers, and carpeting so thick that a piece of cutlery, if accidentally dropped, would make no sound. The food was lavish in the French style, but Bisland was too tired and distraught to eat and only sipped at her wine and absentmindedly crumbled her bread. A reporter from the Paris News Association came to the table to talk to her. Elizabeth Bisland, he would later write, "was very much annoyed to learn that the fast steamer, *Ems,* which she had expected to meet at Southampton for home, had been taken off. Otherwise she would have been sure that her voyage would be a success. Now the *Bothnia,* at Queenstown, is the only boat available and, as it is a very slow one, she fears she will arrive in New York too late." When dinner was over, her helpful friend from the India mail train arrived to accompany her to the Euston station, where the train for Holyhead was scheduled to depart at 8:20. He had brought with him traveling rugs and cushions, a spice cake in case she became hungry, and a stack of books and newspapers; on the train he made sure that her foot warmer was filled with hot water and directed the guard to give her his best care and attention. "There is a vast amount of chivalry and tenderness distributed in the hearts of men," Bisland wrote in that same travel essay, "and while the woman who goes guarded may be quite unaware of it, because nothing in her case calls it forth, the chivalry is there, and ready for almost unlimited draughts upon its patience, devotion, and sympathy."

Bisland settled herself down in the plush of the seat and removed her veil and gloves, readying herself for the journey. Only now, alone in the train, with six hours of traveling ahead of her, could she really take stock of what had happened, the chain of misfortunes that had led her here: the *Prussian* had broken a screw in Hong Kong harbor; *La Champagne,* it seemed, had refused to wait; the *Ems* had been taken off the line; the *Etruria* had been replaced by the *Bothnia.* At this point, she understood, there was little chance of her arriving in New York on time. The inside of the carriage was lit, and in the window she could see herself hanging in the air, as pale and mournful as a ghost. She could have stayed overnight in London enjoying the hospitality of Lady Broome, with whom she had made a fast friendship in Ceylon, could have slept on silk sheets in a large, warm bed. Despite that, she knew she would not have slept comfortably. The idea of racing against Nellie Bly had never appealed to her; she had not even wanted to start on this trip in the first place. But now she had. She had watched the sun come up over the Mediterranean; she had eaten broiled eels, and curry, and mangoes with insides like orange custard; she had seen Mount Fuji at sunrise and the Aden Tanks in the moonlight. Back in New York there were people anxiously awaiting her arrival, and to them was due her best effort. The *Bothnia* was a slow boat, but aboard it she still had a chance. She would push on.

Somewhere along the road to Holyhead she fell asleep, though only for a short while; she was assailed by horrible dreams and awoke with a cry. The train was riding through a wild storm, wind howling and rain drumming against the windows. Indeterminate shapes rose against the sky, darkness etched on greater darkness. Out there stood towns with noble names—Rugby, Stafford, Chester—places she had always imagined, with their medieval cathedrals, castles, libraries, but now sliding by unseen, mile after mile. Deep in the night the train arrived at Holyhead station. Through the window the illuminated faces of the clock tower looked blurry, out of focus. The temperature had dropped and the rain was now mixed with sleet. Gathering up her belongings, Bisland ran down to the pier, the icy drops pelting her cheeks. At the dock the paddle-wheel steamer bobbed madly on the surf, straining against its ties like a wild animal on a leash.

Even in daylight, in the best of weather, the trip across the Irish Sea lasted four hours; and even then the voyage was rough enough that a guidebook of the time could refer to tourists in northern Ireland being "haunted by the dread of the terrible 4 hours between Holyhead and Kingstown." Thirty-seven years earlier another woman journalist, Grace Greenwood, had crossed from Holyhead to Kingstown during a tour of Europe. "Throughout that trip," she wrote, "I felt that I would sooner cross the Styx to the Plutonian shores than attempt it again." Not two months before, the British steamship *Florence* had foundered in a gale on the Irish Sea, and nine lives were lost. It was best, of course, not to speak of such things, and the passengers on the steamer huddled silently together beneath blankets in the cabin. Now and again an especially fierce wave would send the ship into a queasying plunge, and another passenger would rush up to deck to be sick over the side. The engines throbbed steadily beneath them, hour after hour. The sky was already lightening to gray when land was sighted. Coming ashore to the Kingstown jetty, the passengers were immediately hurried onto the waiting train bound for Queenstown.

Bisland felt wretched and grimy—she had not changed her clothes in nearly three days—and so worn down that the remarkable beauty of the passing landscape was scarcely able to revive her spirits. Filmy mists swept across the land like phantoms, the countryside a lush green even in January. It was Sunday now, she realized, watching the peasants tramp the muddy roads to church. These were faces, broad and ruddy, that she recognized from back home. She gazed at the sturdy young men, wondering idly how soon they would be mayors in New York or aldermen in Chicago, at the girls in their bunchy provincial dresses, whose daughters might someday be Washington society ladies wearing gowns made by Worth. The train kept up its incessant rattle. She tried reading one of her books, but the words danced on the page. Her hunger was making it difficult to concentrate. She had not eaten since the previous morning in

Calais, nearly twenty-four hours before. She still had the spice cake, but it was very dry and she had nothing to wash it down with except a bit of brandy in a flask; after a few bites she choked on the cake and set it aside. Due to the late arrival of the Holyhead boat the train was running late and stopped only for the shortest possible time at each station, not long enough for her to get anything to eat. The train passed the beautiful city of Cork, with its fine old mansions and crumbling castles covered with ivy; half an hour later, at noon, it arrived at the railway station, dockside in Queenstown. The *Bothnia,* thankfully, had not yet arrived, the bad weather having delayed it as well, but the steamship was expected in just a few minutes. From the train Bisland's luggage was sent down to the tender, and she went off quickly in search of food. The large and stately Queen's Hotel was not far from the landing, but the bad luck that had followed her for the better part of two days required that the hotel kitchen should be undergoing repairs, and only by "frantic protest" did she manage to obtain from a kitchen worker a cup of cold, bitter tea and a bit of bread as limp and dingy as a scrub rag. Back at the terminal, one of the porters warned her that she should be ready at a moment's notice to be summoned to the tender, for when the steamship was signaled offshore there would be no time to waste. Bisland found the ladies' room and made her toilet as best she could—her toiletries case was in her Gladstone bag, aboard the tender—and then took a seat on a bench in the damp, chilly waiting room.

Hour after hour passed with no summons to the tender. The rain drummed on the roof; the wind whistled through the thin glass of the windows. In her exhaustion, the walls themselves seemed slightly to tremble. In the previous two days she had been in Italy, France, England, Wales, and now Ireland. This was not traveling, as Jules Verne had once observed about Phileas Fogg; it was only describing a circumference. All afternoon Bisland sat in the waiting room, as she later recalled it, "hopeless, helpless, overwhelmed with hunger, lack of sleep, and fatigue." She closed her eyes and tried to summon her strength. Her wool overcoat hung heavily on her shoulders, soaked from the rain and the spray. She felt chilled to the bone; it would take time, she knew, to recover from her night on the Irish Sea, and now she was about to cross the Atlantic Ocean. In those two days she had been on a train, a boat, another train, another boat, and still another train. It was best not to think about those meals on the India mail train, the warming soup, the fresh bread and butter, espe-

cially the strong hot coffee. From the window a line of hills rose an irresolute gray, seeming to blend into the sky churning with low clouds.
The gray and beamless atmosphere, Shelley had written of days like this one.
Outside the station she could hear the cries of beggars imploring newly
arrived travelers for pennies; here was the poverty of Ireland that had
brought so many to New York. There had been beggars at the train stations of the American West, beggars in the harbors of Singapore and
Aden, beggars outside the temples in Colombo. On this trip, as Scripture
said, the poor had always been with her. Slowly the room darkened. Finally, near six o'clock, when her patience was at an end and she was demanding food from one of the station clerks, the long-awaited notice
came: the *Bothnia* had been signaled, and the tender must be off.

The tender put out from shore, but almost immediately the wind
drove it back, whirling the little boat around in the water like an eggshell.
The steamship lay miles offshore. From the far cliffs a lighthouse flashed
and darkened in maddening regularity, seeming never to get any closer.
The tender rolled and pitched on the waves, its engines roaring and then
subsiding, again and again, for fully two and a half hours, until at last it
pulled alongside the *Bothnia*. From somewhere on the steamship instructions were sent down through a speaking trumpet; a gangplank was
tossed aboard and made fast with hawsers. Wearily the passengers lined
up to board the ship. By this time Elizabeth Bisland was dizzy from cold
and hunger and exhaustion, and in the darkness she groped her way un-
steadily up the narrow, slippery gangplank. No sooner had she set foot
on the *Bothnia*'s rain-soaked deck than a shove from an impatient passenger behind her sent her tumbling into the ship's scuppers, raising welts
that would remain for the rest of the voyage. A compassionate stewardess
showed Bisland to her cabin, where she crawled blindly into bed, bruised,
speechless, and on the verge of tears.

That night the *Bothnia* set out into the worst weather that had been
seen on the North Atlantic in many years.

CHAPTER 15

The Special Train

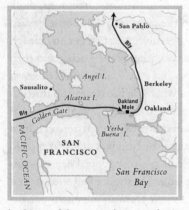

JANUARY 21, 1890
San Francisco Bay

DESPITE THE FOUR-DAY STORM ON THE PACIFIC, THE *OCEANIC* HAD STILL managed to make the crossing in good time, sailing into San Francisco Bay in the early hours of January 21—a day later than Chief Allen's confident prediction, but still a day ahead of schedule. In the morning the revenue officers came aboard to inspect the ship; they brought with them the latest newspapers, all of them heralding Nellie Bly's impending arrival. The other big news story of the day was far less pleasant: a massive blizzard had led to the shutdown of railroad traffic through much of the American West for the better part of a week. "I read of the impassable snow blockade," Bly recalled later, "and my despair knew no bounds."

It was the largest snow blockade in the history of the United States. Seven feet had fallen on the Sierra Nevada mountains of California, more than had ever been recorded, with drifts reaching twenty feet. On the other side of the mountains, in Nevada, the situation was even worse. Local train men reported that in canyons there the drifting snow was anywhere from thirty to sixty feet deep. Stockmen were estimating that by the time the storm was over, four-fifths of the cattle and sheep in Nevada would be dead. The train blockade extended as far north as Washington State, where ten lives had been lost in the blizzard. Fifteen feet of snow had fallen in eastern Oregon, and the conditions were scarcely better in Montana and Colorado. The *New York Herald* declared, "No such storm has been known since the first white man penetrated the Rocky Mountains."

By this time Nellie Bly had traveled more than eighteen thousand miles without a single missed connection or major delay. Now, having returned to her own country, she was facing the most serious threat to her race against time. "Guessers who felt quite sure that all elements of uncertainty would be practically eliminated after Miss Bly reached San Francisco," *The World* advised its readers, "will see that there is more uncertainty now than at any time during the journey." The original plan had been for Bly to take the Central Pacific Railroad's overland route via Ogden and Omaha to Chicago. That route, however, was now totally impassable: no eastbound trains would be able to get through for several days at least, and perhaps for as much as a week. The only alternative was to head south in an attempt to skirt the blockade.

The World cabled General Passenger Agent T. H. Goodman of the Southern Pacific Railroad, asking him to charter a special train to carry Nellie Bly from Oakland to Chicago by a southern route. According to one report, "The New York journal sent instructions to spare no expense in attaining the object desired." Goodman immediately began consultations with officials of the Southern Pacific and Santa Fe Railroads, and at noon on Monday, January 20, the *Queen,* one of the Southern Pacific's fastest locomotives, with the Pullman sleeper car *San Lorenzo* attached to it, was moved to the depot at the Oakland Mole, to be ready as soon as Bly's steamship arrived. It would function as a regular train on the Southern Pacific system down through central California to Mojave, and then proceed east as a special train on the Atlantic and Pacific Railroad's "New Mexico Southern" road east to Albuquerque; there it would switch to the Atchison, Topeka and Santa Fe road, heading briefly northeast to La Junta, Colorado, before resuming a more direct eastward path to Kansas City and then on to Chicago. The Southern Pacific sent telegrams up and down the route instructing local companies to have the fastest engines and best men available as needed; extra engines were placed on side tracks, ready to be called into service in case of an emergency. Bly's train was given a "regardless order," which meant that it would have the right of way over everything else on the road. To make those accommodations from Mojave to Chicago, the Santa Fe railroad charged *The World* a dollar a mile, for a total of $2,190; Nellie Bly's train ride across America thus cost more than all the other parts of her trip put together.

Ever since the very first announcement of Nellie Bly's race, *The World* had been proclaiming that their competitor would not resort to chartered ships or trains; only in this way could *The World* fulfill its self-declared mandate of public service, which was to determine how quickly and easily a typical traveler could circle the globe using "the ordinary lines of commerce." But when presented with the likelihood that Nellie Bly, like thousands of other typical travelers, would be snowbound for days on end in California—when *The World* was faced with a conflict between its stated intention to use only ordinary transportation and its desire to break the around-the-world record (and beat *The Cosmopolitan* in the bargain)—the outcome was never in doubt: a special train was chartered, and no expense spared to make all possible speed. "This was permissible," was all *The World* would say, opaquely, on the matter, "inasmuch as the snow blockade on the Central Pacific made passage by that route impossible and the wide detour and loss of time that the change of programme necessitated justified the deviation." The only public demurral came from a small newspaper in a state through which Nellie Bly's train would not pass. "As we understood it," asked the *Register* of Wheeling, West Virginia, "she was to use only the regular modes of travel, making the regular connections. How is this?"

AMONG THE PASSENGERS trapped on the snowbound trains was a *World* editor by the name of John J. Jennings. Jennings, who had recently joined the *Evening World* after two years as managing editor of Joseph Pulitzer's *St. Louis Post-Dispatch,* had been ordered to San Francisco to serve as one of the "Nellie Bly Escort Corps," to meet Bly when her steamship landed and accompany her back to New York. He set out at once on a fast mail train heading west. The train made excellent time as far as Utah, where the snows began; by the morning of January 16, it was ten hours behind time and the road had become almost impassable. The engineer had no choice but to stop at a train shed in Emigrant Gap, California, a narrow pass in the Sierra Nevada 160 miles from San Francisco. The passengers reconciled themselves to being stuck there for several days at least, and perhaps a good deal longer.

Time passed very slowly. Each day John Jennings and a couple of the others walked back down the railroad tracks to look for the rotary plow. Sometimes they shoveled snow from the tracks, or picked ice from the rails. There was nothing else to do. The men, and three of the ten women on board, did daily exercises in the train shed. Two Dominican nuns sat in the same place day after day, cheerfully reading their prayer books. One passenger set to work with paper and pencil writing a newspaper that he called *The Daily Snow,* providing the latest news of the train; each issue was produced in a single copy that was eagerly read and circulated among the passengers. With each passing day the situation grew increasingly precarious. The train had two Pullman buffet cars with a limited supply of canned food. The shed was damp and dark, and cold all the time, leaving the passengers pale and shivering. By the third day half a dozen had fallen ill, among them the only doctor in the group, the police surgeon of San Francisco, who came down one night with congestion of the lungs that, it was feared, would develop into pneumonia; he was ministered to with quinine from his own supply, and with the little brandy that still remained. Before long the train's oil tanks had also been depleted; at night the cars were plunged into blackness, and all the passengers could do was wait in the cold and dark for morning. They were twenty-six miles from Donner Lake—as the site was now called—the spot in the Sierra Nevada where the snowbound Donner party had met their terrible end.

At five o'clock in the afternoon of the fifth day, January 20, John Jennings received a telegram with instructions from *The World:* Nellie Bly's steamship was about to arrive in Oakland, and he should get there by the following morning and spare no expense in doing so. No train, he knew, would be able to reach them for two days at least; the only way out now was on skis (or, as they were called in the mountains of the American West, "snowshoes," the term "ski" not yet being in wide circulation). The nearest station that a train could reach was in the town of Alta, fifteen miles away. Jennings himself had no experience in the mountains— he had grown up in St. Louis and was a drama critic by trade—but a local miner named J. W. Deuel, who had lived in the Sierra for twenty-five years, agreed to guide him to Alta for a price of twenty-five dollars. At the Western Union office by the train station, Jennings sent a telegram to the division superintendent of the railroad asking that an engine be made available for a trip to Colfax or farther; almost immediately the superintendent cabled back granting the request. The telegraph operators warned Jennings that he was facing a desperate trek across the mountains at night. The summit had received twenty to thirty feet of snow, they reminded him, and there was a risk of snowslide at any time. A telegraph lineman had started out the night before from the nearby town of Summit and was thought to be lost in the snow; a Chinese laborer had perished in Towles, near Alta, within fifty feet of the train station. John Jennings was forty-six years old and had never been on skis in his life, but he would not be dissuaded; Deuel had said that he could get to Alta by two A.M., and Jennings had confidence in his guide and in himself. He returned to the train to get ready, where two other passengers volunteered to join the expedition. At six-fifteen, seventy-five minutes after receiving the telegram from New York, Jennings and the three others set out for Alta to the cheers of the passengers who remained behind.

Darkness had already fallen; J. W. Deuel led the way holding a lantern, the others following in single file. Each man wore a buttoned-up overcoat, leather gloves, and a hat with flaps that covered his ears, and carried his skis on one shoulder and a snow pole on the other; each had on several pairs of socks and wore long rubber boots, keeping his shoes in his coat pockets. Earlier that day a rotary plow had dug out the railroad track from Emigrant Gap almost to Blue Canyon, five miles away, and the men walked in the cuts that the plow had made. The cuts ranged from eight to sixteen feet deep, making high walls of snow as smooth and solid as plaster; it was like walking down a narrow windowless corridor with no end. The great danger, of course, was that a train would come through and the men would be trapped on the track with no way to escape. This was a form of death not unheard of in the mountains. Each man, as he walked, listened for a distant whistle. The only light came from the orange glow of the lantern, which reflected eerily off the walls of snow. The amount of snowfall was almost unimaginable: only the very tops of the pine trees peeked above the snow lines, and the telegraph poles were buried up to their top arms. Once they passed an abandoned two-story house, covered in snow to the chimney. Above them the sky was blue-black; the snow crunched loudly underfoot. Just past midnight they arrived at Shady Run, two miles west of Blue Canyon. There the trail became indistinct: they would have to ski the remaining five miles to Alta.

The skis were made of white ash; they were seven feet long and four inches wide, and turned up at the front ends. Deuel was the only one in the party who had ever skied before, and the going was very slow. Ice formed so quickly under the skis that every hundred yards Jennings needed to stop and scrape it off with his pole. The skis had to be kept parallel at all times or else they would tangle and the skier would fall into a snowbank. This happened to Jennings perhaps twenty times; each time the inside of his coat sleeves filled with snow and his gloves were again encased in ice. Once one of the men, tired of struggling with his skis, took them off and tried walking on top of the snow; almost immediately he fell through and sank out of sight and had to be pulled out by the others. As they moved, drifting snow formed small icicles on their faces; two of the men said that their hats were frozen to their heads. With his every muscle aching and his extremities having passed from painful to numb, facing the prospect of several more hours trekking in the bitter cold, Jennings began to understand why men often decide to lie down in the snow and go to sleep. The only sound was the constant gentle shushing of the skis, like a mother quieting her children at bedtime. Thirty feet below them the railroad track lay like a subterranean river.

It was past four o'clock in the morning when the group, exhausted and chilled to the core, finally reached Alta. J. W. Deuel had suffered frostbite on his left hand, but other than that the men were all right. A train was waiting at the station to take Jennings to Sacramento.

"Thus it was by eight hours' snowshoeing," John Jennings would later report, "the blockade on the Central Pacific was raised and *The World*'s instructions carried out."

JANUARY 21–22, 1890
Oakland to Mojave Desert

At eight o'clock on the morning of January 21 the tugboat *Millen Griffith* pulled up alongside the steamship *Oceanic* lying in San Francisco Bay, and several distinguished-looking men came aboard. They included the deputy collector of the Port of San Francisco, the inspector of customs, the superintendent of the Occidental and Oriental steamship line, and the port's quarantine officer, who had to examine all of the ship's passengers for smallpox before they would be allowed to come ashore. The lone reporter in the group was Charles Low of the *San Francisco Examiner,* who had been asked by *The World* to accompany Nellie Bly to New York in the event that John Jennings did not arrive in time.

Low found Nellie Bly in the *Oceanic*'s saloon, quietly eating her breakfast. Though he was a seasoned reporter, he still could not help but feel slightly starstruck in the presence of the young woman who had lately occupied so much of the nation's attention. She was slender and pretty, smaller of stature than he had imagined, with large gray eyes and an upturned nose, her dark hair braided and tied in two loops at the nape of her neck. Her hands, Low observed, were white and nervous, and on the thumb of her left hand she wore a simple gold band. She was wearing the same blue broadcloth dress in which she had left New York, and was only sixty-eight days older than when she departed, but she looked now like a seasoned traveler, her face deeply browned by the sun—all but her nose, which was burned a bright red.

Low said, "The *World* men are snowbound in the Sierras, Miss Bly, and *The World* is going to let the *Examiner* take care of you."

Bly looked up and smiled. "Is it another rescue expedition?" she asked, gathering up her belongings. "Well, I'm ready to be rescued. My things are packed and I've only got to slip on my ulster." Though her movements were quick and businesslike he thought he could sense a shyness, a hint of self-deprecation in her manner; it occurred to him that she was the sort of girl of whom men say, "God bless her little heart." With Low following behind, Bly hurried down the gangplank to the tugboat ("quick-footed as a schoolboy," he noted admiringly), and then turned to wave to the ship's crew. "They've all been so nice! Oh, the captain—there's the doctor—but *my monkey,*" she cried. "Where's my monkey?"

The monkey in his cage was passed down to a deckhand, and Bly's baggage was tossed in after. The tug started for shore, but before it could get more than a few yards the quarantine officer shouted down to Bly that he had not yet examined her tongue, and that she was not permitted to land until he did so. By this time, though, there would be no delaying the arrival of the famous world traveler. Playfully Bly stuck out her tongue at the doctor, and with a broad smile he called back, "All right!" Everyone on the tug laughed, and Bly waved farewell to the passengers she was leaving behind.

The tugboat set out across San Francisco Bay for the brief trip to the Oakland Mole, where her train awaited. Bly stood by the capstan with her face to the salty breeze, taking in the sights: Goat Island, Angel Island, Alcatraz with its lighthouse and ring of cannons shining in the morning sun. She had seen none of this before, but after so long traveling in the East it all seemed reassuringly familiar. Slowly the dark mass at the end of the long pier differentiated into a crowd of people; as the tugboat drew closer she could see the excited, expectant faces. The tug pulled up and a gangway was thrown across, and shortly before nine o'clock, to the cheers of the onlookers, Nellie Bly set foot again on America. She waved and flashed that dazzling smile; she thought she had never felt a more exquisite happiness.

On the pier Bly was met by Division Superintendent Alvin D. Wilder of the Southern Pacific Railroad, who ushered her quickly to the waiting train with R. A. Donaldson of the railroad's Passenger Department walking ahead, imperiously brushing the crowd aside to let her pass.

At exactly 9:02 A.M. the train set off to more cheers from the crowd. It comprised simply an engine and a vestibuled baggage and sleeper car. The *San Lorenzo,* one of the newest cars in the Pullman fleet, contained a buffet, drawing room, and observation parlor; the wood finishing was of mahogany and bird's-eye maple, the upholstery was purple velvet. Settling in for the ride, Bly arranged the monkey cage with the bars facing outward so that McGinty could watch the country as it passed. Wilder and Donaldson would be escorting her as far as Port Costa, along with William A. Bissell, general freight and passenger agent of the Atlantic and Pacific Railroad. As the train set off, Bissell asked Nellie Bly when she would like to arrive in New York. Bly inquired about Elizabeth Bisland, and looked relieved to hear that Bisland was then struggling with storms over the Atlantic. She considered Bissell's question, her eyes seeming to darken as she furrowed her brows in calculation. "Not later than Saturday evening," she replied after a moment, although privately she doubted they could get her there that quickly.

Bissell nodded. "Very well," he said quietly. "We will put you there on time."

Also on board was a stenographer and a telegraph operator, and as the train set off, Bly dictated a message to be sent back to *The World* in New York; it would be published in the paper the following day:

The saddest sounds that came to me were the farewells called from the Hoboken pier when I started on my trip. The sweetest sounds were the words of welcome and applause which greeted my arrival in San Francisco. Most of my journey has been by water and most of that has been very rough. I have travelled nearly sixteen thousand miles on the seas and am a pretty good sailor by this time. . . . Just think of it! I haven't been seasick once, and am delighted to be able to say in this connection that I have enjoyed good health ever since I left New York.

Of course Bly *had* been seasick, on more than one occasion, while aboard the *Augusta Victoria*. She herself had noted this in her first letter to *The World* back in November; in January, though, more confident and so close to setting the around-the-world speed record, this uncomfortable fact did not comport with the desired image of the intrepid young woman traveler—healthy, lively, unaffected, modest, patriotic: the very embodiment, in the phrase just then coming into vogue, of the New American Girl—and so she preferred to change it.

At ten minutes past eleven the train stopped for lunch in the little town of Lathrop, where the train would begin its journey south through central California. In Lathrop the train was held over in the station for four minutes, an unanticipated development but one that Bly understood when she looked up and saw, coming through the vestibule into the car, *The World*'s own John J. Jennings, just off the train from Sacramento and ready to take his place as Nellie Bly's Escort Corps. As the train sped south, Jennings related to the others the story of his remarkable overnight trek across the mountains. Not surprisingly, he still seemed shaken by the events of the previous days. "I have seen snow and blizzards in New York," he said wonderingly, "but the people back there don't know what snow is." Jennings was by nature self-effacing, but his reputation had been made: in the news stories the reporters sent back east he was already being referred to as "Snowshoe" Jennings.

The next station stop would not be for another two hours. Those in the *San Lorenzo* with Nellie Bly spent the time reading, or counting telegraph poles to gauge the speed of the train, or admiring the San Joaquin Valley from the car's observation parlor. The track here was very smooth and straight as a sunbeam, and even at full speed the carriage rocked from side to side as gently as a cradle. Bly herself felt little inclination to do anything other than sit quietly and rest. There was, she knew, nothing left for her to do. She could change nothing, she could hurry nothing; all she could do now was wait for the train to deliver her to the end of her long journey.

Just before one o'clock the train stopped in Merced. A large crowd, all dressed in their best clothes, had gathered around the station. Bly assumed that the people were having a picnic, and was amazed to hear that they were waiting for her. In answer to the crowd's calls she stepped out to the train's back platform, prompting a cheer so loud that, as she recalled later, it "almost frightened me to death." Immediately the town band struck up a chorus of "My Nellie's Blue Eyes," the popular song that in the coming days she would hear more times than she could count. Afterward, a delegation of fifty townswomen visited Bly in her car to wish her Godspeed. Someone passed her a large tray of fruit and nuts and candy, the tribute of a local newsboy; Bly remarked that she was more grateful than if it had been the gift of a king.

At two minutes after two the train arrived in Fresno, where again a large crowd awaited her at the depot. At this stop men and women alike came into the *San Lorenzo* to meet Nellie Bly. The men asked about the delays she experienced, about the number of miles she had traveled; the women wanted to examine the dress in which she had traveled around the world and to see what she was carrying in her famous gripsack. Four staff members of the *Fresno Evening Expositor* brought aboard a large basket of fruits and wines, all products of Fresno County, to present to Bly. Soon the bell rang and the crowd filed slowly out of the vestibule. As the train pulled away from the depot, Nellie Bly stepped back onto the platform of her car and waved her cap to the crowd standing below; in response the men waved their hats, the women raised their handkerchiefs, and everyone gave a parting cheer.

So it went for the rest of the day as the train made its way south toward Mojave. With each station stop, each crowd waiting to receive her, each brass band playing "My Nellie's Blue Eyes" and "The Girl I Left Behind Me," Bly became more used to the idea of her own fame. Until now she had achieved her journalistic success precisely by being unrecognized, and at first she did not like being looked at by large groups of strangers, but by the end of the first day she felt as comfortable with it as if they were simply looking at the train in which she rode. At Tehachapi a delegation of farmers and lumbermen were waiting at the station for

Bly and were deeply disappointed to learn that she had retired for the evening. These were people who sixty-nine days earlier had never heard of Nellie Bly. Her life, she was beginning to understand, had changed forever.

JANUARY 22–23, 1890

Mojave Desert to New Mexico

The special train rolled on through the night. At Mojave it switched engines and tracks and began the long journey eastward into the desert. There was no moon, and the stands of yucca that interrupted the horizon glowed faintly in the dim light of the stars. Here the absolute silence of the world was broken only by the rumble of the train and the occasional howl of a coyote. Here the train stations were not depots but simple station houses. One of them, deep in the desert, was called Bagdad; another, at what was presumably the hottest place on the line, was called Siberia. Just past dawn the train crossed the border into Arizona, at a town with the unlikely name of Needles.

As the sun rose, the train began to climb into the mountains; by ten o'clock, at Williams, Arizona, the elevation was more than eight thousand feet. After the station stop at Williams, the engineer surprised Nellie Bly by inviting her to ride in the cab, and even to operate the throttle, for much of the thirty-one miles to Flagstaff. Bly was thrilled by the unexpected opportunity and took it for all it was worth, pushing the throttle as far as the engineer would allow; sometimes, when he wasn't looking, she nudged it just a bit further, and on the straight stretches of road she pushed it open as far as it would go, until she was sure that nothing had ever run so fast over the Atlantic and Pacific line. For *The World* Nellie Bly had learned to ride a bicycle, which she called "the most delightfully perfect amusement ever invented or imagined," because it came closer than anything else to satisfying her lifelong desire to fly; but riding a bicycle was nothing compared to this. The air roared in her ears—she had to shout at the engineer, right next to her, just to be heard—and the telegraph poles flashed by like lightning. One man standing near the track, she was delighted to see, had to hold his hat on his head as the train went whizzing past. Ahead of her the snowy crown of Flagstaff Mountain rose in the distance; as the track curved, the mountain would appear first on one side of the engine and then the other, and Bly watched it loom closer and closer all the way to the end of her run. For a woman to operate a locomotive was highly unusual, and it was an achievement of which she was very proud. The next day she told a reporter from the *Philadelphia Inquirer,* "For a new engineer the master mechanic said I was a rushing success."

This was a region of rock and cactus and sagebrush, of sandstone buttes carved into fantastic shapes by eons of wind; in the bright sun the mountains looked brown and scorched, as if a fire had just swept over them. It was a forbidding landscape and sparsely settled: most of the people waiting at a train station to see Nellie Bly had traveled a long distance to get there. The women wore calico dresses; the men wore rawhide cowboy hats and carried pistols in their belts. Bly herself was continually surprised that the residents of these "almost desert places" had even heard of her, but everywhere the train stopped, she reported back to New York, "a crowd is gathered who call for me, and will not be satisfied until I appear on the rear platform to receive their greetings."

At four o'clock in the afternoon the train crossed the state line into New Mexico. The Navajo reservation was about twenty miles south of the railroad tracks, near the town of Gallup, and Bly saw many Indians on horseback riding nearby. The *Rand McNally* guide to the area advised travelers that the Navajos "display their only interest in civilization by looking at the trains. There is no telling what they think of the innovation." Just east of Gallup, railroad men were repairing a bridge that spanned a deep ravine. While the repairs were in progress the bridge was held up only by jackscrews, without the girders that normally helped to support it. Hearing Bly's unscheduled train coming, the workmen frantically tried to flag it down before it reached the bridge, but they were too late and they watched helplessly as it thundered past at fifty miles an hour, over the weakened bridge and safely across to the other side. "The escape is a miraculous one," *The World* marveled the next day, "and section men who witnessed the train flash past on the frail structure regard the escape as one of the most miraculous in railway history."

The fast run across a rickety bridge would seem dramatic enough in itself, but over time, in Nellie Bly's retelling, it became even more so. In her version of the story the bridge not only threatened to fall; in this version it actually fell. "I've had many narrow escapes and no closer call than on my lightning trip across the continent when the railroad bridge fell down the instant we crossed," she related to a reporter two months after her return. It was a story that she told again and again. In her book about the trip, Bly wrote that "my train had run safely across a bridge which was held in place only by jack-screws, and which fell the moment we were across." No one seemed to notice or care that the scene had been lifted directly from *Around the World in Eighty Days,* when Phileas Fogg's train races across a ruined bridge in Wyoming. "But hardly had the train passed the river," Jules Verne wrote, "when the bridge, now completely demolished, crashed noisily down into the rapids of Medicine Bow."

At every station stop Nellie Bly stood on the back platform of the train and shook hands and signed autographs. People held up cards, notebooks, sheets of foolscap, even pine boards, most of the time accompanied by a pencil or a pen freshly dipped in ink, and she always signed until the last request had been satisfied. When the train pulled out of the station the crowds would run after it, grabbing for her hands as long as they could. Bly's arms were sore for several days afterward—"but I did not mind the ache," she would say later, "if by such little acts I could give pleasure to my own people, whom I was so glad to be among once more." As it sped east, the *San Lorenzo* filled with wreaths and bouquets sent by well-wishers; congratulatory telegrams poured in from all over the country, many of them addressed only to *Nellie Bly, Nellie Bly's Special Train.* "It is pardonable in us as Americans to say that your indomitable will and pluck are but characteristic of model young America," read one such telegram. "Get there, Nellie Bly, and God bless you." Later, Bly would remember that trip across the country as "one maze of happy greetings, happy wishes, congratulating telegrams, fruit, flowers, loud cheers, wild hurrahs, rapid hand-shaking and a beautiful car filled with fragrant flowers attached to a swift engine that was tearing like mad through flower-dotted valley and over snow-tipped mountain, on-on-on!"

Everywhere she was received with the sort of fanfare usually reserved for a conquering hero; her race around the world was already being turned from a personal into a national triumph. *The World,* in the days before her return, called it "a tribute to American pluck, American womanhood and American perseverance." This, of course, despite the fact that Bly's success had been made possible by German and British steamships, British coaling stations, a British-owned canal designed by a Frenchman, and a transcontinental railroad largely built by Chinese workers not permitted American citizenship. Bly herself wrote, "They

A drawing of "the rival tourists" that appeared in
Frank Leslie's Illustrated Newspaper *in January 1890. Note that*
only Elizabeth Bisland is referred to as "Miss."

say no man or woman in America ever received ovations like those given me during my flying trip across the continent. The Americans turned out to do honor to an American girl who had been the first to make a record of a flying trip around the world, and I rejoiced with them that it was an American girl who had done it."

JANUARY 23–24, 1890
Kansas to Chicago

The railroad trip through Kansas was, in Bly's own description, "a triumphal march." At one of the train stations a man shouted jubilantly to her, "Come out here and we'll elect you governor." Seeing the crowds that waited at every stop, standing in the January cold just to get a glimpse of her, she could well believe him. In Topeka more than a thousand people were on hand to greet her; they pressed forward so vigorously that the police had to intervene. In Larned she was received by a cheering crowd of several hundred; in Dodge City, where it seemed that nearly every resident was at the train depot, the mayor presented her with a resolution that read:

Vim, enterprise, phenomenal activity and high courage unite in the person of Miss Nellie Bly, the swift messenger of the New York World, now passing through our city on her wonderful journey around the world. She proves that woman leads and man follows; that the earth is none too large for woman's conquest; that whether the earth moves or not, civilization advances, mankind progresses and Nellie Bly is a synonym for success and happy achievements. The people of Dodge City join the procession, toss up their hats and cry God speed.

In Hutchinson, Kansas, the members of the Ringgold Silver Cornet Band, who had been practicing a special number in Nellie Bly's honor, were so awed by the sight of her that they forgot to play and simply joined in cheering with the rest of the crowd.

"The traveller appeared to be in excellent spirits," John Jennings reported from Kansas to the readers of *The World,* "and somewhat surprised at the enthusiasm she had provoked."

Through whirling snow the train roared through a succession of little towns, Halstead at 2:48 and Newton at 2:50 and Florence at 3:42 and Emporia at 4:37. Engines were changed on the fly; long before the train was due into a town, all switches were spiked into position to prevent collisions with slower-moving trains. Upon entering Kansas, Bly's train had been given permission to exceed the state speed limit of 50 miles per hour, and at various times the train was running as fast as 65. The 134 miles between Dodge City and Hutchinson were covered in exactly 134 minutes; east of Ellinwood, seven miles were made in six minutes. "It is doubtful whether such marvelous speed has ever before been made on the Santa Fe line," noted the *Topeka Daily Capital*. Nellie Bly thoroughly enjoyed it. "This is the way I like to travel," she called happily to one of the reporters. The reporter from the *Capital* did a quick calculation and determined that if Bly had been able to maintain her speed across Kansas for the length of her entire trip, she would have circled the globe in less than twenty-four days.

The *Topeka Daily Capital* reporter rode in the railroad car with Nellie Bly from Larned back to Topeka, and indeed throughout her cross-country train trip Bly was accompanied by a large and ever-changing group of newspaper reporters. The reporters from the smaller papers stayed on for only a few train stops, while those from the larger papers stayed for much longer stretches. Each one, though, wanted to hear the story of her journey around the world, and tirelessly Nellie Bly repeated it anew. Bly, who had been anxious and unhappy for much of the Pacific Ocean crossing, now seemed enlivened by the attention of her fellow journalists. Despite the rigors of her long trip, the *Daily Capital* reporter noted, she was "in the very best of spirits and apparently not fatigued in the least," while to the representative of the *Chicago Daily Herald* she was "cordial, frank and sprightly" and, to the *Pittsburg Press,* "very entertaining." From the very beginning of her career Bly had placed herself at the center of her reportage: her exposé of the Blackwell's Island Lunatic Asylum, for instance, had focused in large part on how she managed to get inside the asylum—the women inmates did not even appear until midway through the story. Still, this was something else entirely. As her train barreled east, Bly could not have helped but recognize just how unusual it was for a journalist, much less a female journalist, to be the subject of so many interviews. She was no longer reporting the story; she was the story.

NELLIE BLY'S TRAIN arrived in Chicago at 7:05 A.M. on Friday, January 24; the trip from Oakland had been made in only sixty-nine hours, the fastest time ever recorded for that run. Bly had stayed up until four o'clock in the morning talking with a young newspaperwoman from Nebraska—her name, amusingly, was Miss Muffett—who had traveled six hundred miles to interview her, and afterward dictating an account of her trip for *The World,* a process that was immeasurably slowed by the stenographer being made seasick by the motion of the train. Despite the lack of sleep she was up by six-thirty, when the porter called to her that the train would soon be in Chicago. She got herself dressed, "drank the last drop of coffee there was left on our train," and was surprised, upon opening the door of her stateroom, to see the car filled with good-looking men. They were members of the Chicago Press Club who had boarded the train at Joliet to escort her through their city, and Bly was delighted to sit with them and answer their questions and joke about her sunburned nose and the cleverness of her monkey and the merits of her one dress. By the time the train rolled into the Polk Street Depot she was wishing she could spend all day in the city.

Carriages were waiting for them at the station; Bly rode in a small coupe with the leader of the press delegation, who would write later that he was so charmed by Nellie Bly that he was tempted to steal her. They sat side by side in the carriage's single seat watching through the windows as the city roused itself for the day, the already crowded grip cars lurching past, the newsboys and bootblacks staking out their corners, the men and women in elegant dark clothing hurrying off to work. The tall, ornately carved stone buildings that lined the streets were more reminiscent of New York than any other place she had ever been, and must have impressed on her the idea, pleasing though almost impossible fully to grasp, that by the end of the following day she would be back home with her mother. In the beautifully appointed rooms of the Press Club the president offered Bly congratulations on behalf of all the newspaper men and women of Chicago. All of the men in attendance seem to have been utterly charmed by Nellie Bly; wrote one, "All preconceived notions that she was a sort of man in female attire, that she was something of a tomboy, that she was too adventurous for refined womanhood, that she was a mere 'globe-trotter,' vanished before her winning smile and soft, lightly musical voice. She was feminine in the best sense. She was natural. A free, independent, but gentle product of distinctively American social condition—that was all and everything."

After what she termed a "delightfully informal reception," Bly was driven to Kinsley's, Chicago's most fashionable restaurant, where the club had arranged for her breakfast. Kinsley's had been built in the style of a Moorish castle, though the medieval effect was vitiated somewhat by the red-and-white striped awnings that hung above every window; inside, diners could choose among a French café, a German café, a Gentleman's Restaurant, a Ladies' and Gentlemen's Restaurant, and several banquet rooms of various sizes, one of which is presumably where Bly met the group of Chicago journalists who were waiting for her. Bly, one reported the next day, chatted "charmingly" and "unreservedly" about her trip, and "told of small, pointed incidents which only a woman would remember." She related amusing stories about the Englishmen she had met on her travels, including one especially caddish fellow who flirted with her unconscionably (Bly described how she "dropped him a brief note, telling that if I even so much as caught him looking at me again I would report him to the crew of the first man-of-war we met floating the Stars and Stripes and induce the laddies in blue to resent an insult to the womanhood of their country by boarding our vessel and leading him off in chains"). She joked about her black-and-white checked overcoat, which she claimed was loud enough to have left a continuous echo behind her as she traveled. She recounted how she had seen the American flag only once, flying over the consulate in Canton. When the meal was over the journalists in attendance grandly voted Nellie Bly "one of the boys." This was, in fact, the only way that she might be able to join the Chicago Press Club, as women were allowed as members solely on an honorary basis.

After breakfast the party drove to the Chicago Board of Trade, where Bly was shown to an upstairs viewing gallery. The hall boasted the marble pillars and gilded arches, the enormous plate-glass windows and high tessellated ceilings of a great European gambling house. Downstairs, the trading floor—the "wheat pit," as it was known—was the usual pandemonium, jammed tight with wildly excited men waving their arms, shouting, jostling, apparently engaged in a never-ending struggle to gain one another's attention. Somehow those gestures converted money into more money, an alchemical process utterly mystifying to the uninitiated. "From this gallery," explained an 1891 guidebook, "a perfect view may be had of the operations on the floor, operations which it would be impossible to describe, and impossible for the average visitor to understand." One of the men in the wheat pit, already raising his arm to offer something to someone, happened first to glance up and saw, standing at the railing, a dark-haired young woman in a checked coat and fore-and-aft cap. "There's Nellie Bly!" he shouted.

Instantly all trading stopped. The men crowded into the middle of the floor, where they could better see the gallery, and after a moment of stunned silence, burst into wild cheering. "People can say what they please about Chicago," Bly wrote later, "but I do not believe that anywhere else in the United States can a woman get a greeting which will equal that given by the Chicago Board of Trade." Above the din came cries of "Speech, speech," but Bly just bowed and waved her cap and playfully shook her head, and as she turned to leave the men gave her their best three cheers and a tiger, the final whoop louder than anything heard on the floor on even the busiest trading day.

The scene at the Board of Trade was so tumultuous that Bly had to be escorted to the street through a private hallway; afterward the members of the Press Club drove Bly to the Union Station, where she would switch to a Pennsylvania Railroad train for the last leg of her journey. The news of her presence had by now made its way around the city, and outside the station still another throng had gathered to see her, a seemingly endless stream of brokers and typewriters and clerks pouring out of the surrounding office buildings onto the broad sidewalks wanting to see the young woman who had gone around the world faster than anyone ever had before, surrounding her as she stepped down from her carriage and calling her name and jostling for a better look, and not satisfied until she had shaken all the hands they stretched out to her. Finally Bly managed to make her way inside the station. At the platform she reluctantly said goodbye to the men of the Press Club; thanking them "for the royal manner in which they had treated a little sun-burnt stranger," she boarded her train.

The Pennsylvania Railroad train to New York, known as the Atlantic Express No. 20, departed at ten-thirty in the morning. Nellie Bly had been given exclusive use of the rear parlor car, the *Ilion;* it was, in the words of one reporter aboard the train, "a perfect bower of beauty and comfort." The walls were painted a peacock blue, set off by curtains and lambrequins of fawn gray. The stateroom was already full of flowers sent by well-wishers—so full, in fact, that many more had to be left behind. In one corner of the room sat the red and gold temple chair from Hong Kong; on the wall hung a Japanese mandolin that Bly was saying had been a gift from a prince in Yokohama. Just before the train started east, a telegram intended to have been delivered in San Francisco was handed to her. It read: "Mr. Verne wishes the following message to be handed to Nellie Bly the moment she touches American soil: Monsieur and Madame Jules Verne address their sincere felicitations to Miss Nellie Bly at the moment when that intrepid young lady sets foot on the soil of America."

"Oh, I am so glad to get that," Bly exclaimed.

With the snowstorms behind her and New York only a day away—and Elizabeth Bisland apparently delayed by storms on the Atlantic—there seemed nothing left that could deny her victory. Happily Bly lounged in the *Ilion*'s drawing room, chatting with the reporters on board. Back in Kansas, Nellie Bly had given the first hint of possible ill will toward Elizabeth Bisland when to a reporter's question she answered tartly, "I know nothing of her plans and I care very little about it," and further asserted, "The idea of taking this trip was entirely my own. I suppose the editor of *The Cosmopolitan* thought he could get some good advertising by taking advantage of *The World*'s enterprise, but I don't think they will be able to steal all the thunder." Now she grew more expansive on the subject in a long interview with a reporter from the *Chicago Tribune,* who at one point inquired about "Miss Bisland."

"Miss Bisland?" Bly repeated, with what the reporter described as a "twinkle in her eye." She explained that she had left New York nine hours before Elizabeth Bisland, that Bisland's trip was "suddenly conceived," and that she herself had not even heard about Bisland until she reached Yokohama. (This was a bit of misremembering on either Bly's or the reporter's part, as she had actually learned about Bisland in Hong Kong.) Warming to her story, Bly went on, "Miss Bisland had reached Yokohama two days before me and had then left. I soon found that she had not spent those days idly. She had tried to bribe the officers of the Occidental and Oriental steamship *Oceanic* to make a slow trip with me to San Francisco. I really think she succeeded in fixing the Captain. I do not tell this against Miss Bisland. I merely state it as a fact I discovered. Perhaps anything is fair in a race of this kind, as well as in war, since money counts as much as cleverness.

"But, having discovered it, I went frankly to the officers of the *Oceanic* and told them of it. I said to them that it was their duty to make as fast a trip across the Pacific as they could. I said I would not give them one cent beyond my regular fare to induce them to perform their duty, but I also told them that if they didn't do their duty I would 'roast' them with my pen to the whole world. If they could afford to stand that, and their employers beside, all right. Perhaps that was as much bribery as Miss Bisland had done. At least it was as effective. The steamship reached San Francisco one day late, but it was because of a stormy headwind, and not on account of any dereliction on the officers' part."

This was an astonishing—and entirely unsubstantiated—accusation, made against not only Elizabeth Bisland but also the officers of the *Oceanic,* who had by Bly's own account done everything possible to deliver her to San Francisco as quickly as possible and whom she elsewhere characterized as "perfect, from the captain down." In that regard, it might also be noted that in fact the *Oceanic* arrived in San Francisco one day early, not one day late; the steamship was late only in relation to Chief Engineer William Allen's prediction that Nellie Bly would be brought across the Pacific in record-breaking time—a prediction that he believed so strongly that he had it painted on the ship's engines.

All in all it was, the *Tribune* observed, "a pretty piece of feminine revenge."

ON JANUARY 23, *The World* printed the final coupon for the Nellie Bly Guessing Match, as the paper had already announced that guessing would cease once Bly reached Chicago. The paper now established the rules for the official determination of Bly's final time: her race around the world would be considered at an end when she stepped from the train at Jersey City. (Earlier the finishing point had been the *World* offices in New York, but it was decided that this unnecessarily extended her journey, as she had left from Hoboken, New Jersey, and passed through New York Harbor on her voyage east.) At the moment that both of her feet touched the platform, three official timekeepers, provided with synchronized stopwatches, would record the time to a fifth of a second. Two of the timekeepers were from the Manhattan Athletic Club and one was from the New York Athletic Club, and each, *The World* assured its readers, was "thoroughly experienced in timing all sorts of events." If two of the three stopwatches marked the same time and the third differed, the time marked by the two watches would be accepted as final; if all three differed, the official finishing time would be the one in the middle. This was "strictly in accordance with the rules laid down by the Amateur Athletic Union of the United States, which are conceded to be eminently just and fair."

If Nellie Bly's final time was not guessed exactly, then the closest entry to it would be declared the winner; in the event of a tie, the prize would be given to the submission that had arrived first. If the guesses had been received on the same day, the prize would be awarded to the one that came from farther away, as it had presumably been mailed earlier; if the guesses came from the same distance away, then the winner would be the one that had been taken from its envelope first. It was by no means inconceivable that such an outcome might occur. By this time *The World* had already tabulated more than six hundred thousand ballots.

JANUARY 24–25, 1890
Chicago to Pittsburgh

The Atlantic Express set out from Chicago, the broad belt of parallel tracks that had commenced at the station slowly dwindling, the tracks diverging one by one, like a river branching into tributaries, until finally there was only one, running south toward Indiana. The train rode through endless miles of flat terrain unbroken by any house or tree, a vast grass prairie that a writer once described as having a face but no features. The land was, in the phrase of the day, as level as a ballroom floor, but eventually small undulations could be seen at the horizon, and then patches of bare forest began to appear, and near them farms marked off by knobby fence posts, and then, farther on, small manufacturing towns with foundries and tanneries and mills, and rows of sturdy-looking houses made of wood and brick. It was country that seemed impervious to the passing news of the outside world, but when the train stopped for lunch at Logansport, Indiana, several hundred townspeople were waiting for Nellie Bly at the station. When a young man jumped onto the rear platform of one of the cars and waved his hat and shouted "Hurrah for Nellie Bly!" they laughed and clapped and cheered her on as though she was one of their own. When she stepped down from the train platform the crowd fell back to let her pass, and Bly made her way through to the dining room of Johnston's Hotel, where she was joined by Charles Watts, the local division superintendent for the Pennsylvania Railroad, and his young daughter Hortense, who shyly presented her with a bouquet of flowers. Among the many lunch courses set out before her was a salad on which the inscription *Success, Nellie* had been cut out of beets. Outside, the crowd pressed in front of the windows to watch her eat.

As it happened, Dr. Frank Ingram, the assistant superintendent of the women's lunatic asylum on Blackwell's Island, was originally from Logansport, Indiana. In her *World* exposé Bly had praised the young doctor as the only compassionate official she encountered in the asylum, and in New York, where they were sometimes seen together, it was rumored that they had become romantically involved. Now the local reporters pressed Bly about a new rumor: that she and Ingram were engaged to be married. Bly seemed surprised, and amused, by the claim, and though she acknowledged that she knew Dr. Ingram "intimately," she denied that there was any truth to the rumor. Still, less than a week later, newspapers in both Cincinnati and Philadelphia, quoting "reliable sources" in Logansport, would run an item claiming that Nellie Bly and Dr. Frank Ingram were engaged.

The closer the train got to New York, it seemed, the louder and more demonstrative the crowds became. Though it was after eight o'clock when the train arrived in Columbus, Ohio, more than five hundred men and women were waiting at the station to greet Nellie Bly. It was an outpouring with no precedent in recent memory. The Columbus stationmaster told a reporter from Pittsburgh, "When ex-President Cleveland passed through here in '87, and in '88 when President Harrison utilized the same railway portals, I thought I had seen crowds and heard noise that came near the limit of pandemonium, but this ovation to Nellie Bly tonight tops the record." The people were lined many deep along the entire length of the train platform and into the station itself, and as the train stopped they called to her to come out so they could see her; and when she appeared at the rear of the train they surged toward her with such speed and force that a phalanx of blue-suited policemen formed themselves into a wall in front of the car, and so they had to content themselves with giving three cheers several times as Bly smiled and waved her cap and bowed at them. Noted the *Cincinnati Commercial,* "Miss Bly is about twenty years old, of medium build, with dark hair, piercing eyes, and a bewitching smile. She captured the crowd as soon as she appeared."

The train remained in the station for only a few minutes, just long enough to change engines, and then set off east again. Only three stops remained before Pittsburgh, in Newark, Dennison, and Steubenville. In Steubenville a crowd of two hundred was waiting for her in the cold and dark. It was then 12:34 A.M., the beginning of the last day of her journey. Inside the *Ilion,* a sense of anticipation hung in the air; the talk was carried on in low tones. In the distance, the orange glow from open furnaces and coke ovens seemed to turn the dark river into molten lava. "There is the Ohio," Bly observed at one point, glancing out the window. "I'm nearing dear old Pittsburgh." Before long she excused herself to rest for a couple of hours. It had been an especially long, eventful day—the meeting with the men of the Chicago Press Club already seemed ages ago—and she had gotten almost no sleep the night before. She wanted to be alert for the friends and colleagues she expected would be there to greet her in Pittsburgh.

With that she disappeared into her sleeping compartment, leaving the stateroom to the journalists, railroad officials, and other invited guests along for this part of the journey. She could hear their voices through the curtain. One of them, a manufacturer from Pittsburgh, was saying that her achievement of circling the globe was not merely, as some contended, "a clever play for personal notoriety and the advertising of two metropolitan journals" but was in fact "of incalculable value to the civilized world." To illustrate his point, he explained, he needed only to call to mind his fellow Pittsburgher, Andrew Carnegie, who had recently taken his own around-the-world trip, though of course not against time but simply for pleasure and recreation; supposing Mr. Carnegie were, say, in Hong Kong and had received word by telegram that the Edgar Thomson steel plant in Bessemer had been destroyed by fire and that his presence was needed back in Pittsburgh at the earliest possible moment—would he, in planning his return trip, give even a trifling thought to Jules Verne's imaginary schedule, or would he instead turn to the standard schedule now established by Miss Bly? Eventually the men's voices faded away, replaced by the rhythmic clacking of the wheels beneath her, as unmistakably industrial a sound as the threshing of an automated loom, but somehow musical, too, like the rat-a-tat of a snare drum in one of those bands that had serenaded her all the way across the country. It had been a welcoming party unlike anything she had ever expected, surely the grandest any American woman had ever received.

Years before, she had told Erasmus Wilson, her old friend from the *Dispatch,* that she had four goals in life: to work for a New York newspaper, to reform the world, to fall in love, and to marry a millionaire. The first she had manifestly accomplished; perhaps now she might add the second as well. The world went on little changed from before, of course, but perhaps it had been drawn together just a bit more tightly by the girdle she had thrown around it. And she had shown for all time that a woman with pluck, energy, and independence could find her way to the ends of the earth and back just as well as a man. Later that day, she knew, she would see her mother at last, her mother who had always dressed her in pink as a child so that she would learn how to attract attention and who had struggled so desperately after her husband's death. The family had had a business, real estate, a large house, and then without warning

Judge Cochran had taken ill and died and it all suddenly disappeared. Later on there was another husband, for a while at least, and somehow things got even worse. A woman should not depend on a man for her money: that was the lesson Pink Cochrane had repeated to herself every time she had to wash someone else's dishes or pick up after someone else's children, the refrain she sang in her head as she tramped up and down the streets of Pittsburgh in search of work. Now, as Nellie Bly, she was returning in a private railroad carriage bedecked with flowers.

The train pulled in to Pittsburgh's Union Station at ten minutes past three in the morning. Bly stepped onto the rear platform of her car, and with tears in her eyes she waved to all those who had come in the middle of the night to welcome her; below her was a sea of men in heavy coats and black derby hats. Inside the *Ilion,* she was warmly embraced by relatives and friends, and a delegation of local newspapermen offered hearty congratulations to their former colleague. The reporter from the *Pittsburg Press* gave her his silver press badge to wear; delighted, Bly pinned it to her dress and promised to return it when she got to New York. That was the dress in which she had raced around the world; that dress, the reporter noted silently, was now historical.

CHAPTER 16

"From Jersey to Jersey Is Around the World"

JANUARY 19–29, 1890

Atlantic Ocean

"THE WEATHER ALONG THE TRANS-ATLANTIC STEAMSHIP ROUTES," THE U. S. Signal Service noted in its monthly review for January 1890, "was exceptionally severe." The assessment was, if anything, understated. News reports of ocean crossings that month have the eerie, majestic quality of gothic tales: stories of ships sailing into port with decks encased in ice six inches thick, their riggings hung with icicles like immense crystal chandeliers; glittering ice fields the size of small cities; hurricane-force winds blowing for days on end; hailstones rattling against decks like shotgun pellets; mountainous black waves that appeared without warning, smashing masts and flooding cabins and washing overboard everything that wasn't tied or bolted down. To subdue the ocean's force some of the larger ships hung from their bows large canvas bags filled with an especially heavy, thick oil known as "wave quelling oil"; the oil seeped out of small holes punched in the bags, blanketing the churning water and reducing the crest of the waves. By the judicious use of oil bags one steamer managed to sail safely through a storm for twelve hours, though outside the charmed ring of oil, noted one awestruck correspondent, "the ocean was like a boiling caldron."

Day after day ships straggled into port with cracked shafts, broken masts, split sails, decks swept clear from stem to stern. Nearly every ship had its own frightening tale of wind and water. Two crew members of the bark *Janet Crown* had been washed overboard and drowned; the steamer *Yorkshire* had three seamen blown from its rigging into the sea, only one of whom managed to survive. The Cunard steamship *Catalonia,* sailing to Queenstown from Boston, ran into a hurricane; according to one news report, the ship lost four lifeboats, its bulwarks and deckhouses were badly battered, and its "davits were twisted like wires." Water flooded the funnels, putting out the fires in seven furnaces; and a steam pipe exploded, killing three stokers as they slept.

Another Cunard steamship, the *Gallia,* lost five lifeboats; the ship's staterooms were flooded several feet deep (a London news service reported that "the consternation of the passengers, suddenly aroused from sleep, was awful"); the engine room skylight was smashed; the mainmast and foreyard were sprung loose; part of the starboard rail was broken off and the port rail entirely carried away. The greatest damage to the ship had been caused by a single cataclysmic wave that, in the captain's estimation, was more than one hundred feet high. "He had never seen one like it in thirty-five years' seafaring," a newspaper reported upon his return, "and doesn't want to see another."

The British ship *Loch Moidart,* bound for Hamburg, came ashore instead in Holland, its sturdy hull leaking like a cracked vase; those on board reported that thirty members of the crew had been washed overboard and all but two had drowned.

The French Line steamship *La Champagne,* which Elizabeth Bisland had hoped to meet at Le Havre, ran into the same North Atlantic storms that assailed so many other ships that January. Like the others its decks were swept, its riggings ice-coated, its railings damaged, but the steamer managed to sail through a maddening week of calms and squalls with no loss other than a few lifeboats. On the eighth day at sea, *Harper's Weekly* reported later, "her people were treated to a display of nature's handiwork which they are not likely to forget as long as they live": south of Greenland near the Newfoundland coast, *La Champagne* encountered three massive icebergs amid a vast field of heaving ice. The icebergs were tinted the bluish-green of a tropical sea; the tallest rose some two hundred feet above the waterline, its sides as intricately faceted as a square-cut diamond. On board the passengers marveled at the shifting effects of light and shade as the ship slowly plowed its way through the ice field until the icebergs were out of sight. The weather was fine for the rest of the voyage, and *La Champagne* arrived at Sandy Hook—the spit of land that set the outer limit of New York's waters—at 6:32 P.M. on January 27. The normally fast and reliable steamer was two days overdue; if Elizabeth Bisland had taken *La Champagne,* as planned, her trip would have been completed in seventy-four days and thirty-two minutes.

Instead, Bisland was on board the Cunard steamer *Bothnia*. The ship was still out on the Atlantic Ocean, but no one knew exactly where; it had left Queenstown on January 19 and had not been seen since.

JANUARY 25, 1890
Philadelphia to Jersey City

At 1:24 in the afternoon the crowd inside Philadelphia's Broad Street Station caught the first glimpse of the Atlantic Express No. 20 as it rolled over the Schuylkill River. The news ran like a shiver of electricity through the five thousand people waiting there, who watched in growing excitement as the train came up the raised roadbed beside the massive stone viaduct. It stopped before the Seventeenth Street signal tower, where a shifter engine nimbly detached the rear car of the train and backed it up fifty feet; the Atlantic then rolled in under the iron-roofed train shed to Track 3, coming to a halt with a great wheeze and last puff of white smoke as the shifter pushed the *Ilion* onto a special track. The entire operation took only thirty-six seconds, and Nellie Bly was in the depot just as the electric clocks were indicating 1:25, precisely on time.

Those fortunate enough to have been permitted past the gates of the depot and onto the platform itself immediately surged toward the carriage like river water rushing around a stone, engulfing it on all sides. "The Pennsylvania Railroad Company has never had a train mobbed," the *Philadelphia Inquirer* reported the next day, "but the Nellie Bly special was attacked and captured by an eager crowd as soon as it stopped in the station." There was laughing, shouting, jostling for position. A charge of anticipation had entered the air, and a slight undercurrent of danger; in such close quarters, crowds this size, even the happy ones, could quickly turn ragged and mean. At one edge of the crowd a group of black-helmeted policemen brandishing tasseled batons struggled to clear a path for a man in a silk top hat. When at last the man got to the front platform of the railroad car he jumped aboard and reached back to help up the woman who followed him, a bespectacled older woman wearing a simple black dress with a black velvet wrap. The man was Julius Chambers, managing editor of *The World,* who had been at the pier in Hoboken to see Nellie Bly off and had traveled now to Philadelphia to accompany her on the triumphant last leg of her journey. The woman, who passed through the crowd entirely unrecognized, was Nellie Bly's mother.

Inside, the car was an opulence of brass and leather and polished wood, the air scented with flowers and loud with conversation. Mary Jane Cochrane edged her way through the car, past all the well-dressed men she did not know, until she saw her daughter: wearing the same blue dress as the last time she had seen her, but sun-darkened now and with a splash of pink across her nose, just as when they were traveling together in Mexico. "Oh, Nellie," she said, taking her daughter into her arms.

"Mother!" Bly murmured, in a voice thick with emotion. "I'm so glad!"

The two held each other for long seconds, the men in the car quieting and stepping back from the embrace as a sacred thing. Outside, though, the assembled thousands were calling her name, and soon Nellie Bly appeared, her eyes still filled with tears, and stood at the rear platform of her car smiling and waving as she silently took in the crowd's acclaim; there was, in the din, little else she could do. Then, as always happened, those in the front raised their hands up to her. Immediately below was a man named Harry Heston, who was the cashier of the restaurant in the Broad Street Station, and he beamed and warmly clasped Bly's hand, a reporter observed, "as if they had been friends for years."

Nellie Bly, it seemed, had the essential quality of celebrity: people she did not know felt that they were her friends.

The crowd shook Bly's hands so vigorously that Julius Chambers began to fear that they would pull her off the car, and for several minutes a *World* reporter held Bly from behind as she leaned down from the platform of the train. Then they heard a shout from inside the car to clear a passage for the Reception Committee—the large group that had arrived that morning from New York and which included, in addition to Julius

Chambers and Mary Jane Cochrane, Bly's close friend the writer and feminist Cora Linn Daniels, several reporters (among them James Metcalfe, the violet-eyed journalist from *Life* magazine who had often squired Nellie Bly around town the year before), civic leaders, and prominent business executives. Also in the group was John Montgomery Ward, the popular shortstop for the New York Giants. Like Bly, Ward had grown up in western Pennsylvania, and he had recently completed a barnstorming tour of the world with an all-star baseball team; he had asked that a place be reserved for him on the train, a request that *The World* was happy to grant. The group had come in from New York in the Pullman car *Beatrice,* which had now been attached to the *Ilion* along with a new engine for the final stage of the trip. From the rear platform Bly gave a last wave goodbye and went in to greet her distinguished guests, and within moments the train was moving again, the massed brick spires of Broad Street Station growing smaller and the noise of the crowd replaced by the rumble of steel wheels on steel tracks.

On the way to the junction at Germantown, where the Philadelphia contingent would leave the train, the city's recorder of deeds gathered everyone together and presented Nellie Bly with a huge bouquet of La France roses. "We admire your courage, pluck and endurance," he declared, "and in presenting these flowers I desire to express the wish that your journey through life may be as bright and beautiful and successful as this wonderful one which is just drawing to a close." Bly asked the recorder to tell the people of Philadelphia that she appreciated their kindness and to thank them on her behalf, and he assured her he would. The delegation from Philadelphia came up to shake hands with her and offer their best wishes, and Bly distributed roses to the assembled reporters, joking and answering their questions and signing autographs for them. One of the autographs she signed on copy paper, and a facsimile of it appeared the next day in the *Philadelphia Inquirer.*

After Germantown the train rode through a crest of hills into New Jersey. The trees on the hillside were bare now; at Princeton the clustered blue and gray slate roofs of the College of New Jersey rolled across the window like a moving diorama. The train passed New Brunswick, Rahway, Trenton, suburban towns with wide streets and handsome houses. From the dining car, where lunch was being served, Nellie Bly looked out at the people waiting at each of the stations. The train, they must have known, would not even be stopping; they just wanted to wave hello and call a welcome and perhaps catch a glimpse of the young globe-trotter about whom they had heard so much. "I feel a little like a presidential candidate," Bly had remarked back in New Mexico, when her cross-country trip, with all the bouquets and brass bands, was starting to take on the festive trappings of a whistle-stop tour. Now, though, she was actually drawing crowds as large and enthusiastic as the ones that turned out for presidential candidates, and even for sitting presidents: "Poor Nellie's hand was worked harder than President Harrison's limb was ever pumped," one Philadelphia newspaper had noted. As she sat with her mother and Cora Linn Daniels in the dining car, Bly sipped her champagne and picked at her salad, too excited and exhausted to eat. She had barely slept since setting foot on the western edge of the United States, and now the eastern edge was just ahead. The conversation at the table was desultory; there was so much to say it was difficult to know how to begin. Of course she was delighted to be returning home again—and ahead of time—but this train ride had been so enjoyable she almost hated for it to end. It was approaching three o'clock in the afternoon. She wondered where she would be at this time the next day, and the day after that. For the last two and a half months her only concern had been to keep moving forward; now she had arrived at the bottom of the itinerary, and she wasn't sure what came next.

When lunch was over and the plates were taken away they could hear Julius Chambers, the chairman of the Reception Committee, calling for order in the stateroom next door. Nellie Bly came into the car, smiling almost shyly in the gaze of the crowd; her mother and Cora Linn Daniels took a seat, but Bly herself remained standing. Julius Chambers had kind, dark eyes and a thick mustache beginning to gray; he wore a dark suit and tie with the high shirt collar of the day. As the managing editor of *The World*—where he had just been given a new three-year contract by Joseph Pulitzer—he felt comfortable commanding attention in a large group of men. He thanked everyone for being present on this extraordinary occasion. "Nobody since the sands of time began to run," he said, "has ever had the pleasant and remarkable task of introducing a young lady who has made a tour of the world in seventy-two days." Truly that was a remarkable travel time, but there was nothing more remarkable about the young lady than the great seriousness with which she had accepted and fulfilled her assignment; it had been, for her, always business. "And now," he continued expansively, "she has returned to us again and tens of thousands of people welcome her back. She has sailed over three oceans, traversed two continents. She is here, ladies and gentlemen, here, as ever, the same happy, earnest, faithful Nellie Bly."

The room burst into loud applause, and when it finally subsided Bly said, "I don't know how to thank you for so kind a welcome, except to say that there is one land on this earth and that is America." She spoke in the distinctive Pennsylvania hill town lilt that many in the room had not heard before. "This attention that I am receiving is very much of a surprise to me. I thought there would be just a finishing of the trip at New York and that would be the end of it all, but ever since I arrived at San Francisco I have been delightfully received, and I thank you for this kind attention."

When she finished there was more applause, and three cheers and a tiger. Julius Chambers then gave the floor to Leicester Holme, the private secretary for Mayor Hugh J. Grant of New York, who read a statement from the mayor offering his congratulations and welcoming Nellie Bly most heartily. Afterward they listened to the president of the Mutual Reserve Life Insurance Association, who presented Bly with a miniature inkstand in the shape of the world, followed by the president of the New York Medico-Legal Society, representatives of the Pennsylvania Railroad and the Press News Association, and finally John Montgomery Ward, tall and handsome, who stood up to pay tribute to Nellie Bly as "a representative of the highest type of American Womanhood."

With the speechmaking completed and the outskirts of Jersey City coming into view, John Jennings began to organize Bly's possessions for delivery to her home. He was, she confided in one of the reporters, a "modest little man who doesn't say much but does great work." In the final minutes those in the carriage with Nellie Bly settled into a thoughtful silence. Up ahead was the finish line; something was about to occur, something considerable, but she did not know exactly what it would be. It had been cold in Philadelphia that morning, but the day had grown steadily warmer. The sky was low and gray, with the dramatic dark clouds of a Winslow Homer seascape. Moving dots appeared on the low horizon that, as the train drew closer, turned into gulls circling over the water. The Pennsylvania Railroad depot was right over the horizon, just past the vanishing point of the tracks.

THOSE ON THE TRAIN could sense it before they could see it: a vast dark presence, many thousands of people, ten thousand certainly, perhaps as many as fifteen; it gave off a hum that rose and fell like the swell of cicadas, but deeper-voiced, and more insistent as the train came around the long, gentle curve that led to the western end of the depot. The train appeared and at once all of the wooden barriers that had been erected to keep the crowd organized came down; from afar it looked as though a tidal wave was sweeping across the railroad yard from the ocean behind, drowning everything in its black waters. Inside, the crowd poured in through the baggage room, through the men's and ladies' waiting rooms and the gentlemen's smoking room; the balcony was lined several rows deep. It was the largest gathering in which any of them had ever taken part—any but the Civil War veterans among them. There were men wearing bowlers and derbies and top hats, women in boaters and bonnets, children bareheaded and in caps; they had come on foot and by carriage and ferry and some of them, like Nellie Bly herself, by train, because they wanted to see for themselves the black-and-white checked overcoat and the fore-and-aft cap and the leather gripsack, and to welcome home the daring American girl who had raced around the world speaking only English and taking little more than the clothes on her back and had beaten in reality what an Englishman had done only in a Frenchman's imagination.

On the platform, just where the train's rear car was expected to stop, Mayor Orestes Cleveland of Jersey City stood with a large basket of cut flowers for the guest of honor; he held them high above his head so that they would not get crushed by the crowd that pressed around him. Next to the mayor the timekeepers from the athletic clubs kept their synchronized stopwatches at the ready. Nellie Bly had been instructed by telegram to emerge onto the top step of the carriage as the train came near the station, and with the speed slackening on the last stretch of track she did so. As the train rolled into the depot she grasped the handrail a bit more tightly. The train stopped and she stepped down, lightly, quickly, first one foot, then the other. The moment her second foot hit the ground, the three timekeepers clicked their stopwatches in unison. The race was over.

The time was fifty-one minutes and forty-four seconds past three o'clock in the afternoon. Nellie Bly had completed her trip exactly 72 days, 6 hours, 11 minutes, and 14 seconds after she began it. No one had ever gone around the world as fast.

Instantly the scene dissolved into pandemonium; in the words of one young New Jerseyite, the crowd "ripped the atmosphere up the back." Those inside the depot cheered as loudly as they possibly could, the din reverberating off the walls and back onto itself, a physical force, it seemed, strong enough to rattle the tin roof. A *World* man raised a handkerchief atop an umbrella and someone watching in the station's Western Union office shouted "Now!" A telegraph switch was flipped, sending a signal across the harbor to Battery Park at the southernmost tip of Manhattan, where Captain Hubert Wycherly of the John Pain & Sons Pyrotechnics Company had set up a line of mortars. Moments later the roar of a ten-cannon salute split the air, and then, from farther away, in Fort Greene Park in Brooklyn, where the signal had been transmitted to a telegraph pole on Myrtle Avenue, there was another cannon report, followed by another, and another, and several more in close succession. The call was immediately taken up by the boats in the harbor, the tugs and barges and ferries all sounding their steam whistles; on and on it went, the shrill of the whistles and the deep percussive booms of the cannon, a celebration both thrilling and slightly frightening, like the extended final salvo of a Fourth of July fireworks show, when the pyrotechnicians empty their stocks into the air and the crowd rises to its feet cheering and the explosions seem as if they will never end. "No chieftain returning from a tour of conquest," wrote one of the reporters, "ever received a more royal welcome."

As Nellie Bly stepped off the train, Mayor Cleveland rushed forward to greet her and with a courteous bow handed her the basket of flowers; she in turn nodded and bowed and smiled her thanks. The noise in the depot was too great for any words to be exchanged, and so the ceremony of presentation and acceptance had to be performed in the broad gestures of Kabuki. Someone took the basket from Nellie Bly, and the mayor and a retinue of city officials standing behind him motioned the crowd to quiet so that he might deliver his welcome address. Orestes Cleveland was a large man with a broad pate and mournful bulldog eyes, and he drew himself up to his full height and began to speak. "The American Girl will no longer be misunderstood," he declaimed, his voice pitched somewhere between an oration and a shout. "She will be recognized as pushing, determined, independent, able to take care of herself wherever she may go." He turned to address Nellie Bly directly. "You have added another spark to the great beacon light of American liberty that is leading the people of other nations in the grand march of civilization and progress. Passing rapidly by them, you have cried out in a language they could all understand, 'Forward!' and you have made it the watchword of 1890. The American people from every part of this great and glorious country shouted back to you, 'Forward! And God speed you on your wonderful march!'"

There was a good deal more, enough that the printed transcript of the speech in the next day's newspaper would run to ten paragraphs. But no one could hear Mayor Cleveland, or in any case wanted to listen to him, and eventually he gave up trying to speak and introduced Nellie Bly.

Beneath her cap, Bly's hair was attractively disheveled, and when she smiled, her sun-browned skin set off the brilliant white of her teeth. She looked radiant, triumphant. "From Jersey to Jersey is around the world," she called, "and I am in Jersey now."

Nellie Bly's tumultuous reception in Jersey City

That was all she said, but no more was needed. "Hurrah for Nellie Bly!" the crowd shouted back again and again. Women fluttered their handkerchiefs and men waved their canes; bouquets were tossed down to her from the balcony. Then the march to the ferry terminal began. The police formed a circle around Bly and Mayor Cleveland—Bly's mother and Cora Linn Daniels had already gone on ahead—and by pushing and shouting and waving their batons they tried to navigate the five hundred feet of passageway down to the landau that waited by the terminal. Standing among the policemen Bly was nearly lost from sight; the crowd strained on tiptoes to catch a glimpse as she passed by. Every inch of ground was contested; the farther the group struggled along the passageway the more tightly packed the crowd became, and after no more than one hundred feet progress had ground to a total halt, at which point two of the larger policemen lifted Nellie Bly bodily and, using their shoulders as a kind of battering ram, carried her the rest of the way to the terminal. There she was helped up into the carriage, Mayor Cleveland scrambling onto the seat beside her; the driver took hold of the reins, and the horse—surely spooked by the swirling, noisy crowd—made its way haltingly down the pier. "When the carriage started for the ferryboat the stampede of people in the same direction was something terrible," reported the *Philadelphia Inquirer,* "men, women and children being pushed down and fairly trod upon."

The carriage was driven down the gangplank directly onto the ferry, which a thousand people had already boarded. They had been waiting for a long time, and they were disappointed that they could not see Nellie Bly as she sat inside the landau. As the ferry set off across the harbor someone began a chant; it was modeled on the one from President Cleveland's re-election campaign in 1888, "Four—four—four years more!" except that now it went, "Open—open—open the coach! Open—open—open the coach!" Soon the chant had spread across the top deck of the ferry, becoming so loud and insistent that the driver was ordered to comply, and he stepped down from his seat in the front and threw back the top of the landau—"and when he took the roof off the carriage," a *World* reporter observed, "the crowd nearly took the roof off the ferry-boat." All the way across to New York, Nellie Bly stood in the carriage and waved to the crowd around her, the air filled with happy cheering and the whistles of all the ships in the harbor.

At the Cortlandt Street pier in New York another large crowd had gathered, as loud and enthusiastic as the one that had seen her off in Jersey City. West Street, along the river, was almost impassable, and Cortlandt Street itself was choked with people. The carriage took several minutes to navigate the four blocks to Broadway; there it turned left for the short drive uptown to the *World* office on Park Row. As she had on the ferry, Bly stood all the way, smiling and waving her cap and bowing right and left to the immense throngs on the sidewalks, sometimes handing out flowers to the men and boys who walked or ran alongside. One man, Bly recalled later in some amazement, kept asking her to touch his hand. She called to him that he shouldn't get so close to the wheels or he might be run over. "God bless you, Nellie," he said again and again, "you are kind and thoughtful."

In the tall buildings that lined Broadway, the windows were filled with faces. Traffic had slowed nearly to a standstill; carriages and streetcars were blocked in by the streaming crowds, and the shouts of conductors and clanging of car bells only added to the clamor. Seemingly by general acclamation the rules of the road had been dispensed with, Broadway now less an avenue than a broad pedestrian promenade. The carriage had to push its way through the street like a snowplow, making progress little by little, carefully clearing a path all the way to the newspaper district. Delivery trucks that had made the mistake of attempting to go through Park Row were now completely hemmed in, and some in the crowd had climbed atop them to use their roofs as impromptu viewing platforms. Finally Nellie Bly's carriage arrived in front of the World Building at number 31-32. The police chief of the nearby Oak Street station house had placed twenty-five men in front of the building; the sergeant in charge organized a passage for Bly from the carriage to the doorway, flanking it with police officers on both sides. Stepping down from the landau, Bly called to the crowd, "I am so glad to be home again!" and then gave a last wave of her cap and disappeared inside.

Upstairs, Bly was escorted to an informal reception in the main editorial room, where her colleagues had gathered to welcome her back; the room was piled high with flowers and congratulatory letters and telegrams.

From *The Cosmopolitan,* John Brisben Walker, conceding defeat, sent a basket of rare roses.

JANUARY 30, 1890
New York

The *Bothnia* sighted New York on the morning of Thursday, January 30. It had been a dreadful passage from Queenstown. Across most of the North Atlantic the sea churned and heaved, the waves tossing the ship back and forth like a football. For days Elizabeth Bisland lay wretched and miserable in her berth, too seasick to move. Again and again the ship would climb a green mountain of sea, pause for a moment at the crest of the wave, and then slide back down again on the other side, the back of the ship coming up out of the water, like a bucking bronco kicking its hind legs. After days of this constant pounding all of her joints felt dislocated, and even her teeth had begun to ache in her head. The cot beneath her felt as thin and hard as a coffin. The crew had left the doors to the decks open to prevent them from freezing shut, and a bitterly cold wind blew through the passageways and into the cabins. On the third day of the storm—or perhaps it was the fourth—Bisland was just resolving to get up from her berth when a sudden lurch of the ship sent a water jug flying out of its basin onto her chest, where it broke into pieces and drenched her and the sheets with icy water; afterward she discovered that the key to her steamer trunk, where she had all her dry changes of clothing, had somehow been mislaid. She stood helpless in the cabin, the cold breeze piercing her through her wet and clinging nightdress. Each night she fell asleep telling herself that the morning would be better, but when she awoke everything was just as before. The wind, it began to seem, had always been howling, the waves always raging. The captain of the *Bothnia,* the forty-seven-year-old Scotsman James B. Watt, was a deeply respected veteran commander (so respected, in fact, that at the age of sixty-five, two years past Cunard's normal retirement age, he would be given command of a new steamship—the *Lusitania*), but not even the most skilled seaman could make any speed amid such storms. With each passing day the prospect of catching Nellie Bly became ever more remote; at the end of a trip ruled by the calendar and the clock, time seemed now to slow, and even to run backward, carrying her ever farther from her goal.

On the morning of the eleventh day, when the seas had calmed and the sky began to clear, a thin rim of film appeared on the horizon. On the forward deck, the passengers stood wrapped in their furs, red-nosed and shivering but excited at the prospect of land at last. As the ship moved closer the film thickened and darkened, eventually resolving itself into Coney Island; before long those on deck were seeing a most extraordinary sight. It was the Elephantine Colossus: an immense wooden elephant, twelve stories high, with tusks forty feet long and a hide made from blue tin. Built only a few years before, it was already one of Coney Island's premier attractions. "The work is really an architectural wonder," a writer of the time declared. "It bursts upon the astonished gaze of passengers on the in-coming European steamers, giving them their first idea of the bigness of some things in this country." The forelegs—each of them sixty feet in circumference—contained a cigar store and a diorama, and circular staircases hidden in the hind legs led visitors up to the concert hall, museum, and numerous novelty shops contained inside its immense body. Now, as the *Bothnia* steamed slowly past, the glass eyes of the great elephant seemed to gaze on the ship in reproach, Elizabeth Bisland would later observe, "as if to deprecate our late coming."

The ship sailed through the Narrows into the Upper Bay. On the right the Statue of Liberty held her torch uplifted; to the left was Staten Island, the tidy little villages tucked into the hills, the grand yacht houses down along the water. A young Englishwoman, following her new husband to a foreign country, remarked in surprise that it all looked much like England; apparently, Bisland thought, she had been expecting log cabins in a frontier settlement. In the distance she could see the skyline of lower Manhattan, the new skyscrapers with their domes and spires rising above the mass of older buildings like peaks in a mountain chain; it still inspired a kind of reverence in her, seemed to her just as astonishing as when she first saw it, on a ship coming north from New Orleans. As the city came into view, a wash of familiarity came over her, blotting out all sense of elapsed time; she felt she knew how everything looked at that moment—the streets, the houses, the passersby—as if she had only turned her head away for an instant, when something unexpected caught her attention.

The *Bothnia* entered New York Harbor and began steaming up the West Side of Manhattan. At exactly one-thirty in the afternoon the ship slid into the Cunard pier No. 40, at the foot of Clarkson Street: her journey was over. No official timekeepers were on hand to record the arrival, and indeed Elizabeth Bisland's final time was by no means as definite as Nellie Bly's. The *Bothnia* had crossed the bar at 10:10 that morning, making for a trip of 76 days, 16 hours, and 10 minutes; John Brisben Walker himself put the time at 76 days, 16 hours, and 48 minutes, though he never explained the reasoning behind that calculation. Using one-thirty P.M. as the end point, the trip would have been completed in 76 days, 19 hours, and 30 minutes. In any case, no one cared to dispute Walker's own pronouncement; the runner-up's final time was something of an afterthought. Still, using any of those times, Elizabeth Bisland's trip around the world would have been the fastest one ever recorded—but for the fact that Nellie Bly had arrived four and a half days earlier.

Those days, however, made all the difference. The crowd awaiting Elizabeth Bisland numbered in the hundreds rather than the thousands and was far quieter and less boisterous than the ones that had greeted Nellie Bly both in Jersey City and at the Cortlandt Street pier. Bisland emerged on deck with the rest of the ship's passengers; she was wearing a neatly fitted black traveling suit beneath the same dark Newmarket coat and glazed black sailor's hat that she had been wearing when she first set out from New York. A small pair of binoculars was slung over her shoulder, and her face was deeply sunburned. "She looked," wrote a reporter from the *St. Louis Republic,* "like a veteran yachtswoman." Her sister Molly was waiting at the end of the gangway, and as Bisland stepped onto the dock she fell into her sister's arms; immediately Molly burst into tears, saying, "She has beaten you, but you did well." John Brisben Walker and several colleagues from *The Cosmopolitan* were also on hand with a number of friends to offer their consolation and congratulations.

A handful of newspaper reporters gathered around to ask her about her trip. Bisland told them that she was delighted with her journey and with the courtesy and kindness that had greeted her in all the countries she visited; her only regret, she said, was not having been able to beat the time of Nellie Bly. With that, her sister spirited her off into a carriage waiting on the dock, and the two hurried uptown to their little apartment on Fourth Avenue, which was filled with flowers sent by friends in honor of her safe arrival.

That night, in an article that served as a kind of postmortem of the trip, John Brisben Walker told a reporter from *The World* that "the young woman he sent around the world from west to east was by no means an expert traveller" and had "made several blunders." The only blunder he specifically cited was this: "Instead of taking the steamer *Prussian* at Hong Kong for Brindisi, she took another boat which left three days earlier but reached its destination four days later than the *Prussian*. Then she missed the French steamer *La Champagne,* which had been held for her at Havre, and was forced to take passage on the *Bothnia* from Queenstown."

Elizabeth Bisland, though, had not wanted to abandon the *Prussian* in Hong Kong; the *Prussian*'s screw had broken in the harbor, and Bisland had no choice but to take the slower Peninsular and Oriental steamer in its place. Moreover, even if Bisland *had* boarded *La Champagne* at Havre, the storms on the North Atlantic added several days to the steamship's time, enough to have ensured Bisland's defeat regardless. The day after Elizabeth Bisland's arrival in New York, *La Champagne*'s commander, Captain Boyer, told a reporter that if Bisland had been on board he thought he could have landed her in New York on the afternoon of Sunday, January 26—a far better showing, but still several hours behind Nellie Bly's time. Though John Brisben Walker preferred to lay the blame with Elizabeth Bisland, he might have looked instead to his initial decision to have her travel west rather than east. Going in this direction, Walker believed, Bisland would avoid the headwinds that Nellie Bly would likely encounter on the South China Sea; but that decision in turn brought Bisland onto the North Atlantic in January rather than November, when she was far more likely to encounter weather rough enough to slow a steamship.

Indeed, the outcome would have been little different even if the *Prussian* had not broken its screw in Hong Kong harbor. *The Cosmopolitan*'s original itinerary had the *Prussian* delivering Elizabeth Bisland into Genoa on January 12, four days earlier than the P&O steamer *Britannia* brought her to Brindisi. The earlier arrival would have allowed Bisland enough time to take an express train to Calais, then ferry across the English channel and board a train for Liverpool, where the White Star steamship *Adriatic* departed on January 15. The *Adriatic* was a fast ship; in 1872 it held the Blue Ribbon for a westbound North Atlantic passage, having crossed from Queenstown to New York in 7 days, 23 hours, and 17 minutes. That crossing, however, had taken place in the month of May. In January 1890, like all of the other steamships on the North Atlantic, the *Adriatic* had a very rough passage—which included ice fields and a hurricane that lasted for eight hours—and reached the bar in New

York at 2:06 A.M. on January 26 after an eleven-day crossing. If Elizabeth Bisland had been aboard the *Adriatic,* her final travel time would have been 72 days, 8 hours, and 6 minutes—still nearly two hours behind Nellie Bly.

In the face of hurricanes and ice fields, seven-day steamers turned into eleven-day steamers, and a seventy-two-day trip instead took seventy-six. No matter what route Elizabeth Bisland took across the Continent, and despite her harrowing three-day trip to catch the *Bothnia,* there was not a ship in Europe that would have landed her in New York in time to beat Nellie Bly. It was not the December storms on the South China Sea that ultimately determined the winner, as John Brisben Walker had anticipated, but the January storms on the North Atlantic.

Nellie Bly's triumphant return was announced in newspapers across the United States and Europe; Elizabeth Bisland's later arrival in New York earned scarcely a mention. In New York, the *Times* ran a brief item on page 8; the *Herald*'s story, on page 12, was somewhat longer, but somehow managed to refer to her as "Miss Mary Bisland."

"Miss Bisland's late arrival takes all the glory out of her really meritorious achievement," editorialized the *Philadelphia Inquirer* shortly after her return, before going on to suggest: "The only thing she can do now to recover prestige is to try it again. With the experience of her last trip she should be able to break the record made by her successful rival. It might not pay; but neither did the first trip."

Asked the *Washington Critic,* "Wasn't there a Miss Bisland who started out to do something a long time ago?"

The *Daily Messenger* of St. Albans, Vermont, observed that no crowds were on hand to receive Elizabeth Bisland and noted simply, "It is the winner who wins."

CHAPTER 17

Father Time Outdone

ATHER TIME OUTDONE! PROCLAIMED *THE WORLD*'S HEADLINE FOR SUN-day, January 26, in the largest type the setters in the composition room could find. Below it, seven more headline decks summarized the entire story of Nellie Bly's record-breaking trip, including how "Even Imagination's Record Pales Before the Performance of 'The World's' Globe-Circler," and "The History of Journalism Cannot Parallel This Popular Achievement." Under the masthead a large cartoon drawn by *The World*'s Walt McDougall showed Nellie Bly in her distinctive checked ulster and cap, gripsack in hand, greeting an unhappy-looking group of historical circumnavigators, among them Sir Francis Drake and Captain Cook, and, at the end of the row, a monocled man in full evening dress—Phileas Fogg. The caption below it read: "A Little Pardonable Consternation Among the Globe-Circlers at the Remarkable Achievement of 'The World's' Traveller."

"All Europe Enthusiastic," the paper reported, above commendatory remarks given to *World* correspondents by geographers, scientists, journalists, and even Vicomte de Lesseps, the developer of the Suez Canal, who congratulated Bly on her courage and laughingly added, "I think I should have some share in the ovations, seeing that—thanks to my canal—I have rendered the journey so much shorter." In London, *The World*'s Tracey Greaves paid a visit to the president of the Royal Geographical Society. "While I can't see that her trip will benefit the cause of science," observed the Right Honorable Sir Mountstuart Grant Duff, "it shows what a plucky young woman with a powerful newspaper at her back can do. For my part I think it best in travelling to see foreign countries slowly, but if any more enterprising Americans desire to emulate Miss Bly's example it is much better to travel rapidly than not to travel at all. Miss Bly has proved herself a remarkable young woman, and I hope she will get a good husband."

Upon Bly's arrival in Jersey City, *The World*'s Paris correspondent, Robert H. Sherard, set off at once to Amiens to deliver the good news to Jules Verne in person. "Bravo!" Verne cried three times on hearing the news, and then said delightedly, "This is a most excellent result. I consider the performance wonderful. This great journalistic feat will interest the whole world." Verne told Sherard that every week he received numerous letters asking him about Bly's trip, and that in Amiens he never met anyone who didn't immediately ask, "Well, how is Miss Bly getting on?" (Indeed, in Paris interest in Bly's trip was so widespread that no fewer than ten new editions of *Around the World in Eighty Days* had been issued, and in response to "very general demand," the theatrical version, which had closed eleven years earlier, was now being revived. There was even talk of altering the script to add some lines about Nellie Bly's own race around the world. "We certainly owe her some recognition," explained the stage manager.)

Honorine Verne, too, was delighted with the news. "I always said that Miss Bly was certain to succeed. She looked like one who would not get beaten at anything she might undertake. I am very glad if only for the reason that now my husband will have a little peace of mind. You can't imagine the interest M. Verne has taken in this trip." Often in the evening, she said, he would bring out his globe and point out where Nellie Bly probably was at that moment; on the wall map upstairs he would mark her daily progress with little flags. "Now tell me," Honorine Verne asked Sherard lightly, "did Miss Bly come back alone? Did she not find a husband en route? Remember, we teased her about that."

Sherard assured her that Nellie Bly was still single.

Jules Verne said, "I have thought all the time about Miss Bly, as my wife says. My principal thought was, '*Dieu!* How I wish I were free and young again!' I would have been enchanted to do the same journey, even under the same conditions—rush round the globe without seeing much. I would have set off at once and perhaps offered to escort Miss Bly."

"That wouldn't have suited me," said Honorine. "Besides, one condition of Miss Bly's tour was: do it alone, risking the dangers of the unprotected." With that, she sent down to the cellar for a vintage bottle of Pontet-Canet, and together the three raised glasses in honor of Nellie Bly's success.

Later, Robert Sherard would claim that he "repeatedly" asked *The World* to send Jules Verne a letter thanking him for his kindness in hosting Nellie Bly, but no letter was ever sent; Sherard said he was told that "the old man had got good advertising out of it and had no reason to complain."

THE PRINT RUN for the January 26 issue of *The World* was 280,340 copies, the largest ever for one of the paper's Sunday editions. Even so, newsdealers throughout the city ran short of *The World* that day. In New York's hotels newsboys were offering patrons fifteen cents for a copy of the paper that normally sold for only four, which they then resold for anywhere from twenty-five to fifty cents apiece; and even at those prices, it was reported, there were no copies to be had. To meet the demand, *The World*'s presses ran all through the night printing extra copies, and the following day the city's residents were given the highly unusual sight of newsboys selling the Sunday paper on Monday morning.

On January 26, *The World* received a letter sent by a Mr. and Mrs. G. S. Harding of No. 188 Eldridge Street, on the Lower East Side, giving news of their baby. She had been born the afternoon before, just as the cannonade was going off at the Battery, and they had named her Nellie Bly Harding—"hoping," they wrote, "she may prove a bright light same as her namesake."

Indeed, *The World* reported, "Several ladies who have become mothers since Nellie Bly started on her trip have notified the European Trip Editor that they intend to name their offspring after the young circumnavigator."

The following day *The World* received another letter, from John J. Timmins of New York, who wrote, "I have taken the liberty of naming my four-year-old colt, which promises to trot very fast, Nellie Bly, after your world-renowned globe-trotter. Hoping she will prove as successful, I remain very respectfully yours."

In Burlington, Wisconsin, William W. Storms named one of his prizewinning Buff Leghorn chickens after her, and several show dogs were so named as well, including a pug, an English setter, and a toy spaniel, the latter owned by Mrs. Ferdinand Senn, a champion spaniel breeder in New York. In 1890, at the fourteenth annual dog show of the Westminster Kennel Club, in the category of Japanese spaniels, the red ribbon for second place was awarded to Nellie Bly.

Later on, in recognition of her record-breaking ride on its line from Chicago to Jersey City, the Pennsylvania Railroad named its fastest train after her, and for many years, until 1961, the *Nellie Bly* ran nonstop between New York and Atlantic City.

AT THE AMPHION THEATRE in Brooklyn, the popular music hall team of Hallen and Hart were starring in their musical comedy *Later On!* Now they announced that they would be adding a new song to the show, which they called "Globe Trotting Nellie Bly." To a lively allegro tempo the song's first verse ran:

> *I hold here in my hand a lengthy cablegram,*
> *That came from far across the sea;*
> *It's from Miss Nellie Bly, and its contents I will try*
> *To tell, if you will listen to me.*
> *She's trying very hard to beat the world's record*
> *To round the world in seventy-five days*
> *Of the many funny sights in her cablegram she writes,*
> *Of the people and their very curious ways.*

After describing some imaginary escapades of Bly in Europe (kissing the Blarney stone, telling funny stories to the Prince of Wales, singing "Little Annie Rooney" to Jules Verne), the song concluded:

> *When she landed in Hong Kong, she rang the dinner gong,*
> *And they thought her quite a curiosity.*
> *To see our Nellie hustle, and she did not wear a bustle,*
> *A sight which even here we rarely see.*
> *When she reached Yokohama she met a Jersey farmer,*
> *And together they sipped too-long boo-long tea;*
> *She was courted by a Jap—sat in the old King's lap,*

And he wanted her to marry him, you see.
But when the Oceanic *sailed,*
How that poor fellow wailed,
Now she's on the ocean blue.
She's a box of chewing tu-lu
For each one in Honolu',
I wish she'd bring some back to me and you.

"Globe Trotting Nellie Bly" was not sung until the show's third act, *The World* reported, "but it was worth waiting for. The joint stars rendered the song effectively, and made such a hit that an encore was vigorously and vociferously demanded."

AS THE COUPONS HAD come pouring into its offices in the closing days of the Nellie Bly Guessing Match, *The World* supplemented its regular staff of fourteen tabulators with six clerks from the New York Post Office (two of them said to be "postmark experts" who could "determine at a glance dates of mailing and reception, where a novice would be hopelessly puzzled"), but even these six proved inadequate, and the number was increased first to ten, and then to fourteen, until eventually nineteen additional men from the Post Office had been brought on. The corps was divided into three squads of eleven men, with each squad working a full eight-hour shift, so that the counting and sorting could go on without cease throughout the day, until all 927,422 coupons had been tabulated.

By the following Sunday, February 2, *The World* was finally able to declare a winner: Mr. F. W. Stevens, of 193 Second Avenue in New York City, who had submitted a guess of 72 days, 6 hours, 11 minutes, and 14 2/5 seconds, or two-fifths of a second off the actual time. (The next closest guess came from Thomas Halton, of 1345 Third Avenue, who had guessed 72 days, 6 hours, 11 minutes, and 13 2/5 seconds—just one-fifth of a second away from a claim to the prize.) On the afternoon of the announcement a *World* reporter visited Frank Stevens at his home near Twelfth Street to ask him about his winning strategy.

Every evening after reading *The World,* Stevens explained, he cut out the official coupon and sent in a guess on it; he figured that he had sent in about fifty coupons in all. His earliest guesses had been based on the supposition that Nellie Bly would take the five o'clock train out of Chicago, but when he saw that she would probably reach Chicago in time to take the ten-thirty train on Friday morning, he made a number of guesses based on the scheduled arrival time in Jersey City. "That is about all there was to it," he said modestly. "I didn't go into anything like a close study of time tables."

The *World* reporter described Frank Stevens as "a young man of genial manners and a pleasant, easy address." Stevens worked as the general superintendent at Bill & Caldwell, a manufacturer of hats, furs, and straw goods at 550 Broadway, in the cast-iron district; he had come to the city six years earlier from the upstate town of Dover, and had never been abroad. The reporter asked him, "Will you take the trip yourself or delegate it to some one else?"

"If I can get away from business I shall go myself," he replied, "and if I do I will take Mrs. Stevens with me, and pay her expenses out of my own pocket."

IN THE SAME ISSUE of *The World* that announced the winner of the guessing match, an editorial declared, "The year 1890 opens audaciously for *The World*." Total circulation for the month of January, the paper reported, was well over ten million copies, with a daily average of 333,058; this was a gain of 35,613 copies per day over the previous January. There seemed no denying that the increase in sales was due in large part to the public's intense interest in Nellie Bly—particularly as a front-page notice beneath the masthead of that very issue advised readers: "With Every Copy of To-day's World Will Be Furnished *Free* a Photo-likeness of Nellie Bly. Be Sure That You Receive the Picture with Your Copy."

It was nothing short of astonishing that a newspaper for which a reporter had done her most significant work undercover would give out a photograph of her, but, as *The World* acknowledged elsewhere in the issue, "the public interest in the young lady has become so great that *The World* to-day relieves the intense public curiosity by publishing her portrait." This explanation was contained in the introduction to a feature article in the same issue, "The Story of Nellie Bly," which was touted as "an authentic biography of *The World*'s globe-girdler." (As the paper explained, "at the same time that the public learns what Nellie Bly looks like, it seems well to say something about who and what she is.")

"Miss Cochrane is a good-looking brunette," *The World* informed its readers (this was an upgrade from its earlier assessment of her as "fairly good-looking"), "of medium height, and slight graceful figure, who does not look nearly so old as the records make her. Her appearance is girlish, and while contact with the world in her journalistic capacity has given her thoughts and manners a serious cast, and the far-reaching usefulness of many of her tasks has made her feel that newspaper women have earnest missions in life, still there is a glint of the sunshine of youth in many of her ways and a jolly light-heartedness at times manifests itself, which shows that there is a strong, bright link between her looks and the girlhood that radiates through them." The article described Bly's upbringing in the little Pennsylvania town of "Cochrane's Mills" (*The World,* like young Pink Cochran herself, had unilaterally added an *e* to the end of the surname); her father's sudden death and the struggle over the family estate; her entry into journalism in Pittsburgh; and her "many and brilliant" achievements with *The World,* including her Blackwell's Island exposé. The "authentic biography," though, repeated the canard that Nellie Bly was twenty-three, not twenty-five, years old; moreover, it asserted that as a girl Bly had attended boarding school in Pennsylvania for two full years (in fact it had been only one semester) and that she had withdrawn from the school not because her mother could no longer afford to send her but "on account of threatening heart disease." Even one more year of study, the family doctor was said to have determined, "would probably cost the girl her life."

Probably very few of the paper's readers recalled that on the day Nellie Bly set out from Hoboken a *World* reporter had asked her whether she was bringing any medicine in her bag. Bly, he wrote, had given a smile "of derision at such a question" and replied, "I never was very sick in my life and don't expect to be now."

THE PREVIOUS DECEMBER, Walt McDougall had drawn a cartoon for *The World* entitled "Will It Come to This?" that showed Nellie Bly disembarking from a steamship to an excited crowd waiting to greet her, each person holding up an object for display: a Nellie Bly sewing machine, Nellie Bly hat, Nellie Bly typewriter, Nellie Bly camera, and so forth. Only a few months later McDougall's cartoon proved to be remarkably prescient. It was an age when American companies were beginning to understand that the image of a famous person could be used to sell products; through advertising, the traits generally associated with the person—in Nellie Bly's case, these included pluck, vitality, courage, patriotism, and, most important, success—seemed to be transferred to the product and, by extension, to the person using it. So in 1890 women around the country wore Nellie Bly caps and Nellie Bly dresses and Nellie Bly gloves, modeled on the ones she had made famous (and therefore appealing) during her trip. Children used the Nellie Bly tablet notebook—the cover of which featured a large globe with, incongruously, kittens scampering over it—and carried it to school in a Nellie Bly schoolbag, next to, perhaps, the Nellie Bly doll. At home, one could write on Nellie Bly stationery with the Nellie Bly fountain pen in the light of the Nellie Bly lamp, and afterward relax with the Nellie Bly photograph album (it was, said the industry journal *The American Stationer,* "the biggest seller of the season; two editions have been sold out and still the cry is for more") and "Nellie Bly Globe Circling Embroideries." The W. E. Piaget Company offered a Nellie Bly bonbon box. The George L. Ingerson company of Syracuse, New York, even sold "Nellie Bly Horse Feed."

A series of delicately tinted advertising trade cards, extolling the virtues of numerous products, showed Nellie Bly in her iconic traveling outfit, ubiquitous gripsack in hand, in various whimsical settings—sitting on the crescent moon, standing atop a dragonfly, walking a tightrope between the earth and the moon—each one accompanied by a laudatory verse. ("If Nellie Bly is in the sky / Observing Luna's phases," read the card that showed her perched atop the moon, "It is because the World's applause / Makes light of those it praises.") In one of the most striking images, Bly clutches an American flag with which she waves farewell to Phileas Fogg receding into the distance.

> "O Fogg, goodbye," said Nellie Bly,
> "It takes a maiden to be spry.
> To span the space 'twixt thought and act,
> And turn a fiction to a fact."

The cards sold everything from coffee to tobacco to spices, from baking soda to Dr. Morse's India Root Pills, which promised fast relief for "biliousness, headache, and constipation."

Probably the most popular product associated with Bly's trip was the

A typical example of a Nellie Bly advertising card,
this one selling cream of tartar and baking soda

board game *Round the World with Nellie Bly,* advertised as "A Novel and Fascinating Game with Plenty of Excitement on Land and Sea"; indeed, the game proved so popular that its manufacturer, McLoughlin Brothers, would issue a second edition before the end of the year. Based in New York, McLoughlin Brothers was at the time the leading manufacturer of board games in the country, due in large part to its pioneering use of chromolithography, a printing process that produced richly colored images at low cost. The technology was put to glorious use in *Round the World with Nellie Bly,* in which players moved along a brightly colored spiral path on which each space represented a day of Nellie Bly's trip. (To add variety, some liberties were taken with the actual events: Bly, for instance, was "on a raft" on the sixty-fourth day and "rescued" on the sixty-fifth.) The game came with a spinner and a set of markers; after each spin the player moved his or her marker forward the corresponding number of spaces, with fate determined by the luck of the spin. Thus, on the fifth day one encountered an iceberg and had to go back to port; on the ninth day one met Jules Verne and was granted an additional spin; brigands in Brindisi on the eleventh day sent one back two days; fair weather on the Pacific sent one ahead two days; a steamship collision on the sixty-third day sent one back fifteen days. Catastrophically, becoming snowbound in the Sierra on the sixty-ninth day (a fate Bly herself had avoided by use of a chartered train) forced the player to lose five spins. Having traveled successfully through the seventy-second day, the player landed at the center of the spiral, where a trumpet blared ALL RECORDS BROKEN, moving past the Statue of Liberty onto a Manhattan Island on which the only recognizable structure is the World Building.

IN THE FINAL DAYS of Bly and Bisland's race around the world, John Brisben Walker of *The Cosmopolitan* insisted that he had sent three messages to Elizabeth Bisland while she was aboard the India mail train, instructing her to take the steamship *La Champagne* at Le Havre; those messages, he claimed, had never been delivered. In an article in the *Washington Post,* unnamed friends of Walker attributed Bisland's loss to "the bad faith of the steamship people," who had purposely delayed delivery of the three messages. The *Post* reported, "There will probably be some lively litigation over this matter should Miss Bisland arrive here late and behind time." When the race was over, and Bisland had indeed arrived behind time, another news story reported that "a fair race was spoiled by a foul" and "a suit against the steamship company will follow."

Two years later Allan Forman of *The Journalist* would claim, "It is a fact—which I can prove as I am somewhat intimately connected with the whole affair—that had it not been for a trick which would have disqualified *The World* among sporting men but which, under the very loose code of ethics which governs the conduct of a 'great' newspaper, is perhaps allowable to save the paper from ignominious defeat—had it not

The popular board game Round the World with Nellie Bly, *as it first appeared in the pages of* The World

been for this trick, I say, Miss Bisland would have beaten Miss Bly by three days."

Allan Forman never did "prove" his allegations against *The World*—presumably he was suggesting that the paper had induced the Cook's agent at Villeneuve to provide misinformation to Bisland—nor did John Brisben Walker ever initiate any litigation relating to the race, against the steamship companies or anyone else. Probably he understood that Bisland would have lost the race regardless. In any case, he had received his publicity and the additional revenue that came with it. An article about Walker in *The Review of Reviews* noted of Bisland's trip, "The venture turned out to be one of the most successful strokes of business in the history of the magazine. Mr. Walker estimates its money value to his establishment at a figure which seems incredible."

Elizabeth Bisland herself never addressed any of the rumors surrounding the mysterious travel agent. She did not comment publicly on the trip after the day of her return, other than in the seven articles she wrote about it for *The Cosmopolitan,* where she had resumed work as literary editor. Her account began:

> If, on the thirteenth of November, 1889, some amateur prophet had foretold that I should spend Christmas Day of that year on the Indian Ocean, I hope I should not by any open and insulting incredulity have added new burdens to the trials of a hard-working soothsayer—I hope I should, with the gentleness due a severe case of aberrated predictiveness, have merely called his attention to that passage in the Koran in which it is written, "The Lord loveth a cheerful liar"—and bid him go in peace. Yet I did spend the 25th day of December steaming through the waters that wash the shores of the Indian Empire, and did do other things equally preposterous, of which I would not have believed myself capable if forewarned of them. I can only claim in excuse that these vagaries were unpremeditated, for the prophets neglected their opportunity and I received no augury.

In the articles Bisland always described her seventy-six-day undertaking for *The Cosmopolitan* as a "trip" or a "journey," and never, not even once, as a "race."

In the spring, Lady Broome—whom Elizabeth Bisland had befriended when they stayed at the same hotel in Colombo—sent a letter from England inviting Bisland to spend the upcoming London season with her and her husband, Sir Frederick Broome; the invitation was happily accepted. Quickly Bisland got her work affairs into order: while she was away, it was agreed, she would continue writing the "In the Library" column for *The Cosmopolitan,* and the editors of *Harper's Bazaar* also commissioned her to write a series of five articles entitled "An American Woman's First Season in London." On the afternoon of Wednesday, May 14, Elizabeth Bisland gave a farewell reception at her apartment on Fourth Avenue, where the guest list included the poet and magazine editor R. W. Gilder; former Union Army general Fitz John Porter; and Frances Folsom Cleveland, wife of the former president, who only four years earlier, at the age of twenty-one, had become the youngest First Lady in history. Three days later she boarded the Cunard steamship *Servia* (as it happened, the sister ship of the *Bothnia,* on which she had endured such a miserable Atlantic crossing the previous January), bound for Liverpool. Elizabeth Bisland would spend the following year—the time when the American public's interest in her was at its height—in England.

DURING HER TRIUMPHANT railroad trip across the country, a reporter from the *Philadelphia Inquirer* had asked Nellie Bly what she planned to do next. Bly immediately responded, "I expect to go back to work again. You know I must do something for a living. And I expect to work until I fall in love and get married."

Nellie Bly, however, did not go right back to work, at least not at *The World.* In those first hectic days after her return (made more hectic by the monkey, who, whenever he was let out of his cage, ran around the apartment smashing all the china he could find), Bly received visitors, accepted flowers sent by well-wishers, posed for photos, and fielded offers from theatrical promoters. At this point she was probably the most famous woman in the United States—perhaps even, in *The World*'s estimation, "the best-known and most widely talked-of young woman on earth today"—and as such, it seemed inevitable that she would undertake a lecture tour. The lecture tour was how nineteenth-century Americans got to see and hear famous people, be they scientists, inventors, philosophers, or retired generals, or simply those deemed to have a sufficiently unusual talent or compelling enough personal story. After some deliberation, Bly chose J. M. Hill to represent her, having decided that he presented "the best opportunities." It seemed an obvious choice: Hill was the most prominent theatrical promoter in the country, who owned theaters, produced plays, and managed actors and actresses. In a matter of days he had arranged a forty-city lecture tour for Bly, stretching from New York to California; her first appearance was slated for February 9.

After her four-part account of her trip, which ran each Sunday through the month of February, Nellie Bly's byline stopped appearing in *The World*. "Miss Bly has a vacation from *The World*," the paper informed its readers, "and these lectures have no connection with her journalistic work. The enterprise is her own, and *The World* echoes the wishes of thousands when it says it hopes she will make a fortune on the lecture platform."

NELLIE BLY'S TOUR began auspiciously, at the Union Square Theatre in New York, where J. M. Hill had booked her to lecture for three successive Sunday evenings. (This would not have been especially difficult for him to arrange, as he owned the theater.) The Union Square Theatre was widely considered to be one of the most beautiful in New York. From the entrance, a broad columned portico on Fourteenth Street, patrons passed through a brilliantly lit vestibule to the auditorium, which was painted white and ornamented throughout with gold fluting. Across the ceiling ran a series of frescoes depicting figures from Greek mythology; the proscenium arch had been painted maroon with gold at the bottom edge to simulate drapery. The auditorium held about twelve hundred seats in three steeply rising tiers, and on the evening of February 9 they were all filled with well-dressed New Yorkers. On the stage, furniture had been arranged in a typical drawing-room scene; it was the set for the other show currently playing at the theater, *The County Fair,* a comedy starring the popular female impersonator Neil Burgess as the spinster aunt Abigail Prue. At eight-thirty P.M., J. M. Hill himself walked onto the stage, coming down to the footlights to briefly address the audience. He was a handsome man in his middle years, his most distinguishing feature a pair of bushy sideburns; a few years earlier *The New York Times* had described him as resembling "a particularly good-looking curate."

"It is my pleasure and privilege, ladies and gentlemen," said Hill, "to present to you this evening an American girl who has made the circuit of the globe alone, and she is here to tell you how the trip was made. It is her first appearance before an audience and she does not come as a trained speaker, so that whatever imperfections she may display, you will understand the cause. I feel quite sure, however, that you will extend to her a cordial welcome. Permit me to introduce Miss Nellie Bly."

From the center entrance of the drawing room Nellie Bly appeared and, to a great burst of applause, began to walk downstage. The stage was thirty-five feet deep and she was several seconds in crossing it. She had on the same blue broadcloth dress that she had worn on her trip around the world; on her left wrist was a silver bracelet, on her right a watch in a thick black band, and on her thumb her lucky gold ring. Her hair was cut into bangs at the front and braided in the back. She stepped down to the footlights and took a bow. After a moment the applause died down and the hall grew silent.

"As Mr. Hill has said," she began, "I am not a trained speaker. I am here simply to tell you of my journey around the world, and how I came to make it." Those in the front rows might have noticed that her cheeks were slightly flushed, but her voice was even and steady; if she was feeling any nervousness her voice did not betray it. She continued, "Over a year ago I first got the idea. I went to a railroad office and got some time-tables, and studied them before making the suggestion to the editor of *The World*. I had reached the conclusion that a journey around the earth could be made in less than eighty days. I was rather afraid to offer the idea at first, because I didn't know how it would be received, but I did it finally, and said I thought the trip could be made in less time than it had been made by Phileas Fogg." Bly explained that the editor of *The World* refused to send a woman, because of the number of trunks she would require. " 'Well,' said I, 'send your man, and I'll start out at the same time and beat him.' " The audience laughed at this, which seemed to catch Bly somewhat by surprise, but she continued with even more firmness in her voice, and went on to tell the entire story of her trip, from the traveling dress that was made by William Ghormley in a single day ("I didn't think that he could, but he did, and this is the dress I have on now") to the crowds of thousands that had greeted her on her return. She spoke for ninety minutes, and as she did she shifted from one foot to the other, rarely standing perfectly still. Occasionally she would place her right hand, then both hands behind her, and often left them down at her sides; these were the gestures of an untrained elocutionist, and they seemed only to endear her further to the audience. She told about meeting Jules Verne, about her travel though foggy Italy on the India mail train. Describing her arrival in Brindisi, Bly said, "The people looked at me and when they heard that I was an American they laughed. That made me angry and I told the guard to tell them that the Italians in America were normally seen with a hand-organ. Then they stopped laughing."

As she narrated her travels farther east, the details seemed to have been conjured from an exotic Oriental tale: the snake charmers of Colombo and the dancing girls of Yokohama, the gambling halls of Port Said and the execution grounds of Canton. She told about how, near Singapore, a lazy Englishman had proposed to her and how she in turn had proposed to put him to work—a line that drew laughter and applause from the audience. "Not the least interesting part of the story," noted a reporter from *The World,* "was the sturdy loyalty to the Stars and Stripes that Miss Bly displayed throughout the journey." She would not, Bly said, permit anyone to make unjust reflections upon the United States without receiving prompt and firm retaliation from her. More than one reporter noted with approval that her lecture was shot through with constant assertions of American superiority: America, Nellie Bly liked to say, was "far ahead" of all other nations, a sentiment that she repeated over and over, in every talk and interview she gave.

After an hour and a half Bly had taken her audience around the world and then delivered it back again to New York; when she finished speaking she received a triple ovation. Afterward J. M. Hill was pleased to announce that the evening's receipts had totaled $1,362.75.

IN FEBRUARY THE *Dallas Morning News* noted, "Since Nellie Bly, the journalist, decided to become Nellie Bly the lecturer some of the papers have opened a merciless fire upon her." It was one thing for a young woman to go around the world, and apparently quite another for her to attempt to profit from it. There seemed also to be something distasteful in the notion of a woman presuming to speak, uninterrupted, for an entire evening. From Laramie, Wyoming, the *Daily Boomerang* announced to its readers: "Nellie Bly is going on the lecture platform. We had hoped that she was too sensible a young woman to do that." The *Knoxville Journal* agreed: "It is to be hoped that Nellie Bly won't lecture. The public has some rights." Reporting the news of Bly's contract with J. M. Hill, the

Philadelphia Inquirer remarked, "This is sad, but the affair could have no other ending." After Bly's first lecture the *Chicago Times* had to resort to biblical allusions to find language strong enough for its disapproval: "The flesh-pots of Egypt in the shape of $1400 for a first appearance have proved too strong a temptation, and that young and interesting woman is now chasing after the American public with the same determination that she ran around the world. It is to be hoped that having definitely made up her mind to go after mere money she will find enough of it to justify her in her apostasy."

"She was engaged by a big newspaper to do a big piece of advertising, and she did her duty in a big, spacious sort of way," observed the *Chicago Journal,* before adding sarcastically, "Miss Bly has been made famous, and may now settle down comfortably into the position of a leader, if not a savior, of society."

FROM NEW YORK, Nellie Bly traveled up to Rochester, and to Hartford and Boston; later would come lectures in Philadelphia and Harrisburg, and then Chicago and points west. She had gone around the world, and almost immediately had set out again around the country. She was staying in hotels, most of them very nice, but still not like home; often Bly stayed in her room, writing her book about the trip. While on tour she seemed always to read the articles about herself in the local papers. "Sometimes I am very unhappy," she admitted to a reporter, "because I have been misrepresented by some newspapers as a coarse, unrefined girl, who loves to stir up sensation. Some have poked great fun at me because I have gone on a tour, but I am only making my living. I am only a woman and when unkind things are said of me that the public read and comment upon it makes me unhappy."

She had always been careful to dress well and present herself as a modest, plainspoken American girl; now, for the first time, she seemed to have lost control of her image. She always claimed to be younger than she actually was; now some newspapers were overstating her age. Once Bly complained in print that she had been described as being anywhere "from 30 to 40, and no woman likes to be any older than she is." Already by March some of the novelty seemed to have worn off her lecture tour. In Philadelphia, the *Inquirer* blamed poor advertising for her having been greeted by "anything but a full theatre." In Chicago she had an audience

Nellie Bly in 1890

of only a few hundred, far less than the theater's capacity; one of the local papers, the *Daily Inter Ocean,* referred to the crowd as "small but appreciative." For years, ever since she first became a reporter, Bly had thrived on the fast pace and constantly changing activity of her work—how one week she might be learning how to fence and the next investigating the claims of a faith healer. Now there was always the same blue dress (eventually it must have seemed less outfit than costume), the same ninety-minute lecture, crowds and venues that seemed to vary little from place to place. She told a reporter that while lecturing was much easier, it lacked the excitement of newspaper work, and when the tour was over she figured she would "return to the ranks."

ON THE AFTERNOON of March 5, 1890, shortly before departing for her lecture in Philadelphia, Nellie Bly was walking with her mother on Broadway when a man—Bly described him as "coarse-featured" and "brutal-looking"—approached her and addressed her by name. Recognizing him as a private detective, Bly kept walking and refused to acknowledge his calls. In frustration the man grabbed Bly by the shoulder and tried to force a piece of paper down the neck of her coat, at which point she appealed to a nearby policeman for help.

"That is Nellie Bly," the detective is said to have shouted, "and I am ordered to arrest her."

The policeman allowed Bly to leave, and with her mother she hurried aboard a passing streetcar, shaken and angered by the experience. Later a reporter would write of the encounter with the private detective, "What he wanted Nellie does not know, but she thinks it is a plot to injure her in some way."

Though nothing more of this incident ever came to light, it seems clear that the detective, in forcing the piece of paper on Nellie Bly, was attempting to deliver a subpoena—and there was, at the time, a pending lawsuit in which Bly figured directly. In one of her most celebrated exposés for *The World,* Nellie Bly had posed as the wife of a drug manufacturer, who was hoping to kill an upcoming bill regulating patent medicines. In an Albany hotel room she sought to obtain the help of Edward Phelps, the so-called Lobby King of Albany, who assured her that for the right price he could have the bill killed in the Assembly. On a printed list of the members of the Affairs of Cities Committee he even put marks next to the ones on his payroll; a facsimile of that list was published in *The World* on April 1, 1888. One of the marked names was that of Daniel W. Tallmadge, an assemblyman from Brooklyn, who strongly objected to being implicated in the matter—he .was, his attorney affirmed, "a gentleman who valued his high reputation more than he did his life"—and after the publication of Bly's story he brought a libel suit against *The World,* estimating the damage to his reputation at $50,000. For nearly two years both sides filed a series of motions and countermotions, but in March of 1890 the case was finally ready to go to trial. Nellie Bly's testimony, of course, would be critical to the defense's case, and *The World* sent word to Bly asking her to come at once to Brooklyn. However, according to one published report, "Miss Bly made a response that she was under the management of Mr. Hill and was engaged in a lecture tour and therefore could not obey the summons. In this dilemma Manager Hill was appealed to and he sent for the young woman, requesting her to return to New York and thereupon she most emphatically declined to do anything of the kind."

The *World*'s attorneys requested a postponement of the trial, owing to their inability to subpoena their principal witness—while on tour she was beyond the jurisdiction of the court—but the judge refused to grant a further delay. At this point the defense team withdrew ("in no pleasant humor," a reporter observed), and the Tallmadge libel suit was heard without *The World*'s offering a defense and with Daniel W. Tallmadge himself as the only witness. When the judge charged the jury he indicated that the article was "plainly libelous," and after only five minutes' deliberation the jury found for the plaintiff and assessed damages of $20,000. It was an enormous sum of money—equivalent to the combined annual salary, on average, of thirty-two female journalists.

NELLIE BLY HERSELF never explained why she had refused to testify for *The World*. Others, though, were happy to provide a reason: as one newspaper report observed, "Enemies have been unkind enough to suggest that she had become afflicted with the disease whereby the head weighs much more than the rest of the body and which is popularly supposed to be incurable."

Bly did, however, reveal the bitterness that she felt toward the paper that had sponsored her trip. "*The World* never even said 'thank you' to me after my return," she complained to fellow journalist Frank G. Carpenter in a letter written later that year, though they had "made thousands of dollars clear on their increased circulation during my absence and immediately after my return." She continued, "From them I did not receive one cent and my salary had been a very low one. Mr. Pulitzer cabled his congratulations to me and begged me to accept the present he was sending from India. I accepted the congratulations but then never seen [*sic*] the present. A movement was started in the office to get a medal for me but I have it upon good authority that the medal was given as a prize in a telegrapher's contest." Even the lecture tour—from which the newspaper had demanded she return in order to testify in their libel suit—"came to me through no effort of *The World*."

On the face of it this stinginess would seem difficult to believe, as Joseph Pulitzer was famously generous toward his employees; indeed, after Bly's first success with *The World,* her Blackwell's Island exposé, Pulitzer had made it known that he had rewarded her with "a handsome check." But Pulitzer was also an exceedingly rigorous and demanding employer, and he had always been haunted by the fear of libel suits—so much so that, according to Walt McDougall, "he nightly read most every paragraph in the paper" to examine it for potentially libelous material. When the new World Building opened in December of 1890, signs were hung around the city room that exhorted: "Accuracy! Terseness! Accuracy!" ("Accuracy," a *World* editor recalled Pulitzer as saying, "is to a newspaper what virtue is to a woman.") Something had caused Pulitzer to become suddenly parsimonious with his star reporter, and it certainly seems possible that it was the Tallmadge libel suit. So: Joseph Pulitzer, upset about a pending libel suit arising from Nellie Bly's work, refused to give her a bonus on her return; Bly, bitter about not being rewarded for the profits she brought to *The World,* refused to testify on the paper's behalf; and *The World,* deprived of her testimony, was ordered to pay out $20,000, thus confirming Pulitzer's initial grievance. Nellie Bly, for her part, felt that she could not continue to work at a newspaper that had asked so much of her and given her so little in return. She wrote to Frank Carpenter, "I have a standing invitation from *The World* to go back but it is needless to add that in face of their shabby treatment of me I shall never do so."

IN THE WAKE OF her refusal to testify in the Tallmadge case, Bly had a falling-out with J. M. Hill—the details of the break are not known, but a theatrical promoter would certainly not want to incur the enmity of the city's largest newspaper—and on May 4 the *Philadelphia Inquirer* reported that "the lecture tour has been abandoned."

At least one news report twisted the facts of the Tallmadge libel case, the better to suit the emerging public image of the grasping woman. "Our famous Nellie Bly," sneered the *New Mexican* newspaper of Santa Fe, "has brought a libel suit for $20,000 against the New York World. If she gains it she will be still more famous. A woman is never satisfied it seems." Nellie Bly, observed the *Cincinnati Commercial,* "has discovered that a successful lecture tour in the United States is a far more difficult undertaking than a tour around the world in seventy-three days." The *Michigan Farmer* noted, unkindly, "Nellie Bly is not a success as a lecturer. If she wishes to marry, however, this might be considered a recommendation."

AT THE END OF JULY, Bly's book-length account of her trip, entitled *Nellie Bly's Book: Around the World in Seventy-Two Days,* was published by the Pictorial Weeklies Company of New York. Not only was her name in the title, but her photograph appeared on the front cover as well, a head-and-shoulders portrait of her in ghillie cap and checked overcoat, gazing directly at the reader. The pride Bly took in the speed with which she had circled the globe was evident in the book's final chapter, entitled simply "The Record." It gave the actual itinerary of her trip compared to the one that had been published the day she left; the miles traveled from point to point and the hours spent in traveling and the hours delayed (she had, she calculated, spent 56 days, 12 hours, and 41 minutes in actual travel); her average rate of speed, both including and exclusive of stops; the names of all the steamships and railway lines on which she had traveled; and all the countries and bodies of water through which she had passed. *Nellie Bly's Book* sold for fifty cents; within a month the first edition of ten thousand copies had sold out.

Like many popular books of the time, *Nellie Bly's Book* included advertisements at the front and back. Not surprisingly, it featured an advertisement for William Ghormley, the dressmaker who had so quickly produced Nellie Bly's now-famous blue broadcloth dress, but less predictable were the ads for Pears' Soap and for Bovinine, the "Fluid Food" made from raw beef extract that "creates new and vitalized blood faster than any other preparation" (only twelve ounces, it was asserted, contained the "strength" of ten pounds of meat). The advertisement for Cheque Bank Checks consisted solely of a facsimile of a letter sent by Nellie Bly to the Wall Street agents of the Cheque Bank Limited Company. "Gentlemen," the letter began,

> In response to your inquiry, I will say, that I took the book of Cheque Bank checks with me on my tour round the world, and found them available as ready cash in every port that I visited. I assure you that they are a great convenience to travelers, and are only to be known and understood to be appreciated.

The Eastman Company of Rochester, New York, included a full-page advertisement for its new "Kodak cameras," handheld and loaded with film that the customer could mail in for processing. "You press the button," the company promised, "we do the rest." It could not have been coincidental that in the text of the book itself Bly had written:

> The only regret of my trip, and one that I can never cease to deplore, was that in my hasty departure I forgot to take a Kodak. On every ship and at every port I met others—and envied them—with Kodaks. They could photograph everything that pleased them; the light in those lands is excellent, and many were the pleasant mementos of their acquaintances and themselves they carried home on their plates. I met a German who was spending two years going around the world and he carried two Kodaks, a large and a small, and his collection of photographs was the most interesting I ever saw.

In August 1890, Nellie Bly signed a three-year contract to write serial fiction for Norman L. Munro's weekly magazine *The New York Family Story Paper*. Munro had made a fortune as a publisher of both books and magazines (the year before, he had collected Bly's Mexico reportage into a book entitled Six Months in Mexico), most of it the sort of mass-market fare, thrillers and romances and detective stories, that was then called "dime novel fiction." The New York Family Story Paper was the most popular and profitable of all his publications, advertised as having "the largest circulation of any family paper published in the world." For her work Bly would receive a salary of $10,000 the first year and $15,000 for each of the next two years. This was an astonishing amount of money, more even than Julius Chambers earned as managing editor of The World; according to at least one newspaper report, the contract with Munro made Bly the highest-salaried woman in the United States.

In making the offer, Norman L. Munro was obviously looking to trade on the Nellie Bly name, which he assumed would sell a lot of papers, and it is not hard to understand why Bly would have accepted it. She was continuing to support her mother as well as herself; and, unhappily, her older brother Charles had died earlier that year at the age of twenty-eight, and she may well have assumed some responsibility for the care of his widow and two young children. It is not known how much she was making from the sales of her book. By her own estimation she had earned about $9,500 from her lecture tour, a very good sum but perhaps not as large as she had anticipated. After her return from her around-the-world trip two real estate companies, seeking to capitalize on her fame, had each given her an undeveloped piece of property, one in Brooklyn and the other in the newly incorporated town of Iron City, Tennessee; together the two lots were said to be worth about $1,500. There is no evidence that Bly was paid anything at all by the advertisers who had used her image to sell their products. Most critically, she had left The World and now had no regular income. So it must have been a huge relief not to have to worry about money for the next three years; she had never forgotten how difficult life had been for her family when her father died and the money suddenly ran out.

The problem, however, was that she had only ever written fiction once before, in her novel The Mystery of Central Park, published in the fall of 1889. Though it contained some vivid New York color—scenes set in the city morgue and in a paper-box factory made good use of Bly's skills as a reporter—the novel as a whole was standard-issue melodramatic romance, the sort of story in which the heroine's "brown eyes sparkled like the reflection of the sun in a still, dark pool" while the hero "brooded moodily." Not surprisingly, *The Mystery of Central Park* had received scathing reviews and poor sales. The publisher seems to have envisioned it as the first in a series (the front cover touts "The 'Nellie Bly' Series"), but the public reception proved discouraging enough that no subsequent book ever appeared.

Now she was being paid a great deal of money to write serial stories—a genre that required an injection of suspense at the end of each installment so that the reader will eagerly look forward to the next one—and she didn't have any plot or characters for them. Over the years she had developed a close working relationship with Walt McDougall, *The World*'s staff illustrator; the two of them often went out on stories together so that McDougall could illustrate the scenes about which Bly wrote. ("She was sprightly, yet not frivolous," he once said of Bly. "Not a deep mind but a warm and generous heart.") Sometime after signing the contract with Norman Munro, Bly came to McDougall for help. She was, he could see, deeply distressed; she admitted to him that she didn't know how to begin the story.

"That's perfectly easy," McDougall recalled telling her. "You've merely to start off with a big thrill. Have your hero fall into a deep pit filled with big rattlesnakes, and go on to describe his terrors."

Bly considered this. She asked, "But how'll I keep the snakes from biting him?"

"He had a bottle in his hip pocket. It breaks, and the rattlers all keep their distance—but you don't mention this until you've written three or four thousand words, at least."

"It sounds great. But how am I going to get him out?"

"It doesn't matter. Any old way. Of course the heroine—and to the reader, that means you—must get him out, but the real punch is in his terrible situation. You can get him out with an ordinary barn ladder, a well-rope, or even a hop pole, nobody will notice."

"Yes, well, after that?"

"Keep on getting him, or her, into more just such holes, one in each chapter, until they get married or take out accident insurance, when, of course, the story must stop."

With that, McDougall said, Bly went off, and that was the last he ever heard about it.

Of course, there was another kind of writing at which Nellie Bly genuinely excelled—but she could never go back to doing the undercover reportage that had launched her career in the first place. She was now too famous.

BY THE SUMMER OF 1890, one American newspaper reported, Elizabeth Bisland was "in the very cream of the swim"; through her hosts Lord and Lady Broome, she had been given "entree to the best English society." Bisland attended squash parties and balls and dinners (including one held in the very dining room on the walls of which James McNeill Whistler had painted his famous peacocks), and the Henley boat races, and a socialist meeting, and once a garden party given by the Prince of Wales. She visited artists' studios and, less happily, endured tea parties in drawing rooms where the air was thick, in Bisland's description, with "portentous platitudes," the very solemn sort of affair that mischievously brought up in her "wild desires to whoop and smash china by way of restoring the equilibrium." Going to see her host, Sir Frederick Broome, debate in the House of Lords, she was ushered to an upstairs gallery where women watched from behind grates; afterward, in *Harper's Bazaar,* she wrote tartly, "I wonder if they fear we shall get into mischief that they cage us up like monkeys?"

The Broomes also introduced Bisland into London's literary society, where she met, among others, the philosopher and biologist Herbert Spencer, the popular novelist Rhoda Broughton, and Rudyard Kipling, who seemed as smitten with her as the men in New York had been. "I guess you'll have enough men censer-swinging under your nose to prevent your waving the thurible too markedly under mine," he wrote in a letter to her that summer. "All the same and until you go after something else new I am grateful."

At the close of the London season Bisland left the city for Oxford, where she took lodgings at 26 Holywell Street, a three-story stone house on a narrow medieval lane. Directly across the way was Rhoda Broughton's house, where in the oak-ceilinged drawing room, with her two pugs and Yorkshire terrier sleeping in baskets by the fireplace, friends gathered for tea at four-thirty each afternoon. Broughton also hosted regular gatherings of Oxford's Browning Society, where the guests occasionally included Robert Browning himself. It was the type of literary salon, full of warm hospitality and intelligent, animated conversation, to which Bisland had gravitated since her earliest days in New Orleans.

While Bisland was living in Oxford, she collaborated with Rhoda Broughton on a short novel entitled *A Widower Indeed*. The story concerns Edward Lygon, a bursar from an Oxford college, who is grieving over the recent death of his wife; soon he meets the new lodger at his neighbor's house on Holywell Street, a beautiful young woman from the American South with the unlikely name of Georgia Wrenn. She possesses, as the narrator describes it, "excellent health, pungent curiosity, and untrammeled freedom," and, needless to say, over the course of the book Edward Lygon falls in love with her. Georgia Wrenn seems to have been modeled, at least in part, on Elizabeth Bisland herself, and the general feeling among literary critics was that Bisland's main contribution to the writing of the novel was to provide character details about the young protagonist as well as the occasional odd bit of Southern dialect. (Wrenn once describes herself "slumping in and out of puddles in a kinsfolky way," and elsewhere exclaims, "It makes you feel as if you might whip your weight in wild cats without trying.") *A Widower Indeed* received decidedly mixed reviews: *Godey's Lady's Book,* for instance, said that "The book has much interest and force, so that, once having opened it, one does not know how to leave off reading it," but *The London Gentlewoman* called it "a tedious and disappointing book" in which "neither author is at her best, or even her second best." In New York, *The Independent* split the difference: "We note the peculiarities of Miss Broughton's diction and the impress of her worst style all through the half unnatural, half commonplace composition. We are inclined to credit all the best pages to Miss Bisland."

One of the men who had been very taken with Elizabeth Bisland back in New York was a thirty-five-year-old attorney by the name of Charles Wetmore. Born in Ohio and raised in Michigan, Wetmore had graduated from Harvard Law School and recently taken a job in a Wall Street law firm. His entry in the book *Prominent and Progressive Americans* indicates that he had decided to move to "the great metropolis of the nation"—much like Bisland in leaving New Orleans—because that was where "the competition [was] keenest, the requirements for high success the most exacting, and the possibilities of achievement the most promising." Wetmore was an avid outdoorsman, described by *The New York Times* as "an enthusiastic member of the Seawanhaka Corinthian Yacht Club"; he had a thick mustache that turned up dashingly at the ends and the smoldering dark eyes of a matinee idol. While Elizabeth Bisland was living in Oxford, Charles Wetmore came to visit her, and by the time he left the two were engaged. The following year Bisland returned to New York (she had now become editor of the women's section of the *Illustrated American*), and on October 6, 1891, she married Wetmore in a church crowded with friends and relatives. That same year, Harper & Brothers published *A Flying Trip Around the World,* a collection of the articles Bisland had written about her trip for *The Cosmopolitan*. It was the first book for which she was the sole author, the first of many that she would go on to write.

IN AUGUST 1890 Nellie Bly sent a poignant letter to her old friend Erasmus Wilson of the *Pittsburg Dispatch*. "My dear 'Q. O.,'" she wrote,

> . . . since I'm in luck again I'm hunting up old friends who seemed to have forgotten me. I sent you a newspaper the other day containing a notice of the very good contract I have made with Mr. Munro. It allows me to do newspaper work. I had made up my mind never to work for a newspaper again but I can do serial stories for Mr. Munro and never go out of my own home. I am busy on one now entitled "New York by Night." You know all the great English novelists began in this way, so I hope. The woman who wrote "Booths Baby" which has sold more than 500,000 copies and has been dramatized and played in every city in Europe & America has always written for such story papers. And then Mrs. Burnett wrote for *The Ledger* until she made a hit as a novelist, so I feel encouraged. . . . Why don't you write to me occasionally? How do you like my book? I have sold over 10,000 copies.

As Bly herself would later provide the inspiration for a younger generation of female journalists, so now she looked for encouragement to women who had come before her—women who had worked for story papers before achieving success as a novelist. That form of writing, though, seems always to have been a terrible struggle for her. No issues of *The New York Family Story Paper* survive from those years, but the literary press of the time made reference to only a single story by Bly appearing in Munro's paper.

By the fall of that year Nellie Bly had abandoned New York entirely. In November she moved with her mother to a farmhouse in the town of White Plains, some twenty-five miles north of the city; Mary Jane Cochrane had taken a five-year lease on the house, perhaps to escape the unpleasant talk that had been swirling around her daughter of late, and to provide her with the time and quiet in which to write. (Though in truth the house may not always have been very quiet: in a letter Bly said that she was living with "the cleverest parrot, the most wonderful monkey, and the wisest Skye terrier in the world," but "not one is congenial and friendly with the other, and they live in a constant state of suspended hostilities which may break forth at any moment and obliterate my menagerie.") Sometime in the fall Bly suffered an accident of some sort—she never indicated specifically what it was—and for a long time she was mostly confined to her bed, able to get around only on crutches. She tried her best to write while lying in bed, but she found it tiring and could never do it for very long. She was increasingly depressed. Her handwriting, which in her younger years had been breezy and full of flourishes, had become stiff and cramped, the lines heavy. Early the next year Bly would write to Erasmus Wilson again; the Pittsburgh Press Club was honoring him at their annual banquet, and they had not invited her to attend. Bly confided to him, "I think it was awfully shabby of them to leave me out but then—I suppose I can live with it." Later in the letter she wrote, "I am glad, dear Q, that you always hope for the best. Life cannot be entirely cheerless while hope remains. It is a year since I have entertained such a feeling and, strange to say, I have not the least conception why I am, or should be, blue."

It had been a year, Bly told Wilson, since she last felt hopeful. She wrote that letter on January 26, 1891—a year and a day since she stepped down from the train in Jersey City at the end of her triumphal march. Exactly one year before, she had been sitting in that little New York apartment crowded with flowers sent by well-wishers, exhausted but happy, unable to sleep for the roar of the crowd still ringing in her ears.

Over the course of the following year Nellie Bly had quit her newspaper in a dispute over money, been involved in a libel suit, fallen out with her manager and had her lecture tour cut short, endured the slights of newspaper editors, moved out of New York, become bedridden, and struggled to fulfill a lucrative magazine contract. She had ended up doing a kind of writing for which she had no natural talent and that could not have inspired her the way newspaper work once had. She was living in a lonely, isolated farmhouse, away from the city where she had gained her greatest success. Her romances with James Metcalfe (who had publicly poked fun at her) and Frank Ingram, however serious they might have been, had ended, and nothing else had taken their place. She was twenty-seven years old and still single; her professed goal had been to fall in love and marry a millionaire, but now that must have seemed an increasingly remote possibility. She had sold lots of copies of *Nellie Bly's Book,* but it was the last book she would ever write.

These days she felt, much of the time, listless and weary, and had trouble concentrating; she lay in bed and was gaining weight, and her doctor, she said, blamed it on her "blood." In March 1891, Bly wrote to Erasmus Wilson that she had become "a victim of the most frightful depression that ever beset mortal. You can imagine how severe it is when I tell you that I have not done a stroke of work for four weeks."

How different she had felt when she started out from Hoboken on that gray November morning—frightened, of course, but confident as well, and, as always, hopeful. And she had done what she set out to do: she had gone around the world faster than anyone ever had before her. She had outraced Elizabeth Bisland; but now, looking back, it was not entirely clear which of them had won.

EPILOGUE

—

IN 1890, SHORTLY AFTER NELLIE BLY AND ELIZABETH BISLAND RETURNED home, the superintendent of the U.S. Census declared the American frontier officially closed. The railroad had knitted together the country from coast to coast; the Indian wars were all but over (the massacre at Wounded Knee, South Dakota, the final military encounter between the United States and the Sioux, would take place in December of that year); since 1889 six western states had been admitted to the Union, leaving only Utah, Oklahoma, New Mexico, and Arizona as the last remaining territories in the continental United States. Now, with a renewed sense of patriotism and national pride, the country began to turn its attention outward.

In the decades since the Civil War, the United States had been transformed from a largely agricultural society to a largely industrial one. Over the span of some thirty years, production of wheat rose by 256 percent, steel rails by 523 percent, and coal by an incredible 800 percent; by 1890 the United States had become the leading consumer of energy in the world. That same year Congress approved the funding for the nation's first three battleships. In May 1890 a U.S. Navy captain and War College lecturer by the name of Alfred Thayer Mahan published an enormously influential book with the deceptively narrow title *The Influence of Sea Power upon History, 1660–1783*. Mahan, an unabashed imperialist, believed that a modern nation should seek power and wealth through foreign expansion made possible by a strong navy. That navy, in turn, would require numerous overseas bases and coaling stations; not incidentally, the colonies that supported those bases would also provide cheap raw materials as well as markets for products exported from home. In a review in *The Atlantic Monthly,* a young Washington civil service commissioner named Theodore Roosevelt declared, "Captain Mahan has written distinctly the best and most important, and also by far the most interesting book on naval history which has been produced on either side of the water for many a long year."

A strong navy, a string of overseas bases and coaling stations, colonies providing raw materials and foreign markets: this was, of course, the model presented by Great Britain, which was well on its way to creating the largest and most powerful empire the world had ever known. On their race around the world, Nellie Bly and Elizabeth Bisland had traversed that empire from Hong Kong in the east to Britain itself in the west, sailing on British ships and stopping at British coaling stations along the route, where they slept in British hotels, sent cables from British telegraph stations, and took carriage rides past British cliffside villas overlooking native huts. Elizabeth Bisland (who in one of her letters described herself as "not unduly pro-American") deeply admired the grandeur, tradition, and culture of Great Britain, which she referred to as "the mother soil"; for her part, Nellie Bly despised the British but envied the power of their empire, not to mention the sense of national pride that it bestowed on the citizens of the home country. The two ideas would be neatly combined by Senator Albert Beveridge of Indiana, who proclaimed, two days before the United States declared war on Spain: "The trade of the world must and shall be ours. And we will get it as our mother England has told us how."

By the 1890s Americans had also begun to travel to Europe in much larger numbers—though often, in imperial fashion, they seemed to want to bring their own country with them. In Liverpool they could stay at the Hotel Washington, in Florence at the Hôtel du New York, and in Paris at the Hôtel États-Unis and Hôtel de l'Oncle Tom. Everywhere concierges, waiters, and carriage drivers learned English in order to communicate with American tourists who insisted on speaking only their own language. Throughout Europe, hotels installed extra baths and elevators in the American fashion, and restaurants began offering such American favorites as ice cream and soda; still, it was reported, American travelers often complained when they could not find fried ham or pork and beans on the menu. These were the tourists Henry James dismissed as "vulgar, vulgar, vulgar," who could easily be recognized by their enormous bags, bad French, and demands for pale ale. Henry Adams decried the typical American traveler, "bored, patient, helpless, indulgent to an extreme," who was to be found "in every railway station in Europe carefully explaining to every listener that the happiest day of his life would be the day he should land on the pier in New York." (Nellie Bly herself had told a reporter in Kansas, "There is really not so much for Americans to see in foreign lands. We've got the best of everything here; we lack in nothing; then when you go over there you must be robbed, you get nothing fit to eat and you see nothing that America cannot improve upon wonderfully.") The writer Mary Cadwalader Jones felt obliged to begin her book *European Travel for Women: Notes and Suggestions* by remarking that "unless travellers are willing to leave national prejudices behind them, and ready to see whatever is characteristic and excellent in a foreign country, without finding fault because it is unfamiliar, they had better remain at home.

"Americans," she pointedly added, "are among the worst offenders in this regard."

IN 1892 ELIZABETH BISLAND and Charles Wetmore moved from the city to an estate they had built in Oyster Bay, Long Island. They called the house Applegarth, because it lay nestled between an ancient apple orchard on one side and an equally venerable pear orchard on the other. The design of the house had been adapted to the surrounding trees, "wound and looped between these irreplaceable treasures," Bisland wrote in an article about Applegarth, "pushing out a porch here, or a window there . . . and stepping up and down to rooms of different levels as the grade of the land required, so that roots need not be cut nor branches lopped"; they had not wanted to commit, as she put it, "the too common crime of arboricide." Applegarth was designed in the Tudor style, made of brick, half-timbering, and stucco, with multiple gables and chimneys, leaded windows, and doorways framed in limestone. Inside, many of the rooms had oak-beamed ceilings and walls finished in oak paneling. The stone fireplace in the drawing room was modeled on one belonging to Queen Elizabeth I (whom Bisland had long admired as having "rejected the whole theory of feminine subordination"); in the dining room, the decorated ceiling was adapted from the one in Queen Elizabeth's bedroom at Knole, and the furniture was copied from pieces in the Cluny Museum in Paris and the Victoria and Albert Museum in London.

Elizabeth Bisland and Charles Wetmore never had any children, and they lived, with Bisland's sister Melanie, at Applegarth until 1909; subsequently they moved to Washington, D.C., where Wetmore—who had left the law to become president of a utility company called the North American Company—served on the boards of directors of a number of public utilities. The years at Applegarth had been very productive ones for Bisland. During that time she edited the two-volume *Life and Letters of Lafcadio Hearn,* for which she wrote a long and sensitive remembrance of her old friend from New Orleans. She also wrote a highly regarded autobiographical novel, *A Candle of Understanding,* and two essay collections in which she celebrated the pleasures of literature and forcefully decried the domination of women by men. ("The oldest of all empires is that of man; no royal house is so ancient as his," wrote Bisland. "The Emperors of Japan are parvenus of the vulgarest modernity in comparison, and the claims of long descent of every sovereign in Europe shrivel into absurdity beside the magnificent antiquity of this potentate.") Her collection *At the Sign of the Hobby Horse,* published in 1910, contained essays on literary subjects as varied as garden books, contemporary poetry, and children's stories. The book's opening essay, "The Morals of the Modern Heroine," discussed what Bisland called "the contradictory attitude in the mind of the male—until recently almost the exclusive maker of literature—toward his female." As portrayed in books written by men, female characters had long been reduced to two main types: "the passionless goddess and the greedy child . . . and, tucked in between these extremes of virtues and vices on the heroic scale, an endless chain of rosy, smiling, comfortable young persons, with the morals of rabbits and the mentality of butterflies."

The New York Times, reviewing *At the Sign of the Hobby Horse,* pronounced Elizabeth Bisland's essays "so sane and so charmingly written . . . that the reviewer is tempted to quote from every page. They are wholesome and fresh, striking a distinct note of insistence on the desirability of making the most of life and art, of enjoying a world which is not, on the whole, such a bad place." Bisland's own world, however, would soon darken considerably, and her next essay collection would not appear for another seventeen years.

About 1910, Charles Wetmore was stricken with an illness of some sort; Elizabeth Bisland herself never identified it in any of her essays or letters, noting only that it affected the nerves and "cruelly attacked mind as well as body." It was an illness, as well, for which there was no obvious cure, and in the face of the suddenly uncertain future, Wetmore put aside his work and the two traveled together for a year, from April 1911 to April 1912, through Japan, China, Singapore, Ceylon, and India, revisiting many of the sites Bisland had first seen during her race against Nellie Bly. Much of that year they spent in Japan, their favorite part of the world; they reveled in early-morning strolls through the hills, stopping often to rest amid boughs flowered with crimson, lemon, and white. In the evenings they ate fish and bamboo shoots and salt pickle, and boiled rice in red-lacquered bowls, watching the sun go down over the purple mountains and the little lights sparkling in the dusk of the city below as from frail-looking wooden temples silvery with age bells rang out in single notes, with long vibrations that lingered on the air. The Japanese landscape, Bisland later wrote, is "a heaped mass of green velvet with the rice valleys shining like lakes of intensest emerald between and the cloud shadows race and run in every possible tone of blue and amethyst across, and then it all begins over again and yet is never quite the same." One morning in Yokohama they stood on a rock high among the trees, "breathing the moist saltness of the sea air mingled with faint almond perfumes of the cherry blooms. The mounting sun had burned away the mists of the night, and in the blue, floating far above a gulf of azure vapor, hung a vast shining cone of silver—a ghostly crest like a white flame." It was Fujiyama again, just as she had seen it the first time, on a December morning twenty-two years before.

Elizabeth Bisland was, as she put it, looking for the Japan of the Japanese, "light, fine, frail, with a touch of whimsey; of gay fancifulness; of soft, delicate fairness and flowery quiet." That Japan, though, was becoming increasingly difficult to find; the new trains brought swarms of tourists, and the streets were lined with the modern hotels and teahouses that catered to them. "One wouldn't begrudge the tourist so if he seemed to enjoy it, but his perspiring pervasiveness apparently derives nothing but fatigue from the effort, and one can't but wish he'd leave the places of beauty alone to the few who do get comfort out of them," Bisland wrote from Tokyo to her brother Pressley in New York, adding, "I think China and Japan are the only two countries remaining not utterly destroyed by our loathsome Occidental 'improvements.'"

An older Elizabeth Bisland, in an undated family photograph

By the following year, Charles Wetmore's illness had become serious enough that he was forced into retirement at the age of fifty-nine. In 1913 the couple moved to England, taking a home in the village of West By-fleet in Surrey, southwest of London; there, far from the pressures of work, amid the peaceful English countryside, they hoped that Wetmore might rest and recuperate. Not long afterward, though, on August 4, 1914, Great Britain declared war on Germany, and almost immediately innumerable thousands of young men were returning home blinded and broken. For more than a year Bisland did volunteer work in the local hospitals. From the very beginning she bitterly hated the war and would continue to be haunted by it; caring for those wounded soldiers, she would recall later, "especially those first gassed victims—gave me a sense of its intolerable abominations that never left me waking or sleeping."

With no rest to be found in England, the couple returned to Washington, D.C. Elizabeth Bisland's face was still youthful, her pale skin smooth and her eyes as clear as ever, but her long, wavy hair, formerly chestnut-colored, was now liberally streaked with gray. "Ever since the war began my spirit has been crushed as beneath a huge stone by the horrors and the suffering of this unhappy world," she wrote to Charles Hutson, a poet and editor whom she had befriended back in New Orleans. In April 1917 the United States entered the war, and Bisland threw herself into work for the National Salvage Society, organizing drives in several states to collect tinfoil, cork, paper, rags, leather, and glass to sell for the benefit of the Red Cross. The following year she was diagnosed with anemia, a condition that she attributed to "seven years of stress and strain and long nursing"; though her doctors counseled rest, she was not willing, as she put it, to "forget about war-work and housekeeping and stay in bed mornings and generally be a superfluous slug just when one wishes to be useful to one's country." Instead, she intensified her pace: as she had in England, she began volunteering to help care for the sick and wounded, this time at Washington's Walter Reed Hospital.

She had a patient to look after at home as well, one whose condition, despite all her efforts, seemed only to worsen. Finally, on Christmas Eve 1918, the situation had deteriorated to the point that Charles Wetmore was admitted to a nearby sanitarium. The doctors there insisted that Bisland not visit him, having determined, unaccountably, that her presence would be a hindrance to his recovery. Yet at the same time she felt bound to remain nearby, as "he might need me suddenly and I wish to be where it would be possible to reach him at once." For months Elizabeth Bisland lived in an agony of waiting and worrying. She was, she wrote to Hutson, "wading deep waters."

My poor husband has had to go to a sanitarium at last. For ten years I have been fighting his malady by every means that affection or science could suggest, and am defeated and helpless in the end. With such loss and suffering everywhere one doesn't like to make too much outcry over one's own, but if it had been a sacrifice in a great cause one could bear it with grace. This seems like such a futile, wanton blow—achieving no end. And one asks why with all his gifts and graces and talents this black drop should be squeezed into the cup to poison it.

In her sorrow Bisland turned to gardening for relief. The previous fall she had planted daffodils, jonquils, crocus bulbs, in the fervent hope that a show of blossoms might celebrate peace in the spring; spring came with still no peace, but the blossoms at least had arrived. In the grounds near her house she created a wildflower sanctuary; up early every morning, she worked the soil with basket and spade. Hard work at the beginning of the day, she had found, brought better sleep at the end, and in the meantime it kept her from thinking too much about her own sorrows and those of the wider world. She read every night, turning out the light only reluctantly at midnight, resentful at not being able to plunge into the next chapter. Reading had always been for her a doorway into another world, but now it became something more, an anodyne that dulled aches, an opiate that stilled the incessant turning over of questions that had no answers. She described herself, in those days, as a clock with a broken mainspring. "If you shake me hard I tick for a few moments, but soon relapse into silence and uselessness."

On June 1, 1919, Charles Wetmore died inside the sanitarium; Elizabeth Bisland had not laid eyes on him since Christmas Eve. With her husband's death Bisland plunged into a deep depression. "It seems to me the world grows every day ghastlier and vaguer and more like a dream, in which one moves about doing the accustomed things mechanically," she wrote to her old friend Charles Hutson on stationery bordered in black. "My only comfort now is that he clung to me for help and I was able to help and comfort him along his dark road. But now that he no longer needs me—will never need me—all the meaning and purpose have gone out of life."

She sat in her quiet house with empty hands, the constant, insistent duties of years having suddenly come to an end. Charles had been both husband and, later, child to her, and with his passing she felt she had lost an entire family. Her only consolation was that her husband's death had brought to an end ten years of suffering—suffering that he had borne,

Bisland wrote, "with a patience and gallantry that only made him a thousand times more dear and touching."

For months she made no plans; nothing seemed worthwhile, nothing appealing. She and Charles had been together for almost thirty years; it was the sort of long intimacy that sews together the fibers of two separate lives, so that when one is taken the other is left torn and broken. Her friends did what they could to console her; it was for the best, they said, and someday the two would meet again. These were, Bisland thought, little more than pious conventionalities, but people who were otherwise helpless meant to express sympathy by them, and for that she was grateful. Still, she could see no recourse but to try to bear her sorrows with whatever dignity and courage she was capable of. Her friends reminded her, too, that charitable activities could be a help, as a way of stepping outside oneself, and over time Bisland resumed her longtime work as president of the Women's Evening Clinic. Paid for by private donations, it was the first clinic of its kind in Washington, providing affordable medical treatment for women who worked during the day; in 1920 the Women's Evening Clinic opened another facility, the Good Health Home, for which Elizabeth Bisland had raised much of the funds. In a letter she admitted, "For these ailing women and girls I have been working very hard, hoping that would bring some sense of reality, but sorrowful as their sufferings are they continue to seem just as shadowy as everything else does." But still she continued her efforts: support for working women was a cause that she had cared about at least as far back as 1884, when she had founded the New Orleans Women's Club.

In 1922, now past sixty, Bisland closed up her house in Washington and set off by herself for a seven-month tour of Japan and China; she felt that the rigors of such a long journey would soon be beyond her, and she wanted one more look at that beloved part of the world. She took long solitary walks through mountain forests, visited ancient temples, sought out the company of poets and painters, abbots and musicians. She returned to Washington invigorated by her long immersion in the East, though she confessed that she was "terribly bored at having to fit myself into Western life again. I always did like the Orient best ever since I first laid eyes on it so many years ago."

Wanting now a simpler, quieter life, in 1924 she sold her house in Washington and moved to another, set on twenty-five acres of woods just outside Charlottesville, Virginia. Called Greenway Rise, the property had been long neglected, and with an energy that surprised her, Bisland oversaw a major renovation. The house that emerged was large and square, with a blue-tiled roof and gray stucco walls covered with rose vines that she had planted; she installed a Japanese pergola in the back and created an apple tree walk that reminded her of the house she had built with her husband in Oyster Bay. Greenway Rise was not far from the University of Virginia, the school founded by Thomas Jefferson (Jefferson, like Queen Elizabeth I, was one of her personal heroes), and Bisland enjoyed, at a certain remove, the life of the university. She attended lectures, spoke occasionally to classes. The New Orleans *Times-Democrat,* the newspaper that had published that first Christmas poem when she was twenty, described Elizabeth Bisland in those later years as "a distinguished white-haired lady in regally old-fashioned black velvet and lace."

Living in Virginia, Elizabeth Bisland began to write again in earnest, and in 1927 she published her final essay collection, entitled *The Truth About Men and Other Matters.* In it she considered country living, travels in Japan, and relations between the sexes. (In the title essay she observed, "The record of the race, hitherto accepted as the truth about ourselves, has been the story of facts and conditions as the male saw them—or wished to see them. . . . No secret has been so well-kept as the secret of what women have thought about life.") Much of the book, though, was about growing gracefully old. In an essay called "Toward Sunset," Bisland observed "That old age may be agreeable to others and tolerable to itself no other equipment is so necessary as a vigorous sense of humour." But old age itself, she was quick to point out, "is not an amusing episode":

> Firstly, because one suffers from being forced to dwell in a house steadily falling to decay; a trial to the housekeeper, arousing a sense of some innate incompetence that the beams of the building should sag, doors open difficultly, windows dim with the dust of time, the outer complexion of the house grow streaked and grey with the weathering of many seasons. There is a certain desperation in the realization that no repairs are possible. . . . one braces one's self to accept courageously the wrongs of time; to wear the lichens and mosses with silent gallantry.

As she grew older she had increasingly turned away from the stern religiosity of her parents; now, reading history and philosophy, she discovered that the pre-Christian Stoic point of view most appealed to her. She wrote, "I never can understand why any one should think, because of absence of future rewards or punishments, one should misbehave. I have not the slightest belief in either, and behave myself simply because I find it a thousand times more agreeable than the other thing. Vice always looks to me so atrociously stupid and dull, and there are so many delicious things in the world that I could not imagine myself doing wicked things when the innocent ones are so far more agreeable." She had always found sustenance in nature, and in the autumn she often spent mornings walking the hills around her house, admiring the peaceful countryside in the shadow of the Blue Ridge Mountains. The fields were streaked with goldenrod, ironweed, joe-pye weed, and wild asters; the dark crimson stains of Virginia creeper reminded her of the blood that ran from Casca's dagger: imperial summer lying dead. "The earth is a ripened fruit," she wrote of that season, "lying enfolded in dreams, brooding tenderly, rich with many blossoms aureate, purple, white." The air seemed haunted by delicate unknown perfumes, "the soul of summer passing invisibly in a fragrance." In the mornings, now, the mists hung like smoke in the still air. The frost hardened and crisped the ears of corn ripening in the fields, waiting to be pulled from their stalks and hauled away to nearby cribs and barns. At night the hunter's moon rose large and orange, as in one of her earliest memories, her family's flight from Louisiana during the War. She thought often of New Orleans, that shabby and picturesque place of her youthful dreams; from the distance of years the city seemed to her bathed in golden light and the smell of roses. The year was turning to a close, the days drawing in. *Boughs are daily rifled by the gusty thieves / And the book of Nature getteth short of leaves.* They were lines by Thomas Hood, which she had first read so long ago in a book of British poetry; they had remained with her all this time, even now, in her own winter. "Winter," she wrote in one of her last essays, "like age, robs of the dear illusion of soft outlines; shows all the veins and articulations of the poor skeleton once clothed about with a garment of fair flesh and of tender foliage." The winter skies over Virginia were a hard icy blue; the trees, she thought, looked gaunt and weary, gently lifting their boughs as if to test the brittleness of the frost. At the beginning of the new year, surprising everyone who knew her, Elizabeth Bisland suddenly came down with pneumonia, and on January 6, 1929, she died. She was sixty-seven years old. The funeral services were held in New York, and she was buried in

Woodlawn Cemetery in the Bronx, beside her husband. The epitaph on her gravestone is a line from Robert Browning, written in the voice of a Greek poet: *Wishing thee wholly where Zeus lives the most, within the essential element of calm.*

Elizabeth Bisland's obituary in *The New York Times,* five paragraphs long, noted the plans for her burial; her birth on the Fairfax Plantation in Louisiana; her marriage to Charles Wetmore; her editorial positions on the New Orleans *Times-Democrat* and *The Cosmopolitan;* and the several books she had written. It did not mention her race around the world.

IN HER LATER YEARS the reclusive poet Emily Dickinson composed a cautionary poem on the perils of celebrity. "Fame is a bee," she wrote,

> It has a song—
> It has a sting—
> Ah, too, it has a wing.

By the beginning of the 1890s Nellie Bly had experienced all of fame's attributes—the song, the sting, and the wing. Having left her contract with *The New York Family Story Paper* unfulfilled, she disappeared from sight. For more than a year she published absolutely nothing. Her absence was so striking that in August 1892, Allan Forman of *The Journalist* asked his readers, "Where is Nellie Bly? I don't mean the song, but the girl," and two months later repeated the query: "What is Nellie Bly doing now?"

Her seventy-two-day race around the world was a success from which Nellie Bly had not yet been able to recover. In the meantime, newspapers all over the country were hiring women to pursue the type of undercover participatory journalism, some of it serious, some frivolous, that Bly herself had once undertaken for *The World*. That variety of reporter now even had a name: "stunt girl." Stunt girls begged in the streets, sought illegal abortions, visited opium dens. In 1890 Annie Laurie of the *San Francisco Examiner*—whose very first article for the paper had been an interview with Elizabeth Bisland—set out to investigate the treatment received by poor women in the city's public hospitals. She had a doctor friend put belladonna drops in her eyes to dilate her pupils and then pretended to faint in the street; carried to a public hospital in a wagon used to transport dead bodies, she was forced to drink an emetic of mustard and hot water and was then briskly discharged. The influence of Nellie Bly's earlier insane asylum exposé for *The World* could hardly have been lost on anyone. At *The World,* a stunt girl named Meg Merrilies similarly got herself picked up by an ambulance in City Hall Park, so that she could be taken to the Chambers Street Hospital to find out how poor patients were treated; what she found there, in *The World*'s description, was "abuse, neglect, profanity and filth." Meg Merrilies put on a diving suit and helmet and explored the ocean fifty feet deep off Staten Island; she passed a night surrounded by almost a billion dollars of gold and silver in a local depository of the U.S. Treasury, only to find that the money, in antiquated safes, was not adequately safeguarded; she assisted a circus trainer with his performing lions. Once, astonishingly, she allowed a million volts of electricity to pass through her body, the most powerful current any human had ever taken; later she performed the most hair-raising stunt of all—getting shot in the chest by a .45 caliber Winchester rifle while wearing a bulletproof vest (or, as it was called, "the much-discussed bullet-proof cloth"). In fact, there was no "Meg Merrilies"; *The World* employed a number of stunt girls, all of whom wrote under the same pen name. Clearly the paper's management had realized that anonymous, assembly-line stunt girls would never be able to attain the stature of a Nellie Bly and would thus have little leverage to demand more money or better assignments, as Bly herself once had.

By this time *The World* had moved in to its grand new tower on Park Row, but Joseph Pulitzer himself was still away from the office, continuing his travels through Europe to recuperate and consult with medical experts. He could no longer oversee the day-to-day administration of the newspaper; as was his tendency, he had appointed two men, George W. Turner and John Cockerill, to run the paper together in his absence, and as there was already a good deal of friction between them, he appointed a third man as a kind of referee to mediate disputes. This was Col. William L. Davis, a mining engineer by trade, who had no newspaper experience but at least had the advantage of being Pulitzer's brother-in-law. Pulitzer grandly termed the new managerial structure a "regency," but not surprisingly it proved unworkable, producing conflict and deadlock and a 16 percent decline in circulation; and as Joseph Pulitzer was disinclined to trust his editors anyway ("Every reporter is a hope," he once said, "and every editor is a disappointment"), he fired Turner and shipped

Cockerill back to his old job at the *St. Louis Post-Dispatch*. For the next two years the editorial merry-go-round at *The World* continued apace; in September 1893 Pulitzer reassigned the paper's city editor, Merrill Goddard, to be editor of the Sunday *World*. Goddard was an enterprising twenty-seven-year-old Dartmouth graduate; he had made his reputation when, as a young reporter covering President Grant's funeral, he donned a black suit and posed as the undertaker's assistant, enabling him to sit next to the grieving widow in the front carriage of the funeral procession. Goddard had a brilliant sense of what would sell newspapers—the following year he would begin publishing *The Yellow Kid,* the first of the color Sunday comic strips—and in one of his first acts as Sunday editor he offered Bly her old job back. With no source of regular income other than the small stipend her mother continued to receive, Bly gratefully accepted.

Her very first piece for *The World* was a jailhouse interview with the anarchist Emma Goldman, who was awaiting trial on trumped-up charges of incitement to riot. Later she would interview several politicians from Tammany Hall, the youthful millionaire John Jacob Astor, and the "moral reformer" the Reverend Charles Parkhurst; there was also another jailhouse interview, this one with the labor leader Eugene V. Debs, who, like Goldman, was serving time for his political activities.

As the months went along, Bly's work for *The World* settled into an uncomfortable mix of big-name interviews and, increasingly, follies. She traveled up to White Plains to take the "Keeley cure"—normally meant for women addicted to liquor or morphine—by being injected with a solution said to be bichlorate of gold. She spent a night in a haunted house in New Jersey, supposedly armed with two pistols, waiting for a ghost that never arrived. She visited a gambling house in the city, but her investigation came to an end when she was recognized by one of the players. She spent a day with the wealthy inmates of the Bloomingdale Insane Asylum in upper Manhattan; the article that resulted was decidedly sedate, and suffered in comparison with the danger and outrage that had so animated her earlier asylum exposé—a contrast brought into sharp relief when one of the patients noticeably perked up upon discovering that she was Nellie Bly, who had gone undercover at Blackwell's Island. Indeed, much of Bly's current work seemed like a rehash of her earlier *World* columns, with little of the derring-do so evident in the adventures of her present-day rival "Meg Merrilies." Bly was still only twenty-seven years old, but she seemed to have been doing this kind of work for a long time. An item in *The Journalist* observed that Nellie Bly had left *The World* upon "receiving a better offer from some publishing house" but was now "back again, her copy mutilated, her feelings hurt, herself put in the background, or assigned to do work repulsive or revolting."

In July 1894, Bly traveled to Chicago to report on a strike among the train workers in the company town of Pullman, Illinois. The workers were protesting wage cuts and rent hikes in the "model town"; though she had been initially unsympathetic to their demands, she wrote, "before I had been half a day in Pullman I was the most bitter striker in town." Bly marched with the strikers and was persuaded to deliver a speech at a large rally, but even this excitement—and the cheers of the workers—seemed not to lift her spirits. "How I would like to see you!" she wrote to Erasmus Wilson on her return to New York. "What a long time it is and how little I am doing. And I used to have such hopes!"

Her life, though, was about to undergo a dramatic change. On a train headed to Chicago, Bly met a man named Robert Seamon, and within the week the two had eloped. The marriage took all who knew her by surprise, not only because of its suddenness but also because Seamon was an old man: seventy years old, in fact, forty years older than Bly. He was the owner of the Iron Clad Manufacturing Company of Brooklyn, and he was said to be worth $5 million. Some journalists branded Bly a gold digger, which was unkind, but certainly Seamon represented long-term financial security for Bly, as well as the possibility of giving up increasingly unsatisfying and exhausting newspaper work, and perhaps, too, he served as a kind of replacement for the father she had lost as a girl. In his memoir, Bly's old friend Walt McDougall suggested that Bly was upset that a man to whom she was "deeply attached"—this may have been a reference to James Stetson Metcalfe—had married someone else. In any event, Bly had married a millionaire, and thus fulfilled the fourth of her youthful vows; whether she had fulfilled the third—to fall in love—seemed much less clear. Almost from the beginning there were signs of trouble in the marriage. On numerous occasions Seamon hired private detectives to follow his wife, and at least once to investigate James Metcalfe.

Nellie Bly, though, seemed to take to life as a wealthy woman. She moved in to Seamon's elegant four-story brownstone on West Thirty-seventh Street near Fifth Avenue, which she substantially redecorated, and oversaw the large household staff. She dressed in expensive clothing and became friends with local aristocrats including Hetty Green, widely considered the richest woman in the United States, and Edwin Gould, the brother of Jay. For four years Bly and Seamon traveled in Europe, visiting Paris, London, Rome, Vienna; upon their return, in 1899, Bly became increasingly involved in the operations of the Iron Clad Manufacturing Company, which centered on an immense factory complex in the Bushwick section of Brooklyn. When Robert Seamon died at the age of eighty, in 1904, Bly assumed control of the business.

The Iron Clad company turned sheet metal into milk cans, coal scuttles, fire shovels, wash tubs, water buckets, ice-cream freezers, ash cans, oil cans, garbage cans, and almost every other imaginable metal object, up to and including kitchen sinks. By 1905 the company was doing more than a million dollars a year in sales. Bly was, she liked to say, "the only woman in the world personally managing industries of such a magnitude." The remarkable drive, perseverance, and creativity that had once propelled her to success in journalism she now applied to metal manufacture. She worked twelve-hour days at the factory, devising more efficient work processes and installing more modern machinery. It turned out that she had a talent for industrial design; at one time there were twenty-five patents with her name on them, including one for the first steel barrel made in the United States.

However, Bly was not at all interested in finances ("financial details bored me terribly," she later admitted), and she made the critical mistake of allowing her husband's accountants complete control of the company's books. Some of the employees took advantage of her, embezzling hundreds of thousands of dollars by forging her name on company checks, including $15,000 in political contributions and $25,000 for a yacht. Eventually she was forced to declare bankruptcy; several creditors sued her for breach of contract, and years of expensive, wearying suits and countersuits followed. In 1914, when the court demanded that she open the company's books, Bly refused the order; it was, she claimed, "being put only for the purpose of obtaining information to be used in further depriving me of my rights." As a result, charges were filed against her for obstruction of justice and nonpayment of legal fees. Bly pleaded not guilty to all the charges. She transferred her stock in the company to her mother, asking Mary Jane to transfer them in turn to a wealthy Viennese friend of hers named Oscar Bondy (who would not be subject to her creditors' claims); four days later, she fled the country.

On August 1, 1914, Bly left New York for Austria, sailing on the White Star steamship *Oceanic,* the successor to the ship on which she had crossed the Pacific twenty-four years earlier. War in Europe was imminent; Austria-Hungary had declared war on Serbia only three days earlier. Overseas, Bly lived with Bondy in Vienna and also traveled through Central Europe filing occasional dispatches for William Randolph Hearst's *Evening Journal.* As the war went on, though, she gave up journalism to participate in charitable efforts for Austrian widows and orphans. Her sympathy for the Austro-Hungarian cause was provoked in large part by her longtime enmity for Great Britain; in one story for the *Journal,* Bly wrote that "the English chill one's blood with repulsion," and later Bly told an American official that she had gone to Austria because she hated the English and would do anything against them.

For five years Nellie Bly lived in exile; then, when the war was over, she returned to the United States to face the charges against her. The slender young brunette of popular memory was now gray-haired and stout; dark half-moons had appeared under her eyes, giving her a perpetually sleepless look. The iconic bangs were gone; she wore her hair pulled back in a matronly chignon. A reporter for the *Brooklyn Daily Eagle* described her return: "Charmingly garbed in silks and furs, still as vivacious as the indefatigable investigator of years ago, Nellie Bly still overpowers one with her striking personality."

In New York, Bly surrendered to federal marshals and was set free on $1,000 bail. While she was in Europe, her mother—prompted by her brother Albert—had sued for the return of Mary Jane's shares in the Iron Clad company, claiming that the transfer of stock to Oscar Bondy had been fraudulent. (That suit would be decided in favor of Bly, but by then the company was essentially worthless.) Not long after her return, the court cleared Bly of all the earlier charges. Now almost penniless, she looked to work again as a newspaperwoman in New York, the city where once she had been the toast of the town. Journalism, though, had changed dramatically in the intervening years, and Bly was little remembered, even by the current generation of female reporters. They prided themselves on objective, factual reporting; they were not interested in emotional appeals or undercover work, and they frankly regarded its greatest practitioner as an anachronism, even something of an embarrassment. An old friend of Bly's from *The World,* Arthur Brisbane, who had become editor of the *Evening Journal,* offered Bly a regular column; the pay was $100 a week, less than half of what Norman L. Munro had signed her for thirty years earlier.

No longer welcome at the Brooklyn home of her mother and brother, Bly took a small two-room suite at the Hotel McAlpin, the largest hotel in the world; it was located on Thirty-fourth Street at Broadway, not more than a block from where she had lived with her mother at the time she went around the world. Unexpectedly, Bly flourished at the *Evening Journal,* where she rediscovered her avocation for helping the weak and less fortunate. Sometimes she used her column to dispense marital or career advice, or to advance a favorite cause (she campaigned for the hiring of American seamen and against capital punishment), but her work at the *Journal* was primarily charitable in nature; most often she wrote columns about people in need and solicited help from her readers. One of her subjects, for instance, was an eleven-year-old girl named Maizie, who had been stricken with infantile paralysis and now moved only with great difficulty; Maizie's father had died, and she lived with her two younger siblings and her grandparents, all of whom depended on Maizie's mother, who did factory work for twelve dollars a week, supplemented by another two dollars she made from cleaning offices after hours. "On this $14 these six human creatures live," Bly wrote, suggesting that someone reading her words might be able to hire the grandparents for suitable work, or provide a better-paying job for the beleaguered young mother. "Can anyone resist the unselfishness of little Maizie, the crippled child? I am confident, from all the goodness that poured in upon me in answer to pleas for help before Christmas, that there will be plenty to come forward to aid this poor American family. Immediate aid in the way of clothing for the little hard-working mother and Maizie and her brother of nine and the baby of four, and clothing for the grandmother, who is an enormous woman, and for the grandfather, who is five feet eleven, and takes a number 40 coat."

Thanks to Bly's *Evening Journal* columns, orphaned children received Christmas gifts; a boy with consumption received two suits and three overcoats; a woman with seven children, whose husband was out of work, received money, food, and clothing. Week after week the donations came in to Bly at the Hotel McAlpin and then went back out again, distributed to the poor, the ill, the suffering, the helpless. Bly employed

Nellie Bly circa 1921, at the age of fifty-seven

several unmarried women to open, sort, file, and answer her mail and arrange her interviews. One of her secretaries was a woman who supported her five children and widowed mother—and who, in turn, having been touched by one of the letters sent in to Nellie Bly, bought a railway ticket for a poor young man to return to the home he had left many years before, and arranged for friends to give him a new set of clothes and twelve dollars in pocket money besides. Bly wrote a column to raise money for St. Mark's Hospital at Eleventh Street and Second Avenue, a hospital financed by private donations, that treated its patients at no charge and to which she had directed hundreds of people who came to her in need of medical care but without the means to pay for it: the "hospital with a heart," she called it.

Many of her *Evening Journal* columns were devoted to finding homes for abandoned babies, whom she often cared for herself in the hotel until she could locate suitable foster parents. ("I get in debt each month trying to support them," she once wrote.) Young mothers whose troubled circumstances prevented them from caring for their children brought them to Nellie Bly, and she wrote columns extolling the virtues of little Faith, Gloria, Ralph, Yolanda, all of whom needed only "a chance to be beautiful and clever and great." She asked readers who wanted to adopt a child to write to her, in full confidentiality, giving their reasons and qualifications. "I know there are plenty of people waiting to make their homes happy with a baby," she wrote in one column, "and I want to spread joy in the world and at the same time secure for these blessed little ones comfortable homes and love and devotion and a chance in the world."

Bly collected old clothes from the other residents of the Hotel McAlpin and distributed them to those in need. Over time the hotel's managers grew annoyed by the shabbily dressed individuals who seemed always to be sitting in the plush chairs of the hotel's huge marble lobby; everyone understood that they were waiting to be taken up to see Nellie Bly. Bly's friends often warned her that people were taking advantage of her generosity, but her answer was always the same: "Relieve immediately; investigate afterwards." There was, though, one striking exception to her openheartedness: even years later, those who had known Nellie Bly could still recall how cold and distant she became whenever she met someone from England. Her secretaries knew better than to send up to her any young woman who had even the hint of an English accent.

In those days Bly always wore a large hat with a veil and cultivated the air of mystery that had surrounded her when she was at *The World*. Though she had a private office at the *Evening Journal,* she dictated her columns to a secretary in her hotel room. She hated the telephone, and used it only when her column was given a secondary position on the editorial page; then, with her fingers clenched and her mouth pursed in an angry line, she would call the office and berate everyone from Arthur Brisbane on down.

"The truest happiness and the only forgetfulness come from making others happy," Bly wrote in one of her *Evening Journal* columns. She seemed to have regained at last the enthusiasm of her youth, the satisfaction that came from using her influence to right wrongs and provide help to those who needed it. By now, though, the hard condition of her later years was taking its toll. She had put on a lot of weight, and much of the time she was tired and ill. Still, she persisted in her work; she was constantly rushing in cabs from place to place, sleeping little, eating poorly, going out in all kinds of weather. She refused to take medicine, as though to do so would be to admit personal weakness. In January 1922, Bly caught pneumonia and was taken to St. Mark's Hospital, the very hospital she had once extolled in her column. The doctors were confident of her recovery, but in the second week she suffered a downturn, and on the morning of January 27, Nellie Bly died in her hospital room. She was only fifty-seven.

Nellie Bly, too, was buried in Woodlawn Cemetery, no more than a quarter mile from the grave site of Elizabeth Bisland. Curiously, it was just one of many things the women had in common. Both had married wealthy men, were childless, performed relief work in Europe during the First World War; both were widowed, both died of pneumonia, and both had been writers right up to the very end. Of the two, though, only Nellie Bly had race horses and show dogs and an express train named for her, and a board game with her picture on it, and songs sung of her famous deeds. Of the two, only Nellie Bly would be remembered long after death, and almost always it was for her record-breaking trip around the world.

In 1936, a young Brooklyn-born reporter for the *Evening Journal* named Dorothy Kilgallen embarked on an around-the-world race against two male reporters, Leo Kieran of the *Times* and H. R. Ekins of the *World-Telegram*. At the beginning of her trip Kilgallen wrote, "Nell Bly, watch over me. You may be astonished at what you see—but watch, anyway." Kilgallen crossed the Atlantic not on a steamship but on a zeppelin—the *Hindenburg*—and was the first woman to fly across the Pacific Ocean. But Dorothy Kilgallen, unlike Nellie Bly, finished second.

In 1946 a new musical, *Nellie Bly,* about the race around the world, opened at the Adelphi Theatre on Broadway. Savaged by the critics (the *Journal American* noted that the trip was supposed to take seventy-five days, but in the Adelphi Theatre "it seems a whole lot longer"), the play closed after only sixteen performances. The plot, such as it was, bore only the vaguest resemblance to actual history: scenes took place in an Arabian harem, a Moscow public square, and the Paris Exposition, where Nellie Bly somehow ended up doing a striptease with cancan dancers in a cabaret. And the rival journalist against whom Bly was racing turned out to be a man from the *Herald*—who was, of course, secretly in love with the plucky young reporter from *The World*. Elizabeth Bisland had been removed from the theatrical version of the race, as would surely have pleased her.

Though Nellie Bly lived for another thirty-two years, her life seemed always defined by those seventy-two days of her youth; to the end, her name seemed to resonate with the cheers of distant crowds. Bly's final column for the *Evening Journal* was headlined NELLIE BLY ON PRANKS OF DESTINY. It concerned two imaginary young women who started out on similar career paths but whose lives took them in very different directions. "Is it possible for us to struggle and overcome fate," Bly asked in that column—the very last words she would ever publish—"or are we merely being swept along a course which all our efforts fail to alter or change?"

ACKNOWLEDGMENTS

In Brooklyn, where I live, many older residents remember the late, lamented Nellie Bly Amusement Park (in Bath Beach, right off the Belt Parkway) but little about Bly herself, and even less about the race around the world that made her, for a while, among the most famous women in America. I, too, only vaguely knew who Nellie Bly was when I happened upon a reference to her celebrated race; and I knew nothing at all about her rival Elizabeth Bisland, other than the fact that on that November day in 1889 she had set off around the world as well. Four years ago, I decided to write a book about these two young travelers. It has been, for me, a fascinating and enjoyable journey, and I am deeply grateful to the many people who helped me to complete the trip.

First thanks go to my agent, Henry Dunow, who was the first person after my wife to whom I mentioned the idea for a book about the Bly-Bisland race. From the beginning Henry believed in and enthusiastically supported this book, and near the end, in a moment of crisis, came up with its title; along the way, as always, he has been both an exceptional literary agent and a *gantzer mensch*.

It has been my great good fortune to have had Susanna Porter as an editor. Over and again Susanna carefully read the manuscript, offering countless thoughtful suggestions that improved it enormously; I feel privileged to have been the beneficiary of her intelligence, her wisdom, and her always welcome sense of calm. Also at Ballantine Books, Priyanka Krishnan handled myriad technical details with remarkable grace and good humor. Emily DeHuff's copyediting, so careful and precise, was the sort that any writer would treasure. I've been delighted, as well, to have been able to work with an exceptionally talented and good-spirited production team, among them Loren Noveck, the book's production editor; Barbara Bachman, who oversaw the book's design; Liz Shapiro, who created the lovely cover; and David Lindroth, who drew all of the wonderful maps. To these people, and to all the others at Random House who have been so good to this book and helped to make its production such a pleasure, I offer my heartfelt thanks.

I did the research for this book in many libraries and archives, but primarily at the New-York Historical Society, the New York Public Library, the Butler Library of Columbia University, and the Library of Congress, and many librarians there and elsewhere gave me invaluable assistance. I owe a special debt, though, to several in particular. Arlene Balkansky sent me copies of numerous articles about Bly and Bisland in the collection of the Library of Congress. Frances S. Garrison of Mansfield University in Pennsylvania sent me copies of newspaper articles written by Nellie Bly during her time in Pittsburgh. At the Howard-Tilton Memorial Library of Tulane University, Sean Benjamin provided photos and historical information about New Orleans's old Newspaper Row, and guided me through a collection of letters written by Elizabeth Bisland during the last twenty years of her life.

Piers Brendon, author of *Thomas Cook: 150 Years of Popular Tourism,* offered historical information about Thomas Cook and Son, as did Paul Smith, the Thomas Cook company archivist. I thank them for their help, and of course any errors here regarding the agency are mine alone.

Among Elizabeth Bisland's descendants are several with genealogical expertise, the products of which they freely shared with an outsider who wanted to learn all he could about their illustrious ancestor. Many thanks to Thomas A. H. Scarborough, author of the scholarly essay "The Bislands of Natchez," and Betty Shields McGehee, who sent me her breathtakingly researched unpublished family history, "A Record of the Descendants of John Bisland and Susannah Rucker." I am especially indebted to Elizabeth Bisland's great-grandniece Sara Bartholomew, who was patient and unfailingly generous in answering my many queries, and who provided me a wealth of materials including newspaper clippings, family photographs, surveys of Fairfax and Applegarth, and a trove of never-before-seen letters written by Elizabeth Bisland on a subsequent trip around the world. This would have been a far poorer book without her assistance.

Lenny Benardo, Jennifer Weiss, Deborah Schupack, and Joan Dempsey read the manuscript in various stages and offered many helpful comments and much-needed encouragement; I'm honored by their friendship and their goodwill, and I hope someday to be able to repay them adequately for it.

Finally, I offer this book with love to my children, Ezra and Vivian (with whom I have passed happy hours playing *Round the World with Nellie Bly,* and who joined me for the last piece of research for this book, a trip to Woodlawn Cemetery in the Bronx, where they solemnly laid flowers on the grave sites of both Nellie Bly and Elizabeth Bisland—roses for Bly, daffodils for Bisland), and especially to my wife, Cassie Schwerner, who was from the very beginning this book's most dedicated supporter, its sharpest reader, and its most patient listener, and who has long been my best companion in travels of all kinds.

NOTES

THIS IS A WORK of nonfiction. All of the dialogue in this book, and anything else between quotation marks, has been taken from a written source such as a memoir, letter, or newspaper article. None of the events presented here was imagined, and no thoughts have been ascribed to a character that he or she did not personally claim. In writing this book I have drawn from newspaper and magazine articles, guidebooks, travelers' accounts, letters, histories, and biographies; in the travel sections I drew most heavily on the writing of Nellie Bly and Elizabeth Bisland themselves, especially the books each wrote about the race, respectively *Around the World in Seventy-Two Days* (1890) and *A Flying Trip Around the World* (1891). All direct quotations from these books are cited in the endnotes; in certain other places I have paraphrased the travelers' descriptions as a way of maintaining their distinctive voices and points of view. Bly had a sharp, peppery style and Bisland was erudite and lyrical, and their own books about the "lightning trip" are each wonderful and well worth reading.

PROLOGUE

xiii **the North River, as it was still called then**: Dutch colonists called the Delaware the South River, and the Hudson the North River. King (1892), 68.

xiii *Augusta Victoria*: The ship was actually christened after the German empress Auguste Victoria, but the name was misspelled; oddly enough, it would be many years before the correction was made. Bowen, 198.

xiv **a gigantic hearse with windows**: Fox, 95.

xiv **a pleasing note of sophistication**: Kroeger, 25.

xvi **"Don't worry"**: Bly (1890), 14. The citations for Bly's book of her trip are taken from the paperback reprint *Around the World in Seventy-two Days* (Indialog Publications, 2003).

xvi **Their apartment was on West Thirty-fifth Street**: *Trow's New York City Directory, Vol. CIII, for the Year Ending May 1, 1890* (New York: Trow City Directory Company, 1889), 347. The entry is listed under the name of her mother, Mary J. Cochrane.

xvi **Bly paid her nickel**: *Sun*, 328.

xvii **a one-way ticket, three cents**: Kobbé, 32.

xvii **an unusual rising inflection**: McDougall, 186.

xxi **at the age of twenty she had moved to New Orleans**: Lafcadio Hearn incorrectly remembered Bisland as having moved to New Orleans when she was sixteen, a mistake that subsequently found its way into several histories. In fact, as Susan Millar

Williams notes, Hearn, who first met Bisland when he was working for the New Orleans *Times-Democrat,* did not begin working for the paper until 1881, when Bisland was twenty. Williams, 685.

xxi   **the little apartment she shared with her sister on Fourth Avenue**: *Trow's New York City Directory, Vol. CIV, for the Year Ending May 1, 1891* (New York: Trow City Directory Company, 1890), 111.

xxii   **"a sort of goddess"**: Williams, 686.

xxii   **"a beautiful dangerous leopard"**: Ibid.

xxii   **("After the period of sex-attraction has passed")**: Bisland (1906), 125.

xxii   **working for eighteen hours at a stretch**: Stevenson, 190.

xxii   **Rousseau's *Confessions***: She was inspired to read the *Confessions* because George Eliot had called it the most interesting book she knew. Bisland (1906), 7.

xxii   **"and to this notoriety I most earnestly objected"**: Bisland (1891), 4.

xxiii   **"a wild, crooked, shrieking hodge-podge"**: Bisland (1910), 140.

xxiii   **known to frequent O'Rourke's saloon**: Sante, 117.

CHAPTER ONE: A FREE AMERICAN GIRL

3   **"It is not necessary to be a city of the first class"**: Henry, unpaged.

4   **"So active was the child's brain"**: *The World,* February 2, 1890, 5.

4   **"acquired more conspicuous notice"**: Haughton, 95.

4   **Judge Cochran suddenly fell ill and died**: See Kroeger, 9–12.

5   **"without exception, the blackest place which I ever saw"**: Graham, 31.

5   **nearly five hundred factories**: Ibid., 7.

6   **including as a kitchen girl**: Bly herself made reference to this. "How Bly Was Discovered," *Pittsburg Commercial Gazette,* January 25, 1890, 1.

6   **may also have found work as a nanny**: Kroeger, 33.

6   **corresponding clerk**: Ibid., 30.

6   **ten daily newspapers**: Writers Program of the Works Projects Administration in the Commonwealth of Pennsylvania, *Pennsylvania: A Guide to the Keystone State,* University of Pennsylvania, 1940, 142.

6   ***Pittsburg Dispatch***: At the time, the newspapers of Pittsburgh spelled the city's name without the final *h.* See the discussion in Kroeger, xix.

6   **"who think they are out of their spheres"**: Ibid., 35.

6   **her hair, which she had not yet taken to wearing up**: Ravitch, 13.

7   **"Can they that have full and plenty of this world's goods"**: Kroeger, 41.

8   **"neat and catchy"**: Ibid., 43.

8   **It was late in the afternoon**: Ravitch, 12.

8   **12,308 Americans listed as journalists**: Beasley and Gibbons, 10.

9   **"A man must examine minutely a woman's costume"**: "Women Journalists," *Pittsburg Dispatch,* August 21, 1887, 9.

9   **"I think there is no class of employment"**: J.L.H., "A Woman's Experience of Newspaper Work," *Harper's Weekly,* January 25, 1890, 74.

9   **"one long-drawn-out five o'clock tea"**: Flora McDonald, "The Newspaper Woman," *The Journalist,* January 26, 1889, 13.

9   **"A woman—never!"**: "Young Women in Journalism," *Review of Reviews* 6, no. 34 (November 1892), 452.

10   **"I have never yet seen a girl enter the newspaper field"**: Edward Bok, "Is the Newspaper Office the Place for a Girl?" *Ladies' Home Journal* 18, no. 3 (February 1901), 18.

10   **"Young womanhood"**: Ibid.

10   **"A great deal of the practical training"**: *The Epoch* 5, no. 126 (July 5, 1889), 347.

11   **"He was much surprised"**: Ross (1936), 323.

11   **"They plough, harrow, reap"**: Marzolf, 15.

12   **"Women enjoy a reputation for slipshod style"**: Bennett, 15.

12 **"gush and a tendency to hysteria"**: Ibid., 20.

12 **"women of fluent pen and chaotic mind"**: Julia Ward Howe, "Of Journalism and Woman's Part in It," *The Epoch* 5, no. 126 (July 5, 1889), 350.

12 **"jelly-like inaccuracy of thought and expression"**: Nelly Mackay Hutchinson, "Woman and Journalism," *The Galaxy* 14, no. 4 (April 1872), 503.

12 **the Women's Press Club was not founded until 1889**: Ross (1936), 46. The club was founded by Jane Cunningham Croly ("Jennie June"). In 1891 Croly sponsored Nellie Bly for membership.

12 **"Women in absolutely every other line of work"**: Edward Bok, "Is the Newspaper Office the Place for a Girl?" *Ladies' Home Journal* 18, no. 3 (February 1901), 18.

12 **paid in "compliments" rather than cash**: Agnes Hooper Gottlieb, "Grit Your Teeth, Then Learn to Swear: Women in Journalistic Careers, 1850–1926," *American Journalism* 18, no. 1 (Winter 2001), 63.

12 **wrote for more than two years**: Ibid.

13 **"any well-balanced woman"**: Flora McDonald, "The Newspaper Woman," *The Journalist,* January 26, 1889, 13.

13 **"a place that will offer and give assistance"**: Kroeger, 55.

13 **"too impatient to work along at the usual duties"**: Bly (1889), 5.

13 **listening to two of her family's boarders**: Ravitch, 15.

14 **either working or married**: Her older brothers Albert and Charles were working and married; her younger sister Catherine May married at the age of sixteen and had a child the following year. It is not clear what her younger brother Harry's status was at this time.

15 **"a free American girl"**: Bly (1889), 113.

15 **fifteen dollars a week**: Ross (1936), 49.

16 **four goals in life**: Ross (1965), 205.

16 **"I am off for New York"**: *Pittsburg Commercial Gazette,* January 25, 1890, 7.

CHAPTER TWO: THE NEWSPAPER GODS OF GOTHAM

17 **One and a half million people**: The 1890 federal census placed New York's population at 1,513,501; the city's own census put the number at 1,710,715. Kobbé, 12.

17 **one-fifteenth of the population**: *Sun's Guide,* 1.

17 **Half of all the commerce**: Kobbé, 15.

17 **more than a billion letters**: *Sun's Guide*, 202; Zeisloft, 430.

17 **"the crush of carriages"**: *New York Illustrated,* 9.

17 **"Immense injury is done"**: Still, 208.

18 **he had been lifted sixty-two stories**: Landau and Condit, 110.

18 **a currently debated etiquette question**: The consensus seems to have been that removing one's hat was not required. An elevator, it was decided, was not so much a room as it was a form of public transportation, like a streetcar.

20 **"forever rising to a higher plane of perfection"**: Seitz, 171.

20 **spit on the *Sun***: Burrows and Wallace, 1051.

20 **wearing a flowered hat**: Ross (1965), 205.

20 **West Ninety-sixth Street**: Kroeger, 79.

20 **(the perfect home for one-sided newspapers)**: Golding, 3.

21 **whose influence could not have been as great**: Indeed, other than this single biographical detail Edward Dulzer has been entirely lost to history.

21 **writing freelance articles for the *Dispatch***: Kroeger, 81.

21 **"to obtain the opinion of the newspaper gods of Gotham"**: Ibid.

21 **the third-floor city room**: A description of the *Sun's* city room can be found in Churchill, 12–13.

22 **"If I could have my way"**: Dana, 32.

22 **a daily testimonial to correct English usage**: Churchill, 15.

22 **The room was small and cluttered**: A description of Dana's office can be found in O'Brien, 161–64.

22 **"there the poor editor is left"**: Dana, 95.

22 **"I think if they have the ability"**: All of the editors' quotes are from the *Pittsburg Dispatch*, August 21, 1887, 9.

24 **"We have more women now than we want"**: "Among the Mad," *Godey's Lady's Book*, January 1889, 20.

24 **"Miss Nellie Bly . . . came here from Pittsburg[h]"**: Kroeger, 84.

24 **her purse had been stolen**: This is how Bly herself described the incident. Some later, unsubstantiated accounts describe the purse as having merely been lost. See Rittenhouse, 55; Ross (1936), 49.

24 **borrowed ten cents' carfare**: This was an extraordinary act of generosity on the landlady's part, as Bly was already twenty dollars behind on her board bill. "Among the Mad," 20.

24 **"I had to do a great deal of talking"**: Ibid.

25 **a hundred compositors**: The descriptions of *The World*'s processes of production are from *The History of the World*, 11–18.

26 **she found herself standing before the desk**: This is the story as Bly herself presented it in "Among the Mad" (20), subsequently supported in a *World* story of February 2, 1890. Several later biographical accounts give far more colorful versions. Mignon Rittenhouse wrote that after three hours of waiting, the city editor took Bly to Joseph Pulitzer's office, where he was with Cockerill. Rittenhouse, 55. Ishbel Ross included the detail about a three hours' wait, but had Bly first meeting with Cockerill, who then took her to see Pulitzer; in this account, Pulitzer himself gave her the $25. Ross (1936), 50. Emily Hahn also has Cockerill bringing her in to meet Pulitzer. Hahn, 43.

26 **ashes accumulated like snowdrifts**: Jordan, 20.

26 **"My Dear Sir"**: Smith (1983), 50.

26 **the crackling of a piece of paper**: Milton, 19.

26 **Exalted Ruler of the Elks**: McDougall, 207.

27 **the Slayback scandal**: See King (1965), 100–109.

27 **"so coolly killed"**: McDougall, 104.

27 **"the best man in the world"**: Smith (1983), 50.

27 **"unquestionably the best news editor in the country"**: *The Journalist*, May 8, 1886, 3.

28 *The World* **had received a tip**: Brian, 124.

28 **Blackwell's Island**: In 1921 Blackwell's Island was renamed Welfare Island; in 1973 it was given the name Roosevelt Island, by which it is known today.

28 **"Do you think you can work your way"**: "Among the Mad," 20.

28 **On the morning of September 23, 1887**: The incidents that follow are recounted in "Among the Mad" and Bly (1887).

29 **her real name was Nellie Moreno**: "Nellie Moreno" was thus a pseudonym that cloaked a pseudonym that cloaked a pseudonym.

34 **long-standing abuses had been miraculously corrected**: In the final sentence of her book *Ten Days in a Mad-House*, published shortly after her articles appeared in *The World*, Bly wrote, "I have one consolation for my work—on the strength of my story the committee of appropriation provides $1,000,000 more than was ever before given, for the benefit of the insane." In fact, more than $1.24 million in additional funds had already been requested for the Department of Public Charities and Corrections in that year's city budget, of which $850,000 was eventually allocated, and only $50,000 of which was specifically earmarked for the Blackwell's Island asylum. Kroeger, 97.

34 **"very bright"**: Ibid., 95.

35 **"When a charming young lady comes into your office"**: *Puck*, November 7, 1888, 166.

36 **West Seventy-fourth Street**: *Trow's New York City Directory, Vol. CII, for the Year Ending May 1, 1889* (New York: Trow City Directory Company, 1888), 346. The entry is listed under her mother's name: "Cochrane Mary J. wid. Michael."

36 **West Thirty-fifth Street**: *Trow's New York City Directory, Vol. CIII, for the Year Ending May 1, 1890* (New York: Trow City Directory Company, 1889), 347.

36 **"Dress is a great weapon"**: Kroeger, 283.

36 **"the enterprising and remarkable member"**: *The Epoch,* March 22, 1889, 113.

37 **the satirical magazine** *Life*: *Life* was published weekly until 1932; it continued as a monthly until 1936, when Henry Luce purchased the name for his new weekly magazine. Flautz, 14.

37 **"When first you dropped upon the pave"**: Rittenhouse, 219.

37 **raised and lowered by hydraulic pressure**: Morris (1996), 182.

37 **they shared picnics**: Hahn, 71.

37 **an editor had counseled**: Ibid., 66.

CHAPTER THREE: THE SECRET CUPBOARD

40 **("I've been having chuck steak")**: Caldwell, 154.

40 **scented with patchouli**: Sloat, 25–26.

41 **at Thirty-second Street in genteel Murray Hill**: The apartment was at 475 Fourth Avenue, on the east side of the street, between Thirty-first and Thirty-second Streets. The entry is listed under her sister Mary Louise's name: "M. L. Bisland." *Trow's New York City Directory, Vol. CIII, for the Year Ending May 1, 1890* (New York: Trow City Directory Company, 1889), 111.

41 **located above a candy store**: According to *Wilson's Business Directory of New York City 1889,* the store belonged to A. Davot and C. Stoerckel.

41 **the stucco work alone**: Homberger, 260.

41 **"filled with a better class"**: *New York Illustrated,* 20.

41 **"probably the best location for a magazine"**: *The Journalist,* November 30, 1889, 2. If John Brisben Walker wanted to impress an out-of-town advertiser, he needed only to bring him around the corner to Delmonico's, the city's most venerable and expensive restaurant, where French food was served in a vast dining room swathed in mahogany, with gleaming parquet floors and silver chandeliers hanging from frescoed ceilings.

41 **a manufacturer of office equipment**: "A Successful Magazine," *The Journalist,* April 30, 1892, 2–3.

42 **"her talents have realized for her"**: *The Journalist,* December 8, 1888, 3.

42 **sizzling down into white foam**: This memory, like many others from her childhood, was recounted by Elizabeth Bisland in her autobiographical novel *A Candle of Understanding,* published in 1903.

42 **the baby Thomas Pressley**: It was later decided that the boy should be named Thomas Percival Bisland, and the old family name of Pressley was given to a younger brother, born in 1868. Note by Pressley Bisland, February 20, 1944, to the transcript of a letter written by Thomas Shields Bisland to his wife, Margaret Brownson Bisland, October 11, 1864, provided to the author by Elizabeth Shields McGehee. Pressley Bisland would eventually become the adoptive father of the poet Lawrence Ferlinghetti.

42 **whom everyone called Pressley**: Thomas Bisland wrote in a letter to his wife (see ibid.), "You must call him Pressley for I detest the name of Thomas."

42 **Elizabeth Ker**: Ker was the surname of Margaret's brother-in-law, David Ker.

43 **pillared portico**: See the description of Fairfax in Verdery, 5767.

43 **served as the base of operations**: Scarborough, 42. For a full account of the events leading up to the Battle of Fort Bisland, see Taylor, 120–34.

43 **Confederate general Richard Taylor**: Taylor's father, Zachary, was president of the United States.

44 **Elizabeth Bisland would remember**: See Bisland (1903), 29.

44 **much more interesting than the North**: Ibid.

44 **fled with the two girls in an army ambulance**: Verdery, 5768.

44 **her parents' home in Brooklyn**: Elizabeth Shields McGehee, "A Record of the Descendants of John Bisland and Susannah Rucker, with Emphasis on the Family of Their Son William Bisland," unpublished document, February 1993, 16–17. Margaret's father, John Brownson, was a wealthy attorney in New York. The home was on Sidney Place in Brooklyn Heights.

44 **serving as a quartermaster sergeant**: Hall, 153. Thomas Shields Bisland was captured when Union forces took Vicksburg after the long siege; he would later be released in a prisoner exchange and rejoin his regiment for the remainder of the war. Scarborough, 43.

44 **a semblance of order was restored**: Bisland (1903), 30.

44 **in Attakapas**: Margaret Brownson's grandparents settled in Attakapas (also spelled Attackapas) in 1805. McGehee, 16.

44 **It was strange**: Bisland (1903), 145.

45 **Leicester baronets**: Verdery, 5767.

45 **land grant from the Spanish governor**: Scarborough, 27.

45 **six plantations and nearly four hundred slaves**: Ibid., 24.

45 **Thomas Shields Bisland had left medicine**: Verdery, 5767.

45 **in 1858 he had spent $112,000**: U.S. Army Corps of Engineers, New Orleans District, *Historical and Archeological Investigations of Fort Bisland and Lower Bayou Teche, St. Mary Parish, Louisiana*, Cultural Resources Series Report Number COELMN/PD-90/12, June 1991, 51.

45 **"big hominy"**: Verdery, 5768.

46 **"The conversation impressed me"**: Bisland (1903), 159.

46 **Like many of their neighbors**: Family attitudes in the rural South of the 1860s, Bisland recalled in her essay "The Child in Literature," "still strikingly resembled that of England in the eighteenth century under the Georges." Bisland (1910), 73.

47 *The British Poets*: Ibid., 90.

47 **"I was quite old enough to realize"**: Bisland (1906), 251.

47 **In 1873**: Historical accounts differ about the date of the family's move to Mount Repose. Katherine Verdery wrote that the move occurred in 1873 (Verdery, 5768). Elmo Howell suggests that the family moved two years later than that, in 1875 (Howell, 139). Elizabeth Shields McGehee gives the date as 1879 (McGehee, 18). However, Elizabeth Bisland's younger sister Melanie was born in 1874, and U.S. Census records state that her birthplace was Mississippi, which would seem to indicate that the move to Mount Repose occurred earlier than 1874. Bureau of the Census, *Twelfth Census of the United States, 1900*. Washington, D.C.: National Archives and Records Administration, 1900, roll T623_1079, p. 5B.

47 **her father inherited the house**: Verdery, 5768; Howell, 139. Elizabeth Shields McGehee says that Bisland "bought" Mount Repose from his sister Leonora Goode, but gives no details as to price. In any case, the price could not have been much. McGehee, 18.

47 **a desk once used by Aaron Burr**: Howell, 139.

47 **William had vowed**: Howell, 139.

48 **pushed a grandfather clock down the stairs**: McGehee, 17.

48 **the couple separated**: Ibid.

48 **a newspaper that had recently been founded in New Orleans**: The New Orleans *Times-Democrat* was established in 1881 as the result of the merger of two existing papers, the *Times* and the *Democrat*.

48 **writing in the remotest parts of the garden**: This is conjecture, based on a passage in *A Candle of Understanding*. See Bisland (1903), 13.

48 **she stored her work in a secret cupboard**: Verdery, 5767.

48 **When she was twenty years old**: In her entry about Elizabeth Bisland in the *Library of Southern Literature,* Katherine Verdery claimed that Bisland was sixteen years old when she submitted her Christmas sonnet to the *Times-Democrat* (Ibid., 5768). However, the New Orleans *Times-Democrat* did not begin publication until 1881, when Bisland was twenty.

48 **under the nom de plume of B.L.R. Dane**: What led Elizabeth Bisland to choose this particular name is no longer known.

48 **"O fierce wild wind"**: Tinker, 176.

49 **"exquisite"**: Ibid.

49 **she was a great admirer of his poetry**: In a later essay Bisland referred to the "thrilling vibrations" of Poe's poetry, "those sonorous undertones, that velvety, muffled music." Bisland (1910), 131.

49 **the one entitled "Caged"**: The poem in its entirety can be found in Tinker, 179–80.

49 **"considerable curiosity was aroused"**: Ibid., 176.

49 **Page M. Baker**: It is conjecture on my part that the letter writer was Page M. Baker, as none of the historical sources provide the identity of the writer. However, Katherine Verdery and subsequent sources refer to the writer as "the editor" of the paper, which would seem to indicate the editor in chief rather than a subeditor; Baker himself was a very hands-on editor, and a great lover of literature, so it is not a stretch to suppose that he would have involved himself in this issue. The only other possible letter writer is Lafcadio Hearn, the paper's literary editor, but Hearn and Bisland later became close friends and correspondents, and no mention was ever made of his having written this letter.

49 **an elderly man who had once lived in England**: Verdery, 5769.

50 **with little need of revision**: In the *Times-Democrat,* Lafcadio Hearn wrote, "We afterward discovered" that Bisland's poems had "been written without revision or remodelling of any sort." Tinker, 177.

50 **"mob of gentlewomen who wrote with ease"**: Brady, (1999), 7.

50 **In the winter of 1882**: Bisland (1907), I:77. In the winter of 1882 Elizabeth Bisland was twenty-one years old. Hearn mistakenly described her as being "sixteen years old, or so, when I first met her" (Stevenson, 125), an error that was compounded by later biographers. Edward Larocque Tinker, for instance, called Bisland "a tall, handsome, dark-eyed girl of 18" (Tinker, 175); a later biographer, Jonathan Cott, says that she was seventeen (Cott, 151).

50 **a small whitewashed room**: See the description in Bisland (1903), 224.

50 **vacancies were signaled**: Coleman (1885), 64.

51 **"a wretched little provincial"**: Bisland (1903), 225.

51 **on lower Camp Street**: The exact address was 58 Camp Street. *New Orleans City Directory, 1882* (New Orleans: L. Soards), 819. Today the building would be on the 300 block of Camp Street, between Natchez and Gravier Streets.

52 **a German visitor to the city**: Campanella, 117.

52 **Across Canal, on Camp Street**: See the section called "A Stroll Up Newspaper Row," in ibid., 151.

52 **a far different city**: See the descriptions of New Orleans in Jackson (1969), 16, 26.

52 **of which she was an original member**: King (1932), 57.

52 **(another was Julia Ward Howe)**: Howe was living in the city while she served as chief of the Woman's Department of the 1884 New Orleans World's Fair.

52 **No invitations to the Royal Street salon were ever sent out**: Brady (1992), 155.

53 **"a place of resort for men and women of brains and wit"**: Ibid.

53 **"a little circle of magnetic sunshine"**: Brady (1999), 7.

54 **"to remain on good terms with him"**: Bisland (1907), 79.

54 **"diamond-hard"**: Ibid.

54 *"une jeune fille un peu farouche"*: Bisland (1907), II:475.

54 **who at the age of eighteen**: Margaret Brownson Bisland was born on September 30, 1839, and married on June 24, 1858. McGehee, 16.

54 **in 1884 . . . she inserted a notice**: The notice appeared in the September 9, 1884, edition of the *Times-Democrat*.

55 **"elevated financially, socially, and morally"**: Lindig, 49.

55 **"equal salaries with men"**: Ibid.

55 **twelve women showed up**: Ibid.; Miller, 341.

55 **the New Orleans Woman's Club**: The club's name was not officially established until the following year. Lindig, 51.

55 **"This Louisiana sisterhood"**: Miller, 341.

56 **its aggressive religiosity**: In a later essay, entitled "Amateur Saints," Bisland would write, "If there is any one thing more particularly repulsive to me than another it is the way the average clerical person speaks of religious things. One would suppose that such matters, if one really believed them, would be the profoundest sentiments of one's nature, and be mentioned with the reserve and reverence with which the lay person treats the deeper sentiments, such as love, honour, or patriotism." Bisland (1906), 153.

CHAPTER FOUR: "HOW QUICK CAN A WOMAN GO AROUND THE WORLD?"

57 **She had fifty dollars in her purse**: Tutwiler, 631.

57 **on Madison Avenue**: Bisland is not listed in the city directories of the time. The first record of where she lived came from Lafcadio Hearn, who in 1887 tried to visit her at her previous address of 136 Madison Avenue. By that time, though, she had already moved to Fourth Avenue. McWilliams, 198.

57 **a kind of naturalized citizen of New York**: See Tutwiler, 628.

57 **a European style of building called an apartment house**: See the description of New York apartment houses in *The Strangers Mercantile Guide*, 97. Note, by the way, the distinction between apartment houses and tenements, which had long existed in New York: apartment houses, unlike tenements, provided a bathroom within each dwelling.

57 **only a single rental apartment building**: Nevius, 150.

57 **fourteen stories tall**: Landau and Condit, 112.

57 **"Why not go as high"**: Ibid., 135.

58 **"large and determined"**: The description of him is from Lafcadio Hearn. Bisland (1907), I: 408.

58 **the Hubert Home Club**: Landau and Condit, 135. The building still stands on the northeast corner of Madison Avenue and Thirtieth Street.

58 **coal cost twice as much by the scuttleful**: Tutwiler, 629.

58 **"My dear little girl"**: Verdery, 5770.

58 **"a little sketch of a negro funeral"**: Tutwiler, 633.

59 **"She works for four papers"**: Stevenson, 190. The entry for Elizabeth Bisland in the *Library of Southern Literature* estimates that during this period she was turning out, on average, fifty thousand words a month, and further states that she was earning as much as five thousand dollars a year, a prodigious amount for a freelance writer of the time. Verdery, 5770.

59 **Fourth Avenue between Thirty-first and Thirty-second Streets**: The address was 475 Fourth Avenue. The first listing for the sisters does not appear until the directory for 1890. *Trow's New York City: Directory, Vol. CIV, for the Year Ending May 1, 1891* (New York: Trow City Directory Company, 1890), 111.

59 **"undoubtedly the most beautiful woman in Metropolitan journalism"**: *The Journalist*, December 8, 1888, 3.

59 **"the prettiest writing woman in New York"**: Molly Bawn, "Feminine Bachelors," *Philadelphia Inquirer*, December 1, 1889, 9.

59 **"She was a devilishly beautiful woman"**: Tinker, 317.

59 **"expanded mentally and physically"**: Cott, 234.

59 **"She is a witch—turning heads everywhere"**: Ibid.

60 **"Mentally American women do not interest American men"**: Bisland (1906), 125.

60 **he would leap over a four-barred gate**: Sedgwick, 113.

60 **"English, Philosophy, Sciences"**: McDonald, 57.

61 **a prize of three thousand dollars**: *Dictionary of American Biography,* vol. X (New York: Charles Scribner's Sons, 1936), 347. The prize was given to a Duryea Motor Wagon that covered the sixteen miles in just over an hour.

61 **"representing the highest thought"**: Schneirov, 106.

62 **"How quick can a woman go around the world?"**: "Woman Against Woman" *Daily Picayune,* November 20, 1889, 6.

62 **("This we explained we could readily do")**: "Round the World," *Cook's Excursionist and Tourist Advertiser,* January 1890, 10.

63 **"the stiffest man in New York to work for"**: Sedgwick, 113.

64 **her most recent feature article had caused consternation**: Elizabeth Bisland, "Co-operative Housekeeping in Tenements," *The Cosmopolitan,* November 1889, 35–42.

64 **"the very essence of culture and refinement"**: *New Haven Register,* January 31, 1890, 3.

65 **put the salary at $3,000 a year**: "Miss Bisland and Miss Bly," *Idaho Statesman,* June 6, 1890.

65 **"substantial arguments"**: Bisland (1891), 5.

66 **"a vigorous interview"**: Ibid.

66 **Fifty people had been invited**: "Miss Bisland's Story," *San Francisco Examiner,* November 20, 1889, 1.

66 **a hard-working bee**: Ibid.

66 **a glazed black sailor's hat**: This was apparently the latest style. A *World* editorial of the period remarked, "The shiny black sailor hat has taken possession of the New York girl. Where did she get it? Give us the inventor's name, that we may expose him to the world."

67 **bribery and price manipulation**: See Klein, 39–48.

67 **"Keep the money together, hey"**: Homberger, 17.

68 **the largest enclosed space in the United States**: Burrows and Wallace, 944.

CHAPTER FIVE: "I THINK I CAN BEAT PHILEAS FOGG'S RECORD"

69 **still the brown of a penny**: "For more than twenty years, the Statue of Liberty was dark brown, changing to its familiar hue around the time of America's entry into World War I." Jean Ashton et al., *When Did the Statue of Liberty Turn Green?* (New York: Columbia University Press, 2010), 90.

70 **rejected by Egypt's ruler**: Michael B. Oren, *Power, Faith, and Fantasy: America in the Middle East, 1776 to the Present* (New York: W. W. Norton, 2007), 269.

70 **from 1877 until 1884**: Ellis, 389.

70 **"you are really on your tour around the world"**: Bly (1890), 16.

71 **her great-uncle Thomas Kennedy**: Ross (1936), 48.

73 **"Have you any ideas?"**: This and the succeeding quotations are from Bly (1890), 8.

74 *The World* **received a letter**: The various proposals to race around the world were reported in the *World* article "Around the World," November 14, 1889, 1.

74 **a Washington correspondent**: This was probably Frank G. Carpenter.

74 **the field of record-breaking travel**: See Jules C. Ladenheim, *The Jarrett-Palmer Express of 1876: Coast to Coast in Eighty-three Hours* (Westminster, Maryland: Heritage Books, 2008).

74 **underwrite half the cost of the trip**: Ladenheim, 11.

76 **she and her mother went to the Broadway Theatre**: "Nellie Bly's Story," *The World,* February 2, 1890.

76   **sometime after ten o'clock**: This is one example of numerous inconsistencies in Bly's account. In the initial *World* story about the trip ("Around the World," November 1, 1889), Bly describes how she was at Ghormley's "by 10 o'clock." In her later account of the trip, though, published in *The World* on February 2, 1890, she wrote that "it was 11 o'clock before I started out."

76   **"I want a dress by this evening"**: Bly (1890), 9.

76   **one hundred fifty gowns ordered by Mrs. Vanderbilt**: Morris (1996), 153.

77   **for a final fitting**: Neither Bly nor Ghormley ever mentioned the price he charged her for the dress, but it could not have been much—Bly was not nearly as wealthy as most of Ghormley's clientele—and there is every likelihood that he gave it to her free of charge. Both he and Bly must have been aware of the invaluable publicity her trip would bring him, the countless questions that would be asked about who had made the dress she wore day after day in her race around the world.

77   **Thomas Cook & Son**: There is some confusion about this. *The World*'s announcement of the trip, published November 14, 1889, declared, "Here in New York, by a visit to that friend of all travellers—Cook's Agency—it was possible to plan out a complete itinerary of the trip." No mention was made of Nellie Bly having been present at the meeting. In Bly's book about her trip, however, she wrote that she went with the *World* staff member to plan the itinerary—but stated that they went to "a steamship company's office." Bly (1890), 12. It is possible that she was thinking of the steamship company's office she went to when she first contemplated making the trip.

78   **three dozen steamships had been damaged**: Lieutenant J. D. Jerrold Kelley, "The Ship's Company," in Chadwick et al., 203.

80   **$2,500 in American gold and bills**: In 2010 dollars, this would be worth approximately $60,000.

80   **a suitable companion piece**: Bly (1890), 11.

81   **"will continue to work and propel the ship"**: *Across the Atlantic* (New York: Hamburg-American Line, 1900), 65.

81   **flags of country and company**: The flag of the Hamburg-American Line was diagonally quartered into white and blue fields, with a black anchor and yellow shield at its center.

81   **the largest ship ever built in a German yard**: N. R. P. Bonsor, *North Atlantic Seaway: An Illustrated History of the Passenger Services Linking the Old World with the New* (Newton Abbott, United Kingdom: David & Charles, 1975), I:356.

81   **364 first-class and 116 second-class passengers**: "The Augusta Victoria," *Marine Engineer,* May 1, 1890, 57.

82   **"I wonder that people who wanted to break the souls"**: Fox, 204.

82   **to lie down and to stand up**: Ibid., 203.

82   **"makes the drinker very miserable"**: Hoyt, 95.

82   **"not recommended for daily or long-continued use"**: Lockwood, 298.

82   **"mixed Renaissance"**: "The Augusta Victoria," *Marine Engineer,* May 1, 1890, 57.

83   **the stewards of the second-class dining hall**: William H. Rideing, "The Building of an Ocean Greyhound," in Chadwick et al., 138.

83   **"you must come back every time"**: "Nellie Bly at Sea," *The World,* December 8, 1889.

84   **the air smelled different**: See Fox, 202.

85   **The rail had been torn away**: "A Smashing Wave," *New York Times,* October 13, 1889, 3.

85   **some had sewn weights**: Coleman (1976), 33.

85   **"I am sure we are all going down"**: Bly (1890), 20.

86   **A typical bill of fare**: John H. Gould, "Ocean Passenger Travel," in Chadwick et al., 137.

86   **massive iron doors**: Anderson, 44.

87   **the same basins used to dispose of vomit**: Fox, 333.

87   **"No sick cans are furnished"**: Ibid.

87 **"It needs no imagination"**: Ibid., 143.

88 **"great fun to watch life in the steerage"**: Lockwood, 304.

88 **those up above tossed coins or candy**: Fox, 334.

88 **"The children among us pelt the little ones"**: Lockwood, 304.

89 **the most beautiful scenery in the world**: Bly (1890), 22.

· 89 **the *Augusta Victoria* continued its path**: For the arrival of the *Augusta Victoria* in Southampton, see "Nellie Bly's Trip," *The World,* December 8, 1889; "Nellie Bly's Story," *The World,* February 2, 1890.

90 **"Mr. and Mrs. Jules Verne"**: Bly (1890), 24.

90 **talking to the Southampton postmaster**: See Greaves's account in "Nellie Bly's Trip," *The World,* December 8, 1889.

91 **"Where are your keys?"**: "Nellie Bly's Story," *The World,* February 2, 1890. Bly provided a slightly different version of the dialogue in her book-length account of the trip.

CHAPTER SIX: LIVING BY RAILROAD TIME

93 **designed by Louis Comfort Tiffany himself**: White (1978), 241.

93 **by lightly scorching satinwood in hot sand**: Ibid., 438.

93 **billiard tables and bowling alleys**: Ibid., 241.

93 **"Their duties will be those of a maid"**: "Ladies' Maids on the Pennsylvania Limited," *New York Times,* November 14, 1889, 5.

94 **"futile wrestlings"**: Bisland (1894), 375.

94 **Eventually she managed to undress**: This and the other bedtime preparations became Bisland's nightly ritual aboard a train, the result of which, she would later advise other female travelers, "is that one's body being quite free from compression of clothes, and the lungs fed with adequate oxygen, one wakes in the morning fresh and vigorous after healthful sleep, and is prepared for the new day's trials or pleasures." Ibid., 376.

94 **"An epidemic of globe-galloping"**: *New York Tribune,* November 15, 1889.

94 **"summoned to the office yesterday"**: "Broke the Record!" *New York Herald,* November 17, 1889.

95 **a whimsical editorial**: "Why Not the Moon?" *New York Tribune,* November 17, 1889.

95 **"Miss Nellie Bly and Miss Elizabeth Bisland"**: See "The Two Globe Trotters," *The Journalist,* November 23, 1889, 8.

96 **"When you come to think of it"**: This and the subsequent quotations are from "Success to Nellie Bly," *The World,* November 17, 1889.

96 **"she is trying it in one-third of the time"**: In fact it was much closer to one-half.

97 **"in sending its bright little correspondent"**: Dorothy Maddox, "Nellie Bly's Trip," *Philadelphia Inquirer,* November 18, 1889, 5.

98 **It had been arranged**: Bisland (1891), 8.

99 **a telegraph office was still open**: See the description in Louis Schick, *Chicago and Its Environs: A Handbook for the Traveler* (Chicago: L. Schick, 1891), 47.

99 **"a commiserating adieu"**: Bisland (1891), 8.

99 **only a single restaurant**: Zeisloft, 484.

99 **The train to Omaha**: See the description in August Mencken, *The Railroad Passenger Car* (Baltimore: Johns Hopkins University Press, 1957), 164–65.

99 **"stupefaction of amazement"**: Bisland (1891), 9.

100 **"for some brief space"**: Ibid., 10.

100 **it was a hive of activity**: See the description in Lucius Beebe, *The Overland Limited* (Berkeley, California: Howell-North Books, 1963), 15.

100 **("by chance")**: Bisland (1891), 12.

100 **a new fast mail train**: See ibid., 12–20; White (1910), 123–32; "From Ocean to Ocean," *New York Tribune,* November 20, 1889; "An Ocean-to-Ocean Race," *The World,* No-

vember 20, 1889; "The Fast Mail," *San Francisco Bulletin,* November 20, 1889; "Through on Time," *Daily Inter Ocean* (Chicago), November 20, 1889.

101 **newspaper reporters from some of the cities**: Among them, as it happened, was a reporter from *The World* named Frederick Duneka.

102 **Bill Downing**: In her book about the trip Bisland called him "a certain engineer, whose name was Foley—or words to that effect." Bisland (1891), 15.

103 **hard red clay and sandstone**: *Great Trans-Continental Tourist's Guide* (New York: Geo. A. Crofutt, 1870), 90.

104 **months of hard travel by covered wagon**: Edwards, 40.

104 **"the most important event of modern times"**: Ambrose, 357.

105 **"It carries its own food and water"**: J. Scott Russell, "The Service of Steam," *Good Words for 1876,* edited by Donald Macleod (London: Daldy, Isbister & Co., 1876), 619.

105 **46,844 miles of railroad track**: Alfred D. Chandler, Jr., ed., *The Railroads: The Nation's First Big Business* (New York: Harcourt, Brace & World, 1965), 13.

105 **"This railroad will be built"**: Ambrose, 225.

105 **"The railroad men in Omaha"**: Ibid., 223.

105 **("In no parts of the 250 miles ranged by the buffalo")**: E. D. Cope, "The Life of the Plains," *The Friend* 45, no. 29 (1872), 1.

105 **the railroad was itself the single largest consumer**: See Tony Judt, "The Glory of the Rails," *New York Review of Books,* December 23, 2010, 60.

105 **three-quarters of all the steel produced in America**: Chandler, 22.

106 **The Pennsylvania Railroad employed more workers**: Ward, 129.

106 **"The railroad kings have of late years"**: In Peter d'A. Jones, ed., *The Robber Barons Revisited* (Boston: D. C. Heath, 1968), 29.

106 **they delivered "ultimatums"**: Ward, 153.

106 **"I, of all people, know the problems of empire"**: Robert Sobel, *The Entrepreneurs* (New York: Weybright and Talley, 1974), 113.

106 **"The world of to-day differs from that of Napoleon"**: Ambrose, 25.

106 **a traveler on a stagecoach or canal boat**: Ward, 108.

106 **could now be measured in hours and minutes**: Ibid., 111.

106 **had moved no closer to Philadelphia**: Ibid., 112.

107 **"local mean time"**: See Trachtenberg, 59.

107 **twenty-seven different time zones**: Boardman, 64.

107 **The B&O Railroad**: Cashman, 27.

107 **(ran trains in opposite directions)**: Ward, 107.

107 **the mean sun time at the meridians**: Cashman, 27.

107 **the president, the Congress, or the courts**: Trachtenberg, 60.

107 **"People will have to marry by railroad time"**: Cashman, 27.

108 **"nameless, undefined apprehensions"**: Bisland (1891), 23.

108 **the lilies of the field**: "Miss Bisland's Story," *San Francisco Examiner,* November 20, 1889, 1.

108 **even one hundred fifty miles an hour**: Bisland (1891), 23.

109 **the fine white dust seeped through the windows**: See the description in Fogg, 21.

109 **"peace and composure"**: Bisland (1891), 19.

110 **four days, fifteen hours, and fifteen minutes**: The mail train, which left New York after her, made it in an even shorter time—four days, twelve hours, and forty-five minutes.

111 **the Palace Hotel**: See James R. Smith, *San Francisco's Lost Landmarks* (Sanger, California: Word Dancer Press, 2005), 215–19.

111 **on the front page**: "Miss Bisland's Story," *San Francisco Examiner,* November 20, 1889, 1.

113 **The plan now was for her to sail**: "Phineas [sic] Fogg's Rivals," *San Francisco Examiner,* November 21, 1889.

113 **the North German Lloyd ship *Prussian***: The Norddeutscher Lloyd company called the ship the *Preussen.*

114 **"a delegation"**: Bisland (1891), 29.

114 *How old are you?*: "Phineas [sic] Fogg's Rivals," *San Francisco Examiner,* November 21, 1889.

114 **"a sort of inexpensive freak show"**: Bisland (1891), 29.

114 **she would conduct herself in such a way**: Ibid., 4.

CHAPTER SEVEN: A MAP OF THE WORLD

117 **thought she had run away from home**: "Nellie Bly's Story," *The World,* February 2, 1890, 10.

117 **"If she attempts any description at all"**: "Nellie Bly's Trip," *The World,* December 8, 1889, 1.

117 **"How are these streets"**: Bly (1890), 27.

118 **no word spoken against her country**: Rittenhouse, 154.

118 **a Vandyke beard**: See *Sigma Chi Quarterly* 24 (1904–1905), 250–51.

118 **McCormick asked Greaves to please stand**: That, in any case, was how Nellie Bly recalled the incident; in Tracey Greaves's account it is Bly herself who "lures Mr. Mc-Cormick into a corner so that I shan't hear what she has to say." "Nellie Bly's Trip," *The World,* December 8, 1889, 3.

118 **"There is one question"**: Bly (1890), 27.

119 **"I remember once"**: Ibid., 28.

119 **first to the *World* offices near Trafalgar Square**: "Nellie Meets Verne," *The World,* November 24, 1889, 1. In her book about the trip, Bly indicated that the stop at the *World* offices had preceded the visit to Robert McCormick. Bly (1890), 27.

119 **Not until many years later would it be discovered**: On her passport application Bly gave her date of birth as May 5, 1867. She had actually been born exactly three years earlier. See Kroeger, 145.

119 **"Have I been slaving?"**: Lynch, 54.

120 **on the stone wall that ran along the ancient quay**: Waltz, 13.

120 **he would travel only in his imagination**: Evans, 21.

120 **"I may become a good writer"**: Costello, 44.

122 **the merchant steamer they have hired**: The 1956 movie version takes liberties with the novel in having Fogg and Passepartout triumphantly cross the Atlantic Ocean in a hot-air balloon. This scene appears nowhere in the book, and in fact Verne's narrator explicitly dismisses the notion of a balloon trip across the Atlantic as "highly risky and, in any case, impossible."

122 **noticed a newspaper advertisement**: Some versions of the story refer to it as a brochure.

123 **"one of the most eccentric men in America"**: Thomas W. Herringshaw, *The Biographical Review of Prominent Men and Women of the Day* (Chicago: W. H. Ives, 1888), 178.

123 **alternating lines of red and blue**: McDougall, 173.

123 **the liberator of France**: "George Francis Train," *The Bookman* 19 (March–August 1904), 8.

124 **("When I found 'Fogg' ")**: Costello, 120.

124 **more than a hundred thousand copies**: Ibid., 118.

124 **"Between ourselves, a success?"**: Ibid., 124.

124 **much less than his fair share for the play**: See Butcher's discussion in Verne, 207.

124 **finally secured his fortune**: Costello, 123.

125 **placed by the door exactly at seven**: Waltz, 142.

125 **The paper's managing editor**: According to Julius Chambers, the idea for the meeting with Jules Verne had originally come from the paper's publisher, George W. Turner. "The suggestion was Mr. Turner's; but most of the details of the journey fell to me. I arranged for the call of the young lady on M. Verne, at Amiens." Chambers, 315.

125 **"it would give a good advertisement"**: Sherard, 315.

126 **About to meet one of the world's most famous men**: For descriptions of Nellie Bly's meeting with Jules Verne, see Bly (1890), 33–40; "Nellie Meets Verne," *The World,* November 24, 1889; "Nellie Bly's Trip," *The World,* December 8, 1889; "The Visit to Verne," *The World,* February 9, 1890.

126 **"There they are"**: "Nellie Bly's Story," *The World,* February 9, 1890.

127 **"a girl reporter"**: Sherard, 315.

128 **matching oil portraits of the Vernes**: Butcher, 270.

129 **"the nose of a sleuth"**: Ibid., 239.

129 **"My line of travel"**: Bly (1890), 37.

129 **"I am more anxious to save time"**: This is the version from Bly's book. Tracey Greaves remembered her as saying, "People who cross India in these expeditions come back married and that is just what I do not want to do." "Nellie Meets Verne," *The World,* November 24, 1889.

129 **his wife frequently burst into tears**: Butcher, 270.

129 **"he piles the problems"**: Ibid., 173.

130 **"an immense and irreparable folly"**: Ibid., 270.

130 **"If Monsieur Verne would not consider it impertinent"**: Bly (1890), 37.

130 *Sans dessus dessous*: The book was published in English under the title *The Purchase of the North Pole.*

132 **"I entirely rewrite the whole work"**: "Nellie Meets Verne," *The World,* November 24, 1889.

132 **"If you do it in seventy-nine days"**: Bly (1890), 40.

132 **"Good back"**: "The Visit to Verne," *The World,* February 9, 1890. In his account of the trip, Tracey Greaves remembered Verne as saying "Good duck."

132 **"for once I was able to control my mischievousness"**: Ibid.

132 **"what took the hearts of both myself and Mrs. Verne"**: "Nellie Bly's Admirer," *The World,* December 26, 1889.

132 **"My God, what a shame"**: Butcher, 211.

133 **eventually as far as Japan**: When Nellie Bly arrived in Japan, she was interviewed by a reporter from Tokyo, whose newspaper "had translated and published the story of my visit to Jules Verne." Bly (1890), 160.

134 **"Nellie did nothing but talk"**: "Nellie Bly's Trip," *The World,* December 8, 1889.

135 **it cost more to travel from Calais to Brindisi**: Ibid.

135 **a washstand piled high with dirty towels**: This was described by S. W. Wall, who took the India mail train with George Francis Train shortly after Bly's trip. Wall, 237.

135 **nothing more than coffee and bread**: Ibid.

137 **"If you hurry"**: Bly (1890), 50.

138 **"Can you run?"**: Ibid.

CHAPTER EIGHT: "ET EGO IN ARCADIA"

140 **"the ship which makes possible the concept"**: Johnson, 54.

140 **"424 coolies on board"**: "The *Oceanic* Sails for China," *San Francisco Chronicle,* November 22, 1889, 5.

140 **a foaming flood of emerald water**: Bisland (1891), 40.

141 **float forever in those soundless depths**: Ibid., 45.

141 **a late-night excursion**: The scene is described in ibid., 33–39.

142 **gutted houses and reconstructed the interiors**: Ibid., 35.

142 **feeling that she understood**: See "Miss Bisland's Trip," *Daily Picayune,* February 9, 1890, 12.

142 **"a place that left a sinister, menacing impression on my mind"**: Bisland (1891), 33.

142 **nearly one in three of San Francisco's workers was Chinese**: Gyory, 7.

142 **Chinese miners were forbidden access**: See Ambrose, 150. Much of the discussion in this section is derived from Ambrose, 150–62.

142 **A Chinese-English phrase book of the period**: Benoni Lanctot, *Chinese and English Phrase Book, with the Chinese Pronunciation Indicated in English, Specially Adapted for the Use of Merchants, Travelers and Families* (San Francisco: A. Roman, 1867). See also Ambrose, 151.

143 **"They built the Great Wall, didn't they?"**: Ambrose, 150.

143 **meals involving oysters and cuttlefish**: Ibid., 161–62.

143 **"has a sort of hydrophobia"**: Ibid., 162.

143 **"Good engineers"**: Ibid., 156.

144 **used by both Union and Confederate armies**: Ibid., 158.

144 **even a few thousand votes swayed by fear and hatred**: See Gyory, 15.

144 **characterized Chinese immigrants as "vicious"**: This and the following quotations are from ibid., 3–5.

145 **"we are to keep our hand on the door-knob"**: Ibid., 254.

145 **"Everyone has been charming to me"**: Wm. S. Walsh, "In the Library," *The Cosmopolitan*, January 1890.

147 **"Society people are much interested"**: "Society Topics of the Week," *New York Times*, November 24, 1889, 11.

148 **"Her home is with her sister"**: *Town Topics*, December 5, 1889, 7.

148 **Yure brave gurl**: "Around the Whirled in 60 Seconds," *Town Topics*, November 21, 1889, 14.

149 **"The blue deepens and deepens"**: Bisland (1891), 44.

149 **strolling from promenade deck to saloon deck**: William Rideing, "The Crew of a Transatlantic Liner," *The Cosmopolitan* 12, no. 6 (April 1892), 682.

149 **"quite content with boiled rice"**: Ballou, 24.

150 **"seems afraid to breathe or move"**: Bisland (1891), 49.

151 **the figures marked every day at noon on the map**: "The noon position of the ship is—next to dinner—the great event of the day, and many are the pools and bets made on the figures of the run." Lieutenant J. D. Jerrold Kelley, "The Ship's Company," in Chadwick et al., 179.

151 **"A ship is a world"**: Knox, 67.

151 **"Our small, circumscribed world"**: Bisland (1891), 47.

151 **the ancient storehouse of nautical jokes**: See Hoyt, 111.

152 **"The more complete the transformation"**: Campbell, 178.

152 **"That is Japan"**: Bisland (1891), 51.

153 **The green hills that sloped down to the water**: Curtis, 65.

154 **chanting a strange song as they walked**: Ibid., 69.

154 **"will not be winded at all"**: Bisland (1891), 61.

154 **rarely lasted more than five years**: John D. Ford, *An American Cruiser in the East* (New York: A. S. Barnes, 1905), 60. John Donaldson Ford was a rear admiral in the U.S. Navy long stationed in the Far East. He refused ever to ride in a jinrikisha.

154 **officially designated as the first foreign port**: Hammer, 11.

155 **Fish à la Chambord**: The hotel menu can be found in George Moerlein, *A Trip Around the World* (Cincinnati: M. & R. Burgheim, 1886), 25.

155 **"busy, attentive, hurrying little fellows"**: Ibid.

157 **"the bravest and freest race in Asia"**: Bisland (1891), 71.

157 **a train to Tokyo**: As was the style of the time, Bisland spelled it "Tokio."

157 **"The homes and the habits"**: Henry T. Finck, *Lotos-time in Japan* (New York: Charles Scribner's Sons, 1895), 16.

157 **a porcelain vase standing in the corner**: Caine, 158.

158 **the shopkeepers always bowed in greeting**: See ibid., 156–58.

158 **"Garments of the Dawn"**: Bisland (1891), 74. The gown is also described in "Celestial Triumphs: A Most Beautiful Fabric Miss Bisland Brought from Japan," *Macon Telegraph,* August 28, 1890, 2.

158 **"Let there be a gown"**: "Miss Bisland's Trip: Her Story of Circling the World," New Orleans *Daily Picayune,* February 9, 1890, 12.

159 **"the country of common-sense"**: Bisland (1891), 55.

160 **an agreement between the steamship lines and the Six Companies**: See "Dead Chinamen as Freight," *Medical Record* 48 (October 26, 1895), 612.

CHAPTER NINE: BAKSHEESH

162 **in operation since 1837**: Peninsular and Oriental, 13.

163 *Victoria, Britannia, Oceania,* **and** *Arcadia*: Collectively the ships were known as the "Jubilee class."

163 **"a rather dampening effect"**: "From Jersey Back to Jersey," *The World,* January 26, 1890.

164 **twelve cubic yards in size**: Marlowe, 169.

165 **two hundred tons per hour**: Chadwick et al., 266.

165 **"having an idea"**: Bly (1890), 61.

165 **"The men in the party used their sticks"**: Ibid., 62.

166 **"Here's Mrs. Maybrick!"**: In April 1889, Florence Maybrick, an American socialite living in Great Britain, was charged with poisoning her husband with arsenic. The case caused a sensation in Great Britain. Florence Maybrick was convicted of murder and sentenced to death; she ended up serving fourteen years in prison.

166 **bouncing up and down in the saddles**: Bly (1890), 63.

166 **the town wore the gray, greasy look**: See Wall, 208.

167 **"indicating a colony from Europe's far West"**: T. G. Appleton, *Syrian Sunshine* (Boston: Roberts Brothers, 1877), 6.

167 **"I do not think that any one of us knew anything about the game"**: Bly (1890), 63.

167 **the barge in the fading light**: Ibid., 65. See also the description in Richard Harding Davis, *The Rulers of the Mediterranean* (New York: Harper and Brothers, 1893), 92–95.

168 **"How suddenly it has gotten dark"**: Seitz, 177.

168 **"Find a breeze"**: Ibid., 24.

168 **never adequately diagnosed**: One of Pulitzer's biographers, W. A. Swanberg, suggested that Pulitzer was manic depressive and may have suffered from Tourette's syndrome. Swanberg, 131.

168 **world-renowned specialists**: Among them was Dr. S. Weir Mitchell, whose "rest cure" for the writer Charlotte Perkins Gilman would inspire her classic story "The Yellow Wallpaper."

169 **"His face is repulsive"**: Swanberg, 162.

169 **"a renegade Jew"**: Ibid.

169 **"Jewseph Pulitzer"**: Brian, 88.

169 **a one-story annex**: See Swanberg, 360; Seitz, 14; Milton, 19.

169 **"The room was so still as to be uncanny"**: Seitz, 14.

170 **a will of iron**: Brendon (1983), 90.

170 **prizes for the best news ideas**: Swanberg, 130.

170 **bag of gold**: Ibid., 162.

170 **fear of being ruined**: McDougall, 103; Swanberg, 130.

170 **hired office spies**: Brendon (1983), 92.

170 **"a condition of suspicion"**: McDougall, 107.

171 **"It was a strange complex"**: Craven, 125.

171 **it required a ton of coal per day to heat**: Morris (2010), 257.

171 **the Whitney mansion**: See Craven, 281–84.

172   "the very carmagnole of display": Logan, 193.

172   commuted to his Manhattan office: Painter, xxvii.

172   "authority ought not to rest": Mott (1962), 423.

172   "a spitefulness that is peculiarly feminine": Milton, 17.

172   the top 12 percent of American families: Painter, xx.

172   "you realize that a change has taken place in *The World*": Swanberg, 81.

172   "a complete antithesis to that splendid thoroughfare": M. F. Sweetser, *The Middle States: A Handbook for Travellers* (Boston: J. R. Osgood and Company, 1874), 18.

173   on which no church would ever be built: Sante, 12.

173   Four out of five people in New York: Emery and Emery, 259.

173   "Condense! Condense!": Burrows and Wallace, 1151.

173   "The first object of any word": Juergens, 58.

174   much as a display window did for a department store: Arthur Brisbane, a former *World* editor who later went on to edit the *New York Journal,* once said: "Perhaps headlines do take up too much space. The display windows of the big stores take up too much space also. But in a busy nation the first necessity is to attract attention." Ibid., 48.

175   his American Museum: Barnum's museum burned down in 1865 and was replaced on the site by the new office building of the *New York Herald.*

175   oddities and wonders from the world over: Some, of course, had been created by Barnum himself.

176   the paper's Sunday circulation stood at 15,770: On May 10, 1885, *The World* published a week-by-week breakdown of its circulation for the previous two years.

176   it had increased tenfold, to 153,213: Juergens, 50.

176   frescoed ceilings and leather-covered walls: Burrows and Wallace, 1051.

176   "Laffan, that begins to look serious": Seitz, 173.

176   down by more than 51,000 from September: On September 8, 1889, *The World* gave its weekly circulation figure as 2,312,370; on November 10 the corresponding number was 2,261,270.

176   a building that would ultimately cost $2 million: Landau and Condit, 197.

177   "who think that night is the best part of the day": Bly (1890), 14.

178   "Our passengers are mostly English people": "Under Summer Skies," *The World,* December 29, 1889.

178   "How much time have you spent in studying the United States?": See ibid.; "Round the World," *Chicago Tribune,* January 27, 1890.

180   Since leaving Hoboken she had traveled 6,905 miles: Bly provided a table of distances as an appendix to her book about the trip.

180   seven hundred troops: R. J. Gavin, *Aden under British Rule, 1839–1967* (London: C. Hurst, 1975), 1.

181   ("They claim that a shark will not attack a black man"): Bly (1890), 79.

182   "As I traveled on": Ibid., 75.

182   "Though born and bred a staunch American": Ibid., 80.

CHAPTER TEN: AN ENGLISH MARKET TOWN IN CHINA

184   on November 21 she would set sail from San Francisco: Apparently, at the time of Wilson's interview, John Brisben Walker had not yet begun his efforts to bribe officials of the Occidental and Oriental steamship line to move up the *Oceanic*'s departure date.

185   despite the confidence of A. D. Wilson's assertions: And even here Wilson had one of his dates wrong: Bisland was hoping to catch the transatlantic steamer out of Havre on January 18, not January 21.

186   ghostly white French frigates: See the description in Duncan, 181.

186   like the hide of a lion: Bisland (1891), 86.

187 **"Conveyance in the East"**: Ibid., 119.

187 **to inform *The Cosmopolitan* of her arrival**: "Miss Bisland Leads," *San Jose Mercury News,* December 18, 1889, 2.

188 **"cool and unhasting repose"**: Bisland (1891), 96.

189 **More than 160,000 people lived there**: Caine, 236.

189 **"buzzing and humming"**: Bisland (1891), 107.

189 **"loath that I should lose a single pleasure"**: Ibid., 100.

190 **"Docks, hospitals, wharves"**: Verne, 96.

191 **"Is it an emperor?"**: Bisland (1891), 92.

191 **"exceedingly tall"**: H. W. Warren, "Canton on the Pearl River," *The Chautauquan* 8 (October 1887–July 1888), 547.

191 **"It gives me my first real impression of the power of England"**: Bisland (1891), 92.

192 **"wicked wounds"**: Donald Featherstone, *Tel El-Kebir 1882: Wolseley's Conquest of Egypt* (London: Osprey, 1993), 34.

192 **inspirational stories about General Gordon**: See the discussion in Wilson (2002), 493.

193 **"it was not superior virtue"**: Max Boot, *War Made New: Technology, Warfare, and the Course of History, 1500 to Today* (New York: Gotham Books, 2006), 153.

193 **"It is almost impossible to over-estimate"**: Edward Vibart, *The Sepoy Mutiny as Seen by a Subaltern* (London: Smith, Elder & Co., 1898), 248.

193 **"The electric telegraph has saved India"**: Ibid., 252.

193 **A telegraph message could be sent from London to Bombay**: Standage, 102.

193 **"that new and dangerous magic"**: Ibid., 156.

194 **"Time itself is telegraphed out of existence"**: Ibid., 102.

194 **"annihilated both space and time"**: Ibid., 90.

194 **"it has been their pleasing custom"**: "Two Days Are Gained: How Miss Bisland May Beat the Around the World Record," *San Francisco Examiner,* November 21, 1889.

194 *The Cosmopolitan* **sent a cable**: Ibid.

195 **the *Prussian* broke its screw**: "Miss Bisland's Trip: Her Story of Circling the World," *Daily Picayune,* February 9, 1890, 12.

195 **"render a single screw steamship helpless"**: Henry Fry, *The History of North Atlantic Steam Navigation* (London: Sampson Low, Marston and Company, 1896), 50.

195 **"I am advised to go in her as far as Ceylon"**: Bisland (1891), 108.

CHAPTER ELEVEN: "THE GUESSING MATCH HAS BEGUN IN BEAUTIFUL EARNEST"

197: **"Nellie Bly Guessing Match"**: See, for instance, the following *World* articles: "Make Your Guess!" December 1, 1889; "The Guessing Match," December 3, 1889; "Nellie Bly's Guessers," December 5, 1889; "Guess and Guess Again!" December 6, 1889; "Many Thousand Guessers," December 8, 1889.

199 **business mail was delivered as many as four times a day**: "The United States Postal Service: An American History, 1775–2006." United States Postal Service, http://about.usps.com/publications/pub100.pdf, 21.

200 **more than one hundred thousand guesses**: "The Guessing Match," *The World,* December 3, 1889.

203 **"Nellie Bly's trip around the world excites great interest"**: "Nellie Bly's Time," *The World,* December 11, 1889.

203 **"The entire press of the country is discussing the trip"**: *The Journalist,* November 30, 1889, 2.

204 **the longshore winds**: Willis, 15.

205 **"the island of jewels"**: Ferguson, 120.

205 **("now made in all sorts of tweed-like patterns")**: Willis, 246.

205 **they never bit Europeans**: Wilson (1989), 239.

206 **stained their mouths a vampirish red**: See Bisland (1891), 156.

207   **cut on corundum wheels**: Willis, 6.
207   **"We can call 'steward!' "**: Bly (1890), 85.
208   **"palpitation of the heart"**: Ibid., 86.
208   **"I had a shamed feeling"**: Ibid., 95.
208   **"drift out on dreams"**: Ibid., 87.
209   **"brutal and unkind"**: Bly, *Mystery of Central Park,* 56.
210   **"Have you any reason for feeling depressed"**: "Nellie Bly's Doctors," *The World,* October 27, 1889.
210   **twenty-five cents for eight words**: Willis, unpaged.
211   **"The gorgeous Buddhist temples of the Singhalean"**: "Nellie Sails To-Day," *The World,* December 13, 1889.
211   **"little of interest"**: Bly (1890), 96.
211   **a fungus had blighted the fields**: Willis, 40.
211   **"is a very docile and obedient labourer"**: Ibid., 54.
211   **"Both men and women"**: Ibid.
212   **"To these Tamils Ceylon is a heaven upon earth"**: Caine, 295.
212   **"but far from what it is claimed to be"**: Bly (1890), 98.
213   **"When will we sail?"**: Ibid., 100.
214   **"a great relief to be again on the sweet, blue sea"**: Ibid., 102.

CHAPTER TWELVE: THE OTHER WOMAN IS GOING TO WIN

215   **"the languorous, voluptuous sleep of the tropics"**: Bisland (1891), 111.
215   **intelligent curiosity**: See Bisland (1894), 371.
215   **"I go to bed exhaustedly happy"**: Bisland (1891), 111.
216   **"If one refuses to adapt"**: Bisland (1894), 381.
216   **"a charming little old lady from Boston"**: Bisland (1891), 111.
216   **"Everything pleases, everything amuses me"**: Ibid.
217   **"fine creatures"**: Ibid., 112.
217   **"There is a sea rumor"**: Elizabeth Bisland, "An American Woman's First Season in London (I)," *Harper's Bazaar,* July 19, 1890, 567.
217   **"I never saw such splendid figures"**: "Miss Bisland's Trip: Her Story of Circling the World," *Daily Picayune,* February 9, 1890, 12.
218   **"Only those who travel to these Eastern ports"**: Bisland (1891), 118.
218   **"It must be regarded as proved beyond all doubt"**: Adams, 5–6.
218   **"air of superiority"**: Ibid., 16.
218   **"English travellers and writers"**: Ibid., 17.
219   **"In every emergency"**: Ibid., 11.
219   **"seed of civilization"**: Lears, 107.
219   **America's own future of imperial expansion**: "The very word *England* connoted imperial mastery, which American expansionists found attractive." Painter, 142.
219   **"The Briton and the American are too much alike"**: Andrew Carnegie, "Do Americans Hate England? No!" *Review of Reviews* 2, no. 7 (July 1890), 34.
220   **"prolific in enthusiasm"**: "Britain's Honored Queen," *New York Times,* June 22, 1887.
220   **"a memorial demonstration"**: "They See No Cause for Joy," *New York Times,* June 21, 1887.
220   **Robert and Catherine Risher Cochran**: Kroeger, 529.
220   **a dry-goods merchant in Glasgow**: Scarborough, 27; McGehee, 1.
221   **"It fills my soul with a passion of pride"**: Bisland (1891), 193.
221   **an Episcopalian**: See, for instance, Bisland's entry in *Who Was Who in America,* vol. 1 (1897–1942) (Chicago: Marquis, 1968), 1325.
221   **Lady Broome**: Lady Broome (Mary Ann Barker) later invited Bisland to spend the 1890 season with her as her guest, a season Bisland would write about in a series of

articles for *Harper's Bazaar* entitled "An American Woman's First Season in London."
Verdery, 5771.

221 **as she herself preferred,** *flavour*: "She can discern a little the play of character, the
flavour of the contrasts of existence." Bisland (1910), 170.

221 **an occasional sighting of a sea turtle**: See the description in Ballou, 126.

222 **nestled into the rocks and foliage**: See the description in J. Thomson, *The Straits of
Malacca, Indo-China and China* (London: Marston, Low & Searle, 1875), 3.

222 **"The picturesque waterfall is nothing marvelous"**: Bly (1890), 103.

223 **"dire chattering, wringing of hands"**: Ibid., 106.

223 **"We all gathered to see the sight"**: Ibid.

224 **"The mail contract made it compulsory"**: Ibid., 108.

225 **the hills were composed primarily of laterite**: Reith, 35.

225 **fifteen acres of greensward**: Reith, 47.

225 **the newly opened Raffles Museum**: Bly herself referred to it only as "a most interesting museum," but given its location and prominence, it seems very likely to have been
the Raffles Museum.

225 **"That's a funeral"**: Bly (1890), 111.

227 **donate him to the menagerie in Central Park**: "Likes Globe-Trotting," *The World,*
January 27, 1890.

227 **a price of three dollars**: "Two Days to Spare," *Chicago Tribune,* January 25, 1890.

227 **"as strong as a man"**: Ibid.

227 **numerous accounts portraying him**: For example: "Before leaving she picked up a
monkey that sat on her shoulder at subsequent press appearances, for she was now
interviewed at every stop." Ross (1965), 199.

227 **("It is a savage little fellow")**: "Beating Her Time," *Milwaukee Sentinel,* January 25,
1890.

227 **Solaris, Tajmahal, and Jocko**: See "The Arrival and Start," *The World,* January 22,
1890; "Nellie Bly," *San Francisco Daily Bulletin,* January 21, 1890; "Two Days to
Spare," *Chicago Tribune,* January 25, 1890.

227 **a name suggested to her by a reporter**: "Beating Her Time," *Milwaukee Sentinel,*
January 25, 1890.

227 **given to her by a rajah in Singapore**: See, for example, "Snowshoe Jennings," *Pittsburg Press,* January 25, 1890.

228 **"quite attentive to me"**: Bly (1890), 116.

229 **"Do you think life is worth living?"**: This scene is described in ibid., 116–17.

231 **"dirty fellows"**: Bly (1890), 125.

231 **"Will you tell me the date"**: This and the succeeding quotations are from ibid.,
126–29.

232 **"Yes, the other woman"**: It is not clear exactly when Bly learned Elizabeth Bisland's
name. She does not record having been told it in Harmon's office. Presumably
Fuhrmann, as purser of the *Oceanic* (the steamship on which Bisland had crossed the
Pacific), knew Bisland's name and told it to Bly during the time they spent together
in Hong Kong. In any case, Bly knew the name by the time she arrived in San Francisco. See, for example, "Nellie Bly," *San Francisco Daily Bulletin,* January 21, 1890.

232 **"She left here three days ago"**: In Bly's account, Harmon told her that Elizabeth
Bisland had left Hong Kong three days earlier. In fact Bisland had left five days earlier,
on December 18.

CHAPTER THIRTEEN: THE TEMPLE OF THE DEAD

235 **"creeping chills"**: Bisland used this phrase in "Miss Bisland's Trip: Her Story of Circling the World," *Daily Picayune,* February 9, 1890, 12.

236 **"an elaborate apology"**: Bisland (1891), 119.

236 **like brides or debutantes**: Ibid., 123.

236   **the mothers and wives of conquerors**: Ibid., 145.

236   **"the sappy red of English beef"**: Ibid., 123.

237   **"He has no enthusiasms"**: Ibid., 124.

237   **something moving inside the room**: This scene is described in ibid., pp. 125–26.

237   **one Chinaman per day**: See, for example, Charles Burton Buckley, *An Anecdotal History of Old Times in Singapore* (Singapore: Fraser & Neave, 1902), II:565; Hugh Craig, ed., *The Animal Kingdom,* vol. 1 (New York: Johnson & Bailey, 1897), 190. It should be noted that Elizabeth Bisland herself amended this to "carry off on average one person a day." Bisland (1891), 125.

238   **rats were tossed into pits**: Sante, 107.

239   **"He has learned in his score of years"**: Bisland (1891), 127.

239   **"Massa, massa, massa!"**: See the description in "With Opium to Hong-Kong," *Every Saturday* 2, no. 27 (July 7, 1866), 11.

240   **"If I feed them"**: Charles Mayer, "Long Chances in the Animal Dealer's Game," *Asia* 21 (February 1921), 157.

240   **"calm and dominant"**: Bisland (1891), 131.

240   **wore an expression of stolid despair**: Ibid., 132.

241   **forty-year-old Canadian**: "Capt. W. M. Smith Is Dead in Hoboken," *New York Times,* December 10, 1932.

241   **"to see all of them I could while in their land"**: Bly (1890), 137.

241   **the nearby city of Canton**: Bly described her experiences in Canton in ibid., 140–51.

241   **Captain Goggin**: Nellie Bly identified him as "Captain Grogan," but his actual name was S. W. Goggin. *The Chronicle and Directory for China, Corea, Japan, the Philippines . . .* (Hong Kong, 1892), 446, 535.

242   **"I have always said to critics"**: Bly (1890), 138.

242   **"These ships carry, each trip"**: Jackson (1899), 26.

242   **Several years earlier, a band of Chinese pirates**: A book published in 1882 described the incident as having occurred "not long before." John Miller Strachan, *From East to West* (London: Wells Gardner, Darton & Co., 1882), 42.

243   **an iron gate guarded by an armed sentry**: "China and the Chinese—Canton," *Cook's Excursionist* (January 1892), 14.

243   **"To sit on a quiet deck"**: Bly (1890), 138.

243   **"princes and statesmen"**: Jackson (1899), 29.

244   **educated in an American mission**: "Her Last Chapter," *The World,* February 23, 1890.

244   **"I made such an effort to sit straight"**: Bly (1890), 143.

244   **Longevity Street**: Gray, 17.

245   **"the foreigner lies down to sleep"**: Rounsevelle Wildman, *China's Open Door: A Sketch of Chinese Life and History* (Boston: Lothrop, 1900), 238.

245   **"Having it entirely under their own control"**: John MacGowan, *Pictures of Southern China* (London: Religious Tract Society, 1897), 496.

246   **"That is the most beautiful flag in the world"**: Bly (1890), 141.

246   **one of them had to step into a doorway**: "Medical Impressions of the Far East," *Boston Medical and Surgical Journal* 148, no. 17 (April 23, 1903), 457.

246   **Horses were unknown**: Ballou, 93.

247   **European women pinched their waists**: See "China and the Chinese—Canton," *Cook's Excursionist* (January 1892), 14.

247   **"It's blood"**: Bly (1890), 144.

247   **discernible from half a mile away**: Gray, 473.

247   *ling-chi*: See, for instance, Walter Beverley Crane, "The Hip Shing Tong of China-town and Chinese Secret Societies," *Broadway Magazine* 13, no. 12 (March 1905), 15; Charles Denby, *China and Her People* (Boston: L. C. Page, 1905), I:88.

248   **"Would you like to see some heads?"**: Bly (1890), 144.

248   **the company's early expansion into the Far East**: See Harcourt, 6.

249 **"the best food in the world, rice"**: Fay, 53.

249 **the new mechanized looms of Lancashire**: Ibid.

249 **the number of opium smokers in China to be four million**: Beeching, 66.

249 **"so wicked as to be a national sin"**: Brian Inglis, *The Opium War* (London: Hodder and Stoughton, 1976), title page.

249 **three 74-gun warships**: Beeching, 112.

249 **unemployed tea porters**: Ibid., 99.

249 **"forced the accursed drug upon the Chinese"**: Fogg, 30.

250 **("all male")**: Bly (1890), 148.

251 **"an inward feeling of emptiness"**: Ibid., 150.

251 **"will be pleasantly spent in Hong Kong"**: "Nellie's Christmas," *The World,* December 25, 1889.

252 **suspended between two heavens**: See Bly (1890), 136.

252 *Success to your novel enterprise*: "Two Days to Spare," *Chicago Tribune,* January 25, 1890.

252 **packs of chewing gum for sale**: Ibid.

253 **"We have met"**: Bly (1890), 153.

253 **"The most rigid discipline"**: Oldham, 34.

253 **the White Star chartered the *Oceanic***: In so doing, the *Oceanic*'s route was moved from the North Atlantic to the Pacific Ocean.

253 **"You were so different"**: Bly (1890), 132.

254 **"familiar negro melodies"**: Ibid., 154.

CHAPTER FOURTEEN: THE MYSTERIOUS TRAVEL AGENT

255 **one of the P&O's "Jubilee" steamships**: Howarth, 111.

255 **two funnels and four masts**: Divine, 148.

256 **"like Hong Kong, Singapore"**: Ibid., 167.

256 **"with the persistent industry of coral insects"**: "Thomas Stevens in Aden," *The World,* 1889.

256 **a long black paling**: Walter B. Harris, *A Journey Through the Yemen* (Edinburgh: William Blackwood and Sons, 1893), 123.

257 **the dust and bones of a dead land**: Bisland (1891), 167.

257 **lines to Suez, Bombay, and Durban**: A. E. B., "Aden," *Electrical Journal* 6 (March 26, 1881), 228.

257 **lime-washed to the whiteness of snow**: Bisland (1891), 168.

257 **Soon the Tanks came into view**: Bisland's visit to the Tanks is described in ibid., 169–72.

258 **enormous thirsty mouths**: Ibid., 169.

258 **no evening mistiness of vision**: Ibid.

258 *At one stride comes the dark*: Ibid., 170.

259 **white as a pearl**: Ibid., 172.

259 **unsolvable riddles of existence**: Ibid., 171.

259 *Lord of the senses five*: Ibid., 174.

259 **the light of night and day**: Ibid.

259 **to have thus once really lived**: Ibid., 175.

260 *For Nellie Bly*: Bly (1890), 168. In an article Bly wrote for *The World,* the lines were reversed as "We'll Win or Die / For Nellie Bly" and no date was included. "Her Last Chapter," *The World,* February 23, 1890.

260 **110 miles ahead of the pace**: "From Jersey Back to Jersey," *The World,* January 25, 1890.

260 **"Typhoon Bill"**: "Capt. W. M. Smith Is Dead in Hoboken," *New York Times,* December 10, 1932.

261 **"If I fail"**: Bly (1890), 168.

262 **sailors sought to make sense of a life filled with random misfortunes**: See Fox, 213.

262 **Sneezing to the left was unlucky**: Hoyt, 132.

262 **"Always a head wind"**: Fox, 213.

262 **her monkey's life was saved**: Bly (1890), 170.

263 **"It is better to be comfortable for seven days"**: Fox, 343.

263 **"faced with a competition"**: A. E. Seaton, "Speed in Ocean Steamers," *Scribner's Magazine* 10, no. 1 (July 1891), 3.

263 **117,000 men working the oars**: William H. Rideing, "The Building of an Ocean Greyhound," in Chadwick et al., 109.

263 **58 tons of coal per day**: Oldham, 50.

263 **"almost appalling"**: "The Ocean 'Record,'" *New York Times,* May 21, 1889.

263 **"and if they could burn more"**: William Rideing, "The Crew of a Transatlantic Liner," *The Cosmopolitan* 12, no. 6 (April 1892), 682.

264 **"the dirtiest and shabbiest"**: "Nellie Bly," *Topeka Daily Capital,* January 24, 1890.

264 **"The Japanese are the direct opposite to the Chinese"**: Bly (1890), 157.

265 **iron ladders smeared with oil**: Fox, 321.

265 **167 degrees Fahrenheit**: George Henry Rohé, *A Text-book of Hygiene* (Baltimore: Thomas & Evans, 1884), 206.

265 **banging their shovels on the furnace doors**: See the description in Fox, 321–22.

266 **two tons of coal a day**: Ibid., 214.

266 **"Shove it back!"**: "Flesh and Blood Cannot Stand It," *The Engineer* 19, no. 1 (January 4, 1890), 101.

266 **"These are horrible suggestions of ours"**: Ibid.

266 **"It was interesting to learn"**: "A Look at the Majestic," *New York Times,* April 12, 1890. See also Fox, 322.

266 **in their dungarees**: See the description in Fox, 322.

266 **"They were tough-looking characters"**: Ibid.

267 **"Working, as these men do"**: Hobart Amory Hare, *New and Altered Forms of Disease, Due to the Advance of Civilization in the Last Half Century* (Philadelphia: P. Blakiston, Son & Co., 1886), 13.

267 **"a cavern of torture"**: "Roasting a Stoker," *The Lancet* 1, no. 1 (January 1860), 78.

267 **"dyspneic and short lived"**: W. Gilman Thompson, *The Occupational Diseases* (New York: D. Appleton, 1914), 417.

267 **driven temporarily insane**: Hoyt, 119; Wall, 235.

268 **the first *out* of Brundisium**: Bisland (1891), 182.

269 **"All baggage by this service"**: Wall, 235.

269 **A. D. Wilson**: The article identified him as "A. D. Turner," but his surname was in fact Wilson. *The World* had a business manager by the name of George Turner. "A Close Finish Likely," *St. Louis Republic,* January 17, 1890.

270 **"I hope I did not forget the dignity"**: Bisland (1891), 184.

270 **"the luggage and some few tattered remnants"**: Ibid., 185.

271 **"after each one's kin"**: Ibid., 186.

271 **the fast steamship *La Champagne***: In her book Bisland erroneously referred to the ship as "the *Transatlantique.*" The steamship's name was *La Champagne;* the name of the steamship line was the Compagnie Générale Transatlantique.

272 **its chartered train could cover the distance in three hours**: "Miss Bisland's Disappointment," *New York Times,* January 19, 1890.

272 **"especially courteous"**: Bisland (1891), 189.

272 **was waiting with her veil and gloves on**: "Miss Bisland's Trip," *Daily Picayune,* February 9, 1890, 12.

272 **the evils of ale**: See the discussion in Brendon (1991), 5.

273 **twenty-one pounds per soldier**: Ibid., 191.

273 **(enclosed in a leather or cloth case)**: Withey, 160.

273 **opened its first Paris office**: This and other information about the Cook's Paris office

is from an email sent to the author by Paul Smith, Thomas Cook company archivist, September 6, 2011.

273 **The steamship *La Champagne*, the agent told Bisland**: See Bisland (1891), 189; "Miss Bisland's Trip," *Daily Picayune*, February 9, 1890, 12.

273 **frantically cabling the Compagnie Générale Transatlantique**: "Miss Bisland's Disappointment," *New York Times*, January 19, 1890.

273 **for a price of $2,000**: Ibid.

274 **for more than three hours**: See Bisland (1891), 190; "The Story of a Tour," *The World*, January 26, 1890; "Miss Bisland Arrives," *Philadelphia Inquirer*, January 31, 1890, 2.

274 **chartered from the Western Railroad**: "Miss Bisland's Disappointment," *New York Times*, January 19, 1890.

274 **"a czar in his own world"**: Towne, 42.

274 **"firm that his orders should be carried out"**: Ibid., 28.

274 **a cable from one of the Paris welcoming party**: "Miss Bisland's Disappointment," *New York Times*, January 19, 1890.

274 **"The cause of this false information"**: Bisland (1891), 190.

275 **Nothing on this trip had moved her quite as much**: "Miss Bisland's Trip," *Daily Picayune*, February 9, 1890, 12.

275 **started out from a continent**: See Bisland (1891), 192.

275 **"It fills my soul with a passion of pride"**: Ibid. 193.

275 **"the mother soil"**: Ibid., 194.

275 **everything compact, solid, durable**: Ibid., 195.

275 **The land seemed to swarm with phantoms**: Ibid.

276 **the clang of their armor**: Ibid.

276 **the *Ems* had been suddenly withdrawn**: Ibid., 196; "Miss Bisland's Disappointment," *New York Times*, January 19, 1890; "Over Four Days Late," *Chicago Herald*, January 31, 1890, 3.

276 **"a bitter disappointment"**: "Over Four Days Late," *Chicago Herald*, January 31, 1890, 3.

277 **six days and five hours**: Chadwick, 77.

277 **replaced it with the *Bothnia***: Bisland (1891), 197; "Miss Bisland's Hard Luck," *Cincinnati Commercial*, January 19, 1890, 1.

277 **the slowest vessel in the entire Cunard fleet**: "Miss Bisland's Disappointment," *New York Times*, January 19, 1890; "The Story of a Tour," *The World*, January 26, 1890.

277 **"The woman who knows how to accept a favor"**: Bisland (1894), 383.

277 **He arranged for her to have dinner**: Bisland (1891), 197.

277 **carpeting so thick**: Eduardo A. Gibbon, *Nocturnal London* (London: S. E. Stanesby, 1890), 56.

277 **"was very much annoyed to learn"**: "All Around the World," *New York Times*, January 19, 1890.

278 **scheduled to depart at 8:20**: Ibid.

278 **"There is a vast amount of chivalry"**: Bisland (1894), 382.

278 **little chance of her arriving in New York on time**: "Over Four Days Late," *Chicago Herald*, January 31, 1890, 3.

279 **"haunted by the dread of the terrible 4 hours"**: John Murray, *Handbook for Travellers in Ireland* (London: John Murray, 1864), 53.

279 **"I would sooner cross the Styx"**: Grace Greenwood, "Haps and Mishaps of a Tour in Europe in 1853," *Bentley's Miscellany* 35 (1854), 380. "Grace Greenwood," it should be noted, was a pen name; the writer's real name was Sara Jane Clarke.

279 **mayors in New York**: Bisland (1891), 199.

280 **"frantic protest"**: Ibid., 200.

280 **"hopeless, helpless, overwhelmed"**: Ibid.

281 **tumbling into the ship's scuppers**: Ibid., 201; "Miss Bisland's Trip," *Daily Picayune*, February 9, 1890, 12.

CHAPTER FIFTEEN: THE SPECIAL TRAIN

282 **"I read of the impassable snow blockade"**: Bly (1890), 172.

282 **the largest snow blockade in the history of the United States**: See, for instance, "The Great Snow Blockade," *New York Sun,* January 22, 1890; "The Big Snow Blockade," *New York Sun,* January 23, 1890; "Behind a Wall of Crystal Drifts," *New York Herald,* January 21, 1890.

283 **"No such storm has been known"**: "Behind a Wall of Crystal Drifts," *New York Herald,* January 21, 1890.

283 **General Passenger Agent T. H. Goodman**: "To Break Fogg's Record," *Trenton Times,* January 22, 1890.

283 **"The New York journal sent instructions"**: "Nellie Bly," *San Francisco Daily Bulletin,* January 21, 1890.

284 **"regardless order"**: "Nellie Bly's Fast Ride," *Chicago Herald,* January 24, 1890.

284 **a dollar a mile**: "'Round the World," *Chicago Tribune,* January 27, 1890.

284 **"This was permissible"**: "On Time!" *The World,* January 22, 1890.

284 **"As we understood it"**: *Wheeling* (WV) *Register,* January 22, 1890, 2.

284 **John J. Jennings**: For a description of Jennings's overnight trek across the Sierra, see "Raising the Blockade," *The World,* January 22, 1890; "The Great Snow Blockade," *The World,* February 2, 1890.

285 **would be able to reach them for two days at least**: In fact the passengers were not rescued until January 26, after more than ten days in the train shed.

287 **The skis were made of white ash**: "On Snowshoes," *Daily Alta California,* January 22, 1890. Jennings himself indicated that his own skis were made of pine.

287 **"Thus it was by eight hours' snowshoeing"**: "Raising the Blockade," *The World,* January 22, 1890.

288 **Low found Nellie Bly in the *Oceanic*'s saloon**: See "Nellie Bly Hastens On," *San Francisco Examiner,* January 22, 1890.

288 **"God bless her little heart"**: Ibid.

288 **"They've all been so nice!"**: Ibid.

288 **Bly stuck out her tongue**: Ibid.; Bly (1890), 172.

289 **she had never felt a more exquisite happiness**: "Two Days to Spare," *Chicago Tribune,* January 25, 1890.

289 **imperiously brushing the crowd aside**: "Nellie Bly," *San Francisco Daily Bulletin,* January 21, 1890.

289 **"Not later than Saturday evening"**: Ravitch, 38.

290 **"I have seen snow and blizzards in New York"**: "Nellie Bly's Fast Run," *Chicago Herald,* January 22, 1890.

290 **straight as a sunbeam**: Bly (1890), 174.

291 **"almost frightened me to death"**: Ibid.

291 **looking at the train in which she rode**: "Likes Globe-Trotting," *The World,* January 27, 1890.

292 **inviting her to ride in the cab**: "Nellie Comes A-Rushing," *Philadelphia Inquirer,* January 24, 1890; "The Nell for Bisland," *Pittsburg Press,* January 24, 1890.

292 **"the most delightfully perfect amusement"**: "Nellie Bly on a Bicycle," *The World,* June 23, 1889.

293 **"For a new engineer"**: "Nellie Comes A-Rushing," *Philadelphia Inquirer,* January 24, 1890.

293 **"almost desert places"**: "Nellie Bly Talks," *The World,* January 23, 1890.

293 **"display their only interest in civilization"**: Steele, 109.

293 **"The escape is a miraculous one"**: "Flying Home," *The World,* January 23, 1890.

293 **"I've had many narrow escapes"**: "Around the World," *Philadelphia Inquirer,* March 7, 1890.

294 **"my train had run safely across a bridge"**: Bly (1890), 176.

294 **"But hardly had the train passed the river"**: Verne, 158.

294 **People held up cards**: "Two Days to Spare," *Chicago Tribune*, January 25, 1890.

294 **"but I did not mind the ache"**: Bly (1890), 176.

294 **"one maze of happy greetings"**: Ibid., 173.

294 **Bly's success had been made possible**: See Edwards, 54.

294 **"They say no man or woman in America"**: Bly (1890), 173.

295 **"a triumphal march"**: "A Day More," *The World*, January 24, 1890.

295 **In Topeka more than a thousand people were on hand**: "Nellie Bly," *Topeka Daily Capital*, January 24, 1890. In her book about the trip, Bly put the number at "over ten thousand." Bly (1890), 176.

296 **"Vim, enterprise, phenomenal activity"**: "Nellie Bly," *Topeka Daily Capital*, January 24, 1890.

297 **"drank the last drop of coffee"**: Bly (1890), 177.

298 **"All preconceived notions"**: "Two Days to Spare," *Chicago Tribune*, January 25, 1890.

298 **"delightfully informal reception"**: Bly (1890), 177.

298 **Kinsley's had been built in the style of a Moorish castle**: Emmett Dedmon, *Fabulous Chicago* (New York: Atheneum, 1981), 116.

298 **"told of small, pointed incidents"**: "Two Days to Spare," *Chicago Tribune*, January 25, 1890.

298 **"dropped him a brief note"**: "'Round the World," *Chicago Tribune*, January 27, 1890.

299 **flying over the consulate in Canton**: The story mistakenly states that it was the consulate in Ceylon. It also refers to the Englishmen she met "in India"; she did not, of course, travel in India. "Two Days to Spare," *Chicago Tribune*, January 25, 1890.

299 **"one of the boys"**: "'Round the World," *Chicago Tribune*, January 27, 1890.

299 **a great European gambling house**: See the description in "The Wheat Pit," *Flaming Sword* 5, no. 1 (January 7, 1893), 61.

299 **"From this gallery"**: Lears, 55.

299 **"There's Nellie Bly!"**: "Beating Her Time," *Milwaukee Sentinel*, January 25, 1890; Bly (1890), 178.

299 **"People can say what they please about Chicago"**: Bly (1890), 178.

299 **through a private hallway**: "Luxurious Traveling," *Pittsburg Press*, January 25, 1890.

300 **"for the royal manner"**: Bly (1890), 178.

300 **"a perfect bower of beauty and comfort"**: "Luxurious Traveling," *Pittsburg Press*, January 25, 1890.

300 **a gift from a prince in Yokohama**: "Snowshoe Jennings," *Pittsburg Press*, January 25, 1890.

300 **"Mr. Verne wishes the following message"**: "Beating Her Time," *Milwaukee Sentinel*, January 25, 1890.

301 **"I know nothing of her plans"**: "Nellie Bly," *Topeka Daily Capital*, January 24, 1890.

301 **"Miss Bisland?"**: "Two Days to Spare," *Chicago Tribune*, January 25, 1890.

301 **"perfect, from the captain down"**: "'From Jersey Back to Jersey,'" *The World*, January 25, 1890.

302 **guessing would cease once Bly reached Chicago**: The paper acknowledged that "Due allowance will be made for the distance between the post-office address of the sender and *The World* office."

302 **The paper now established the rules**: "Guess Early and Often," *The World*, January 23, 1890.

302 **more than six hundred thousand ballots**: Ibid.

303 **a face but no features**: See Cook, 97.

303 **"Hurrah for Nellie Bly!"**: "Home Again," *The World*, January 25, 1890.

303 **Dr. Frank Ingram**: See the discussion in Kroeger, 169.

304 **"When ex-President Cleveland passed through here"**: "Luxurious Traveling," *Pittsburg Press*, January 25, 1890.

304 **"Miss Bly is about twenty years old"**: "Nellie Bly in Chicago," *Cincinnati Commercial*, January 25, 1890.

304 **seemed to turn the dark river into molten lava**: See the description in "On the Youghiogheny," *Methodist Magazine* 32, no. 1, (July 1890), 18.

304 **"There is the Ohio"**: "Snowshoe Jennings," *Pittsburg Press*, January 25, 1890.

305 **"a clever play for personal notoriety"**: "Luxurious Traveling," *Pittsburg Press*, January 25, 1890.

306 **that dress . . . was now historical**: Ibid.

CHAPTER SIXTEEN: "FROM JERSEY TO JERSEY IS AROUND THE WORLD"

307 **"The weather along the trans-Atlantic steamship routes"**: United States Signal Service, *Monthly Weather Review* 18 (January 1890), 7.

307 **News reports of ocean crossings that month**: See, for example, "Awful Atlantic Gales," *New York Sun*, January 22, 1890; "A Frightful Voyage," *The World*, January 22, 1890; "On the Stormy Atlantic," *New York Times*, January 24, 1890; "Lashed by an Angry Sea," *The World*, January 25, 1890; "Shipwreck and Death," *The World*, January 27, 1890; "Buffeted by Wind and Waves," *The World*, January 28, 1890; "Tossed in Ocean Gales," *New York Times*, January 28, 1890.

308 **"the ocean was like a boiling caldron"**: "Ocean's Fierce Fury," *The World*, January 23, 1890.

308 **"davits were twisted like wires"**: "A Frightful Voyage," *The World*, January 22, 1890.

308 **("the consternation of the passengers")**: "Flooded the Gallia's Cabin," *The World*, January 23, 1890.

308 **her people were treated to a display of nature's handiwork"**: "'La Champagne' among Icebergs," *Harper's Weekly* (February 8, 1890), 107.

309 **Philadelphia's Broad Street Station**: For descriptions of Bly's trip from Philadelphia to Jersey City, see "Her Reception in This City," *Philadelphia Inquirer*, January 26, 1890; "On the Homestretch," *The World*, January 26, 1890; "At the Finish," *The World*, January 26, 1890.

310 **"I'm so glad!"**: "On the Homestretch," *The World*, January 26, 1890.

310 **"as if they had been friends for years"**: "Her Reception in This City," *Philadelphia Inquirer*, January 26, 1890.

311 **a facsimile of it appeared the next day**: See "What Nellie Said," *Philadelphia Inquirer*, January 26, 1890.

312 **"I feel a little like a presidential candidate"**: "Nellie Bly Talks," *The World*, January 23, 1890.

312 **"Poor Nellie's hand was worked harder"**: "Her Reception in This City," *Philadelphia Inquirer*, January 26, 1890.

312 **"Nobody since the sands of time began to run"**: The excerpts of the speeches delivered on the train are from "On the Homestretch," *The World*, January 26, 1890.

314 **perhaps as many as fifteen**: The estimate of fifteen thousand is from "Nellie Bly Beats Time," *Chicago Herald*, January 26, 1890.

315 **Captain Hubert Wycherly**: "Announcing the Finish," *The World*, January 26, 1890.

315 **"No chieftain returning from a tour of conquest"**: "Nellie Bly Beats Time," *Chicago Herald*, January 26, 1890.

316 **"From Jersey to Jersey is around the world"**: "On the Homestretch," *The World*, January 26, 1890.

317 **Every inch of ground was contested**: See "At the Finish," *The World*, January 26, 1890.

317 **At the Cortlandt Street pier**: For Bly's return to New York, see ibid.

318 **"God bless you, Nellie"**: "Likes Globe-Trotting," *The World*, January 27, 1890.

318 **a basket of rare roses**: "Editor Walker's Compliment," *The World*, January 26, 1890.

319 **tossing the ship back and forth like a football**: Bisland (1891), 201.

319 **the forty-seven-year-old Scotsman James B. Watt**: Mitch Peeke et al., 33.

320 **resolving itself into Coney Island**: Bisland (1891), 204.

320 **the Elephantine Colossus**: Michael Immerso, *Coney Island: The People's Playground* (New Brunswick, New Jersey: Rutgers University Press, 2002), 38, 57. Sadly, the Elephant burned down in 1896.

320 **"as if to deprecate our late coming"**: Bisland (1891), 204.

320 **a wash of familiarity came over her**: Ibid.

321 **John Brisben Walker himself put the time**: "Bright Bessie Bisland," *St. Louis Republic,* January 31, 1890.

321 **numbered in the hundreds rather than the thousands**: "Over Four Days Late," *Chicago Herald,* January 31, 1890.

321 **glazed black sailor's hat**: "Bright Bessie Bisland," *St. Louis Republic,* January 31, 1890; "Over Four Days Late," *Chicago Herald,* January 31, 1890.

321 **"like a veteran yachtswoman"**: "Bright Bessie Bisland," *St. Louis Republic,* January 31, 1890.

321 **Her sister Molly was waiting**: This is conjecture. Molly was the sister with whom Elizabeth Bisland was then living; it is possible that this was Elizabeth's younger sister Maggie, who was eighteen at the time and later came to live in New York as well. The *St. Louis Republic* article identified the sister as "Miss Rebecca Bisland," but there was no sister by that name. Ibid.

321 **"She has beaten you, but you did well"**: Ibid.

321 **"the young woman he sent around the world"**: "Very Close Guessing," *The World,* January 31, 1890.

322 **7 days, 23 hours, and 17 minutes**: Fox, 243.

322 **a hurricane that lasted for eight hours**: " 'La Champagne' among Icebergs," *Harper's Weekly* (February 8, 1890), 107.

323 **"Miss Mary Bisland"**: "Miss Bisland Completes Her Long Trip," *New York Herald,* January 31, 1890.

323 **"Wasn't there a Miss Bisland"**: *Washington Critic,* February 1, 1890.

323 **"It is the winner who wins"**: St. Albans (Vermont) *Daily Messenger,* February 1, 1890.

CHAPTER SEVENTEEN: FATHER TIME OUTDONE

325 **"Bravo!"**: "Verne's 'Bravo,' " *The World,* January 26, 1890.

325 **("We certainly owe her some recognition")**: "Nellie Bly's Fame," *The World,* January 9, 1890.

326 **"no reason to complain"**: Sherard, 316. In his memoir *Twenty Years in Paris,* Robert Sherard described how he had visited Verne only a few weeks before his death in 1905, and the two were reminiscing about old times, and during the conversation, Verne "said that it was very strange that after he had served the purpose of the paper not a word of acknowledgment had been made to him."

327 **second place was awarded to Nellie Bly**: "New York Dog Show," *Forest and Stream* 34, no. 4 (February 13, 1890), 70.

327 **"Globe Trotting Nellie Bly"**: "A Song of Nellie Bly," *The World,* January 12, 1890; "They Sang of Nellie Bly," *The World,* January 14, 1890.

329 **in the cast-iron district**: Today it is SoHo.

329 **"the public interest in the young lady"**: "The Story of Nellie Bly," *The World,* February 2, 1890.

330 **"I never was very sick in my life"**: "Around the World," *The World,* November 14, 1889.

331 **the Nellie Bly tablet notebook**: *American Stationer* 28 (December 18, 1890), 1415.

331 **"the biggest seller of the season"**: *American Stationer* 28 (October 30, 1890), 994.

333 **would issue a second edition**: Wong, 320.

333 **the leading manufacturer of board games**: See Hofer, 15–17; Wong, 320. McLough-

lin Brothers would continue to be so until 1920, when it was acquired by the Springfield, Massachusetts, game company Milton Bradley.

333 **the World Building**: Indeed, *The World* must have made a deal with McLoughlin Brothers to produce *Round the World with Nellie Bly*, as it was essentially a colorized version of a game offered by the newspaper on the front page of its second section on January 26, 1890, the issue celebrating Bly's arrival.

333 **"the bad faith of the steamship people"**: "Cause of Miss Bisland's Delay," *Washington Post*, January 24, 1890.

334 **"a fair race was spoiled by a foul"**: *New Mexican* (Santa Fe), January 28, 1890, 2.

334 **"It is a fact"**: "A Successful Magazine," *The Journalist* 15, no. 7 (April 30, 1892), 3.

335 **"The venture turned out"**: "The Cosmopolitan Magazine—Its Methods and Its Editors," *Review of Reviews* 5 (1892), 608.

335 **"If, on the thirteenth of November"**: Bisland (1891), 1.

336 **"I expect to go back to work again"**: "What Nellie Said," *Philadelphia Inquirer*, January 26, 1890.

337 **"the best opportunities"**: "The Winner," *The World*, February 2, 1890.

337 **the most prominent theatrical promoter in the country**: See, for instance, "Chat from the Theatres," *New York Times*, November 6, 1885.

337 **one of the most beautiful in New York**: See the description in John W. Frick, *New York's First Theatrical Center: The Rialto at Union Square* (Ann Arbor, Michigan: UMI Research Press, 1985), 34.

337 **"a particularly good-looking curate"**: "Gossip of the Theatres," *New York Times*, January 18, 1885.

337 **"It is my pleasure and privilege"**: "Nellie Bly Lectures," *The World*, February 10, 1890.

338 **"As Mr. Hill has said"**: Ibid. Descriptions of Bly's lecture can also be found in "Nellie Bly: The Young Lady Relates Her Experience in Going Around the World," *Boston Morning Journal*, March 3, 1890; "Around the World," *Philadelphia Inquirer*, March 7, 1890; "Nelly Bly's Story," *Daily Inter Ocean* (Chicago), March 24, 1890.

339 **the evening's receipts**: "Nellie Bly Succeeding," *The World*, February 16, 1890.

339 **"Since Nellie Bly, the journalist"**: *Dallas Morning News*, February 20, 1890.

339 **"Nellie Bly is going on the lecture platform"**: *Daily Boomerang* (Laramie, Wyoming), February 7, 1890.

339 **"It is to be hoped that Nellie Bly won't lecture"**: *Knoxville Journal*, February 12, 1890.

340 **"This is sad"**: "The Chat of New York," *Philadelphia Inquirer*, February 2, 1890.

340 **"She was engaged by a big newspaper"**: "The Story of Two Young Women," *Chicago Journal*, February 15, 1890.

340 **hotels, most of them very nice**: In Philadelphia, for instance, Bly stayed at the Continental Hotel, on the corner of Ninth and Chestnut Streets; it was described by a contemporary guidebook as "one of the best hotels in America."

340 **"Sometimes I am very unhappy"**: "Around the World," *Philadelphia Inquirer*, March 7, 1890.

342 **"coarse-featured" and "brutal-looking"**: A description of the incident can be found in "Around the World," *Philadelphia Inquirer*, March 7, 1890.

343 **"Miss Bly made a response"**: "Gossip of New York," *Philadelphia Inquirer*, May 4, 1890.

343 **("in no pleasant humor")**: "Tallmadge Gets $20,000," *Brooklyn Daily Eagle*, March 17, 1890.

343 **thirty-two female journalists**: An 1892 article in the *Minneapolis Tribune* reported that the average weekly salary for a newspaperwoman in New York was $12, though a few earned as much as $80. Kroeger, 195.

343 **she had refused to testify**: Bly did subsequently testify when the case was reheard in November 1890. In the end, the original verdict was affirmed and Tallmadge awarded

$6,500. See "In the Tallmadge Libel Suit," *Brooklyn Daily Eagle,* November 12, 1890; "Tallmadge's Verdict Affirmed," *Brooklyn Daily Eagle,* January 26, 1892.

343 **"Enemies have been unkind enough to suggest"**: "Gossip of New York," *Philadelphia Inquirer,* May 4, 1890.

344 **"*The World* never even said 'thank you'"**: Letter to Frank G. Carpenter, August 12, 1890, Sophia Smith Collection, Smith College. Carpenter—a respected journalist, photographer, and writer of geography textbooks—was conducting a survey of notable women on issues such as women in politics, women in the military, women and work, marriage, and suffrage.

344 **"he nightly read most every paragraph in the paper"**: Brian, 109.

344 **"Accuracy! Terseness! Accuracy!"**: Kroeger, 187.

344 **("Accuracy . . . is to a newspaper what virtue is to a woman")**: Barrett, 11.

344 **Something had caused Pulitzer to become suddenly parsimonious**: In her biography of Bly, Brooke Kroeger suggested a similar line of reasoning, though attributed the cause to "a libel suit threatened by the seven doctors whose conflicting diagnoses and prescriptions she had published" after she went to them for treatment of migraines. This idea was suggested in a 1931 letter to a graduate student from someone who had known Bly, but Kroeger indicated that "no documentation could be found" for it. Ibid.

345 **"the lecture tour has been abandoned"**: "Gossip of New York," *Philadelphia Inquirer,* May 4, 1890.

345 **"Our famous Nellie Bly"**: *New Mexican* (Santa Fe), March 24, 1890.

345 **"a successful lecture tour"**: *Cincinnati Commercial,* April 20, 1890.

345 **"Nellie Bly is not a success as a lecturer"**: *Michigan Farmer,* May 24, 1890.

345 **At the end of July**: The first advertisement for Nellie Bly's book appeared in *Life* magazine on July 31, 1890, and the book was reviewed in the August 9 issue of *The Critic.*

346 **"The only regret of my trip"**: Bly (1890), 166.

347 **detective stories**: In 1883, for instance, Munro began publishing the *Old Cap. Collier Library,* the first magazine devoted to detective fiction. J. Randolph Cox, *The Dime Novel Companion: A Source Book* (Westport, Connecticut: Greenwood Press, 2000), 180.

347 **"the largest circulation of any family paper"**: Kroeger, 190.

347 **more even than Julius Chambers earned**: In 1889 Chambers signed a three-year contract with *The World* paying $250 per week, or about $39,000 for the duration of the contract. Swanberg, 187. Bly, by comparison, would make $40,000.

347 **the highest-salaried woman in the United States**: "Women Money Makers," *Morning Oregonian,* September 7, 1890.

347 **her older brother Charles had died**: Kroeger, 186.

347 **she had earned about $9,500 from her lecture tour**: Letter to Frank G. Carpenter, August 12, 1890. Her estimate of the value of the two lots is contained in this letter as well.

348 **("She was sprightly, yet not frivolous")**: McDougall, 187.

348 **"That's perfectly easy"**: Ibid., 188–89.

349 **"in the very cream of the swim"**: "Women Money Makers," *Morning Oregonian,* September 7, 1890.

349 **a garden party given by the Prince of Wales**: Ibid.

349 **"portentous platitudes"**: Elizabeth Bisland, "An American Woman's First Season in London (III)," *Harper's Bazaar,* September 6, 1890, 686.

349 **"I wonder if they fear we shall get into mischief"**: Elizabeth Bisland, "An American Woman's First Season in London (I)," *Harper's Bazaar,* July 19, 1890, 23.

349 **"enough men censer-swinging under your nose"**: Letter from Rudyard Kipling, January 1890, Syracuse University Special Collections Research Center.

349 **Rhoda Broughton's house**: See the description in Wood (1993), 52.

350 **"the great metropolis of the nation"**: "Charles Whitman Wetmore," *Prominent and Progressive Americans: An Encyclopædia of Contemporaneous Biography,* vol. 2 (New York: New York Tribune, 1904), 226.

350 **"an enthusiastic member"**: "Miss Elizabeth Bisland Married," *New York Times,* October 7, 1891.

350 **he had a thick mustache**: See the photograph of Wetmore in *Prominent and Progressive Americans,* 224.

351 **(she had now become editor of the women's section)**: "People in General," *Washington Post,* August 21, 1891.

351 **"My dear 'Q. O.'"**: Letter to Erasmus Wilson, August 22, 1890, William R. Oliver Special Collections Room, Carnegie Library of Pittsburgh.

351 **only a single story by Bly**: See "Periodical Palaver," *The Newsdealer* 1 (March–December 1890), 11.

352 **a five-year lease on the house**: Kroeger, 191.

352 **"the cleverest parrot"**: George Swetnam, "Forgotten Friendship," *Pittsburgh Press Sunday Magazine,* January 15, 1967, unpaged.

352 **able to get around only on crutches**: Kroeger, 188.

352 **breezy and full of flourishes**: See Swetnam's description in "Forgotten Friendship."

352 **"I think it was awfully shabby of them"**: Ibid.

353 **"the most frightful depression"**: Ibid.

EPILOGUE

355 **production of wheat**: Calhoun, 262.

355 **the leading consumer of energy**: Zimmerman, 25.

355 **the nation's first three battleships**: Calhoun, 263.

355 **numerous overseas bases**: See the discussion in Herrick, 50.

356 **"Captain Mahan has written"**: Zimmerman, 100.

356 **("not unduly pro-American")**: Letter written aboard the SS *Macedonia,* March 3, 1912, private collection of Sara Bartholomew.

356 **"The trade of the world"**: Bartlett, 2.

356 **the Hotel Washington**: Dulles, 103.

356 **fried ham or pork and beans**: Plesur, 110.

356 **"vulgar, vulgar, vulgar"**: Dulles, 106.

357 **"bored, patient, helpless"**: Ibid., 112.

357 **("There is really not so much for Americans to see")**: "Nellie Bly," *Topeka Daily Capital,* January 24, 1890.

357 **"unless travellers are willing"**: Jones, 1.

357 **"wound and looped between"**: Elizabeth Bisland, "The Building of Applegarth," *Country Life in America* 18, no. 6 (October 1910), 657.

357 **Applegarth was designed in the Tudor style**: See ibid.; Robert B. Mackay et al., 374–75.

357 **("rejected the whole theory of feminine subordination")**: Bisland (1906), 192.

358 **lived, with Bisland's sister Melanie**: *Twelfth Census of the United States, 1900,* Washington, D.C.: National Archives and Records Administration, roll T623_1079, 5B. Bisland is misidentified as "Elizabeth Whetmore."

358 **("The oldest of all empires")**: Bisland (1906), 189.

358 **"the passionless goddess and the greedy child"**: Bisland (1910), 5.

358 **"so sane and so charmingly written"**: "A Side-Saddled Hobby-Horse," *New York Times,* June 11, 1910.

359 **"cruelly attacked mind as well as body"**: Letter to Charles Hutson, July 1, 1919, Elizabeth Bisland Wetmore papers, Manuscripts Collection 574, Louisiana Research Collection, Howard-Tilton Memorial Library, Tulane University.

359 **boughs flowered with crimson**: See the descriptions in Bisland (1927), 87–88.

359 **"a heaped mass of green velvet"**: Letter of August 3, 1911, private collection of Sara Bartholomew.

359 **"breathing the moist saltness of the sea air"**: Bisland (1927), 88.

359 **"light, fine, frail"**: Ibid.

359 **"One wouldn't begrudge the tourist so"**: Letter of April 27, 1911, private collection of Sara Bartholomew.

360 **the village of West Byfleet**: "News from the Classes," *Harvard Graduates' Magazine* 28 (September 1919), 135.

361 **"especially those first gassed victims"**: Letter to Charles Hutson, October 8, 1918, Elizabeth Bisland Wetmore papers.

361 **"Ever since the war began"**: Ibid.

361 **"seven years of stress and strain"**: Ibid., July 11, 1918.

361 **"he might need me suddenly"**: Ibid., January 29, 1919.

361 **"My poor husband has had to go"**: Ibid., January 19, 1919.

362 **"If you shake me hard"**: Ibid., March 11, 1919.

362 **"the world grows every day ghastlier"**: December 27, 1919.

363 **"with a patience and gallantry"**: Ibid., July 1, 1919.

363 **sews together the fibers of two separate lives**: Ibid.

363 **the Good Health Home**: *Evening Star* (Washington, D.C.), July 14, 1920.

363 **"For these ailing women and girls"**: Letter to Charles Hutson, December 27, 1919, Elizabeth Bisland Wetmore papers.

363 **Greenway Rise**: Today a private school occupies the site.

364 **"a distinguished white-haired lady"**: "Woman Writer's Death Is Sudden," *Times-Democrat,* January 8, 1929.

364 **("The record of the race")**: Bisland (1927), 1.

364 **"That old age may be agreeable"**: Ibid., 17.

364 **"Firstly, because one suffers"**: Ibid., 18–19.

365 **Stoic point of view**: Letter to Charles Hutson, November 8, 1926, Elizabeth Bisland Wetmore papers.

365 **"I never can understand why"**: Ibid., November 16, 1922.

365 **"The earth is a ripened fruit"**: Bisland (1927), 235.

365 **"the soul of summer"**: Ibid.

365 **"robs of the dear illusion"**: Ibid., 238.

365 **suddenly came down with pneumonia**: "Woman Writer's Death Is Sudden," *Times-Democrat,* January 8, 1929.

366 **obituary in *The New York Times***: "Mrs. E. B. Wetmore, Author, Dies in South," *New York Times,* January 9, 1929.

366 **"Where is Nellie Bly?"**: Kroeger, 188.

366 **Stunt girls**: See the discussion in Lutes, 2, 13.

366 **She had a doctor friend put belladonna drops**: Ibid., 33.

367 **Col. William L. Davis**: Seitz, 170.

367 **a 16 percent decline in circulation**: Morris (2010), 290.

367 **("Every reporter is a hope")**: Ibid., 33.

367 **shipped Cockerill back to his old job**: Cockerill resigned rather than accept the demotion.

368 **posed as the undertaker's assistant**: Brian, 198.

369 **"receiving a better offer"**: Kroeger, 226.

369 **"How I would like to see you!"**: Kroeger, 241.

369 **long-term financial security**: See the discussion in ibid., 264.

369 **"deeply attached"**: McDougall, 189.

370 **Hetty Green**: *Story of Nellie Bly,* 38.

370 **"the only woman in the world personally managing industries"**: Kroeger, 309.

370 **twenty-five patents with her name on them**: Ibid., 305.

370 **("financial details bored me")**: Ibid., 329.

370 **$15,000 in political contributions**: *Story of Nellie Bly*, 51.

370 **"being put only for the purpose of obtaining information"**: Ibid., 55.

371 **"the English chill one's blood"**: Kroeger, 422, 438.

371 **"Charmingly garbed in silks and furs"**: *Story of Nellie Bly*, 57.

371 **Bly was little remembered**: Ross (1965), 215.

372 **the pay was $100 a week**: Kroeger, 452.

374 **"Relieve immediately; investigate afterwards"**: Ravitch, 50.

374 **the hint of an English accent**: Ibid., 55.

374 **a large hat with a veil**: Ross (1936), 59.

374 **from Arthur Brisbane on down**: Ravitch, 55.

375 **in the second week she suffered a downturn**: Ibid., 56.

375 **buried in Woodlawn Cemetery**: Bly was buried in a crowded section of the cemetery, with no headstone; a stone would not be installed until 1978, when the New York Press Club paid for one.

375 **"Nell Bly, watch over me"**: Kilgallen, 32.

375 **Dorothy Kilgallen . . . finished second**: The race was won by the *World-Telegram*'s H. R. Ekins; Leo Kieran of the *Times* was third.

375 **a new musical**: See *New York Theatre Critics' Reviews* 7, no. 26 (1946), 481–84.

SELECTED BIBLIOGRAPHY

―

Adams, George Burton. *Why Americans Dislike England*. Philadelphia: Henry Altemus, 1896.

Allotte de la Fuÿe, Marguerite. *Jules Verne*. Translated by Erik de Mauny. London: Staples, 1954.

Ambrose, Stephen E. *Nothing Like It in the World: The Men Who Built the Transcontinental Railroad, 1863–1869*. New York: Simon and Schuster, 2000.

Anderson, Roy. *White Star*. Prescot, United Kingdom: T. Stephenson and Sons, 1964.

Armstrong County, Pennsylvania: Her People Past and Present. 2 vols. Chicago: J. H. Beers, 1914.

Aurand, Harold W. *Coalcracker Culture: Work and Values in Pennsylvania Anthracite, 1835–1935*. Selinsgrove, Pennsylvania: Susquehanna University Press, 2003.

Ballou, Maturin M. *Due West; or, Round the World in Ten Months*. Boston: Houghton Mifflin, 1885.

Barrett, James Wyman. *Joseph Pulitzer and His World*. New York: Vanguard Press, 1941.

Bartlett, C. J., ed. *Britain Pre-eminent: Studies of British World Influence in the Nineteenth Century*. London: Macmillan, 1969.

Beasley, Maurine H., and Sheila J. Gibbons. *Taking Their Place: A Documentary History of Women and Journalism*. Washington: American University Press, 1993.

Beeching, Jack. *The Chinese Opium Wars*. London: Hutchinson, 1973.

Beer, Thomas. *The Mauve Decade: American Life at the End of the Nineteenth Century*. Garden City, New York: Garden City Publishing, 1926.

Bell, Duncan. *The Idea of Greater Britain: Empire and the Future of World Order, 1860–1900*. Princeton: Princeton University Press, 2007.

Bennett, Arnold. *Journalism for Women: A Practical Guide*. London: John Lane, 1898.

Bisland, Elizabeth. "The Art of Travel." In *The Woman's Book: Dealing Practically with the Modern Conditions of Home-Life, Self-Support, Education, Opportunities, and Every-Day Problems*. Vol. 1. New York: Charles Scribner's Sons, 1894. 371–400.

―――. *At the Sign of the Hobby Horse*. Boston: Houghton Mifflin, 1910.

―――. *A Candle of Understanding*. New York: Harper and Brothers, 1903.

―――. *A Flying Trip Around the World*. New York: Harper and Brothers, 1891.

————, editor. *The Life and Letters of Lafcadio Hearn*. 2 vols. Boston: Houghton Mifflin, 1907.

————. *The Secret Life: Being the Book of a Heretic*. New York: John Lane, 1906.

————. *The Truth About Men and Other Matters*. New York: Avondale Press, 1927.

Blake, David Haven. *Walt Whitman and the Culture of American Celebrity*. New Haven: Yale University Press, 2006.

Bleyer, Willard Grosvenor. *Main Currents in the History of American Journalism*. Boston: Houghton Mifflin, 1927.

Bly, Nellie. *The Mystery of Central Park*. New York: G. W. Dillingham, 1889.

————. *Nellie Bly's Book: Around the World in Seventy-two Days*. New York: Pictorial Weeklies, 1890.

————. *Six Months in Mexico*. New York: John W. Lovell, 1889.

————. *Ten Days in a Mad-House*. New York: Munro, 1887.

Boardman, Fon W., Jr. *America and the Gilded Age, 1876–1900*. New York: Henry Z. Walck, 1972.

Bowen, Frank C. *A Century of Atlantic Travel, 1830–1930*. Boston: Little, Brown, 1930.

Boylan, James. "Morrill Goddard." *American Newspaper Journalists, 1901–1925*, edited by Perry J. Ashley. *Dictionary of Literary Biography*, vol. 25. Detroit: Gale Research Company, 1983. 90–92.

Brady, Patricia. "Around the World in 76 Days: Louisiana's Intrepid Bessie Bisland." *Historic New Orleans Collection Quarterly*, Winter 1999, 7.

————. "Literary Ladies of New Orleans in the Gilded Age." *Louisiana History* 33, no. 2 (Spring 1992). 147–56.

Brendon, Piers. *The Life and Death of the Press Barons*. New York: Atheneum, 1983.

————. *Thomas Cook: 150 Years of Popular Tourism*. London: Seckel and Warburg, 1991.

Brian, Denis. *Pulitzer: A Life*. New York: John Wiley and Sons, 2001.

Broughton, Rhoda, with Elizabeth Bisland. *A Widower Indeed*. New York: D. Appleton, 1891.

Brown, Georgina. *The Shining Mountains*. Leadville, Colorado: Brown, 1976.

Burrows, Edwin G., and Mike Wallace. *Gotham: A History of New York City to 1898*. New York: Oxford University Press, 1999.

Burt, Elizabeth, ed. *Women's Press Organizations, 1881–1999*. Westport, Connecticut: Greenwood Press, 2000.

Butcher, William. *Jules Verne: The Definitive Biography*. New York: Thunder's Mouth Press, 2006.

Caine, W. S. *A Trip Round the World in 1887–8*. London: George Routledge and Sons, 1888.

Caldwell, Mark. *New York Night: The Mystique and Its History*. New York: Scribner, 2001.

Calhoun, Charles W., ed. *The Gilded Age: Essays on the Origins of Modern America*. Wilmington, Delaware: Scholarly Resources, 1996.

Campanella, Richard. *Time and Place in New Orleans: Past Geographies in the Present Day*. Gretna, Louisiana: Pelican Publications, 2002.

Campbell, Gertrude Elizabeth, Lady. *Etiquette of Good Society*. London: Cassell and Company, 1893.

Carnegie, Andrew. *Notes of a Trip Round the World*. New York: Carnegie, 1879.

Cartlidge, Oscar. *Fifty Years of Coal Mining*. Charleston, West Virginia: Rose City Press, 1936.

Cashman, Sean Dennis. *America in the Gilded Age: From the Death of Lincoln to the Rise of Theodore Roosevelt*. New York: New York University Press, 1993.

Chadwick, F. E., et al. *Ocean Steamships: A Popular Account of Their Construction, Development, Management and Appliances*. New York: Charles Scribner's Sons, 1891.

Chambers, Julius. *News Hunting on Three Continents*. New York: Mitchell Kennerly, 1921.

Churchill, Allen. *Park Row*. New York: Rinehart, 1958.

Coleman, Terry. *The Liners: A History of the North Atlantic Crossing*. London: Allen Lane, 1976.

Coleman, William Head. *Historical Sketch Book and Guide to New Orleans and Environs*. New York: W. H. Coleman, 1885.

Cook, Joel. *America, Picturesque and Descriptive*. Philadelphia: Henry T. Coates & Co., 1900.

Costello, Peter. *Jules Verne: Inventor of Science Fiction*. London: Hodder and Stoughton, 1978.

Cott, Jonathan. *Wandering Ghost: The Odyssey of Lafcadio Hearn*. New York: Alfred A. Knopf, 1991.

Craven, Wayne. *Gilded Mansions: Grand Architecture and High Society*. New York: W. W. Norton, 2009.

Curtis, Benjamin Robbins. *Dottings Round the Circle*. Boston: J. R. Osgood, 1876.

Dabney, Thomas Ewing. *One Hundred Great Years: The Story of the Times-Picayune from Its Founding to 1940*. 1944. New York: Greenwood Press, 1968.

Dana, Charles A. *The Art of Newspaper Making: Three Lectures*. New York: D. Appleton, 1900.

Divine, David. *These Splendid Ships: The Story of the Peninsular and Oriental Line*. London: F. Muller, 1960.

Dulles, Foster Rhea. *Americans Abroad: Two Centuries of European Travel*. Ann Arbor: University of Michigan Press, 1964.

Duncan, Sara Jeannette. *A Social Departure: How Orthodocia and I Went Round the World by Ourselves*. New York: D. Appleton, 1890.

Eaton, John P., and Charles A. Haas. *Falling Star: Misadventures of White Star Line Ships*. Wellingborough, United Kingdom: Patrick Stephens, 1989.

Edwards, Rebecca. *New Spirits: Americans in the Gilded Age, 1865–1905*. New York: Oxford University Press, 2006.

Ellis, Edward Robb. *The Epic of New York City*. New York: Coward-McCann, 1966.

Emery, Edwin, and Michael Emery. *The Press and America: An Interpretive History of the Mass Media*. 5th ed. Englewood Cliffs, New Jersey: Prentice-Hall, 1984.

Evans, I. O. *Jules Verne and His Work*. London: Arco, 1965.

Fay, Peter Ward. *The Opium War, 1840–1842*. Chapel Hill: University of North Carolina Press, 1997.

Federal Writers' Project of the Works Progress Administration. *Mississippi: The WPA Guide to the Magnolia State*. 1938. Jackson: University Press of Mississippi, 1988.

Ferguson, John. *Ceylon in 1893*. London: John Haddon, 1893.

Flautz, John. *Life: The Gentle Satirist*. Bowling Green, Ohio: Bowling Green University Popular Press, 1972.

Fogg, William Perry. *Round the World: Letters from Japan, China, India, and Egypt*. Cleveland, 1872.

Fox, Stephen. *Transatlantic: Samuel Cunard, Isambard Brunel, and the Great Atlantic Steamships*. New York: HarperCollins, 2003.

Golding, Louis Thorn. *Memories of Old Park Row, 1887–1897*. Brookline, Massachusetts, 1946.

Graham, Laurie. *Singing the City: The Bonds of Home in an Industrial Landscape*. Pittsburgh: University of Pittsburgh Press, 1998.

Gray, John Henry. *Walks in the City of Canton*. Hong Kong: De Souza, 1875.

Gyory, Andrew. *Closing the Gate: Race, Politics, and the Chinese Exclusion Act*. Chapel Hill: University of North Carolina Press, 1998.

Hahn, Emily. *Around the World with Nellie Bly*. Boston: Houghton Mifflin, 1959.

Hall, Winchester. *The Story of the 26th Louisiana Infantry, in the Service of the Confederate States*. [n.p., 1890?]

Hammer, Joshua. *Yokohama Burning: The Deadly 1923 Earthquake and Fire That Helped Forge the Path to World War II*. New York: Free Press, 2006.

Harcourt, Freda. *Flagships of Imperialism: The P&O Company and the Politics of Empire from Its Origins to 1867*. Manchester, United Kingdom: Manchester University Press, 2006.

Haughton, Ida Cochran. *Chronicles of the Cochrans: Being a Series of Historical Events and Narratives in Which the Members of This Family Have Played a Prominent Part*. Vol. 2. Columbus, Ohio: F. J. Heer, 1925.

Henry, T. J. *1816–1916: History of Apollo, Pennsylvania*. Apollo, Pennsylvania: News-Record Publishing Company, 1916.

Herrick, Walter R., Jr. *The American Naval Revolution*. Baton Rouge: Louisiana State University Press, 1966.

The History of the World. New York: The World, 1886.

Hobsbawm, E. J. *The Age of Empire 1875–1914*. London: Weidenfeld and Nicolson, 1987.

Hofer, Margaret K. *The Games We Played: The Golden Age of Board and Table Games*. New York: Princeton Architectural Press, 2003.

Hofstadter, Richard. *Social Darwinism in American Thought*. 1944. Boston: Beacon Press, 1992.

Homberger, Eric. *Mrs. Astor's New York: Money and Social Power in a Gilded Age*. New Haven: Yale University Press, 2002.

Howarth, David. *The Story of P&O: The Peninsular and Oriental Steam Navigation Company*. London: Weidenfeld and Nicolson, 1986.

Howell, Elmo. *Mississippi Home-Places: Notes on Literature and History.* Memphis: Elmo Howell, 1988.

Hoyt, John Colgate. *Old Ocean's Ferry: The Log of the Modern Mariner, the Trans-Atlantic Traveler, and Quaint Facts of Neptune's Realm.* New York: Bonnell, Silver and Company, 1900.

Hungerford, Edward. *Men and Iron: The History of New York Central.* New York: Thomas Y. Crowell, 1938.

Jackson, Joy J. *New Orleans in the Gilded Age: Politics and Urban Progress, 1880–1896.* Baton Rouge: Louisiana State University Press, 1969.

Jackson, S. C. F. *A Jaunt in Japan.* Calcutta: Thacker, Spink, and Co., 1899.

James, Lawrence. *The Rise and Fall of the British Empire.* London: Little, Brown, 1994.

Johnson, Howard. *The Cunard Story.* London: Whittet Books, 1987.

Jones, Mary Cadwalader. *European Travel for Women: Notes and Suggestions.* New York: Macmillan, 1900.

Jonnes, Jill. *Eiffel's Tower: And the World's Fair Where Buffalo Bill Beguiled Paris, the Artists Quarreled, and Thomas Edison Became a Count.* New York: Viking, 2009.

Jordan, Elizabeth. *Three Rousing Cheers.* New York: D. Appleton–Century, 1938.

Juergens, George. *Joseph Pulitzer and the New York World.* Princeton: Princeton University Press, 1966.

Kern, Stephen. *The Culture of Time and Space 1880–1918.* Cambridge, Massachusetts: Harvard University Press, 1983.

Kilgallen, Dorothy. *Girl Around the World.* Philadelphia: David McKay, 1936.

King, Grace. *Memories of a Southern Woman of Letters.* New York: Macmillan, 1932.

King, Homer W. *Pulitzer's Prize Editor: A Biography of John A. Cockerill, 1845–1896.* Durham, North Carolina: Duke University Press, 1965.

King, Moses. *King's Handbook of New York City: An Outline History and Description of the American Metropolis.* Boston: Moses King, 1892.

Kinross, Lord. *Between Two Seas: The Creation of the Suez Canal.* New York: William Morrow, 1969.

Klein, Aaron E. *New York Central.* Greenwich, Connecticut: Bison Books, 1985.

Knox, Thomas W. *How to Travel: Hints, Advice, and Suggestions to Travelers by Land and Sea All Over the Globe.* Revised Edition. New York: G. P. Putnam's Sons, 1888.

Kobbé, Gustav. *New York and Its Environs.* New York: Harper and Brothers, 1891.

Kroeger, Brooke. *Nellie Bly: Daredevil, Reporter, Feminist.* New York: Times Books, 1994.

Landau, Sarah Bradford, and Carl W. Condit. *Rise of the New York Skyscraper, 1865–1913.* New Haven: Yale University Press, 1996.

Lears, Jackson. *Rebirth of a Nation: The Making of Modern America, 1877–1920.* New York: HarperCollins, 2009.

Lindig, Carmen. *The Path from the Parlor: Louisiana Women, 1879–1920.* Lafayette: University of Southwestern Louisiana Press, 1986.

Lockwood, Allison. *Passionate Pilgrims: The American Traveler in Great Britain, 1800–1914.* New York: Cornwall Books, 1981.

Logan, Andy. *The Man Who Robbed the Robber Barons.* 1965. Pleasantville, New York: Akadine Press, 2001.

Lutes, Jean Marie. *Front-Page Girls: Women Journalists in American Culture and Fiction, 1880–1930.* Ithaca, New York: Cornell University Press, 2006.

Lynch, Lawrence. *Jules Verne.* New York: Twayne, 1992.

Mackay, Robert B., Anthony K. Baker, and Carol A. Traynor, eds. *Long Island Country Houses and Their Architects, 1860–1940.* New York: W. W. Norton, 1997.

Marks, Jason. *Around the World in 72 Days: The Race Between Pulitzer's Nellie Bly and Cosmopolitan's Elizabeth Bisland.* New York: Gemittarius Press, 1993.

Marlowe, John. *The Making of the Suez Canal.* London: Cresset Press, 1964.

Marzolf, Marion. *Up from the Footnote: A History of Women Journalists.* New York: Hastings House, 1977.

McAllister, Ward. *Society as I Have Found It.* New York: Cassell Publishing Company, 1890.

McDonald, Susan Waugh. "From Kipling to Kitsch: Two Popular Editors of the Gilded Age." *Journal of Popular Culture* 15, no. 2 (Fall 1981). 50–61.

McDougall, Walt. *This Is the Life!* New York: Alfred A. Knopf, 1926.

McKerns, Joseph P., ed. *Biographical Dictionary of American Journalism.* Westport, Connecticut: Greenwood Press, 1989.

McPherson, L. G. *The Hand-book of the Pennsylvania Lines.* Chicago: Poole Bros., 1888.

McWilliams, Vera Seeley. *Lafcadio Hearn.* Boston: Houghton Mifflin, 1946.

Miller, Olive Thorne. "The Woman's Club of New Orleans." *The Epoch* 4, no. 97 (December 14, 1888). 341–42.

Milton, Joyce. *The Yellow Kids: Foreign Correspondents in the Heyday of Yellow Journalism.* New York: Harper and Row, 1989.

Mitton, G. E. *The Peninsular and Oriental.* London: Adam and Charles Black, 1913.

Moreno, Barry. *The Statue of Liberty Encyclopedia.* New York: Simon and Schuster, 2000.

Morris, James McGrath. *Pulitzer: A Life in Politics, Print, and Power.* New York: HarperCollins, 2010.

Morris, Lloyd. *Incredible New York: High Life and Low Life from 1850 to 1950.* 1951. Syracuse, New York: Syracuse University Press, 1996.

Mott, Frank Luther. *American Journalism: A History, 1690–1960.* Third Edition. New York: Macmillan, 1962.

———. *A History of American Magazines.* 5 vols. Cambridge, Massachusetts: Harvard University Press, 1957.

Nevin, Adelaide Mellier. *The Social Mirror: A Character Sketch of Pittsburg and Vicinity During the First Century of the County's Existence.* Pittsburgh: T. W. Nevin, 1888.

Nevius, Michelle, and James Nevius. *Inside the Apple: A Streetwise History of New York City.* New York: Free Press, 2009.

New York Illustrated. New York: D. Appleton, 1882.

O'Brien, Frank M. *The Story of the Sun.* New York: D. Appleton, 1928.

Official Guide and Album of the Cunard Steamship Company. Rev. ed. London: Sutton Sharpe and Company, 1878.

Oldham, Wilton J. *The Ismay Line: The White Star Line, and the Ismay Family Story.* Liverpool: Journal of Commerce, 1961.

Oppel, Frank, ed. *Gaslight New York Revisited.* Secaucus, New Jersey: Castle, 1989.

Pacific Mail Steam Ship Company. *Instructions to Captains.* New York: Slote and Janes, 1874.

Painter, Nell Irvin. *Standing at Armageddon: The United States, 1877–1919.* New York: W. W. Norton, 1987.

Parsons, Timothy. *The British Imperial Century, 1815–1914: A World History Perspective.* Lanham, Maryland: Rowman and Littlefield, 1999.

Peeke, Mitch, et al. *The Lusitania Story.* Annapolis, Maryland: Naval Institute Press, 2002.

Peninsular and Oriental Steam Navigation Company. *The P. & O. Pocket Book.* Second issue. London: Head Office, 1900.

Plesur, Milton. *America's Outward Thrust: Approaches to Foreign Affairs, 1865–1890.* DeKalb: Northern Illinois University Press, 1971.

Ravitch, Irene. *Nellie Bly: A Biographical Sketch.* Master's thesis, School of Journalism, Columbia University, 1931.

Reith, G. M. *Handbook to Singapore, with Map, and a Plan of the Botanical Gardens.* Singapore: Singapore and Straits Printing Office, 1892.

Richter, Amy G. *Home on the Rails: Women, the Railroad, and the Rise of Public Domesticity.* Chapel Hill: University of North Carolina Press, 2005.

Riis, Jacob A. *How the Other Half Lives: Studies Among the Poor.* London: Sampson Low, Marston, Searle, and Rivington, 1891.

Rittenhouse, Mignon. *The Amazing Nellie Bly.* New York: E. P. Dutton, 1956.

Robbins, Sara E. *Jefferson County, Colorado: The Colorful Past of a Great Community.* Lakewood, Colorado: Jefferson County Bank, 1962.

Roggenkamp, Karen. *Narrating the News: New Journalism and Literary Genre in Late Nineteenth-Century American Newspapers and Fiction.* Kent, Ohio: Kent State University Press, 2005.

Ross, Ishbel. *Charmers and Cranks: Twelve Famous American Women Who Defied the Conventions.* New York: Harper and Row, 1965.

———. *Ladies of the Press: The Story of Women in Journalism by an Insider.* New York: Harper and Brothers, 1936.

Sante, Luc. *Low Life: Lures and Snares of Old New York.* New York: Vintage, 1992.

Scarborough, Thomas A. H. "The Bislands of Natchez: Sugar, Secession, and Strategies for Survival." *Journal of Mississippi History* 58, no. 1 (Spring 1996). 23–62.

Schickel, Richard. *Intimate Strangers: The Culture of Celebrity.* Garden City, New York: Doubleday, 1985.

Schlereth, Thomas J. *Victorian America: Transformations in Everyday Life, 1876–1915.* New York: HarperCollins, 1991.

Schneirov, Matthew. *The Dream of a New Social Order: Popular Magazines in America 1893–1914.* New York: Columbia University Press, 1994.

Schriber, Mary Suzanne. *Writing Home: American Women Abroad, 1830–1920*. Charlottesville: University Press of Virginia, 1997.

Schulten, Susan. *The Geographical Imagination in America, 1880–1950*. Chicago: University of Chicago Press, 2001.

Sedgwick, Ellery. *The Happy Profession*. Boston: Little, Brown, 1946.

Seitz, Don C. *Joseph Pulitzer: His Life and Letters*. New York: Simon and Schuster, 1924.

Sherard, Robert Harborough. *Twenty Years in Paris: Being Some Recollections of a Literary Life*. London: Hutchinson, 1905.

Sloat, Warren. *A Battle for the Soul of New York: Tammany Hall, Police Corruption, Vice, and Reverend Charles Parkhurst's Crusade Against Them, 1892–1895*. New York: Cooper Square Press, 2002.

Smith, Eugene W. *Trans-Atlantic Passenger Ships Past and Present*. Boston: George H. Dean, 1947.

Smith, Jo Anne. "John A. Cockerill." *American Newspaper Journalists, 1873–1900*, edited by Perry J. Ashley. *Dictionary of Literary Biography*, vol. 23. Detroit: Gale Research Company, 1983. 47–56.

Standage, Tom. *The Victorian Internet: The Remarkable Story of the Telegraph and the Nineteenth Century's On-line Pioneers*. New York: Walker and Company, 1998.

Steele, James W. *Rand, McNally & Co.'s New Guide to the Pacific Coast: Santa Fé Route*. Chicago: Rand, McNally, 1893.

Stevenson, Elizabeth. *The Grass Lark: A Study of Lafcadio Hearn*. New Brunswick, New Jersey: Transaction, 1999.

Stilgoe, John R. *Train Time: Railroads and the Imminent Reshaping of the United States Landscape*. Charlottesville: University of Virginia Press, 2007.

Still, Bayrd. *Mirror for Gotham: New York as Seen by Contemporaries from Dutch Days to the Present*. New York: New York University Press, 1956.

The Story of Nellie Bly. New York: American Flange and Manufacturing Co., 1951.

The Strangers Mercantile Guide to the City of New York. New York: Willis McDonald, 1890.

The Sun's Guide to New York. Jersey City: Jersey City Printing Company, 1892.

Swanberg, W. A. *Pulitzer*. New York: Charles Scribner's Sons, 1967.

Tate, E. Mowbray. *Transpacific Steam: The Story of Steam Navigation from the Pacific Coast of North America to the Far East and Antipodes, 1867–1941*. New York: Cornwall Books, 1986.

Taylor, Richard. *Destruction and Reconstruction: Personal Experiences of the Late War*. New York: D. Appleton, 1879.

Tebbel, John. *The Compact History of the American Newspaper*. New and rev. ed. New York: Hawthorn Books, 1969.

Tinker, Edward Larocque. *Lafcadio Hearn's American Days*. New York: Dodd, Mead, 1924.

Towne, Charles Hanson. *Adventures in Editing*. New York: D. Appleton, 1926.

Trachtenberg, Alan. *The Incorporation of America: Culture and Society in the Gilded Age*. New York: Hill and Wang, 1982.

Turner, Hy B. *When Giants Ruled: The Story of Park Row, New York's Great Newspaper Street*. New York: Fordham University Press, 1999.

Tutwiler, Julia R. "The Southern Woman in New York." *The Bookman* 18, no. 6 (February 1904). 624–34.

The Union Pacific Railroad: A Trip Across the North American Continent from Omaha to Ogden. New York: T. Nelson and Sons, 1871.

Verdery, Katherine. "Elizabeth Bisland Wetmore." *Library of Southern Literature.* Vol. 13. New Orleans: Martin and Hoyt, 1913. 5767–72.

Verne, Jules. *Around the World in Eighty Days.* 1873. Translated by William Butcher. New York: Oxford University Press, 1999.

Walker, John Brisben. *The Church and Poverty.* Washington, D.C.: 1891.

Wall, S. W. *Round the World with Train—A Typhoon: Being the Confessions of a Private Secretary Concerning a Tour of the World in Sixty-Seven Days.* Boston: Round the World Publishing Company, 1891.

Waltz, George H. *Jules Verne: The Biography of an Imagination.* New York: Henry Holt, 1943.

Ward, James A. *Railroads and the Character of America, 1820–1887.* Knoxville: University of Tennessee Press, 1986.

White, James E. *A Life Span and Reminiscences of Railway Mail Service.* Philadelphia: Deemer and Jaisohn, 1910.

White, John H., Jr. *The American Railroad Passenger Car.* Baltimore: Johns Hopkins University Press, 1978.

Williams, Susan Millar. "*L'Enfant terrible:* Elizabeth Bisland and the South." *Southern Review* 22, no. 4 (October 1986). 680–96.

Willis, J. C. *Ceylon: A Handbook for the Resident and the Traveller.* Colombo, 1907.

Wilson, A. N. *The Victorians.* London: Hutchinson, 2002.

Wilson, Derek. *The Circumnavigators.* London: Constable, 1989.

Wingate, Charles F., ed. *Views and Interviews on Journalism.* 1875. New York: Arno, 1970.

Withey, Lynne. *Grand Tours and Cook's Tours: A History of Leisure Travel, 1750 to 1915.* New York: William Morrow, 1997.

Women's Rest Tour Association. *A Summer in England: A Hand-Book for the Use of American Women.* Boston: Alfred Mudge and Son, 1892.

Wong, Edlie L. "Around the World and Across the Board: Nellie Bly and the Geography of Games." In *American Literary Geographies: Spatial Practice and Cultural Production 1500–1900,* edited by Martin Brückner and Hsuan L. Hsu. Newark: University of Delaware Press, 2007. 296–324.

Wood, Marilyn. *Rhoda Broughton (1840–1920): Profile of a Novelist.* Stamford, United Kingdom: Paul Watkins, 1993.

Wood, Stanley. *Over the Range to the Golden Gate.* 1894. Chicago: R. R. Donnelley and Sons, 1908.

Zeisloft, E. Idell, ed. *The New Metropolis: Memorable Events of Three Centuries, from the Island of Mana-hat-ta to Greater New York at the Close of the Nineteenth Century.* New York: D. Appleton, 1899.

Zimmerman, Warren. *First Great Triumph: How Five Americans Made Their Country a World Power.* New York: Farrar, Straus and Giroux, 2002.

ILLUSTRATION CREDITS

—

xix Library of Congress Prints and Photographs Division, reproduction number LC-USZ62-59924

19 Library of Congress Prints and Photographs Division, reproduction number LC-D4-12492

25 Library of Congress Prints and Photographs Division, reproduction number LC-USZ62-136891

46 Library of Congress Prints and Photographs Division, reproduction number LC-DIG-ppmsca-3237

50 Library of Congress Prints and Photographs Division, reproduction number LC-D4-5738

61 General Research Division, The New York Public Library, Astor, Lenox and Tilden Foundations

65 Library of Congress, General Collections

67 Picture Collection, The New York Public Library, Astor, Lenox and Tilden Foundations

81 Library of Congress Prints and Photographs Division, reproduction number LC-D4-22337

112 Library of Congress Prints and Photographs Division, reproduction number LC-USZ62-53135

127 Library of Congress Prints and Photographs Division, reproduction number LC-USZ61-2204

150 Print Collection, Miriam and Ira D. Wallach Division of Arts, Prints and Photographs, The New York Public Library, Astor, Lenox and Tilden Foundations

165 Library of Congress Prints and Photographs Division, reproduction number LC-USZ62-103021

170 Library of Congress Prints and Photographs Division, reproduction number LC-USZ62-41668

186 Library of Congress Prints and Photographs Division, reproduction number LC-USZ62-98424

199 Milstein Division of United States History, Local History & Genealogy, The New York Public Library, Astor, Lenox and Tilden Foundations

206 Library of Congress Prints and Photographs Division, reproduction number LC-USZ62-137734

223 Library of Congress Prints and Photographs Division, reproduction
     number LC-DIG-matpc-22025

245 Library of Congress Prints and Photographs Division, reproduction
     number LC-D426-847

295 The New-York Historical Society

316 Library of Congress Prints and Photographs Division, reproduction
     number LC-USZ61-2126

332 Author's collection

334 Library of Congress Prints and Photographs Division, reproduction
     number LC-DIG-ppmsca-02918

341 Library of Congress Prints and Photographs Division, reproduction
     number LC-USZ62-75620

360 Courtesy of Sara Bartholomew

373 © Bettmann/CORBIS

INDEX

—

Page numbers of illustrations appear in italics.

Adams, George Burton, 218
Adams, Henry, 357
Aden, Yemen, 180–81
    Bisland in, 256–59
    Bly in, 181–82
    as British colony, 180–81, 256
    gharry, 257
    gharry-wallahs, 256
    Gulf of, 256
    Parsees in, 257
    street life of, 257
    Tanks, 257–59
Adriatic (steamship), 322–23
Adriatic Sea, 270
Albers, Adolph, xvii, xx, 83
Allen, William, 260, 261, 262, 302
American Commonwealth, The (Bryce), 106
"American Woman's First Season in London, An" (Bisland), 336, 399n 221
Amiens, France, 125, 126, 325
    Bly arrives in, 126
    India mail train and, 126, 130, 135, 178
    Verne home in. 90, 125, 126–32, 133, 325
Anthony, Susan B., 36
Apollo, Pennsylvania, 3–4
Appleton, Thomas Gold, 167
Arabic (steamship), 262
Arizona, 292–93
Army and Navy Gazette, The, 192
Arnold, Thomas, 249
Around the World in Eighty Days (Verne), ix, 119, 121–23, 131, 280, 294
    Bly's goal to beat Phileas Fogg's time, 72, 116
    Bly's success and sales of, 326
    Hong Kong in, 190
    itinerary of, 131
    movie, 393n 122
    as newspaper serial, 124
    Phileas Fogg, 72, 74, 121–22, 123, 124, 249
    as a stage play, 124, 325
Astor, John Jacob, 368
Atchison, Topeka & Santa Fe Railroad (AT&SF), 283
Atlanta Constitution, 146
Atlantic & Pacific Railroad (A&P), 283, 289, 292
Atlantic Ocean
    Bisland's transatlantic voyage, 319–20
    Bly's transatlantic voyage, 82–89
    dangers of North Atlantic crossing, xiv, xx, 78, 307
    exceptionally severe weather and ship damage (Jan. 1890), 307–9, 322
    icebergs of, 308–9
At the Sign of the Hobby Horse (Bisland), 358
Augusta Victoria (steamship), *81,* 381n xiii
    accommodations and passengers, 81
    arrival in Southampton, 75, 89–90
    Bly departs (Nov. 14, 1889), xiii, xvii–xviii, xxiii, 62, 69–71
    Bly's transatlantic journey, 82–89
    captain, xvii, xx, 83
    coal consumption, 263
    crew and staff, 86
    design and amenities, xiv, 80–81, 85

Augusta Victoria (steamship) (*cont'd*)
 meals, snacks, and dining areas, 82–83,
  85–86
 shipboard life and activities, 84–88
 steerage travel, 81, 86–88

B&O Railroad, 107
Baker, Page M., 49, 387n 49
Barnum, P. T., 175, 176, 397n 175
Bartholdi, Frédéric-Auguste, 70
Beard, George M., 82
Bennett, Arnold, 12
Bennett, James Gordon, Jr., 74
Beveridge, Albert, 356
Bisland, Elizabeth Ker, 40–56, 385n 42
 appearance and beauty, xxi, xxii, 53,
  59, 60, *65*, 147, *295*, *360*, 361, 364
 Applegarth, Oyster Bay home, 357–
  58
 articles for *Harper's Bazaar,* 217, 336,
  349, 399n 221
 articles for *The Cosmopolitan* on her
  journey, 335–36, 351
 books and collections by, 351, 358,
  364
 character and personality, xxii–
  xxiii, 64, 114, 145, 192
 childhood and early years, xxi, 42–
  48, *46*, 188, 386n 46, 386n 47
 as childless, 357
 columnist at *The Cosmopolitan,* xxi,
  41, 42, 60, 145, 336
 death of, 365–66
 death of husband, 362
 editor, *Illustrated American,* 351
 education and reading, xxii, 44, 46–
  47, 113, 362, 382n xxii, 387n 49
 England, affection for, 216–17, 218,
  220, 275, 356, 357, 400n 221
 England residence (1913–1914), 360–
  61
 England visit (1891), following
  journey around the world, 335–
  36, 349–51
 essay for solitary women travelers,
  277
 family and social class of, 42–43, 45,
  147–48, 216–17, 336, 349, 385n 42,
  386n 47
 fiction collaboration with
  Broughton, 350
 as freelance writer, 59, 388n 59

 friendship with Lady Broome, 221,
  335–36, 349
 gardening by, 362
 grave and epitaph, 365–66
 Greenway Rise, home in
  Charlottesville, Virginia, 363–66
 husband's illness and death, 358–62
 as independent woman, 54–56
 inequality and, xxiii
 as journalist, xxi, xxii
 last years, 363–66
 lifestyle, 63
 literary club and salon in New
  Orleans, 52–54
 male admirers, xxi–xxii, 59–60
 married life, 356–62
 meets and marries Charles Wetmore,
  350–51
 in New Orleans, xxi, 49–56, 190,
  365, 381n xxi, 387n 50
 New Orleans Woman's Club
  founded by, 54–56
 in New York, xxi, 57–60, 351
 New York literary salon of, xxi, 59,
  148
 New York residences, xxi, 41, 59,
  321, 385n 41, 388n 57, 388n 59
 obituary, 366
 personal heroes for, 357, 364
 poetry published, 48–49, 386n 48,
  387n 48
 as reporter, New Orleans *Times-
  Democrat,* 50–56, 381n xxi, 387n
  50
 self-image of, 56
 sister living with, xxi, 358, 408n
  321
 travel in 1922, tour of Japan and
  China, 363
 travels with husband (1911–1912),
  359–60
 in Washington, D.C., 361–63
 wealth of, 357–58
 work for women's organizations,
  363
 World War I and, 360–61
 race around the world:
  1st leg, New York to San Francisco
   via train, 67–68, 92–94, 97–111
  2nd leg, San Francisco to Yokohama
   via ship, 110–14, *139*, 139–41, 149–
   53

3rd leg, Yokohama to Brindisi via ship, 113, 160, 185–96, *215,* 215–18, 221, 235–40, 268

4th leg, Brindisi to Le Havre via train, re-routed at Villeneuve–St. Georges to Queenstown, Ireland, 113, 269–81, 397n 185

5th leg, Queenstown to New York via ship, 113–14, 281, *307,* 307–9, 319–21

in Aden and visits to the Tanks, 256–59

age at time of race, xxi, 95

ahead of schedule and Bly, arrival in Hong Kong, 185

Black Watch in Hong Kong described, 191–92

Bly learns of rival, 231–33

book about, 351

Bothnia and Atlantic crossing, 277, 278, 281, 309, 319–20

in Brindisi, Italy, 268–69

Britannia voyage, 255–56

cable sent from Brindisi about predicted arrival, 269

cable sent from Hong Kong, 187

in Calais, 275

celebrity and public reaction to, 112, 114–15, 139–40

chartered trains and ships for, 113, 133

Chinese prisoner observed, 239–40

chivalry of fellow passenger, 277–78

Christmas Eve and Day (1889), 240, 335

coast-to-coast time recorded, 110

delay in Hong Kong departure, 194–95

departure on train bound for Chicago (Nov. 14, 1889), xxii, 67–68

Ems as alternate Atlantic steamship, 272, 274, 276

in England, 275–78

English Channel crossing Calais to Dover, England, 275

false information given to and missed connection, 272–74, 333–35

Fast Western Express cross-country trip, 67–68, 92–94, 97–111, 391n 94, 392n 110

food and beverages, 216–17, 236, 271, 280–81

in France, 271, 274–75

goal of seventy-four days, 185

hair-raising train ride to Ogden, Utah, 102–4

in Hong Kong, 186–96

India mail train and, 268–72

in Ireland, 279–81

in Italy, 270–71

itinerary, 184–85, 194, *215, 235, 255,* 271, *282, 307,* 322, 397n 184, 397n 185

in Japan, 152, 153–60

journey to go westward vs. Bly's eastward, 62

La Champagne sailing from Le Havre and, 269, 271–72, 273–74

length of trip, 321

loneliness during, 98, 99, 145, 151

love of travel, 215

misgivings about, xxii, 67, 98–99

money for, 113

New York City arrival, expected, 194

New York City reached (Jan. 30, 1890), 319–21

night mail train to Holyhead, Wales, 276, 278–79

noteworthy sights, 99–100, 102, 108–10, 112–13, 149, 152, 157, 159–60, 189–90, 236, 257–59

Oceanic and crossing the Pacific, 139–41, 149–52, 395n 151

offer and acceptance of Walker's plan, 61–68

physical demands and toll of, 108, 139, 140–41, 279, 281

postmortem: impossible to have beaten Bly, 322–23

press coverage of, 111–12, 114, 147, 184–85, 277, 321–22, 323

purchases made during, 158

salary for, 65

in San Francisco, 110–14

in Singapore, 235–39

special train booked for by Walker, 274

Thames voyage to Singapore, 215–18, 221

traveling outfits and luggage, 66, 92, 270, 321, 389n 66

Bisland, Elizabeth Ker (cont'd)
  race around the world (cont'd)
    trip as meaningful, 259, 278
    tropics' effect on the nervous
      system, 238
    Walker admits mistakes made, 321–22
    welcome back, 321, 408n 321
Bisland, John, 220–21
Bisland, Maggie, 408n 321
Bisland, Margaret Cyrilla Brownson, 45,
    46, 48, 54, 385n 43, 386n 44, 388n
    54
Bisland, Mary Louise "Molly," 42, 59, 66,
    321, 408n 321
Bisland, Melanie, 358, 386n 47
Bisland, Thomas Pressley, 42, 359, 385n
    43
Bisland, Thomas Shields, 45–46, 385n 43,
    386n 44, 386n 47
Bissell, William A., 289
Blackwell's Island Insane Asylum, xv, 27–
    34, 37, 367, 384n 28, 384n 34
Blaine, James G., 77, 144
Bly, Nellie (Elizabeth "Pink" Cochrane),
    xiv–xv, 4, 5
    agent for, J. M. Hill, 337–38, 339,
      343, 345
    appearance, xiii, xvii, xix, 6, 25, 36,
      129, 132, 146, 288, 295, 341, 371,
      373, 375
    background and childhood, 3–6,
      220, 305–6
    bicycle riding, 292
    birth date and disguising of her age,
      118, 119, 340, 393n 118
    board game Round the World with
      Nellie Bly, 331, 333, 334
    celebrity and public reaction to, xv,
      35, 38, 146, 291–92, 293, 294, 295–
      97, 299–300, 303–4, 310, 312, 326–
      27, 336–40, 342, 366, 375
    championing of Austrian widows
      and orphans, 371
    championing of New York's poor
      citizens and abandoned children,
      372–75
    character and personality, xv, xviii,
      xx, xxii–xxiii, 4, 6, 85, 132, 146,
      212, 213, 234, 261, 340, 343, 374–75
    chewing gum and, 134, 252
    children and animals named after,
      326–27

columnist at the Evening Journal,
    372–75
contract for serial fiction (1890),
    346–47
death of, 375
disappearance from public view
    (1891–1892), 366
earnings, 7, 15, 339, 340, 344, 347,
    372, 410n 347
eccentricity, 374
the English and, dislike for, 178,
    181–83, 218–19, 246, 356, 371,
    374
exile and living with Oscar Bondy
    in Vienna, 371
family supported by, 347, 370–71
fiction writing, 347–48, 351, 352–53,
    366
final column, final written words,
    376
as a "free American girl," 15, 183
goals in life, 16, 305, 353, 369
good luck ring, 24, 80, 262, 288,
    338
grave of, 375, 413n 375
headaches, 71, 118, 210, 212, 244
health problems, 352, 353, 374–75
inequality and, xxiii
Iron Clad Manufacturing Company
    and, 370–71
as late riser, 161–62, 177
lecture tour, 336–40, 342, 345, 409n
    340
letters to Erasmus Wilson, 351, 352,
    369
marriage to Robert Seamon, 369–70
maxim she lived by, 24
in Mexico, as correspondent, 13–15
misfortune and accidents following
    race, 352–53
mother in New York with, xvi, 36
mystery novel by, 209
myths and rumors about, 4, 330
as New American Girl, 290, 294,
    295, 298, 313, 316, 331
New York City, arrival and search
    for a job (1887), 20–28, 384n 24
New York City, final years at Hotel
    McAlpin, 371–75
New York City residences, xvi, 20,
    36, 40, 384n 24
nickname of "Pink," 4, 305

patriotism of, 118, 146, 181, 246
pen name chosen, 8
in Pittsburgh, 5–8, 13–16
products named after, 204, 330–33, 347
property given to, 347
prose and style of, 7
quits *The World,* 344–45, 410n 344
rehired by *The World* (1893), 368
as reporter for the *Pittsburg Dispatch,* 6–7, 13–16, 21–24
as reporter for *The World,* xv, 24–39, 73–74, 297, 344–45, 368–69
romances and men linked to, 36–37, 209–10, 303–4, 353, 369
song about race composed, 327–38
suffragettes and, 36
supporters and detractors, 146–47, 148–49, 339–40, 342, 345
Tallmadge libel suit and, 342–45, 409n 343
undercover investigations, xv, 146, 212, 329, 342, 344, 348–49 (*see also World, The*)
voice of, xvii, 313
as wealthy woman and widow, 369–75
in White Plains, New York, 352–53
Women's Press Club and, 383n 12
work schedule, 71
The World's biographical article on, 329–30
writing on women's issues, 7–8, 13, 16, 21, 27–34, 36
race around the world, xvii, xx, 128
1st leg, Hoboken to Southampton via ship, 69, 75, 77, 82–89
2nd leg, Southampton to Calais to Brindisi via ship and train, 75, 77, 90–91, 116, 130, 134–37
3rd leg, Brindisi to Egypt, Ceylon, Penang, Singapore, and Hong Kong via ship, 77, 119, 138, 161, 161–67, 177–83, 184, 204–14, 221–34
4th leg, Hong Kong to San Francisco via ship, 77, 253–54, 260–62, 282, 287–89
5th leg, San Francisco to Jersey City via train, 77, 282, 282, 289–306, 309–14
in Aden, Yemen, 180–83

age at time of race, 36, 95, 119, 134, 393n 118
American flag and, 245–46
Augusta Victoria and transatlantic crossing, 82–89
awareness of rival Bisland, 116, 231–33, 289, 301, 400n 232
bias and racial generalizations by, 264–65
book about, 294, 345–46, 353, 391n 90
cable from Brindisi, 137–38
cable from train car, feelings about return to the U.S., 289–90
in Canton, 241–51
chair purchased in Hong Kong, 252, 300
Christmas Eve and Day, 241–48, 250–51
in Colombo, Ceylon, 204, 205–14, 206
commendatory remarks on success of, 324–26
crowds waiting for, 291–92, 293, 294, 295–97, 299–300, 303–4, 309–12, 314–18, 316, 406n 295
December 2, 1889, miles traveled in 18 days, 180, 397n 180
departure (Hoboken, Nov. 14, 1889), xiii, xv, xvii–xviii, xxiii, 69–71
disinterest in reporting on social issues during, 88–89, 212, 264
East China Sea, 253–54
encounter with a madman, 228–29
end of the race, Jersey City (Jan. 25, 1890), 314–16, 316
English Channel crossing to Boulogne, France, 126
exaggerations and fabricated events, 227, 290, 293–94, 301–2
exotic food and, 207–8
friend, Dr. Brown, 225–30, 233
goal to beat Phileas Fogg's eighty days, 72, 116, 132, 146, 233
Guessing Match promotion, 197–204, 199, 251–52, 302, 328–29, 406n 302
halfway point, 224
in Hong Kong, 230–33, 241, 252–53
idea for the trip, first declined then accepted by *The World,* xv–xvi, 71–74

Bly, Nellie (Elizabeth "Pink" Cochrane)
  (cont'd)
  race around the world (cont'd)
    ill will toward Bisland, 300–301
    on the India mail train, 135–37, 394n
      135
    itinerary, xvii, xviii, xx, 69, 77, 116,
      129, 131–32, 161, 197, 198, 210, 282,
      390n 77
    Jennings and, 284, 290, 296, 313
    Kilgallen emulates (1936), 375, 413n
      375
    laundry problem, 79–80
    loneliness during, 178, 209
    loyalty to America, 118, 246, 313,
      339, 357
    luggage in a single bag, xvi, 78–79,
      121, 133
    Mediterranean Sea, 161–64
    mixed feelings about, xvi–xvii,
      xviii, xxiii
    money for, 80, 167
    monkey (McGinty) carried with, 227,
      233, 262, 288, 289, 336, 400n 227
    musical written about, 375–76
    "Nellie Bly Escort Corps," 284
    New Year's Eve, 253–54
    noteworthy sights and reflections,
      128, 177, 225–26, 243, 247–48
    obstacles faced, xx
    Oceanic and crossing the Pacific,
      253–54, 260–62
    Oriental voyage, 221–24, 228–30
    other people's proposals to race
      around the world, 74–75
    passport obtained for, 77, 80, 118–19,
      393n 118
    in Penang, 222
    physical demands and toll of, 126,
      131, 134–35, 304
    in Port Said, 164–67, 165
    predicted date of return, 198, 210–11
    preparation for departure, xvi–xvii,
      76–80
    press coverage of, 94–97, 132–34,
      146–47, 203–4, 293, 296–97, 304,
      394n 132
    Reception Committee boards Bly's
      train, 310–11, 312–13
    record-breaking times, 315, 324
    rules and days allotted for, xv, 77–
      78, 133

    seasickness, 82–84, 290
    in Singapore, 225–27
    South China Sea, 221, 224, 228–30
    special train for transcontinental rail
      journey, 283–84, 289–300
    special train has close call on bridge,
      293–94
    Straits of Malacca, 221–22, 228
    Suez Canal, 177–80
    suitors and admirers during, 163–64,
      228–29, 298–99
    timekeepers for, xviii, xxiii, 302,
      314–15
    train from Chicago to Jersey City,
      Atlantic Express No. 20, 300,
      303–6, 309–14
    train to Amiens, 126
    transcontinental journey, Oakland
      to Jersey City, 289–306
    traveling dress, coat, and hat, xvi,
      xviii, xix, 76–77, 78, 163, 227,
      288, 306, 324, 338, 342, 390n 76
    Verne meeting with, in Amiens, 90,
      116, 125–32, 133, 134, 339, 393n
      125, 394n 132
    Verne sends greeting, 300
    Victoria, voyage on, 137–38, 161–65,
      167–68, 177–82
    welcome home reception in New
      York City, 315–17
Bondy, Oscar, 371
Booth, Edwin, 76
Boston Herald, 146
Bothnia (steamship), 277, 278, 336
  Bisland arrival in New York (Jan. 30,
    1890), 319–21
  Bisland departure from Queensland
    (Jan. 19, 1890), 280–81
  Bisland's transatlantic voyage, 309, 319–
    20
  captain, 319
Brindisi, Italy
  as ancient Brundisium, 137, 268
  Bisland's arrival and departure (Jan. 16,
    1890), 268
  Bisland's cable about predicted arrival,
    269
  Bly's arrival and departure (Nov. 25,
    1889), 137–38
  Bly's cable from, 137–38
  reaction to Bly in, 339
Brisbane, Arthur, 372, 374, 397n 174

Britannia (steamship), 322
  Bisland debarks (Jan. 16, 1890), 268–69
  Bisland on, 255–56
  design and amenities, 255
  as P&O "Jubilee" steamship, 255
  shipboard life and activities, 255–56
British Empire, xxiii, 256, 356
  Aden, Yemen, 180–81
  Bisland's admiration of, 218
  Bly's envy of, 181, 356
  Ceylon, 181, 204–5
  currency of, 181
  Egypt and, 181, 191, 192
  Forty-Second Royal Highland
      Regiment ("Black Watch"), 191–
      92, 196
  gatling gun and firepower of, 192–93
  Hong Kong, 181, 188, 190, 249
  island colonies of, 181
  in the Mediterranean, 162–63, 181
  as model for the U.S., 356
  opium trade and Opium War, 248–50
  privilege and power of, 181–82
  Sepoy Mutiny, 193
  Singapore, 236–37, 239
Brooklyn Daily Eagle, 58, 371
Broome, Lady (Mary Anne Barker), 221,
      278, 335–36, 349, 399n 221
Broome, Sir Frederick, 336, 349
Broughton, Rhoda, 349–50
Brown, C. E., 104
Brown, Dr. (Welsh friend of Nellie Bly),
      225–30, 233
Browning, Robert, 349, 366
Brownson, John, 386n 44
Bryce, James, 106, 218
Burgess, Neil, 337
Burr, Aaron, 47

Cable, George Washington, 53
Caine, W. S., 211–12
Calais, France
  Bisland Channel crossing at, 275
  Bly in, 134–35
  India mail train run and, 135, 274–75
California. *See also* San Francisco,
      California
  Bly's special train passes through, 290–
      92
  Fresno County, 291
  Oakland Mole, 110
  Sacramento Valley, 110

San Francisco Bay, 110, *282*, 289
snow blockade of 1890, stranded
      passengers at Emigrant Gap, 284–
      87, 405n 285
Calkins, William, 144–45
Campbell, Lady Gertrude Elizabeth, 152
Candle of Understanding, A (Bisland), 358
Canton, China, 241–51, 264
  American flag in, 245–46, 406n 299
  Bly's tour of and guide, Ah Cum, 243–
      48, 250–51
  Buddhist temples in, 250
  executions in, 247–48
  foreigners as rarity in, 247
  opium use in, 248
  population of, 1880s, 246
  sedan chair, 244
  Shameen (foreign residential area), *245*,
      245–46
  sights of, 246–47
  streets of, 244–45
Carnegie, Andrew, 219–20, 304
Carpenter, Frank G., 203, 344–45, 410n
      344
Catalonia (steamship), 308
Central Pacific Railroad
  Chinese workers, 143–44
  "Golden Spike" at Promontory
      Summit, 104
  snow blockade shutting down railroad
      traffic in American West and, 283
Ceylon. *See also* Colombo, Ceylon
  agricultural products, 212
  beauty of, 204
  as British colony, 181, 204–5
  British population of, 205
  coffee and tea exports, 211
  flora and fauna, 205
  Tamil tea pickers, 211–12
Chambers, Julius, xviii, 310, 311, 312, 393n
      125
  salary at *The World,* 347, 410n 347
Charlottesville, Virginia, 363–66
Chautauquan magazine, 191
Cheque Bank Checks, 346
Chicago, Illinois
  Bisland arrives and departs (Nov. 16,
      1889), 98–99
  Bly arrives and departs (Jan. 24, 1890),
      297, 300
  Bly given escort and reception, 297–
      300

Chicago, Illinois (*cont'd*)
  Board of Trade, 299–300
  General Time Convention, 107
  Kinsley's restaurant, 298
  Union Depot, 92, 98
Chicago Daily Herald, 297
Chicago Press Club, 298
  Bly admitted as "one of the boys," 299
  escorting Nellie Bly, 297–300, 304
  women excluded, 299
Chicago Times, 145, 340
Chicago Tribune, 58, 105, 302
China. *See also* Canton, China; Hong
    Kong; immigration; Singapore
  Bisland tours (1922), 363
  Bly's generalizations about people, 264–65
  civil service, 250
  opium trade and Opium War, 248–50
  Treaty of Nanking, 249
China (steamship), 262
Chinese Exclusion Act, 145, 241
Chopin, Kate, 53
chromolithography, 333
Cincinnati Commercial, 304, 345
City of Paris (steamship), 75
Civil War
  Battle of Fort Bisland, 43, 385n 43
  the Bisland family and, 42, 43–44, 385n 43, 386n 44
  Britain and, 219
  memories of battlefields, 144
  Pulitzer in, 171
  U.S. as agricultural society and, 355
Clarke, Thomas Curtis, 106
Clay, Henry, 47, 51
Cleveland, Orestes, 314, 315–16, 317
Cleveland Leader, 124
Cochran, Albert, 383n 14
Cochran, Catherine May, 383n 14
Cochran, Charles, 347, 383n 14
Cochran, Harry, 383n 14
Cochran, Michael, 4
Cochran, Robert and Catherine Risher, 220
Cochrane, Elizabeth Jane. *See* Bly, Nellie
Cochrane, Mary Jane, 4–6
  on Bly's train from Philadelphia to Jersey City, 310, 311, 312, 317
  Bly supports, 347
  breech with Bly over money, 370–72

  living with Bly in New York, xvi, 36, 76
  in Mexico with Bly, 13–14
Cockerill, John, 26, 73
  assigns Bly to the Blackwell Island exposé, 27–28
  Bly interviews on women reporters, 24
  Bly's race around the world story idea, 73
  Bly talks her way into seeing him, 24–27, 384n 26
  as co-editor of *The World,* 367
  as editor at *The World,* 24, 26–28
  Pulitzer fires, 368, 412n 368
  Slayback scandal, 27
  at the St. Louis *Post-Dispatch,* 27
Coleridge, Samuel, 190
Colombo, Ceylon, 180, *197, 206*
  beggars of and poverty, 281
  Bisland transfer at (Jan. 1, 1890), 195, 255
  Bly and food of, 207–8
  Bly delay in, 210–11
  Bly's arrival (Dec. 8, 1889), 204
  Bly's departure (Dec. 13, 1889), 214
  Bly's stay in, 205–14, 406n 299
  as British colony, 204–5
  Galle Face Hotel, 208–9
  gems of, 207
  Grand Oriental Hotel, 206–7
  jinrikishas (ricksaws), 208
  newspapers in, 211
  Singhalese of, 206
Columbus, Ohio, 304
Compagnie Générale Transatlantique (the French Line), 185, 271, 403n 271
Confessions (Rousseau), xxii, 382n xxii
Cook, Thomas, 272–73
Cooley's Weekly, Norwich, Connecticut, 133
"coolie," 143, 211
Cork, Ireland, 280
Cosmopolitan, The, xxi, 41–42, 146, 351.
    See also Walker, John Brisben
  Bisland and her "In the Library" column, xxi, 41, 42, 60, 145, 336
  Bisland's articles on her journey, 335–36, 351
  Bisland's cable from Brindisi, 269
  Bisland's cable from Hong Kong, 187
  Bisland's note from the *Oceanic,* 145

Bisland's race around the world, xxi, xxii, 61–68, 98–99, 145–46, 184–85, 194, 269, 335–36

Bisland welcomed home by colleagues, 321

concedes defeat to Bly, 318

offices, xxii, 41, 62, 99, 385n 41

prizes and publicity stunts, 60–61, 389n 61

ships' use of coal discussed, 263

travel stories in, 42

Country Fair, The (play), 337

Croly, Jane Cunningham "Jennie June," 383n 12

Cummings, Amos J., 96

Cunard Line, 276–77, 308, 319, 336

Curzon, Wyndham, 163

Daily Boomerang, Laramie, Wyoming, 339

Daily Inter Ocean, 342

Daily Messenger, St. Albans, Vermont, 323

Dallas Morning News, 339

Dana, Charles A., 21–23, 169, 172, 176

Daniels, Cora Linn, 311, 312, 317

Davis, Col. William L., 367

Davis, Mollie Moore, 52, 59

Debs, Eugene V., 368

"Deep-Sea Cables, The" (Kipling), 194

Delmonico's, New York, 194, 385n 41

D'Ennery, Adolphe, 124

Detroit Commercial, 146

Deuel, J. W., 285–87

Dickens, Charles, xiv, 105, 131

Dickinson, Edward, 100, 104

Dickinson, Emily, 366

Dodge City, Kansas, 295–96

Donaldson, R. A., 289

Dover, England, 275

Downing, "Cyclone" Bill, 102–4, 108, 143, 392n 102

Duff, Sir Mountstuart Grant, 325

Dulzer, Edward, 21, 383n 21

dungaree, 166

Duquesnel, Félix, 124

East China Sea, 253–54

Eastman Company, 346

Egypt

  baksheesh and beggars in, 165, 179

  British conquest of, 191, 192

  Port Said, 164–67

  Suez Canal, 123, 164, 177–80

Ekins, H. R., 375, 413n 375

"Elegy Written in a Country Churchyard" (Gray), 47

Elizabeth I, Queen, 357

Emerson, Ralph Waldo, 107–8

Emigrant Gap, California, 284–86

Ems (steamship), 272, 276, 277

Engineer, The, 266

England, 116. *See also* British Empire

  American attitudes toward, 218–20, 356

  American tourism and, 356

  Bisland and husband move to Surrey (1913–1914), 351

  Bisland arrives and departs (Jan. 18–19, 1890), 275–78

  Bisland crosses the Channel from Calais to Dover (Jan. 18, 1890), 275

  Bisland's affection for the English, 216–17, 220, 275, 349–50

  Bisland spends year in (1890–1891), 335–36, 349–51

  Bly crosses the Channel from Folkestone to Boulogne (Nov. 22, 1889), 116, 119, 126

  Bly lands in Southampton (Nov. 21, 1889), 89–91

  Bly rushes to London and obtains her passport, 116–19

  Bly's dislike of the English, 178, 181–83, 218–19, 246, 356, 371, 374

  Kent, 275

  "this other Eden," 190

  Victoria's golden jubilee, 163

  World War I, 360–61

Epoch, The, 10, 36, 54

Et in Arcadia Ego, 159–60

Etiquette of Good Society (Campbell), 152

Etruria (steamship), 276–77

European Travel for Women (Cadwalader), 357

Ferlinghetti, Lawrence, 385n 43

Ficklen, John Rose, 52

Fillmore, Millard, 11

Five Weeks in a Balloon (Verne), 120

Florence (steamship), 279

Flying Trip Around the World, A (Bisland), 351

Fogg, William Perry, 124

Ford, John Donaldson, 395n 154

Forman, Allen, 334–35, 366

Foster, Stephen, 8, 254
France
  Bisland en route to Calais, 274–75
  Bisland en route to Villeneuve–St.
    Georges, 271
  Bly in Amiens, 125–32
  Bly in Calais, 134–35
Franz Joseph, Emperor, 106
Free Press, Waverly, New Jersey, 203–4
Fresno Evening Expositor, 291
Friend, The, 105

Galaxy, The, magazine, 12
Gallia (steamship), 308
Genoa, Italy, 113
gharry, 225, 236, 257
Ghormley, William, 63, 76, 338, 346, 390n
  76
Gibraltar, 181
Gilman, Charlotte Perkins, 396n 168
"Girl I Left Behind Me, The," 291
"Globe Trotting Nellie Bly" (Hallen and
  Hart), 327–38
Godey's Lady's Book, 350
Goggin, S. W., 241–42, 401m 241
Goldman, Emma, 368
González, Manuel, 15
Goode, Leonora, 386n 47
Good Health Home, 363
Goodman, T. H., 283
Gordon, Charles, 273
Gould, Edwin, 370
Gould, Jay, 38, 172, 173, 370
Grand Central Depot, New York City,
  67, 98
  Bisland's departure on the Fast Western
    Express (Nov. 14, 1889), xxii,
    67–68
  first run of transcontinental fast mail
    train leaves (Nov. 14, 1889), 100–
    110
Grant, Hugh J., 96, 313
Gray, Thomas, 47
Great Northern Telegraph Company, 187
Greaves, Tracey, 89–91, 116–19, 125–26,
  134–35, 324–25, 393n 118
  Bly-Verne meeting and, 90, 125–27,
    133, 394n 129, 394n 132
Greeley, Horace, 11
Green, Hetty, 370
Greenwood, Grace, 279, 404n 279
Grozier, Edwin, 170

Hamburg-American Packet Company,
  xiii, xvii, 80, 81, 390n 81. *See also
  Augusta Victoria*
Hare, Hobart Amory, 267
Harper's Bazaar, 58
  "An American Woman's First Season in
    London" (Bisland), 336, 399n 221
  Bisland's articles in, 217, 349
Harper's Weekly, 9, 12, 308
Harriman, Edward H., 106
Harris, Townsend, 154
Hawley, Joseph R., 219
Hazelton, George, 144
Hearn, Lafcadio, xxi–xxii, 49, 53–54,
  59–60, 358, 381n xxi, 387n 49,
  387n 50
Hearst, William Randolph, xxi
Heston, Harry, 310
Hetzel, Pierre-Jules, 119, 121
Hill, J. M., 337–38, 339, 343, 345
Hindenburg (zeppelin), 375
Hoboken, New Jersey, Bly departs on the
  Augusta Victoria, xiii, xv, xvii–
  xviii, xxiii, 69–71
Holme, Leicester, 313
Holyhead, Wales, 279
Hong Kong, *184, 186*
  Bay, 186
  Bisland arrival (Dec. 15, 1889), 185
  Bisland delayed and ship change, 194–
    95
  Bisland departure (Dec. 18, 1889), 195,
    400n 232
  Bisland in, 186–96
  Black Watch stationed in, 191–92, 196
  Bly arrival (Dec. 23, 1889), 210, 230
  Bly delayed in, 232–33, 241, 252–53
  Bly purchases chair in, 252
  Bly's connection in, 224
  Bly's departure (Dec. 28, 1889), 184,
    210–11, 252–53
  Bly's disapproval of, 231, 264
  Bly's sightseeing, 241, 252
  Botanical Gardens, 189–90
  as British colony, 181, 188, 190, 249
  English residential section, 187–88
  fashion and culture, 187
  "Happy Valley," 241
  native section, 189
  Parsees in, 187, 195, 257
  Queen's Road, shops on, 252
  sedan chair, 186–88, 230–31, 233

Sikh policemen, 190–91
  Verne on, 190
  Victoria Peak, 252
Hood, Thomas, 365
Hopkins, Gerard Manley, 110
Hotel McAlpin, New York City, 372–75
Howard, Joseph, 95
Howe, Julia Ward, 12, 52, 387n 52
How to Travel (Knox), 79
Hugo, Victor, 127
Hutchinson, Kansas, 296
Hutchinson, Nelly Mckay, 12
Hutson, Charles, 361, 362

Illustrated American, 58, 351
immigration
  anti-Chinese laws and bias, 142–45, 241
  Chinese, 140, 141–45
  Irish Catholic, 219
  New York City and, 173
  steerage travel and, 88, 140
  U. S. tradition of exclusion, 145
India
  Parsees, 195–96
  Sepoy Mutiny, 193
  telegraph and British in, 193
India mail train, 126, 130, 178
  Bisland on, 268–72, 274–75,
  Bly on, 135–37, 394n 135
Influence of Sea Power upon History, 1660–1783, The (Mahan), 355
Ingram, Frank G., 36–37, 303–4, 353
International Sleep-Car Company, 134
Ireland
  beggars of and poverty, 281
  Bisland arrival and departure (Jan. 19, 1890), 279–81
  Bisland crossing of Irish Sea, Holyhead to Queenstown, 279
  Queenstown, 276
Irish Sea, 279
Iron Clad Manufacturing Company, 369–71
Italy. *See also* Brindisi, Italy
  American tourism and, 356–57
  Bisland traveling through, 270–71
  Bly traveling through, 136–37
  British subsidy of mails, 271
  railway employees, 136, 271

James, Henry, 356
Janet Crown (ship), 308

Japan
  Bisland in Tokyo, 158–60
  Bisland in Yokohama, 153–58
  Bisland returns (1911–1912), 359–60
  Bisland returns (1922), 363
  Bisland sights land and Mount Fuji from the *Oceanic,* 152
  Bisland's love of, 159–60, 359, 363
  Bly's generalizations about people, 264–65
  countryside, 158–59
  fashion and culture, 154, 157
  jinrikishas (ricksaws), 153, 154, 186
  Mount Fuji (Fujiyama), 152
  press coverage of Bly's race, 394n 132
Jarrett, Henry C., xvii, 74–75, 77
Jefferson, Thomas, 364
Jennings, John J.
  as aide to Bly, 313
  meets Bly's special train in Lathrop, 290
  "Nellie Bly Escort Corps" and, 284, 290
  reporting on Bly's train journey, 296
  skis out of snow blockade, 284–87, 290, 405n 285, 405n 287
Jersey City, New Jersey
  Bly arrives (Jan. 25, 1890), 314–16
  Pennsylvania Railroad terminal, 93, 314
Jewish South, 51
jinrikishas (ricksaws), 222, 395n 154
  in Ceylon, 208
  in Japan, 153, 154, 186
Johns Hopkins University, 96
Johnson, Samuel, 215
Jones, Mary Cadwalader, 357
Journalism for Women: A Practical Guide (Bennett), 12
Journalist, The, 9, 12–13, 24, 27, 169, 203, 334
  on Bly's rehiring by *The World,* 369
  "Where is Nellie Bly?," 366
Journey to the Center of the Earth, A (Verne), 120–21
Joy, Sally or "Penelope Penfeather," 8

Kandy, Ceylon, 212, 264
Kansas
  Bly's train passes through, 295–97
  Bly's train permitted to exceed state speed limit, 296
Keats, John, 113, 215
Keller, Helen, xv
Kennedy, Thomas, 72

Kent, England, 275
Kieran, Leo, 375, 413n 375
Kilgallen, Dorothy, 375, 413n 375
King, Grace, 53
Kinglake, A. W., 193
Kipling, Rudyard, 194
Knox, Thomas W., 79
    circumnavigation of the globe and, 96
    guide for travelers, 151
Knoxville Journal, 339

La Champagne (steamship), 114, 403n 271
    arrival in New York City behind Bly,
        322
    Bisland booked on, 194, 195
    Bisland given false information about,
        273–74
    importance of Bisland connecting
        with, 269, 271–72
    transatlantic crossing missed by
        Bisland, 308–9
    Walker pays for delayed sailing for
        Bisland, 273–74
Laffan, William L., 176
Lahore Chronicle, 193
Lake Shore Railroad line, 97–98
Lancet, The, 267
Later On! (musical comedy), 327–38
Laurie, Annie, 111, 366–67
Lazarus, Emma, 145
Le Havre, France, 113, 185, 194, 195, 269,
    271, 272, 274, 308, 333
Lehr, Elizabeth, 171
Lemoinne, M. Georges, 273
Lesseps, Count Ferdinand de, 164, 324
Lewis, Sir William, 277
Life and Letters of Lafcadio Hearn (ed.
    Bisland), 358
Life magazine, 37, 311, 385n 37, 410n 345
Little Lord Fauntleroy (play), 63
Lives (Plutarch), 268
Loch Moidart (ship), 308
Logansport, Indiana, 303
London, England
    Bisland and literary society in, 349
    Bisland and the London season, 349
    Bisland arrives and departs (Jan. 18,
        1890), 276
    Bly arrives and departs (Nov. 22, 1889),
        116–19
    Bly asked to compare it to New York,
        117

    Charing Cross Station, 276
    cityscape and weather, 117–18
    commendatory remarks on Bly's
        success from, 324–25
    Euston Station, 277
    Grand Hotel, 277
    newspaper account of Bly-Verne
        meeting, 132
London *Daily Telegraph,* 194
London Gentlewoman, The, 350
London Southwestern Railway, 90
Long Island Times, 133
Lord, Cheste, 58
Low, Charles, 288
Lusitania (steamship), 319

Madden, George A., 6, 7–8, 13, 15
Maddox, Dorothy, 97
Mahan, Alfred Thayer, 355–56
Majestic (steamship), 266
Malta, 162, 181
Master of Ballantrae, The (Stevenson), 63
Maybrick, Florence, 166, 396n 166
McCormick, Robert S., 118–19, 393n 118
McDonald, Flora, 9, 13
McDougall, Walt, 324, 330, 344, 348, 369
McLoughlin Brothers, 333, 408–09n 333
Mediterranean Sea, Bly's crossing, 161–64
Merrilies, Meg, 367
Metcalfe, James Stetson, 37, 209–10, 311,
    353, 369
Mexico, 13–15
Michigan Farmer, 345
Midsummer's Night Dream, A
    (Shakespeare), 123
Minneapolis Tribune, 409n 343
Missouri Pacific Railroad, 173
Mitchell, S. Weir, 396n 168
Mojave Desert, 292
Morse, Samuel, 194
Mount Repose, Natchez, Mississippi, 46,
    47, 188, 386n 47
Munro, Norman L., 346–47, 351, 410n
    347
Murray, Digby, 253
"My Nellie's Blue Eyes," 291
Mystery of Central Park, The (Bly), 209,
    347–48

National Salvage Society, 361
National Woman Suffrage Convention,
    36

Native Americans
  as beggars, 109
  Indian Wars, 355
  Navajos, 293
  railroads and, 105, 109
  of the Southwest, 109
Nellie Bly (musical), 375–76
Nellie Bly's Book: Around the World in Seventy-Two Days (Bly), 345–46, 353, 391n 90, 410n 345
  advertisements in, 346
"Nelly Bly" (Foster), 8, 254
Nepaul, 210, 212, 213
Nevada, 109–10
New and Altered Forms of Disease, Due to the Advance of Civilization in the Last Half Century (Hare), 267
New Mexican, Santa Fe, 345
New Orleans
  Bisland in, xxi, 49–56, 190, 365, 381n xxi
  Bisland's room in, 50, 51
  Camp Street, 51, 52
  Canal Street, 51, 52
  culture of, 51
  French Quarter, 50
  Monkey Wrench corner, 51
  Newsboys' Home, 52
  "Newspaper Row," 51
  newspapers of, 51–52, 386n 48
  Royal Street (Rue Royal), 50, 50, 51, 52
  Royal Street salon and literary personages, 52–54, 59
New Orleans *Daily Picayune*, 51, 53, 54
  Bisland interview in, 217–18
  coverage of Bisland's journey, 184–85
New Orleans *Ledger*, 51
New Orleans *Times-Democrat*, 48, 386n 48. *See also* Hearn, Lafcadio
  Bisland as reporter at, 50–56, 381n xxi
  on Bisland in her later years, 364
  Bisland's "Literary Bric-a-Brac" column, 59
  Bisland's poetry in, 48–49, 387n 49, 387n 50
  offices of, 51
New Orleans Woman's Club, 54–56, 363
newspapers
  Bly as inspiration for female journalists, 351
  effect of Bly-Bisland race on reporting by women, 97

errors in coverage of around the world races, 95
  first Sunday comic strip published, 368
  as the fourth estate, 11
  front page of, 174, 397n 174
  inequality for female journalists, 8–13
  Mexican, 15
  New Orleans's, 51–52
  newsroom for men only, 9–10, 21
  New York's, 19, 19–20
  number of journalists 1880 census, 8
  Pittsburgh's, 6
  Pulitzer's innovations, 174–76
  "stunt girl," 366–67
  training of reporters, 10
  undercover investigations, 366
  women reporters, xv, 8–13, 21–24, 97, 111, 366–67, 371–72, 409n 343
  women's page and society reporting, 8–9, 21, 52
  The World as largest, xv
New York Athletic Club, xviii, xxiii, 302
New York Central Railroad
  Bisland departs on the Fast Western Express (Nov. 14, 1889), xxii, 67–68
  Bisland's trip to Chicago, 92–94, 97–98
  Chicago Depot, 98–99
  Grand Central Depot, New York City, 67, 67, 98
  opulent cars and amenities, 93–94
  sleeper cars, 94
  Vanderbilts and, 67, 174
New York City
  apartment houses in, 57–58, 388n 57
  Barnum's American Museum, 175, 397n 175
  Bisland and high society, 147–48
  Bisland arrival on the *Bothnia* (Jan. 30, 1890), 320–21
  Bisland arrives in and begins work (1885), 57–60, 388m 59
  Bisland's literary salon, xxi, 59
  Bisland's residences in, xxi, 41, 57, 59, 385n 41, 388n 57, 388n 59
  Blackwell's Island, 384n 28
  Bly arrives in and seeks a job (1887), 20–28
  Bly speaks at the Union Square Theatre, 337–39
  Bly's race around the world, interest in, 96

New York City (cont'd)
  Bly's residences in, xvi, 20, 36, 40, 371–
    75, 384n 24
  Bly's welcome home, 315–18
  boat traffic, Hudson River, xiii
  the Bowery, 172–73
  Bowling Green, 72
  Delmonico's, 194, 385n 41
  Elephantine Colossus, Coney Island,
    320
  environment, architecture, and
    everyday life, 17–19, 20
  exposé of Chambers Street Hospital,
    367
  fall of 1889, weather, xiii–xiv
  Fifth Avenue, 40–41
  Grand Central Depot, 67, 67–68, 98
  great blizzard of 1888, 37
  Hotel McAlpin as Bly residence, 371–
    75
  Hubert Home Club, 58, 388n 58
  immigrants in, 173
  invention of the elevator and, 18, 383n
    18
  life in (1889), 63
  local transportation, xvi–xvii, 20
  Madison Square Park, 41
  mansions and displays of wealth, 171–
    72
  Murray Hill, xxi, 41
  "Nellie Bly Guessing Match" and, 197–
    203, 199
  newspapers, 19–20
  Nineteenth Street commercial district,
    76
  North River, xiii, 381n xiii
  only one restaurant where women
    could eat at the counter, 99
  Park Row (newspaper district), 19, 19–
    20, 26, 72, 76
  population of, 1880s, 17, 383n 17
  Printing-House Square, 72
  Pulitzer's dislike of the elite, 171
  Pulitzer's residence, 169
  Queen Victoria's golden jubilee and,
    220
  Rialto, 40
  society and class in, 171–72
  Statue of Liberty, 69–70
  Tenderloin district, xvi, 40
  theater and arts, 63, 76
  Trinity Church, 19
  wealthy families of, 41, 171–72
  Western Union, 17
  Whitney mansion, 171
  winner of "Nellie Bly Guessing
    Match," 328–29
New York Commercial Advertiser, 72
New York Daily News, 72
New York Evening Journal
  Bly as columnist for, 372–75
  Bly's final column, 376
  Kilgallen's race around the world
    (1936), 375
New York Evening Post, 171
New York Family Story Paper, The, 346–47,
  351, 366
New York Herald, 23
  Bisland's return noted, 323
  coverage of Bly's and Bisland's race,
    94–95
  Jarrett's around the world race proposal
    and, 74–75
  office building, 72, 397n 175
  price of an issue, 176
  rumor of reporter sent on rival
    circumnavigation, 94
  story on snow blockade shutting down
    railroad traffic in American West
    (Jan., 1890), 283
New York Independent, 350
New York Journal American, 375
New York Mail and Express, 23, 72
New York Morning Journal, 72
New York Press, 95
New York Press Club, 413n 375
New York Sun, 20
  Bisland writing for, 58
  Dana and women journalists, 21–23
  Dana as opposing all social change,
    172
  Dana's antipathy toward Pulitzer, 169
  Riis's exposés of slum life in, 174
  rivalry with The World, 20, 176
New York Telegram, 9
  race around the world (1936), 375
  on women reporters, 23–24
New York Times, 72
  biographical item on Bisland, 147
  Bisland's obituary, 366
  Bisland's return noted, 323
  editorial on ships' use of coal, 263
  "Flying Trips of Two Young Women,"
    95

office building, *19*, 19–20, 72
price of an issue, 176
race around the world (1936), 375, 413n 375
on record-setting voyage of the *Majestic,* 266
review of Bisland's collection, 358
on Wetmore, 350
on women reporters, 23
New York Tribune, 11
anti-Chinese bias, 144
anti-labor stance, 172
clock tower, 19, *19*, 69, 72, 76
coverage of Bly's and Bisland's race, 95
misinformation about third reporter racing around the world, 94
office building, *19*, 19
New York *World-Telegram,* 375, 413n 375
Norddeutscher Lloyd line, 194, 272, 276, 392n 113
North German Lloyd lines, 113

Oakland Mole, 110
Bly departure (Jan. 21, 1890), *282*, 288
Occidental and Oriental Steamship Company (O&O), 108, 114, 139, 195, 231, 241, 253, 287. *See also* *Oceanic*
Oceanic (steamship)
Bisland and storm at sea, 140–41
Bisland's arrival in Hong Kong (Dec. 15, 1889), 185
Bisland's departure from San Francisco, (Nov. 21, 1889), 114–15
Bisland's life aboard, 149–52, *150*, 395n 151
Bisland's westbound crossing and arrival in Hong Kong, speed of, 185
Bly departure from Hong Kong (Dec. 28, 1889), 252–53
Bly's accusation of favoritism to Bisland, 301–2
Bly's arrival in San Francisco (Jan. 21, 1890), *282*, 287–89
Bly's voyage on, 184, 253–54, 260–62
Chief Allen's support of Bly and couplet written, 260, 261, 262, 402n 260
Chinese immigrants aboard, 140, 149–51, 153
Chinese passenger's death, 160

coal consumption, 263
design and amenities, 140
first class on, 253
first-class staterooms, 140
New Year's Eve aboard, 253–54
purser, Mr. Fuhrman, 233
record crossing by, 262
steerage, 140, 149–50
stop in Yokohama, 154–60, 185
storm and search for a Jonah, 261–62
Walker's attempt to move up departure of, 108, 111, 114, 185, 232, 397n 184
William "Typhoon Bill" Smith as captain, 241, 253–54, 260
Omaha, Nebraska, 123
Bisland arrives in, 100
train station in, 100
Oriental (steamship)
Bly aboard, 221–24, 228–30
Bly arrives in Hong Kong on (Dec. 23, 1889), 230
Bly boards in Colombo, Ceylon (Dec. 13, 1889), 213–14
Bly encounters a madman aboard ship, 228–29
Bly scheduled on, 180
Colombo to Penang in three days, 222
Penang refueling, 222–24
port in Singapore, 224–27
Singapore to Hong Kong at record speed, 230
South China Sea crossing, 228–30
strange passengers, 229–30
Oxford, England, 349–51
Oyster Bay, Long Island, 357–58

Pacific Mail, 262
Pacific Ocean, 113
Bisland and storm at sea, 140–41
Bisland's crossing, 149–52
Bisland's description of, 149
Bly's crossing, 184, 253–54, 260–62
record-breaking crossings of, 262–63
storms on, 260–61
Palace Hotel, San Francisco, 111, *112*, 139
Pall Mall Gazette, 132
Paris, France, 120, 122, 124, 202, 271, 272, 326, 370
American Legation in, 273–74
American travel to, 356
Bly's trip, widespread interest in, 325
Cook & Son office in, 273, 403n 273

Paris, France (cont'd)
  Ghormley's agents in, 76
  The World's correspondent in, 125, 127,
      128, 129, 132, 325, 408n 326
Paris News Association, 277
Parkhurst, Rev. Charles, 368
Penang, 181, 210
  Bly's arrival on the Oriental (Dec. 16,
      1889), 222
  Hindu temples of, 264
  Oriental refueling and Bly in, 222–24
  as Prince of Wales Island, 222
  prisons of, 240
Peninsular and Oriental Steam
      Navigation Company (the P&O),
      137, 162–63, 185, 195. See also
      Oriental; Thames; Victoria
  British atmosphere aboard ships, 216
  "Jubilee" steamships, 163, 195, 255,
      396n 163
  Lascars as crew, 195
  opium trade and, 248–50
Pennsylvania Railroad
  Beatrice Pullman car, 311
  Bly's final leg of race on Atlantic
      Express No. 20, 300, 303–6, 309–14
  Ilion parlor car, 300, 311
  Jersey City terminal, 93, 314
  number of workers, 106
  opulent cars and amenities, 93
  Pullman sleepers on, 94
  train named after Nellie Bly, 327
Phelps, Edward R., 35, 342–43
Philadelphia
  Bly's lecture tour and, 340, 409n 340
  Bly's message to people of, 311
  Bly's mother and managing editor of
      the World board Bly's train, 310,
      311
  Bly's train reaches (Jan. 25, 1890), 309–
      11
  Reception Committee boards Bly's
      train, 310–11
Philadelphia Inquirer, 293
  Bly interview, 336
  on Bly's lecture tour, 339–40, 345
  Bly's race end reported, 317
  Bly's signature reproduced in, 311
  on Bly's train reaching Philadelphia,
      309
  editorial on Bisland's late arrival, 323
  Maddox editorial on Bly race, 97

Pittsburg Dispatch, 6–7, 13–16, 382n 6
  Bly as Mexican correspondent, 13–15
  Bly's articles in, 13
  Bly's coverage of a woman journalist in
      New York, 21–24
  Bly's pen name created, 8
  hires Pink Cochrane (Nellie Bly), 6–7
  Wilson writing in, 6
Pittsburgh, Pennsylvania, 5
  Bly greeted in, 306
  Bly living in, 5–8, 13–16, 117
  Bly's train reaches (Jan. 25, 1890),
      304–6
  newspapers, 6, 382n 6
  population of (1880s), 6
  Union Station, 306
Pittsburgh Press, 297, 306
Pittsburgh Press Club, 352
Plutarch, 268
Poe, Edgar Allan, 49, 387n 49
Ponsby, Claude, 168
Port Said, Egypt, 164–67, 165, 181
  beggars of, 166, 264
  Bly in (Nov. 27, 1889), 165–67
  as coaling station, 164–65
  street life of, 166–67
  tourists in, 166
Poussin, Nicolas, 159
Powan (river steamer), 241–43
Practical Treatise on Sea-Sickness (Beard),
      82
Prominent and Progressive Americans, 350
Prussian (steamship), 113, 194–95, 322,
      392n 113
Puck magazine, 35, 58
Pulitzer, Joseph, xv, xxi, 20, 26, 38, 312,
      384n 26
  absentee administration of The World,
      367–68
  appearance, 168–69, 170
  attempted trip around the world, 168
  on Bly, 34
  Bly quits The World and, 344, 410n 344
  Cockerill and, 26–28
  detached retina, 168
  enemies of, 169
  family heritage and background, 169,
      171
  fear of libel suits, 170, 344, 410n 344
  first editorial for The World, 173
  front page of papers and, 174, 397n 174
  generosity to employees, 170, 344

health of, 168, 367, 396n 168
newspaper writing and, 173
New York residences, 169
number 10 and, 169, 251
office spies used by, 170–71
raising funds for the Statue of Liberty, 70
success of *The World* and, 176
vision for his newspaper, 172, 175–76
The World's office building and, 20, 176
yacht of, 169–70
Pulitzer, Joseph, Jr., 20

Queenstown, Ireland, 276, 280–81

Raffles, Sir Stamford, 225
railroads, 193. *See also* Bisland, Elizabeth,
    race around the world; Bly,
    Nellie, race around the world;
    specific railroads
    American vs. European trains, 126, 136,
        218
    assets of, 106
    Bly covers strike, 369
    buffalo herds and, 105
    Chinese workers, 143–44
    closing of frontier and, 355
    derailments and speed, 103
    eating stations, 110
    first-class customers, 93
    "Golden Spike" at Promontory
        Summit, 104
    industry as America's first big business,
        106
    labor unrest and strikes, 144, 172, 369
    miles of track in the U.S., 105
    Native Americans and, 105
    opulent cars and amenities, 93
    power of the industry, 106
    prize money for reaching Ogden, Utah
        on schedule and hair-raising ride,
        100, 102–4
    record-breaking cross-country train
        trip, 74
    as representing progress and
        modernity, 107–8
    snow blockade, shutting down railroad
        traffic in American West (Jan.,
        1890), 283–87
    snow blockade, stranded passengers at
        Emigrant Gap, 284–87, 405n 285
    speed and, 263, 392n 110
    speeds of, 103–4, 105
    steam locomotive as an "Iron Horse,"
        105
    steel for tracks, 105–6
    time zones created by, 106–7, 194
    train from Pittsburgh to Mexico City,
        14
    train stations as social center, 100
    transcontinental mail, 63, 100–104,
        392n 110
    transcontinental passengers, 79, 93
    transcontinental railroad completed,
        104, 105, 144
    transformation of travel and life by,
        104–8
    uniforms for employees, 136
    U.S. Mail and Railway Mail Service,
        100–101
Reid, Whitelaw, 172
Reporter, Towanda, Pennsylvania, 133
Richardson, Leander, 169
Riis, Jacob A., 87–88, 174
Rock Island Railroad, 99–100
Roosevelt, Theodore, 356
*Round the World: Letters from Japan, China,
    India, and Egypt* (Fogg), 124
Round the World with Nellie Bly board
    game, 331, 333, 409n 333
Rousseau, Jean-Jacques, xxii, 382n xxii

Said Pasha, Mohammed, 164
San Francisco, California, 108, 110, 112
    Bisland arrival (Nov. 19, 1889), 110
    Bisland departure (Nov. 21, 1889), 114–
        15
    Bisland in, 110–14, 139
    Bly arrival and departure (Jan. 21,
        1890), 282, *282*, 287–89
    Bly's predicted arrival in, 269
    Chinese Quarter, 141–42, 155
    Cliff House, 112–13
    Palace Hotel, 111, *112*, 139
San Francisco Chronicle, 140
San Francisco Examiner
    "Annie Laurie" as reporter for, 111,
        366–67
    Bisland and, 111–13, 114, 147, 194
    reporter Low sent to meet Bly, 288
Sans dessus dessous (Verne), 130, 394n 130
Santa Fe Railroad, 283–84, 296
Scribner's Magazine, 263
Seamon, Robert, 369–70

Servia (steamship), 336
Shelley, Percy Bysshe, 281
Sherard, Robert H., 125
   Bly-Verne meeting and, 125, 127, 128,
      129, 132
   carries news of Bly's success to Jules
      Verne, 325
   requests for *The World* to thank Verne
      unanswered, 326, 408n 326
Sherman, William Tecumseh, 104, 105
ships. *See also Augusta Victoria*; *Oceanic*;
    Oriental; *Thames*
   Blue Ribbon of the Atlantic, 263, 276–
      77
   coaling of, 164–65, 167, 222–24, *223,*
      263–64
   coaling stations, 164, 181, 193
   departure activities, xiv
   design for speed, 263
   Irish Sea crossing, dangers of, 279
   laundries aboard transoceanic, 79–80
   life aboard, 151–52
   loss of a ship's screw, 195
   luxury and first-class, 82–83, 85–86
   New York City's steamship offices, 72
   North Atlantic crossing, dangers of,
      xiv, xx, 78, 307
   North Atlantic crossing, Jan. 1890,
      severe weather of, 307–9, 322
   Pacific crossing, dangers of, 78
   pirates, 222, 242–43, 401n 242
   record-breaking times, 262–63, 266
   sailors' superstitions, 261–62
   seasickness aboard, 81, 82–84
   shipboard life and activities, 84–88,
      149–52, 215–16, 255–56, 395n 151
   speed and noise, fuel consumption,
      263–64, 266
   steerage travel, 86–88, 140, 149–50
   stokers, 265–68, 308
   technological advances, 193
   transatlantic travel, advances in, xiv
Singapore, 196, *235*
   Bisland departure (Dec. 24, 1889), 239
   Bisland hotel room and rat, 236–38
   Bisland in, 235–39
   Bisland's arrival (Dec. 23, 1889), 221,
      235
   Bly observes funeral in, 225–26
   Bly's arrival (Dec. 16, 1889), 224
   Bly's departure (Dec. 17, 1889), 227

   Bly sightseeing and buys monkey in,
      225–27
   as British colony, 181, 236–37, 239
   dhobies (laundrymen), 226
   esplanade, 225
   gharry, 225, 236
   Hôtel de l'Europe, 225
   Malays in, 236, 239
   Raffles Museum, 225, 400n 225
   tigers killing Chinese in, 237, 401m 237
Six Months in Mexico (Bly), 347
Slayback, Alonzo W., 27
Smith, William, 241, 253–54
Southampton, England
   Bly arrives and departs (Nov. 21–22,
      1889), 89–91
   special mail train to London, 90, 91, 116
South China Sea, 216
   Bly and Bisland pass each other on, 221
   Bly crossing of, 228–30
   Bly halfway point, 224
Southern Pacific Railroad
   Bly given cab ride and operates the
      locomotive, 292–93
   Bly's train, Chicago to Pittsburgh,
      303–6
   Bly's train, Kansas to Chicago, 295–302
   Bly's train, Mojave Desert to New
      Mexico, 292–95
   Bly's train, Oakland to Arizona border,
      287–92
   Bly's train breaks speed record, 297
   Bly's train has close call on bridge,
      293–94
   the *Queen* locomotive, 283
   San Lorenzo Pullman sleeper car, 283,
      289, 290
   special train for Nellie Bly, 283–84,
      289–306
   special train for Nellie Bly, cost, 284
   speeds through Kansas, 296
Southwestern Christian Advocate, 51–52
Spalding, Albert G., 96
Spencer, Herbert, 17
Star, Wilmington, North Carolina, 204
Statue of Liberty, 69–70, 320
   Lazarus poem on, 145
   Pulitzer and *The World* and, 70
Steubenville, Ohio, 304
Stevens, Frank W., 328–29
Stevenson, Robert Louis, 63

Stewart, A. T., 41
St. Louis Post-Dispatch, 27, 169, 284, 368
St. Louis Republic, 269, 321
Stowe, Harriet Beecher, 82
Straits of Malacca, 221–22, 228
Suez Canal, 123, 164, 177–80
  gares, 177–78
  history, 177
  passage of Bly's ship (Nov. 28, 1889),
    167–68, 177–80
Sullivan, John L., xv
Swisshelm, Jane Grey, 11

Tallmadge, Daniel W., 342–43, 409n 343
Taylor, Richard, 43, 386n 43
Taylor, Zachary, 386n 43
telegraph, xxiii
  Aden office, 257
  Bisland's cable from Brindisi, 269
  Bisland's cable from Hong Kong, 187
  Bly's cable from Brindisi, 137–38
  Bly's cable from her train car about her
    reaction to U.S. return, 289–90
  Bly's race ending announced, 315
  making time disappear, 193–94
  warfare and, 193
Ten Days in a Mad-House (Bly), 34, 384n
  34
Tennyson, Alfred Lord, 259
Thames (steamship)
  Bisland's arrival in Singapore on (Dec.
    23, 1889), 221, 235
  Bisland booked on, 195
  Bisland departs Hong Kong on (Dec.
    18, 1889), 215
  Bisland's fellow passengers, 235–36, 238
  Bisland's observations of the men
    aboard, 217–18
  Bisland's voyage on, 215, 215–18, 221,
    235
  as British mail ship, 195
  Chinese prisoner aboard, 239–40
  design and amenities, 216
  Lascars as crew, 195, 240
  nearing the equator, 235
  refueling in Singapore, 235
  shipboard life and activities, 215–16
Thomas Cook & Son, 122, 272–73
  Bisland's race around the world and,
    62–63
  "Cook's tour," 273

mysterious agent gives Bisland false
    information, 272–74
  Nellie Bly's race around the world and,
    77, 390n 77
  Paris office, 273, 403n 273
Thoreau, Henry David, 108, 244
Tiffany, Louis Comfort, 93
tiffin, 207
time
  General Time Convention and division
    of the U.S. into four zones, 107
  "local mean time," 107
  railroad time, 106–7
  telegraph's vanquishing of, 193–94
  "To a Locomotive in Winter" (Whitman),
    107
Tokyo, Japan
  Bisland in (Dec. 9, 1889), 158–60
  Bisland returns (1911–1912), 359
  tomb of Iemitsu, 159–60
Topeka, Kansas, 295, 406n 295
Topeka Daily Capital, 296, 297
Town Topics, 147–49
Train, George Francis, 123
travel. *See also* railroads; ships
  aggressive boatmen in Egypt, 165–66
  American currency and, 80
  American travel to Europe, 356–57
  baksheesh and begging in the Middle
    East, 166
  Bly makes fastest circumnavigation of
    the globe, 315
  Bly's race around the world promoted
    as travel story, 78, 146
  circumnavigation of the globe, 96,
    122–24, 304
  "globe girdlers," 123–24
  illness during, xx
  Kodak cameras, 346
  local, in New York City, xvi–xvii, 20
  physical demands and toll of, 108
  public interest in travel stories, 42
  race around the world (1936), 375
  railroads and transformation of, 104–8
  record-breaking Atlantic crossings,
    263, 276–77
  record-breaking cross-country train
    trip, 74
  record-breaking Pacific crossings, 262–
    63
  sickness en route, 77–78

travel *(cont'd)*
   "Special Advice to Ladies," 79
   Suez Canal and direct water route
      between Europe and Asia, 123
   time zones and the railroad, 106–7
   transatlantic travel, advances in, xiv
   transcontinental, 104–8
   transcontinental, in 108 hours, 100
   travelers' checks, 346
   U.S. tourists abroad, 356–57
   women, restrictions on, 136
Trollope, Anthony, 5
Truth About Men and Other Matters, The
   (Bisland), 364
Turner, George, 73, 74, 367, 393n 125,
   403n 269
Twenty Thousand Leagues Under the Sea
   (Verne), 121
Twenty Years in Paris (Sherard), 408n 326
Tyler, Fannie A., 88

Union Pacific Railroad, 123
   Bisland as only woman passenger on
      mail run, 101
   Bisland's trip to San Francisco, 93, 100–
      110
   as empire, 106
   "Golden Spike" at Promontory
      Summit, 104
   Irish workers, 143
   prize money for reaching Ogden, Utah
      on schedule and hair-raising ride,
      102–4
   transcontinental mail and, 100–101
   western landscape and, 101–2
Union Square Theatre, New York, 337
   Bly's lecture at, 337–39
United States
   advertisements in books, 346
   advertising using celebrities, 330–31
   agricultural society replaced by
      industrial, 355
   American travel to Europe, 356–57
   attitudes toward England in, 218–20
   Bly as most famous woman in, 336
   Bly as New American Girl, 290, 294,
      295
   Bly as the highest-salaried woman, 347
   Bly's success as national triumph, 294–
      95
   class distinctions in, 172
   energy consumption in, 355
   frontier, 101–2
   frontier officially closed, 355
   immigration, 88, 140, 141–45, 173, 219
   imperialism, 219, 356, 399n 219
   income tax, 173–74
   Indian Wars, 355
   as industrial society, 355
   largest snow blockade in history (Jan.,
      1890), 283–84
   lecture tours in, 336
   "Nellie Bly Guessing Match" and,
      203–4, *199*
   Nellie Bly products, 204, 330–33
   occupational diseases of, 265–68
   railroads as America's first big business,
      106
   railroads linking coast to coast, 104,
      355
   Spanish-American War, 356
   states and territories, 355
   tourists abroad, 356–57
   values and child-raising, rural South,
      46, 386n 46, 388n 56
   World War I, 361
U.S. Mail
   contract offered for 108 hour
      transcontinental trip, 100, 102
   one and two cent stamps, 199
   Railway Mail Service, 100–101
   tons of mail on transcontinental trains,
      101
   transcontinental mail, 63, 100–101,
      392n 110
U.S. Navy, 355–56
Utah territory, 102
   hair-raising train ride to Ogden, Utah,
      102–4
   Ogden train depot, 102, 104
   Promontory Summit, 104

Vanderbilt, Alva, 171
Vanderbilt, Cornelius, 67
Vanderbilt, Mrs. Cornelius, 58
Vanderbilt, William H., 67, 174
Van Zile, Edward S., 77, 80
Verne, Honorine de Viane, 120, 126, 127–
   32, 134, 325–26
Verne, Jules, 72, 90, 116
   Amiens mansion of, 125, 128
   appearance, 126–27, *127*, 128–29
   Around the World in Eighty Days and,
      119, 121–23, 124, 131, 190

Bly meeting with, 125–32, 133, 339, 393n 125, 394n 132, 408n 326
childhood and favorite books, 120
congratulations sent to Nellie Bly, 300
daily routine, 125
literary career, 119–21
as literary celebrity, 124–25
in local politics, 125
marriage to Honorine de Viane, 120, 129–30
news of Bly's success and reaction, 325–26
shot by his nephew, 125
study of, 130–31
yacht of and travel, 124–25, 128, 131
Victoria (steamship), 194
at Aden, Yemen, 180–81
Bly and fellow travelers, 163–64, 178–80
Bly's arrival in Ceylon (Dec. 8, 1889), 204
Bly's departure on from Brindisi (Nov. 25, 1889), 137–38
Bly's first morning aboard, 161–62
Bly's writing about the English on, 181–82
coaling of, Port Said, 164–65, 167
conjurer comes aboard, 179–80
English servants on, 162
Suez Canal passage, 177–80
Victoria, Queen
British Empire and, 181
golden jubilee, 163, 255
golden jubilee and America, 220
loyalty of subjects, 182
Victorian Age, xxiii
colonial wars of, 192
occupational diseases of, 265–68
virtues of, 122
"Victory, The," 194
Vienna, Austria, 371
Villard, Henry, 171
Villeneuve–St. Georges, France, 272

Wade, Elizabeth Wilkinson or "Bessie Bramble," 8
Walden (Thoreau), 108
Walker, John Brisben, xx–xxi, *61*
attempt to move up departure of the *Oceanic*, 108, 111, 114, 232, 397n 184

background, 41
Bisland's telegram about predicted arrival, 269
Bisland welcomed home by, 321
business ventures, 60–61
character and personality, xxii, 60
The Cosmopolitan and, 41, 60–61, 385n 41
as demanding employer, 63–64
false information given to and to Elizabeth Bisland attributed to "bad faith," 333–35
idea for a race around the world to compete with Bly's, xxi, xxii, 61–68
La Champagne paid to wait for Bisland, 273–74
publicity sought by, 95–96
residence, 62
sends roses to Bly and concedes race, 318
special train booked for Bisland, 274
wager on race with *The World*, 62, 95–96, 145
wealth and accomplishments, 65–66
The World interviews about Bisland's race, 321–22
Walsh, William S., 145, 146
Walter Reed Hospital, 361
Ward, John Montgomery, 311
Washington Critic, 323
Watt, James B., 319
Watts, Charles, 303
Western Railroad of France, 272, 274
Western Union, 17
Wetmore, Charles, 350–51
illness and death, 358–62
marries Elizabeth Bisland, 351
Whistler, James McNeill, 349
White, James E., 103
White Star Line, 139, 140, 253, 262, 322
Whitman, Walt, 107
Why Americans Dislike England (Adams), 218
Widower Indeed, A (Bisland and Broughton), 350
Wilde, Oscar, 127
Wilder, Alvin D., 289
Williams, Arizona, 292
Willis, Sara Boyson or "Fanny Fern," 8
Wilson, A. D., 62, 184–85, 269, 272, 397n 185, 403n 269

Wilson, Erasmus, 6, 305, 351, 352, 353, 369
women
Bisland's charity work and, 363
Bisland's organizing of, 54–56
Bisland writing on literary heroines, 358
Blackwell's Island Insane Asylum, treatment of, 28–34, 384n 34
Bly as inspiration for female journalists, 351, 366
Bly as the highest-salaried in U.S., 347
Bly's championing of poor women and children, 372–75
Bly's lecture tour meets disapproval, 339–40, 342
chaperones for, 126
clothing of 1880s, xvi, 85
criticism of Nellie Bly and, 147
effect of Bly-Bisland race on, 97
excluded from Hindu temple, Singapore, 226
exposé of medical treatment of poor, 366–67
first woman seated in Senate gallery, 11
inequality and, xxiii, 8–13
makeup of 1880s, xvi
Nellie Bly's view on personal appearance, vs. suffragettes, 36
new type of or New American Girl, 54, 96, 147, 290, 294, 295, 313, 316, 331
as reporters, xv, 8–13, 21–24, 111, 366–67, 371–72, 409n 343
single women eating in restaurants, 99
travel and, 82, 85, 136, 357
Women's Evening Clinic, 363
"Women's Experience of Newspaper Work, A" (J.L.H.), 9, 12
Women's Press Club, 12, 383n 12
Woodlawn Cemetery, 366, 375, 413n 375
World, The
Bisland's reviews in, 58
Bly as reporter at, xv, 24–39
Bly-Jules Verne meeting arranged, 125
Bly-Jules Verne meeting reported, 133
Bly meets John Cockerill, 24
Bly quits following wage dispute, 344–45, 410n 344

Bly rehired (1893), 368–69
Bly's exposé of Blackwell's Island Insane Asylum, xv, 27–34, 344, 367
Bly's exposé of sexual predator, 35
Bly's exposé of the "Lobby King," 35, 342–43
Bly's exposé of white slave trade, xv, 35
Bly's lighter stories, 37–38
Bly talks her way into, 24–27, 384n 26
Bly undercover at a paper-box factory, 35
"cat smothers child" story, 197
Chambers as managing editor, xviii, 312, 347, 393n 125, 410n 347
circulation, 38, 75, 176, 202, 329, 397n 176
Cockerill as editor, 24, 26–28, 73
crime stories in, 175–76
editorial shake-up at (1893), 367–68
exposés as specialty of, 28, 174, 367
first Sunday comic strip published, 368
front page, 174–75, 397n 174
Gould as owner, 172
"Meg Merrilies" (stunt girls), 367, 368
office building, 19, 20, 25, 72–73, 169, 176
poor and working class championed by, 173–74
price of an issue, 173, 176
Pulitzer as publisher, xv, 26, 38, 367–68
Pulitzer's first editorial, 173
Pulitzer's generosity to employees, 170
Pulitzer's office spies, 170–71
Pulitzer's purchase of, 169, 172
Pulitzer's vision for, 172, 173
raising funds for the Statue of Liberty, 70
readership of, 173, 174
serialization of novels, 63
"The Story of Nellie Bly," 329–30
Tallmadge libel suit and, 342–43, 409n 343
women reporters and, 24, 367
writing style, 173, 175–76

race around the world
Bly's bitterness about lack of compensation, 344
Bly's Christmas described to readers, 251
Bly's delay in Ceylon announced, 210–11
Bly's photo given as premium, 329
Bly's success as national triumph, 294–95
Bly's telegram about arrival in U.S., 289–90
Bly's telegram from Brindisi, 138
Chambers and Reception Committee on Bly's train, 310, 311, 312–13
"Excursion Editor" for "Nellie's Rush Around," 133–34
false information given to Bisland and, 334–35
Greaves and, 89–91, 116–19, 125–27, 133–35
headlines for Sunday, Jan. 26, 324–25
interview with Walker about Bisland's race, 321–22
itinerary for, xviii, xx, xxi, 77, 129, 131–32, 198
January 26 issue sold out, reprinted, 326, 409n 333
Jennings reports on Bly's transcontinental journey, 296
London correspondent (Greaves) meets Bly and reports, 89–91, 116–19, 125–26, 134–35, 324–25
"Nellie Bly Escort Corps," 284, 290
"Nellie Bly Guessing Match," 177, 197–204, *199*, 251–52, 283, 302, 328–29, 406n 302

Paris correspondent (Sherard) and Bly, 125, 127, 128, 129, 132, 325, 408n 326
predicted date of return, 198, 210–11
preparations for, 77–78
publicity from and circulation increase, 146, 176–77, 197–204, 326, 329
reception for Bly's return, 317
Round the World with Nellie Bly board game, 331, 333, *334,* 409n 333
special train for final leg, 283–84, 289–306
stories on, 79, 133–34
story proposal presented by Bly, 38–39, 73–75
Verne-Bly meeting, 125–32, 393n 125, 394n 132
World War I, 360–61
Bisland war work in England and U.S., 360–61, 375
Bly champions Austrian women and orphans, 371, 375
Wycherly, Hubert, 315
Wyoming, 102

Yokohama, Japan, 185
Bisland in, 153–58
Bisland's arrival (Dec. 8, 1889), 153
Bisland's departure (Dec. 10, 1889), 160
Bisland's return to (1911–1912), 359
Bly's departure (Jan. 7, 1890), 260
the Bund, 153, 155
city life, 155–57
as foreign port, 154
Grand Hotel, 155, 157
merchandise and goods, 157–58
population of, 1889, 154–55
Yorkshire (steamship), 308

Matthew Goodman

Eighty Days

A Reader's Guide

A Conversation with Matthew Goodman

Random House Readers Circle: How did the idea for *Eighty Days* originate?

Matthew Goodman: My previous book, *The Sun and the Moon,* had featured only male characters, so when I began looking around for a new book topic I knew that I wanted the next one to be about a woman. Then one day, during my book explorations, I stumbled across a reference to Nellie Bly; I recognized that name (in part because there used to be a Nellie Bly Amusement Park not far from where I live in Brooklyn), but I didn't know much about her beyond the fact that she had been a journalist. I began to read more about her, and as I did, I discovered that she wasn't just any journalist—she was this *amazing* journalist, who had feigned madness to expose the inner workings of an insane asylum, and so forth. I mean, in an era when the vast majority of female journalists were writing for the women's pages of newspapers, she was an undercover investigative reporter for the most widely read newspaper of her time.

So I kept on reading, and when I read about how Nellie Bly had undertaken a race around the world in 1889, I knew right away that this was the story I wanted to tell. I thought it was absolutely remarkable that a young woman, unaccompanied and carrying only a single bag, would be daring enough to race around the world, through Europe and the Middle East and Far East, during the Victorian era—and do it faster than anyone ever had before her. (Frankly, I found it almost equally remarkable that no one had written a book about the race before.) I was thrilled to have found such a compelling main character, but as a writer, I was also thrilled by the prospect of being able to write about all those exotic locales. But then, as I continued my research, I discovered something even more astonishing: that in fact Nellie Bly was competing against another young female journalist, by the name of Elizabeth Bisland—a detail that is almost never included in the historical record. I was captivated by the notion of these two young women racing each other around the world, one traveling east, the other west.

RHRC: What was the most fun in writing the story of this incredible journey? What do you hope readers take away from the book?

MG: To be honest, I don't often experience writing as "fun" (usually there's too much worry, doubt, and plain old hard work wrapped up in it for me to think of it in quite that way!), but certain scenes in *Eighty Days* were in fact a great deal of fun to write. I loved writing the story of Elizabeth Bisland's wild train ride across Utah with Cyclone Bill Downing, for instance; and the scene where Nellie Bly gets to meet Jules and Honorine Verne in their Amiens estate was really fun, because *they* were all having so much fun with each other. And I took a lot of satisfaction from the pages that described the stokers shoveling coal down in their sweltering fire room; that was a section that I knew I wanted to write from the very beginning, because it was material that I felt very strongly about and hadn't ever seen described in quite that way before.

Much of the fun that I had with *Eighty Days* came from the research for the book, from discovering things that I hadn't known before (who could have ever guessed that Wisconsin used to have thirty-eight time zones?) and which I felt confident would help to make a better story. As you would expect, a lot of this research involved the lives of the two main characters, Nellie Bly and Elizabeth Bisland, both of which proved to be more complicated and surprising than I had originally anticipated. Lots had already been written about Nellie Bly, of course—much of it, as it turns out, not entirely accurate—but very little was known about Elizabeth Bisland (no one had ever written a book about her before), and I very much enjoyed the process of ferreting out old books and other documents that contained odd bits of information that could add a piece to the puzzle, and help me come to know her across the decades. After the book was published I got an e-mail from Elizabeth Bisland's grandnephew that said, in part, "Thank you so much for sharing Elizabeth with the public, since she was indeed so reticent to do that herself." I found that incredibly gratifying.

And I guess—and this is a long way around to answering your question—what I most hope that readers take away from this book is a deeper understanding of these two remarkable women. Though they were very different from each other in many ways, they were both independent and committed to their work, and they were able to support themselves as writers at a time when that was very unusual for women. If by writing *Eighty Days* I can introduce a new generation of readers to Elizabeth Bisland, and reintroduce them to Nellie Bly, then I'll be very pleased.

RHRC: As you unraveled their story, did you find yourself relating to (or rooting for!) either woman in particular?

MG: This is actually a question I hear a lot from readers—who was I rooting for to win the race? The thing is, unlike readers (or most of them, anyway), I knew right from the beginning who had won! So for me, it wasn't really a question of rooting for either Nellie Bly or Elizabeth Bisland to win the race; rather, when I began work on the book I was rooting for them to turn out to be characters as complex and as compelling as possible. And in that respect, both women ably fulfilled my wishes for them.

As I've met readers, at book events and so forth, it's been enjoyable for me to hear about how some of them were rooting for Nellie Bly while others were rooting for Elizabeth Bisland. That's very much what I wanted for *Eighty Days*; I certainly didn't want to be writing a book about a race between a hero and a villain—then you're verging on melodrama—or even a book in which one of the characters is clearly more sympathetic or more interesting than the other. So I've been pleased to discover that the audience's sympathies have been pretty well divided. I think that's because each woman had certain admirable qualities that the other tended not to have. Nellie Bly was physically courageous (her stint inside the Blackwell's Island Insane Asylum made that very clear), independent, ambitious, socially concerned, and fully determined that as a female journalist she could do anything her male colleagues did; Elizabeth Bisland was erudite (the number of subjects about which she could write intelligently was truly astonishing), artistically inclined, sensitive, deeply curious about the world and its inhabitants. And they each had a number of flaws as well—among those flaws, certainly, a kind of reflexive, unconscious racism that was pretty endemic in the society of the time. So I think that a reader will tend to like one or the other woman depending on the particular set of qualities he or she tends to prefer generally.

RHRC: What was your research process like in preparing to write *Eighty Days*?

MG: I spent eighteen months basically living in libraries before I wrote a single sentence of *Eighty Days*. In writing this book I wanted readers not just to *know* what had happened during the race, but to *experience* it as well—to feel like they were right there with Nellie Bly or Elizabeth Bisland on the back of a rickshaw, or in the stateroom of a steamship during a storm, or walking along the Tanks in Aden in the moonlight. I needed the world in which they were living to be as vivid as possible in my mind, so that I could make it as vivid as possible on the page.

Not surprisingly, the first thing I did was to read the books that the two women wrote about the race: Nellie Bly's *Around the World in Seventy-two Days* and Elizabeth Bisland's *A Flying Trip Around the World*. It was a great boon to me that each wrote a book about the race, not only because it allowed me to hear their respective voices, but also because it gave me access to their internal worlds as well as the external world through which they were racing. From there I read everything else that they had ever written, or at least everything that I could get my hands on—books, essays, articles, reviews; this helped me to gain a clearer sense of what they cared about, how they thought, how they changed over the course of their lives. I immersed myself in the newspapers of the time. (Interestingly, I found that the most useful parts of the newspapers were not the news sections, but rather the advertisements. Advertisements, after all, give a sense of the daily life of a society—they tell what people ate and wore, and what they read and how they furnished their house; they tell how much commodities cost; they tell the kinds of things people liked to do in their spare time.) I read biographies of the other significant characters in the book, such as Jules Verne and Joseph Pulitzer; I read everything I could about all the places that the two women visited during the race, including other travelers' accounts, histories, guidebooks. Guidebooks are especially helpful, because they're designed to acquaint the traveler with an unfamiliar destination—and a historian is very much like a traveler, except that you're journeying through time as well as space.

RHRC: This is your third book. Was the experience of writing *Eighty Days* new or different in any way? Did it present more of a challenge?

MG: Well, my first book was a cookbook, so that doesn't count—there wasn't much in the way of recipe testing that I had to do for *Eighty Days*. But my second book, *The Sun and the Moon,* was a narrative history as well, and that book presented its own unique challenges, because it was the first full-scale work of history that I had ever written, and I was sort of teaching myself how to do it as I went along. With *Eighty Days* I had a clearer understanding at the very beginning of how to write a book like this: how best to conduct research, how to structure a narrative, and so forth.

The Sun and the Moon was set a bit further back in time than *Eighty Days*—it tells the true story of a newspaper hoax in the year 1835, in which *The Sun* convinced New Yorkers that life had been discovered on the moon—and there was much less available material, especially about the author of the hoax stories, Richard Adams Locke. (It's frankly a bit disconcerting to a narrative historian when other historical accounts always refer to your main character as "enigmatic.") There was much more to work with for *Eighty Days* (even about Elizabeth Bisland, about whom not very much had been written), which in turn entailed more research, more decisions about what to keep in and what to leave out, and that sort of thing. But ultimately I found it a great boon, because it meant that I had access to enough historical detail to make *Eighty Days* even more novelistic in style than *The Sun and the Moon* had been, which is what I wanted.

For me, the central challenge with *Eighty Days* was not so much in writing about two female protagonists (as I had initially anticipated), but rather in finding the right structure for the book. The fact that the two women were racing in opposite directions was helpful, because it meant that while one was in London, say, the other was in San Francisco—so they weren't constantly seeing the same places at the same time, which might have gotten tedious. But there was still the question of how to handle the sections of the race where not much was going on, like during a long ocean voyage or an extended stay in a particular location. So rather than have the book just be a kind of travelogue—this happened, then that happened—I found that I could use those sections as a kind of stepping-off place to explore larger historical questions naturally raised by that section of the race itself. So, for instance, Elizabeth Bisland's train trip across the American West provided an opportunity to discuss the power of the railroads at the time, while Nellie Bly's voyage across the Pacific led naturally into a discussion of the horrendous working conditions endured by the stokers who were shoveling the coal that allowed her steamship to go as fast as it did. What I was trying to create was almost a kind of symphonic structure, where the two central themes (the women's narratives) were occasionally broken up by slower, more reflective passages that provide a bit of breathing room. Ultimately, I thought, this would both tell a more complete story and produce a more satisfying experience for the reader.

RHRC: Aside from Nellie Bly or Elizabeth Bisland, who among the characters in *Eighty Days* would you have most liked to meet?

MG: Well, as your question indicates, I'd of course most like to have met Bly and Bisland. After spending years thinking so intently about some historical figure, you can't help but wish that you could somehow meet that person in real life: hear her actual voice, watch her gestures, listen to her talk about subjects beyond those in the materials you've already read. It's a kind of perpetually unfulfilled longing, and one that I'd guess is shared by pretty much any historian. Beyond those two, though, my research for *Eighty Days* leads me to think that Joseph Pulitzer would have made a pretty fascinating dinner companion. He adored the novels of George Eliot, read widely in history, was interested in all the current political debates, loved music and the arts, and could recite long passages of his favorite works from memory. Plus, he had a yacht.

RHRC: Nellie Bly carried only a single handbag for her trip around the world. How would you pack for such a trip? What would you consider the essentials to be brought along?

MG: I have to say, every time I packed a bag in preparation for an *Eighty Days* book event, and then schlepped it aboard a plane or train, I thought about Nellie Bly! Invariably, even if I were going only for a single night, my bag would be far larger than the one Bly brought along for a trip lasting two and a half months. (By the way, Bly's leather gripsack—the actual one that she brought with her on the race around the world—is on display at the Newseum in Washington, D.C. I've seen it, and I found it incredibly moving and poignant; that bag is *tiny*.) So I'm hardly a model of Bly-like efficient packing. But if I could take only a single bag for a trip around the world (assuming that it's a trip of some duration, involving some sightseeing in various cities along the way), I think I'd be sure to bring along an extra pair of comfortable walking shoes, a pair of khakis, and a lightweight sports jacket that could be rolled up in the bag. And while I only ever read printed books—that's just my preference—I think that for a trip around the world I'd probably spring for an e-reader of some sort. You can read a lot of books while you're traveling around the world, and I'd just as soon not have them weighing down the bag—the ones I love I'd buy in hard copy upon my return.

RHRC: What's the longest journey you've ever taken?

MG: Many years ago I was fortunate enough to be part of an American delegation invited to China by the Chinese government. We spent a couple of weeks there, visiting Beijing, Hangzhou, and Shanghai. (The train on which we traveled from Hangzhou to Shanghai, with its wood paneling and lace curtains and afternoon tea served in porcelain cups, reminds me now of the ones on which Bly and Bisland rode across the United States.) Coming back, we flew from Beijing to San Francisco on China Air. In those days you could still smoke inside a plane—at least you could on China Air—and it seemed that just about everybody on board, other than me, was a smoker. We crossed the Pacific Ocean in a thick blue haze. *That* was the longest journey I've ever taken!

RHRC: Who are your writing influences? What are you currently reading?

MG: To the extent that I have any "training" as a writer, it's as a fiction writer. (I got an MFA in fiction writing, though now, when I teach, it's in creative nonfiction.) And even now I still find that I tend to divide my reading up pretty evenly between fiction and nonfiction. For instance, I've just finished re-reading Janet Malcolm's books of reportage *In the Freud Archives* and *The Journalist and the Murderer,* and before that I read Steven Millhauser's amazing novel *Martin Dressler*; and right now on my desk I've got Matthew Pearl's novel *The Dante Club,* Tony Horwitz's narrative history *Midnight Rising* (about John Brown), and *Russ & Daughters,* a memoir by my buddy, the New York herring maven Mark Russ Federman. So it's pretty eclectic—though I guess these books do tend to share a sense of engagement with American history and politics, as I hope my own work does as well.

My writing influences also tend to be pretty evenly divided between fiction and nonfiction. Right off the bat I'd mention James Agee's astonishing and beautiful *Let Us Now Praise Famous Men* (Agee was, as one critic memorably said, "a born, sovereign prince of the English language"); almost anything by Joan Didion (though especially her nonfiction, and perhaps most especially *Slouching Towards Bethlehem,* her exhilarating takedown of the excesses and false promises of the American Dream); Grace Paley's wonderfully funny and big-hearted short stories; E. L. Doctorow's historical novel *Ragtime* (I learned a great deal from him about the establishment of tone, and how one puts large observations into short sentences); and Robert Caro's magisterial *The Power Broker,* which presents the sort of scholarship to which all historians should aspire.

If I had to name just one single book as the most influential to me, though, I think I'd choose a book I first read a long, long time ago: Jean Merrill's novel for young people *The Pushcart War.* Set in the then far-off year of 1986, it describes the war between pushcarts and trucks for control of the streets of New York; along the way Merrill creates such unforgettable characters as Maxie Hammerman, the "Pushcart King"; movie star Wenda Gambling; and Mayor Emmet P. Cudd, who in his famous "Peanut Butter Speech" declaimed that as his opponent was against trucks he was against progress, and if he was against progress he might even be *against peanut butter*. In this book Jean Merrill pulled off the trick of being at once uproariously funny and deeply wise about life in New York. When I was in sixth grade I loved *The Pushcart War* so much that my wonderful teacher, Maureen Miletta, suggested I adapt it into a play, which my class performed for the entire school; it remains to this day the most unalloyed pleasure I have ever gotten from a piece of writing.

RHRC: What are you working on next?

MG: Tough question! At the moment, I haven't actually figured out my next book project. I know that I want to do another book of narrative history, like *Eighty Days,* and it's been my experience (and this has been confirmed for me by other narrative historians) that finding a book topic is in some ways the hardest, most harrowing part of the entire process. Before anything else, of course, it has to be a great story—something with drama, tension, excitement, what have you—and ideally it's one that has a clearly defined beginning, middle, and end. And it should feature a compelling, fascinating main character or characters, someone who will maintain a reader's interest over the course of the book. Because I'm telling the story novelistically, with as much richness and vivid detail as possible, there has to be a lot of historical material available on the subject. (Diaries and letters are invaluable for any historian, but especially for the narrative historian.) But even as one requires a lot of available material to tell the story, one also requires a story that hasn't been told before, or at least not told in this way before—and that's a tricky combination. And as if that's not hard enough, I'd also like the story to be about something more than just itself—that is to say, to reveal something larger about the politics or culture of the time.

So that's what I'm looking for: a story as good as that of Nellie Bly and Elizabeth Bisland, and that's a tall order indeed.

Questions for Discussion

1. In the book's prologue Matthew Goodman writes, "Nellie Bly and Elizabeth Bisland were not only racing around the world; they were also racing through the very heart of the Victorian age." What do you think he meant by this? In what way did Bly and Bisland's race illustrate some of the larger social issues of the time?

2. In what ways were Elizabeth and Nellie similar, and in what ways were they dissimilar? Did they have differing views of themselves as women, as writers, as Americans? How might this have colored their attitudes about the around-the-world race?

3. Almost every story of the time mentioned the fact that Nellie Bly carried only a single handbag for her trip around the world. How do you think *you* would pack for such a trip? What would you consider the essentials to bring along?

4. How might other female journalists of the time have viewed Bly and Bisland's race around the world? Do you think they would have been supportive or critical?

5. Throughout the book Goodman intersperses the narrative of the race with discussions of historical issues—such as the hardships faced by women journalists, the power of the railroads, and the working

conditions of stokers on the steamships. Why do you think he did this? Did you feel that this added to or detracted from the book as a whole?

6. Did you find yourself rooting for one of the women to win the race? Which of the women would you rather have as a traveling companion? In what ways would you say each of the women changed over the course of the race?

7. How do you think that Nellie Bly's difficult childhood might have helped to shape some of the choices she made as an adult?

8. *Eighty Days* is an example of the genre called "narrative history"— that is to say, a work of history that adopts some of the techniques generally associated with fiction writing. In what ways does this book read like a novel? How was Matthew Goodman able to accomplish this? Did you ever find yourself momentarily forgetting that it was a true story?

9. Visiting the Tanks of Aden in the moonlight, Elizabeth Bisland has a profound moment in which she comes to understand what the trip has given her: "the vividness of a new world, where one was for the first time, as Tennyson had written, *Lord of the senses five,* where the light of night and day had a new meaning, where years of indifference could fall away like a dried-up husk and every sense respond with the keenness of faculties newborn." Have you ever had an experience like that while traveling? Which of the places described in the book would you most like to visit?

10. The very first story that Bly proposed to *The World* was to sail across the Atlantic in steerage, so that she could report firsthand on the conditions endured by the passengers there. Yet during her around-the-world race, when she had the opportunity, she did not write about steerage passengers. Why do you think this was? Do you think that she had changed as a journalist, and if so, in what ways?

11. Might *Eighty Days* be viewed as a kind of cautionary tale about celebrity? How so?

12. The book's epilogue describes the very different lives led by Nellie Bly and Elizabeth Bisland in the decades after the race. Were you surprised by the way that things turned out for them? Why or why not? How would you answer the question posed about Nellie Bly at the end of the final chapter: "She had outraced Elizabeth Bisland; but now, looking back, it was not entirely clear which of them had won."

13. The story told in *Eighty Days* took place more than 120 years ago. An around-the-world trip that once required two and a half months to complete could be accomplished today in a matter of days. Are there other ways in which society has changed far less dramatically since 1889?

Matthew Goodman is the author of two other nonfiction books, *The Sun and the Moon: The Remarkable True Account of Hoaxers, Showmen, Dueling Journalists, and Lunar Man-Bats in Nineteenth-Century New York* and *Jewish Food: The World at Table*. The recipient of two MacDowell fellowships and one Yaddo fellowship, he has taught creative writing at numerous universities and workshops. He lives in Brooklyn, New York, with his wife and children.

Chat.
Comment.
Connect.

Visit our online book club community at
Facebook.com/RHReadersCircle

Chat
Meet fellow book lovers and discuss what you're reading.

Comment
Post reviews of books, ask—and answer—thought-provoking
questions, or give and receive book club ideas.

Connect
Find an author on tour, visit our author blog, or invite one of
our 150 available authors to chat with your group on the phone.

Explore
Also visit our site for discussion questions, excerpts, author
interviews, videos, free books, news on the latest releases,
and more.

Books are better with buddies.
Facebook.com/RHReadersCircle

RANDOM HOUSE
READER'S CIRCLE ®

THE RANDOM HOUSE PUBLISHING GROUP